SECOND EDITION

The Presence of Others

Voices That Call for Response

SECOND EDITION

The Presence of Others

Voices That Call for Response

ANDREA A. LUNSFORD

The Ohio State University

JOHN J. RUSZKIEWICZ

The University of Texas at Austin

ST. MARTIN'S PRESS

New York

Key to Cover Photographs:
(From left to right, top to bottom) Mike Rose, Zora Neale Hurston,
Douglas Coupland, Lynne V. Cheney, Maxine Hong Kingston,
Pope John Paul II, Joan Didion, Newt Gingrich, Martin Luther King Jr.

Publisher: Marilyn Moller
Development editor: Kristin Bowen
Editorial assistant: Griff Hansbury
Manager, Publishing services: Emily Berleth
Publishing services associate: Meryl Gross
Project management: Books By Design, Inc.
Production supervisor: Scott Lavelle
Text design: Anna George
Cover design: Lucy Krikorian

Library of Congress Catalog Card Number: 95-73167
Manufactured in the United States of America.
1   0   9   8   7
f   e   d   c   b   a

For information, write:
St. Martin's Press, Inc.
175 Fifth Avenue
New York, NY 10010

ISBN: 0-312-13295-6

Acknowledgments

Maya Angelou, "Champion of the World" from *I Know Why the Caged Bird Sings.* Copyright © 1969
   by Maya Angelou. Reprinted with the permission of Random House, Inc.
Dave Barry, "Guys vs. Men" from *Dave Barry's Complete Guide to Guys.* Copyright © 1995 by Dave
   Barry. Reprinted with the permission of Random House, Inc.
Richard Bernstein, "Dérapage" from *Dictatorship of Virtue: Multiculturalism and the Battle for America's
   Future.* Copyright © 1994 by Richard Bernstein. Reprinted with the permission of Alfred
   A. Knopf, Inc.

*(Acknowledgments and copyrights are continued at the back of the book on pages 610–14, which
constitute an extension of the copyright page. It is a violation of the law to reproduce these selections by
any means whatsoever without the written permission of the copyright holder.)*

Contents

"If then a practical end must be assigned to a University course, I say it is that of training good members of society."

"What does a woman need to know to become a self-conscious, self-defining human being?"

....

PART FOUR   HOW WE LIVE

Preface

"For excellence," writes philosopher Hannah Arendt, "the presence of others is always required." Not genius, she tells us, not divine inspiration, not even good old-fashioned hard work, but *others*. In choosing a title for this text, we thought of Arendt's statement, because this book aims to lead composition students toward excellence in reading and writing, toward excellence in thinking through difficult ideas and topics, toward excellence in articulating their own positions on issues and providing good reasons for supporting those positions—always in relation to other people's thoughts and words.

Given these aims, we have been delighted at the response from those using the first edition of *The Presence of Others:* teachers and students report that they have indeed been moved to respond to the many perspectives presented in the text, saying yes to some, and no or even maybe to others. Most important, they note, they have been moved to think hard about these perspectives—and about their own positions. In preparing a second edition of *The Presence of Others,* we have therefore changed the subtitle to *Voices That Call for Response* for this is a book that offers multiple (and sometimes competing) voices and views, ones that call for and even provoke response.

Two of those voices belong to us, the editors, John Ruszkiewicz and Andrea Lunsford. Like the co-anchors in the cartoon on the next page, we take very different views on most issues, and we make many of those views and opinions known in *The Presence of Others.* But disagreement, conflict, and agonism are *not* guiding principles of this book. It is not a tennis match of ideas, one that will yield winners and losers. Rather, we are interested in how we all come to know and to take positions on various issues, how to nurture open and realistic exchanges of ideas.

Equally important, we invite readers to join the conversation, to question and challenge the many points of view—including our own. For this second edition, we've tried our best to select a balanced set of readings that represent widely varying points of view on a range of topics, from education to cultural legends, from science to the world of work. Many of these readings are likely to surprise anyone who believes that attitudes can be predicted by labels as equivocal as "liberal" or "conservative."

The Presence of Others aims to open and sustain animated conversation among the 75 readings, the editors and students whose commentary accompanies the readings, and all the teachers and students we hope will enter the conversation. To encourage active and informed response, we offer a variety of pedagogical features.

"Now here's my co-anchor, Nancy, with a conflicting account of that very same story."

(Drawing by Ziegler; © 1995 by The New Yorker Magazine.)

NOTABLE FEATURES

• A *balance of viewpoints* gives every student ideas to support and to argue against. Readings represent many genres—stories, speeches, sermons, prayers, poems, personal memoirs, interviews, as well as essays and articles—and they take a wide range of varying and often competing perspectives. In chapter 3, for instance, on education, John Henry Newman rubs conversational shoulders with bell hooks, Mike Rose, and Gwendolyn Brooks. Cross-references throughout lead readers back and forth among the readings, drawing them into the conversation.

• *Explicit editorial apparatus* draws students into the conversation. Each readings chapter opens with a page of *brief quotations* from the readings and a *visual text,* giving a glimpse of what's to come. *Headnotes* to each reading provide background information and offer some explanation for our editorial choices. Because these introductions also offer our own strong opinions about the selection, each one is signed. Each selection is followed by a sequence of *questions* that ask students to question the text (and sometimes the headnote), to make connections with other readings, and to join the conversation by articulating their own response in writing. Each reading includes one or more questions designed for group work, which we hope will encourage further conversation and make concrete the presence of others. *A list of other readings* (including some from the Internet) concludes each chapter.

- *An annotated reading in each chapter* includes commentary by the editors and one student commentator, demonstrating what it is to ask critical questions and to read with a critical eye.

- Chapters 1 and 2 provide strategies on *reading and thinking critically* and on moving *from reading to writing*.

NEW TO THIS EDITION

- *Fifty-three new readings* offer more pragmatic, broader-based views than the ones they replace. Among the authors newly represented are Stephen Carter, Andrea Lee, Stanley Crouch, Terry Tempest Williams, John Paul II, Ayn Rand, and Douglas Coupland.

- *A new chapter on work* addresses the understandable concerns college students have about the professional worlds they may soon be entering, with readings on downsizing, finding first jobs, and the impact of technology on the workplace.

- Each chapter now opens with a *visual text*—a photo, an advertisement, a Web page, or a cartoon—along with questions and guidelines (in chapter 1) to help students read visual texts.

- *Guidelines for writing a critical response essay* and an annotated student example have been added to chapter 2, showing students how to respond in writing to what they read.

The accompanying instructor's notes by Melissa Goldthwaite provide detailed advice for teaching this book, including commentary on each selection, sequenced reading and writing assignments, and a selection of essays and articles regarding current controversies over the college curriculum.

ACKNOWLEDGMENTS

This anthology has changed considerably in the six years since we first began exploring its possibilities, primarily because of the presence of many, many others whose perspectives and voices echo in these pages. Of great importance have been the extensive support and ongoing spirited conversation we have received from the St. Martin's staff, and particularly from Kristin Bowen, who has cheerfully and carefully guided the development of this second edition. We also thank Emily Berleth for her efficient management, turning manuscript into bound book. And we have once again enjoyed the extraordinary energy of Marilyn Moller's editorial acumen during the entire project.

In addition to these friends at St. Martin's, we are indebted to many colleagues at our home institutions—especially Melissa Goldthwaite at The Ohio State University. Melissa assisted in the hunt for the best possible readings and prepared the instructor's manual. This manual we believe to be thoroughly informed by contemporary reading theory as well as by Melissa's practical experience from having taught the materials in this book. We owe sincere thanks as well to Jean Williams, Chris DeVinne, Jennifer Cognard-Black, and Matthew Taylor for helping us run down many obscure items.

We are particularly grateful to the students who agreed to add their voices to this text: Teresa Essman and Carrie Ann Laposki from The Ohio State University and Joshua G. Rushing from the University of Texas. For this edition, we are also indebted to the members of Andrea's 1995 first-year writing seminar, who provided insightful readings of and responses to the first edition of this text: Lindsay Anderson, Benjamin Basil, Steve Buckshaw, Suzanne Harris, Mark Holtman, Kimberly Johnson, Aimee Keck, Eugene Khasilev, Michelle Knox, Amanda Linder, Alexander Marcus, John McMillin, Matt Orr, Charlene Roehl, Sean Shipley, Julie Tarrant, Niki Tolani, and Anne Will. And we salute as well the many other students who have taught us over the years how to be better classroom colleagues. In many subtle ways, their voices are everywhere present in this text.

Finally, we have been instructed and guided by extraordinarily astute reviewers, with whom we have been in conversation throughout this project. We thank Linda Adler-Kassner, University of Minnesota; Janice Albert, Las Positas College; Marilyn L. Allison, Vanderbilt University; Kit Andrews, Western Oregon State College; Leslie Babcox, Lehigh University; Beulah P. Baker, Taylor University; Janet D. Ball, University of Southern California; James E. Barcus, Baylor University; Jeanette Struble Blair, Gannon University; Joanna Brooks, University of California at Los Angeles; Addison Bross, Lehigh University; Tiem Brown, Las Positas College, Jane L. Burgstaler, Rochester Community College; Audrey Caldwell, Alvernia College; Andrew Conrad, Mercer County Community College; Sandra Creech, Palomar College; L. L. Dickson, Northern Kentucky University; Michael G. Ditmore, Pepperdine University; Donna Dunbar-Odom, East Texas State University; Kaye Foster, Pitzer College; Gregory W. Fowler, Pennsylvania State University at Erie-Behrend College; Judith G. Gardner, University of Texas at San Antonio; Bruce Gatenby, Idaho State University; Karen Gersten, Roosevelt University; Carol Golliher, Victor Valley College; Margaret Baker Graham, Iowa State University; Paul Hanstedt, Ohio State University; Paul Heilker, Virginia Polytechnic Institute and State University; Will Hochman, University of Southern Colorado; Maurice Hunt, Baylor University; Susan Hunter,

Kennesaw State College; Darryl Johnson, St. Cloud State University; Michael Keller, South Dakota State University; Katy Koenen, Seattle University; Miriamne Krummel, Lehigh University; Lita Kurth, Santa Clara University; Carla La Greca, Marist College; Barbara M. Langheim, University of Cincinnati; Anne Lawday, Manhattanville College; Ed Lotto, Lehigh University; Paul D. Mahaffey, University of Montevallo; Sandra Mahoney, University of the Pacific; Darrin McGraw, University of California at Los Angeles; Patrick McKercher, Las Positas College; Holly Mickelson, Purdue University; Cynthia Moore, University of Louisville; Rolf Norgaard, University of Colorado at Boulder; Elizabeth Pittenger, Florida International University; Judith Remmes, Las Positas College; Cynthia Scheinberg, Mills College; Juanita M. Smart, Washington State University; Penny L. Smith, Gannon University; Helen Strait, University of Texas at San Antonio; Mark Vogel, Appalachian State University; Michele S. Ware, Wake Forest University; Jerri Lynn Williams, West Texas A & M University; Kenneth Wolfskill, Chowan College; Lorna Wood, Auburn University; John Woznicki, Lehigh University; and Joseph Zepetello, Ulster County Community College. They have consistently joined in and talked back to us, providing a richly textured dialogue we hope these pages reflect.

Andrea A. Lunsford
John J. Ruszkiewicz

Profiles of the Editors
and Student Commentators

Throughout *The Presence of Others,* you will read the comments of the editors who chose the selections and wrote the introductions. You will also meet two student editors—one from The Ohio State University, the other from The University of Texas at Austin—and learn their opinions. To give perspective to their sometimes strong, sometimes controversial remarks, we include the following brief self-portraits of Andrea A. Lunsford (A.L.), John J. Ruszkiewicz (J.R.), Teresa Essman (T.E.), and Joshua G. Rushing (J.G.R.). Use these biographies to help you read particular introductions, commentaries, or afterwords with more awareness of the editors' experiences, sensitivities, and blind spots. Think, too, about how your own ideas and beliefs have been shaped by your upbringing, communities, and education.

ANDREA A. LUNSFORD I was born in Oklahoma and have lived in Maryland, Florida, Texas, Washington, Ohio, and British Columbia, yet when I think of "home" I think of the soft rolling foothills of the Smoky Mountains in eastern Tennessee. The hills there are full of Cunninghams, and my granny, Rosa Mae Iowa Brewer Cunningham, and her husband, William Franklin, seemed to know all of them. Like many people in this region, my mother's folks claimed Scottish descent. Indeed, when I later traveled to Scotland, I discovered that many of the songs we sang on my grandparents' big porch were Scottish.

The only one of her large family to enjoy postsecondary education, my Mom graduated with training in teaching and in French from Maryville College in Tennessee. An uncle helped pay her way to school, and it was on a visit to see him that she met my father, another Scottish descendant, Gordon Grady Abernethy. His college education cut short by World War II, Dad gave up his goal of following his father into dentistry and instead took examinations to become a certified public accountant. In hard times, he and my mother left Oklahoma and settled near her family, where Dad got a job with a defense contractor at Oak Ridge. Mama taught briefly and then stayed home with me and, later, with my two sisters and brother. I played in a special playhouse I built in the woods, spent weekends with my grandparents and dozens of Cunningham cousins, and alternated attending my grandparents' Baptist Church (where they baptized my cousins by plunging them into a river) and my parents' Presbyterian Church, where baptisms seemed like a snap. On occasional Sundays, I got to visit a sister church whose congregation was black, where the music was mesmerizing, and where I first began to recognize this country's legacy of segregation and racism. My family, I learned, was proud to have fought for the North, although supporting the Union's cause did not exempt them—or me—from that legacy.

We read a lot in Sunday School and at Summer Bible School, and at home as well. There I had the luxury of receiving books as gifts, especially from my father's sister, and of being read to often: *Gulliver's Travels* as it appeared in *The Book of Knowledge* (our family's one encyclopedia), Joseph and His Coat of Many Colors from Hurlbut's *Stories of the Bible,* Tigger and Roo and Christopher Robin from A. A. Milne, and poems from *A Child's Garden of Verses* are among my earliest memories of texts that grew, over the years, into an animated chorus of voices I still carry with me. Later, I read all of the Nancy Drew, Hardy Boys, and Cherry Ames Senior Nurse series, to be regularly punished for reading in school when I should have been doing something else. Like many young women, I was often "lost in a book," living in a world of heroines and heroes and happy endings. Only slowly and painfully did I come to question the master plot most of these stories reproduced, to realize that endings are never altogether happy and that the roles I play in my own story have been in some important senses scripted by systems beyond my control.

My father wanted me to begin secretarial work after high school, but when I won a small scholarship and got a student job, he and my mother agreed to help me attend our state school, the University of Florida. I graduated with honors but was encouraged by my (male) advisor not to pursue graduate school but rather to "go home and have babies." Instead, I became a teacher, a reasonable job for a woman to aspire to in 1965. Only seven years later did I gather my courage to apply to graduate school after all—and to pursue a Ph.D. Teaching in high school, at a two-year college (Hillsborough Community College in Tampa), and as a graduate assistant helped me reaffirm my commitment to a career in education and introduced me to the concerns that have occupied my professional life ever since: What can I know and learn through my relationships with others? How do people develop as readers and writers? What is the connection between teaching and learning? What does it mean, as the twentieth century draws to a close, to be fully literate?

I pursued these questions in graduate school at Ohio State and beyond, all the while trying to live through two marriages and the loss of my granny, of both my parents, of my younger brother, and, most recently, of a much-loved aunt, Elizabeth McKinsey. Such experiences have led me to think hard not only about the burdens every human life entails but also about the privileges my status as a white, relatively middle class woman has afforded me. These privileges are considerable, and I do not wish to forget them. In addition, I have enjoyed the support of a vital network of women friends and colleagues. Thanks in large measure to them, I am now a professor in a large research university, and I savor the time I can spend with those I love (especially Lisa Ede, my sisters, their children, and my friend and partner William), and I am somewhat able to indulge my desire to experience as much of the world as possible. I even have season tickets to Ohio State basketball and football games (no mean feat in the state of Ohio), which I attend regularly with my colleague and friend Beverly Moss. These relationships—and my very special relationship with my students—have added to the chorus of animated voices I carry with me always.

These and other formative relationships and experiences have helped me learn a lesson that informs my teaching, my life, and my work on this book: that where you stand influences in great measure what you can see. My college advisor, standing as he did in an all-white male professoriate, couldn't quite "see" a young woman joining this elite group, even as a student. My parents, standing as they did in a lower middle class, single-income family with vivid memories of the depression, couldn't easily "see" beyond the desire for their oldest daughter to get a good, steady job as soon as possible. And I, standing where *I* do now, am not able to "see" through my students' eyes, to experience the world as they experience it.

Keeping this point in mind leads me to two acts that are by now habitual with me: examining where I stand, with all that implies about inevitably partial vision and perspective; and asking myself where others stand as well. So I came to this textbook project with John, my friend of almost 25 years now, with at least one specific agenda item: to look as carefully and respectfully as I could at his perspective, at where he stands, and to do the same thing for myself and for every voice included in this text. Such acts are necessary, I believe, before I can say that my opinions are fully considered. My view will always be heavily informed by where I stand. But insofar as I am able to entertain other points of view, I have a chance to understand my own better and to broaden my point of view as well.

JOHN J. RUSZKIEWICZ   My grandparents never spoke much about their reasons for emigrating from eastern Europe earlier this century; their grounds for starting new lives in the United States must have seemed self-evident. Moreover, like the immigrants Crèvecoeur describes in this anthology, they did willingly abandon those "old countries." Only rarely would I hear them talk nostalgically about the lands they left behind. So I'm a second-generation American with roots in, but no strong ties to, Slovakia, Poland, and Ukraine.

My father and mother were both born in rural Pennsylvania, my dad with five brothers and sisters, my mom with seven—eight if you count the infant boy who died of measles. Both my grandfathers mined coal in western Pennsylvania, as did several uncles—a dangerous and difficult living. After World War II, my parents moved to Cleveland, where jobs were more plentiful, and my Dad began a thirty-year stretch at Carling's Brewery. I did my share of manual labor, too, for a short time working in a tool-and-die factory, even paying dues to the Teamsters.

But my blue-collar stints were merely summer jobs between college semesters. Education would be my generation's ticket to the American dream. My parents never allowed my brother (who became a physician) or me to think we had any choice but college. We attended parochial schools, where headstrong nuns and priests introduced us to learning, moral responsibility, and culture. (By eighth grade, students at Saint Benedict's elementary school could sing three High Masses and two Requiems, one of those services in Gregorian chant. We knew what most of the Latin words meant, too.) As grade-schoolers, we had homework—hours of it—every night. High school was the same, only tougher. I didn't have a free period in high school until the semester I graduated, and I'm still thankful for that rigor.

The ethnic neighborhood in Cleveland where I grew up in the 1950s is now considered inner city. It was very much *in the city* when I lived there, too, but a nine- or ten-year-old could safely trudge to church alone at 6:00 A.M. to serve Mass or ride the rapid transit downtown to see a baseball game. I did so, often. In the long, hot summer of 1966, however, Cleveland erupted in racial riots. From my front porch, I could watch the fires.

I come from a family of Democrats—my gregarious mother, far more interested in people than issues, a party worker in Cleveland's Twenty-ninth Ward. One of my first political memories is that of watching John F. Kennedy parade down Euclid Avenue in 1960 during his presidential campaign. But frankly, I was more interested in the new Chrysler convertible ferrying the portly governor of Ohio. I have retained my fondness for old Chryslers—and just about anything else with four wheels.

The first presidential candidate I voted for was George McGovern, in 1972, but what could you expect from a kid who spent high school listening to Bob Dylan and who went to college in the 1960s? In fact, it was during an antiwar rally at St. Vincent College in Latrobe, Pennsylvania, that my drift to the political right began. I had read enough about the history of Vietnam to know that the communist Viet Cong were no angels, but the people at that demonstration believed they were. A professor of physics delivered an impassioned anti-American speech filled with what I knew to be falsehoods, but no one seemed to care. That moment still resonates, after all these years.

Despite the activist times, my college days remained focused on academic subjects—philosophy, history, literature, and cinema. St. Vincent's was small enough to nurture easy commerce among disciplines. I knew faculty from every field, and my roommates were all science majors with views of the world different from my own. Debate was intense, frequent, and good-natured. Emotionally I leaned left, but intellectually I found, time and again, that conservative writers described the world more accurately for me. They still do.

Politics didn't matter much in graduate school at Ohio State in the mid-1970s—although I was the only Ph.D. candidate in English who would admit to voting for Gerald Ford. My interests then were *Beowulf,* Shakespeare, and rhetoric. I met my coauthor, Andrea Lunsford, during my first term at Ohio State in an Old English class; we graduated on the same day five years later.

Today I consider myself an academic and political conservative. Where I work, that makes me a member of the counterculture, a role I now frankly enjoy. There aren't many conservatives among humanities professors in American universities, and that's a shame because the academy would be a richer place were it more genuinely diverse. Politically and intellectually, I find myself in much greater sympathy with Jefferson, Madison, and Burke (Edmund, not Kenneth) than with Rousseau, Marx, Freud, or Foucault. I voted twice for Ronald Reagan, and in my office hangs a poster of Margaret Thatcher given to me by a student. It scares the daylights out of some colleagues. My professional friends are mainly Democrats or worse, but I respect them. They sometimes tell me that they are surprised to find me so reasonable, being a Republican and all. I tell them they need to meet—and hire—more Republicans.

Like any good conservative, I prefer to keep my life simple; I could be content with a good truck, a sensible dog, and a capable racquetball partner. But for the past twenty years, I've been teaching at the University of Texas at Austin, where life is rarely dull or simple. In the past I've been embroiled in controversies over political correctness; today my campus concerns are chiefly technological, as the new Division of Rhetoric and Composition where I work moves toward offering a majority of its courses in networked electronic environments. Never have I seen more rapid or exciting change in the classroom for both students and faculty.

And it's on classroom matters that my coeditor Andrea and I are most likely to agree, even if, from abortion to higher taxes on productive people, our politics differ. So when I proposed an anthology for writing classes that would broaden the range of readings available to students and make the political persuasion of the editors a part of the package, Andrea agreed to the project. She said it embodied the feminist concept of "situated knowledge." Well, sure, if that makes her happy. I'm no theorist. I was just glad to have the privilege and pleasure of working with my good friend and political other.

TERESA ESSMAN   Someone once said, "Curiosity killed the cat." That makes me very glad I'm not a cat, for as long as I can remember, I have possessed an innate curiosity about the things around me. As a child, I plagued my Mom with questions like "Why are skillets black?" She would laugh and reply, "To make little girls ask questions." Now, as I finish my first year at Ohio State University, I realize my curiosity has yet to fade.

This curiosity is the driving force behind my desire to learn about the people around me, especially about what they value most. One of my pet peeves is people who believe in something simply because they think they should or because their parents believed it. My parents encouraged me to think for myself and form my own opinions, and hardly ever pushed their own viewpoints on me. Perhaps it is because of this upbringing that I have little patience with people who cling self-righteously to an idea but are unable to back it up with evidence.

When I arrived at college, I was eager to learn the thoughts and beliefs of people around me. In my dormitory, my friends and I often get into some very interesting debates about anything and everything from abortion to women's roles in the church. I come from a town in central Ohio that, at the risk of making an understatement, is not a very diverse place. There was one African American in the district while I was in high school, and the rest of the population consisted primarily of white, middle-class farmers. Beginning my college education was a wonderful experience; suddenly I encountered people from many backgrounds who held many different perspectives on issues I had previously considered cut and dried. For instance, I had thought it was commonly accepted that women becoming Catholic priests was a step in the right direction. Personally, if I wanted to become a priest, I would be rather annoyed with anyone who told me I wasn't competent for the position simply because I was a woman. However, a friend I met in college completely disagrees with the concept, declaring that it goes against tradition. In any case, these and other debates have helped reinforce or led me to revise my own views and better understand the views of others.

Now, as a college student, I am working toward a career I have been curious about since I was a child. Through numerous early-life encounters with hospital emergency rooms, I earned great respect for the medical profession. And at age nine, I spent a few weeks in the hospital recovering from an emergency appendectomy. While there I met a wonderful intern; he did song and dance and magic shows, and even brought me a toy pinball game. Nothing is more wonderful to a kid in a hospital than someone who cares enough to make his or her day a little brighter. Ever curious, I asked him on one visit what made him want to be a doctor. He said he had always wanted to help people out, and medicine was where he could be the best at making a difference. Looking back, I think his answer had a profound effect on me. I have always wanted to help people, and I find medicine intriguing. Once again, my curiosity about the world around me changed the course of my life. However, the same hospital stay bred a gripping fear of needles, so I decided to find a career that did not involve such instruments.

My curiosity about medicine prompted me to become a volunteer at Children's Hospital in Columbus. There I had the opportunity to watch a physical therapist work with a five-year-old burn patient who suffered from severe muscle damage. The therapist was painstakingly gentle with the girl, and watching her in action sparked an interest in me. Since then, my goal has been to become a physical therapist, ultimately to work with children.

In my desire to try everything imaginable, I have found a few other loves. I absolutely adore my alto saxophone, affectionately named Bertha. She has been with me for years, and I plan to play her for many more to come. I also sing with the Symphonic Choir at Ohio State and enjoy acting in small theater plays and musicals. I would like to continue the family tradition and try out for the Ohio State marching band; unfortunately, the all-brass organization refuses to recognize the wonderful qualities of woodwinds. Another dream is to one day own and operate my own llama ranch. When I mention this, most people graciously inform me that llamas spit (as if I didn't already know). I would rather look on the bright side and remember that llamas hum when happy and are very affectionate animals. I once read an article about a llama rancher who owned a llama that could hum a perfect B-flat when content. I would also love to marry a wonderful person and have two or three children. How I will ever find time to do it all, I don't know yet.

One of my favorite pastimes is to curl up with a good book. When I was a child, stories helped pass the time on long trips to Grandma's house. Not surprisingly, the *Curious George* books were some of my favorites. I also loved the whimsical poems of Shel Silverstein, and the world lost a wonderful storyteller when Dr. Seuss left us. Since then, my horizons have expanded to mysteries, most likely because of my ongoing desire to figure things out. I love trying to uncover the culprit before the hero or heroine does. Books will always be my old friends, and I know I will love to read as long as I am capable of doing so.

I have no idea exactly what the future holds. But as I have grown older, my curiosity has led me in several different directions, and that trend will undoubtedly continue.

JOSHUA G. RUSHING Although I was made in Japan (conceived on a parental vacation), I cannot claim to be anything other than a pure Texan—as well as a father, husband, marine, and full-time college student. That may sound like a great deal for a twenty-four-year-old to bear, but the truth is I don't bear the load at all—*they,* my family and corps, carry me. During my short time in the corps, six years, I have been fortunate to be granted extended visits to exotic locations such as Europe, the Middle East, and the Arctic Circle. In addition to getting to see the world, I have enjoyed long stays in coastal North Carolina, where I was stationed for almost four years, and New Orleans, my last duty station before I moved to Austin. But no matter where I am, in my soul a neon Lone Star perpetually flashes to the rhythm of a Willie Nelson tune.

That I refer to my "soul" seems strange, considering my pragmatic agnosticism. Having previously staked claims on both sides of the divine fence (for which I wish there were a saddle), I have been forced between a rock (the lack of empirical evidence for the existence of God, hence the need for faith) and a hard place (the same void of conclusive proof that there is not a God, hence the same need for faith).

Although I do not necessarily believe in a God, I do believe that I have been blessed with a fabulous family. My wife makes me look forward to waking up in the morning next to her, and my four-year-old son is a well-spring of new ideas and perspectives (for example: "What kind of animal is Gumby?"). Speaking of animals, our family also includes a yellow Labrador puppy named Cuervo.

I tend to be no more polar in politics than I am in religion. My centrist beliefs might make it seem as though I lead a fairly dull life when it comes to opinions, but, on the contrary, I have found that practicing the fine and delicate art of fence-riding allows me to take sides in more arguments than William F. Buckley Jr. My niche affords me the freedom to play the incessant devil's advocate. One would be hard pressed to find an issue on which I could not disagree with people—no matter what side of the argument they're on. Much to my wife's frustration, daily debating has become my mental aerobics. Having said that, I must admit that the inevitable responsibilities of life have been swaying me from my well-worn tracks down the middle. As I grow older, my political views are starting to lean to the right—a predictable trend that, in my experience, affects most people.

Glancing to the future, I still wonder what I will be when I grow up. I have no clue and, truthfully, not even a desire for a particular profession. I have always been envious of peers who have known since they were four that they wanted to be doctors and at my age are now graduating from medical school. My strongest hopes are to be a good father and husband; besides that I think I will abide by the old Scottish proverb: "Be happy while you're living for you're a long while dead."

On Reading
and Thinking Critically

Introduction

THIS IS A BOOK for and about reading. Its pages contain voices joined in conversation and debate over issues important to all of us: What, how, and under what circumstances should we learn and become educated? Who are we as individuals and as members of various groups and cultures? What do we believe? How do we choose to live? In the conversations surrounding these issues, the editors of this book have joined in, and you will find our reasons for choosing particular selections and our thoughts about these selections running throughout this text. Its primary aim, however, is to invite *you* to join in this conversation, to add your voice to the discussion in these pages. Doing so invites you to assume the perspective of a critical reader.

*   *   *

WHAT IS CRITICAL READING?

If you've been wondering what critical reading is, you're already demonstrating one of the hallmarks of a critical reader: a questioning attitude, one that probes for definitions, explanations, proofs, and assumptions. Perhaps we can further clarify what we mean by critical reading by focusing on two everyday uses of the word *critical*. In its most common usage, *critical* means acting like a critic, as in "many voters have been highly critical of Clinton's economic policies," or "some members of the African American community have been critical of what they see as Spike Lee's appropriation of Malcolm X." In this sense of the word, *critical* suggests that you have explored an issue (like an economic policy or a particular movie) and are ready to evaluate it, to see whether and how it meets your standards. But *critical* is also used to denote something of singular importance, as in "critical care unit" or a "critical point in negotiations." In this sense of the word, *critical* suggests that you attach importance to what you are examining and to your own critical responses to it. For the purposes of this text, then, critical readers are those who bring all their powers to bear on understanding, analyzing, and evaluating some important question, issue, or perspective contained in a piece of writing. Critical readers, in other words, do not accept things blindly or "at face value," but instead look at them from a variety of perspectives, saying both *yes* and *no* to them until they are ready to take their own stance on the issues.

Saying Yes, No, and Maybe

The chapters of this text will allow you many chances to practice saying *yes* and *no*—and sometimes *maybe*—to ideas. As you read the selections in chapter 3, Education, for example, you will encounter widely varying perspectives on whom and what higher education is for as well as what its content should be. When you read Adrienne Rich's "What Does a Woman Need to Know?" her answers to this question may seem perfectly reasonable to you; you find you can understand her point of view and say *yes* to her ideas. But then you begin to wonder about them and to say, well, *maybe,* or even to say *no.* Are Rich's ideas appropriate for the 1990s, and do they respond to the problems you think women need to confront? Are the charges she brings fair and accurate? All of these acts—saying *yes, maybe,* and/or *no*— are necessary for critical reading, for the kind of reading that is open to new ideas but that insists on thinking them through from every perspective.

Thus, critical reading is what you do when you need to understand the terms of a contract you are about to sign, decide which of several automobile financing plans will be best for you, master the material necessary to shine on an important examination, evaluate the arguments for or against a political proposal or candidate, or compare doctors' opinions about whether you should undergo surgery. It is the kind of reading Mortimer Adler is talking about when he says, "When [people] are in love and are reading a love letter, they read for all they are worth. They read every word three ways; they read between the lines and in the margins; they read the whole in terms of the parts, and each part in terms of the whole."

WHY BECOME A CRITICAL READER?

Given our definition of critical reading, the answer to this question is probably already obvious to you. Critical readers are "in on" the conversation surrounding any issue. They resist ready-made or hand-me-down opinions whenever they can. Much in our society makes such critical reading difficult; we are, after all, inundated with ready-made opinions on television and in other mass media as well as in educational, religious, political, and even family institutions. In fact, so many forces are at work to make up our minds for us that many people question whether we aren't fooling ourselves to think that we can control and use language at all, rather than the other way around.

You can probably think of instances in your own life that support this view. The bombardment of commercials at the movies, for example, tempts you to buy popcorn and Coca-Cola. Or you may be aware that educational labels like "honors" or "remedial" have dramatically affected your life. Many studies suggest that we tend to live up (or down) to such labels—for better or worse. This fact of modern life led one theorist of language to say that words we try to use or control are already "half-way in someone else's mouth," meaning that the words we use are already so weighed down with the meanings our society has given them that it is hard to do anything other than accept those meanings. It's hard, that is, for any one person to resist the lure of advertising or to reject the power of educational or social labels.

To some extent, this theory clearly rings true: we do not absolutely control the language we use or read. But the result of such a position is to give up trying to make your voice heard or to bring about any change. Why become a critical reader, then? To resist being controlled by other people's language, to exert some control of your own, to test your wits, to define for yourself your perspective on any issue, to contribute to the thoughts and actions related to those issues. You become a critical reader, in short, **to get involved in the conversation and to make your voice count.**

ARE YOU A CRITICAL READER?

Our guess is that you are already a critical reader when you need to be. You may want to take stock of your general reading habits, however, by answering the following questions. As a rule, when you are reading important material, do you

1. Read carefully, either with or without skimming first?
2. "Talk back" to what you are reading, noting what does or doesn't make sense, what seems right or wrong?
3. Ask questions as you read?
4. Take notes in the margins or on a separate sheet of paper?
5. Ask yourself why the writer takes the position he or she does?
6. Think about the writer's perspective—what his or her interests are in writing the piece?
7. Ask what larger social, economic, political, or other conditions may have influenced the creation of this piece of writing?
8. Consider what in your experience and background leads you to agree with or like, or to disagree with or dislike, the piece of writing?
9. Imagine other ways of looking at the subjects or ideas presented?
10. Summarize the gist of what you have read?
11. Compare what you're reading with other things you have read about the subject?

If you've answered "yes" to most of these questions, you are already reading with a critical eye, and you will understand what we mean when we say reading is a partnership: the text in front of you has words set down, but you are the one who realizes the ideas in those words, tests them against what you know, and puts them to use in your life.

Examining Your Reading Habits   Take five or ten minutes to write a description of yourself as a reader. How do you usually approach a text that you want or need to understand? Do you usually practice critical reading habits? Why, or why not? Bring your description to class for discussion. Compare your description with those of two or three other students in your class, noting the ways in which your reading strategies are similar and/or different.

HOW CAN YOU BECOME A MORE CRITICAL READER?

If you have compared your notes on how you typically read with those of friends or classmates, you will probably have noticed some differences. Indeed, reading practices vary widely, and even highly skilled readers may differ dramatically in the approaches they take. The most effective and satisfying critical reading strategies for you may differ from those for your friends. In particular, your reading strategies are undoubtedly related to who you are, to your gender, age, cultural background, life experiences, prior reading experiences, even your eyesight. In addition, strategies for reading vary widely depending on purpose and situation: you might skim the ingredients listed on a food package just to check that it doesn't contain something you are allergic to, or you might pore slowly over the directions for connecting a modem to make sure that you don't make a mistake.

Thus, part of your job as a critical reader is to get to know your own preferred strategies, your own strengths and weaknesses, and to build on your strengths. While we can't know exactly what will be most effective for any one individual reader, then, we can offer some general guidelines you can experiment with. From them you should be able to design an individual blueprint for reading. We hope that these guidelines will help you when you tackle difficult reading material or material for which you have almost no background. In the annotated essays in chapters 3 through 10 of this book, you will find examples of most of these guidelines, written in the margins and in responses to those essays.

Previewing

- Determine your purpose for reading. Is it to gather information for a writing assignment? to determine whether a source will be useful for a research project? to study for an examination? to prepare for class discussion? to determine your own stance toward the topic—and what in your experience and background leads you to take that stance?

- Consider the title. What does it tell you about what is to come?
- Think about what you already know about the subject. What opinions do you hold on this subject? What major topics do you anticipate? What do you hope to learn? What other things about this topic have you read?
- What do you know about the author? What expertise does he or she have in the subject? What particular perspective on the subject might he or she hold?
- Look at how the text is structured. Are there subdivisions? Read over any headings. Skim the opening sentences of each paragraph.
- Decide what you think the main point or theme of the text will be.

Annotating

- Read carefully, marking places that are confusing or that you want to reread.
- Identify key points or arguments, important terms, recurring images, and interesting ideas, either by underlining them in the text or by making notes in the margin.
- Note any statements you question or disagree with and any counter-evidence or counterarguments that occur to you.
- Note any sources used in the text.

Summarizing

- Summarize the main points. Do they match your expectations?
- Jot down any points you want to remember, questions you want to raise, and ideas for how you may use this material.

Analyzing

- Identify evidence that supports the main argument or illustrates the main point. Is it sufficient to convince you? Is there any evidence that seems to contradict the author's point?
- Identify the writer's underlying assumptions about the subject, where he or she is "coming from" on this issue.
- Ask what may have led the author to this position.

- Question the sources used. Ask yourself whether the source is timely, whether it has sufficient expertise, and whether its perspective or position on the subject is different from yours or from others you know and respect. If so, why?
- Think of other points of view on this topic, perhaps from other things you have read or seen. Is the author's perspective the most persuasive— and why?

Rereading

- Reread quickly to be sure you have understood the reading.
- Identify the author's purpose(s). Were those purposes accomplished?
- Determine whether the questions you had during the first reading have been answered.

Responding

- What one question would you like to ask the writer? How do you think the writer might respond?
- Think about the reading as a whole. What did you like best about it? What puzzled or irritated you? What caused you to like or dislike the piece? Were your expectations met? If not, why not? What more would you like to know about the subject?
- Note what you have learned about effective writing from this reading.
- If you keep a reading log, record these notes there. (For three example reading log entries, turn to p. 192.)

Examining Your Critical Literacy   To practice reading a text critically, turn to one of the texts in this book that is *not* annotated and analyze the piece using the guidelines for thinking and reading critically. For an example of one student's critical response to a reading, see pp. 32–34.

READING VISUAL TEXTS

- If the visual text is a chart, graph, illustration, or advertisement, what information does it convey?
- Does it present numbers or statistics? Are these numbers easier to comprehend because of the visual presentation?

- Does it illustrate a trend or change? Emphasize the change fairly or exaggerate it?
- Does it highlight particular information (a name, a face) to attract your attention?
- How does the ad make you notice and perhaps remember the product or idea it is selling?
- How is the visual text composed?
- What is your eye drawn to? Why?
- What is in the foreground? What is in the background?
- What is in focus, what out of focus? Is the central part of the image blended into the visual text, or is it greatly contrasted?
- What is placed high in the image? What is placed low? to the left? to the right? (Remember that our eyes are trained to "read" from top to bottom, left to right.)
- How is light used? color?
- What details are included or emphasized? What details are omitted or deemphasized?
- What values does the visual text express? What ideals is the image conveying? Consider family values, the good life, love and harmony, success, beauty, power, pleasure, sex appeal, youth, adventure—what else? Is the visual text reinforcing or questioning these values?
- Does the image evoke individuals or ideas that are either very positive or very negative?
- What emotions does the visual text evoke—desire, envy, empathy, guilt? What else? What effect does the image have on you?
- Is anything repeated, intensified, or exaggerated? Look for anything in the image that is made to seem "supernormal" or idealized. What effects does the exaggeration have on you as a reader?
- Is anything downplayed or ambiguous, confusing or distracting, in the visual text?
- Does the image use humor or excess emotion? How does this downplay or distract you from the image's larger purpose?
- What role does ambiguity or suggestion play in the image? Does such ambiguity call on the viewer to fill in some gaps? If so, to what effect?
- What is the role of any printed text that accompanies the image? How does it clarify or reinforce (or perhaps *not* reinforce) the message of the visual text?
- Why was the visual text created in the first place?

- What is the intent(s) of the image's producer?
- How effective or persuasive is the visual for you as a reader?

Examining Your Visual Literacy   To try reading a visual text critically, turn to the advertisement illustrated on p. 293. Then use the guidelines for reading visuals to guide you in a thorough analysis of this particular visual text. Take careful notes during your analysis and bring them to class for discussion.

WHAT DOES READING HAVE TO DO WITH WRITING?

In one sense, critical reading *is* writing. That is, as you read carefully, asking questions and talking back to a text, you inevitably create your own version of the text. Even if that interpretation is not written down on paper, it is "written" in your mind, composed and put into words you can understand and remember. And if you add some of your own ideas—or those you and classmates develop together—to what you read, you can build a new text altogether, one you may later write down.

As our society uses electronic texts more often, in fact, reading and writing will almost certainly become even more intertwined. The "reader" of interactive fiction or a hypertext, for instance, may write part of the text. Those on electronic bulletin boards or conferences may write their own ideas and responses into what they are reading on the screen, something first written by another reader.

But critical reading is also closely related to your own writing, because it enables you to assess what you have written, to say *yes* and *no* and *maybe* to your own ideas—to evaluate the logic of your prose, the effectiveness of your word choice, the degree to which you have gotten your points across. In short, you can apply these same reading strategies to your own writing, to see your own words with a critical eye. Thus, reading critically and writing effectively become reciprocal activities, strengthening each other as you learn to use language more powerfully.

Because we are convinced that reading and writing are closely related, we want this text to offer you many opportunities for moving back and forth from reading to writing to reading. We will, in fact, invite you to experiment with a number of kinds of writing as you read your way into the conversations taking place in the chapters that follow. We turn now, therefore, to chapter 2, From Reading to Writing, for an overview of the writing practices this book invites you to experience.

From Reading to Writing

Introduction

IN SPITE OF ALL the social forces that influence and shape your reading practices, no one can predict precisely how you will respond to what you read. A pamphlet arriving in the mail may persuade you to vote for or against a ballot proposition; a slick brochure might convince you to buy a health insurance policy or to complain about false advertising to a state regulatory agency. A dull book could provide exercise for your throwing arm. A great book might change your life. Clearly, reading can lead to action.

One action that evolves naturally from reading is writing. When you react to something you read by writing something of your own, you preserve and extend ideas. You enter a conversation someone else has started and invite still other readers to join you. Sometimes the connections you'll make between your reading and yourself will be close and personal. At other times, you'll be bridging much wider gaps, linking remote historical epochs, examining works from different cultures, or reconciling positions that at first seem incompatible.

• • •

WRITING TO LEARN

You will have many occasions in college to write. Almost every class requires some written work, although some tasks may seem so routine that you may not even think of them as "writing." Yet even the most routine forms of writing can help fix ideas in your mind or suggest relationships you hadn't considered before. Here are some types of writing common to college work, writing that can help you be a more effective student: class notes, lab notes, reading notes and annotations, comments on other students' work, reading or writing log entries, abstracts of articles, summaries, outlines, and essay examinations. These writings, if you are systematic and careful about them, can help you learn course material—and retain what you learn.

LEARNING TO WRITE EFFECTIVELY

Many of your college courses will ask you to prepare formal essays or other extended pieces of writing related to what you read, hear, or learn. The following guidelines are designed to help you respond effectively to such assignments.

Considering the Assignment

Find out as much as you can about an assignment before starting to write.

- Analyze a writing project carefully. Look for key words in the assignment, such as *analyze, summarize, compare, contrast, illustrate, argue, defend, refute, persuade,* and so on.
- If you don't understand an assignment, ask your instructor for clarification.
- Pay attention to limits on length and time. The length of an assignment will surely influence the focus and thesis of any paper. In general, the shorter the piece, the narrower its focus will need to be.
- Plan your time to allow for all necessary reading, thinking, drafting, and editing.

Considering Purpose and Audience

Beyond what the assignment itself dictates, consider the larger purpose of the writing. A piece that is largely informative (such as a report) will be somewhat different from one that takes an argumentative stance (such as an editorial). What does the writing have to accomplish to be successful? Your responses to that question will help determine the form, organization, tone, style, and length of your writing. Here are some other questions to help you think about purpose:

- Does the assignment itself specify a purpose?
- What does your instructor expect you to do in this assignment? What do you need to do to meet those expectations?
- How do you want readers to react to your writing? Do you want them to be entertained? Should they learn something? Should they be moved to action?
- Where might you like to have this piece published?

Consider also who will read your piece. The primary audience for your college writing may be your instructors, but *they* may have in mind some other specific audience—your classmates, for example, or the general public.

Following are some questions that can help identify key characteristics of your audience:

- Do your readers belong to some identifiable group: college students, Democrats, women, parents, sociologists?
- How would you characterize your readers? What values and principles do you hold in common with them? What differences are there between you?
- Are your readers likely to know more or less than you do about your subject? What background information do you need to provide?
- Are your readers likely to be engaged by your subject, or do you have to win their attention?
- Are your readers likely to be favorable, neutral, or hostile to your positions?
- Should you use simple, general, or technical language?
- Are you addressing more than one audience? If so, do any of the audiences seem incompatible?

Generating Ideas and Making Plans

You don't need to know what you are going to say before you begin writing. Many experienced writers, in fact, report that their best ideas emerge *during* writing, and others say they make elaborate plans only to see them go awry as they write. Even so, all writers must start somewhere. You may find some of the following techniques helpful in discovering ideas:

- Read any assigned material carefully, annotating key information, summarizing main points, and noting connections among readings.
- Try specific techniques for developing ideas, such as freewriting, brainstorming, or journal writing.
- Get more information—from the library, from data banks, from professional organizations, from friends or instructors, and so on.
- Do field research. Conduct a survey or some interviews.
- Get involved in discussions about your subject. Talk to people. Listen to their ideas and opinions.
- Draw on your personal experiences, especially when dealing with social, cultural, and political issues. *Your* experience counts.

Once you have ideas, sketch out a plan, a scheme to make a project manageable. Here are some ways of working out a plan:

- Fix on a tentative thesis statement or main point you want to prove, defend, or illustrate. Think of it as a promise to your readers.
- Prepare a scratch outline by listing the major ideas you want to cover and then arranging them in an order that makes sense to you.
- Construct a formal outline if you find such devices useful.
- Try a "zero draft"—a quick, discardable version of an essay to help you focus on the major issues.

Drafting

Drafting is the point in the writing process when words are put down on the page or up on the screen. The cold swimming hole approach works best for some writers: just plunge in. After all, you can't do much as a writer until you produce some words. In case you don't much like cold water, however, here's some other advice for getting started on a first draft:

- Control your expectations. No one expects a first draft to be perfect. In fact, no one expects a final draft to be the last word on any subject. So take it easy.
- Skip the introduction if you find yourself stuck on the opening sentences. Start somewhere else, perhaps with an idea you are especially eager to develop. Then write another portion of the essay, and then another. You can put all the parts together later; if you are working on a computer, you'll need only a few keystrokes.
- Set some reasonable production goals, especially for longer projects. Commit yourself to writing one or two pages before getting up from your desk, and try to stop at a point where you feel confident about what comes next. That way, beginning again will be easier. Reward yourself when you meet your goal.
- Try a quick draft: sketch out the full essay without stopping.

Getting—and Giving—Feedback

Seek responses from other readers. Within whatever guidelines your instructor establishes, ask classmates, friends, or any potential readers for their reactions to your drafts. Here are some guidelines you can ask your readers to use in reviewing your draft:

- Begin by describing objectively what you think the draft is saying. That description might prove enlightening to the author.
- Point out anything that is confusing or unclear.

- What is the writer's attitude toward the topic? How do you know?
- Describe what is most memorable.
- Focus initially on big issues: What is its intended purpose? Who is its desired audience? How is it organized? What are its arguments? its examples and illustrations?
- List the strengths of the draft. How can they be enhanced?
- List the weaknesses. How might they be eliminated or minimized?
- Suggest specific revisions. What more do you as one reader want or need to know? Which other arguments or ideas should be considered?

Revising

Respond to comments on a first draft by looking at the entire project anew. Reshape the project as much as necessary to serve your purpose, your subject matter, and your readers. Here are some specific suggestions for revising:

- To gain perspective, put the draft aside for a day or two.
- Be as tough minded as you can about the condition of a draft. Discard whole paragraphs or pages when they simply don't work. Don't just tinker or look for the easiest way of salvaging weak material. You may need a new thesis or a completely different structure.
- Consider very carefully any response you've received.
- Consider alternative plans for organization. Be flexible.
- Consider the overall strategy of the essay. Might a different point of view or tone make it more effective?
- Review your thesis or main idea. Does it achieve the purpose you had in mind? Is the thesis fully explained and supported?
- Reconsider whether you know enough about your subject to write about it with authority. If not, go back to your sources or do more reading.
- Pay attention to transitions. You can help your readers with a few careful phrases that point to where you're going—or where you've been.

Editing

Once you've revised your draft, it's time to edit your work by attending carefully to the structure of paragraphs, the shape of sentences, the choice of words, and the conventions of punctuation and mechanics.

- Reconsider openings and closings. In academic writing, openings should capture the reader's attention and identify key points, while conclusions should summarize ideas and draw implications.
- Read your draft aloud, paying attention to the length, variety, rhythm, and coherence of sentences.
- Look for wordiness. Stylistically, nothing hurts an essay more than empty phrases.
- Consider your vocabulary for appropriateness. Is it appropriate to use contractions or slang or dialect? Do any technical terms need defining?
- Check any documentation of sources for the correct form. Reconsider also the way you incorporate sources—do you quote, paraphrase, and summarize appropriately? Do you weave quotations smoothly into your own text?
- Check for problems of grammar and usage, particularly any that have caused you problems in the past.
- For detailed examples and answers to questions of grammar, usage, and style, check a handbook.
- Find a suitable title. For most academic work, titles should provide clear descriptions of the contents.

Preparing the Final Copy

Now is the time to assemble and check your final copy.

- Review the assignment to be sure you have met all requirements of form. Does your instructor want a title page? an outline? Must the paper be typed?
- Be sure your name is on the essay in the proper place(s).
- Paginate, and clip the pages together. (Do not staple them.)
- Proofread one last time for typographical errors, spelling errors, and other slips. If you have a spell checker, run it for a final check. If necessary, make minor last-minute corrections by hand.
- Make sure the essay is neatly written, typed, or printed.

AN ALPHABETICAL CATALOG OF THE WRITING ASSIGNMENTS IN THIS BOOK

Throughout *The Presence of Others* we invite you to respond to the readings we've selected, to join in conversation with all the people who've collaborated to write this book—writers, editors, reviewers, and students. Following is an alphabetical catalog of guidelines to the writing assignments you may be asked to do as you use this book.

Analyzing

Analytical writing puts ideas under scrutiny. To analyze a reading, examine its ideas systematically, questioning the validity of arguments, the accuracy of facts, the logical relationship of ideas, the fairness of conclusions, and the assumptions underlying them. Here are some suggestions for analyzing a reading:

- To begin, identify exactly what you want to analyze, from a paragraph to a full work.
- Note any preconceptions or assumptions you bring to the topic of your analysis. Think about how they may affect your analysis.
- Mark the text you are analyzing thoroughly. Annotate its margins, highlight key quotations, and circle terms you think are especially important.
- Divide the text into its main ideas, and look at each one carefully. What support exists for each idea?
- Look for connections between ideas. Are these connections clear and logical to you?
- Try to think of opposing points of view or alternative perspectives on the topic. Has the writer considered them fairly?

For an example of analysis, see the essay by Adrienne Rich (p. 44).

Writing a Rhetorical Analysis   A specific kind of analytical writing useful for scrutinizing a reading's purposes and strategies is rhetorical analysis. In its simplest form, rhetorical analysis explores two basic questions: what is the writer's purpose, and how is that purpose presented to an intended audience? Answers to these important contextual questions help readers appreciate the options that writers face and the possible reasons behind particular rhetorical choices. A rhetorical analysis looks at the particular strategies a writer uses to attain his or her goals and gauges their overall success. Rhetorical analysis can consider a writer's cultural, economic, social, or political contexts, and how they affect the reading and writing of the text.

Here are tips for examining a text rhetorically:

- Try to define the major purpose of the text, but understand that it may be composed for more than one reason. Identify these multiple purposes when you can, pointing out in your analysis where they may conflict. When possible, show where such conflicts may have affected the writer's choice of arguments, evidence, vocabulary, examples, and so on.

- Try to identify a primary audience and describe its expectations. What do members of the primary audience know about the subject and what do they need to know? How does the text address their expectations or needs?

- Identify any secondary audiences. How do their needs differ from those of the primary audience?

- Explore the author's attitude toward the topic. What is the author's stake in the subject?

- Explore the relationship of the author to the audience. Does he or she maintain a position of distance and authority or seek to "come close to" readers?

- Explain how the piece has been shaped by rhetorical concerns, including the complexity of the discussion, the detail, the author's tone and voice, the vocabulary choices, and the kinds of sentences.

For an example of a rhetorical analysis, see the essay by P. J. O'Rourke (p. 424).

Writing a Critical Analysis   A critical analysis may examine many of the same issues as those in a rhetorical analysis. But a critical analysis usually makes value judgments about the integrity of a text—its power and its reach.

Critical analysis looks carefully at the logic of a text, identifying its claims and assessing the premises and evidence that support those claims. Critical analysis seeks to answer questions such as these: Does the piece make a coherent claim? Are the assumptions behind the claim defensible? Are the connections among assumptions, claims, and evidence logical? Is the evidence presented sufficient and reliable? Is the text fair or is the author biased in a way that undermines the credibility of the piece?

Critical analysis also looks at the *success* of a text, at how persuasive it is, how well it makes emotional or ethical appeals, how successfully it moves or delights readers.

Here are some tips for examining a text critically:

- Understand the intended audience(s) and purpose(s). Consider the work's historical, social, and political contexts in some detail.

- Identify the claims, both stated and implied.

- Identify the premises behind the claims, and determine how those assumptions would be received by the intended reader(s).

- Examine the evidence for each claim. What are the sources of information? Study any statistics and how they are used. Consider the sources and reliability of polls and surveys.

- Explore the logic of the argument. Has the writer engaged in any logical fallacies? Consider, too, the rhetorical force of the evidence—is it sufficient? overwhelming?

- Consider the way the writer presents himself or herself. Does the writer make a persuasive, appealing case? Is he or she appropriately engaged in or deliberately removed from the piece?

- Consider the way the text makes its overall appeal. Is the format appropriate to its audience? Is it appropriately serious? humorous? academic? colloquial?

For an example of critical analysis, see the essay by Christina Hoff Sommers (p. 328).

Arguing

Among a writer's toughest jobs is making a persuasive argument, one that moves readers to reaffirm a commitment—or to consider changing their minds or taking action. Almost all the readings in this book contain arguments. As you work at reading these pieces, you may want to construct arguments of your own. Here are some suggestions for writing an effective academic argument:

- Develop a clear, carefully limited thesis to defend. This thesis will often evolve gradually as you learn more about your subject.

- Find various good reasons for someone to agree with the thesis. Support all statements with specific and appropriate evidence.

- Show that any evidence you have gathered is fair, appropriate, and accurate; that your various arguments support one another; and that they outweigh possible counterarguments.

- When building an argument from something you've read, regard that text and everything connected with it as potential evidence. This would include the language and style of the writer, his or her background and reputation, the time and place of publication, the reputation of the publisher, and so on.

- Quote from the piece carefully to demonstrate the points you are making. Bring the writer's voice into your side of the conversation.

- Appeal to the readers you are trying to convince by connecting your argument to subjects they are likely to know and care about. An effective argument stimulates thinking and conversation. It doesn't close off discussion or create instant enemies.

For examples of effective arguments, see the essays by Christian Zawodniak (p. 124) and J. Michael Bishop (p. 255).

Brainstorming

Brainstorming is an activity that can help start you thinking, record thoughts and impressions, and stockpile material for more formal kinds of writing. Basically, it consists of putting down ideas—about a reading, a writing topic, a problem to solve, whatever—as they come to mind.

You can certainly brainstorm alone, although it probably works better in a group. If you are working with a group, assign one person to jot down notes. You can brainstorm either as you read or immediately afterward. Here are some specific tips for brainstorming:

- List your thoughts as they occur to you. Put down whatever comes to mind; let your ideas flow. Prune and reorder ideas *later.*
- Try to include examples from your reading to develop your thoughts.
- Don't judge the quality of your brainstorming prematurely. Record your intuitions. Give yourself slack to explore ideas—even silly or out-landish ones.
- Once you've written all your thoughts down, look for connections among them. What conclusions can you draw about your position on the subject by looking at these connections?

Comparing and Contrasting

Strictly speaking, when you compare things, you are looking for similarities; when you contrast them, you are pointing out differences. Here are some suggestions for comparing and contrasting:

- Break your subject into parts or aspects that can be studied profitably. As the old saying goes, you don't want to compare apples and oranges.
- Pursue your analysis systematically, point by point. Group the comparisons or contrasts purposefully so that they make or support a point about your subject.
- Use appropriate transitional words and phrases. Readers can easily get lost if a writer jumps from one point of comparison or contrast to another without providing the necessary bridges.
- Be fair. Even when you are inclined to favor one side over another, be sure to consider the other side fairly.

The selections by Shelby Steele (p. 63) and Newt Gingrich (p. 576) provide examples of comparing and contrasting.

Defining

When asked to define a word or concept in a paragraph, you're usually expected to write an extended explanation of the term, accompanied by illustrations and examples. Terms can also be defined through descriptions of their components, descriptions of processes (how something works), or any appropriate combination of these methods. Here are some suggestions for defining:

- To define a term, place it within a larger category and then list features or characteristics that distinguish it from other items in that category: "A skyscraper is a building of unusual height."

- Then expand the simple definition by providing additional distinguishing details: "A skyscraper is a building of unusual height, most often supported by a steel skeleton and having many stories. The earliest skyscrapers appeared in American cities, especially Chicago and New York, late in the nineteenth century. The height of buildings was confined at first by construction techniques that required massive masonry walls and by the limits of elevator technology. The invention of steel skeletons that supported both floors and walls and the development of high-speed elevators made much taller buildings possible. Among the most famous skyscrapers are the Empire State Building in New York and the Sears Tower in Chicago."

- In most cases, try to keep the tone of a definition factual and impersonal.

Differences over definitions often give rise to the disagreements that people have about important political and social issues. Therefore, always be sensitive to the key words in a text. Quite often, while you and other readers agree on the core meanings of such important terms (their denotations), you may not share the feelings, images, and associations that these words evoke (their connotations). For examples of definition, see the essays by Hector St. Jean De Crèvecoeur (p. 361), Richard Bernstein (p. 372), and Joan Didion (p. 493).

Describing

Descriptions provide a snapshot of an object—explaining what it looks like at a particular moment.

- Consider your perspective on the object. From what angle are you observing it? Share this point of view with readers.

- Record the most distinctive features and details, those that will enable readers to visualize what you are describing. In most types of writing, your goal is to convey an accurate *impression* of what you have seen, be it person, thing, or even idea.

- Descriptions depend heavily on modifiers—words that specify shape, size, color, smell, and so on. Modifiers should be chosen very deliberately—and used sparingly.

For effective examples of description, see the selections by Andrea Lee (p. 196) and Terry Tempest Williams (p. 513).

Writing a Dialogue

A dialogue is a conversation between two or more people—as in an interview, where ideas and opinions are exchanged, or in fiction or nonfiction writing, where a conversation is reproduced or imagined. To write such a conversation, you need to know something about the way the participants think, how they view the world, even the way they speak. Writing a fictional dialogue thus requires—and allows—imaginative role playing. Here are some suggestions for creating one:

- Try to put yourself within the minds of the characters and consider how they might respond to each other. Look closely at the typical attitudes, interests, habits, and expressions used by your characters. Try to reproduce them.

- It's not enough just to have characters "talk"; you have to figure out a subject for them to talk about. The liveliest dialogues usually feature some exchange of ideas or opinions.

- Set the dialogue in a particular place and time.

- A dialogue can be a stimulating way to respond to a reading. Imagine a dialogue among yourself and some friends on the reading—or place yourself in conversation with the writer. What would you like to say to Mary Shelley, bell hooks, or Allan Bloom? What might they say to you?

For an example of dialogue, see the selection by Kevin Kelly (p. 243).

Evaluating

Writing an evaluation involves making and justifying judgments. First, you need to determine the appropriate criteria for the evaluation. Obviously, you wouldn't use the same standards in evaluating an elementary school play that you would in reviewing a Broadway production. In most cases, it is best to take a clear position in a review. Don't make your evaluation so subtle that no one can tell what your stance is. Here are some suggestions for writing an evaluation:

- Determine the appropriate criteria for the evaluation. Sometimes these standards will be obvious or given. In other cases, you will have to establish and define them. Readers will want to know why you are applying certain measures so that they can determine whether to trust your opinions.
- Measure your subject according to these standards.
- Base your evaluation on clear and sufficient evidence. A good evaluation is based on tangible facts and compelling arguments.
- Let readers see how you arrived at your judgment. For example, if you raise doubts about the competence of an author, make clear what led you to that conclusion.
- Arrange your arguments in logical order—perhaps in order of increasing importance. Sometimes you can bolster your argument by comparing and contrasting your subject with objects or ideas already familiar to your readers.

For an example of evaluation, see the essay by P. J. O'Rourke (p. 424).

Exploring

The point of exploratory writing is to examine subjects imaginatively, so such essays are often more tentative than reports or more purely argumentative writing. Exploratory pieces allow you to take risks, to jump into controversies too complex to be resolved easily. So when you want to explore an issue in writing, try to go beyond predictable and safe positions. Following are some strategies for doing so:

- Read a series of provocative articles from various perspectives. Talk with friends or classmates. Reach for dialogue, discussion, and debate.
- Be prepared for multiple drafts. Your best ideas are likely to emerge during the composing process.
- Be open to alternative views and marginalized voices. Bring other writers into the discussion.
- As the piece evolves, show it to interested readers and ask for their frank response. Incorporate questions, debates, or other material into the discussion. Dialogue can be a particularly stimulating technique for exploration.
- Don't expect to wrap up this kind of writing with a neat bow. Be prepared for gaps. Exploratory writing often produces more questions than answers.

For examples of exploratory writing, see the essays by Andrew Sullivan (p. 302), Zora Neale Hurston (p. 366), and William F. Buckley Jr. (p. 525).

Freewriting

Freewriting is a technique for generating ideas. When you freewrite about something, you follow ideas to see where they lead. Freewriting in response to reading might be prompted by particular words, phrases, or passages that you have highlighted while reading. It can also be useful for exploring connections between two or three different selections. Here are some specific tips for freewriting:

- One way to get started is by answering a question—for instance, "This topic makes me think of . . ." or "When I think of this topic, I feel . . ."
- Write nonstop for a fixed period of time—five or ten minutes, perhaps. Don't stop during that time; the point is to generate as much material as you can.
- If you can't think of anything to write, put down a nonsense phrase or repeat a key word just to keep your pen or cursor moving.
- Don't stop to question or correct your work while freewriting. Forget about style and correctness. Get the intellectual juices flowing.
- After freewriting, read the words you have produced to recover the ideas you may have generated. If you have come up with observations worthy of more exploration, make those ideas the focus of more freewriting.

Interviewing

We routinely ask people questions to satisfy our curiosity, but to turn a conversation with an interesting and knowledgeable person into a useful interview, you need to do your homework. The first step is to decide who you wish to interview—and you don't have to limit yourself to experts only. Friends and classmates have knowledge and opinions you might tap by interviewing them. Think of an interview as a high-powered conversation, a new way to learn. Here are some suggestions for arranging, conducting, and recording an interview:

- Call or write ahead for an appointment.
- Prepare your questions in advance, perhaps brainstorming a preliminary list, then augmenting it with who-what-where-when-why-how items.

Arrange your queries in a sensible order, perhaps beginning with more factual questions and then moving to more complex questions of opinion.

- Prepare some open-ended questions—the kind that can't be answered in a word or phrase. Give yourself leeway to take the conversation down any paths that open up.

- Record your subject's responses carefully, double-checking with him or her later any direct quotations you might want to use. Use a tape recorder if your subject approves.

- Record time, date, place, and other pertinent information about the conversation for your records.

- After an interview, summarize the information briefly in your own words.

This book includes a published interview with Kirkpatrick Sale, by Kevin Kelly (p. 243).

Writing a Letter to the Editor

A familiar kind of persuasive writing is the letter to the editor, in which writers explain why they agree or disagree with something they've read. Such letters are typically composed in response to positions taken by newspapers, magazines, or journals. In most cases, letters to the editor are spirited arguments, somewhat personal, and carefully targeted.

Letters to the editor follow the conventions of business letters and should be dated and signed. Here are some suggestions for writing one:

- Think about who reads the periodical to which the letter will be sent. Because such a letter is intended for publication, it is usually written more to win the support of other readers than to influence editors or publishers.

- Identify your target article within the first line or two. Let readers know exactly what piece provoked your ire or admiration.

- Make your case quickly. Since space for letters is very limited in most publications, expect to make only one or two points. Execute them powerfully and memorably, using the best examples and reasons you can.

- When appropriate, use irony, satire, or humor.

For an example, see the letter to the editor written by Florence Hoff (p. 567).

Narrating

Whereas descriptions usually refer to stationary objects, narratives depict motion, whether it be the action of a single person or the unfurling of a complex historical event, such as a war or social movement. When you narrate, you usually tell a story of some kind. But narratives may also explain *how something occurred* (analyzing a process) or *why something happened* (tracing cause and effect). Here are some suggestions for narrating:

- Place the events you are discussing in a meaningful order, usually chronological—first this happened, then this, then this, and so on.
- Provide necessary background information by answering the questions who, what, where, when, why, and how the events occurred.
- Most narrative calls for some description. Flesh out any characters and describe any scenic details necessary to the narrative.
- Use transitional phrases (*then, next, on the following day*) and sequences (*in the spring, during the summer, later in the year*) to keep the sequence of the narrative clear. Remember, however, that the sequence doesn't always have to be chronological (you've certainly seen flashbacks in movies).

For examples of narration, see the selections by Mary Shelley (p. 230) and Maxine Hong Kingston (p. 313).

Parodying

Your appreciation of a written work can't be tested better than by parody. A parody is an imitation, either of an author, a work, or an attitude, written with a critical and usually humorous edge. Parody succeeds when readers recognize both your target and your criticism; they should laugh at the wit in your mimicking something they too have experienced.

When you write a parody, you are in certain ways collaborating with other writers. You will necessarily learn much about the way they think and use language. Here are some suggestions for writing a parody:

- Choose a distinctive idea or work to parody. The more recognizable an attitude or famous a work is, the easier it will be to poke fun at. But even the most vapid work can be mocked for its dullness.
- Look for familiar subjects, motifs, or opinions, and distort them enough to be funny but not so much that the original idea becomes unrecognizable.
- When parodying a well-known work or writer, try shifting from a serious theme to a frivolous one; for example, imagine a pompous opera

critic reviewing Janet Jackson's latest video or a dour news commentator interviewing the ghost of Elvis.

- Pinpoint the habits of language ordinarily used to discuss your subject—typical sentence openers, preferred jargon, distinctive patterns of repetition, favorite sentence patterns, unusual punctuation. Then exaggerate those habits.

- Don't make your parody too long. Parody is a form of wit, and brevity is its soul.

- Above all, have fun. When a parody ceases being funny, it becomes simply bad imitation.

For an example of parody, see the selection by Dave Barry (p. 343).

Writing a Position Paper

A position paper is a short (often one-page) argument that can sometimes be exploratory. In it, you will usually present a thesis—a statement that needs to be proved or defended. But such a paper is often assigned to jump-start discussions or to get various points of view on the table, so feel free to take risks and examine new approaches. A position paper need not have the gloss of a polished argument, and its language can be livelier than that of more formal academic arguments. It should stimulate your readers—often your classmates—to respond actively to your ideas. Here are some suggestions for writing a position paper:

- Begin by taking a stand on a subject. Find a statement you can defend reasonably well.

- Support your thesis with various kinds of evidence—arguments, examples, statistics, illustrations, expert opinions, and so on.

- If the position paper is very brief, suggest the direction a fuller argument might take.

- Write an open-ended conclusion, qualifying your original thesis or pointing to avenues for further study.

For two papers that take different positions on the same topic, see the selections by Susan Faludi (p. 324) and Christina Hoff Sommers (p. 328).

Proposing Solutions

Proposals identify a problem and suggest action that will remedy the problem. You need to convince readers first that a problem exists and is serious, then that your solution is a feasible remedy. Often you will try as well to inspire your readers to take some action.

- To demonstrate that the problem exists, give examples and cite evidence such as statistics or the testimony of experts.
- To convince readers to accept your solution, you need to show that it is feasible—and that it is better than other solutions that might reasonably be proposed.
- Consider your audience. Are they likely to be aware of the problem? Try to connect the problem to concerns they might have.

For examples of writing that proposes solutions, see the essays by Adrienne Rich (p. 44) and Allan Bloom (p. 52).

Keeping a Reading Log

Many writers use reading logs to record their feelings and detailed impressions about what they're reading and thinking. Your instructor may ask you to keep one and turn it in as part of your work for a course. Here are some suggestions for keeping a reading log:

- If you want to remember what you've read, take time to summarize or list its main ideas.
- Then write out your immediate reactions to the reading. These may include memorable images, things that made you angry, sad, puzzled, or delighted, or things that you want to know more about. Later, in a more extended comment, summarize your thoughts about the reading. Reflect on what in the reading and in your experience may have shaped your reactions.
- Make some notes about the author's perspective, where he or she seems to be coming from, noting places in the reading that provide clues to the perspective.
- Write in an informal, exploratory style, almost as if you were talking to yourself.
- Date your entries, and be sure to identify the reading.
- Look at your commentary in the context of your notes on other readings. Do you see any useful or interesting connections?

For examples of reading log entries, see the editors' responses to Anthony Brandt's essay (p. 192).

Reporting

Doing a report is one of the most common academic assignments. Reports are explanations that transfer information from writers to readers. That information may come directly from the writers' minds or from other sources of information—from traditional libraries to field research to computer networks.

- Focus a report around a thesis, a clear statement of purpose. The thesis is the point or controlling idea of a piece. A thesis statement makes a promise to readers, telling them what to expect, and it limits the subject matter and scope of your report.
- Acknowledge any sources you use.
- Define any terms your readers may not know.
- Arrange information according to a plan your readers can easily follow. For example, a report on the major events of the Cold War could follow a chronological organization: first, second, third. A report on the Cold War policies of Joseph Stalin and Harry Truman might use a structure comparing and contrasting the two leaders.
- Conclude by summarizing your work and exploring its implications.
- Give the report a concise, factual, and descriptive title.

For an example of a report, see the selection by Paul Osterman (p. 558).

WORKING WITH SOURCES

Much of the college writing you will do will involve the use of source materials. Here are some guidelines for evaluating, quoting, paraphrasing, and summarizing sources.

Evaluating Sources

Not all sources are equally authoritative or useful. Here are some general tips for evaluating sources; consult your instructor, librarian, or writing handbook for further advice.

- Note whether a source is a primary or secondary one.
- Learn the differences between scholarly and trade books, and choose sources appropriate to your work. The claims in scholarly books are systematically documented and carefully reviewed; trade books may be just as factual and reliable, but they typically lack formal documentation.

- Understand the differences between scholarly journals and popular magazines. Both may serve your research needs, but in different ways. Journals written for specialists will often be highly technical and, consequently, difficult for people outside a profession to read; popular magazines serve wider audiences and present more accessible—if less authoritative—information.
- Understand the limits of online Internet sources. World Wide Web sites, for example, vary enormously in quality, from those carefully maintained by institutions and professional organizations to playful home pages posted by individuals. Be especially careful with sites associated with familiar figures or institutions but not actually maintained or authorized by them.

Quoting

Quoting involves noting down a source's *exact words*. You will have many occasions in working with the readings in this book to use direct quotation. Many of the headnotes that introduce each reading show examples of direct quotation.

- Copy quotations *carefully,* with punctuation, capitalization, and spelling exactly as in the original.
- Bracket any words of your own you need to add to the quotation.
- Use ellipses to indicate any omitted words.
- Enclose the quotation in quotation marks.

Paraphrasing

A paraphrase accurately states all the relevant information from a passage *in your own words and phrasing,* without any additional comment or elaboration. Use paraphrases when you want to cite ideas from a source but have no need to quote exact words.

- Include the main points and some important details from the original, in the same order in which they were presented.
- Use your own words and sentence structures. If you want to include especially memorable language from the original, enclose it in quotation marks.
- Leave out your own comments and reactions.
- Recheck the paraphrase against the original to be sure that the words and structures are your own and that they express the author's meaning accurately.

Summarizing

A summary concisely restates key ideas *in your own words*. Sometimes you may need to summarize something in a sentence or two: "P. J. O'Rourke's 'The Death of Communism' describes the euphoria he feels the moment he realizes that the West has won the Cold War." Often a more detailed synopsis is necessary. Preparing such a summary takes some planning. Here are some suggestions:

- Outline the text you are summarizing. Identify its main points, sub-points, and key bits of supporting evidence.
- Flesh out the outline with necessary details, taking care to show the connections between key ideas.
- Check that your concise version of a longer work can stand on its own. Remember that your readers may not have access to the original piece, so all references need to be clear.
- Double-check against the piece you are summarizing to make sure the wording in your summary is your own.

For an example of summary, see portions of Neil Postman's essay (p. 133).

Deciding Whether to Quote, Paraphrase, or Summarize

- *Quote*
  Wording that is so memorable or expresses a point so perfectly that you cannot improve or shorten it without weakening the meaning you need
  Authors' opinions you wish to emphasize
  Respected authorities whose opinions support your own ideas
  Authors whose opinions challenge or vary from others in the field
- *Paraphrase*
  Passages that you do not wish to quote but whose details you wish to note *fully*
- *Summarize*
  Long passages whose *main points* you wish to record *selectively*

Incorporating Sources

Incorporate quotations, paraphrases, and summaries into your own writing carefully, often by using a signal phrase ("he said" or "she remarks"). Choose the verbs you use to introduce source material carefully; be sure they express your thoughts accurately. Notice, for instance, the difference between saying someone "said," "claimed," or "asserted." For effective incorporation of sources, see the many quotations in Lynne V. Cheney's essay (p. 112).

Acknowledging Sources

When quoting, paraphrasing, or summarizing sources in formal essays, reports, or research projects, be sure to acknowledge all sources according to the conventions required by your field or instructor.

WORKING WITH OTHERS

The title for this text recalls a remark by philosopher Hannah Arendt that "for excellence, the presence of others is always required." Nowhere is Arendt's observation more accurate than in the college community. Your college coursework will call on you to read, write, and research a vast amount of material. But you will not—or need not—do all that reading, writing, and researching alone. Far from it. Instead, you can be part of a broad conversation that includes all the texts you read; all the writing you produce; all the discussions you have with teachers, friends, family members, and classmates; all the observations and interviews you conduct. Throughout this book, we draw on Arendt's concept—from our title to the way we group readings in conversation with one another to the many assignments that ask you to work with others.

Collaboration can play an important part in all the writing you do, first if you talk with others about your topic and your plans for approaching it, then if you seek responses to your draft and gather suggestions for improving it. In much the same way, reading can be done "with others"—first by entering into mental conversation with the author and with the social and historical forces at work shaping the author's text, then by comparing your understanding of the text with that of other readers and using points of agreement or disagreement as the basis for further analysis.

As you read this book, the most immediate and valuable of your collaborators may be your classmates. Indeed, you can learn a great deal by listening carefully both to them and to your instructor. You can profit even more by talking over issues with them, by comparing notes and ideas with them, and by using them as a first and very important audience for your writing. They will inevitably offer you new perspectives, new ways of seeing and knowing.

- Once you establish a group, trade phone numbers, e-mail addresses, and schedules, and set a time to meet.
- Set an agenda for each meeting. If you intend to study or compare certain readings, be sure everyone knows in advance and brings the essay

or book to the meeting. Perhaps begin by brainstorming major questions you have about the reading.

- Use the group to work through difficult readings. If a reading is especially long, have each member take one section to explain and "teach" to the others.

- If you need to prepare something as a group, decide on a fair and effective means of dividing the task. Assign each group member specific duties. Arrange for a time to meet when those individual duties will have been accomplished. At the meeting, work to review the various parts and put them together.

- If a project involves a group presentation or report, figure out what each member will contribute. Plan all the work that is to be done and schedule any necessary meetings. For the presentation, make sure every group member is involved in some way. Decide on any visual aids or handouts in advance and prepare them carefully. Finally, *practice the presentation.* Everyone will benefit from a "dress rehearsal."

- Most important, listen to every member of the group carefully and respectfully; everyone's ideas must be taken into consideration. If conflict arises—and in any lively and healthy collaboration, it will—explore all areas of the conflict openly and fairly before seeking resolution.

- Take time each meeting to assess the effectiveness of the group. Consider these questions: What has the group accomplished so far? With what has it been most helpful? With what has it been least helpful? What have you contributed? What has each of the others contributed? How can you all make the group more effective?

A SAMPLE CRITICAL RESPONSE ESSAY

We have outlined in this chapter some of the ways you may be asked to respond to selected readings in your writing classes. A type of response you are most likely to be asked to do is a critical response essay (guidelines for writing a critical analysis begin on p. 16.) Read the following critical response essay by Carrie Ann Laposki to see how one student responds to the selection in this book by Christina Hoff Sommers, "Figuring Out Feminism" (p. 328).

CARRIE ANN LAPOSKI
Refiguring Feminism: Gender and Equity

CARRIE ANN LAPOSKI is a first-year student at The Ohio State University. She wrote "Refiguring Feminism: Gender and Equity" after her instructor asked the class to choose one essay from the chapter on gender in this text and respond critically to it. We have annotated Laposki's essay to highlight her responses to the piece by Christina Hoff Sommers.

In "Figuring Out Feminism," Christina Hoff Sommers alerts readers to the sometimes erroneous and exaggerated statistics about women's issues presented in the media. In Sommers's opinion, these statistics are the ammunition that gender feminists use to prove that males work "to keep women cowering and submissive."

Laposki formulates what she sees as Sommers's claim. — J.R.

Sommers cites several clear examples to show that many such statistics are misrepresented. After researching these statistics, often going all the way to their points of origin to examine their credibility, she concludes that some statistics were the result of misunderstanding (the March of Dimes domestic violence report), that some were pure myth (the "Super Bowl domestic violence" statistic), and that some were misquotes of otherwise credible reports (Gloria Steinem's anorexia statistics). Because she uses more than one example and her research was in-depth, I find her evidence quite convincing.

Here Laposki assesses some examples Sommers uses as evidence to support her claim. — A.L.

Sommers also poses an important question: "Why are certain feminists so eager to put men in a bad light?" I feel that Sommers offers a reasonable response to this question, citing the beliefs of different feminist groups. She explains that two types of feminists—gender feminists and equity feminists—are currently at work in the United States. Gender feminists seek to persuade us that our nation is a patriarchal society that constantly oppresses women. Their ideology holds that "physical menace toward women is the norm." According to Sommers, gender feminists often use unsubstantiated or exaggerated statistics to persuade us that male dominance is a founding principle of our society.

Equity feminists, on the other hand, point to the gains women have recently made in education, wages, and male-dominated fields as signs of progress toward the goal of total equality. Sommers says that these feminists allow women's success to speak for itself rather than use propaganda to falsely persuade Americans to join the feminist movement.

Laposki brings her perspective to the analysis, looking for a way to reconcile gender and equity feminists.
— J.R.

I believe that in order to establish gender equality in the United States, we must first find the correct balance of gender feminism and equity feminism, a possibility that Sommers does not explore. It is important to be aware of the patriarchal tendencies in our society, but it is equally important to understand the gains made by women as a source of empowerment. Then women must invite men to join the feminist cause so that they may work together toward equality rather than work against one another. Sommers seems to present gender feminism and equity feminism as either–or issues rather than issues that can be blended to create a unified solution for gender equality.

Laposki notes an omission in Sommers's argument.
— A.L.

Sommers devotes only a few paragraphs to positive, correctly reported statistics. Her article, written for sophisticated readers able to understand the importance and magnitude of her research, could lead someone less educated about gender equality to assume that *all* statistics about women's issues are bogus. If Sommers had used more "correct" statistics, a better basis of comparison would have been established, thus getting beyond easy dismissal of all women's statistics.

Laposki suggests that Sommers's selection of statistics may mislead some audiences.
—A.L.

In general, I feel that Sommers's article serves as a thought-provoking warning for both women and men. It teaches us that we should not

Laposki concludes by approving the message of the piece: examine claims carefully.
— J.R.

always believe what we read to be honest or factual—indeed, that we must do research on our own to ensure the accuracy of our information. Sommers's article should serve as a "wake-up call" to us all as we work to build a gender-sensitive America.

Education:
The Idea of a University

Look carefully at this cover of a recent university catalogue. What is the center of attention in this illustration? What draws your eye to that point? Why might the university have chosen this particular picture for their cover? What does the illustration seek to suggest about a college education?

If then a practical end must be assigned to a University course, I say it is that of training good members of society.

JOHN HENRY NEWMAN, *The Idea of a University*

What does a woman need to know to become a self-conscious, self-defining human being?

ADRIENNE RICH, *What Does a Woman Need to Know?*

The university has to stand for something.

ALLAN BLOOM, *The Student and the University*

What has emerged on campus in recent years . . . is a *politics of difference,* a troubling, volatile politics in which each group justifies itself, its sense of worth and its pursuit of power, through difference alone.

SHELBY STEELE, *The Recoloring of Campus Life*

Studying at Stanford, I began to think seriously about class differences. To be materially underprivileged at a university where most folks . . . are materially privileged provokes such thought.

BELL HOOKS, *Keeping Close to Home: Class and Education*

If the canon itself is the answer to our educational inequities, why has it historically invited few and denied many?

MIKE ROSE, *Lives on the Boundary*

One male student instructs another on how to succeed in a feminist classroom. "Pretend to be a male chauvinist, then have a conversion. You're bound to get an A."

LYNNE V. CHENEY, *PC: Alive and Entrenched*

It is important for undergraduates to write about teaching because it is what "happens" to us as college students.

CHRISTIAN ZAWODNIAK, *"I'll Have to Help Some of You More Than I Want To": Teacher Power, Student Pedagogy*

I realize that I am beginning to sound like E. D. Hirsch, Jr., but I find it truly astonishing that the great story of humanity's perilous and exciting romance with technology is not told in our schools.

NEIL POSTMAN, *The Word Weavers/The World Makers*

We real cool. We left school.

GWENDOLYN BROOKS, *We Real Cool*

Introduction

YOU MAY BE SURPRISED to learn that until fairly recently in the United States most people either did not have the resources to attend college or were excluded from the majority of colleges for other reasons (such as race or gender). Today, however, nearly half of all high school graduates extend their education at a two-year or four-year college or university. And many older individuals who had never pursued higher education or had left college for some reason are now returning to the classroom. More and more people are attending college these days—but what kind of education are they receiving?

In fact, questions about the purpose of education have been under scrutiny at least since Socrates was put on trial in 399 B.C.E. on charges of corrupting the youth of Athens by his teaching of philosophy. But no one seems to agree these days in the United States, any more than in ancient Greece, about what the role of higher education should be. Who should be allowed to attend colleges and universities—and who should not be? Should education be a mechanism for advancing the welfare of the nation—augmenting its productivity, management skills, and technology and preserving the quality of its workforce? Should it be an instrument of social change—teaching ideas of social justice, adjusting to new demographics in the population it serves, and providing the rationale for radical reforms of the economic order? Should it exist primarily to stimulate the intellect and the imagination of students? Or should schooling serve other or multiple purposes?

In this chapter, we have selected readings that bring different perspectives—and offer very different answers—to these central questions about the purposes of higher education. We hope these readings will lead you to consider such questions yourself, to think hard and long about what higher education is for and what it *should* be for in the future. Before you begin reading, however, you may want to think over some of the issues raised in this chapter. Here are some questions to get you started thinking:

- What are your reasons for coming to college? Do you think your reasons correspond to your college's or university's goals for its students?

- In what ways was your decision to attend college shaped or influenced by factors outside your control?

- What should be the goals of higher education? If you were president of your college or university, what would you list as the school's aims? What would be your top priorities?

- Have you ever felt excluded in any way from school? Have you ever experienced anything that discouraged you from going to school? On the other hand, what particular encouragement have you had to go to school?

- What metaphor, simile, or analogy seems to you most appropriate for college? To get started, complete the following sentence: College is like a _____.

- What role should a college or university play in any of the following areas: shaping students' moral character? providing students with intellectual stimulation and satisfaction? preparing people for jobs? preparing citizens to participate in a democracy? preparing workers to compete in a global economy? preparing people to advance the frontiers of scientific research and to understand technology? You may find it interesting to discuss with a few classmates which of these goals they consider most important.

•   •   •

JOHN HENRY NEWMAN
The Idea of a University

JOHN HENRY NEWMAN's The Idea of a University *is among the most famous attempts to define a liberal arts education. Originally written in 1852 in response to a papal proposal for a Roman Catholic university in Ireland,* The Idea of a University *served as an intellectual manifesto for Catholics, who had long been an oppressed minority in the British Isles. Full emancipation occurred for them only in 1829; prior to that date, Catholics had been denied political rights in England and Ireland as well as admission to the great British universities, Oxford and Cambridge.*

Newman (1801–90), a well-known Anglican priest who had converted to the Roman church, wrote The Idea of a University *to explore what a Catholic university would be like—how it might merge religious and secular concerns. He was also responding to a world growing ever more secular in its interests, more scientific in its methods, more utilitarian in its philosophy. Revolutions in technology and industrial organization seemed to be reshaping every human endeavor, including the academy.*

Newman had reservations about these changes, many of which we take for granted today, such as the division of universities into various "schools" (arts, sciences, professional schools), the selection by students of their own programs of study, and the establishment of areas of specialization (what we would call "majors"). His aim is to defend the value of learning for its own sake.

The Idea of a University *is an example of deliberative rhetoric: Newman is both recommending and defending the proposal for a Catholic university. He faces both an entrenched Anglican tradition and a scholarly community leaning in the direction of what is today called "secular humanism." The following excerpts from this book-length work do not focus on religious issues, however. Instead, they explain several of Newman's goals for the liberal arts university.* − J.R.

DISCOURSE V
KNOWLEDGE ITS OWN END

1

I have said that all branches of knowledge are connected together, because the subject-matter of knowledge is intimately united in itself, as being the acts and the work of the Creator. Hence it is that the Sciences, into which our knowledge may be said to be cast, have multiplied bearings one on another, and an internal sympathy, and admit, or rather demand, comparison and adjustment. They complete, correct, balance each other. This consideration, if well-founded, must be taken into account, not only as regards the attainment of truth, which is their common end, but as regards the influence which they exercise upon those whose education consists in the study of them. I have said already, that to give undue prominence to one is to be unjust to another; to neglect or supersede these is to divert those from their proper object. It is to unsettle the boundary lines between science and science, to disturb their action, to destroy the harmony which binds them together. Such a proceeding will have a corresponding effect when introduced into a place of education. There is no science but tells a different tale, when viewed as a portion of a whole, from what it is likely to suggest when taken by itself, without the safeguard, as I may call it, of others.

Let me make use of an illustration. In the combination of colors, very different effects are produced by a difference in their selection and juxtaposition; red, green, and white, change their shades, according to the contrast to which they are submitted. And, in like manner, the drift and meaning of a branch of knowledge varies with the company in which it is introduced to the student. If his reading is confined simply to one subject, however such division of labor may favor the advancement of a particular pursuit, a point into which I do not here enter, certainly it has a tendency to contract his mind. If it is incorporated with others, it depends on those others as to the kind of influence which it exerts upon him. Thus the Classics, which in England are the means of refining the taste, have in France subserved the spread of revolutionary and deistical doctrines. In Metaphysics, again, *Butler's Analogy of Religion** which has had so much to do with the conversion to the Catholic faith of members of the University of Oxford, appeared to Pitt* and others, who had received a different training, to operate only in the direction of infidelity. And so again, Watson, Bishop of Llandaff,* as I think he tells us in the narrative of his life, felt the science of Mathematics to indispose the mind to religious belief, while others see in its investigations the best parallel, and thereby defense, of the Christian Mysteries. In like manner, I suppose, Arcesilas* would not have handled logic as Aristotle, nor Aristotle have criticized poets as Plato; yet reasoning and poetry are subject to scientific rules.

It is a great point then to enlarge the range of studies which a University professes, even for the sake of the students; and, though they cannot pursue

---

Butler's Analogy of Religion: a defense of Christian revelation (1736) by Joseph Butler (1692–1752)

Pitt: William Pitt (1708–78), British parliamentarian and orator

Watson, Bishop of Llandaff: Richard Watson (1737–1816), a professor of chemistry and divinity

Arcesilas: Greek philosopher (c. 316–241 B.C.E.) who advocated rational skepticism

every subject which is open to them, they will be the gainers by living among those and under those who represent the whole circle. This I conceive to be the advantage of a seat of universal learning, considered as a place of education. An assemblage of learned men, zealous for their own sciences, and rivals of each other, are brought, by familiar intercourse and for the sake of intellectual peace, to adjust together the claims and relations of their respective subjects of investigation. They learn to respect, to consult, to aid each other. Thus is created a pure and clear atmosphere of thought, which the student also breathes, though in his own case he only pursues a few sciences out of the multitude. He profits by an intellectual tradition, which is independent of particular teachers, which guides him in his choice of subjects, and duly interprets for him those which he chooses. He apprehends the great outlines of knowledge, the principles on which it rests, the scale of its parts, its lights and its shades, its great points and its little, as he otherwise cannot apprehend them. Hence it is that his education is called "Liberal." A habit of mind is formed which lasts through life, of which the attributes are, freedom, equitableness, calmness, moderation, and wisdom; or what in a former Discourse I have ventured to call a philosophical habit. This then I would assign as the special fruit of the education furnished at a University, as contrasted with other places of teaching or modes of teaching. This is the main purpose of a University in its treatment of its students.

And now the question is asked me, What is the *use* of it? and my answer will constitute the main subject of the Discourses which are to follow.

• • •

Discourse VII
Knowledge Viewed in Relation to Professional Skill

10

But I must bring these extracts to an end. Today I have confined myself to saying that that training of the intellect, which is best for the individual himself, best enables him to discharge his duties to society. The Philosopher, indeed, and the man of the world differ in their very notion, but the methods, by which they are respectively formed, are pretty much the same. The Philosopher has the same command of matters of thought, which the true citizen and gentleman has of matters of business and conduct. If then a practical end must be assigned to a University course, I say it is that of training good members of society. Its art is the art of social life, and its end is fitness for the world. It neither confines its views to particular professions on the one hand, nor creates heroes or inspires genius on the other. Works indeed of genius fall under no art; heroic minds come under no rule; a University is not a birthplace of poets or of immortal authors, of founders of schools, leaders of colonies, or conquerors of nations. It does not promise a generation of Aristotles or Newtons, of Napoleons or Washingtons, of Raphaels or Shakespeares, though such miracles of nature it has before now contained within its precincts. Nor is it content on the other hand with forming the critic or the experimentalist, the economist or the engineer, though such too it includes within its scope. But a University training is the great ordinary means to a great but ordinary end; it aims at raising the intellectual tone of society, at cultivating the public mind, at purifying the national taste, at supplying true principles to popular enthusiasm and fixed aims to popular aspiration, at giving enlargement and sobriety to the ideas of the age, at facilitating the exercise of political power, and refining the intercourse of private life. It is the education which gives a man a clear conscious view of his own opinions and judgments, a truth in developing them, an eloquence in expressing them, and a force in urging them. It teaches him to see things as they are, to go right to the point, to disentangle a skein of thought, to detect what is sophistical, and to discard what is irrelevant. It prepares him to fill any post with credit, and to master any subject with facility. It shows him how to accommodate himself to others, how to throw himself into their state of mind, how to bring before them his own, how to influence them, how to come to an understanding with them, how to bear with them. He is at home in any society, he has common ground with every class; he knows when to speak and when to be silent; he is able to converse, he is able to listen; he can ask a question pertinently, and gain a lesson seasonably, when he has nothing to impart himself; he is ever ready, yet never in the way; he is a pleasant companion, and a comrade you can depend upon; he knows when to be serious and when to trifle, and he has a sure tact which enables him to trifle with gracefulness and to be serious with effect. He has the repose of a mind which lives in itself, while it lives in the world, and which has resources for its happiness at home when it cannot go abroad. He has a gift which serves him in public, and supports him in retirement, without which good fortune is but vulgar, and with which failure and disappointment have a charm. The art which tends to make a man all this, is in the object which it pursues as useful as the art of wealth or the art of health, though it is less susceptible of method, and less tangible, less certain, less complete in its result.

QUESTIONING THE TEXT

1. Examine the goals Newman explicitly provides for the university in the passage from Discourse VII. Do these goals still seem relevant today? Why, or why not? If you keep a reading log, answer this question there.

2. As you reread Newman's essay, record your reactions to his style in the margins. Does it feel stuffy or solemn? Does it move you or impress you? When you are finished, draw some conclusions from your comments.
3. The introduction emphasizes that Newman's *The Idea of a University* was written in response to changes occurring in the United Kingdom in the nineteenth century. Do any of these changes seem relevant to events in the United States as the twenty-first century approaches?

MAKING CONNECTIONS

4. Would Mike Rose or the students he describes in "Lives on the Boundary" (p. 97) fit into the university Newman describes? Write a two- or three-page essay exploring this issue.
5. One of the major complaints made against contemporary universities by Allan Bloom (p. 52) is that they fragment knowledge into many separate disciplines and then give students no guidance through or sense of connection among them. Discuss the underlying principle in Newman and Bloom that a good liberal education approaches knowledge as a whole, not as a collection of separate courses, fields, or career paths.

JOINING THE CONVERSATION

6. Can Newman's concept of "liberal arts" survive in our world today? Does it deserve to? Why, or why not? Write a position paper on this subject.
7. For a national news magazine, write an evaluation of American higher education as you imagine Newman might regard it if he were living today. What might he admire? What would he criticize?
8. With a group of classmates, discuss the "usefulness" of the education you have had in high school and college. Which courses of study seem to have the most direct application to daily life? Which, if any, seem designed primarily as learning for its own sake?

ADRIENNE RICH
What Does a Woman Need to Know?

44

I have been very much moved that you, the class of 1979, chose me for your commencement speaker. It is important to me to be here, in part because Smith is one of the original colleges for women, but also because she has chosen to continue identifying herself as a women's college. We are at a point in history where this fact has enormous potential, even if that potential is as yet unrealized. The possibilities for the future education of women that haunt these buildings and grounds are enormous, when we think of what an independent women's college might be: a college dedicated both to teaching women what women need to know and, by the same token, to changing the landscape of knowledge itself. The germ of those possibilities lies symbolically in The Sophia Smith Collection, an archive much in need of expansion and increase, but which by its very existence makes the statement that women's lives and work are valued here and that our foresisters, buried and diminished in male-centered scholarship, are a living presence, necessary and precious to us.

Suppose we were to ask ourselves simply: What does a woman need to know to become a self-conscious, self-defining human being? Doesn't she need a knowledge of her own history, of her much-politicized female body, of the creative genius of women of the past—the skills and crafts and techniques and visions possessed by women in other times and cultures, and how they have been rendered anonymous, censored, interrupted, devalued? Doesn't she, as one of that majority who are still denied equal rights as citizens, enslaved as sexual prey, unpaid or underpaid as workers, withheld from her own power—doesn't she need an analysis of her condition, a knowledge of the women thinkers of the past who have reflected on it, a knowledge, too, of women's world-wide individual rebellions and organized movements against economic and social injustice, and how these have been fragmented and silenced?

Doesn't she need to know how seemingly natural states of being, like heterosexuality, like motherhood, have been enforced and institutionalized to deprive her of power? Without such education, women have lived and continue to live in ignorance of our collective context, vulnerable to the projections of men's fantasies about us as they appear in art, in literature, in the sciences, in the media, in the so-called humanistic studies. I suggest that not anatomy, but enforced ignorance, has been a crucial key to our powerlessness.

There is—and I say this with sorrow—there is no women's college today which is providing young women with the education they need for survival as whole persons in a world which denies women wholeness—that knowledge which, in the words of Coleridge, "returns again as power." The existence of Women's Studies courses offers at least some kind of life line. But even Women's Studies can amount simply to compensatory history; too often they fail to challenge the intellectual and political structures that must be challenged if women as a group are ever to come into collective, nonexclusionary freedom. The belief that established science and scholarship—which have so relentlessly excluded women from their making—are "objective" and "value-free" and that feminist studies are "unscholarly," "biased," and "ideological" dies hard. Yet the fact is that all science, and all scholarship, and all art are ideological; there is no neutrality in culture. And the ideology of the education you have just spent four years acquiring in a women's college has been largely, if not entirely, the ideology of white male supremacy, a construct of male subjectivity. The silences, the empty spaces, the language itself, with its excision of the female, the methods of discourse tell us as much as the content, once we learn to watch for what is left out, to listen for the unspoken, to study the patterns of established science and scholarship with an outsider's eye. One of the dangers of a privileged education for women is that we may lose the eye of the outsider and come to believe that those patterns hold for humanity, for the universal, and that they include us.

And so I want to talk today about privilege and about tokenism and about power. Everything I can say to you on this subject comes hard-won, from the lips of a woman privileged by class and skin color, a father's favorite daughter, educated at Radcliffe, which was then casually referred to as the Harvard "Annex." Much of the first four decades of my life was spent in a continuous tension between the world the Fathers taught me to see, and had rewarded me for seeing, and the flashes of insight that came through the eye of the outsider. Gradually those flashes of insight, which at times could seem like brushes with madness, began to demand that I struggle to connect them with each other, to insist that I take them seriously. It was only when I could finally affirm the outsider's eye as the source of a legitimate and coherent vision, that I began to be able to do the work I truly wanted to do, live the kind of life I truly wanted to live, instead of carrying out the assignments I had been given as a privileged woman and a token.

For women, all privilege is relative. Some of you were not born with class or skin-color privilege; but you all have the privilege of education, even if it is an education which has largely denied you knowledge of yourselves as women. You have, to begin with, the privilege of literacy; and it is well for us to remember that, in an age of increasing illiteracy, 60 percent of the world's illiterates are women. Between 1960 and 1970, the number of illiterate men in the world rose by 8 million, while the number of illiterate women rose by 40 million.[1] And the number of illiterate women is increasing. Beyond literacy, you have the privilege of training and tools which can allow you to go beyond the content of your education and re-educate yourselves—to debrief yourselves, we might call it, of the false messages of your education in this culture, the messages telling you that women have not really cared about power or learning or creative opportunities because of a psychobiological need to serve men and produce children; that only a few atypical women

5

---

[1] United Nations, Department of International Economic and Social Affairs, Statistical Office, *1977 Compendium of Social Statistics* (New York: United Nations, 1980).

have been exceptions to this rule; the messages telling you that woman's experience is neither normative nor central to human experience. You have the training and the tools to do independent research, to evaluate data, to criticize, and to express in language and visual forms what you discover. This is a privilege, yes, but only if you do not give up in exchange for it the deep knowledge of the unprivileged, the knowledge that, as a woman, you have historically been viewed and still are viewed as existing, not in your own right, but in the service of men. And only if you refuse to give up your capacity to think as a woman, even though in the graduate schools and professions to which many of you will be going you will be praised and rewarded for "thinking like a man."

The word *power* is highly charged for women. It has been long associated for us with the use of force, with rape, with the stockpiling of weapons, with the ruthless accrual of wealth and the hoarding of resources, with the power that acts only in its own interest, despising and exploiting the powerless—including women and children. The effects of this kind of power are all around us, even literally in the water we drink and the air we breathe, in the form of carcinogens and radioactive wastes. But for a long time now, feminists have been talking about redefining power, about that meaning of power which returns to the root—*posse, potere, pouvoir:* to be able, to have the potential, to possess and use one's energy of creation—*transforming power.* An early objection to feminism—in both the nineteenth and twentieth centuries—was that it would make women behave like men—ruthlessly, exploitatively, oppressively. In fact, radical feminism looks to a transformation of human relationships and structures in which power, instead of a thing to be hoarded by a few, would be released to and from within the many, shared in the form of knowledge, expertise, decision making, access to tools, as well as in the basic forms of food and shelter and health care and literacy. Feminists—and many nonfeminists—are, and rightly so, still concerned with what power would mean in such a society, and with the relative differences in power among and between women here and now.

Which brings me to a third meaning of power where women are concerned: the false power which masculine society offers to a few women, on condition that they use it to maintain things as they are, and that they essentially "think like men." This is the meaning of female tokenism: that power withheld from the vast majority of women is offered to a few, so that it appears that any "truly qualified" woman can gain access to leadership, recognition, and reward; hence, that justice based on merit actually prevails. The token woman is encouraged to see herself as different from most other women, as exceptionally talented and deserving, and to separate herself from the wider female condition; and she is perceived by "ordinary" women as separate also, perhaps even as stronger than themselves.

Because you are, within the limits of all women's ultimate outsiderhood, a privileged group of women, it is extremely important for your future sanity that you understand the way tokenism functions. Its most immediate contradiction is that, while it seems to offer the individual token woman a means to realize her creativity, to influence the course of events, it also, by exacting of her certain kinds of behavior and style, acts to blur her outsider's eye, which could be her real source of power and vision. Losing her outsider's vision, she loses the insight which both binds her to other women and affirms her in herself. Tokenism essentially demands that the token deny her identification with women as a group, especially with women less privileged than she: if she is a lesbian, that she deny her relationships with individual women; that she perpetuate rules and structures and criteria and methodologies which have functioned to exclude women; that she renounce or leave undeveloped the critical perspective of her female consciousness. Women unlike herself—poor women, women of color, waitresses, secretaries, housewives in the supermarket, prostitutes, old women—become invisible to her; they may represent too acutely what she has escaped or wished to flee.

President Conway tells me that ever-increasing numbers of you are going on from Smith to medical and law schools. The news, on the face of it, is good: that, thanks to the feminist struggle of the past decade, more doors into these two powerful professions are open to women. I would like to believe that any profession would be better for having more women practicing it, and that any woman practicing law or medicine would use her knowledge and skill to work to transform the realm of health care and the interpretations of the law, to make them responsive to the needs of all those—women, people of color, children, the aged, the dispossessed—for whom they function today as repressive controls. I would like to believe this, but it will not happen even if 50 percent of the members of these professions are women, unless those women refuse to be made into token insiders, unless they zealously preserve the outsider's view and the outsider's consciousness.

For no woman is really an insider in the institutions fathered by masculine consciousness. When we allow ourselves to believe we are, we lose touch with parts of ourselves defined as unacceptable by that consciousness; with the vital toughness and visionary strength of the angry grandmothers, the shamanesses, the fierce marketwomen of the Ibo Women's War, the marriage-resisting women silkworkers of prerevolutionary China, the millions of widows, midwives, and women healers tortured and burned as witches for three centuries in Europe, the Beguines of the twelfth century, who formed independent women's orders outside the domination of the Church, the women of the Paris Commune who marched on Versailles, the uneducated housewives of the Women's Cooperative Guild in England who memorized poetry over the washtub and organized against their oppression as mothers, the women thinkers discredited as "strident," "shrill," "crazy," or "deviant" whose courage to be heretical, to speak their truths, we so badly need to draw upon in our own lives. I believe that every woman's soul is haunted by the spirits of earlier women who fought for their unmet needs and those of their children and their tribes and their peoples, who refused to accept the prescriptions of a male church and state, who took risks and resisted, as women today—like Inez Garcia, Yvonne Wanrow, Joan Little, Cassandra Peten—are fighting their rapists and batterers. Those spirits dwell in us, trying to speak to us. But we can choose to be deaf; and tokenism, the myth of the "special" woman, the unmothered Athena sprung from her father's brow, can deafen us to their voices.

In this decade now ending, as more women are entering the professions (though still suffering sexual harassment in the workplace, though still, if they have children, carrying two full-time jobs, though still vastly outnumbered by men in upper-level and decision-making jobs), we need most profoundly to remember that early insight of the feminist movements as it evolved in the late sixties: *that no woman is liberated until we all are liberated.* The media flood us with messages to the contrary, telling us that we live in an era when "alternate life styles" are freely accepted, when "marriage contracts" and "the new intimacy" are revolutionizing heterosexual relationships, that shared parenting and the "new fatherhood" will change the world. And we live in a society leeched upon by the "personal growth" and "human potential" industry, by the delusion that individual self-fulfillment can be found in thirteen weeks or a weekend, that the alienation and injustice experience by women, by Black and Third World people, by the poor, in a world ruled by white males, in a society which fails to meet the most basic needs and which is slowly poisoning itself, can be mitigated or dispersed by Transcendental Meditation. Perhaps the most succinct expression of this message I have seen is the appearance of a magazine for women called *Self*. The insistence of the feminist movement, that each woman's selfhood is precious, that the feminine ethic of self-denial and self-sacrifice must give way to a true woman identification, which would affirm our connectedness with all women, is perverted into a commercially profitable and politically debilitating narcissism. It is important for each of you, toward whom many of these messages are especially directed, to discriminate clearly between "liberated life style" and feminist struggle, and to make a conscious choice.

It's a cliché of commencement speeches that the speaker ends with a peroration telling the new graduates that however badly past generations have behaved, their generation must save the world. I would rather say to you, women of the class of 1979: Try to be worthy of your foresisters, learn from your history, look for inspiration to your ancestresses. If this history has been poorly taught to you, if you do not know it, then use your educational privilege to learn it. Learn how some women of privilege have compromised the greater liberation of women, how others have risked their privileges to further it; learn how brilliant and successful women have failed to create a more just and caring society, precisely because they have tried to do so on terms that the powerful men around them would accept and tolerate. Learn to be worthy of the women of every class, culture, and historical age who did otherwise, who spoke boldly when women were jeered and physically

harassed for speaking in public, who—like Anne Hutchinson, Mary Wollstonecraft, the Grimké sisters, Abby Kelley, Ida B. Wells-Barnett, Susan B.
Anthony, Lillian Smith, Fannie Lou Hamer—broke taboos, who resisted
slavery—their own and other people's. To become a token woman—
whether you win the Nobel prize or merely get tenure at the cost of denying
your sisters—is to become something less than a man indeed, since men are
loyal at least to their own world view, their laws of brotherhood and male
self-interest. I am not suggesting that you imitate male loyalties; with the
philosopher Mary Daly, I believe that the bonding of women must be utterly
different and for an utterly different end: not the misering of resources and
power, but the release, in each other, of the yet unexplored resources and
transformative power of women, so long despised, confined, and wasted. Get
all the knowledge and skill you can in whatever professions you enter; but remember that most of your education must be self-education, in learning the
things women need to know and in calling up the voices we need to hear
within ourselves.

QUESTIONING THE TEXT

1. Rich says that the term *power* is "highly charged for women," and she
   uses it in several different senses in this essay. Look carefully at these different meanings of *power*. Which meaning fits best with your own understandings—and would you agree that *power* is "highly charged for
   women"?
2. Rich lists three broad areas of knowledge that, she argues, women most
   need. What reasons and evidence does she offer to explain why women
   need such knowledge?
3. How does A.L.'s reference to her own school experience affect your
   reading of Rich's essay, if at all? Why do you think A.L. included this
   information in the introduction?

MAKING CONNECTIONS

4. Do you agree with Rich that women's educational needs are different
   from men's? Why, or why not? In "The Idea of a University" (p. 39),
   John Henry Newman seems to suggest that all students have the same
   basic needs. How might Rich respond to him on this point?
5. Writing about fifteen years after Rich, Lynne V. Cheney, in "PC: Alive
   and Entrenched" (p. 112), has a very different perspective on the ways
   in which colleges do not teach students what they most need to know.
   Would Rich be likely to agree with Cheney? Write a one-page dia-

logue between the two women on the subject of "what a university should teach its students."

JOINING THE CONVERSATION

6. What, if any, changes has your school made in the last ten years or so to accommodate the needs and interests of women students? Consider such factors as increased hiring of women faculty, the opening of a women's student center or a women's studies program or department, speakers on women's issues, improvements in campus safety. Write a brief editorial intended for your campus newspaper in which you reflect on the extent to which your school is "user-friendly" for women and whether women at your school can learn what they most "need to know."

7. Try your own hand at writing a brief essay answering the question "What Does a Woman [or Man] Need to Know?" You may want to compare your essay with those of other classmates, noting points of agreement and disagreement—particularly among women and men.

ALLAN BLOOM
The Student and the University

IN THE LAST DECADE, *perhaps no book on the academy has been more widely read, debated, and attacked than* The Closing of the American Mind *(1987) by Allan Bloom (1930–92), who taught at the University of Chicago as Professor in the Committee on Social Thought and the College. Bloom recommended the same sort of visionary liberal education that John Henry Newman had championed more than a century earlier in* The Idea of a University. *His book, a wide-ranging assault on many modern assumptions about education, calls for a return—at least at the schools he considers "first-rank"—to a traditional curriculum centered on Great Books deeply read and understood.*

Newman wrote The Idea of a University *in the midst of a debate similar to that initiated by Bloom's book in the United States; both authors argue against those who would reshape education along more utilitarian lines. Yet while they have much in common, I am struck by their differences in tone. Newman portrays his version of liberal education as a true engine of progress, the best way of achieving a better world. Bloom, on the other hand, seems more pessimistic, offering his Great Books curriculum as a slim hope for recapturing a paradise already quite lost, an academic garden where dedicated faculty and serious students might ponder enduring philosophical questions.*

I've included a section from The Closing of the American Mind *titled "Liberal Education" partly because Bloom's work remains so controversial and partly because I think he was right in arguing that a college degree these days often certifies little more than that a student has sat through a specified number of unrelated courses. The university has become a supermarket stuffed with trendy subjects and majors. Like shoppers grabbing fast foods and seduced by slick advertising and eye-catching displays, too many students choose classes for all the wrong reasons—to get their fifteen hours, to meet a core requirement, to accommodate their work schedules.*

Surely, we can do better.

The line I remember best from Bloom is the one I've highlighted in the opening to this chapter: "The university has to stand for something." Need I add, besides football? — J.R.

LIBERAL EDUCATION

What image does a first-rank college or university present today to a teen-ager leaving home for the first time, off to the adventure of a liberal education? He has four years of freedom to discover himself—a space between

the intellectual wasteland he has left behind* and the inevitable dreary professional training that awaits him after the baccalaureate. In this short time he
must learn that there is a great world beyond the little one he knows, experience the exhilaration of it and digest enough of it to sustain himself in the intellectual deserts he is destined to traverse. He must do this, that is, if he is to
have any hope of a higher life. These are the charmed years when he can, if
he so chooses, become anything he wishes and when he has the opportunity
to survey his alternatives, not merely those current in his time or provided by
careers, but those available to him as a human being. The importance of these
years for an American cannot be overestimated. They are civilization's only
chance to get to him.

In looking at him we are forced to reflect on what he should learn if he
is to be called educated; we must speculate on what the human potential to
be fulfilled is. In the specialties we can avoid such speculation, and the avoidance of them is one of specialization's charms. But here it is a simple duty.
What are we to teach this person? The answer may not be evident, but to attempt to answer the question is already to philosophize and to begin to educate. Such a concern in itself poses the question of the unity of man and the
unity of the sciences. It is childishness to say, as some do, that everyone must
be allowed to develop freely, that it is authoritarian to impose a point of view
on the student. In that case, why have a university? If the response is "to provide an atmosphere for learning," we come back to our original questions at
the second remove. Which atmosphere? Choices and reflection on the reasons for those choices are unavoidable. The university has to stand for something. The practical effects of unwillingness to think positively about the contents of a liberal education are, on the one hand, to ensure that all the
vulgarities of the world outside the university will flourish within it, and, on
the other, to impose a much harsher and moral illiberal necessity on the student—the one given by the imperial and imperious demands of the specialized disciplines unfiltered by unifying thought.

The university now offers no distinctive visage to the young person. He
finds a democracy of the disciplines—which are there either because they are
autochthonous or because they wandered in recently to perform some job
that was demanded of the university. This democracy is really an anarchy, because there are no recognized rules for citizenship and no legitimate titles to
rule. In short there is no vision, nor is there a set of competing visions, of
what an educated human being is. The question has disappeared, for to pose
it would be a threat to the peace. There is no organization of the sciences,
no tree of knowledge. Out of chaos emerges dispiritedness, because it is

---

four years of . . . intellectual wasteland: For a different perspective on what a student brings
to his or her undergraduate experience, see bell hooks, "Keeping Close to Home: Class and Education" (p. 85).

impossible to make a reasonable choice. Better to give up on liberal education and get on with a specialty in which there is at least a prescribed curriculum and a prospective career. On the way the student can pick up in elective courses a little of whatever is thought to make one cultured. The student gets no intimation that great mysteries might be revealed to him, that new and higher motives of action might be discovered within him, that a different and more human way of life can be harmoniously constructed by what he is going to learn.

Simply, the university is not distinctive. Equality for us seems to culminate in the unwillingness and incapacity to make claims of superiority, particularly in the domains in which such claims have always been made—art, religion and philosophy. When Weber* found that he could not choose between certain high opposites—reason vs. revelation, Buddha vs. Jesus—he did not conclude that all things are equally good, that the distinction between high and low disappears. As a matter of fact he intended to revitalize the consideration of these great alternatives in showing the gravity and danger involved in choosing among them; they were to be heightened in contrast to the trivial considerations of modern life that threatened to overgrow and render indistinguishable the profound problems the confrontation with which makes the bow of the soul taut. The serious intellectual life was for him the battleground of the great decisions, all of which are spiritual or "value" choices. One can no longer present this or that particular view of the educated or civilized man as authoritative; therefore one must say that education consists in knowing, really knowing, the small number of such views in their integrity. This distinction between profound and superficial—which takes the place of good and bad, true and false—provided a focus for serious study, but it hardly held out against the naturally relaxed democratic tendency to say, "Oh, what's the use?" The first university disruptions at Berkeley were explicitly directed against the multiversity smorgasbord and, I must confess, momentarily and partially engaged my sympathies. It may have even been the case that there was some small element of longing for an education in the motivation of those students. But nothing was done to guide or inform their energy, and the result was merely to add multilife-styles to multidisciplines, the diversity of perversity to the diversity of specialization. What we see so often happening in general happened here too; the insistent demand for greater community ended in greater isolation. Old agreements, old habits, old traditions were not so easily replaced.

Thus, when a student arrives at the university, he finds a bewildering variety of departments and a bewildering variety of courses. And there is no official guidance, no university-wide agreement, about what he *should* study. Nor

5

Weber: Max Weber (1864–1920), German social scientist and author of *The Protestant Ethic and the Spirit of Capitalism*

does he usually find readily available examples, either among students or professors, of a unified use of the university's resources. It is easiest simply to make a career choice and go about getting prepared for that career. The programs designed for those having made such a choice render their students immune to charms that might lead them out of the conventionally respectable. The sirens sing *sotto voce* these days, and the young already have enough wax in their ears* to pass them by without danger. These specialties can provide enough courses to take up most of their time for four years in preparation for the inevitable graduate study. With the few remaining courses they can do what they please, taking a bit of this and a bit of that. No public career these days—not doctor nor a lawyer nor politician nor journalist nor businessman nor entertainer—has much to do with humane learning. An education, other than purely professional or technical, can even seem to be an impediment. That is why a countervailing atmosphere in the university would be necessary for the students to gain a taste for intellectual pleasures and learn that they are viable.

The real problem is those students who come hoping to find out what career they want to have, or are simply looking for an adventure with themselves. There are plenty of things for them to do—courses and disciplines enough to spend many a lifetime on. Each department or great division of the university makes a pitch for itself, and each offers a course of study that will make the student an initiate. But how to choose among them? How do they relate to one another? The fact is they do not address one another. They are competing and contradictory, without being aware of it. The problem of the whole is urgently indicated by the very existence of the specialties, but it is never systematically posed. The net effect of the student's encounter with the college catalogue is bewilderment and very often demoralization. It is just a matter of chance whether he finds one or two professors who can give him an insight into one of the great visions of education that have been the distinguishing part of every civilized nation. Most professors are specialists, concerned only with their own fields, interested in the advancement of those fields in their own terms, or in their own personal advancement in a world where all the rewards are on the side of professional distinction. They have been entirely emancipated from the old structure of the university, which at least helped to indicate that they are incomplete, only parts of an unexamined and undiscovered whole. So the student must navigate among a collection of carnival barkers, each trying to lure him into a particular sideshow. This undecided student is an embarrassment to most universities, because he seems to be saying, "I am a whole human being. Help me to form myself in my wholeness and let me develop my real potential," and he is the one to whom they have nothing to say.

---

wax in their ears: an allusion to Homer's *Odyssey,* in which the hero, Odysseus, orders his sailors to put wax in their ears to escape the seductive song of the Sirens

Cornell was, as in so many other things, in advance of its time on this issue. The six-year Ph.D. program, richly supported by the Ford Foundation, was directed specifically to high school students who had already made "a firm career choice" and was intended to rush them through to the start of those careers. A sop was given to desolate humanists in the form of money to fund seminars that these young careerists could take on their way through the College of Arts and Sciences. For the rest, the educators could devote their energies to arranging and packaging the program without having to provide it with any substance. That kept them busy enough to avoid thinking about the nothingness of their endeavor. This has been the preferred mode of not look- ing the Beast in the Jungle in the face—structure, not content. The Cornell plan for dealing with the problem of liberal education was to suppress the stu- dents' longing for liberal education by encouraging their professionalism and their avarice, providing money and all the prestige the university had available to make careerism the centerpiece of the university.

The Cornell plan dared not state the radical truth, a well-kept secret: the colleges do not have enough to teach their students, not enough to justify keeping them four years, probably not even three years. If the focus is careers, there is hardly one specialty, outside the hardest of the hard natural sciences, which requires more than two years of preparatory training prior to graduate studies. The rest is just wasted time, or a period of ripening until the students are old enough for graduate studies. For many graduate careers, even less is really necessary. It is amazing how many undergraduates are poking around for courses to take, without any plan or question to ask, just filling up their college years. In fact, with rare exceptions, the courses are parts of specialties and not designed for general cultivation, or to investigate questions important for human beings as such. The so-called knowledge explosion and increasing specialization have not filled up the college years but emptied them. Those years are impediments; one wants to get beyond them. And in general the persons one finds in the professions need not have gone to college, if one is to judge by their tastes, their fund of learning or their interests. They might as well have spent their college years in the Peace Corps or the like. These great universities—which can split the atom, find cures for the most terrible dis- eases, conduct surveys of whole populations and produce massive dictionaries of lost languages—cannot generate a modest program of general education for undergraduate students. This is a parable for our times.

There are attempts to fill the vacuum painlessly with various kinds of fancy packaging of what is already there—study abroad options, individual- ized majors, etc. Then there are Black Studies and Women's or Gender Stud- ies, along with Learn Another Culture. Peace Studies are on their way to a similar prevalence. All this is designed to show that the university is with it and has something in addition to its traditional specialties. The latest item is computer literacy, the full cheapness of which is evident only to those who think a bit about what literacy might mean. It would make some sense to promote literacy literacy, inasmuch as most high school graduates nowadays have difficulty reading and writing. And some institutions are quietly undertaking this worthwhile task. But they do not trumpet the fact, because this is merely a high school function that our current sad state of educational affairs has thrust upon them, about which they are not inclined to boast.

Now that the distractions of the sixties are over, and undergraduate education has become more important again (because the graduate departments, aside from the professional schools, are in trouble due to the shortage of academic jobs), university officials have had somehow to deal with the undeniable fact that the students who enter are uncivilized, and that the universities have some responsibility for civilizing them. If one were to give a base interpretation of the schools' motives, one could allege that their concern stems from shame and self-interest. It is becoming all too evident that liberal education—which is what the small band of prestigious institutions are supposed to provide, in contrast to the big state schools, which are thought simply to prepare specialists to meet the practical demands of a complex society—has no content, that a certain kind of fraud is being perpetrated. For a time the great moral consciousness alleged to have been fostered in students by the great universities, especially their vocation as gladiators who fight war and racism, seemed to fulfill the demands of the collective university conscience. They were doing something other than offering preliminary training for doctors and lawyers. Concern and compassion were thought to be the indefinable X that pervaded all the parts of the Arts and Sciences campus. But when that evanescent mist dissipated during the seventies, and the faculties found themselves face to face with ill-educated young people with no intellectual tastes—unaware that there even are such things, obsessed with getting on with their careers before having looked at life—and the universities offered no counterpoise, no alternative goals, a reaction set in.

Liberal education—since it has for so long been ill-defined, has none of the crisp clarity or institutionalized prestige of the professions, but nevertheless perseveres and has money and respectability connected with it—has always been a battleground for those who are somewhat eccentric in relation to the specialties. It is in something like the condition of churches as opposed to, say, hospitals. Nobody is quite certain of what the religious institutions are supposed to do anymore, but they do have some kind of role either responding to a real human need or as the vestige of what was once a need, and they invite the exploitation of quacks, adventurers, cranks and fanatics. But they also solicit the warmest and most valiant efforts of persons of peculiar gravity and depth. In liberal education, too, the worst and the best fight it out, fakers vs. authentics, sophists vs. philosophers, for the favor of public opinion and for control over the study of man in our times. The most conspicuous participants in the struggle are administrators who are formally responsible for presenting some kind of public image of the education their colleges offer, persons with a political agenda or vulgarizers of what the specialties know, and real teachers of the humane disciplines who actually see their relation to the whole and urgently wish to preserve the awareness of it in their students' consciousness.

So, just as in the sixties universities were devoted to removing requirements, in the eighties they are busy with attempts to put them back in, a much more difficult task. The word of the day is "core." It is generally agreed that "we went a bit far in the sixties," and that a little fine-tuning has now become clearly necessary.

There are two typical responses to the problem. The easiest and most administratively satisfying solution is to make use of what is already there in the autonomous departments and simply force the students to cover the fields, i.e., take one or more courses in each of the general divisions of the university: natural science, social science and the humanities. The reigning ideology here is *breadth*, as was *openness* in the age of laxity. The courses are almost always the already existing introductory courses, which are of least interest to the major professors and merely assume the worth and reality of that which is to be studied. It is general education, in the sense in which a jack-of-all-trades is a generalist. He knows a bit of everything and is inferior to the specialist in each area. Students may wish to sample a variety of fields, and it may be good to encourage them to look around and see if there is something that attracts them in one of which they have no experience. But this is not a liberal education and does not satisfy any longing they have for one. It just teaches that there is no high-level generalism, and that what they are doing is preliminary to the real stuff and part of the childhood they are leaving behind. Thus they desire to get it over with and get on with what their professors do seriously. Without recognition of important questions of common concern, there cannot be serious liberal education, and attempts to establish it will be but failed gestures.

It is a more or less precise awareness of the inadequacy of this approach to core curricula that motivates the second approach, which consists of what one might call composite courses. There are constructions developed especially for general-education purposes and usually require collaboration of professors drawn from several departments. These courses have titles like "Man in Nature," "War and Moral Responsibility," "The Arts and Creativity," "Culture and the Individual." Everything, of course, depends upon who plans them and who teaches them. They have the clear advantage of requiring some reflection on the general needs of students and force specialized professors to broaden their perspectives, at least for a moment. The dangers are trendiness, mere popularization and lack of substantive rigor. In general, the natural scientists do not collaborate in such endeavors, and hence these courses tend to be unbalanced. In short, they do not point beyond themselves and do not provide the student with independent means to pursue permanent questions independently, as, for example, the study of Aristotle or Kant as wholes once did. They tend to be bits of this and that. Liberal education should give the student the sense that learning must and can be both synoptic and precise. For this, a very small, detailed problem can be the best way, if it is framed so as to open out on the whole. Unless the course has the specific intention to lead to the permanent questions, to make the student aware of them and give him some competence in the important works that treat of them, it tends to be a pleasant diversion and a dead end—because it has nothing to do with any program of further study he can imagine. If such programs engage the best energies of the best people in the university, they can be beneficial and provide some of the missing intellectual excitement for both professors and students. But they rarely do, and they are too cut off from the top, from what the various faculties see as their real business. Where the power is determines the life of the whole body. And the intellectual problems unresolved at the top cannot be resolved administratively below. The problem is the lack of any unity of the sciences and the loss of the will or the means even to discuss the issue. The illness above is the cause of the illness below, to which all the good-willed efforts of honest liberal educationists can at best be palliatives.

Of course, the only serious solution is the one that is almost universally rejected: the good old Great Books approach, in which a liberal education means reading certain generally recognized classic texts, just reading them, letting them dictate what the questions are and the method of approaching them—not forcing them into categories we make up, not treating them as historical products, but trying to read them as their authors wished them to be read. I am perfectly well aware of, and actually agree with, the objections to the Great Books cult. It is amateurish; it encourages an autodidact's self-assurance without competence; one cannot read all the Great Books carefully; if one only reads Great Books, one can never know what a great, as opposed to an ordinary, book is; there is no way of determining who is to decide what a Great Book or what the canon is; books are made the ends and not the means; the whole movement has a certain coarse evangelistic tone that is the opposite of good taste; it engenders a spurious intimacy with greatness; and so forth. But one thing is certain: wherever the Great Books make up a central part of the curriculum, the students are excited and satisfied, feel they are doing something that is independent and fulfilling, getting something from the university they cannot get elsewhere. The very fact of this special experience, which leads nowhere beyond itself, provides them with a new alternative and a respect for study itself. The advantage they get is an awareness of the classic—particularly important for our innocents; an acquaintance with what big questions were when there were still big questions; models, at the very least, of how to go about answering them; and, perhaps most important of all, a fund of shared experiences and thoughts on which to ground their friendships with one another. Programs based upon judicious use of great texts provide the royal road to students' hearts. Their gratitude at learning of Achilles or the categorical imperative is boundless. Alexandre Koyré, the late historian of science, told me that his appreciation for America was great when—in the first course he taught at the University of Chicago, in 1940 at the beginning of his exile—a student spoke in his paper of Mr. Aristotle, unaware that he was not a contemporary. Koyré said that only an American could have the naive profundity to take Aristotle as living thought, unthinkable for most scholars. A good program of liberal education feeds the student's love of truth and passion to live a good life. It is the easiest thing in the world to devise courses of study, adapted to the particular conditions of each university, which thrill those who take them. The difficulty is in getting them accepted by the faculty.

None of the three great parts of the contemporary university is enthusiastic about the Great Books approach to education. The natural scientists are benevolent toward other fields and toward liberal education, if it does not steal away their students and does not take too much time from their preparatory studies. But they themselves are interested primarily in the solution of the questions now important in their disciplines and are not particularly concerned with discussions of their foundations, inasmuch as they are so evidently successful. They are indifferent to Newton's conception of time or his disputes with Leibniz about calculus; Aristotle's teleology is an absurdity beneath consideration. Scientific progress, they believe, no longer depends on the kind of comprehensive reflection given to the nature of science by men like Bacon,* Descartes, Hume, Kant and Marx. This is merely historical study, and for a long time now, even the greatest scientists have given up thinking about Galileo and Newton. Progress is undoubted. The difficulties about the truth of science raised by positivism, and those about the goodness of science raised by Rousseau and Nietzsche, have not really penetrated to the center of scientific consciousness. Hence, no Great Books, but incremental progress, is the theme for them.

Social scientists are in general hostile, because the classic texts tend to deal with the human things the social sciences deal with, and they are very proud of having freed themselves from the shackles of such earlier thought to become truly scientific. And, unlike the natural scientists, they are insecure enough about their achievement to feel threatened by the works of earlier thinkers, perhaps a bit afraid that students will be seduced and fall back into the bad old ways. Moreover, with the possible exception of Weber and Freud, there are no social science books that can be said to be classic. This may be interpreted favorably to the social sciences by comparing them to the natural sciences, which can be said to be a living organism developing by the addition of little cells, a veritable body of knowledge proving itself to be such by the very fact of this almost unconscious growth, with thousands of parts oblivious to the whole, nevertheless contributing to it. This is in opposition

---

The natural scientists . . . men like Bacon: For a different assessment of the "comprehensive reflection given to the nature of science by men like Bacon," see Emily Martin, "The Body at War," especially pp. 275–77.

to a work of imagination or of philosophy, where a single creator makes and surveys an artificial whole. But whether one interprets the absence of the classic in the social sciences in ways flattering or unflattering to them, the fact causes social scientists discomfort. I remember the professor who taught the introductory graduate courses in social science methodology, a famous historian, responding scornfully and angrily to a question I naively put to him about Thucydides with "Thucydides was a fool!"

More difficult to explain is the tepid reaction of humanists to Great Books education, inasmuch as these books now belong almost exclusively to what are called the humanities. One would think that high esteem for the classic would reinforce the spiritual power of the humanities, at a time when their temporal power is at its lowest. And it is true that the most active proponents of liberal education and the study of classic texts are indeed usually humanists. But there is division among them. Some humanities disciplines are just crusty specialties that, although they depend on the status of classic books for their existence, are not really interested in them in their natural state—much philology, for example, is concerned with the languages but not what is said in them—and will and can do nothing to support their own infrastructure. Some humanities disciplines are eager to join the real sciences and transcend their roots in the now overcome mythic past. Some humanists make the legitimate complaints about lack of competence in the teaching and learning of Great Books, although their criticism is frequently undermined by the fact that they are only defending recent scholarly interpretation of the classics rather than a vital, authentic understanding. In their reaction there is a strong element of specialist's jealousy and narrowness. Finally, a large part of the story is just the general debilitation of the humanities, which is both symptom and cause of our present condition.

To repeat, the crisis of liberal education is a reflection of a crisis at the peaks of learning, an incoherence and incompatibility among the first principles with which we interpret the world, an intellectual crisis of the greatest magnitude, which constitutes the crisis of our civilization. But perhaps it would be true to say that the crisis consists not so much in this incoherence but in our incapacity to discuss or even recognize it. Liberal education flourished when it prepared the way for the discussion of a unified view of nature and man's place in it, which the best minds debated on the highest level. It decayed when what lay beyond it were only specialties, the premises of which do not lead to any such vision. The highest is the partial intellect; there is no synopsis.

QUESTIONING THE TEXT

1. How would you characterize Bloom's tone, especially at the beginning of the essay? What does he assume about the quality of a person's life both before and after the college experience? Cite examples from the

essay to support your response. If you keep a reading log, answer this question there.

2. Bloom distinguishes between prestigious private liberal arts colleges and state universities. What mission does he ascribe to each? How do you react to that distinction? What are its implications?

3. Explore Bloom's analogy that likens liberal arts colleges to churches. What are the strengths of the analogy? the weaknesses? After exploring the comparison, try to suggest an analogy of your own.

4. Do you agree or disagree with J.R.'s rationale in the introduction for including this reading in this chapter? Explain your reasoning.

MAKING CONNECTIONS

5. Imagine that you are Allan Bloom. Now annotate the margins of the reading by Mike Rose (especially his comments on the Great Books). How did assuming Bloom's perspective affect your reading of Rose? If you keep a reading log, answer this question there.

6. Bloom finally suggests that the best approach to a liberal arts education is "the good old Great Books approach." Who else in this chapter might support Bloom? Why?

JOINING THE CONVERSATION

7. Bloom claims that a liberal arts education should give a student the feeling that learning can be both *synoptic* and *precise*. Examine the meaning of those terms in a dictionary, and then explore in writing why it is that Bloom believes that a smattering of introductory college courses in different disciplines provides an inadequate perspective on learning.

8. Are you satisfied with your own education? Write an essay exploring this important question. Where do you think Bloom hits the mark in his criticisms? Do any groups seem to be excluded from his program of study? Do any aspects of life seem neglected?

9. Working together with some classmates, list works you have individually read that you believe should be on a list of Great Books. Then discuss what makes a book "great." Can people in a culture as diverse as that in the United States agree on a core of Great Books? If so, explain the criteria you would use to determine such a list.

SHELBY STEELE
The Recoloring of Campus Life

Shelby Steele's book on race relations in the United States, The Content of Our Character *(1990), takes its title from Martin Luther King Jr.'s "I Have a Dream" speech, delivered at a civil rights demonstration in Washington, D.C., in 1963. In that address, King called for the eradication of racial prejudices: "I have a dream my four little children will one day live in a nation where they will not be judged by the color of their skin but by the content of their character." A generation later, Steele (b. 1946) poses the painful question of whether the civil rights establishment has abandoned King's dream. Has the goal of desegregation, he asks, been supplanted by ethnic and racial separation? Has the ideal of equal opportunity been tainted by quotas?*

The lengthy chapter of the book reprinted here examines the sensitive subject of race relations on campus frankly and openly. Steele, a professor of English at San Jose State University in California, is a controversial figure, a black man whose views, like those of Clarence Thomas and the economist Thomas Sowell, challenge the agenda of many civil rights organizations. Steele confronts the anxieties of both blacks and whites with uncommon directness. It is a measure of the national discomfort we feel in talking about race and racism that some people regard views like Steele's as politically "incorrect." Judge for yourself whether he is raising issues that ought not to be matters of debate. – J.R.

[handwritten margin note: Why is this the only reading in this chapter that includes notes by the editors in the margins?]

[handwritten margin note: ✓]

[left margin note:] The U.S. has about 3,000 colleges and universities. Do 80 incidents a year—most involving ethnic "insensitivity"—really constitute an increase in racial tensions? Was there a time when such incidents were fewer? – J.R.

In the past few years, we have witnessed what the National Institute Against Prejudice and Violence calls a "proliferation" of racial incidents on college campuses around the country. Incidents of on-campus "intergroup conflict" have occurred at more than 160 colleges in the last two years, according to the institute. The nature of these incidents has ranged from open racial violence—most notoriously, the October 1986 beating of a black student at the University of Massachusetts at Amherst after an argument about the World Series turned into a racial bashing, with a crowd of up to three thousand whites chasing twenty blacks—to the harassment of minority students and acts of racial or ethnic insensitivity, with by far the greatest number of episodes falling in the last two categories. At Yale last year, a swastika and the words

[right margin note:] What is this institute—and what is its agenda? – A.L.

63

"white power" were painted on the university's Afro-American cultural center. Racist jokes were aired not long ago on a campus radio station at the University of Michigan. And at the University of Wisconsin at Madison, members of the Zeta Beta Tau fraternity held a mock slave auction in which pledges painted their faces black and wore Afro wigs. Two weeks after the president of Stanford University informed the incoming freshman class last fall that "bigotry is out, and I mean it," two freshmen defaced a poster of Beethoven—gave the image thick lips—and hung it on a black student's door.

In response, black students around the country have rediscovered the militant protest strategies of the sixties. At the University of Massachusetts at Amherst, Williams College, Penn State University, University of California–Berkeley, UCLA, Stanford University, and countless other campuses, black students have sat in, marched, and rallied. But much of what they were marching and rallying about seemed less a response to specific racial incidents than a call for broader action on the part of the colleges and universities they were attending. Black students have demanded everything from more black faculty members and new courses on racism to the addition of "ethnic" foods in the cafeteria. There is the sense in these demands that racism runs deep. Is the campus becoming the battleground for a renewed war between the races? I don't think so, not really. But if it is not a war, the problem of campus racism does represent a new and surprising hardening of racial lines within the most traditionally liberal and tolerant of America's institutions—its universities.

As a black who has spent his entire adult life on predominantly white campuses, I found it hard to believe that the problem of campus racism was as dramatic as some of the incidents seemed to make it. The incidents I read or heard about often seemed prankish and adolescent, though not necessarily harmless. There is a meanness in them but not much menace; no one is proposing to reinstitute Jim Crow on campus. On the California campus where I now teach, there have been few signs of racial tension.

And, of course, universities are not where racial problems tend to arise. When I went to college in the mid-sixties, colleges were oases of calm and understanding in a racially tense society; campus life—with its traditions of tolerance and fairness, its very distance from the "real" world—imposed a degree of broad-mindedness on even the most provincial students. If I met whites who were not anxious to be friends with blacks, most were at least vaguely friendly to the cause of our freedom. In any case, there was no guerrilla activity against our presence, no "mine field of racism" (as one black student at Berkeley recently put it to me) to negotiate. I wouldn't say that the phrase "campus racism" is a contradiction in terms, but until recently it certainly seemed an incongruence.

I was in college at this same time and this does not describe my experience on a very racist and often hostile campus. — A.L.

But a greater incongruence is the generational timing of this new problem on the campuses. Today's undergraduates were born after the passage of the 1964 Civil Rights Act. They grew up in an age when racial equality was for the first time enforceable by law. This too was a time when blacks suddenly appeared on television, as mayors of big cities, as icons of popular culture, as teachers, and in some cases even as neighbors. Today's black and white college students, veterans of "Sesame Street" and often of integrated grammar and high schools, have had more opportunities to know each other than any previous generation in American history. Not enough opportunities, perhaps, but enough to make the notion of racial tension on campus something of a mystery, at least to me.

He's now assuming it's a "new" problem, but he hasn't proven it. — A.L.

To look at this mystery, I left my own campus with its burden of familiarity and talked with black and white students at California schools where racial incidents had occurred: Stanford, UCLA, and Berkeley. I spoke with black and white students—not with Asians and Hispanics—because, as always, blacks and whites represent the deepest lines of division, and because I hesitate to wander onto the complex territory of other minority groups. A phrase by William H. Gass—"the hidden internality of things"—describes, with maybe a little too much grandeur, what I hoped to find. But it is what I wanted to find, for this is the kind of problem that makes a black person nervous, which is not to say that it doesn't unnerve whites as well. Once every six months or so someone yells "nigger" at me from a passing car. I don't like to think that these solo artists might soon make up a chorus, or worse, that this chorus might one day soon sing to me from the paths of my own campus.

I don't follow him here. What does he mean by "hidden internality"? — A.L.

I have long believed that the trouble between the races is seldom what it appears to be. It was not hard to see after my first talks with students that racial tension on campus is a problem that misrepresents itself. It has the same look, the archetypal pattern, of America's timeless racial conflict—white racism and black protest. And I think part of our concern over it comes from the fact that it has the feel of a relapse, illness gone and come again. But if we are seeing the same symptoms, I don't believe we are dealing with the same illness. For one thing, I think racial tension on campus is more the result of racial equality than inequality.

Maybe this is what he means— the old appearance/reality binary. — A.L.

Has racism ever really "gone"? — T.E.

Is this the main point he is arguing? — A.L.

How to live with racial difference has been America's profound social problem. For the first hundred years or so following emancipation it was controlled by a legally sanctioned inequality that kept the races from each other. No longer is this the case. On campuses today, as throughout society, blacks enjoy equality under the law—a profound social advancement. No student may be kept out of a class or a dormitory or an extracurricular activity because of his or her race. But there is a paradox here: on a campus where members of all races are gathered, mixed together in the classroom as well as socially, differences are more exposed than ever. And this is where the trouble starts. For members of each race—young adults coming into their own, often away from home for the first time—bring to this site of freedom, exploration, and (now, today) equality, very deep fears, anxieties, inchoate feelings of racial shame, anger, and guilt. These feelings could lie dormant in the home, in familiar neigh-

He's right: higher education challenges the comfortable assumptions most students bring to campus. — J.R.

I've never experienced such feelings where race is concerned, and I come from a predominantly white community. — T.E.

borhoods, in simpler days of childhood. But the college campus, with its structures of interaction and adult-level competition—the big exam, the dorm, the mixer—is another matter. I think campus racism is born of the rub between racial difference and a setting, the campus itself, devoted to interaction and equality. On our campuses, such concentrated micro-societies, all that remains unresolved between blacks and whites, all the old wounds and shames that have never been addressed, present themselves for attention—and present our youth with pressures they cannot always handle.

I have mentioned one paradox: racial fears and anxieties among blacks and whites, bubbling up in an era of racial equality under the law, in settings that are among the freest and fairest in society. But there is another, related paradox, stemming from the notion of—and practice of—affirmative action. Under the provisions of the Equal Employment Opportunity Act of 1972, all state governments and institutions (including universities) were forced to initiate plans to increase the proportion of minority and women employees and, in the case of universities, of students too. Affirmative action plans that establish racial quotas were ruled unconstitutional more than ten years ago in *University of California v. Bakke,* but such plans are still thought by some to secretly exist, and lawsuits having to do with alleged quotas are still very much with us. But quotas are only the most controversial aspect of affirmative action; the principle of affirmative action is reflected in various university programs aimed at redressing and overcoming past patterns of discrimination. Of course, to be conscious of past patterns of discrimination—the fact, say, that public schools in the black inner cities are more crowded and employ fewer top-notch teachers than a white suburban public school, and that this is a factor in student performance—is only reasonable. But in doing this we also call attention quite obviously to difference: in the case of blacks and whites, racial difference. What has emerged on campus in recent years—as a result of the new equality and of affirmative action

The beneficiaries of affirmative action are usually middle-class students—not poor minority youth from inner cities. Do middle-class whites resent that fact? — J.R.

This idealistic view of a university as "free and fair" would be contested by many. — A.L.

that's not what he says.

and, in a sense, as a result of progress—is a *politics of difference,* a troubling, volatile politics in which each group justifies itself, its sense of worth and its pursuit of power, through difference alone.

In this context, racial, ethnic, and gender differences become forms of sovereignty, campuses become balkanized, and each group fights with whatever means are available. No doubt there are many factors that have contributed to the rise of racial tension on campus: What has been the role of fraternities, which have returned to campus with their inclusions and exclusions? What role has the heightened notion of college as some first step to personal, financial success played in increasing competition, and thus tension? But mostly, what I sense is that in interactive settings, fighting the fights of "difference," old ghosts are stirred and haunt again. Black and white Americans simply have the power to make each other feel shame and guilt. In most situations, we may be able to deny these feelings, keep them at bay. But these feelings are likely to surface on college campuses, where young people are groping for identity and power, and where difference is made to matter so greatly. In a way, racial tension on campus in the eighties might have been inevitable.

I would like, first, to discuss black students, their anxieties and vulnerabilities. The accusation black Americans have always lived with is that they are inferior—inferior simply because they are black. And this accusation has been too uniform, too ingrained in cultural imagery, too enforced by law, custom, and every form of power not to have left a mark. Black inferiority was a precept accepted by the founders of this nation; it was a principle of social organization that relegated blacks to the sidelines of American life. So when young black students find themselves on white campuses surrounded by those who have historically claimed superiority, they are also surrounded by the myth of their inferiority.

Of course, it is true that many young people come to college with some anxiety about not being good enough. But only blacks come wearing a

Identity politics (I get my identity solely and only through one characteristic, such as race) to me is different from politics of difference, which seeks to honor differences among all *people while not ignoring commonalities.*
— A.L.

Black shame and white guilt? Steele's analysis looks simplistic. Can he sustain it?
— J.R.

Steele implies that college students are shallow, that they would immediately focus on race if any problem arose. This is not my experience.
— T.E.

When he uses "of course" I always wonder whether I'll agree with what comes next!
— A.L.

color that is still, in the minds of some, a sign of inferiority. Poles, Jews, Hispanics, and other groups also endure degrading stereotypes. But two things make the myth of black inferiority a far heavier burden—the broadness of its scope and its incarnation in color. There are not only more stereotypes of blacks than of other groups, but these stereotypes are also more dehumanizing, more focused on the most despised human traits: stupidity, laziness, sexual immorality, dirtiness, and so on. In America's racial and ethnic hierarchy, blacks have clearly been relegated to the lowest level—have been burdened with an ambiguous, animalistic humanity. Moreover, this is made unavoidable for blacks by sheer visibility of black skin, a skin that evokes the myth of inferiority on sight. Today this myth is sadly reinforced for many black students by affirmative action programs, under which blacks may often enter college with lower test scores and high school grade point averages than whites. "They see me as an affirmative action case," one black student told me at UCLA. This reinforces the myth of inferiority by implying that blacks are not good enough to make it into college on their own.

So when a black student enters college, the myth of inferiority compounds the normal anxiousness over whether he or she will be good enough. This anxiety is not only personal but also racial. The families of these students will have pounded into them the fact that blacks are not inferior. And probably more than anything it is this pounding that finally leaves the mark. If I am not inferior, why the need to say so?

This myth of inferiority constitutes a very sharp and ongoing anxiety for young blacks, the nature of which is very precise: it is the terror that somehow, through one's actions of by virtue of some "proof" (a poor grade, a flubbed response in class), one's fear of inferiority—inculcated in ways large and small by society—will be confirmed as real. On a university campus where intelligence itself is the ultimate measure, this anxiety is bound to be triggered.

A black student I met at UCLA was disturbed a little when I asked him if he ever felt vulnerable—

I have often wondered if any blacks felt affirmative action projects were just racist and belittling.   T.E.

Test scores reflect biased test designs, and grades can too. I don't buy this argument.
— A.L.

anxious about "black inferiority"—as a black student. But after a long pause, he finally said, "I think I do." The example he gave was of a large lecture class he'd taken with over three hundred students. Fifty or so black students sat in the back of the lecture hall and "acted out every stereotype in the book." They were loud, ate food, came in late—and generally got lower grades than whites in the class. "I knew I would be seen like them, and I didn't like it. I never sat by them." Seen like what, I asked, though we both knew the answer. "As lazy, ignorant, and stupid," he said sadly.

he has a choice in this association —

Had the group at the back been white fraternity brothers, they would not have been seen as dumb whites, of course. And a frat brother who worried about his grades would not worry that he [had] been seen "like them." The terror in this situation for the black student I spoke with was that his own deeply buried anxiety would be given credence, that the myth would be verified, and that he would feel shame and humiliation not because of who he was but simply because he was black. In this lecture hall his race, quite apart from his performance, might subject him to four unendurable feelings—diminishment, accountability to the preconceptions of whites, a powerlessness to change those preconceptions, and finally, shame. These are the feelings that make up his racial anxiety, and that of all blacks on any campus. On a white campus a black is never far from these feelings, and even his unconscious knowledge that he is subject to them can undermine his self-esteem. There are blacks on any campus who are not up to doing good college-level work. Certain black students may not be happy or motivated or in the appropriate field of study—*just like whites*. (Let us not forget that many white students get poor grades, fail, drop out.) Moreover, many more blacks than whites are not quite prepared for college, may have to catch up, owing to factors beyond their control: poor previous schooling, for example. But the white who has to catch up will not be anxious that his being behind is a matter of his whiteness, of his being racially inferior. The black student may well have such a fear.

Steele makes a convincing distinction here. Growing up, I heard Polish jokes and slurs, but not often enough to think that society really believed the stereotype. That makes a difference. — J.R.

Do Asian American students feel similarly pressured by a stereotype that marks them all as diligent, hardworking, and extraordinarily smart? — J.R.

Perhaps, but there's a big difference in living up to a positive stereotype and disproving a negative one.

Or smart but bored? — A.L.

I don't buy this— the fraternity stereotype is quite strong, too. Why wouldn't a frat brother be disturbed? — T.E.

I'm irritated by his continued attempts to speak for all African Americans. — A.L.

This, I believe, is one reason why black colleges in America turn out 37 percent of all black college graduates though they enroll only 16 percent of black college students. Without whites around on campus, the myth of inferiority is in abeyance and, along with it, a great reservoir of culturally imposed self-doubt. On black campuses, feelings of inferiority are personal; on campuses with a white majority, a black's problems have a way of becoming a "black" problem.

Going to an all-black college doesn't shut out the rest of the world. I don't buy this. — T.E.

But this feeling of vulnerability a black may feel, in itself, is not as serious a problem as what he or she does with it. To admit that one is made anxious in integrated situations about the myth of racial inferiority is difficult for young blacks. It seems like admitting that one is racially inferior. And so, most often, the student will deny harboring the feelings. This is where some of the pangs of racial tension begin, because denial always involves distortion.

Do all blacks feel this way? Steele is generalizing. — T.E.

In order to deny a problem we must tell ourselves that the problem is something different from what it really is. A black student at Berkeley told me that he felt defensive every time he walked into a classroom of white faces. When I asked why, he said, "Because I know they're all racists. They think blacks are stupid." Of course it may be true that some whites feel this way, but the singular focus on white racism allows this student to obscure his own underlying racial anxiety. He can now say that his problem—facing a classroom of white faces, *fearing* that they think he is dumb—is entirely the result of certifiable white racism and has nothing to do with his own anxieties, or even that this particular academic subject may not be his best. Now all the terror of his anxiety, its powerful energy, is devoted to simply *seeing* racism. Whatever evidence of racism he finds—and looking this hard, he will no doubt find some—can be brought in to buttress his distorted view of the problem while his actual deep-seated anxiety goes unseen.

This helps explain the dilemma of many black students on mainly white campuses. — J.R.

Denial, and the distortion that results, places the problem *outside* the self and in the world. It is not that I have any inferiority anxiety because of my race; it is that I am going to school with people

this seems to a racism . . . make psychological problem that blacks have

This seems a kind of false either/or argument to me. Either the problem is all external (white racists) or all internal (deep-seated anxieties). — A.L.

who don't like blacks. This is the shift in thinking that allows black students to reenact the protest pattern of the sixties. *Denied racial anxiety–distortion–reenactment* is the process by which feelings of inferiority are transformed into an exaggerated white menace—which is then protested against with the techniques of the past. Under the sway of this process, black students believe that history is repeating itself, that it's just like the sixties, or fifties. In fact, it is not-yet-healed wounds from the past, rather than the inequality that created the wounds, that is the real problem.

Obsessive attention to race can breed racist feelings. That's one reason I'm uneasy with multicultural curriculums that emphasize difference.   —J.R.

This process generated an unconscious need to exaggerate the level of racism on campus—to make it a matter of the system, not just a handful of students. Racism is the avenue away from the true inner anxiety. How many students demonstrating for black theme dorms—demonstrating in the style of the sixties, when the battle was to win for blacks a place on campus—might be better off spending their time reading and studying? Black students have the highest dropout rate and the lowest grade point average of any group in American universities. This need not be so. And it is not the result of not having black theme dorms.

People said the same thing to the '60s civil rights protesters.   —A.L.

It was my very good fortune to go to college in 1964, when the question of black "inferiority" was openly talked about among blacks. The summer before I left for college, I heard Martin Luther King speak in Chicago, and he laid it on the line for black students everywhere: "When you are behind in a footrace, the only way to get ahead is to run faster than the man in front of you. So when your white roommate says he's tired and goes to sleep, you stay up and burn the midnight oil." His statement that we were "behind in a footrace" acknowledged that, because of history, of few opportunities, of racism, we were, in a sense, "inferior." But this had to do with what had been done to our parents and their parents, not with inherent inferiority. And because it was acknowledged, it was presented to us as a challenge rather than a mark of shame.

Of the eighteen black students (in a student body of one thousand) who were on campus in my freshman year, all graduated, though a number of us were not from the middle class. At the university where I currently teach, the dropout rate for black students is 72 percent, despite the presence of several academic support programs, a counseling center with black counselors, an Afro-American studies department, black faculty, administrators, and staff, a general education curriculum that emphasizes "cultural pluralism," an Educational Opportunities Program, a mentor program, a black faculty and staff association, and an administration and faculty that often announce the need to do more for black students.

At my university, these programs are tiny and underfunded. At Ohio State, only 3.2% of faculty are African American. – A.L.

It may be unfair to compare my generation with the current one. Parents do this compulsively and to little end but self-congratulation. But I don't congratulate my generation. I think we were advantaged. We came along at a time when racial integration was held in high esteem. And integration was a very challenging social concept for both blacks and whites. We were remaking ourselves—that's what one did at college—and making history. We had something to prove. This was a profound advantage; it gave us clarity and a challenge. Achievement in the American mainstream was the goal of integration, and the best thing about this challenge was its secondary message—that we *could* achieve.

Integration is a goal rarely mentioned in campus discussions of racial problems these days. – J.R.

Is "achievement in the American mainstream" another way of saying "being like white people"? – A.L.

There is much irony in the fact that black power would come along in the late sixties and change all this. Black power was a movement of uplift and pride, and yet it also delivered the weight of pride—a weight that would burden black students from then on. Black power "nationalized" the black identity, made blackness itself an object of celebration, an allegiance. But if it transformed a mark of shame into a mark of pride, it also, in the name of pride, required the denial of racial anxiety. Without a frank account of one's anxieties, there is no clear direction, no concrete challenge. Black students today do not get as clear a message from their racial identity as my generation got. They are not filled with the same urgency to prove them-

This may be true, but it's another one of those either/or arguments I'm always leery of. – A.L.

selves because black pride has said, *You're already proven, already equal, as good as anybody.*

The "black identity" shaped by black power most forcefully contributes to racial tensions on campuses by basing entitlement more on race than on constitutional rights and standards of merit. With integration, black entitlement derived from constitutional principles of fairness. Black power changed this by skewing the formula from rights to color—if you were black, you were entitled. Thus the United Coalition Against Racism (UCAR) at the University of Michigan could "demand" two years ago that all black professors be given immediate tenure, that there [be] a special pay incentive for black professors, and that money be provided for an all-black student union. In this formula, black becomes the very color of entitlement, an extra right in itself, and a very dangerous grandiosity is promoted in which blackness amounts to specialness.

Race is, by any standard, an unprincipled source of power. And on campuses the use of racial power by one group makes racial, ethnic, or gender difference a currency of power for all groups. When I make my *difference* into power, other groups must seize upon their difference to contain my power and maintain their position relative to me. Very quickly a kind of politics of difference emerges in which racial, ethnic, and gender groups are forced to assert their entitlement and vie for power based on the single quality that makes them different from one another.

On many campuses today academic departments and programs are established on the basis of difference—black studies, women's studies, Asian studies, and so on—despite the fact that there is nothing in these "difference" departments that cannot be studied within traditional academic disciplines. If their rationale is truly past exclusion from the mainstream curriculum, shouldn't the goal now be complete inclusion rather than separateness? I think this logic is overlooked because those groups are too interested in the power their difference can bring, and they insist on separate departments and programs as tribute to that power.

I agree. It's just as racist (and negative) to have all-black unions as it is to have all-white ones.
— T.E.

I agree. Balkanization can present a danger, but that doesn't mean we should reject difference. — A.L.

I agree—the I have the same problem with these specialized depts.— they are "fads" and the money to support them will probably go when the fad passes —

*Is this happening — is
what is
now at
Ber U.*

This politics of difference makes everyone on campus a member of a minority group. It also makes racial tension inevitable. To highlight one's difference as a source of advantage is also, indirectly, to inspire the enemies of that difference. When blackness (and femaleness) become power, then white maleness is also sanctioned as power. A white male student I spoke with at Stanford said, "One of my friends said the other day that we should get together and start up a white student union and come up with a list of demands."

It is certainly true that white maleness has long been an unfair source of power. But the sin of white male power is precisely its use of race and gender as a source of entitlement. When minorities and women use their race, ethnicity, and gender in the same way, they not only commit the same sin but also, indirectly, sanction the very form of power that oppressed them in the first place. The politics of difference is based on a tit-for-tat sort of logic in which every victory only calls one's enemies to arms.

This elevation of difference undermines the communal impulse by making each group foreign and inaccessible to others. When difference is celebrated rather than remarked, people must think in terms of difference, they must find meaning in difference, and this meaning comes from an endless process of contrasting one's group with other groups. Blacks use whites to define themselves as different, women use men, Hispanics use whites and blacks, and on it goes. And in the process each group mythologizes and mystifies its difference, puts it beyond the full comprehension of outsiders. Difference becomes inaccessible preciousness toward which outsiders are expected to be simply and uncomprehendingly reverential.* But beware: in this world, even the insulated world of the college campus, preciousness is a balloon asking for a needle. At Smith College graffiti appears: "Niggers, spics, and chinks. Quit complaining or get out."

Quite true—but does one lead to the other? — T.E.

Another either/or. I don't accept the notion that we must honor only one or the other— difference or community. — A.L.

Difference becomes . . . reverential: For another critical look at "elevation of difference," see Richard Bernstein, "Dérapage," (p. 372).

I think that those who run our colleges and universities are every bit as responsible for the politics of difference as are minority students. To correct the exclusions once caused by race and gender, universities—under the banner of affirmative action—have relied too heavily on race and gender as criteria. So rather than break the link between difference and power, they have reinforced it. On most campuses today, a well-to-do black student with two professional parents is qualified by his race for scholarship monies that are not available to a lower-middle-class white student. A white female with a private school education and every form of cultural advantage comes under the affirmative action umbrella. This kind of inequity is an invitation to backlash.

In a decision startling to many, a federal court has ruled that affirmative action programs at my school based on race and ethnicity are unconstitutional. —J.R.

These generalizations simply are not true. Affirmative action at my school does nothing to advantage the students described here. —A.L.

What universities are quite rightly trying to do is compensate people for past discrimination and the deprivations that followed from it. But race and gender alone offer only the grossest measure of this. And the failure of universities has been their backing away from the challenge of identifying principles of fairness and merit that make finer and more equitable distinctions. The real challenge is not simply to include a certain number of blacks, but to end discrimination against all blacks and to offer special help to those with talent who have also been economically deprived.

I agree. —A.L.

I agree. These special funds make me uncomfortable. — T.E.

With regard to black students, affirmative action has led universities to correlate color with poverty and disadvantage in so absolute a way as to encourage the politics of difference. But why have they gone along with this? My belief is that it is due to the specific form of racial anxiety to which whites are most subject.

Most of the white students I talked with spoke as if from under a faint cloud of accusation. There was always a ring of defensiveness in their complaints about blacks. A white student I spoke to at UCLA told me: "Most white students on this campus think the black student leadership here is made up of oversensitive crybabies who spend all their time looking for things to kick up a ruckus about." A white student at Stanford said, "Blacks do nothing but complain and ask for sympathy when everyone really knows that they don't do well because they don't try. If they worked harder, they could do as well as everyone else."

That these students felt accused was most obvious in their compulsion to assure me that they were not racist. Oblique versions of some-of-my-best-friends-are stories came ritualistically before or after critiques of black students. Some said flatly, "I am not a racist, but . . ." Of course, we all deny being racist, but we only do this compulsively, I think, when we are working against an accusation of bias. I think it was the color of my skin itself that accused them.

This was the meta-message that surrounded these conversations like an aura, and it is, I believe, the core of white American racial anxiety. My skin not only accused them; it judged them. And this judgment was a sad gift of history that brought them to account whether they deserved such accountability or not. It said that wherever and whenever blacks were concerned, they had reason to feel guilt. And whether it was earned or unearned, I think it was guilt that set off the compulsion in these students to disclaim. I believe it is true that, in America, black people make white people feel guilty.

Guilt is the essence of white anxiety just as inferiority is the essence of black anxiety. And the terror that it carries for whites is the terror of discovering that one has reason to feel guilt where blacks are concerned—not so much because of what blacks might think but because of what guilt can say about oneself. If the darkest fear of blacks is inferiority, the darkest fear of whites is that their better lot in life is at least partially the result of their capacity for evil—their capacity to dehumanize an entire people for their own benefit and then to be indifferent to the devastation their dehumanization has wrought on successive generations of their victims. This is the terror that whites are vulnerable to regarding blacks. And the mere fact of being white is sufficient to feel it, since even whites with hearts clean of racism benefit from being white—benefit at the expense of blacks. This is a conditional guilt

Too bad Steele deliberately avoided talking with Hispanic and Asian minorities. Their perspectives on the matter of "guilt" would have enriched the discussion here.

—J.R.

true!

having nothing to do with individual intentions or actions. And it makes for a very powerful anxiety because it threatens whites with a view of themselves as inhuman, just as inferiority threatens blacks with a similar view of themselves. At the dark core of both anxieties is a suspicion of incomplete humanity.

So, the white students I met were not just meeting me; they were also meeting the possibility of their own inhumanity. And this, I think, is what explains how some young white college students in the late eighties could so frankly take part in racially insensitive and outright racist acts. They were expected to be cleaner of racism than any previous generation— they were born into the Great Society. But this expectation overlooks the fact that, for them, color is still an accusation and judgment. In black faces there is a discomforting reflection of white collective shame. Blacks remind them that their racial innocence is questionable, that they are the beneficiaries of past and present racism, and the sins of the father may well have been visited on the children.

He isn't saying that comment this supports his point.

Steele overgeneralizes. All whites are not racists.
— T.E.

And yet young whites tell themselves that they had nothing to do with the oppression of black people. They have a stronger belief in their racial innocence than any previous generation of whites and a natural hostility toward anyone who would challenge that innocence. So (with a great deal of individual variation) they can end up in the paradoxical position of being hostile to blacks as a way of defending their own racial innocence.

I think this is what the young white editors of the *Dartmouth Review* were doing when they harassed black music professor William Cole. Weren't they saying, in effect, I am so free of racial guilt that I can afford to attack blacks ruthlessly and still be racially innocent? The ruthlessness of these attacks was a form of denial, a badge of innocence. The more they were charged with racism, the more ugly and confrontational their harassment became (an escalation unexplained even by the serious charges against Professor Cole). Racism became a means of rejecting racial guilt, a way of showing that they were not, ultimately, racists.

The politics of difference sets up a struggle for innocence among all groups. When difference is the currency of power, each group must fight for the innocence that entitles it to power. To gain this innocence, blacks sting whites with guilt, remind them of their racial past, accuse them of new and more subtle forms of racism. One way whites retrieve their innocence is to discredit blacks and deny their difficulties, for in this denial is the denial of their own guilt. To blacks this denial looks like racism, a racism that feeds black innocence and encourages them to throw more guilt at whites. And so the cycle continues. The politics of difference leads each group to pick at the vulnerabilities of the other.

Men and women who run universities—whites, mostly—participate in the politics of difference because they handle their guilt differently than do many of their students. They don't deny it, but still they don't want to *feel* it. And to avoid this feeling of guilt they have tended to go along with whatever blacks put on the table rather than work with them to assess their real needs. University administrators have too often been afraid of guilt and have relied on negotiation and capitulation more to appease their own guilt than to help blacks and other minorities. Administrators would never give white students a racial theme dorm where they could be "more comfortable with people of their own kind," yet more and more universities are doing this for black students, thus fostering a kind of voluntary segregation. To avoid the anxieties of integrated situations blacks ask for theme dorms; to avoid guilt, white administrators give theme dorms.

When everyone is on the run from their anxieties about race, race relations on campus can be reduced to the negotiation of avoidances. A pattern of demand and concession develops in which both sides use the other to escape themselves. Black studies departments, black deans of student affairs, black counseling programs, Afro houses, black theme dorms, black homecoming dances and graduation ceremonies—black students and white administrators have slowly engineered a machinery of sepa-

Steele is lumping all administrators together; this makes me skeptical of the following argument.
— T.E.

This is undoubtedly often true.
— A.L.

ratism that, in the name of sacred difference, re-draws the ugly lines of segregation.

Black students have not sufficiently helped themselves, and universities, despite all their con-cessions, have not really done much for blacks. If both faced their anxieties, I think they would see the same thing: academic parity with all other groups should be the overriding mission of black students, and it should also be the first goal that uni-versities have for their black students. Blacks can only *know* they are as good as others when they are, in fact, as good—when their grades are higher and their dropout rate lower. Nothing under the sun will substitute for this, and no amount of conces-sions will bring it about.

Universities can never be free of guilt until they truly help black students, which means leading and challenging them rather than negotiating and capit-ulating. It means inspiring them to achieve aca-demic parity, nothing less, and helping them to see their own weaknesses as their greatest challenge. It also means dismantling the machinery of separatism, breaking the link between difference and power, and skewing the formula for entitlement away from race and gender and back to constitutional rights.

As for the young white students who have redis-covered swastikas and the word "nigger," I think that they suffer from an exaggerated sense of their own innocence, as if they were incapable of evil and beyond the reach of guilt. But it is also true that the politics of difference creates an environ-ment that threatens their innocence and makes them defensive. White students are not invited to the negotiating table from which they see blacks and others walk away with concessions. The pre-sumption is that they do not deserve to be there be-cause they are white. So they can only be defensive, and the less mature among them will be aggressive. Guerrilla activity will ensue. Of course this is wrong, but it is also a reflection of an environment where difference carries power and where whites have the wrong "difference."

I think universities should emphasize commonal-ity as a higher value than "diversity" and "plural-

White professors who make compa-rable observations are sometimes charged with racism. What does such an accusation reveal about the advocates of a campus "politics of difference"?
— J.R.

Basing affirmative action programs (if we must have them) on economic need, not race and gender, would do more to ease ten-sions on campus than most current solutions. — J.R

Not an exagger-ated sense of their own importance and power?
— A.L.

ism"—buzzwords for the politics of difference. Difference that does not rest on a clearly delineated foundation of commonality is not only inaccessible to those who are not part of the ethnic or racial group, but also antagonistic to them. Difference can enrich only the common ground.

Integration has become an abstract term today, having to do with little more than numbers and racial balances. But it once stood for a high and admirable set of values. It made difference second to commonality, and it asked members of all races to face whatever fears they inspired in each other. I doubt the word will have a new vogue, but the values, under whatever name, are worth working for.

I want to value commonality and diversity without establishing a hierarchy where one must always be on top. — A.L.

Afterwords

The most striking line to me in this selection is Steele's almost casual observation that "every six months or so someone yells 'nigger' at me from a passing car." I admire the courageous way he reacts to such racist acts, refusing to dwell on the pain and insult he must certainly feel. Taking no pleasure in the convincing evidence he has that racism endures in the United States, Steele patiently searches for solutions to the problem, exempting no one from scrutiny, treating no one with contempt. That search is what "The Recoloring of Campus Life" is all about.

In the years since Steele wrote "The Recoloring of Campus Life," the racial issues he explores have been debated intensely in the United States—especially the fairness of affirmative action policies, which had been imposed chiefly by executive order and judicial fiat without the deliberative scrutiny of the legislative process. Despite demagoguery on both sides, the debate has at least made it possible to talk more openly about the enmities Steele records in his groundbreaking chapter. Such honesty will be required in order to open up American education to once-excluded groups without discriminating and segregating anew. The key to success may well be keeping bureaucrats and politicians, especially those in Washington, out of the loop when it comes to decisions about college admissions and enrollment. — J.R.

While I agree with many individual points Steele makes (all students should be challenged to achieve their full potential; commonalities among us are important and should be nurtured), I came away disappointed in this article for several reasons. First, Steele seems too glib in his dismissal of affirmative action, which for all its flaws helped him to achieve and to prosper. In addition, his tendency to locate the source of racial tension in individual anxieties—inferiority for African Americans, guilt for Caucasians—tends to put the blame for problems on campus onto individuals or on "a handful of students." In doing so, Steele ignores the degree to which the system of higher education and much else in American society—with its hypercompetition, rank-ordering, and glorification of the kind of extreme individualism that breeds alienation—work to fuel racism that ends up harming all students. Finally, I find that Steele thinks, ironically, in black-and-white terms: either commonality or difference; either affirmative action or equality for all; either black studies, women's studies, and so on or a fair and "common" core. My own experience tells me that such polarized thinking is usually oversimplified and that "both/and" is preferable to "either/or." I want to celebrate and value and understand differences among people and those common ties that bind us together. I want to know and appreciate what makes me unique, as well as what makes me like other folks, including Shelby Steele. The college campus, I believe, is just the place to enact such a "both/and" philosophy. That's why I like being there. And that's why I have a more hopeful reading of "the recoloring of campus life" than does Steele.   — A.L.

As a college student reading Steele's article, I believe that many of his points make sense. I agree that many affirmative action programs lead some whites to resent the extra aid given to black students. It is difficult to see someone who is not as qualified receive special benefits based on an externality, especially with financial aid, when money matters are often a determining factor in the ability to attend college. However, these special programs never led me to believe black students were unqualified or could not earn scholarships any other way.

Steele overgeneralizes. I do not like to be told, as a Caucasian student, the way in which my race affects how I view my African American classmates. I am sure that some students feel the way Steele believes I should, but to imply that all white students feel guilt seems ludicrous to me. I think, in most cases, generalizations are harmful to the proposed argument; they force readers like me to be skeptical of the arguments.

I personally feel very boxed in by Steele's argument. Blacks think one way, whites think another, according to him. We either have affirmative action or complete equality (if such a thing is possible). This mode of thinking bothers me, because the world operates in such vast terms that gray areas are unavoidable. Such polar arguments make it seem as if all campuses are alive with inescapable racial tensions and that noticing differences brings out the racist in everyone. I disagree: college is a place of learning and discovery. It is possible to see differences in background (or color) and understand that those differences do not have to alienate us from others. All people possess qualities that are innately different from or the same as those of others. We can recognize and appreciate these differences without considering them obstacles to be overcome before any similarities can be discovered.   — T.E.

QUESTIONING THE TEXT

1. J.R.'s introduction suggests that blacks—like Shelby Steele, Clarence Thomas, and Thomas Sowell—who challenge mainstream civil rights policies (such as affirmative action) become controversial. Should the headnote offer more specific evidence for this claim?
2. "The Recoloring of Campus Life" contains a great number of "cause and effect" analyses. Identify one example of an effect that Steele traces to its root causes, and then write a paragraph assessing the persuasiveness of his reasoning.
3. Steele notes that about once every six months, someone yells a racial epithet at him from a passing car. Freewrite about such an incident, perhaps describing a similar experience and/or considering how it would feel to be a victim of one.
4. Look at the use of quotation marks in the annotations next to Steele's text. Which ones are used to mark direct quotations, and which ones are used for some other purpose? What other purposes do A.L., T.E., and J.R. have for placing certain words in quotes?

MAKING CONNECTIONS

5. Compare the perspectives on education offered by bell hooks in "Keeping Close to Home" (p. 85) and Shelby Steele and the language they use to make their cases. How do they differ in tone and language? What audience do you believe each is trying to reach? Do you find one author more successful than the other? Why, or why not?
6. Would John Henry Newman's concept of the university, as described starting on p. 39, be able to accommodate the kinds of problems with "difference" that Steele describes? Explore the question in a brief essay.

JOINING THE CONVERSATION

7. Steele seems to blame affirmative action programs for many of the racial problems on campuses. Talk to officials on your campus or use the library to augment your understanding of such programs. How do they operate? What is their relationship to the sensitive issue of quotas? Bring your findings to class for discussion.
8. Steele inveighs against the establishment of black "theme" dorms. In a brief column such as might appear in a student newspaper, argue for or against the establishment of dormitories, student unions, or campus cultural programs designed to serve particular ethnic or racial groups.

9. Steele deliberately does not explore the status of other minorities on campus—notably Hispanic and Asian students. With a group of class-mates, discuss the problems faced by these groups or others on your campus, such as women, homosexuals, older students, men, Christians, Jews, and so on. Then write a report applying what Steele observes about black-white relationships to the relationship between one of these groups and other students.

BELL HOOKS
Keeping Close to Home: Class and Education

BELL HOOKS (b. 1952), like Adrienne Rich and Mike Rose, gives us ways to know what it means to see education as the practice of exclusion. Her own education was both difficult and hard-won. As she says, "To a southern black girl from a working-class background who had never been on a city bus, who had never stepped on an escalator, who had never travelled by plane, leaving the comfortable confines of a small town Kentucky life to attend Stanford University was not just frightening; it was utterly painful."

In fact, hooks drafted her first book, Ain't I a Woman: black women and feminism, *when she was a Stanford undergraduate. She has since written several other volumes:* Feminist Theory: from margin to center *(1984);* Talking Back *(1989), from which the following selection is taken;* Yearning: Race, Gender, and Cultural Politics *(1990); and* Teaching to Transgress: Education as the Practice of Freedom *(1994). In "Keeping Close to Home," hooks talks about her experiences as an undergraduate and offers an implicit argument for the role a university should play in the life of a nation. She also offers an implicit response to Shelby Steele by explaining why she wanted to acquire the "mainstream" education Stanford had to offer and to retain her own separate background and values as well. "Both/and," hooks says, in response to Steele's "either/or."*

A few years ago I heard hooks speak about her experiences as a teacher in largely white universities. I was struck by how open and responsive hooks was to her again almost all white audience, and I particularly noted a gesture that she made. In signaling to one questioner after another, hooks never once pointed her finger. Instead, she extended an open palm, issuing an invitation rather than a command (or an accusation). I've never forgotten that gesture, or her passion as she spoke about her own need for an education and her determination to gain that education without giving up her own voice and style. Thus, I jumped at a chance to include her voice in these pages. — A.L.

We are both awake in the almost dark of 5 A.M. Everyone else is sound asleep. Mama asks the usual questions. Telling me to look around, make sure I have everything, scolding me because I am uncertain about the actual time the bus arrives. By 5:30 we are waiting outside the closed station. Alone together, we have a chance to really talk. Mama begins. Angry with her children, especially the ones who whisper behind her back, she says bitterly, "Your childhood could not have been that bad. You were fed and clothed. You did not have to do without—that's more than a lot of folks have and I just can't stand the way y'all go on." The hurt in her voice saddens me. I have always wanted to protect mama from hurt, to ease her burdens. Now I am part of what troubles. Confronting me, she says accusingly, "It's not just the other children. You talk too much about the past. You don't just listen." And I do talk. Worse, I write about it.

Mama has always come to each of her children seeking different responses. With me she expresses the disappointment, hurt, and anger of betrayal: anger that her children are so critical, that we can't even have the sense to like the presents she sends. She says, "From now on there will be no presents. I'll just stick some money in a little envelope the way the rest of you do. Nobody wants criticism. Everybody can criticize me but I am supposed to say nothing." When I try to talk, my voice sounds like a twelve year old. When I try to talk, she speaks louder, interrupting me, even though she has said repeatedly, "Explain it to me, this talk about the past." I struggle to return to my thirty-five year old self so that she will know by the sound of my voice that we are two women talking together. It is only when I state firmly in my very adult voice, "Mama, you are not listening," that she becomes quiet. She waits. Now that I have her attention, I fear that my explanations will be lame, inadequate. "Mama," I begin, "people usually go to therapy because they feel hurt inside, because they have pain that will not stop, like a wound that continually breaks open, that does not heal. And often these hurts, that pain has to do with things that have happened in the past, sometimes in childhood, often in childhood, or things that we believe happened." She wants to know, "What hurts, what hurts are you talking about?" "Mom, I can't answer that. I can't speak for all of us, the hurts are different for everybody. But the point is you try to make the hurt better, to heal it, by understanding how it came to be. And I know you feel mad when we say something happened or hurt that you don't remember being that way, but the past isn't like that, we don't have the same memory of it. We remember things differently. You know that. And sometimes folk feel hurt about stuff and you just don't know or didn't realize it, and they need to talk about it. Surely you understand the need to talk about it."

Our conversation is interrupted by the sight of my uncle walking across the park toward us. We stop to watch him. He is on his way to work dressed in a familiar blue suit. They look alike, these two who rarely discuss the past. This interruption makes me think about life in a small town. You always see someone you know. Interruptions, intrusions are part of daily life. Privacy is difficult to maintain. We leave our private space in the car to greet him. After the hug and kiss he has given me every year since I was born, they talk about the day's funerals. In the distance the bus approaches. He walks away knowing that they will see each other later. Just before I board the bus I turn, staring into my mother's face. I am momentarily back in time, seeing myself eighteen years ago, at this same bus stop, staring into my mother's face, continually turning back, waving farewell as I returned to college—that experience which first took me away from our town, from family. Departing was as painful then as it is now. Each movement away makes return harder. Each separation intensifies distance, both physical and emotional.*

To a southern black girl from a working-class background who had never been on a city bus, who had never stepped on an escalator, who had never travelled by plane, leaving the comfortable confines of a small town Kentucky life to attend Stanford University was not just frightening; it was utterly painful. My parents had not been delighted that I had been accepted and adamantly opposed my going so far from home. At the time, I did not see their opposition as an expression of their fear that they would lose me forever. Like many working-class folks, they feared what college education might do to their children's minds even as they unenthusiastically acknowledged its importance. They did not understand why I could not attend a college nearby, an all-black college. To them, any college would do. I would graduate, become a school teacher, make a decent living and a good marriage. And even though they reluctantly and skeptically supported my educational endeavors, they also subjected them to constant harsh and bitter critique. It is difficult for me to talk about my parents and their impact on me because they have always felt wary, ambivalent, mistrusting of my intellectual aspirations even as they have been caring and supportive. I want to speak about these contradictions because sorting through them, seeking resolution and reconciliation has been important to me both as it affects my development as a writer, my effort to be fully self-realized, and my longing to remain close to the family and community that provided the groundwork for much of my thinking, writing, and being.

Studying at Stanford, I began to think seriously about class differences.   5 To be materially underprivileged at a university where most folks (with the exception of workers) are materially privileged provokes such thought. Class differences were boundaries no one wanted to face or talk about. It was easier to downplay them, to act as though we were all from privileged backgrounds, to work around them, to confront them privately in the solitude of one's room, or to pretend that just being chosen to study at such an institution meant that those of us who did not come from privilege were already in transition toward privilege. To not long for such transition marked one as rebellious, as unlikely to succeed. It was a kind of treason not to believe that it was better to be identified with the world of material privilege than with the world of the working class, the poor. No wonder our working-class parents

---

Departing was . . . physical and emotional: For another account of the emotions stirred by revisiting one's family, see Joan Didion, "On Going Home" (p. 493).

from poor backgrounds feared our entry into such a world, intuiting perhaps that we might learn to be ashamed of where we had come from, that we might never return home, or come back only to lord it over them.

Though I hung with students who were supposedly radical and chic, we did not discuss class. I talked to no one about the sources of my shame, how it hurt me to witness the contempt shown the brown-skinned Filipina maids who cleaned our rooms, or later my concern about the $100 a month I paid for a room off-campus which was more than half of what my parents paid for rent. I talked to no one about my efforts to save money, to send a little something home. Yet these class realities separated me from fellow students. We were moving in different directions. I did not intend to forget my class background or alter my class allegiance. And even though I received an education designed to provide me with a bourgeois sensibility, passive acquiescence was not my only option. I knew that I could resist. I could rebel. I could shape the direction and focus of the various forms of knowledge available to me. Even though I some-times envied and longed for greater material advantages (particularly at vacation times when I would be one of few if any students remaining in the dormitory because there was no money for travel), I did not share the sensibility and values of my peers. That was important—class was not just about money; it was about values which showed and determined behavior. While I often needed more money, I never needed a new set of beliefs and values. For example, I was pro-foundly shocked and disturbed when peers would talk about their parents with-out respect, or would even say that they hated their parents. This was especially troubling to me when it seemed that these parents were caring and concerned. It was often explained to me that such hatred was "healthy and normal." To my white, middle-class California roommate, I explained the way we were taught to value our parents and their care, to understand that they were obligated to give us care. She would always shake her head, laughing all the while, and say, "Missy, you will learn that it's different here, that we think differently." She was right. Soon, I lived alone, like the one Mormon student who kept to himself as he made a concentrated effort to remain true to his religious beliefs and values. Later in graduate school I found that classmates believed "lower class" people had no beliefs and values. I was silent in such discussions, disgusted by their ig-norance.

Carol Stack's anthropological study, *All Our Kin,* was one of the first books I read which confirmed my experiential understanding that within black culture (especially among the working class and poor, particularly in southern states), a value system emerged that was counter-hegemonic, that challenged notions of individualism and private property so important to the maintenance of white-supremacist, capitalist patriarchy. Black folk created in marginal spaces a world of community and collectivity where resources were shared. In the preface to *Feminist Theory: from margin to center,* I talked about how the point of difference, this marginality, can be the space for the forma-tion of an oppositional world view. That world view must be articulated, named if it is to provide a sustained blueprint for change. Unfortunately, there has existed no consistent framework for such naming. Consequently both the experience of this difference and documentation of it (when it occurs) gradually loses presence and meaning.

Much of what Stack documented about the "culture of poverty," for example, would not describe interactions among most black poor today irrespective of geographical setting. Since the black people she described did not acknowledge (if they recognized it in theoretical terms) the oppositional value of their world view, apparently seeing it more as a survival strategy determined less by conscious efforts to oppose oppressive race and class biases than by circumstance, they did not attempt to establish a framework to transmit their beliefs and values from generation to generation. When circumstances changed, values altered. Efforts to assimilate the values and beliefs of privileged white people, presented through media like television, undermine and destroy potential structures of opposition.

Increasingly, young black people are encouraged by the dominant culture (and by those black people who internalize the values of this hegemony) to believe that assimilation is the only possible way to survive, to succeed. Without the framework of an organized civil rights or black resistance struggle, individual and collective efforts at black liberation that focus on the primacy of self-definition and self-determination often go unrecognized. It is crucial that those among us who resist and rebel, who survive and succeed, speak openly and honestly about our lives and the nature of our personal struggles, the means by which we resolve and reconcile contradictions. This is no easy task. Within the educational institutions where we learn to develop and strengthen our writing and analytical skills, we also learn to think, write, and talk in a manner that shifts attention away from personal experience. Yet if we are to reach our people and all people, if we are to remain connected (especially those of us whose familial backgrounds are poor and working-class), we must understand that the telling of one's personal story provides a meaningful example, a way for folks to identify and connect.

Combining personal with critical analysis and theoretical perspectives 10 can engage listeners who might otherwise feel estranged, alienated. To speak simply with language that is accessible to as many folks as possible is also important. Speaking about one's personal experience or speaking with simple language is often considered by academics and/or intellectuals (irrespective of their political inclinations) to be a sign of intellectual weakness or even anti-intellectualism. Lately, when I speak, I do not stand in place—reading my paper, making little or no eye contact with audiences—but instead make eye contact, talk extemporaneously, digress, and address the audience directly. I have been told that people assume I am not prepared, that I am anti-intellectual, unprofessional (a concept that has everything to do with class as it determines actions and behavior), or that I am reinforcing the stereotype of black as non-theoretical and gutsy.

Such criticism was raised recently by fellow feminist scholars after a talk I gave at Northwestern University at a conference on "Gender, Culture, Politics" to an audience that was mainly students and academics. I deliberately chose to speak in a very basic way, thinking especially about the few community folks who had come to hear me. Weeks later, KumKum Sangari, a fellow participant who shared with me what was said when I was no longer present, and I engaged in quite rigorous critical dialogue about the way my presentation had been perceived primarily by privileged white female academics. She was concerned that I not mask my knowledge of theory, that I not appear anti-intellectual. Her critique compelled me to articulate concerns that I am often silent about with colleagues. I spoke about class allegiance and revolutionary commitments, explaining that it was disturbing to me that intellectual radicals who speak about transforming society, ending the domination of race, sex, class, cannot break with behavior patterns that reinforce and perpetuate domination, or continue to use as their sole reference point how we might be or are perceived by those who dominate, whether or not we gain their acceptance and approval.

This is a primary contradiction which raises the issue of whether or not the academic setting is a place where one can be truly radical or subversive. Concurrently, the use of a language and style of presentation that alienates most folks who are not also academically trained reinforces the notion that the academic world is separate from real life, that everyday world where we constantly adjust our language and behavior to meet diverse needs. The academic setting is separate only when we work to make it so. It is a false dichotomy which suggests that academics and/or intellectuals can only speak to one another, that we cannot hope to speak with the masses. What is true is that we make choices, that we choose our audiences, that we choose voices to hear and voices to silence. If I do not speak in a language that can be understood, then there is little chance for dialogue. This issue of language and behavior is a central contradiction all radical intellectuals, particularly those who are members of oppressed groups, must continually confront and work to resolve. One of the clear and present dangers that exists when we move outside our class of origin, our collective ethnic experience, and enter hierarchical institutions which daily reinforce domination by race, sex, and class, is that we gradually assume a mindset similar to those who dominate and oppress, that we lose critical consciousness because it is not reinforced or affirmed by the environment. We must be ever vigilant. It is important that we know who we are speaking to, who we most want to hear us, who we most long to move, motivate, and touch with our words.

When I first came to New Haven to teach at Yale, I was truly surprised by the marked class divisions between black folks—students and professors— who identify with Yale and those black folks who work at Yale or in surrounding communities. Style of dress and self-presentation are most often the central markers of one's position. I soon learned that the black folks who spoke on the street were likely to be part of the black community and those who carefully shifted their glance were likely to be associated with Yale. Walking with a black female colleague one day, I spoke to practically every black person in sight (a gesture which reflects my upbringing), an action which disturbed my companion. Since I addressed black folk who were clearly not associated with Yale, she wanted to know whether or not I knew them. That was funny to me. "Of course not," I answered. Yet when I thought about it seriously, I realized that in a deep way, I knew them for they, and not my companion or most of my colleagues at Yale, resemble my family. Later that year, in a black women's support group I started for undergraduates, students from poor backgrounds spoke about the shame they sometimes feel when faced with the reality of their connection to working-class and poor black people. One student confessed that her father is a street person, addicted to drugs, someone who begs from passersby. She, like other Yale students, turns away from street people often, sometimes showing anger or contempt; she hasn't wanted anyone to know that she was related to this kind of person. She struggles with this, wanting to find a way to acknowledge and affirm this reality, to claim this connection. The group asked me and one another what we [should] do to remain connected, to honor the bonds we have with working-class and poor people even as our class experience alters.

Maintaining connections with family and community across class boundaries demands more than just summary recall of where one's roots are, where one comes from. It requires knowing, naming, and being ever-mindful of those aspects of one's past that have enabled and do enable one's self-development in the present, that sustain and support, that enrich. One must also honestly confront barriers that do exist, aspects of that past that do diminish. My parents' ambivalence about my love for reading led to intense conflict. They (especially my mother) would work to ensure that I had access to books, but would threaten to burn the books or throw them away if I did not conform to other expectations. Or they would insist that reading too much would drive me insane. Their ambivalence nurtured in me a like uncertainty about the value and significance of intellectual endeavor which took years for me to unlearn. While this aspect of our class reality was one that wounded and diminished, their vigilant insistence that being smart did not make me a "better" or "superior" person (which often got on my nerves because I think I wanted to have that sense that it did indeed set me apart, make me better) made a profound impression. From them I learned to value and respect various skills and talents folk might have, not just to value people who read books and talk about ideas. They and my grandparents might say about somebody, "Now he don't read nor write a lick, but he can tell a story," or as my grandmother would say, "call out the hell in words."

Empty romanticization of poor or working-class backgrounds under- 15 mines the possibility of true connection. Such connection is based on understanding difference in experience and perspective and working to mediate and negotiate these terrains. Language is a crucial issue for folk whose movement outside the boundaries of poor and working-class backgrounds changes the nature and direction of their speech. Coming to Stanford with my own version of a Kentucky accent, which I think of always as a strong sound quite different from Tennessee or Georgia speech, I learned to speak differently while maintaining the speech of my region, the sound of my family and community. This was of course much easier to keep up when I returned home to stay often. In recent years, I have endeavored to use various speaking styles in the classroom as a teacher and find it disconcerts those who feel that the use of a particular patois excludes them as listeners, even if there is translation into the usual, acceptable mode of speech. Learning to listen to different voices, hearing different speech challenges the notion that we must all assimilate— share a single, similar talk—in educational institutions. Language reflects the culture from which we emerge. To deny ourselves daily use of speech patterns that are common and familiar, that embody the unique and distinctive aspect of our self is one of the ways we become estranged and alienated from our past. It is important for us to have as many languages on hand as we can know or learn. It is important for those of us who are black, who speak in particular patois as well as standard English, to express ourselves in both ways.

Often I tell students from poor and working-class backgrounds that if you believe what you have learned and are learning in schools and universities separates you from your past, this is precisely what will happen. It is important to stand firm in the conviction that nothing can truly separate us from our pasts when we nurture and cherish that connection. An important strategy for maintaining contact is ongoing acknowledgment of the primacy of one's past, of one's background, affirming the reality that such bonds are not severed automatically solely because one enters a new environment or moves toward a different class experience.

Again, I do not wish to romanticize this effort, to dismiss the reality of conflict and contradiction. During my time at Stanford, I did go through a period of more than a year when I did not return home. That period was one where I felt that it was simply too difficult to mesh my profoundly disparate realities. Critical reflection about the choice I was making, particularly about why I felt a choice had to be made, pulled me through this difficult time. Luckily I recognized that the insistence on choosing between the world of family and community and the new world of privileged white people and privileged ways of knowing was imposed upon me by the outside. It is as though a mythical contract had been signed somewhere which demanded of us black folks that once we entered these spheres we would immediately give up all vestiges of our underprivileged past. It was my responsibility to formulate a way of being that would allow me to participate fully in my new environment while integrating and maintaining aspects of the old.*

---

too difficult to mesh . . . new environment: For a perspective on assimilation in Latino communities, see Linda Chavez, "Toward a New Politics of Hispanic Assimilation" (p. 415).

One of the most tragic manifestations of the pressure black people feel to assimilate is expressed in the internalization of racist perspectives. I was shocked and saddened when I first heard black professors at Stanford downgrade and express contempt for black students, expecting us to do poorly, refusing to establish nurturing bonds. At every university I have attended as a student or worked at as a teacher, I have heard similar attitudes expressed with little or no understanding of factors that might prevent brilliant black students from performing to their full capability. Within universities, there are few educational and social spaces where students who wish to affirm positive ties to ethnicity—to blackness, to working-class backgrounds—can receive affirmation and support. Ideologically, the message is clear—assimilation is the way to gain acceptance and approval from those in power.

Many white people enthusiastically supported Richard Rodriguez's vehement contention in his autobiography, *Hunger of Memory,* that attempts to maintain ties with his Chicano background impeded his progress, that he had to sever ties with community and kin to succeed at Stanford and in the larger world, that family language, in his case Spanish, had to be made secondary or discarded. If the terms of success as defined by the standards of ruling groups within white-supremacist, capitalist patriarchy are the only standards that exist, then assimilation is indeed necessary. But they are not. Even in the face of powerful structures of domination, it remains possible for each of us, especially those of us who are members of oppressed and/or exploited groups as well as those radical visionaries who may have race, class, and sex privilege, to define and determine alternative standards, to decide on the nature and extent of compromise. Standards by which one's success is measured, whether student or professor, are quite different from those of us who wish to resist reinforcing the domination of race, sex, and class, who work to maintain and strengthen our ties with the oppressed, with those who lack material privilege, with our families who are poor and working-class.

When I wrote my first book, *Ain't I a Woman: black women and feminism,*   20 the issue of class and its relationship to who one's reading audience might be came up for me around my decision not to use footnotes, for which I have been sharply criticized. I told people that my concern was that footnotes set class boundaries for readers, determining who a book is for. I was shocked that many academic folks scoffed at this idea. I shared that I went into working-class black communities as well as talked with family and friends to survey whether or not they ever read books with footnotes and found that they did not. A few did not know what they were, but most folks saw them as indicating that a book was for college-educated people. These responses influenced my decision. When some of my more radical, college-educated friends freaked out about the absence of footnotes, I seriously questioned how we could ever imagine revolutionary transformation of society if such a small shift in direction could be viewed as threatening. Of course, many folks warned that the absence of footnotes would make the work less credible in academic circles. This information also highlighted the way in which class informs our choices. Certainly I did feel that choosing to use simple language, absence of footnotes, etc. would mean I was jeopardizing the possibility of being taken seriously in academic circles but then this was a political matter and a political decision. It utterly delights me that this has proven not to be the case and that the book is read by many academics as well as by people who are not college-educated.

Always our first response when we are motivated to conform or compromise within structures that reinforce domination must be to engage in critical reflection. Only by challenging ourselves to push against oppressive boundaries do we make the radical alternative possible, expanding the realm and scope of critical inquiry. Unless we share radical strategies, ways of rethinking and revisioning with students, with kin and community, with a larger audience, we risk perpetuating the stereotype that we succeed because we are the exception, different from the rest of our people. Since I left home and entered college, I am often asked, usually by white people, if my sisters and brothers are also high achievers. At the root of this question is the longing for reinforcement of the belief in "the exception" which enables race, sex, and class biases to remain intact. I am careful to separate what it means to be exceptional from a notion of "the exception."

Frequently I hear smart black folks, from poor and working-class backgrounds, stressing their frustration that at times family and community do not recognize that they are exceptional. Absence of positive affirmation clearly diminishes the longing to excel in academic endeavors. Yet it is important to distinguish between the absence of basic positive affirmation and the longing for continued reinforcement that we are special. Usually liberal white folks will willingly offer continual reinforcement of us as exceptions—as special. This can be both patronizing and very seductive. Since we often work in situations where we are isolated from other black folks, we can easily begin to feel that encouragement from white people is the primary or only source of support and recognition. Given the internalization of racism, it is easy to view this support as more validating and legitimizing than similar support from black people. Still, nothing takes the place of being valued and appreciated by one's own, by one's family and community. We share a mutual and reciprocal responsibility for affirming one another's successes. Sometimes we have to talk to our folks about the fact that we need their ongoing support and affirmation, that it is unique and special to us. In some cases we may never receive desired recognition and acknowledgment of specific achievements from kin. Rather than seeing this as a basis for estrangement, for severing connection, it is useful to explore other sources of nourishment and support.

I do not know that my mother's mother ever acknowledged my college education except to ask me once, "How can you live so far away from your people?" Yet she gave me sources of affirmation and nourishment, sharing the legacy of her quilt-making, of family history, of her incredible way with words. Recently, when our father retired after more than thirty years of work as a janitor, I wanted to pay tribute to this experience, to identify links between his work and my own as writer and teacher. Reflecting on our family past, I recalled ways he had been an impressive example of diligence and hard work, approaching tasks with a seriousness of concentration I work to mirror and develop, with a discipline I struggle to maintain. Sharing these thoughts with him keeps us connected, nurtures our respect for each other, maintaining a space, however large or small, where we can talk.

Open, honest communication is the most important way we maintain relationships with kin and community as our class experience and backgrounds change. It is as vital as the sharing of resources. Often financial assistance is given in circumstances where there is no meaningful contact. However helpful, this can also be an expression of estrangement and alienation. Communication between black folks from various experiences of material privilege was much easier when we were all in segregated communities sharing common experiences in relation to social institutions. Without this grounding, we must work to maintain ties, connection. We must assume greater responsibility for making and maintaining contact, connections that can shape our intellectual visions and inform our radical commitments.

The most powerful resource any of us can have as we study and teach in   25
university settings is full understanding and appreciation of the richness, beauty, and primacy of our familial and community backgrounds. Maintaining awareness of class differences, nurturing ties with the poor and working-class people who are our most intimate kin, our comrades in struggle, transforms and enriches our intellectual experience. Education as the practice of freedom becomes not a force which fragments or separates, but one that brings us closer, expanding our definitions of home and community.

QUESTIONING THE TEXT

1. Hooks contends that "[w]ithin universities, there are few educational and social spaces where students who wish to affirm positive ties to ethnicity—to blackness, to working-class backgrounds—can receive affirmation and support. Ideologically, the message is clear—assimilation is the way to gain acceptance and approval from those in power." What is hooks's attitude toward assimilation? What in the text reveals that attitude? Freewrite for 10 or 15 minutes on how your own school is leading you to assimilate to some things, such as academic language, grading standards, or ways of behaving—both in and out of class.

2. In this essay, hooks describes several occasions when she was accused of writing or speaking in ways that were unacceptable according to academic standards. Does this essay meet the criteria for academic writing as you understand it? Give examples to illustrate what you find "academic" about this essay.

3. Look at the quotation A.L. chooses to use in her introduction about hooks. Why do you think she chose that quotation in particular?

MAKING CONNECTIONS

4. A.L. chose both this reading and the one by Mike Rose (p. 97). What do these pieces have in common that might have appealed to A.L.? What, on the other hand, might hooks and Rose be expected to disagree on?

5. In the previous reading, Shelby Steele represents African American students as affected by a "myth of inferiority." Would hooks agree? Why, or why not?

JOINING THE CONVERSATION

6. Hooks says that after arriving at college a person may find it difficult to stay connected to her or his home community, especially if that community is quite different from the academic community. Do you agree? Has coming to college changed your relationship with your family and/or home community? If you keep a reading log, answer this question there.

7. Hooks suggests that her experiences with people who were different from her—her white, middle-class roommate, for example—strengthened her sense of herself as a black, working-class person. How has your involvement with people who are different from you affected your sense of who you are? Write a paragraph or two about some memorable character who has shaped your sense of self.

8. Working with two or three classmates, come up with a list of characteristics of an "academic" style of speaking or writing. What kinds of language use does your group think the university would consider unacceptable? What arguments would you make for—or against—such academic writing? Together prepare a brief letter to incoming students explaining how the university defines "academic writing."

MIKE ROSE
Lives on the Boundary

AS A CHILD, MIKE ROSE (b. 1944) never thought of going to college. The son of Italian immigrants, he was placed in the "vocational track" in school (through a clerical error, as it turns out) and, as he says, "lived down to expectations beautifully." He was one of those who might well have been excluded from the university. In his prize-winning volume Lives on the Boundary (1989), Rose recalls those circumstances that opened up the university to him, and he argues forcefully that education in a democracy must be truly open to all, a theme he pursues in his latest book, Possible Lives (1996).

In the excerpt from Lives that follows, Rose describes several students he has known, considering the ways in which the "idea of a university" either includes or excludes them. In an extended discussion of what he calls the "canonical curriculum," he concludes that "books can spark dreams," but "appeals to elevated texts can also divert attention from the conditions that keep a population from realizing its dreams."

I wanted to include this passage from Rose's book because he explicitly addresses the call made by Allan Bloom and others for a university curriculum based on "Great Books," books that by definition exclude the experiences of the students Rose describes. In addition, I chose this selection because Rose is a graceful prose stylist, a gifted scholar, and a much-valued friend.

Professor of Education at UCLA, Rose is also a truly extraordinary teacher. His own story, and the stories of those students whose lives he has touched, attest to the transformational power of the kind of educational experience he advocates. To "have any prayer of success" at making such experiences possible, Rose says, "we'll need many . . . blessings." We'll also need many more teachers and writers like Mike Rose. — A.L.

I have a vivid memory of sitting on the edge of my bed—I was twelve or thirteen maybe—listening with unease to a minute or so of classical music. I don't know if I found it as I was turning the dial, searching for the Johnny Otis Show or the live broadcast from Scribner's Drive-In, or if the tuner had simply drifted into another station's signal. Whatever happened, the music caught me in a disturbing way, and I sat there, letting it play. It sounded like the music I heard in church, weighted, funereal. Eerie chords echoing from another world. I learned over, my fingers on the tuner, and, in what I remember as almost a twitch, I turned the knob away from the melody of these strange instruments. My reaction to the other high culture I encountered— *The Iliad* and Shakespeare and some schoolbook poems by Longfellow and

Lowell—was similar, though less a visceral rejection and more a rejecting disinterest, a sense of irrelevance. The few Shakespearean scenes I did know—saw on television, or read or heard in grammar school—seemed snooty and put-on, kind of dumb. Not the way I wanted to talk. Not interesting to me.

There were few books in our house: a couple of thin stories read to me as a child in Pennsylvania (*The Little Boy Who Ran Away,* an *Uncle Remus* sampler), the *M* volume of the *World Book Encyclopedia* (which I found one day in the trash behind the secondhand store), and the Hollywood tabloids my mother would bring home from work. I started buying lots of Superman and Batman comic books because I loved the heroes' virtuous omnipotence—comic books, our teachers said, were bad for us—and, once I discovered them, I began checking out science fiction novels from my grammar school library. Other reading material appeared: the instructions to my chemistry set, which I half understood and only half followed, and, eventually, my astronomy books, which seemed to me to be magical rather than discursive texts. So it was that my early intrigue with literacy—my lifts and escapes with language and rhythm—came from comic books and science fiction, from the personal, nonscientific worlds I created with bits and pieces of laboratory and telescopic technology, came, as well, from the Italian stories I heard my uncles and parents tell. It came, too, from the music my radio brought me: music that wove in and out of my days, lyrics I'd repeat and repeat—"gone, gone, gone, jumpin' like a catfish on a pole"—wanting to catch that sound, seeking other emotional frontiers, other places to go. Like rocker Joe Ely, I picked up Chicago on my transistor radio.

Except for school exercises and occasional cards my mother made me write to my uncles and aunts, I wrote very little during my childhood; it wasn't until my last year in high school that Jack MacFarland* sparked an interest in writing. And though I developed into a good reader, I performed from moderately well to terribly on other sorts of school literacy tasks. From my reading I knew vocabulary words, and I did okay on spelling tests—though I never lasted all that long in spelling bees—but I got C's and D's on the ever-present requests to diagram sentences and label parts of speech. The more an assignment was related to real reading, the better I did; the more analytic, self-contained, and divorced from context, the lousier I performed. Today some teachers would say I was a concrete thinker. To be sure, the development of my ability to decode words and read sentences took place in school, but my orientation to reading—the way I conceived of it, my purpose for doing it—occurred within the tight and untraditional confines of my home. The quirks and textures of my immediate environment combined with my escapist fantasies to draw me to books. "It is what we are excited about that educates us," writes social historian Elizabeth Ewen. It is what taps our

---

Jack MacFarland: a teacher, currently at a California community college, whom Rose calls "the teacher who saved [my] life"

curiosity and dreams. Eventually, the books that seemed so distant, those Great Books, would work their way into my curiosity, would influence the way I framed problems and the way I wrote. But that would come much later—first with Jack MacFarland (mixed with his avant-garde countertradition), then with my teachers at Loyola and UCLA—an excitement and curiosity shaped by others and connected to others, a cultural and linguistic heritage received not from some pristine conduit, but exchanged through the heat of human relation.

A friend of mine recently suggested that education is one culture embracing another. It's interesting to think of the very different ways that metaphor plays out. Education can be a desperate, smothering embrace, an embrace that denies the needs of the other. But education can also be an encouraging, communal embrace—at its best an invitation, an opening.* Several years ago, I was sitting in on a workshop conducted by the Brazilian educator Paulo Freire. It was the first hour or so and Freire, in his sophisticated, accented English, was establishing the theoretical base of his literacy pedagogy—heady stuff, a blend of Marxism, phenomenology, and European existentialism. I was two seats away from Freire; in front of me and next to him was a younger man, who, puzzled, finally interrupted the speaker to ask a question. Freire acknowledged the question and, as he began answering, he turned and quickly touched the man's forearm. Not patronizing, not mushy, a look and a tap as if to say: "You and me right now, let's go through this together." Embrace. With Jack MacFarland it was an embrace: no-nonsense and cerebral, but a relationship in which the terms of endearment were the image in a poem, a play's dialogue, the winding narrative journey of a novel.

More often than we admit, a failed education is social more than intellectual in origin. And the challenge that has always faced American education, that it has sometimes denied and sometimes doggedly pursued, is how to create both the social and cognitive means to enable a diverse citizenry to develop their ability. It is an astounding challenge: the complex and wrenching struggle to actualize the potential not only of the privileged but, too, of those who have lived here for a long time generating a culture outside the mainstream and those who, like my mother's parents and my father, immigrated with cultural traditions of their own. This painful but generative mix of language and story can result in clash and dislocation in our communities, but it also gives rise to new speech, new stories, and once we appreciate the richness of it, new invitations to literacy.

Pico Boulevard, named for the last Mexican governor of California, runs an immense stretch west to east: from the wealth of the Santa Monica

---

* For a related discussion of education as "smothering" or "an invitation," see Christian Zawodniak, "Teacher Power, Student Pedagogy," p. 124.

beaches to blighted Central Avenue, deep in Los Angeles. Union Street is comparatively brief, running north to south, roughly from Adams to Temple, pretty bad off all the way. Union intersects Pico east of Vermont Avenue and too far to the southwest to be touched by the big-money development that is turning downtown Los Angeles into a whirring postmodernist dreamscape. The Pico-Union District is very poor, some of its housing as unsafe as that on Skid Row, dilapidated, overcrowded, rat-infested. It used to be a working-class Mexican neighborhood, but for about ten years now it has become the concentrated locale of those fleeing the political and economic horror in Central America. Most come from El Salvador and Guatemala. One observer calls the area a gigantic refugee camp.

As you move concentrically outward from Pico-Union, you'll encounter a number of other immigrant communities: Little Tokyo and Chinatown to the northeast, Afro-Caribbean to the southwest, Koreatown to the west. Moving west, you'll find Thai and Vietnamese restaurants tucked here and there in storefronts. Filipinos, Southeast Asians, Armenians, and Iranians work in the gas stations, the shoe-repair stores, the minimarts. A lawnmower repair shop posts its sign in Korean, Spanish, and English. A Korean church announces "Jesus Loves You" in the same three languages. "The magnitude and diversity of immigration to Los Angeles since 1960," notes a report from UCLA's Graduate School of Architecture and Urban Planning, "is comparable only to the New York-bound wave of migrants around the turn of the century." It is not at all uncommon for English composition teachers at UCLA, Cal-State L.A., Long Beach State—the big urban universities and colleges—to have, in a class of twenty-five, students representing a dozen or more linguistic backgrounds: from Spanish and Cantonese and Farsi to Hindi, Portuguese, and Tagalog. Los Angeles, the new Ellis Island.

On a drive down the Santa Monica Freeway, you exit on Vermont and pass Rick's Mexican Cuisine, Hawaii Discount Furniture, The Restaurant Ecuatoriano, Froggy's Children's Wear, Seoul Autobody, and the Bar Omaha. Turn east on Pico, and as you approach Union, taking a side street here and there, you'll start seeing the murals: The Virgin of Guadalupe, Steve McQueen, a scene resembling Siqueiros's heroic workers, the Statue of Liberty, Garfield the Cat. Graffiti are everywhere. The dreaded Eighteenth Street gang—an established Mexican gang—has marked its turf in Arabic as well as Roman numerals. Newer gangs, a Salvadoran gang among them, are emerging by the violent logic of territory and migration; they have Xed out the Eighteenth Street *placas* and written their own threatening insignias in place. Statues of the Blessed Mother rest amid potted plants in overgrown front yards. There is a rich sweep of small commerce: restaurants, markets, bakeries, legal services ("Income Tax y Amnestia"), beauty salons ("Lolita's Magic Touch—Salon de Belleza—Unisex"). A Salvadoran restaurant sells teriyaki burgers. A "Discoteca Latina" advertises "great rap hits." A clothing store has a Dick Tracy sweatshirt on a half mannequin; a boy walks out wearing a blue t-shirt that announces "Life's a Beach." Culture in a Waring blender.

There are private telegram and postal services: messages sent straight to "domicilio a CentroAmerica." A video store advertises a comedy about immigration: *Ni de Aqui/Ni de Alla,* "Neither from Here nor from There." The poster displays a Central American Indian caught on a wild freeway ride: a Mexican in a sombrero is pulling one of the Indian's pigtails, Uncle Sam pulls the other, a border guard looks on, ominously suspended in air. You see a lot of street vending, from oranges and melons to deco sunglasses: rhinestones and plastic swans and lenses shaped like a heart. Posters are slapped on posters: one has rows of faces of the disappeared. Santa Claus stands on a truck bumper and waves drivers into a ninety-nine cent outlet.

Families are out shopping, men loiter outside a cafe, a group of young girls collectively count out their change. You notice, even in the kaleidoscope you pick out his figure, you notice a dark-skinned boy, perhaps Guatemalan, walking down Pico with a cape across his shoulders. His hair is piled in a four-inch rockabilly pompadour. He passes a dingy apartment building, a *pupuseria,* a body shop with no name, and turns into a storefront social services center. There is one other person in the sparse waiting room. She is thin, her gray hair pulled back in a tight bun, her black dress buttoned to her neck. She will tell you, if you ask her in Spanish, that she is waiting for her English class to begin. She might also tell you that the people here are helping her locate her son—lost in Salvadoran resettlement camps—and she thinks that if she can learn a little English, it will help her bring him to America.

The boy is here for different reasons. He has been causing trouble in school, and arrangements are being made for him to see a bilingual counselor. His name is Mario, and he immigrated with his older sister two years ago. His English is halting, unsure; he seems simultaneously rebellious and scared. His case worker tells me that he still has flashbacks of Guatemalan terror: his older brother taken in the night by death squads, strangled, and hacked apart on the road by his house. Then she shows me his drawings, and our conversation stops. Crayon and pen on cheap paper; blue and orange cityscapes, eyes on billboards, in the windshields of cars, a severed hand at the bus stop. There are punks, beggars, piñatas walking the streets—upright cows and donkeys—skeletal homeboys, corseted girls carrying sharpened bones. "He will talk to you about these," the caseworker tells me. "They're scary, aren't they? The school doesn't know what the hell to do with him. I don't think he really knows what to do with all that's in him either."

In another part of the state, farther to the north, also rich in immigration, a teacher in a basic reading and writing program asks his students to interview one another and write a report, a capsule of a classmate's life. Caroline, a black woman in her late forties, chooses Thuy Anh, a Vietnamese woman many years her junior. Caroline asks only five questions—Thuy Anh's English is still difficult to understand—simple questions: What is your name? Where were you born? What is your education? Thuy Anh talks about her childhood in South Vietnam and her current plans in America. She is the oldest of nine children, and she received a very limited Vietnamese education, for she had to spend much of her childhood caring for her brothers and sisters. She married a serviceman, came to America, and now spends virtually all of her time pursuing a high school equivalency, struggling with textbook descriptions of the American political process, frantically trying to improve her computational skills. She is not doing very well at this. As one of her classmates observed, she might be trying too hard.

Caroline is supposed to take notes while Thuy Anh responds to her questions, and then use the notes to write her profile, maybe something like a reporter would do. But Caroline is moved to do something different. She's taken by Thuy Anh's account of watching over babies. "Mother's little helper," she thinks. And that stirs her, this woman who has never been a mother. Maybe, too, Thuy Anh's desire to do well in school, her driven eagerness, the desperation that occasionally flits across her face, maybe that moves Caroline as well. Over the next two days, Caroline strays from the assignment and writes a two-and-a-half page fiction that builds to a prose poem. She recasts Thuy Anh's childhood into an American television fantasy.

Thuy Anh is "Mother's little helper." Her five younger sisters "are happy and full of laughter . . . their little faces are bright with eyes sparkling." The little girls' names are "Hellen, Ellen, Lottie, Alice, and Olie"—American names—and they "cook and sew and make pretty doll dresses for their dolls to wear." Though the family is Buddhist, they exchange gifts at Christmas and "gather in the large living room to sing Christmas carols." Thuy Anh "went to school every day she could and studied very hard." One day, Thuy Anh was "asked to write a poem and to recite it to her classmates." And, here, Caroline embeds within her story a prose poem—which she attributes to Thuy Anh:

> My name is Thuy Anh I live near the Ocean. I see the waves boisterous and impudent bursting and splashing against the huge rocks. I see the white boats out on the blue sea. I see the fisher men rapped in heavy coats to keep their bodies warm while bringing in large fishes to sell to the merchants, Look! I see a larg white bird going on its merry way. Then I think of how great God is for he made this great sea for me to see and yet I stand on dry land and see the green and hillie side with flowers rising to the sky. How sweet and beautiful for God to have made Thuy Anh and the sea.

I interview Caroline. When she was a little girl in Arkansas, she "would   15 get off into a room by myself and read the Scripture." The "poems in King

Solomon" were her favorites. She went to a segregated school and "used to write quite a bit" at home. But she "got away from it" and some years later dropped out of high school to come west to earn a living. She's worked in a convalescent hospital for twenty years, never married, wishes she had, comes, now, back to school and is finding again her love of words. "I get lost . . . I'm right in there with my writing, and I forget all my surroundings." She is classified as a basic student—no diploma, low-level employment, poor test scores—had been taught by her grandmother that she would have to earn her living "by the sweat of my brow."

Her work in the writing course had been good up to the point of Thuy Anh's interview, better than that of many classmates, adequate, fairly free of error, pretty well organized. But the interview triggered a different level of performance. Caroline's early engagement with language reemerged in a lyrical burst: an evocation of an imagined childhoood, a curious overlay of one culture's fantasy over another's harsh reality. Caroline's longing reshaped a Vietnamese girlhood, creating a life neither she nor Thuy Anh ever had, an intersection of biblical rhythms and *Father Knows Best*.

Over Chin's bent head arches a trellis packed tight with dried honey-suckle and chrysanthemum, sea moss, mushrooms, and ginseng. His elbow rests on the cash register—quiet now that the customers have left. He shifts on the stool, concentrating on the writing before him: "A young children," he scribbles, and pauses. "Young children," that doesn't sound good, he thinks. He crosses out "children" and sits back. A few seconds pass. He can't think of the right way to say it, so he writes "children" again and continues: "a young children with his grandma smail . . ." "Smail." He pulls a Chinese-English dictionary from under the counter.

In front of the counter and extending down the aisle are boxes of dried fish: shark fins, mackerel, pollock. They give off a musky smell. Behind Chin are rows of cans and jars: pickled garlic, pickled ginger, sesame paste. By the door, comic books and Chinese weeklies lean dog-eared out over the thin retaining wire of a dusty wooden display. Chin has found his word: It's not *smail,* it's *smile.* "A young children with his grandma smile . . ." He reaches in the pocket of his jeans jacket, pulls out a piece of paper, and unfolds it. There's a word copied on it he has been wanting to use. A little bell over the door jingles. An old man comes in, and Chin moves his yellow pad aside.

Chin remembers his teacher in elementary school telling him that his writing was poor, that he didn't know many words. He went to middle school for a few years but quit before completing it. Very basic English—the ABCs and simple vocabulary—was, at one point, part of his curriculum, but he lived in a little farming community, so he figured he would never use it. He did, though, pick up some letters and a few words. He immigrated to America when he was seventeen, and for the two years since has been living with his uncle in Chinatown. His uncle signed him up for English classes at the community center. He didn't like them. He did, however, start hanging out in the recreation room, playing pool and watching TV. The English on TV intrigued him. And it was then that he turned to writing. He would "try to learn to speak something" by writing it down. That was about six months ago. Now he's enrolled in a community college literacy program and has been making strong progress. He is especially taken with one tutor, a woman in her mid-thirties who encourages him to write. So he writes for her. He writes stories about his childhood in China. He sneaks time when no one is in the store or when customers are poking around, writing because he likes to bring her things, writing, too, because "sometime I think writing make my English better."

The old man puts on the counter a box of tea guaranteed to help you stop   20
smoking. Chin rings it up and thanks him. The door jingles and Chin returns to his writing, copying the word from his folded piece of paper, a word he found in *People* magazine: "A young children with his grandma smile *gleefully*."

Frank Marell, born Meraglio, my oldest uncle, learned his English as Chin is learning his. He came to America with his mother and three sisters in September 1921. They came to join my grandfather who had immigrated long before. They joined, as well, the millions of Italian peasants who had flowed through Customs with their cloth-and-paper suitcases, their strange gestural language, and their dark, empty pockets. Frank was about to turn eight when he immigrated, so he has faint memories of Calabria. They lived in a one-room stone house. In the winter, the family's scrawny milk cow was brought inside. By the door there was a small hole for a rifle barrel. Wolves came out of the hills. He remembers the frost and burrs stinging his feet as he foraged the countryside for berries and twigs and fresh grass for the cow. *Chi esce riesce,* the saying went—"he who leaves succeeds"—and so it was that my grandfather left when he did, eventually finding work amid the metal and steam of the Pennsylvania Railroad.

My uncle remembers someone giving him bread on the steamship. He remembers being very sick. Once in America, he and his family moved into the company housing projects across from the stockyard. The house was dirty and had gouges in the wood. Each morning his mother had to sweep the soot from in front of the door. He remembers rats. He slept huddled with his father and mother and sisters in the living room, for his parents had to rent out the other rooms in order to buy clothes and shoes and food. Frank never attended school in Italy. He was eight now and would enter school in America. America, where eugenicists were attesting, scientifically, to the feeblemindedness of his race, where the popular press ran articles about he immorality of these swarthy exotics. Frank would enter school here. In many ways, you could lay his life like a template over a current life in the Bronx, in Houston, in Pico-Union.

He remembers the embarrassment of not understanding the teacher, of not being able to read or write. Funny clothes, oversize shoes, his hair slicked down and parted in the middle. He would lean forward—his assigned seat, fortunately, was in the back—and ask other Italian kids, ones with some English, to tell him what for the love of God was going on. He had big, sad eyes, thick hands, skin dark enough to yield the nickname Blacky. Frank remembers other boys—Carmen Santino, a kid named Hump, Bruno Tucci—who couldn't catch on to this new language and quit coming to school. Within six months of his arrival, Frank would be going after class to the back room of Pete Mastis's Dry Cleaners and Shoeshine Parlor. He cleaned and shined shoes, learned to operate a steam press, ran deliveries. He listened to the radio, trying to mimic the harsh complexities of English. He spread Pete Mastis's racing forms out before him, copying words onto the margins of newsprint. He tried talking to the people whose shoes he was shining, exchanging tentative English with the broken English of Germans and Poles and other Italians.

Eventually, Frank taught his mother to sign her name. By the time he was in his teens, he was reading flyers and announcements of sales and legal documents to her. He was also her scribe, doing whatever writing she needed to have done. Frank found himself immersed in the circumstance of literacy.

With the lives of Mario and Caroline and Chin and Frank Marell as a   25
backdrop, I want to consider a current, very powerful set of proposals about literacy and culture.

There is a strong impulse in American education—curious in a country with such an ornery streak of antitraditionalism—to define achievement and excellence in terms of the acquisition of a historically validated body of knowledge, an authoritative list of books and allusions, a canon. We seek a certification of our national intelligence, indeed, our national virtue, in how diligently our children can display this central corpus of information. This need for certification tends to emerge most dramatically in our educational policy debates during times of real or imagined threat: economic hard times, political crises, sudden increases in immigration. Now is such a time, and it is reflected in a number of influential books and commission reports. E. D. Hirsch* argues that a core national vocabulary, one oriented toward the English literate tradition—Alice in Wonderland to zeitgeist—will build a knowledge base that will foster the literacy of all Americans. Diane Ravitch* and Chester Finn* call for a return to a traditional historical and literary curriculum: the valorous historical figures and the classical literature of the once-elite

---

E. D. Hirsch: author of *Cultural Literacy: What Every American Needs to Know,* which argues for a standard national public school curriculum that would ensure that all Americans share a common cultural vocabulary

Diane Ravitch: author of *Developing National Standards in Education* and an Education Department official in the Reagan administration

Chester Finn: undersecretary of education in the Reagan administration

course of study. Allan Bloom, Secretary of Education William Bennett, Mortimer Adler* and the Paideia Group, and a number of others have affirmed, each in their very different ways, the necessity of the Great Books: Plato and Aristotle and Sophocles, Dante and Shakespeare and Locke, Dickens and Mann and Faulkner. We can call this orientation to educational achievement the canonical orientation.

At times in our past, the call for a shoring up of or return to a canonical curriculum was explicitly elitist, was driven by a fear that the education of the select was being compromised. Today, though, the majority of the calls are provocatively framed in the language of democracy. They assail the mediocre and grinding curriculum frequently found in remedial and vocational education. They are disdainful of the patronizing perceptions of student ability that further restrict the already restricted academic life of disadvantaged youngsters. They point out that the canon—its language, conventions, and allusions—is central to the discourse of power, and to keep it from poor kids is to assure their disenfranchisement all the more. The books of the canon, claim the proposals, the Great Books, are a window onto a common core of experience and civic ideals. There is, then, a spiritual, civic, and cognitive heritage here, and *all* our children should receive it. If we are sincere in our desire to bring Mario, Chin, the younger versions of Caroline, current incarnations of Frank Marell, and so many others who populate this book—if we truly want to bring them into our society—then we should provide them with this stable and common core. This is a forceful call. It promises a still center in a turning world.

I see great value in being challenged to think of the curriculum of the many in the terms we have traditionally reserved for the few; it is refreshing to have common assumptions about the capacities of underprepared students so boldly challenged. Many of the people we have encountered in these pages have displayed the ability to engage books and ideas thought to be beyond their grasp. There were the veterans: Willie Oates* writing, in prison, ornate sentences drawn from *The Mill on the Floss*.* Sergeant Gonzalez* coming to understand poetic ambiguity in "Butch Weldy."* There was the parole aide Olga who no longer felt walled off from *Macbeth*. There were the EOP* students at UCLA, like Lucia who unpackaged *The Myth of Mental Illness* once she had an orientation and overview. And there was Frank Marell who, later in his life, would be talking excitedly to his nephew about this guy Edgar Allan

---

Mortimer Adler: educator and philosopher, author of many books, including three volumes on the Paideia Proposal, an educational framework based on ancient Greek concepts

Willie Oates, Sergeant Gonzalez: students in a veterans' program that Rose worked in

The Mill on the Floss: a novel (1860) by George Eliot (1819–80)

"Butch Weldy": a poem in *Spoon River Anthology* (1915) by Edgar Lee Masters (1869–1950)

EOP: Equal Opportunity Program

Poe. Too many people are kept from the books of the canon, the Great
Books, because of misjudgments about their potential. Those books eventually proved important to me, and, as best I know how, I invite my students to
engage them. But once we grant the desirability of equal curricular treatment
and begin to consider what this equally distributed curriculum would contain,
problems arise: If the canon itself is the answer to our educational inequities,
why has it historically invited few and denied many? Would the canonical
orientation provide adequate guidance as to how a democratic curriculum
should be constructed and how it should be taught? Would it guide us in
opening up to Olga that "fancy talk" that so alienated her?

Those who study the way literature becomes canonized, how linguistic
creations are included or excluded from a tradition, claim that the canonical
curriculum students would most likely receive would not, as is claimed, offer
a common core of American experience. Caroline would not find her life
represented in it, nor would Mario. The canon has tended to push to the
margin much of the literature of our nation: from American Indian songs and
chants to immigrant fiction to working-class narratives. The institutional messages that students receive in the books they're issued and the classes they take
are powerful and, as I've witnessed since my Voc. Ed. days, quickly internalized. And to revise these messages and redress past wrongs would involve
more than adding some new books to the existing canon—the very reasons
for linguistic and cultural exclusion would have to become a focus of study in
order to make the canon act as a democratizing force. Unless this happens,
the democratic intent of the reformers will be undercut by the content of the
curriculum they propose.

And if we move beyond content to consider basic assumptions about   30
teaching and learning, a further problem arises, one that involves the very nature of the canonical orientation itself. The canonical orientation encourages a
narrowing of focus from learning to that which must be learned: It simplifies
the dynamic tension between student and text and reduces the psychological
and social dimensions of instruction. The student's personal history recedes as
the what of the classroom is valorized over the how. Thus it is that the encounter of student and text is often portrayed by canonists as a transmission.
Information, wisdom, virtue will pass from the book to the student if the student gives the book the time it merits, carefully traces its argument or narrative or lyrical progression. Intellectual, even spiritual, growth will *necessarily*
result from an encounter with Roman mythology, *Othello,* and "I heard a Fly
buzz—when I died—,"* with biographies and historical sagas and patriotic
lore. Learning is stripped of confusion and discord. It is stripped, as well, of
strong human connection. My own initiators to the canon—Jack MacFarland, Dr. Carothers, and the rest—knew there was more to their work than

---

*"I heard a Fly buzz—when I died—": poem by Emily Dickinson (1830–86)

their mastery of a tradition. What mattered most, I see now, were the relationships they established with me, the guidance they provided when I felt inadequate or threatened. This mentoring was part of my entry into that solemn library of Western thought—and even with such support, there were still times of confusion, anger, and fear. It is telling, I think, that once that rich social network slid away, once I was in graduate school in intense, solitary encounter with that tradition, I abandoned it for other sources of nurturance and knowledge.

The model of learning implicit in the canonical orientation seems, at times, more religious than cognitive or social: Truth resides in the printed texts, and if they are presented by someone who knows them well and respects them, that truth will be revealed.* Of all the advocates of the canon, Mortimer Adler has given most attention to pedagogy—and his Paideia books contain valuable discussions of instruction, coaching, and questioning. But even here, and this is doubly true in the other manifestos, there is little acknowledgement that the material in the canon can be not only difficult but foreign, alienating, overwhelming.

We need an orientation to instruction that provides guidance on how to determine and honor the beliefs and stories, enthusiasms, and apprehensions that students reveal. How to build on them, and when they clash with our curriculum—as I saw so often in the Tutorial Center at UCLA—when they clash, how to encourage a discussion that will lead to reflection on what students bring and what they're currently confronting. Canonical lists imply canonical answers, but the manifestos offer little discussion of what to do when students fail. If students have been exposed to at least some elements of the canon before—as many have—why didn't it take? If they're encountering it for the first time and they're lost, how can we determine where they're located—and what do we do then?

Each member of a teacher's class, poor or advantaged, gives rise to endless decisions, day-to-day determinations about a child's reading and writing: decisions on how to tap strength, plumb confusion, foster growth. The richer your conception of learning and your understanding of its social and psychological dimensions, the more insightful and effective your judgments will be. Consider the sources of literacy we saw among the children in El Monte: shopkeepers' signs, song lyrics, auto manuals, the conventions of the Western, family stories and tales, and more. Consider Chin's sources—television and *People* magazine—and Caroline's oddly generative mix of the Bible and an American media illusion. Then there's the jarring confluence of personal horror and pop cultural flotsam that surfaces in Mario's drawings, drawings that would be a rich, if volatile, point of departure for language instruction. How

model of learning . . . truth will be revealed: For another comparison of education to religion, see Allan Bloom, "The Student and the University" (p. 52).

would these myriad sources and manifestations be perceived and evaluated if viewed within the framework of a canonical tradition, and what guidance would the tradition provide on how to understand and develop them? The great books and central texts of the canon could quickly become a benchmark against which the expressions of student literacy would be negatively measured, a limiting band of excellence that, ironically, could have a dispiriting effect on the very thing the current proposals intend: the fostering of mass literacy.

To understand the nature and development of literacy we need to consider the social context in which it occurs—the political, economic, and cultural forces that encourage or inhibit it. The canonical orientation discourages deep analysis of the way these forces may be affecting performance. The canonists ask that schools transmit a coherent traditional knowledge to an ever-changing, frequently uprooted community. This discordance between message and audience is seldom examined. Although a ghetto child can rise on the lilt of a Homeric line—books *can* spark dreams—appeals to elevated texts can also divert attention from the conditions that keep a population from realizing its dreams. The literacy curriculum is being asked to do what our politics and our economics have failed to do: diminish differences in achievement, narrow our gaps, bring us together. Instead of analysis of the complex web of causes of poor performance, we are offered a faith in the unifying power of a body of knowledge, whose infusion will bring the rich and the poor, the longtime disaffected and the uprooted newcomers into cultural unanimity. If this vision is democratic, it is simplistically so, reductive, not an invitation for people truly to engage each other at the point where cultures and classes intersect.

I worry about the effects a canonical approach to education could have   35
on cultural dialogue and transaction—on the involvement of an abandoned underclass and on the movement of immigrants like Mario and Chin into our nation. A canonical uniformity promotes rigor and quality control; it can also squelch new thinking, diffuse the generative tension between the old and the new. It is significant that the canonical orientation is voiced with most force during times of challenge and uncertainty, for it promises the authority of tradition, the seeming stability of the past. But the authority is fictive, gained from a misreading of American cultural history. No period of that history was harmoniously stable; the invocation of a golden age is a mythologizing act. Democratic culture is, by definition, vibrant and dynamic, discomforting and unpredictable. It gives rise to apprehension; freedom is not always calming. And, yes, it can yield fragmentation, though often as not the source of fragmentation is intolerant misunderstanding of diverse traditions rather than the desire of members of those traditions to remain hermetically separate. A truly democratic vision of knowledge and social structure would honor this complexity. The vision might not be soothing, but it would provide guidance as to how to live and teach in a country made up of many cultural traditions.

We are in the middle of an extraordinary social experiment: the attempt to provide education for all members of a vast pluralistic democracy. To have any prayer of success, we'll need many conceptual blessings: A philosophy of language and literacy that affirms the diverse sources of linguistic competence and deepens our understanding of the ways class and culture blind us to the richness of those sources. A perspective on failure that lays open the logic of error. An orientation toward the interaction of poverty and ability that undercuts simple polarities, that enables us to see simultaneously the constraints poverty places on the play of mind and the actual mind at play within those constraints. We'll need a pedagogy that encourages us to step back and consider the threat of the standard classroom and that shows us, having stepped back, how to step forward to invite a student across the boundaries of that powerful room. Finally, we'll need a revised store of images of educational excellence, ones closer to egalitarian ideals—ones that embody the reward and turmoil of education in a democracy, that celebrate the plural, messy human reality of it. At heart, we'll need a guiding set of principles that do not encourage us to retreat from, but move us closer to, an understanding of the rich mix of speech and ritual and story that is America.

QUESTIONING THE TEXT

1. What do you think Rose means when he says that "a failed education is social more than intellectual in origin"? Look back to A.L.'s profile on pp. xxiii–xxv. Does anything there suggest a time when her education failed for social—or intellectual—reasons? Describe a time when your education failed—or succeeded—largely because of social reasons. If you are keeping a reading log, record your answers there.

2. Rose quotes a friend who says that education can be thought of as "one culture embracing another." Give a few examples from his essay that illustrate this embrace, and then give an example from your own educational experience.

3. Why do you think Rose includes the stories of Mario, Caroline, Chin, and Frank Marell as a backdrop for his discussion about current concepts of literacy in America? What do their stories have in common? What kinds of students does he leave unmentioned?

MAKING CONNECTIONS

4. Imagine Rose responding to Allan Bloom's arguments (p. 52) about what a university should teach the students he's concerned with. What would Rose and Bloom agree on? Where would they disagree—and why?

5. Spend some time thinking about one of the students Rose describes. Then write a brief poem (using Gwendolyn Brooks as a model, perhaps; see p. 147) that would characterize that student's attitude toward school.

JOINING THE CONVERSATION

6. Try to remember a time when your relationship with someone (teacher, parent, coach, religious leader) made it easier (or harder) for you to learn what that person was trying to teach you. Write a brief description of this event for your class, concluding by summarizing those things about another person that most *help* you to learn from him or her.

7. Rose remembers that his earliest interest in literacy came from "comic books and science fiction, from the personal, nonscientific worlds I created with bits and pieces of laboratory and telescopic technology, came, as well, from the Italian stories I heard my uncles and parents tell." Brainstorm with two or three other students about your earliest out-of-school experiences with reading and writing. How were they like or unlike your experiences of reading and writing in school?

LYNNE V. CHENEY
PC: Alive and Entrenched

WHEN DO COLLEGE COURSES become political? I think it occurs when in-structors use their classes deliberately to shape or change the political beliefs of students. Lynne V. Cheney (b. 1941), a Ph.D. in English and chair of the National Endowment for the Humanities (1986–92), believes that such courses distort the fundamental mission of higher education, which is to search for truth. Indeed, she offers evidence in her book Telling the Truth *(1995) that many students today find more freedom of thought outside their colleges than in them. I've included this piece from her chapter "PC: Alive and En-trenched" because I fear Cheney may be right: the champions of difference in our academic communities—especially those who insist on analyzing everything according to the categories of race, class, and gender—sometimes forget that prin-ciples of diversity should extend to political choices too. If you don't feel free to speak your mind in some classes these days, perhaps Cheney's report will open your eyes.* — J.R.

There are many reasons to be silent rather than speak out on campuses today. Undergraduates have to worry not only about the power of professors to de-termine grades but also about faculty members' ability to make the classroom a miserable place for the dissenting student. In 1991, Michelle Colitsas, a se-nior at Mount Holyoke College in Massachusetts, wrote a critique in a stu-dent newspaper of a philosophy class in which she was enrolled. As Colitsas described it, students in the course read *Plato, Nietzsche, Mill*—and Patricia J. Williams's *The Alchemy of Race and Rights.** Although Williams's book presents a very limited (and entirely positive) view of affirmative action, it was one for which the professor "exhibited a strong affinity . . . ," Colitsas wrote, "both through her own statements, as well as through her unquestioned support of those student comments similar to Ms. Williams' in sharp contrast with her challenges to those student comments raised in opposition to or in skepticism of Ms. Williams' view." Colitsas maintained that such teaching violated a trust: Students rely on teachers to give them a complete view of controversial issues, not a partial one based on their preferences. "When the teacher pro-

---

Plato, Nietzsche, Mill . . . Rights: three philosophers more commonly studied in college courses than Patricia J. Williams

fesses opinion as fact, subjective concepts and definitions as the truth," Colitsas wrote, "the contract [between teacher and student] is violated."[1]

Although Colitsas did not name the course or the professor, one can well imagine the faculty member's irritation at a student's writing about the problem in the campus press. Still, the professor's response was extraordinary. As a student newspaper described it, the professor "announced that she would be leaving early in order to provide the 20–30 members of the class with the opportunity to share their views." What followed was, in the newspaper's words, a "verbal lynching":

> The "discussion" quickly degenerated into an *ad hominem* denunciation of a single student. As Colitsas put it, "They were no longer attacking my political beliefs, they were attacking my character.[2]

Marc Shachtman, an undergraduate at Ohio's Oberlin College, described a similar incident at that campus:

> In a course I took last year a maverick student said he agreed with a Supreme Court justice's view that a particular affirmative action program would unconstitutionally discriminate on the basis of race. During the next few minutes a couple of students vehemently objected. One raised her voice significantly, the other began to yell at him. In the following fifteen minutes, the professor did not speak; instead, he took other volunteers. Almost all of these students jumped on the bandwagon, berating the one maverick student. The professor gave him one more chance to speak. By this time the student was quite flustered and incoherent.

Noted Shachtman, "The class learned that bringing out such controversial views would carry a high social cost. They would be less likely to repeat the 'error' of their fellow student."[3]

When students do speak their minds, their complaints may have little 5
effect. A feminist professor teaching at the University of Wisconsin listed some of the objections that students had made to feminist teaching in composition and introduction to literature sections. Wrote one student, "I feel this course was dominated and overpowered by feminist doctrines and ideals." Wrote another:

> Feminism is an important issue in society—but a very controversial one. It needs to be confronted on a personal basis, not in the classroom. I didn't appreciate feminist comments on papers or expressed about a work.

---

[1]Michelle Colitsas, "Education Based on Violated Trust," *Catalyst* (September 1991), 3.
[2]"From the Editor: Dubious Dialogue," *Catalyst* (November/December 1991), 11.
[3]Marc Shachtman, "Learning and Losing: The Need for a Balance in Political Views," *Oberlin Forum* (October 1990), 3.

Another student complained, "My professor . . . is a feminist and she incorporates her ideas and philosophy into her grading scale."[4]

The professor quoting these complaints did not accord them any legitimacy. She did not ask whether it might be reasonable for a student to object when a course that is supposed to be about how to write is turned into a course on overcoming patriarchy. To her, the complaints were examples of what feminists have to put up with in the classroom. They were simply a starting point for discussing the "resistance" that must be overcome "in order to get our students to identify with the political agenda of feminism."[5]

A professor from the University of Massachusetts at Boston, who used a freshman writing course to teach, as she put it, "leftist politics" and "feminist thought," found herself the subject of a complaint from a young woman named Minnie, whom the professor described as "a young working class woman from Puerto Rico." What Minnie wanted was to learn how to write. She wanted model essays to pattern her work after; she wanted the professor to correct her papers and tell her how to write better; and when these things did not happen, she complained to the writing director. As the professor described Minnie's grievance:

> She made it clear that . . . notions of gender politics, notions of student empowerment did not touch her need for the proper style, the proper accent, the Doolittle makeover she had signed up for. It was not that Minnie did or did not wish to embrace her race and her class; it was that she wished to define them otherwise. That is, to define herself as American, middle-class, conservative, genderless: the student, the worker, the citizen.

Even though the professor is trying to disparage Minnie's ideas with this description, it seems quite clear that the young woman knew exactly what she needed—and had every right to expect—from a freshman writing class. And it is equally clear that the professor was determined to see her as a misguided ingrate for wanting to make her way in this society rather than become an expert in its faults. "Minnie's tuition dollar is buying plastic surgery, not literacy," the professor concluded.[6]

Composition courses have become particularly susceptible to ideological teaching. Writing in such periodicals as the *Journal of Advanced Composition* and *College English,* composition teachers offer advice on how to inform such courses with "political consciousness and social action"[7] so that students will

---

[4]Quoted in Dale M. Bauer, "The Other 'F' Word: The Feminist in the Classroom," *College English* (April 1990), 385–86.

[5]Ibid., 387.

[6]Elizabeth A. Fay, "Anger in the Classroom: Women, Voice, and Fear," *Radical Teacher* (Fall 1992), 14–15.

[7]James N. Laditka, "Semiology, Ideology, *Praxis:* Responsible Authority in the Composition Classroom," *Journal of Advanced Composition* (Fall 1990), 366.

become "social and political activists."[8] They discuss how to tailor "liberatory pedagogy" so as to bring students from different social and economic backgrounds to "a critical awareness of the constrictions in their own class position." One would not want, for example, to use the same methods on students from upper-class backgrounds who "have the financial and emotional security to be open to progressive pedagogy and even radical politics" that one would use on middle-class students who "reflect the reflex conservatism of uncritical subordination to established social order and authority."[9]

Maxine Hairston, former chair of the Conference on College Composition and Communication, identifies the new model for freshman writing programs as one "that puts dogma before diversity, politics before craft, ideology before critical thinking, and the social goals of the teacher before the educational needs of the student."[10] Two of the most widely used textbooks for freshman composition, *Racism and Sexism,* edited by Paula S. Rothenberg, and *Rereading America,* edited by Gary Colombo, Robert Cullen, and Bonnie Lisle, support her assessment.[11] Both present essay after essay portraying the United States as mired in racism, sexism, and elitism—not to mention that most hopeless of all states, capitalism. According to the publisher of *Rereading America,* the book was used at almost five hundred colleges and universities the first year it was published.

As politicized as many composition classes are, women's studies classes are typically worse. When Karen Lehrman visited women's studies classes on four different campuses for *Mother Jones* magazine, she was struck by the amount of consciousness-raising she found. Time and again, students were urged to talk about their personal experiences of oppression and their emotions about being oppressed, rather than to consider the status of women in any objective fashion. At the University of California at Berkeley, after the screening of a film, a professor asked her class: "How do you *feel* about the film?" In another class at Berkeley, students took up the topic of faked orgasms. "Many in women's studies consider personal experience the only real source of truth," Lehrman writes.[12]

Professors themselves report on their techniques for consciousness-raising. A professor at the University of North Carolina at Charlotte describes

10

---

[8]James A. Berlin, "Freirean Pedagogy in the U.S.: A Response," *Journal of Advanced Composition* (Winter 1992), 419.

[9]Donald Lazere, "Back to Basics: A Force for Oppression or Liberation?" *College English* (January 1992), 17–18.

[10]Maxine Hairston, "Diversity, Ideology, and Teaching Writing," *College Composition and Communication* (May 1992), 180.

[11]Paula S. Rothenberg, *Racism and Sexism: An Integrated Study* (New York: St. Martin's, 1988); Gary Colombo, Robert Cullen, and Bonnie Lisle, *Rereading America: Cultural Contexts for Critical Thinking and Writing* (Boston: St. Martin's, 1992).

[12]Karen Lehrman, "Off Course," *Mother Jones* (September/October 1993), 48.

in an article how she encourages students in her women's studies class to tell "life stories," particularly on Mondays, and how she uses anecdotes from her own life to spur them on.[13] A professor at the State University of New York at Brockport informs other members of the Women's Studies List on the Internet of the positive results for her women's studies class of her having confessed her own previously repressed memories of child abuse. An English professor and two psychologists at a small college in Michigan worry about faculty members in a variety of courses urging students to reveal intimate details of their lives. One faculty member, they report, holds special sessions after class for students who reveal they are victims of sexual abuse.[14]

Some students buy into the ideology they find in classrooms. A women's studies major at San Francisco State University proudly tells two visiting researchers that she "got her politics" at State.[15] These students work not only to make sure that their peers conform, but also that faculty members do not stray from the party line. Daphne Patai and Noretta Koertge report on three professors who have decided to abandon women's studies because of their experiences with militant students.[16]

Other students, whether they support the ideology or not, are affected by the thinking that permits the ideology in classrooms: the idea that there is no truth and no reality, that there are only different stories told by different groups in order to advance their interests. One of the clearest examples of this in recent years occurred at Duke University when the student newspaper published a paid advertisement setting forth what has become the standard line among those who deny that the Jewish Holocaust occurred, which is that the gas chambers, the photographs of dead and starving concentration camp prisoners, and the eyewitness accounts of death and suffering were all a fraud.[17] Student newspapers across the country had received the same advertisement, and while many refused to accept it (Harvard, Yale, MIT) on the very sensible grounds that newspapers have no obligation to publish advertisements that are misleading and fail to meet elementary standards of evidence and logic, many had run the ad (Cornell, Northwestern, the University of Michigan). Administrators at these schools typically cited First Amendment

[13]Kathleen Weiler, *Women Teaching for Change: Gender, Class & Power* (New York: Bergin & Garvey, 1988), 63.

[14]Susan Swartzlander, Diana Pace, and Virginia Lee Stamler, "The Ethics of Requiring Students to Write About Their Personal Lives," *Chronicle of Higher Education* (17 February 1993), B1.

[15]Quoted in Frances A. Maher and Mary Kay Thompson Tetreault, *The Feminist Classroom: An Inside Look at How Professors and Students Are Transforming Higher Education for a Diverse Society* (New York: Basic Books, 1994), 54.

[16]Patai and Koertge, *Professing Feminism,* 13–17.

[17]Bradley R. Smith, "The Holocaust Controversy: The Case for Open Debate," *Chronicle* (5 November 1991), 14, Advertisement.

reasons, though as Deborah E. Lipstadt, who has written about Holocaust denial, notes, many of these papers had policies in place prohibiting racist and sexist advertising; and some of them had also refused to run cigarette advertising.[18]

But the Duke editor offered a unique defense of her decision: namely, that the deniers are simply revisionists who are "reinterpreting history, a practice that occurs constantly, especially on a college campus."[19] The Duke History Department, to its credit, rose up in protest at the idea that Holocaust denial is simply a new perspective on the past. Revisionism is not about the "actuality" of events; it is about their "interpretation," a department statement said.[20] But the distinction is one that postmodern thinkers, with talk about how facts themselves are "situated," often honor in the breach. The Duke editor's decision may well have revealed less about her misunderstanding of ideas that are now common on campuses than it did about what can happen when truth and reason are dismissed. As Deborah Lipstadt observes, "The deniers are plying their trade at a time when much of history seems to be up for grabs and attacks on the Western rationalist tradition have become commonplace."[21]

Some students—and it may well be the majority—simply try to cope with what they find going on in classrooms. A student at Smith College in Massachusetts told Karen Lehrman that she "quickly discovered that the way to get A's [in a feminist anthropology course] was to write papers full of guilt and angst about how I'd bought into society's definition of womanhood and now I'm enlightened and free."[22] When I visited the University of Pennsylvania, a student told me that she had discovered, "If you write about misogyny, you'll do great."[23] The same idea informs an exchange that made its way into a learned journal not long ago. One male student instructs another on how to succeed in a feminist classroom. "Pretend to be a male chauvinist, then have a conversion. You're bound to get an A."[24]

Upon encountering a teaching assistant "with wild ideas," most undergraduates, a University of Pennsylvania student told me, will "just do whatever is necessary to get a good grade. . . . They'll talk the talk and walk the walk that the TA wants them to." What this produces, the undergraduate

15

---

[18]See Deborah E. Lipstadt, *Denying the Holocaust: The Growing Assault on Truth and Memory* (New York: Free Press, 1993), 194–95.

[19]Ann Heimberger, "First Amendment Protects Controversial Advertisers, Too," *Chronicle* (5 November 1991), 9.

[20]"The History Department Responds to Holocaust Ad," *Chronicle* (13 November 1991), 7.

[21]Lipstadt, *Denying the Holocaust,* 17.

[22]Quoted in Lehrman, "Off Course," 49–50.

[23]Conversation with author, 27 April 1993.

[24]Susan C. Jarratt, "Rhetorical Power: What Really Happens in Politicized Classrooms," *ADE Bulletin* (Fall 1992), 36.

went on to explain, is "the conviction that it is not the pursuit of truth [that college is about], it's just getting out."[25]

A student at the University of North Carolina at Chapel Hill told me, "You learn to read professors when you're in college, and you know exactly what they want to hear. . . . You just go ahead and say what they want to hear, which, in my case, was [to] bash Reagan and Bush." When I asked him if he personally had done this, he answered, "Yes. That's totally against my personal beliefs, to bash Reagan and Bush . . . but I'm not here to philosophize my beliefs in Pol Sci 41, I'm here to get a decent grade in the class."[26]

Anyone fortunate enough to have gone to college in years when literature and philosophy and political science classes were indisputably places for expressing views and testing beliefs realizes how much this student and so many of his peers are missing. While it is gratifying that they do not buy into the politics they find in classrooms and heartening that they are usually good-humored about their situation, it is dismaying to think how little they know of the excitement of learning and how well versed they are becoming in dissembling—and in the cynicism that a system that encourages dissembling produces.

A student at the University of Pennsylvania observed to me that the classroom is not the only place that students encounter ideology. Describing a university administration that "has its own agenda and is accountable to no one," he noted that while "there are problems in the classroom," there are worse problems "outside the classroom" where administrators' control is more certain.[27] He was specifically pointing to the world of diversity training that has grown up on college and university campuses across the nation. At the University of Pennsylvania, as at scores of institutions, incoming freshmen (or first-year students, in politically correct terminology) get a massive infusion of what University of Pennsylvania history professor Alan C. Kors calls the "ideological analysis" of the "heirs of the sixties."[28] The guiding assumption of this extracurricular training is that the attitudes and beliefs with which students arrive on campus are unsatisfactory and must be changed. "Families have not socialized their children in good values," declared a speaker at a 1995 conference in Washington, D.C., on how to transform not only the classroom but student life outside it as well.[29] Typical lessons in this co-curriculum are that only whites can be racist because only white people have

---

[25]Conversation with author, 27 April 1993.

[26]Conversation with author, 1 April 1993.

[27]Conversation with author, 27 April 1993.

[28]Alan Charles Kors, "The Politicization of the University, In Loco Parentis," The World & I (May 1991), 486.

[29]Beverly Guy-Sheftall quoted in Candace de Russy, "Whole-Campus Multiculturalization (Brought to You by Ford)," Measure (January 1995), 6–7.

power and that "institutional racism" exists whenever institutions like universities do not produce equal outcomes for all races. Students learn how deeply racist is the college or university they have chosen to attend—even when the facts have to be altered to support that conclusion.

The "Facilitator's Guide" for diversity training distributed at the University of Pennsylvania in 1989 called for facilitators to read to students "incidents of harassment that have taken place at the University over the past few years."[30] One of those to whom the guide was distributed, Michael Cohen, a professor of physics, recognized that in at least three cases, the so-called incidents of harassment had been exaggerated to the point of fabrication. In one instance, facilitators were to describe the following events to students:

> A University professor continually referred to African-American students in his class as "ex-slaves" and said that their comments would be particularly useful when the class discussed the Thirteenth Amendment. It was later discovered that other African-American students who had taken the professor's class had had similar experiences.[31]

Cohen pointed out that the facts in this case were well known. In widely publicized hearings it had been established that the professor had made a one-time reference to African-American students as ex-slaves and had done so in a statement in which he expressed surprise that while he, a Jew, celebrated his liberation from slavery at Passover,* African-American students, likewise "ex-slaves," did not celebrate the Thirteenth Amendment.* The "Facilitator's Guide" also failed to mention the harsh punishment meted out to the professor: He was suspended and forced to undergo sensitivity training. Concluded Cohen, "I don't know who compiled the list of incidents and who approved the final text, but I do know that they are people with little regard for the truth."[32]

Above all, diversity training emphasizes that students must think of themselves and others in racial terms. Professor Kors observes that when students have their "first contact with the university, before they get into a classroom, they're taught that race and gender are the primary parts of human personality."[33] At diversity training sessions at Penn, freshmen have been asked

20

---

[30]"Diversity Education Labor Day Program: Facilitator's Guide" (Philadelphia: University of Pennsylvania, 1989), 11.

Passover: Jewish religious festival commemorating the Israelites' departure from slavery in Egypt as chronicled in Exodus

Thirteenth Amendment: "Neither slavery nor involuntary servitude, except as a punishment for a crime whereof the party shall have been duly convicted, shall exist within the United States, or any place subject to their jurisdiction."

[31]Ibid., 12.

[32]Michael Cohen, "What Is Happening and Why?" *Daily Pennsylvanian* (2 October 1989), 6.

[33]Conversation with author, 26 April 1993.

to label themselves by race and gender so that they can play "human bingo"—before they introduce themselves by name. At Bryn Mawr College in Pennsylvania, freshmen have been asked to construct a "cultural coat of arms" for themselves, filling it in with "their cultural group's greatest accomplishment, a favorite food of their cultural group, a piece of clothing that is symbolic of their cultural group, and an artifact of their cultural group in their home."[34]

At the State University of New York at Binghamton, orientation group leaders have been given definitions of various stages of racial sensitivity, the most unenlightened of which is the stage in which "majority members . . . do not perceive themselves as 'racial beings' and tend to assume that racist and cultural differences are unimportant."[35] To liberate incoming freshmen from this stage, orientation leaders break them up into small groups and have them play "Wheel of Oppression," a game that shows how prejudice combined with social power leads to sexism, ableism, ageism, classism, heterosexism, and racism. One group leader reported on the results of the orientation:

> Most of them didn't know what we were talking about. It was kind of sad. When we first got together they were all friendly, drawn together because they were new. But as we got into the game playing, especially the "Wheel of Oppression" part, they began to split up and draw away into little cliques.[36]

A recent graduate of Skidmore College in New York wrote in the school's alumni paper about how divisive her experience with a student-led diversity effort had been:

> One of my closest friends at that time was from Texas. . . . But then it happened. . . . At the [diversity awareness] meeting a student took the podium and announced her belief that all whites are racist. She then demanded that the audience respond: those in agreement were to raise their hands. I was shocked when I saw my friend raise hers. The instant she raised her hand, a line was drawn. We were no longer simply two friends. Now, she was black and I was white.[37]

Two graduate students at the University of Cincinnati have written about an orientation session required of residence hall staff members. Those attending were separated into groups, given a bag of Tinkertoys, and in-

---

[34]"Building Pluralism at Bryn Mawr College" (Bryn Mawr, Penn.: Bryn Mawr College, 1988), 44.

[35]W. Terrell Jones and Art Costantino, "Agent of Oppression Group Awareness," handout circulated at State University of New York at Binghamton, 1.

[36]Quoted in David Rossie, "SUNY-B's First Lesson: Get Correct," *Press & Sun-Bulletin* (4 August 1991), E1.

[37]Jennifer George, letter to the editor, *Skidmore Scope* (June 1994), 2.

structed to "build the tallest free-standing structure." One group had only two white males; and they were the only members of their group to work on the project, "the others showing no interest whatsoever," according to the graduate students. These two white males managed to build a structure taller than any other group's—for which the diversity training instructor berated them. They had "personified all the characteristics of white-male oppression," by being concerned "only with building the tallest structure and of listening only to the other white male in the group."[38]

Many students do not buy into the ideas that have become the staples of diversity training: In a survey done of Stanford University students by political scientist John Bunzel, the overwhelming majority of white students defined *racism* in the traditional way—as either prejudice ("preconceived and unfavorable judgments about people") or discrimination ("selective mistreatment"). A high percentage of black students, on the other hand, defined racism as diversity educators have come to talk about it: in terms of power, so that the phrase "white racism" becomes a redundancy.[39]

From this latter definition flows one of the most disturbing features of college and university life in the 1990s: self-segregation. Minority students demand separate clubs, yearbooks, dorms, and commencement ceremonies, arguing that they provide a zone of comfort and encourage racial and ethnic awareness. Some maintain that group power is the primary goal. Asked why black students choose to separate themselves at Stanford, a black student responded:

> My answer begins with our history of subjugation. Whites have had the power ever since this country got started, and they abused it. The rest of my answer is that they still have the power and they still abuse it. How do you fight against the misuse of power? With your own power.[40]

If one accepts the idea that racism is impossible for minorities, then acts of separatism by minorities cannot be defined as racist. As a black student leader at Stanford declared, "There is no such thing as reverse racism, reverse sexism, because those people don't have the wherewithal to act out their prejudices.[41]

But to white students who do not accept the idea that only they can be racist, black separatism is cause for resentment. Writes Bunzel, "Apart from feeling that they can and deserve to be trusted, [white students] resent the fact that at the same time that blacks are adamant in opposing racism, they con-

---

[38]Nicholas A. Damask and Craig T. Cobane, "Our Little Workshop in Thought Control on Campus in Ohio," *Washington Times* (20 October 1993), A23.

[39]John H. Bunzel, *Race Relations on Campus: Stanford Students Speak* (Stanford, Calif.: Stanford Alumni Association, 1992), 36, 38.

[40]Quoted in Bunzel, *Race Relations,* 65–66.

[41]Ibid., 54.

tinue to segregate themselves from whites. Self-segregation is precisely the kind of action and behavior that whites consider discriminatory."[42] Thus, it should not be surprising that many white students come away from their college years with less sympathy for minority causes than when they started. Almost one-third of the white students in Bunzel's survey reported that their experience at Stanford had made them "more suspicious of the 'anti-racism' of minorities."[43] A student at the University of Pennsylvania described his experience this way, "I have always considered myself an open-minded person, but being inundated with this day after day after day, and seeing how the University is divided, I have much less tolerance than I ever had before."[44]

For students who do not accept the premises on which most diversity training is based, it oftentimes has exactly the opposite result of that intended. For all students, it has the effect of increasing consciousness of race and decreasing consciousness of people as individuals. Instead of bringing us closer to the world that Martin Luther King, Jr., envisioned—a world in which people are judged not by color but by character—diversity training often brings the message that race matters most.

In every part of the university, the range of permitted thought and expression is narrowing. Faculty are constrained in their research and teaching, students in their academic and personal lives. Surely it is one of the sad spectacles of our time to watch great institutions that once encouraged the search for truth seeking now instead to ensure ideological conformity.

QUESTIONING THE TEXT

1. Have you taken part in a diversity training or orientation program such as those Cheney describes? If so, write a letter to Cheney comparing or contrasting your experiences with those of the students she describes.
2. J.R.'s introduction suggests that colleges should be as attentive to political diversity as they are to racial and gender difference. What might the consequences be for faculty and curriculum if schools insisted on political balance in the classroom?
3. What kinds of evidence does Cheney use to make her case? Which evidence do you find most compelling? Which evidence, if any, do you question?
4. Cheney suggests that "There are many reasons to be silent rather than speak out on campus today." Discuss an experience of your own that relates to this claim. Do you usually feel free to speak in college classes, or have you sometimes felt coerced into silence?

---

[42]Ibid., 74.
[43]Ibid., 45.
[44]Conversation with author, 27 April 1993.

MAKING CONNECTIONS

5. Read Cheney's piece back to back with the selection from Mike Rose's *Lives on the Boundary* (p. 97). Then look for common ground between them. How might you reconcile Cheney's call for a freer pursuit of truth in college with Rose's championing of a cultural literacy that rejects universal truth as a principle? What values might Cheney and Rose ultimately share?

6. Cheney claims that women's studies courses are quite politicized and that instruction in these courses relies heavily on consciousness-raising, "life stories," and tales of abuse. Adrienne Rich's "What Does a Woman Need to know?" in this chapter (p. 44) is a feminist text that might be used in a women's studies course. Reread it carefully in light of Cheney's criticisms, and then write a position paper about the politics of Cheney's and Rich's essays.

JOINING THE CONVERSATION

7. Cheney suggests that English composition classes have become some of the most ideological courses in higher education. Write a report describing any political currents and attitudes you have sensed in your writing class. In what ways do your experiences reinforce or contradict Cheney's observations?

8. Working in a group, outline a proposal for a school orientation program that might foster community among students of different races, classes, religions, sexual orientation, and political persuasions, but that also might avoid the "diversity training" pitfalls that Cheney describes. Write your proposal in the form of a one-page report.

9. Write an exploratory essay for a campus or local newspaper attempting to define how political an instructor may be in a college course. You might limit your subject by focusing on a particular course and level— that is, does it make a difference if an instructor is teaching in a required freshman English course rather than in an upper-division government class?

CHRISTIAN ZAWODNIAK

"I'll Have to Help Some of You More Than I Want To": Teacher Power, Student Pedagogy

CHRISTIAN ZAWODNIAK (b. 1975) grew up in New Jersey, the youngest of twelve children. Now pursuing a double major in French and English at Ohio State, Zawodniak plans to become a teacher. He is, then, interested in the issues this chapter raises, and, like several other selections in this chapter, Zawodniak's essay explores the issue of power in higher education. More specifically, he is interested in how power can be "balanced" in the college classroom, particularly since he knows that "a careful balance is hard to achieve, and no one knows how the power issues will play out until class starts."

Zawodniak speaks from firsthand knowledge, reporting on his own experiences in first-year writing at a large midwestern university, describing the class and his teacher, and striving to understand how to "overcome the isolation that often exists between teachers and students." From these reflections emerge a complex picture of one English composition classroom—warts and all—as seen by an extremely thoughtful student. What kind of essay might you write about your own class? About your own participation in it? About the ways in which teachers and students "have to get personal"? About how you and a teacher can work together to make learning happen? I chose Zawodniak's essay because it raises all these questions for me and because it reminds me of how much I love teaching: who wouldn't love a job that calls forth people like Christian Zawodniak? — A.L.

Teachers always have power in a class. They hold the grades, and, usually, students perceive them as holding the knowledge, too. The way teachers use this power is perhaps the defining characteristic of their pedagogy. Some teachers may work with students to create the class environment; others may force a class environment upon students. Regardless of their approach or intent, teachers have the power even before they step into the class. Their syllabus is already made, though not necessarily fixed; students already have perceptions of or attitudes toward the role of the teacher, the course, the school, or maybe even the specific teacher; we students have already been educated throughout our lives on how to treat teachers and how they will treat us. None of this may be explicitly meant by a teacher; perhaps it may not even be implicitly considered, but the power is there. This power is no easy burden for teachers: Those who ignore lines of power within the class often reinforce them; those who meet power issues by being too controlling often narrow the space for student creativity. A careful balance is hard to achieve, and no one knows how the power issues will play out until class starts.

I write this essay to offer a student perspective on the issues of power in the classroom. And although it is only one perspective, I've done a lot of thinking about teaching styles, about writing, and about conducting classes in my first year of college.

It is the first day of class in my first quarter of freshman English.[1] Jeff, my teacher, has already passed out the syllabus. Some words are spoken, but I don't remember them. Then, from my teacher I hear, "I'll have to help some of you more than I want to." And recall thinking, "This is radical—*not* what I expected." I don't quite understand what Jeff's comment means. It seems rebellious, yet official. Jeff was admitting that teachers, like everyone, get tired. Teachers aren't machines that never run out of energy, but sometimes they have to help students even more than they want to, even when they have been working with students all day. Jeff's directness gave him validity as a person (like us), not a teacher who could do everything. Jeff won't just fit into a teacher "mold," he won't pretend that teachers can just go through a routine; rather he seems like a teacher who will shake things up, breaking that mold.

The course description, directly from the syllabus:

> Since writing is an activity rather than a subject area in itself, you will be learning by doing and becoming more self-aware about what you are now doing and what some of your other options might be. For this reason, much of our time in class will be spent in activities, not in lectures; therefore, it is more than usually important that you come to class faithfully and that you keep up with your assignments.

The syllabus was one of my first impressions of the course. Reading it   5
now, I would say that student awareness of "options" (a word that still means little to me in the syllabus) is the course goal. But Jeff's description seemed so vague to me that I couldn't grasp what the course plan or his vision was. The syllabus didn't tell me what Jeff wanted, but that only intensified Jeff's mystery. He was like a puzzle with dazzling pieces, but not a whole picture could be made out of them. Syllabi are not as revealing as a teacher's day-to-day instruction, so I don't expect too much from a syllabus. However, Jeff didn't expand much on his course description. The most he did was tell us his office hours and office phone number. But the syllabus does show the ideology at work in this case: that students should be left to work by themselves. When teachers leave us students alone, we have the best chances for freedom to find

---

[1]The purpose of the class was for students to write—we had no literature text, only instruction books, *The Concise Guide to Writing*, *A Writer's Reference*, and *Re:Visions*, a collection of the best freshman essays from the year before.

our own voices, and, perhaps, creativity. Our independence allows us to make the class; this was Jeff's silent motto. And it fit perfectly with what he had said on the first day: "I'll have to help some of you more than I want to."

Most English teachers often have similar goals—to teach students how to read a text critically or how to write well—but the means and methods of achieving those goals are what count in the classroom, in practice. In my freshman composition class, I experienced the complications of participating in what Jeff considered a "student pedagogy." I am still gaining an under-standing of what happened in the class. In this paper, I will show snapshots of the class structure and day-to-day activities. Most of all, I will reflect on what continues to puzzle me most: my affection for the teacher and my shifting views of his attempts at a student-centered pedagogy.

I will start with my first impressions of Jeff and give some of my thoughts of those impressions. Early in the process of writing the paper, I wrote in my journal:

> I think what turned me on to Jeff was what he said in the first week of class, and that I wrote at the top of the syllabus: "The five-paragraph essay is not only old and silly; it's a rule for a rule's sake." Who couldn't love that? It says "break the rules" and it went against most of what I had been taught in high school. . . . I also liked Jeff 'cause he wore sneakers and jeans and was an inconsistent shaver. I guess I saw him as not being a snobby academic—he seemed to fit in with us.
>
> — 13 February 95

I liked Jeff from the start because of his style. Dressing casually and sit-ting on a table cast him in the role of "outsider." Of course, his views about the five-paragraph essay, which I knew well from high school, showed that he liked writing for writing's sake, not to fit a formula. Jeff didn't follow the rules; he questioned them. His style seemed to refute the formal power teachers usually show by dressing up or by standing behind a podium giving a lecture.

I also liked things about Jeff's teaching and what he taught. His "scien-tific method" made sense. When I say scientific method, I do not refer to the formal scientific method used by scientists. I mean that Jeff seemed to think we could and should have what he referred to as a "scientific approach" to writing. When he talked about forms of arguments, he said that there are three basic appeals that arguments can make: to emotions, reason, character. Appeals to emotions, he said, were things like TV commercials. I thought of those fabric softener commercials where the world, and individuals' lives, are bright and sunny, all because of Downy. Jeff plainly stated that appeals to rea-son were the best kinds of arguments. Arguments about character were what politicians did, but that was my thought, not Jeff's. I didn't use this "thesis tri-angle," as it was called, in my own writing, but it does show Jeff's scientific pedagogical bent.

Aristotle

Jeff's pedagogy, as I experienced it, was to interfere as little as possible with   10
class activities, leaving the students to run the class. He gave prompts, but once
conversation started, he didn't speak. Rather, he would sit there, looking at us
or into space, and we would talk and then look at him, looking for some kind of
guidance. There was a lot of silence. I didn't think it was good silence usually,
but the silence of our uncertainty, intimidation, and confusion. I felt intimidated
because we were risking our ideas when we spoke, and the best response we
could get from the teacher would be an evaluation—a judgment of our ideas. It
wasn't what Jeff did that bothered me—all teachers give prompts and want student participation; it was how he did it that was bad.

Perhaps he thought that in that room, we—students and teacher—could
be equals and have an ideal class. However, to achieve the ideal class I think
Jeff wanted, students would have needed to leave our experiences with teaching and with the power teachers hold at the door. He wanted students to be
observers of the world from his isolated classroom, once saying that to understand a system you have to get outside of it.

But this pedagogy didn't work for the class theme, which was *personal*
essays. Students wrote various types of essays: personal experience, profile,
problem-solution, concept explanation, but all were to come from our own
experiences. In writing personal essays, we go into the world, as observers *and*
participants. In my concept paper, for example, I talked about something I
knew about. For my profile, I talked about a lady who worked at the cafeteria, because I already had experience with her and impressions of her. I
couldn't understand the nuances of preparing for the morning cafeteria rush
or of running meal cards through the machine, if I had not known something
of her firsthand. For my personal experience paper, I revisited a move from
New Jersey to Ohio in third grade. By getting inside that experience, not remaining outside it, I could give rich details. Good writing takes us into a
place, and we can't create it by trying to remain outside.

Jeff's method seemed to be based on the assumption that we can't comment on what we do not know and we don't know what we cannot prove.
This often meant that he didn't speak much in class, because when we speak
we usually make some sort of claim or assertion. He once told us about a student who asserted that the Bible's story of creation was correct, and Jeff said
he couldn't prove the student wrong. I took Jeff to mean that we cannot
comment on that which we do not know, we can only move to higher levels
of probability. Jeff's silence in class discussions, therefore, isn't too surprising.
Perhaps he saw silence as an occasion to investigate—and he didn't want to
do the investigating for us. He didn't want to do our thinking for us. This approach to teaching resulted in a "laissez-faire" pedagogy. Jeff's job was made
easier because he could just watch us work, but it was difficult for me and
many of my classmates to understand what he wanted.

As the quarter progressed, I viewed Jeff with admiration, soon joined
with intimidation. I began to question his motive for saying he'd probably

have to help some of us more than he wanted to. Shouldn't he help us to be as good as we could be? Perhaps, I thought, all teachers have to help some students more than they want to, and of course all teachers get tired. I began to realize how much Jeff's statement reflected both dispassion and fatigue. He didn't give enough constructive guidance. I often felt alone and mean-spirited in the class. In fact, I think I felt alone *because* of the mean-spiritedness, which I felt because we students were always subject to Jeff's judgment.

Too often Jeff seemed to present "knowledge" or ask questions of us,   15 and then to assume the role as judge of our ideas. Critical pedagogy teaches that teachers are not the sole possessors of knowledge, and Jeff's pedagogy gave us ourselves to start on. Yet, he did not welcome self-reflection; indeed, it usually met with judgment from him. We could speak our minds, but he was still the guard of knowledge, evaluating our responses, rather than encouraging further dialogue.

By presenting and analyzing one particular day in Jeff's class, I can illustrate the intimidating effect of his judgment. On that day Jeff started class by saying something like "How are your papers going?" It wasn't a threatening question, but he spoke in a dispassionate and distant tone. His delivery enacted what he had said on the first day of class: "I'll probably have to help some of you more than I want to."

For a moment, no one spoke. Then I complained that I was having trouble with my concept paper. Specifically, I was having trouble showing my thesis, that football was an outlet for violence (a subject I later abandoned). My classmates asked me questions: "What are you trying to show?" "What do you have down already?" "Is that exactly what you mean?" I tried to respond productively. Then another classmate spoke: "That's my problem, too. I know what I mean to say, but don't know how to say it." Then another, and so on. Soon, many of us were talking about our papers, trying to help one another.

Then Jeff spoke—and the class got silent. In a serious tone, he asked me, "Do you want an extension?" "Yes," I said. He gave another person who spoke up early in the discussion an extension, too. I felt like I had risked Jeff's judgment, and felt great anxiety doing so. I think the extension had the effect of punishing the other students, just because I spoke up in a moment of boldness and no one else did. Even here, when Jeff's pedagogy appeared student-centered (when we ran the discussion ourselves) it had the effect of rewarding a few instead of helping everyone.

As much as Jeff might have tried to leave his power outside the class by speaking only when necessary, the students wouldn't let him. We expected him to do things that he didn't do, such as giving strong, constructive guidance, not just critical comments. To some extent, I think my classmates and I wanted to *obey* Jeff. As my critical writing teacher said on the first day of class last week, "I know that part of acclimating yourself to a new class is trying to figure out what a professor wants." We wanted to know what Jeff wanted, but he wouldn't let us. We students had to do too much guessing.

Paradoxically, Jeff gave us nothing to obey yet forced us to obey him. This practice is not totally bad. Students need to risk our own thoughts, and some of us can do this only if we don't have the safety net of a teacher telling us what to do. Still, we need to know that our ideas will be welcomed, and since Jeff's student-centered pedagogy relied so much on his silence, we hardly had vibrant discussions of any kind in his class.

At different times, Jeff fulfilled his position of power in two ways: by being rigid—and laid back. This paradoxical approach made for some tender, shocking, and always peculiar days.

Jeff was laid back when he tried to bond with us by telling us that he had to clean up his kid's "shit" or that he played basketball with friends. When he talked about basketball, he kind of smiled. I don't know why this sort of communication didn't take place more often. One day, when we were talking about our personal experience papers, Jeff mentioned that once he found a human carcass—but then he said, "it's too early in the morning for that story." And it was, but at the time I felt like the class was together, and Jeff was just "one of us." This intimate, relaxed approach brought out the best in him. Yet, I think the class was a little suspicious of these times, for we never knew what the next day would bring. Here's an example of Jeff's strictness.

My most vivid memory of Jeff's rigidness was the day he responded to our criticisms of the class. Students were given a chance anonymously to write our biggest criticisms one Monday, and the following Wednesday Jeff responded, staunchly answering all criticisms of his teaching: "Some of you complained that I didn't come to class prepared. It took me five years to learn all of this." Then he pointed to the blackboard on which he had written all the concepts we had discussed that quarter. His responses didn't seem genuine or aimed at improving his teaching or helping the students to understand him. He thought he was always right. Jeff's position gave him responsibilities that he officially met. But he didn't take responsibility in all the ways he had led us to expect.

Jeff's rigidness and sense of correctness silenced a lot of us, and he unintentionally kept his power by maintaining silence. His own silence didn't open opportunities for us taking power, though it may have been an invitation to do just that. We can fill silence, but we didn't have a good power structure to do so. It's a nice idea for students to be self-motivated, but sometimes we aren't. Jeff tried to guide us, but his guidance was paradoxically both too formal and too informal. He wanted to follow a plan, which most teachers do, but his plan revealed itself by his simply not telling students what to do—at all.

Jeff seemed unable to respond when the look on a student's face or the silence in the classroom meant he needed to be more inviting or to explain himself more. Our subject was personal essays, yet his aloofness didn't encourage our emotions to come out. He showed us good writing, but the passion and concern for *our* writing seemed lacking. If we couldn't meet his ways of teaching writing, it was very difficult for him to help us produce good writing.

One thing that has become so clear to me and frightened me in writing this essay is how much I liked Jeff and how much sympathy I have for him *because* of his misguided approach. Throughout the quarter, I was almost as caught up in Jeff's ideas as he himself was. During that quarter I had horrible roommates, and Jeff's class was an escape from the chaos of my own dormitory. His rigid teaching became a spot where I (almost) knew the rules. But the rules just didn't work. Even late in the quarter, I felt like I was asking him permission for something—approval perhaps?—when I would show him my rough drafts. I was always checking with Jeff to make sure my writing and reasoning were right, and that constant, nervous checking now shows itself to me as a sign that something in Jeff's pedagogy *wasn't* right.

Since my class with Jeff, I have had several different teachers who have taken different approaches to writing instruction, approaches that have proven more beneficial than the fear of judgment I experienced in Jeff's class, which had the effect of constraining my writing. While I no longer operate under Jeff's pedagogy or his paradigms, my current studies in rhetoric and composition only make me more aware of how delicious a temptation those reductive paradigms can be. It seems so pretty and easy, the notion that we can just follow the rules and everything will work out. But it is the most destructive thing we can do to students' voices. In freshman composition—and in all writing courses—we students need to create our own identities, and only through our own voices can our own identities emerge, not by pretending foreign voices are our own. This goal may not be very easy to reach, but it's the only way to achieve growth. Students cannot fake a discourse and have it contribute to long-term writing growth, if only because faking discourse robs us of our own voices. Moreover, students know when teachers are lying. It sometimes takes us a long time—I am one example—but we do find it out. Then the unlearning of poor instruction can be difficult, but we do unlearn and relearn.

Rather than making students jump through compositional hoops, as Jeff did, teachers should from the start help students find their own voices. This can be dangerous, and is probably always difficult, but not more so than overcoming another teacher's poor instruction. Despite Jeff's belief that he should vacate the class in order to bring out student voices, this paradox remains: students must have active teacher involvement at the core of any student-centered classroom. We need to be welcomed—not left to attempt masterpieces with post–high school hands. Teacher involvement is the key not only to starting conversations, but also to guiding them along their meandering paths. In Jeff's class, we were too often required to play the role of teacher. But when a teacher's "power" acts as a welcoming embrace, rather than as a vacuum, students come to develop creatively. Paradigms cannot embrace us, nor can cold confessions about how much teachers have to "help" students.

Finally, students and teachers have to get personal: students have to get into the personal to write about it, and teachers have to talk about the personal to help us talk about it. Teacher and student must work and continue conversations together because, as Paulo Freire says, "Men are not built in silence, but in word, in work, in action-reflection" (69). When we realize the classroom implications of Freire's wisdom we can overcome the isolation that often exists between teacher and students. When we recognize the necessity of mutual involvement, students and teachers can work together to achieve a pedagogy that is truly student-centered.

WORKS CITED

Axelrod, Rise B., and Charles R. Cooper. *The Concise Guide to Writing.* New York: St. Martin's, 1993.

Freire, Paulo. *Pedagogy of the Oppressed.* New York: Continuum, 1990.

Hacker, Diana. *A Writer's Reference.* 2nd ed. Boston: Bedford, 1992.

Re:Visions: Essays from Freshman Writers. 2nd ed. Cincinnati: U of Cincinnati Dept. of English and Comparative Lit., 1992.

QUESTIONING THE TEXT

1. Where does Zawodniak's title come from? Why does the speaker not want to "help some of you more"?
2. What does A.L. do in her introduction to build Zawodniak's "credentials" to tell this story? Are these credentials convincing to you?
3. Throughout the essay, Zawodniak refers to his teacher as "Jeff." What effect does this use of the first name have on you? How does it help to create a portrait of the teacher?

MAKING CONNECTIONS

4. Lynne V. Cheney (p. 112) charges that English composition classes in particular have become "politicized." In what ways does Zawodniak's description support or refute Cheney's charge?
5. At the end of his essay, Zawodniak calls for a "student-centered" university and pedagogy. How would John Henry Newman (p. 39) be likely to react to such a call? Would he be supportive of the kind of relationship between teachers and students that Zawodniak calls for?

JOINING THE CONVERSATION

6. Zawodniak says that the power of the classroom is "no easy burden for teachers: those who ignore lines of power within the class often reinforce them; those who meet power issues by being too controlling often narrow the space for student creativity." Does your experience as a student support this observation? In a brief essay, explain why or why not.

7. Working with one other classmate, do a little research on Paulo Freire, whom Zawodniak quotes. What is Freire's background? What are his achievements and his philosophy of education? Prepare a brief joint report for your class on Freire and his importance to the goals of education today.

NEIL POSTMAN
The Word Weavers / The World Makers

NEIL POSTMAN (b. 1931), a professor at New York University, is a prolific writer on education, culture, and language. You can measure his intellectual vigor just by surveying several of his book titles: Education as a Subversive Activity *(1969);* Education as a Conserving Activity *(1979);* Amusing Ourselves to Death: Public Discourse in the Age of Show Business *(1985);* Technopoly: The Surrender of Culture to Technology *(1992). Concerned now with the state of American popular culture and the relationship of technology to learning, Postman believes that schools must deal more directly with the impact of television and the computer. The chapter I have selected from his most recent book,* The End of Education *(1995), takes up this technological theme and offers specific suggestions for reforming school curricula. Like John Henry Newman and Allan Bloom, Postman suggests that schools don't so much teach facts as provide perspectives on a world shaped by language. As important as silicon chips and Pentium processors may be, they're inert without ideas.* — J.R.

In an effort to clear up confusion (or ignorance) about the meaning of a word, does anyone ask, What is *a* definition of this word? Just about always, the way of putting the question is, What is *the* definition of this word? The difference between *a* and *the* in this context is vast, and I have no choice but to blame the schools for the mischief created by an inadequate understanding of what a definition is. From the earliest grades through graduate school, students are given definitions and, with few exceptions, are not told whose definitions they are, for what purposes they were invented, and what alternative definitions might serve equally as well. The result is that students come to believe that definitions are *not* invented; that they are not even human creations; that, in fact, they are — how shall I say it?—part of the natural world, like clouds, trees, and stars.

In a thousand examinations on scores of subjects, students are asked to give definitions of hundreds of things, words, concepts, procedures. It is to be doubted that there are more than a few classrooms in which there has been any discussion of what a definition is. How is that possible?

Let us take the equally strange case of questions. There will be no disagreement, I think, to my saying that all the answers given to students are the end products of questions. Everything we know has its origin in questions. Questions, we might say, are the principal intellectual instruments available to human beings. Then how is it possible that no more than one in one hundred students has ever been exposed to an extended and systematic study of the art and science of question-asking? How come Allan Bloom* didn't mention this, or E. D. Hirsch, Jr.,* or so many others who have written books on how to improve our schools? Did they simply fail to notice that *the principal intellectual instrument available to human beings is not examined in school?*

We are beginning to border on absurdity here. And we cross the line when we consider what happens in most schools on the subject of metaphor. Metaphor does, in fact, come up in school, usually introduced by an English teacher wanting to show how it is employed by poets. The result is that most students come to believe metaphor has a decorative function and only a decorative function. It gives color and texture to poetry, as jewelry does to clothing. The poet wants us to see, smell, hear, or feel something concretely, and so resorts to metaphor. I remember a discussion, when I was in college, of Robert Burns's lines:* "O, my love is like a red, red rose / That's newly sprung in June. / O my love is like the melodie / That's sweetly play'd in tune."

The first questions on the test were: "Is Burns using metaphors or similes? Define each term. Why did Burns choose to use metaphors instead of similes, or similes instead of metaphors?"   5

I didn't object to these questions at the time except for the last one, to which I gave a defiant but honest answer: How the hell should I know? I have the same answer today. But today, I have some other things to say on the matter. Yes, poets use metaphors to help us see and feel. But so do biologists, physicists, historians, linguists, and everyone else who is trying to say something about the world. A metaphor is not an ornament. It is an organ of perception. Through metaphors, we see the world as one thing or another. Is light a wave or a particle? Are molecules like billiard balls or force fields? Is history unfolding according to some instructions of nature or a divine plan? Are our genes like information codes? Is a literary work like an architect's blueprint or a mystery to be solved?

Questions like these preoccupy scholars in every field. Do I exaggerate in saying that a student cannot understand what a subject is about without some understanding of the metaphors that are its foundation? I don't think so. In fact, it has always astonished me that those who write about the subject of education do not pay sufficient attention to the role of metaphor in giving form to the subject. In failing to do so, they deprive those studying the subject of the opportunity to confront its basic assumptions. Is the human mind, for example, like a dark cavern (needing illumination)? A muscle (needing exercise)? A vessel (needing filling)? A lump of clay (needing shaping)? A garden (needing cultivation)? Or, as so many say today, is it like a computer that

---

How come Allan Bloom: See the selection by Allan Bloom on p. 52.
E. D. Hirsch, Jr.: author of *Cultural Literacy: What Americans Need to Know* (1987)
Robert Burns's lines: from the poem "A Red, Red Rose" (1796)

[handwritten margin note: business metaphor— our products or our clients?]

processes data? And what of students? Are they patients to be cared for? Troops to be disciplined? Sons and daughters to be nurtured? Personnel to be trained? Resources to be developed?

There was a time when those who wrote on the subject of education, such as Plato, Comenius, Locke, and Rousseau, made their metaphors explicit and in doing so revealed how their metaphors controlled their thinking.[1] "Plants are improved by cultivation," Rousseau wrote in *Emile,* "and man by education." And his entire philosophy rests upon this comparison of plants and children. Even in such ancient texts as the Mishnah,* we find that there are four kinds of students: the sponge, the funnel, the strainer, and the sieve. It will surprise you to know which one is preferred. The sponge, we are told, absorbs all; the funnel receives at one end and spills out at the other; the strainer lets the wine drain through it and retains the dregs; but the sieve—that is the best, for it lets out the flour dust and retains the fine flour. The difference in educational philosophy between Rousseau and the compilers of the Mishnah is precisely reflected in the differences between a wild plant and a sieve.

Definitions, questions, metaphors—these are three of the most potent elements with which human language constructs a worldview. And in urging, *[handwritten check mark]* as I do, that the study of these elements be given the highest priority in school, I am suggesting that world making through language is a narrative of power, durability, and inspiration. It is the story of how we make the world known to ourselves, and how we make ourselves known to the world. It is different from other narratives because it is about nouns and verbs, about grammar and inferences, about metaphors and definitions, but it is a story of creation, nonetheless. Even further, it is a story that plays a role in all other narratives. For whatever we believe in, or don't believe in, is to a considerable extent a function of how our language addresses the world. Here is a small example:

Let us suppose you have just finished being examined by a doctor. In   10 pronouncing his verdict, he says somewhat accusingly, "Well, you've done a very nice case of arthritis here." You would undoubtedly think this is a strange diagnosis, or more likely, a strange doctor. People do not "do" arthritis. They "have" it, or "get" it, and it is a little insulting for the doctor to imply that you have produced or manufactured an illness of this kind, especially since arthritis will release you from certain obligations and, at the same time, elicit sympathy from other people. It is also painful. So the idea that you have done arthritis to yourself suggests a kind of self-serving masochism.

---

[1]See Eva Berger, "Metaphor, Mind & Machine: An Assessment of the Sources of Metaphors of Mind in the Works of Selected Education Theorists" (Ph.D. dissertation, New York University, 1991).

the Mishnah: the first part of the Talmud; a commentary on the scriptures important in Judaic tradition

Now, let us suppose a judge is about to pass sentence on a man convicted of robbing three banks. The judge advises him to go to a hospital for treatment, saying with an air of resignation, "You certainly have a bad case of criminality." On the face of it, this is another strange remark. People do not "have" criminality. They "do" crimes, and we are usually outraged, not saddened, by their doings. At least that is the way we are accustomed to thinking about the matter.

The point I am trying to make is that such simple verbs as *is* or *does* are, in fact, powerful metaphors that express some of our most fundamental conceptions of the way things are. We believe there are certain things people "have," certain things people "do," even certain things people "are." These beliefs do not necessarily reflect the structure of reality. They simply reflect an habitual way of talking about reality. In his book *Erewhon,** Samuel Butler depicted a society that lives according to the metaphors of my strange doctor and strange judge. There, illness is something people "do" and therefore have moral responsibility for; criminality is something you "have" and therefore is quite beyond your control. Every legal system and every moral code is based on a set of assumptions about what people are, have, or do. And, I might add, any significant changes in law or morality are preceded by a reordering of how such metaphors are employed.

I am not, incidentally, recommending the culture of the people of Erewhon. I am trying to highlight the fact that our language habits are at the core of how we imagine the world. And to the degree that we are unaware of how our ways of talking put such ideas in our heads, we are not in full control of our situation. It needs hardly to be said that one of the purposes of an education is to give us greater control of our situation.

School does not always help. In schools, for instance, we find that tests are given to determine how smart someone *is* or, more precisely, how much smartness someone *has*. If, on an IQ test, one child scores a 138 and another a 106, the first is thought to *have* more smartness than the other. But this seems to me a strange conception—every bit as strange as "doing" arthritis or "having" criminality. I do not know anyone who *has* smartness. The people I know sometimes *do* smart things (as far as I can judge) and sometimes *do* dumb things—depending on what circumstances they are in, how much they know about a situation, and how interested they are. Smartness, so it seems to me, is a specific performance, done in a particular set of circumstances. It is not something you *are* or *have* in measurable quantities. In fact, the assumption that smartness is something you *have* has led to such nonsensical terms as *over-* and *underachievers*. As I understand it, an overachiever is someone who

---

Erewhon: a satire (1872) on English life in which the laws and mores of the time are reversed

doesn't *have* much smartness but does a lot of smart things. An underachiever is someone who *has* a lot of smartness but does a lot of dumb things.

The ways in which language creates a worldview are not usually part of   15
the schooling of our young. There are several reasons for this. Chief among them is that in the education of teachers, the subject is not usually brought up, and if it is, it is introduced in a cavalier and fragmentary fashion. Another reason is that it is generally believed that the subject is too complex for schoolchildren to understand, with the unfortunate result that language education is mostly confined to the study of rules governing grammar, punctuation, and usage. A third reason is that the study of language as "world maker" is, inescapably, of an interdisciplinary nature, so that teachers are not clear about which subject ought to undertake it.

As to the first reason, I have no good idea why prospective teachers are denied knowledge of this matter. (Actually, I have *some* ideas, but a few of them are snotty and all are unkind.) But if it were up to me, the study of the subject would be at the center of teachers' professional education and would remain there until they were done—that is, until they retire. This would require that they become well acquainted with the writings of Aristotle and Plato (among the ancients), Locke and Kant (among recent "ancients"), and (among the moderns) I. A. Richards, Benjamin Lee Whorf, and, especially, Alfred Korzybski.*

Of course, there are plenty of "other places" from which profound ideas about language may come. The work of I. A. Richards* (generally) and what he says, specifically, on definition and metaphor are good introductions to language as world maker. On definition (from his *Interpretation in Teaching*):

> I have said something at several places . . . about the peculiar paralysis which the mention of definitions and, still more, the discussion of them induces. It can be prevented, I believe, by stressing the purposive aspect of definitions. We want to do something and a definition is a means of doing it. If we want certain results, then we must use certain meanings (or definitions). But no definition has any authority apart from a purpose, or to bar us from other purposes. And yet they endlessly do so. Who can doubt that we are often deprived of very useful thoughts merely because the words which might express them are being temporarily preempted by other meanings? Or that a development is often frustrated merely because we are sticking to a former definition of no service to the new purpose?[2]

What Richards is talking about here is how to free our minds from the tyranny of definitions, and I can think of no better way of doing this than to

---

Aristotle . . . *Korzybski:* philosophers and theorists of language
I. A. *Richards* (1893–1979): influential English theorist of language and literature
[2]I. A. Richards, *Interpretation in Teaching* (New York: Harcourt Brace), 384.

provide students, as a matter of course, with alternative definitions of the important concepts with which they must deal in a subject. Whether it be molecule, fact, law, art, wealth, genes, or whatever, it is essential that students understand that definitions are instruments designed to achieve certain purposes, that the fundamental question to ask of them is not, Is this the real definition? or Is this the correct definition? but What purpose does the definition serve? That is, Who made it up and why?

I have had some great fun, and so have students, considering the question of definition in a curious federal law. I refer to what you may not say when being frisked or otherwise examined before boarding an airplane. You may not, of course, give false or misleading information about yourself. But beyond that, you are also expressly forbidden to joke about any of the procedures being used. This is the only case I know of where a joke is prohibited by law (although there are many situations in which it is prohibited by custom).

Why joking is illegal when you are being searched is not entirely clear   20
to me, but that is only one of several mysteries surrounding this law. Does the law distinguish, for example, between good jokes and bad jokes? (Six months for a good one, two years for a bad one?) I don't know. But even more important, how would one know when something is a joke at all? Is there a legal definition of a joke? Suppose, while being searched, I mention that my middle name is Milton (which it is) and that I come from Flushing (which I do). I can tell you from experience that people of questionable intelligence sometimes find those names extremely funny, and it is not impossible that a few of them are airport employees. If that were the case, what would be my legal status? I have said something that has induced laughter in another. Have I, therefore, told a joke? Or look at it from the opposite view: Suppose that, upon being searched, I launch into a story about a funny thing that happened to me while boarding a plane in Chicago, concluding by saying, "And then the pilot said, 'That was no stewardess. That was my wife.'" Being of questionable intelligence myself, I think it is a hilarious story, but the guard does not. If he does not laugh, have I told a joke? Can a joke be a story that does *not* make people laugh?

It can, of course, if someone of authority says so. For the point is that in every situation, including this one, someone (or some group) has a decisive power of definition. In fact, to have power means to be able to define and to make it stick. As between the guard at the airport and me, he will have the power, not me, to define what a joke is. If his definition places me in jeopardy, I can, of course, argue my case at a trial, at which either a judge or a jury will then have the decisive authority to define whether or not my words qualified as a joke. But it is also worth noting that even if I confine my joke-telling to dinner parties, I do not escape the authority of definition. For at parties, popular opinion will decide whether or not my jokes are good ones, or even jokes at all. If opinion runs against me, the penalty is that I am not invited to many parties. There is, in short, no escaping the jurisdiction of definitions. Social order requires that there be authoritative definitions and though you may search from now to doomsday, you will find no system without official definitions and authoritative sources to enforce them. And so we must add to the questions we ask of definition, What is the source of power that enforces the definition? And we may add further the question of what happens when those with the power to enforce definitions go mad. Here is an example that came from the Prague government several years ago. I have not made this up and produce it without further comment:

> Because Christmas Eve falls on a Thursday, the day has been designated a Saturday for work purposes. Factories will close all day, with stores open a half day only. Friday, December 25, has been designated a Sunday, with both factories and stores open all day. Monday, December 28, will be a Wednesday for work purposes. Wednesday, December 30, will be a business Friday. Saturday, January 2, will be a Sunday, and Sunday, January 3, will be a Monday.

As for metaphor, I pass along a small assignment which I. A. Richards used on an occasion when I attended a seminar he conducted. (It is but one of a hundred ways to introduce the subject.) Richards divided the class into three groups. Each group was asked to write a paragraph describing language. However, Richards provided each group with its first sentence. Group A had to begin with "Language is like a tree"; Group B with "Language is like a river"; Group C with "Language is like a building." You can imagine, I'm sure, what happened. The paragraphs were strikingly different, with one group writing of roots and branches and organic growth; another of tributaries, streams, and even floods; another of foundations, rooms, and sturdy structures. In the subsequent discussion, we did not bother with the question, Which is the "correct" description? Our discussion centered on how metaphors control what we say, and to what extent what we say controls what we see.

As I have said, there are hundreds of ways to study the relationship between language and reality, and I could go on at interminable length with ideas on how to get into it. Instead, I will confine myself to three further suggestions. The first is, simply, that the best book I know for arousing interest in the subject is Helen Keller's *The Story of My Life*.* It is certainly the best account we have—from the inside, as it were—of how symbols and the abstracting process work to create a world.

Second, I would propose that in every subject—from history to biology to mathematics—students be taught, explicitly and systematically, the universe

---

The Story of My Life (1903): autobiography of an author sightless and deaf from early childhood

of discourse that comprises the subject. Each teacher would deal with the structure of questions, the process of definition, and the role of metaphor as these matters are relevant to his or her particular subject. Here I mean, of course, not merely what are the questions, definitions, and metaphors of a subject but also *how* these are formed and how they have been formed in the past.

Of special importance are the ways in which the forms of questions 25 have changed over time and how these forms vary from subject to subject. The idea is for students to learn that the terminology of a question determines the terminology of its answer; that a question cannot be answered unless there are procedures by which reliable answers can be obtained; and that the value of a question is determined not only by the specificity and richness of the answers it produces but also by the quantity and quality of the new questions it raises.

Once this topic is opened, it follows that some attention must be given to how such terms as *right, wrong, truth,* and *falsehood* are used in a subject, as well as what assumptions they are based upon. This is particularly important, since words of this type cause far more trouble in students' attempts to understand a field of knowledge than do highly technical words. It is peculiar, I think, that of all the examinations I have ever seen, I have never come across one in which students were asked to say what is the basis of "correctness" or "falsehood" in a particular subject. Perhaps this is because teachers believe the issue is too obvious for discussion or testing. If so, they are wrong. I have found that students at all levels rarely have thought about the meaning of such terms in relation to a subject they are studying. They simply do not know in what sense an historical fact is different from a biological fact, or a mathematical "truth" is different from the "truth" of a literary work. Equally astonishing is that students, particularly those in elementary and secondary schools, rarely can express an intelligible sentence on the uses of the word *theory.* Since most subjects studied in school consist largely of theories, it is difficult to imagine exactly what students are in fact studying when they do their history, biology, economics, physics, or whatever. It is obvious, then, that language education must include not only the serious study of what truth and falsehood mean in the context of a subject but also what is meant by a theory, a fact, an inference, an assumption, a judgment, a generalization.

In addition, some attention must obviously be given to the style and tone of the language in a given subject. Each subject is a manner of speaking and writing. There is a rhetoric of knowledge, a characteristic way in which arguments, proofs, speculations, experiments, polemics, even humor, are expressed. One might even say that speaking or writing a subject is a performing art, and each subject requires a somewhat different kind of performance from every other. Historians, for example, do not speak or write the way biologists do. The differences have much to do with the kind of material they are dealing with, the degree of precision their generalizations permit, the type of facts they marshal, the traditions of their subject, the type of training they receive, and the purposes for which they are making their inquiries. The rhetoric of knowledge is not an easy matter to go into, but it is worth remembering that some scholars—one thinks of Veblen* in sociology, Freud in psychology, Galbraith* in economics—have exerted influence as much through their manner as their matter. The point is that knowledge is a form of literature, and the various styles of knowledge ought to be studied and discussed.

What we are after here is to tell the story of language as an act of creation. This is what Socrates meant when he said, "When the mind is thinking, it is talking to itself." Twenty-five hundred years later, the great German philologist Max Müller said the same: "... thought cannot exist without signs, and our most important signs are words." In between, Hobbes, Locke, and Kant said the same thing. So did Bertrand Russell, Werner Heisenberg, Benjamin Lee Whorf, I. A. Richards, Alfred Korzybski, and everyone else who has thought about the matter, including Marshall McLuhan.*

McLuhan comes up here because he is associated with the phrase "the extensions of man." And my third and final suggestion has to do with inquiries into the ways in which humans have extended their capacities to "bind" time and control space. I am referring to what may be called "technology education." It is somewhat embarrassing that this needs to be proposed as an innovation in schools, since Americans never tire of telling themselves that they have created a technological society. They even seem to be delighted about this and many of them believe that the pathway to a fulfilling life is through continuous technological change. One would expect then that technology education would be a familiar subject in American schools. But it is not. Technology may have entered the schools but *not* technology education. Those who doubt my contention might ask themselves the following questions: Does the average high school or college graduate know where the alphabet comes from, something of its development, and *anything* about its psychic and social effects? Does he or she know anything about illuminated manuscripts, about the origin of the printing press and its role in reshaping Western culture, about the origins of newspapers and magazines? Do our students know where clocks, telescopes, microscopes, X rays, and computers come from? Do they have any idea about how such technologies have changed the economic, social, and political life of Western culture? Could they say who Morse, Daguerre, Bell, Edison, Marconi, De Forest, Zworykin,

---

Veblen: Thorstein Bunde Veblen (1857–1929), an economist and social critic of capitalism, author of *The Theory of the Leisure Class*

Galbraith: John Kenneth Galbraith (1908–), leftist economist, author of *The Affluent Society* (1958)

Hobbes . . . McLuhan: theorists of language and culture

Pulitzer, Hearst, Eisenstein, and Von Neumann* were? After all, we might say these men invented the technological society. Is it too much to expect that those who live in such a society will know about them and what they thought they were creating?

I realize I am beginning to sound like E. D. Hirsch, Jr., but I find it truly   30
astonishing that the great story of humanity's perilous and exciting romance with technology is not told in our schools. There is certainly no shortage of writers on the subject. McLuhan, while an important contributor, was neither the first nor necessarily the best who has addressed the issue of how we become what we make. One thinks, for example, of Martin Heidegger, Lewis Mumford, Jacques Ellul, Paul Goodman, Walter Ong, Walter Benjamin, Elizabeth Eisenstein, Alvin Toffler, Theodore Roszak, Norbert Wiener, Sherry Turkle, Joseph Weizenbaum, Seymour Papert, and Herbert Schiller.* One may also find ideas about the subject in the "science fiction" writers I have previously alluded to—Huxley, Orwell, and Bradbury, for example. It would seem that everywhere one turns these days, there are books, articles, films, and television shows on the subject of how our technology has remade the world, and continues to remake it. It is among the leading topics of everyday conversation, especially among academics. There is, for example, hardly a school superintendent anywhere, or a college dean, who cannot give us a ready-made sermon on how we now live in an "information age." Then why do we not have a subject in which students address such questions as these: How does information differ in symbolic form? How are ideographs different from letters? How are images different from words? Paintings from photographs? Speech from writing? Television from books? Radio from television? Information comes in many forms, and at different velocities and in different quantities. Do the differences matter? Do the differences have varying psychic and social effects? The questions are almost endless. This is a serious subject.

I do not know the reasons why there is no such subject in most schools, although I have one suspect under surveillance. It is that educators confuse the teaching of how to use technology with technology education. No objection

---

Morse . . . Von Neumann: Samuel Morse (1791–1872), credited as inventor of the telegraph; Louis Daguerre (1789–1851), inventor of the daguerreotype, an early type of photograph; Alexander Graham Bell (1847–1922), inventor of the telephone; Thomas Alva Edison (1847–1931), inventor of the incandescent light, phonograph, and other items; Guglielmo Marconi (1874–1937), inventor of the wireless radio; Lee De Forest (1873–1961), pioneer in radio and television technology; Vladimir Zworykin (1889–1982), developer of the electron microscope and cathode ray tube used in television; Joseph Pulitzer (1847–1911), American journalist, competitor to William Randolph Hearst; William Randolph Hearst (1862–1951), influential American publisher and journalist; Sergei Eisenstein (1898–1948), Russian director of *Potemkin* and *Ivan the Terrible;* John Von Neumann (1903–57), mathematician and early theorist of the computer.

Martin Heidegger . . . Schiller: writers and thinkers who have explored various aspects of human knowledge, meaning, and technology

can be raised against students' learning how to use television and movie cameras, Xerox machines, and computers. (I most certainly believe students ought to be taught how to use the alphabet.) I have no intention of quarrelling with Seymour Papert, Bill Gross, or Alan Kay about the possibility that the intelligent use of computer technology can increase students' competence in mathematics or stimulate their interest in other subjects. And I endorse those attempts (for example, in New Mexico) to have students make their own television programs so that they will gain insights into the technical problems involved. These are not trivial matters, but they are only a small part of the way in which I define technology education. As I see it, the subject is mainly about how television and movie cameras, Xerox machines, and computers reorder our psychic habits, our social relations, our political ideas, and our moral sensibilities. It is about how the meanings of information and education change as new technologies intrude upon a culture, how the meanings of truth, law, and intelligence differ among oral cultures, writing cultures, printing cultures, electronic cultures. Technology education is not a technical subject. It is a branch of the humanities. Technical knowledge can be useful, but one does not need to know the physics of television to study the social and political effects of television. One may not own an automobile, or even know how to drive one, but this is no obstacle to observing what the automobile has done to American culture.

It should also be said that technology education does not imply a negative attitude toward technology. It does imply a critical attitude. To be "against technology" makes no more sense than to be "against food." We can't live without either. But to observe that it is dangerous to eat too much food, or to eat food that has no nutritional value, is not to be "antifood." It is to suggest what may be the best uses of food. Technology education aims at students' learning about what technology helps us to do and what it hinders us from doing; it is about how technology uses us, for good or ill, and about how it has used people in the past, for good or ill. It is about how technology creates new worlds, for good or ill.

But let us assume that we may overcome any obstacles to making the story of technology a core subject in schools. What is it we would want students to know? Well, for one thing, we would want them to know the answers to all the questions I have cited. But in addition, I would include the following ten principles.

1. All technological change is a Faustian bargain. For every advantage a new technology offers, there is always a corresponding disadvantage.
2. The advantages and disadvantages of new technologies are never distributed evenly among the population. This means that every new technology benefits some and harms others.
3. Embedded in every technology there is a powerful idea, sometimes two or three powerful ideas. Like language itself, a technology predisposes us to favor and value certain perspectives and accomplishments and to sub-

ordinate others. Every technology has a philosophy, which is given expression in how the technology makes people use their minds, in what it makes us do with our bodies, in how it codifies the world, in which of our senses it amplifies, in which of our emotional and intellectual tendencies it disregards.

4. A new technology usually makes war against an old technology. It competes with it for time, attention, money, prestige, and a "worldview."

5. Technological change is not additive; it is ecological. A new technology does not merely add something; it changes everything.

6. Because of the symbolic forms in which information is encoded, different technologies have different *intellectual* and *emotional* biases.

7. Because of the accessibility and speed of their information, different technologies have different *political* biases.

8. Because of their physical form, different technologies have different *sensory* biases.

9. Because of the conditions in which we attend to them, different technologies have different *social* biases.

10. Because of their technical and economic structure, different technologies have different *content* biases.

All of these principles being deeply, continuously, and historically investigated by students, I would then propose the following final examination, which is in two parts.

Part I: Choose one pre–twentieth century technology—for example,   35 the alphabet, the printing press, the telegraph, the factory—and indicate what were the main intellectual, social, political, and economic advantages of the technology, and why. Then indicate what were the main intellectual, social, political, and economic disadvantages of the technology, and why.

Part II: Indicate, first, what you believe are or will be the main advantages of computer technology, and why; second, indicate what are or will be the main disadvantages of computer technology, and why.

Any student who can pass this examination will, I believe, know something worthwhile. He or she will also have a sense of how the world was made and how it is being remade, and may even have some ideas on how it *should* be remade.

QUESTIONING THE TEXT

1. Postman claims that each discipline has its characteristic way of speaking, its own language. Do your experiences in college courses tend to confirm or refute Postman's claim? If you keep a reading log, explore this question there.

2. Postman states that, despite a celebration of technology in our culture, most school curricula do not provide opportunities to study technology itself—either its history or implications. What is the difference between learning how to use technology (a video camera, a computer) and learning about the role that technology plays in our world? Should either, both, or neither subject be taught in school?

3. Postman believes that habits of language shape our understanding of the world, that the way we describe things in language is the way we imagine them to be. Apply this principle to the verbs we use to talk about education: *make* a grade; *take* a test; *fail* a course; *earn* a degree; *enter* college; *drop out* of school; and so on. Then write a short essay reporting on the language of education.

4. J.R. asserts in his introduction that the titles of Postman's books on education and culture suggest his "intellectual vigor." What do the titles cited on p. 133 suggest to you?

MAKING CONNECTIONS

5. Postman complains about "the tyranny of definitions"—the notion that we can know *the* definition of a thing rather than just *a* definition. He also observes that definitions are usually established and enforced by people with power. In a short essay, use Postman's ideas to explore some potential differences between these two phrases, the first borrowed from Newman: *The* Idea of a University and *An* Idea of a University.

6. Postman suggests that metaphors actually shape the way we see things. Read another selection from this chapter. Then, working in a group, characterize the metaphors the author uses to describe the process of learning. Write a brief essay reporting your group's findings or conclusions.

JOINING THE CONVERSATION

7. In class, try the exercise from I. A. Richards that Postman describes on (p. 139). Divide the class into three groups. Each group should then write a paragraph beginning with one of the following sentences:
   Group A: Language is like a tree.
   Group B: Language is like a river.
   Group C: Language is like a building.

   When the paragraphs are complete, share them in class and discuss how the initial similes shaped the descriptions of language that followed.

8. What does Postman mean when he describes technological change as a "Faustian bargain" (p. 143)? Discuss that concept with classmates, then write an essay presenting one current technology as a Faustian bargain.

9. Postman ends his essay by describing a final examination for students taking his proposed course in the "story of technology." Using library and Internet resources, write an essay in response to either Part I or Part II of this examination (p. 144).

GWENDOLYN BROOKS
We Real Cool

WHEN GWENDOLYN BROOKS *(b. 1917) was a little girl, her mother said "You're going to be the first* lady *Paul Laurence Dunbar," a powerful and well-known black poet. Brooks met her mother's challenge and then some, becoming the first African American writer to win the Pulitzer Prize (for* Annie Allen *in 1950) and the first African American woman to be elected to the National Institute of Arts and Letters or to serve as Consultant in Poetry to the Library of Congress. A 1936 graduate of Chicago's Wilson Junior College, Brooks has received over seventy honorary degrees.*

In her most distinguished career, Brooks has drawn on the traditions of African American sermons and musical forms—especially the blues, jazz, and the spiritual—to explore the American condition and, in particular, the realities of African American life. Her brief poem "We Real Cool" depicts a group of young hookey players who have rejected—or been rejected by—their schools. This is the first poem by Brooks I ever read, and it inspired me to seek out her other poetry and prose and to be a lifelong fan of her work. It also made me think about what my life would have been like if I had "left school." — A.L.

The Pool Players.
Seven at the Golden Shovel.

We real cool. We
Left school. We

Lurk late. We
Strike straight. We

Sing sin. We
Thin gin. We

Jazz June. We
Die soon.

IN RESPONSE

1. What message do you take away from Brooks's poem? In what ways does it speak personally to you? If you keep a reading log, answer this question there.
2. How do you think the students in the reading by Mike Rose on p. 97 might respond to the poem?
3. Brooks's poem was written in 1960, and it refers to and uses the style of an even earlier jazz tradition. Write your own 1990s version of "We Real Cool," calling on contemporary music and culture to do so.

OTHER READINGS

Hill, Patrick J. "Multiculturalism: The Crucial Philosophical and Organizational Issues." *Change* July–Aug. 1991. Lays out a rationale for multicultural education.

hooks, bell. "Eros, Eroticism, and the Pedagogical Process." *Teaching to Transgress: Education as the Practice of Freedom.* New York: Routledge, 1994. Discusses the centrality of the body and the importance of passion in teaching.

Keller, Helen. *The Story of My Life.* Rpt. in *The Norton Book of Women's Lives.* Ed. Phyllis Rose. New York: Norton, 1993. Keller's reflections on her first teacher, Anne Sullivan.

MacDonald, Heather. "Why Johnny Can't Write." *The Public Interest* Summer 1995: 3–13. Examines theories used by writing teachers.

McNamara, Patrick H. "All Is Not Lost: Teaching Generation X." *Commonweal* 21 Apr. 1995. Teaching the traditional Western canon works with students today.

Orenstein, Peggy. *School Girls: Young Women, Self-Esteem, and the Confidence Gap.* New York: Doubleday, 1994. Explores issues of self-esteem among female adolescents.

Pratt, Mary Louise. "Humanities for the Future: Reflections on the Western Culture Debate at Stanford." *The South Atlantic Quarterly,* Winter 1990, vol. 89, no. 1, pp. 7–25. On revising the Stanford humanities course to include more on cultural diversity.

Rorty, Richard. "The Unpatriotic Academy." *New York Times,* 13 Feb. 1994: E15. Urges the political left to consider the virtues of patriotism.

Sowell, Thomas. *Inside American Education: The Decline, the Deception, the Dogmas.* New York: Free, 1993. Examines the failures and corruption of the American educational establishment.

ELECTRONIC RESOURCES

American Universities:
> http://www.clas.ufl.edu/CLAS/american-universities.html
> Lists web sites for many American colleges and universities.

The Chronicle of Higher Education: Academe This Week:
> http://chronicle.merit.edu/
> Outlines the content of current issues of a weekly newspaper covering higher education issues.

Community College Web:
> http://www.mcli.dist.maricopa.edu/cc/
> Lists web sites for many two-year schools.

4

Faith: One Nation, Under God

Look closely at this photograph of a church choir. Why do you think the photographer chose this particular angle of vision, with its resulting placement and focus? What ideals and emotions does this image convey to viewers? What thoughts, ideas, or questions might this image raise about issues of faith?

At times we may feel that we do not need God, but on the days when the storms of disappointment rage, the winds of disaster blow, and the tidal waves of grief beat against our lives, if we do not have a deep and patient faith our emotional lives will be ripped to shreds.

MARTIN LUTHER KING JR., *Our God Is Able*

The American Way of Life is a middle-class way, just as the American people in their entire outlook and feeling are a middle-class people.

WILL HERBERG, *This American Way of Life*

. . . every person has both a bad heart and a good heart. No matter how good a man seems, he has some evil. No matter how bad a man seems, there is some good about him.

JOHN ELDER and HERTHA D. WONG, *The Creation*

. . . we have created a political and legal culture that presses the religiously faithful to be other than themselves, to act publicly, and sometimes privately as well, as though their faith does not matter to them.

STEPHEN L. CARTER, *The Culture of Disbelief*

"Maybe there is a heaven," I said, "and that's where they are." Yeah, maybe. And maybe not.

ANTHONY BRANDT, *Do Kids Need Religion?*

Just then Aunt Bessie gave me a little shake and whispered sharply, "Go on up and accept Jesus!"

ANDREA LEE, *New African*

Always and everywhere the Gospel will be a challenge to human weakness.

JOHN PAUL II, *A Minority by the Year 2000*

There are Sikh mayors in Britain and Muslim mayors in Texas. The Buddha would smile at the collapse of our reifications.

DIANA L. ECK, *In the Name of Religions*

A man must always greet his fellow man.

YAFFA ELIACH, *Good Morning, Herr Müller*

In the name of God, the merciful, the compassionate.

THE QUR'AN, *Prayer*

I stood rooted to the spot,
looked up, and believed.

KATHLEEN NORRIS, *Little Girls in Church*

Introduction

ABOUT FAITH, humans have had perhaps the longest and most intense of ongoing conversations, for every people in the world, every culture we know of, enjoys some form(s) of faith or religion, beliefs that are often carried in the myths, stories, or key texts of those cultures. If you take a moment to think of some of the world's great religions, you may list Buddhism, Christianity, Islam, Judaism, Shinto, or the pantheisms of Native Americans. All these religions—and many others—are practiced today in the United States. Thus, our religious landscape, like our ethnic and linguistic heritages, reflects the rich variety of peoples who are part of American culture.

Yet faith goes well beyond organized religion, beyond church, temple, or ritual. People in this country have, if we're lucky, faith in themselves. More subtly, perhaps, we have faith in what rhetorician Richard Weaver called "God terms," those values that guide our lives, even if we are not fully aware of them. Weaver argued that in the middle of the twentieth century, the supreme American God term was "progress," that we as a people had faith in and even might be said to have "worshiped" progress. Others have suggested "democracy," "health," or "financial security" as God terms for Americans, ideas or ideals we tend to put great faith in.

Thus, whether or not you belong to or practice an organized religion, we are guessing that you have faith—perhaps a number of faiths. This chapter invites you to begin examining how you have developed such faith, how you have accepted, rejected, or challenged religions, religious creeds, or other cultural values. To do so, we have chosen articles that take very different perspectives on the subject of faith. Is Christianity, for instance, a wellspring of salvation for all? Or is it a system that inevitably oppresses and excludes some? Is all life on earth sacred? Or is human life somehow privileged over other forms? Do Americans of whatever creed hold any faiths in common?

We hope the selections in this chapter will prompt you to join the age-old conversation these questions are part of. Following are some questions you may want to ponder as you read this chapter.

- What are the three things you *most* believe in? What makes these things important to you?

- What makes a particular belief "religious"? What do the terms "religion" and "God" mean to you? to people with religious views different from yours?

- Where did you get your major beliefs? From family? From friends? From an institution such as a church or school?

- How are people shaped by what they believe? Does religion make for a better society?

- How important is religion to Americans? Have we become a secular society? What, in addition to (or instead of) God, do you think some Americans tend to "worship" or have great faith in? Why do you think they do so? You may want to discuss these issues with a group of classmates.

• • •

MARTIN LUTHER KING JR.
Our God Is Able

THE REVEREND MARTIN LUTHER KING JR. (1929–68) is remembered today for many accomplishments: his leadership of the movement for civil rights for African Americans in the 1950s and 1960s, his advocacy of nonviolent resistance to oppressive systems, his influential writings (such as "Letter from Birmingham Jail"), his powerful and moving speeches, and his Christian ministry. In King, all these elements came together in a figure who changed the face of American public life and reframed the questions any society striving for justice must seek to address. When he was assassinated in Memphis on April 4, 1968, the world lost a major spokesperson for the power that religious faith can exert in people's lives. Shortly before his death, in fact, King spoke of the extreme strife in Memphis, of the challenges facing both black and white communities there, and he called on all people of goodwill to keep the faith. Of his own faith, King seemed secure and sure. In a speech delivered the night before his assassination, he said,

> Well, I don't know what will happen now. We've got some difficult days ahead. But it doesn't matter with me now. Because I've been to the mountaintop. And I don't mind. Like anybody, I would like to live a long life. Longevity has its place. But I'm not concerned about that now. I just want to do God's will. And He's allowed me to go up to the mountain. And I've looked over. And I've seen the promised land. I may not get there with you. But I want you to know tonight, that we, as a people will get to the promised land. And I'm happy tonight. I'm not worried about anything. I'm not fearing any man. Mine eyes have seen the glory of the coming of the Lord.

The following sermon was published in the collection Strength to Love in 1963, the year that King joined other civil rights leaders in the March on Washington. There, at the foot of the Lincoln Memorial, he delivered one of his most memorable and moving speeches, "I Have a Dream," to some 250,000 people, the largest protest demonstration in American history up to that time. In "Our God Is Able," King speaks of another kind of dream, one that shows us the challenges that evil in a variety of forms presents to Christianity. But faith, he tells us, has seen him through the dark days of bigotry and prejudice, through the Montgomery bus boycott, through personal threats and attacks on him, his family, and his home. His advice and his experience are well worth attending to, whatever your religious affiliation or beliefs. – A.L.

Now unto him that is able to keep you from falling.
                                    Jude 24

At the center of the Christian faith is the conviction that in the universe there is a God of power who is able to do exceedingly abundant things in nature and in history. This conviction is stressed over and over in the Old and the New Testaments. Theologically, this affirmation is expressed in the doctrine of the omnipotence of God. The God whom we worship is not a weak and incompetent God. He is able to beat back gigantic waves of opposition and to bring low prodigious mountains of evil. The ringing testimony of the Christian faith is that God is able.

There are those who seek to convince us that only man is able. Their attempt to substitute a man-centered universe for a God-centered universe is not new. It had its modern beginnings in the Renaissance and subsequently in the Age of Reason, when some men gradually came to feel that God was an unnecessary item on the agenda of life. In these periods and later in the industrial revolution in England, others questioned whether God was any longer relevant. The laboratory began to replace the church, and the scientist became a substitute for the prophet. Not a few joined Swinburne in singing a new anthem: "Glory to Man in the highest! for Man is the master of things."

The devotees of the new man-centered religion point to the spectacular advances of modern science as justification for their faith. Science and technology have enlarged man's body. The telescope and television have enlarged his eyes. The telephone, radio, and microphone have strengthened his voice and ears. The automobile and airplane have lengthened his legs. The wonder drugs have prolonged his life. Have not these amazing achievements assured us that man is able?

But alas! something has shaken the faith of those who have made the laboratory "the new cathedral of men's hopes." The instruments which yesterday were worshiped today contain cosmic death, threatening to plunge all of us into the abyss of annihilation. Man is not able to save himself or the world. Unless he is guided by God's spirit, his new-found scientific power will become a devastating Frankenstein monster that will bring to ashes his earthly life.

At times other forces cause us to question the ableness of God. The 5 stark and colossal reality of evil in the world—what Keats calls "the giant agony of the world"; ruthless floods and tornadoes that wipe away people as though they were weeds in an open field; ills like insanity plaguing some individuals from birth and reducing their days to tragic cycles of meaninglessness; the madness of war and the barbarity of man's inhumanity to man— why, we ask, do these things occur if God is able to prevent them? This problem, namely, the problem of evil, has always plagued the mind of man. I would limit my response to an assertion that much of the evil which we experience is caused by man's folly and ignorance and also by the misuse of his freedom. Beyond this, I can say only that there is and always will be a penumbra of mystery surrounding God. What appears at the moment to be evil may have a purpose that our finite minds are incapable of comprehending. So in spite of the presence of evil and the doubts that lurk in our minds, we shall wish not to surrender the conviction that our God is able.

I

Let us notice, first, that God is able to sustain the vast scope of the physical universe. Here again, we are tempted to feel that man is the true master of the physical universe. Man-made jet planes compress into minutes distances that formerly required weeks of tortuous effort. Man-made space ships carry cosmonauts through outer space at fantastic speeds. Is not God being replaced in the mastery of the cosmic order?

But before we are consumed too greatly by our man-centered arrogance, let us take a broader look at the universe. Will we not soon discover that our man-made instruments seem barely to be moving in comparison to the movement of the God-created solar system? Think about the fact, for instance, that the earth is circling the sun so fast that the fastest jet would be left sixty-six thousand miles behind in the first hour of a space race. In the past seven minutes we have been hurtled more than eight thousand miles through space. Or consider the sun which scientists tell us is the center of the solar system. Our earth revolves around this cosmic ball of fire once each year, traveling 584,000,000 miles at the rate of 66,700 miles per hour or 1,600,000 miles per day. By this time tomorrow we shall be 1,600,000 miles from where we are at this hundredth of a second. The sun, which seems to be remarkably near, is 93,000,000 miles from the earth. Six months from now we shall be on the other side of the sun—93,000,000 miles beyond it—and in a year from now we shall have been swung completely around it and back to where we are right now. So when we behold the illimitable expanse of space, in which we are compelled to measure stellar distance in light years and in which heavenly bodies travel at incredible speeds, we are forced to look beyond man and affirm anew that God is able.

II

Let us notice also that God is able to subdue all the powers of evil. In affirming that God is able to conquer evil we admit the reality of evil. Christianity has never dismissed evil as illusory, or an error of the mortal mind. It reckons with evil as a force that has objective reality. But Christianity contends that evil contains the seed of its own destruction. History is the story of evil forces that advance with seemingly irresistible power only to be crushed by the battling rams of the forces of justice. There is a law in the moral world—a silent, invisible imperative, akin to the laws in the physical world—which reminds us that life will work only in a certain way. The Hitlers and the Mussolinis have their day, and for a period they may wield great power, spreading themselves like a green bay tree, but soon they are cut down like the grass and wither as the green herb.

In his graphic account of the Battle of Waterloo in *Les Misérables,* Victor Hugo wrote:

> Was it possible that Napoleon should win this battle? We answer no. Why? Because of Wellington? Because of Blücher? No. Because of God. . . . Napoleon had been impeached before the Infinite, and his fall was decreed. He vexed God. Waterloo is not a battle; it is the change of front of the universe.

In a real sense, Waterloo symbolizes the doom of every Napoleon and is   10 an eternal reminder to a generation drunk with military power that in the long run of history might does not make right and the power of the sword cannot conquer the power of the spirit.

An evil system, known as colonialism, swept across Africa and Asia. But then the quiet invisible law began to operate. Prime Minister Macmillan* said, "The wind of change began to blow." The powerful colonial empires began to disintegrate like stacks of cards, and new, independent nations began to emerge like refreshing oases in deserts sweltering under the heat of injustice. In less than fifteen years independence has swept through Asia and Africa like an irresistible tidal wave, releasing more than 1,500,000 people from the crippling manacles of colonialism.

In our own nation another unjust and evil system, known as segregation, for nearly one hundred years inflicted the Negro with a sense of inferiority, deprived him of his personhood, and denied him his birthright of life, liberty, and the pursuit of happiness. Segregation has been the Negroes' burden and America's shame. But as on the world scale, so in our nation, the wind of change began to blow. One event has followed another to bring a gradual end to the system of segregation. Today we know with certainty that segregation is dead. The only question remaining is how costly will be the funeral.

These great changes are not mere political and sociological shifts. They represent the passing of systems that were born in injustice, nurtured in inequality, and reared in exploitation. They represent the inevitable decay of any system based on principles that are not in harmony with the moral laws of the universe. When in future generations men look back upon these turbulent, tension-packed days through which we are passing, they will see God

---

Prime Minister Macmillan: Harold Macmillan, British prime minister from 1957 to 1963

working through history for the salvation of man. They will know that God was working through those men who had the vision to perceive that no nation could survive half slave and half free.

God is able to conquer the evils of history. His control is never usurped. If at times we despair because of the relatively slow progress being made in ending racial discrimination and if we become disappointed because of the undue cautiousness of the federal government, let us gain new heart in the fact that God is able. In our sometimes difficult and often lonesome walk up freedom's road, we do not walk alone. God walks with us. He has placed within the very structure of this universe certain absolute moral laws. We can neither defy nor break them. If we disobey them, they will break us. The forces of evil may temporarily conquer truth, but truth will ultimately conquer its conqueror. Our God is able. James Russell Lowell was right:

> Truth forever on the scaffold, Wrong forever on the throne,—
> Yet that scaffold sways the future, and, behind the dim unknown,
> Standeth God within the shadow, keeping watch above his own.

III

Let us notice, finally, that God is able to give us interior resources to confront the trials and difficulties of life. Each of us faces circumstances in life which compel us to carry heavy burdens of sorrow. Adversity assails us with hurricane force. Glowing sunrises are transformed into darkest nights. Our highest hopes are blasted and our noblest dreams are shattered.   15

Christianity has never overlooked these experiences. They come inevitably. Like the rhythmic alternation in the natural order, life has the glittering sunlight of its summers and the piercing chill of its winters. Days of unutterable joy are followed by days of overwhelming sorrow. Life brings periods of flooding and periods of drought. When these dark hours of life emerge, many cry out with Paul Laurence Dunbar:

> A crust of bread and a corner to sleep in,
> A minute to smile and an hour to weep in,
> A pint of joy to a peck of trouble,
> And never a laugh but the moans come double;
>   And that is life!

Admitting the weighty problems and staggering disappointments, Christianity affirms that God is able to give us the power to meet them. He is able to give us the inner equilibrium to stand tall amid the trials and burdens of life. He is able to provide inner peace amid outer storms. This inner stability of the man of faith is Christ's chief legacy to his disciples. He offers neither material resources nor a magical formula that exempts us from suffering and persecution, but he brings an imperishable gift: "Peace I leave with thee." This is that peace which passeth all understanding.

At times we may feel that we do not need God, but on the day when the storms of disappointment rage, the winds of disaster blow, and the tidal waves of grief beat against our lives, if we do not have a deep and patient faith our emotional lives will be ripped to shreds. There is so much frustration in the world because we have relied on gods rather than God. We have genuflected before the god of science only to find that it has given us the atomic bomb, producing fears and anxieties that science can never mitigate. We have worshiped the god of pleasure only to discover that thrills play out and sensations are short-lived. We have bowed before the god of money only to learn that there are such things as love and friendship that money cannot buy and that in a world of possible depressions, stock market crashes, and bad business investments, money is a rather uncertain deity. These transitory gods are not able to save us or bring happiness to the human heart.

Only God is able. It is faith in him that we must rediscover. With this faith we can transform bleak and desolate valleys into sunlit paths of joy and bring new light into the dark caverns of pessimism. Is someone here moving toward the twilight of life and fearful of that which we call death? Why be afraid? God is able. Is someone here on the brink of despair because of the death of a loved one, the breaking of a marriage, or the waywardness of a child? Why despair? God is able to give you the power to endure that which cannot be changed. Is someone here anxious because of bad health? Why be anxious? Come what may, God is able.

As I come to the conclusion of my message, I would wish you to permit a personal experience. The first twenty-four years of my life were years packed with fulfillment. I had no basic problems or burdens. Because of concerned and loving parents who provided for my every need, I sallied through high school, college, theological school, and graduate school without interruption. It was not until I became a part of the leadership of the Montgomery bus protest that I was actually confronted with the trials of life. Almost immediately after the protest had been undertaken, we began to receive threatening telephone calls and letters in our home. Sporadic in the beginning, they increased day after day. At first I took them in stride, feeling that they were the work of a few hotheads who would become discouraged after they discovered that we would not fight back. But as the weeks passed, I realized that many of the threats were in earnest. I felt myself faltering and growing in fear.

After a particularly strenuous day, I settled in bed at a late hour. My wife had already fallen asleep and I was about to doze off when the telephone rang. An angry voice said, "Listen, nigger, we've taken all we want from you. Before next week you'll be sorry you ever came to Montgomery." I hung up, but I could not sleep. It seemed that all of my fears had come down on me at once. I had reached the saturation point.

I got out of bed and began to walk the floor. Finally, I went to the kitchen and heated a pot of coffee. I was ready to give up. I tried to think of a way to move out of the picture without appearing to be a coward. In this state of exhaustion, when my courage had almost gone, I determined to take my problem

20

to God. My head in my hands, I bowed over the kitchen table and prayed aloud. The words I spoke to God that midnight are still vivid in my memory. "I am here taking a stand for what I believe is right. But now I am afraid. The people are looking to me for leadership, and if I stand before them without strength and courage, they too will falter. I am at the end of my powers. I have nothing left. I've come to the point where I can't face it alone."

At that moment I experienced the presence of the Divine as I had never before experienced him. It seemed as though I could hear the quiet assurance of an inner voice, saying, "Stand up for righteousness, and stand up for truth. God will be at your side forever." Almost at once my fears began to pass from me. My uncertainty disappeared. I was ready to face anything. The outer situation remained the same, but God had given me inner calm.

Three nights later, our home was bombed. Strangely enough, I accepted the word of the bombing calmly. My experience with God had given me a new strength and trust. I know now that God is able to give us the interior resources to face the storms and problems of life.

Let this affirmation be our ringing cry. It will give us courage to face the   25
uncertainties of the future. It will give our tired feet new strength as we continue our forward stride toward the city of freedom. When our days become dreary with low-hovering clouds and our nights become darker than a thousand midnights, let us remember that there is a great benign Power in the universe whose name is God, and he is able to make a way out of no way, and transform dark yesterdays into bright tomorrows. This is our hope for becoming better men. This is our mandate for seeking to make a better world.

QUESTIONING THE TEXT

1. King argues that God is able to overcome evil, to "beat back gigantic waves of opposition." What examples or reasons or proof can you offer to support *or* to refute King's claim?
2. Paraphrase the verse from Paul Laurence Dunbar on p. 158. Do you agree with this assessment of life? Why, or why not?
3. A.L.'s introduction to this speech presents King in a very positive light. Yet some have criticized him for his advocacy of nonviolence as well as for other perceived failings. What do you know about King? Does your own knowledge support the introduction's perspective? What other perspectives might be possible? Spend 5 minutes jotting down notes in response to these questions, and bring them to class for discussion.

MAKING CONNECTIONS

4. King links what he calls a "man-centered religion" to a Frankenstein monster. Does the monster represented in the excerpt from Mary Shelley's novel beginning on p. 230 seem to be a product of a "man-

centered religion"? Why, or why not? How compelling do you find King's analogy of science without God to a "Frankenstein monster"? Explain your answers to the questions in a paragraph or two.

5. In the next selection, Will Herberg argues that middle-class values constitute a common religion in America. Would King agree? Who is likely to be left out of such a "common religion"—and why?

JOINING THE CONVERSATION

6. King says that in times of dark despair and disappointment, if we do not have faith our "emotional lives will be ripped to shreds." Does your experience bear out King's assertion? Explore this question in writing—in a reading log, if you keep one.

7. Do you see evidence of a "man-centered religion" in the United States today? In a one- or two-page letter to members of your class, explain your reasons for answering this question as you have.

8. Writing in the early 1960s, King uses "man" to refer to human beings in general and masculine pronouns (*he, his,* etc.) to refer to God and to individual humans. Working with one or two classmates, look carefully through this essay, noting any uses of language that might be criticized today for excluding women. Then write a brief report to your class describing any exclusionary language and recommending ways to revise it if you believe revision is necessary.

WILL HERBERG
This American Way of Life

WILL HERBERG's Protestant—Catholic—Jew: An Essay in American Religious Sociology *is regarded as something of a classic. Although the book was published in 1955, its descriptions of American faith and religion still illuminate essential aspects of our national character. We are not the same people we were when Herberg (1902–77) wrote, yet we are not so different either.*

At first glance, the following excerpt from Protestant—Catholic—Jew *may seem to have little to do with religion. But the "American Way of Life" that Herberg sketches out tentatively here is a set of beliefs powerful enough to forge a national identity that transcends differences of culture, race, and creed. Americans' religious convictions are shaped, in part, by a secular faith in democracy and individualism. So we can talk sensibly about American Protestants, American Jews, and American Catholics, knowing that we are describing people with a strong bond of shared beliefs despite their deep religious differences. I think that bond is worth exploring.* − J.R.

What is this American Way of Life that we have said constitutes the "common religion" of American society? An adequate description and analysis of what is implied in this phrase still remains to be attempted, and certainly it will not be ventured here; but some indications may not be out of place.

The American Way of Life is the symbol by which Americans define themselves and establish their unity. German unity, it would seem, is felt to be largely racial-folkish, French unity largely cultural; but neither of these ways is open to the American people, the most diverse in racial and cultural origins of any in the world. As American unity has emerged, it has emerged more and more clearly as a unity embodied in, and symbolized by, the complex structure known as the American Way of Life.

If the American Way of Life had to be defined in one word, "democracy" would undoubtedly be the word, but democracy in a peculiarly American sense. On its political side it means the Constitution; on its economic side, "free enterprise"; on its social side, an equalitarianism which is not only compatible with but indeed actually implies vigorous economic competition and high mobility. Spiritually, the American Way of Life is best expressed in a certain kind of "idealism" which has come to be recognized as characteristically American. It is a faith that has its symbols and its rituals, its holidays and its liturgy, its saints and its sancta; and it is a faith that every American, to the degree that he is an American, knows and understands.

162

The American Way of Life is individualistic, dynamic, pragmatic. It affirms the supreme value and dignity of the individual; it stresses incessant activity on his part, for he is never to rest but is always to be striving to "get ahead"; it defines an ethic of self-reliance, merit, and character, and judges by achievement: "deeds, not creeds" are what count. The American Way of Life is humanitarian, "forward looking," optimistic. Americans are easily the most generous and philanthropic people in the world, in terms of their ready and unstinting response to suffering anywhere on the globe. The American believes in progress, in self-improvement, and quite fanatically in education. But above all, the American is idealistic. Americans cannot go on making money or achieving worldly success simply on its own merits; such "materialistic" things must, in the American mind, be justified in "higher" terms, in terms of "service" or "stewardship" or "general welfare." Because Americans are so idealistic, they tend to confuse espousing an ideal with fulfilling it and are always tempted to regard themselves as good as the ideals they entertain: hence the amazingly high valuation most Americans quite sincerely place on their own virtue. And because they are so idealistic, Americans tend to be moralistic: they are inclined to see all issues as plain and simple, black and white, issues of morality. Every struggle in which they are seriously engaged becomes a "crusade." To Mr. Eisenhower, who in many ways exemplifies American religion in a particularly representative way, the second world war was a "crusade" (as was the first to Woodrow Wilson); so was his campaign for the presidency ("I am engaged in a crusade . . . to substitute good government for what we most earnestly believe has been bad government"); and so is his administration—a "battle for the republic" against "godless Communism" abroad and against "corruption and materialism" at home. It was Woodrow Wilson who once said, "Sometimes people call me an idealist. Well, that is the way I know I'm an American: America is the most idealistic nation in the world"; Eisenhower was but saying the same thing when he solemnly affirmed: "The things that make us proud to be Americans are of the soul and of the spirit."

The American Way of Life is, of course, anchored in the American's vision of America. The Puritan's dream of a new "Israel" and a new "Promised Land" in the New World, the *"novus ordo seclorum"** on the Great Seal of the United States reflect the perennial American conviction that in the New World a new beginning has been made, a new order of things established, vastly different from and superior to the decadent institutions of the Old World. This conviction, emerging out of the earliest reality of American history, was continuously nourished through the many decades of immigration into the present century by the residual hopes and expectations of the immigrants, for whom the New World had to be really something new if it was to

5

---

novus ordo seclorum: Latin for "a new order of the ages"

be anything at all. And this conviction still remains pervasive in American life, hardly shaken by the new shape of the world and the challenge of the "new orders" of the twentieth century, Nazism and Communism. It is the secret of what outsiders must take to be the incredible self-righteousness of the American people, who tend to see the world divided into an innocent, virtuous America confronted with a corrupt, devious, and guileful Europe and Asia. The self-righteousness, however, if self-righteousness it be, is by no means simple, if only because virtually all Americans are themselves derived from the foreign parts they so distrust. In any case, this feeling about America as really and truly the "new order" of things at last established is the heart of the outlook defined by the American Way of Life.

In her *Vermont Tradition,* Dorothy Canfield Fisher lists as that tradition's principal ingredients: individual freedom, personal independence, human dignity, community responsibility, social and political democracy, sincerity, restraint in outward conduct, and thrift. With some amplification—particularly emphasis on the uniqueness of the American "order" and the great importance assigned to religion—this may be taken as a pretty fair summary of some of the "values" embodied in the American Way of Life. It will not escape the reader that this account is essentially an idealized description of the middle-class ethos. And, indeed, that is just what it is. The American Way of Life is a middle-class way, just as the American people in their entire outlook and feeling are a middle-class people. But the American Way of Life as it has come down to us is not merely middle-class; it is emphatically inner-directed. Indeed, it is probably one of the best expressions of inner-direction in history. As such, it now seems to be undergoing some degree of modification—perhaps at certain points disintegration—under the impact of the spread of other-direction in our society. For the foreseeable future, however, we may with some confidence expect the continuance in strength of the American Way of Life as both the tradition and the "common faith" of the American people.

QUESTIONING THE TEXT

1. How does Herberg define democracy? Do we abide by the same definition today?

2. Identify five to ten key words that Herberg uses to characterize the American way of life—terms like *democracy* and *individualism.* Then explain whether those terms make sense in defining the American experience as you have known it.

3. Underline three or four specific sentences that Herberg would likely rewrite were his book being published today instead of in 1955. Then rewrite them, entering the rewritten versions in your reading log if you keep one.

4. In the introduction, J.R. claims that Americans are not completely different today from when Herberg wrote "This American Way of Life" (1955). Do you think you know enough about the 1950s to evaluate J.R.'s claim? Why, or why not?

MAKING CONNECTIONS

5. Where might the secular values Herberg describes in his essay conflict with the religious principles articulated in the previous selection, Martin Luther King Jr.'s "Our God Is Able"?
6. Write an essay arguing for or against this statement: The version of American life described by Herberg in the 1950s indicates that the American people were, in most respects, better off in the Eisenhower era than they are today. Be sure to back up your arguments with specific examples and illustrations.

JOINING THE CONVERSATION

7. Write a brief response to "This American Way of Life," reflecting on how well you fit into the description today.
8. In the way that Herberg has written an essay defining the "American Way of Life," write an equally serious analysis of a class of American experience with which you are personally knowledgeable: the Italian American way of life, the evangelical way of life, the Southern California way of life, the suburban way of life, and so on.
9. Herberg insists that Americans typically see themselves as different from the rest of the world, a more idealistic people not tainted by the corruption and guile of Europe and Asia. Be prepared to discuss whether this is still a representative view. What events since 1955 might have confirmed Americans in this opinion or altered it?

JOHN ELDER and HERTHA D. WONG
The Creation

ALL CULTURES WE KNOW OF *tell stories that aim to answer the question of origin: Where did we come from? Who or what created the earth and everything it contains? And certainly all of the world's religions contain powerful creation stories, many of them bearing striking similarities to one another. In fact, curiosity about the source of and reason for the earth and its inhabitants may be one universal characteristic.*

Like the Mohawk creation story you are about to read here, some of the oldest creation stories of this hemisphere come from oral Native American traditions, and it is important to remember that they were meant to be listened to—in their original language—and that the storyteller was a very significant part of the story. This story has been "translated" in many ways: from oral to written language; from Mohawk to English through any number of translators; from a Native American cultural community to a multicultural and multiethnic community; and from a communal performance tradition to a more solitary textual one. As you read "The Creation," think about how it might have been experienced before its multiple "translations."

As this introduction indicates, John Elder and Hertha D. Wong are not the authors of "The Creation." They are scholars and editors who have gathered a large group of narratives from around the world to illuminate the relationship between people and the planet they inhabit. Elder (professor of English and environmental studies at Middlebury College) and Wong (professor of English at the University of California at Berkeley) are both members of the faculty at the Bread Loaf School of English, where I often teach as well. I have learned from them new ways of listening to stories that the earth and the earth's cultures have to tell. As they say in the introduction to the book from which this selection is taken, "Reimagining notions of nature and our relation to it and telling stories that awaken and sustain our relationship to the earth are necessary acts of survival as we all struggle to transform ourselves from twentieth- to twenty-first-century global citizens." Certainly faith—in its multiple manifestations—will play a crucial role in our ability to achieve these goals. — A.L.

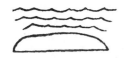

Many Winters in the past (arrow going backward)

the Earth was entirely covered by a great blanket of water. There was no sun, moon, or stars and so there was no light. All was darkness.

At that time, the only living creatures of the world were water animals such as the beaver, muskrat, duck and loon.

Far above earth was the Land of Happy Spirits where lived Rawennio, the Great Ruler. In the center of this upper world was a giant tree.

This great tree was an apple tree whose roots sank deep into the ground.

One day, Rawennio pulled this giant tree up by its roots.

The Great Spirit called his daughter who lived in the Upper World and commanded her to look into the pit caused by the uprooted tree.

This woman, who was to be the mother of the Good and Evil Spirits, came and looked into the hole by the uprooted tree.

She saw far below her the Lower World covered with water and surrounded by heavy clouds.

"You are to go to this world of darkness," said the Great Spirit. Gently lifting her, he dropped her into the hole.

She floated downward.

Far below on the dark water floated the water animals. Looking upward, they saw a great light, which was the Sky Woman, slowly falling toward them.

Because her body shone as a great light they were at first frightened.

Fear filled their hearts and they dove beneath the deep waters.

But upon coming to the surface again, they lost their fear. They began to plan what they would do for the woman when she reached the water.

"We must find a dry place for her to rest on," said the beaver, and he plunged beneath the water in search of some earth. After a long time, the beaver's dead body floated to the top of the water.

The loon tried next, but his body never came to the surface of the water. Many of the other water creatures dived, but all failed to secure any earth.

Finally, the muskrat went below and after a long time, his dead body floated to the surface of the water. His little claws were closed tight. Upon opening them, a little earth was found.

The water creatures took this earth, and calling a great turtle, they patted the earth firmly on her broad back. Immediately, the turtle started to grow larger. The earth also increased.

This earth became North America, a great island. Sometimes the earth cracks and shakes, and waves beat hard against the seashore. White people say, "Earthquake." The Mohawk say, "Turtle is stretching."

The Sky Woman had now almost reached the earth. "We must fly up and let her rest upon our backs so as to make her landing easy," said the chief of the white swans. Flying upward, a great flock of white swans allowed the Sky Woman to rest upon their backs. Gently, they bore her to earth.

After a time, the Sky Woman gave birth to twins. One who became the Good Spirit was born first. The other, the Evil Spirit, while being born, caused his mother so much pain that she died during his birth.

The Good Spirit immediately took his mother's head and hung it in the sky. It became the sun. The Good Spirit, from his mother's body, fashioned the moon and stars and placed them in the sky.

The rest of his mother's body he buried under the earth. That is why living things find nourishment from the soil. They spring from Mother Earth.

The Evil Spirit put darkness in the west sky to drive the sun before it.

The Good Spirit created many things which he placed upon the earth. The Evil Spirit tried to undo the work of his brother by creating evil. The Good Spirit made tall and beautiful trees such as the pine and hemlock.

The Evil Spirit stunted some trees. In others, he put knots and gnarls. He covered some with thorns, and placed poison fruit on them.

The Good Spirit made animals such as the deer and the bear.

The Evil Spirit made poisonous animals, lizards, and serpents to destroy the animals of the Good Spirit's creation.

The Good Spirit made springs and streams of good, pure water.

The Evil Spirit breathed poison into many of the springs. He put snakes into others.

The Good Spirit made beautiful rivers protected by high hills.

The Evil Spirit pushed rocks and dirt into the rivers causing the current to become swift and dangerous. Everything that the Good Spirit made, his wicked brother tried to destroy.

Finally, when the earth was completed, the Good Spirit fashioned man out of some red clay. He placed man upon the earth, and told him how he should live. The Evil Spirit, not to be outdone, fashioned a creature out of the white foam of the sea. What he made was the monkey.

After mankind and the other creatures of the world were created, the Good Spirit bestowed a protecting spirit upon each of his creations.

He then called the Evil Spirit, and told him that he must cease making trouble upon the earth. This the Evil Spirit refused to do. The Good Spirit became very angry with his wicked brother. He challenged his brother to combat, the victor to become ruler of the earth. They used the thorns of a giant apple tree as weapons.

They fought for many suns (days).

Finally, the Evil Spirit was overcome.

The Good Spirit now became ruler over the earth. He banished his wicked brother to a dark cave under the earth. There he must always remain.

But the Evil Spirit has wicked servants who roam the earth. These wicked spirits can take the shape of any creature that the Evil Spirit desires them to take. They are constantly influencing the minds of men, thus causing men to do evil things.

That is why every person has both a bad heart and a good heart. No matter how good a man seems, he has some evil. No matter how bad a man seems, there is some good about him. No man is perfect.

The Good Spirit continues to create and protect mankind. He controls the spirits of good men after death. The Evil Spirit takes charge of the souls of wicked men after death.

QUESTIONING THE TEXT

1. What is the effect of the pictograms in "The Creation"? How do they complement the words used to tell the story?
2. "The Creation" is one of three kinds of creation myths common in Native North America—the Earth-Diver myth. Using this story as an example, list the characteristics of Native American Earth-Diver myths.
3. In her introduction, A.L. says that "Certainly faith . . . will play a crucial role in our ability to achieve" the goals of sustaining ourselves and our relation to nature. What is the effect of A.L.'s choice of the word *certainly* here? What proof do you find that this is "certain"?

MAKING CONNECTIONS

4. In the next selection, Stephen L. Carter uses an example of Native American religious practices in his discussion of contemporary conflicts between religious and spiritual values and government regulations. "Evidently, a small matter like the potential destruction of a religion is no

reason to halt a logging project," he says (p. 182). What values revealed in "The Creation" might support the halting of a logging project?

5. What value might Anthony Brandt (p. 186) find in this Native American story? In what ways might it help answer his question "Do Kids Need Religion?"

JOINING THE CONVERSATION

6. Try your hand at writing a creation story. You may retell a story you have heard or believe (the Genesis account of creation or the big bang theory, for example) or tell a story from your own imagination. Bring your story to class for discussion.

7. With two or three classmates, investigate some creation stories from cultures or religions you are unfamiliar with. You may want to talk with friends or acquaintances who come from other countries or who worship in different settings. Or you may decide to use the resources of the library or the Internet. Try to find at least two stories of creation that were new to you, and bring them to class for discussion.

8. Try recasting "The Creation" in another genre, such as a song, a poem, or a story told by a famous person or character. What must you change to adapt the story to another genre? What can you keep? Bring the results to class for discussion.

STEPHEN L. CARTER
The Culture of Disbelief

FOR YEARS, *conservatives in the United States have complained that religion is being purged from schools, public spaces, and political debates. Schools, they point out, frown on the mere mention of religious topics; courts compel municipalities to disassemble Christmas crèches in town squares; and people opposed to abortion on religious grounds are routinely treated as extremists by the news media. The First Amendment guarantee that Congress should pass no law "prohibiting the free exercise" of religion often now seems more a device to dislodge religious belief from the public square than to protect it.*

The place of religion in American society received more attention after a fiery speech by Patrick Buchanan at the 1992 Republican Convention declaring a cultural war in the United States. But the mainstream media operating out of New York, Washington, D.C., and Atlanta really took notice only after the publication of Stephen L. Carter's The Culture of Disbelief *(1993). The book explores many themes already heavily mined by conservative essayists, but with an important difference: its author is a political liberal teaching at Yale, and his views have been read—and endorsed—by Bill Clinton, the first Democrat to win the presidency since Jimmy Carter did in 1976. Finally, the place of religion in American culture had gained rhetorical presence; it became an issue worth serious consideration.*

To his credit, Carter (b. 1954) makes even skeptical readers appreciate what may be at stake when a culture pressures people with strong beliefs not to act on their principles. Like Andrew Sullivan's selection from Virtually Normal *reproduced in chapter 6, Carter's piece is an example of how to make a compelling civil argument that wins agreement by being inclusive rather than by declaring war. For that reason especially, I was eager to include it in this anthology. —* J.R.

Contemporary American politics faces few greater dilemmas than deciding how to deal with the resurgence of religious belief. On the one hand, American ideology cherishes religion, as it does all matters of private conscience, which is why we justly celebrate a strong tradition against state interference with private religious choice. At the same time, many political leaders, commentators, scholars, and voters are coming to view any religious element in public moral discourse as a tool of the radical right for reshaping American society. But the effort to banish religion for politics' sake has led us astray: In our sensible zeal to keep religion from dominating our politics, we have created a political and legal culture that presses the religiously faithful to be other than themselves, to act publicly, and sometimes privately as well, as though their faith does not matter to them.

Recently, a national magazine devoted its cover story to an investigation of prayer: how many people pray, how often, why, how, and for what. A few weeks later came the inevitable letter from a disgruntled reader, wanting to know why so much space had been dedicated to such nonsense.[1]

Statistically, the letter writer was in the minority: by the magazine's figures, better than nine out of ten Americans believe in God and some four out of five pray regularly.[2] Politically and culturally, however, the writer was in the American mainstream, for those who do pray regularly—indeed, those who believe in God—are encouraged to keep it a secret, and often a shameful one at that. Aside from the ritual appeals to God that are expected of our politicians, for Americans to take their religions seriously, to treat them as ordained rather than chosen, is to risk assignment to the lunatic fringe.

Yet religion matters to people, and matters a lot. Surveys indicate that Americans are far more likely to believe in God and to attend worship services regularly than any other people in the Western world. True, nobody prays on prime-time television unless religion is a part of the plot, but strong majorities of citizens tell pollsters that their religious beliefs are of great importance to them in their daily lives. Even though some popular histories wrongly assert the contrary, the best evidence is that this deep religiosity has always been a facet of the American character and that it has grown consistently through the nation's history.[3] And today, to the frustration of many opinion leaders in both the legal and political cultures, religion, as a moral force and perhaps a political one too, is surging. Unfortunately, in our public life, we prefer to pretend that it is not.

Consider the following events: 5

- When Hillary Rodham Clinton was seen wearing a cross around her neck at some of the public events surrounding her husband's inauguration as President of the United States, many observers were aghast, and one television commentator asked whether it was appropriate for the First Lady to display so openly a religious symbol. But if the First Lady

---

[1]"Talking to God," *Newsweek,* Jan. 6, 1992, p. 38; Letter to the Editor, *Newsweek,* Jan. 1992, p. 10. The letter called the article a "theocratic text masquerading as a news article."

[2]"Talking to God," p. 39. The most recent Gallup data indicate that 96 percent of Americans say they believe in God, including 82 percent who describe themselves as Christians (56 percent Protestant, 25 percent Roman Catholic) and 2 percent who describe themselves as Jewish. (No other faith accounted for as much as 1 percent.) See Ari L. Goldman, "Religion Notes," *New York Times,* Feb. 27, 1993, p. 9.

[3]See, for example, Jon Butler, *Awash in a Sea of Faith* (Cambridge: Harvard University Press, 1990).

can't do it, then certainly the President can't do it, which would bar from ever holding the office an Orthodox Jew under a religious compulsion to wear a yarmulke.*

- Back in the mid-1980s, the magazine *Sojourners*—published by politically liberal Christian evangelicals—found itself in the unaccustomed position of defending the conservative evangelist Pat Robertson against secular liberals who, a writer in the magazine sighed, "see[m] to consider Robertson a dangerous neanderthal because he happens to believe that God can heal diseases."[4] The point is that the editors of *Sojourners*, who are no great admirers of Robertson, also believe that God can heal diseases. So do tens of millions of Americans. But they are not supposed to say so.

- In the early 1980s, the state of New York adopted legislation that, in effect, requires an Orthodox Jewish husband seeking a civil divorce to give his wife a *get*—a religious divorce—without which she cannot remarry under Jewish law. Civil libertarians attacked the statute as unconstitutional. Said one critic, the "barriers to remarriage erected by religious law . . . only exist in the minds of those who believe in the religion."[5] If the barriers are religious, it seems, then they are not real barriers, they are "only" in the woman's mind—perhaps even a figment of the imagination.

- When the Supreme Court of the United States, ostensibly the final refuge of religious freedom, struck down a Connecticut statute requiring employers to make efforts to allow their employees to observe the sabbath, one Justice observed that the sabbath should not be singled out because all employees would like to have "the right to select the day of the week in which to refrain from labor."[6] Sounds good, except that, as one scholar has noted, "It would come as some surprise to a devout Jew to find that he has 'selected the day of the week in which to refrain from labor,'" since the Jewish people have been under the impression for some 3,000 years that this choice was made by God."[7] If the sabbath is just another day off, then religious choice is essentially arbitrary and

---

yarmulke: a skull cap worn by Jewish men, especially in the Orthodox or Conservative traditions

[4]Collum, "The Kingdom and the Power," *Sojourners,* Nov. 1986, p. 4. Some 82 percent of Americans believe that God performs miracles today. George Gallup, Jr., and Jim Castelli, *The People's Religion: American Faith in the '90s* (New York: Macmillan, 1989), p. 58.

[5]Madeline Kochen, "Constitutional Implications of New York's 'Get' Statute," *New York Law Journal,* Oct. 27, 1983, p. 32.

[6]*Estate of Thornton v. Caldor, Inc.,* 472 U.S. 703, 711 (1985) (Justice Sandra Day O'Connor, concurring).

[7]Michael W. McConnell, "Religious Freedom at a Crossroads," *University of Chicago Law Review* 59 (1992): 115.

unimportant; so if one sabbath day is inconvenient, the religiously devout employee can just choose another.

• When President Ronald Reagan told religious broadcasters in 1983 that all the laws passed since biblical times "have not improved on the Ten Commandments one bit," which might once have been considered a pardonable piece of rhetorical license, he was excoriated by political pundits, including one who charged angrily that Reagan was giving "short shrift to the secular laws and institutions that a president is charged with protecting."[8] And as for the millions of Americans who consider the Ten Commandments the fundaments on which they build their lives, well, they are no doubt subversive of these same institutions.

These examples share a common rhetoric that refuses to accept the notion that rational, public-spirited people can take religion seriously. It might be argued that such cases as these involve threats to the separation of church and state, the durable and vital doctrine that shields our public institutions from religious domination and our religious institutions from government domination. I am a great supporter of the separation of church and state . . . but that is not what these examples are about.

What matters about these examples is the *language* chosen to make the points. In each example, as in many more that I shall discuss, one sees a trend in our political and legal cultures toward treating religious beliefs as arbitrary and unimportant, a trend supported by a rhetoric that implies that there is something wrong with religious devotion. More and more, our culture seems to take the position that believing deeply in the tenets of one's faith represents a kind of mystical irrationality, something that thoughtful, public-spirited American citizens would do better to avoid. If you must worship your God, the lesson runs, at least have the courtesy to disbelieve in the power of prayer; if you must observe your sabbath, have the good sense to understand that it is just like any other day off from work.

The rhetoric matters. A few years ago, my wife and I were startled by a teaser for a story on a network news program, which asked what was meant to be a provocative question: "When is a church more than just a place of worship?" For those to whom worship is significant, the subtle arrangement of words is arresting: *more than* suggests that what follows ("just a place of worship") is somewhere well down the scale of interesting or useful human activities, and certainly that whatever the story is about is *more than* worship; and *just*—suggests that what follows ("place of worship") is rather small potatoes.

---

[8]Robert G. Kaiser, "Hypocrisy: This Puffed-Up Piety Is Perfectly Preposterous," *Washington Post,* March 18, 1984, p. C1.

A friend tells the story of how he showed his résumé to an executive search consultant—in the jargon, a corporate headhunter—who told him crisply that if he was serious about moving ahead in the business world, he should remove from the résumé any mention of his involvement with a social welfare organization that was connected with a church, but not one of the genteel mainstream denominations. Otherwise, she explained, a potential employer might think him a religious fanatic.

How did we reach this disturbing pass, when our culture teaches that   10
religion is not to be taken seriously, even by those who profess to believe in it? Some observers suggest that the key moment was the Enlightenment, when the Western tradition sought to sever the link between religion and authority. One of the playwright Tom Stoppard's characters observes that there came "a calendar date—*a moment*—when the onus of proof passed from the atheist to the believer, when, quite suddenly, the noes had it."[9] To which the philosopher Jeffrey Stout appends the following comment: "If so, it was not a matter of majority rule."[10] Maybe not—but a strong undercurrent of contemporary American politics holds that religion must be kept in its proper place and, still more, in proper perspective. There are, we are taught by our opinion leaders, religious matters and important matters, and disaster arises when we confuse the two. Rationality, it seems, consists in getting one's priorities straight. (Ignore your religious law and marry at leisure.) Small wonder, then, that we have recently been treated to a book, coauthored by two therapists, one of them an ordained minister, arguing that those who would put aside, say, the needs of their families in order to serve their religions are suffering from a malady the authors call "toxic faith"—for no normal person, evidently, would sacrifice the things that most of us hold dear just because of a belief that God so intended it.[11] (One wonders how the authors would have judged the toxicity of the faith of Jesus, Moses, or Mohammed.)

We are trying, here in America, to strike an awkward but necessary balance, one that seems more and more difficult with each passing year. On the one hand, a magnificent respect for freedom of conscience, including the freedom of religious belief, runs deep in our political ideology. On the other hand, our understandable fear of religious domination of politics presses us, in our public personas, to be wary of those who take their religion too seriously. This public balance reflects our private selves. We are one of the most religious nations on earth, in the sense that we have a deeply religious citizenry; but we are also perhaps the most zealous in guarding our public institutions

---

[9]Tom Stoppard, *Jumpers,* quoted in Jeffrey Stout, *The Flight from Authority: Religion, Morality and the Quest for Autonomy* (South Bend, Indiana: University of Notre Dame Press, 1981), p. 150.

[10]Ibid.

[11]Stephen Arterburn and Jack Felton, *Toxic Faith: Understanding and Overcoming Religious Addiction* (Nashville, Tenn.: Oliver-Nelson Books, 1991).

against explicit religious influences. One result is that we often ask our citizens to split their public and private selves, telling them in effect that it is fine to be religious in private, but there is something askew when those private beliefs become the basis for public action.

We teach college freshmen that the Protestant Reformation began the process of freeing the church from the state, thus creating the possibility of a powerful independent moral force in society. As defenders of the separation of church and state have argued for centuries, autonomous religions play a vital role as free critics of the institutions of secular society. But our public culture more and more prefers religion as something without political significance, less an independent moral force than a quietly irrelevant moralizer, never heard, rarely seen. "[T]he public sphere," writes the theologian Martin Marty, "does not welcome explicit Reformed witness—or any other particularized Christian witness."[12] Or, for that matter, any religious witness at all.

Religions that most need protection seem to receive it least. Contemporary America is not likely to enact legislation aimed at curbing the mainstream Protestant, Roman Catholic, or Jewish faiths. But Native Americans,* having once been hounded from their lands, are now hounded from their religions, with the complicity of a Supreme Court untroubled when sacred lands are taken for road building or when Native Americans under a bona fide religious compulsion to use *peyote** in their rituals are punished under state antidrug regulations.[13] (Imagine the brouhaha if New York City were to try to take St. Patrick's Cathedral by eminent domain to build a new convention center, or if Kansas, a dry state, were to outlaw the religious use of wine.) And airports, backed by the Supreme Court, are happy to restrict solicitation by devotees of Krishna Consciousness, which travelers, including this one, find irritating.[14] (Picture the response should the airports try to regulate the wearing of crucifixes or yarmulkes on similar grounds of irritation.)

The problem goes well beyond our society's treatment of those who simply want freedom to worship in ways that most Americans find troubling. An analogous difficulty is posed by those whose religious convictions move them to action in the public arena. Too often, our rhetoric treats the religious impulse to public action as presumptively wicked—indeed, as necessarily oppressive. But this is historically bizarre. Every time people whose vision of God's will moves them to oppose abortion rights are excoriated for purportedly trying to impose their religious views on others, equal calumny is implic-

---

[12]Martin E. Marty, "Reformed America and America Reformed," *Reformed Journal* (March 1989): 8, 10.

Native Americans: For a perspective on Native American belief, see John Elder and Hertha D. Wong, "The Creation," p. 166.

peyote: a plant with hullicinatory effects

[13]*Employment Division, Department of Human Resources v. Smith,* 494 U.S. 872 (1990).

[14]*International Society for Krishna Consciousness v. Lee,* 112 S. Ct. 2701 (1992).

itly heaped upon the mass protest wing of the civil rights movement, which was openly and unashamedly religious in its appeals as it worked to impose its moral vision on, for example, those who would rather segregate their restaurants.

One result of this rhetoric is that we often end up fighting the wrong   15
battles. Consider what must in our present day serve as the ultimate example of religion in the service of politics: the 1989 death sentence pronounced by the late Ayatollah Ruhollah Khomeini upon the writer Salman Rushdie for his authorship of *The Satanic Verses,* which was said to blaspheme against Islam. The death sentence is both terrifying and outrageous, and the Ayatollah deserved all the fury lavished upon him for imposing it. Unfortunately, for some critics the facts that the Ayatollah was a religious leader and that the "crime" was a religious one lends the sentence a particular monstrousness; evidently they are under the impression that writers who are murdered for their ideas are choosy about the motivations of their murderers, and that those whose writings led to their executions under, say, Stalin,* thanked their lucky stars at the last instant of their lives that Communism was at least godless.

To do battle against the death sentence for Salman Rushdie—to battle against the Ayatollah—one should properly fight against official censorship and intimidation, not against religion. We err when we presume that religious motives are likely to be illiberal, and we compound the error when we insist that the devout should keep their religious ideas—whether good or bad—to themselves. We do no credit to the ideal of religious freedom when we talk as though religious belief is something of which public-spirited adults should be ashamed.

The First Amendment to the Constitution, often cited as the place where this difficulty is resolved, merely restates it. The First Amendment guarantees the "free exercise" of religion but also prohibits its "establishment" by the government. There may have been times in our history when we as a nation have tilted too far in one direction, allowing too much religious sway over politics. But in late-twentieth-century America, despite some loud fears about the influence of the weak and divided Christian right, we are upsetting the balance afresh by tilting too far in the other direction—and the courts are assisting in the effort. For example, when a group of Native Americans objected to the Forest Service's plans to allow logging and road building in a national forest area traditionally used by the tribes for sacred rituals, the Supreme Court offered the back of its hand. True, said the Justices, the logging "could have devastating effects on traditional Indian religious practices." But that was just too bad: "government simply could not operate if it were required to satisfy every citizen's religious needs and desires."[15]

Stalin: Joseph Stalin (1879–1953), Soviet premier and successor to Lenin
[15]*Lyng v. Northwest Indian Cemetery Protective Association,* 485 U.S. 439 (1988).

A good point: but what, exactly, are the protesting Indians left to do? Presumably, now that their government has decided to destroy the land they use for their sacred rituals, they are free to choose new rituals. Evidently, a small matter like the potential destruction of a religion is no reason to halt a logging project. Moreover, had the government decided instead to prohibit logging in order to preserve the threatened rituals, it is entirely possible that the decision would be challenged as a forbidden entanglement of church and state. Far better for everyone, it seems, for the Native Americans to simply allow their rituals to go quietly into oblivion. Otherwise, they run the risk that somebody will think they actually take their rituals seriously.

THE PRICE OF FAITH

When citizens do act in their public selves as though their faith matters, they risk not only ridicule, but actual punishment. In Colorado, a public school teacher was ordered by his superiors, on pain of disciplinary action, to remove his personal Bible from his desk where students might see it. He was forbidden to read it silently when his students were involved in other activities. He was also told to take away books on Christianity he had added to the classroom library, although books on Native American religious traditions, as well as on the occult, were allowed to remain. A federal appeals court upheld the instruction, explaining that the teacher could not be allowed to create a religious atmosphere in the classroom, which, it seems, might happen if the students knew he was a Christian.[16] One wonders what the school, and the courts, might do if, as many Christians do, the teacher came to school on Ash Wednesday* with ashes in the shape of a cross imposed on his forehead— would he be required to wash them off? He just might. Early in 1993, a judge required a prosecutor arguing a case on Ash Wednesday to clean the ashes from his forehead, lest the jury be influenced by its knowledge of the prosecutor's religiosity.

Or suppose a Jewish teacher were to wear a yarmulke in the classroom.   20 If the school district tried to stop him, it would apparently be acting within its authority. In 1986, after a Jewish Air Force officer was disciplined for wearing a yarmulke while on duty, in violation of a military rule against wearing headgear indoors, the Supreme Court shrugged: "The desirability of dress regulations in the miliary is decided by the appropriate military officials," the Justices explained, "and they are under no constitutional mandate to abandon their considered professional judgment."[17] The Congress quickly enacted leg-

---

[16]*Roberts v. Madigan,* 921 F. 2d 1047 (10th Cir. 1990).

Ash Wednesday: The first day of Lent. In Catholic tradition, ashes on the forehead remind believers of their physical mortality.

[17]*Goldman v. Weinberger,* 475 U.S. 503 (1986).

islation permitting the wearing of religious apparel while in uniform as long as "the wearing of the item would [not] interfere with the performance of the member's military duties," and—interesting caveat!—as long as the item is "neat and conservative."[18] Those whose faiths require them to wear dreadlocks and turbans, one supposes, need not apply to serve their country, unless they are prepared to change religions.

Consider the matter of religious holidays. One Connecticut town recently warned Jewish students in its public schools that they would be charged with *six* absences if they missed two days instead of the officially allocated one for Yom Kippur, the holiest observance in the Jewish calendar. And Alan Dershowitz of Harvard Law School, in his controversial book *Chutzpah,* castigates Harry Edwards, a Berkeley sociologist, for scheduling an examination on Yom Kippur, when most Jewish students would be absent. According to Dershowitz's account, Edwards answered criticism by saying: "That's how I'm going to operate. If the students don't like it, they can drop the class." For Dershowitz, this was evidence that "Jewish students [are] second-class citizens in Professor Edwards's classes."[19] Edwards has heatedly denied Dershowitz's description of events, but even if it is accurate, it is possible that Dershowitz has identified the right crime and the wrong villain. The attitude that Dershowitz describes, if it exists, might reflect less a personal prejudice against Jewish students than the society's broader prejudice against religious devotion, a prejudice that masquerades as "neutrality." If Edwards really dared his students to choose between their religion and their grade, and if that meant that he was treating them as second-class citizens, he was still doing no more than the courts have allowed all levels of government to do to one religious group after another—Jews, Christians, Muslims, Sikhs, it matters not at all. The consistent message of modern American society is that whenever the demands of one's religion conflict with what one has to do to get ahead, one is expected to ignore the religious demands and act . . . well . . . *rationally.*

Consider Jehovah's Witnesses, who believe that a blood transfusion from one human being to another violates the biblical prohibition on ingesting blood. To accept the transfusion, many Witnesses believe, is to lose, perhaps forever, the possibility of salvation. As the Witnesses understand God's law, moreover, the issue is not whether the blood transfusion is given against the recipient's will, but whether the recipient is, at the time of the transfusion, actively protesting. This is the reason that Jehovah's Witnesses sometimes try to impede the physical access of medical personnel to an unconscious Witness: lack of consciousness is no defense. This is also the reason that Witnesses try to make the decisions on behalf of their children: a child cannot be trusted to protest adequately.

---

[18]45 U.S.C. 774, as amended by Pub. L. No. 100–80, Dec. 4, 1987.
[19]Alan M. Dershowitz, *Chutzpah* (Boston: Little, Brown, 1991), pp. 329–30.

The machinery of law has not been particularly impressed with these arguments. There are many cases in which the courts have allowed or ordered transfusions to save the lives of unconscious Witnesses, even though the patient might have indicated a desire while conscious not to be transfused.[20] The machinery of modern medicine has not been impressed, either, except with the possibility that the Witnesses have gone off the deep end; at least one hospital's protocol apparently requires doctors to refer protesting Witnesses to psychiatrists.[21] Although the formal text of this requirement states as the reason the need to be sure that the Witness knows what he or she is doing, the subtext is a suspicion that the patient was not acting rationally in rejecting medical advice for religious reasons. After all, there is no protocol for packing *consenting* patients off to see the psychiatrist. But then, patients who consent to blood transfusions are presumably acting rationally. Perhaps, with a bit of gentle persuasion, the dissenting Witness can be made to act rationally too— even if it means giving up an important tenet of the religion.

And therein lies the trouble. In contemporary American culture, the religions are more and more treated as just passing beliefs—almost as fads, older, stuffier, less liberal versions of so-called New Age—rather than as the fundaments upon which the devout build their lives. (The noes have it!) And if religions *are* fundamental, well, too bad—at least if they're the *wrong* fundaments— if they're inconvenient, give them up! If you can't remarry because you have the wrong religious belief, well, hey, believe something else! If you can't take your exam because of a Holy Day, get a new Holy Day! If the government decides to destroy your sacred lands, just make some other lands sacred! If you must go to work on your sabbath, it's no big deal! It's just a day off! Pick a different one! If you can't have a blood transfusion because you think God forbids it, no problem! Get a new God! And through all of this trivializing rhetoric runs the subtle but unmistakable message: pray if you like, worship if you must, but whatever you do, do not on any account take your religion seriously.

QUESTIONING THE TEXT

1. What effect does the personal tone of Carter's piece have on your willingness to consider his argument? For example, he begins one paragraph "A few years ago, my wife and I . . ." and another "A friend tells the

---

[20]In every decided case that I have discovered involving efforts by Jehovah's Witness parents to prevent their children from receiving blood transfusions, the court has allowed the transfusion to proceed in the face of parental objection. I say more about transfusions of children of Witnesses, and about the rights of parents over their children's religious lives, in chapter 11 [of my book].

[21]See Ruth Macklin, "The Inner Workings of an Ethics Committee: Latest Battle over Jehovah's Witnesses," *Hastings Center Report* 18 (February/March 1988): 15.

story of how. . . ." Would you take "The Culture of Disbelief" more seriously if Carter removed himself from the essay?

2. Carter points out that "nobody prays on prime-time television" even though the vast majority of Americans profess a belief in God. How are faith and religion usually depicted on television and in the movies? Are they fairly and appropriately represented?

3. In the introduction to Carter's essay, J.R. suggests that the mainstream media pay attention to religion only under certain conditions. What are those conditions (according to J.R.)? Do you agree with J.R.'s assertion?

MAKING CONNECTIONS

4. In "Our God Is Able" (p. 154), Martin Luther King Jr. suggests that God has influenced the progress of history, ultimately destroying individuals and systems not compatible with "the moral laws of the universe." Given Carter's description of the politics of a later generation, would King be able to make such arguments in the political arena today? Why, or why not?

5. Read Carter's essay along with Anthony Brandt's "Do Kids Need Religion?" later in this chapter. Then explore whether Brandt's essay confirms Carter's observations about religion in American society today.

JOINING THE CONVERSATION

6. Carter cites several instances in which professionals (teachers or lawyers) had to mute their public expression of religious belief. In a group, choose one example, discuss it, and then brainstorm both sides of the case as if you were preparing to write a column for a newspaper exploring the dilemma.

7. Carter points to the Jehovah's Witnesses' refusal of blood transfusions as an example of religious belief conflicting with the norms of secular ("rational") society. Review the paragraphs dealing with transfusion (para. 22–23), and then write an essay that examines when, if ever, the state should interfere in the practice of religion. You'll probably wish to consult secondary sources.

8. Have you or someone you know been involved in a conflict between religious values and secular values? If so, write a narrative explaining the conflict.

ANTHONY BRANDT
Do Kids Need Religion?

ANTHONY BRANDT, a contributing editor at Parenting *magazine, focuses on the relationship of children to religious faith. Brandt speaks as a parent, one concerned about how best to help his children face the losses and traumas life always brings. In this essay, published in 1991 in the progressive* Utne Reader, *he describes himself as a "run-of-the-mill modern skeptic," without faith or belief, and asks us to consider the uses of religion in what he terms a largely secular society. Might religion serve as a unifying cultural force, even for people who don't "believe"? Even more important, Brandt asks, "What sort of meaning does a secular society offer a child?" These questions suggest that Brandt is searching for a basis on which he can make some very hard choices about how he will (and should) raise his children.*

I admire Brandt's straightforward approach here, his willingness to consider various options, and his refusal to argue that his *way to spirituality is the only or even the best way. In addition, I find that Brandt finally establishes some common ground for* all *people, regardless of differences in religious faith or creed, when he says, "The longing for meaning is something we all share. . . ."*

— A.L.

This happened nearly 20 years ago, so I may not have all the details right. As I remember, my daughter was about 10 years old. She had spent the weekend with her grandparents, and while she was gone, a house down the road from ours burned to the ground. Three children died in the fire. One was a houseguest. The other two were my daughter's closest friends.

My wife went to see the bereaved parents. They were devout Catholics and they took their loss amazingly well. They talked to her about their two girls being angels in heaven now, and they really believed it. At the funeral, they were strong and brave, braver than many others there, including myself.

My tears were bitter. I didn't think their children were angels, I thought they were dead. I had little confidence in any sort of existence beyond that. I was not a devout Catholic or a devout anything. I was your run-of-the-mill modern skeptic who long before had stopped going to church, thought most religious doctrine absurd, and was resolved to live without the illusions of belief.

What does your run-of-the-mill modern skeptic tell his 10-year-old daughter when her closest friends have just died in a fire? My wife and I told her what had happened when she got home from her grandparents' house. I was crying and so was my wife, but my daughter just sat there, stunned, in shock. I wanted so much to console her, to find something to say that would explain, would justify these deaths and give them meaning. But I didn't think these deaths had any meaning. All I could come up with was something I didn't believe. "Maybe there is a heaven," I said, "and that's where they are." Yeah, maybe. And maybe not.

I'm old enough to know now that there's no living without illusions of some sort, that we all need to find or generate some kind of meaning for our lives if life is not to become unbearable. But what kind? It goes without saying that we are no longer a religious society in the conventional sense of the word. Religion no longer stands at the center of our culture as it did a hundred or so years ago. Rather, we are a thoroughly secularized society. The miracles we marvel at are the miracles of technology. For the answers to our questions about the meaning of things, we look not to the elders of a church, but to science.

An event like the cruel and pointless death of three little girls, however, presents a fundamental challenge. What sort of meaning does a secular society offer a child? What do parents with no religious beliefs do when their children start asking those difficult questions about where Grandpa has gone, Grandpa having just died, or why Jesus was crucified, and why people are so mean, and what will happen to them when they die?

For some parents, to be sure, questions like these present no problem. Either they have religious beliefs and are confident they can transmit them to their kids, or they have no religious beliefs at all and see no reason to raise their children to have any. I

Doesn't Brandt underestimate the influence of religion in the U.S.A here? — J.R.

It might, in fact, be harder for a believer to explain to children why a benevolent God would allow such a tragedy to befall the faithful. — J.G.R.

I know children who have experienced the death of a loved one "up close and personal." Our society holds death so much at arm's length and tries to deny it in so many ways that we don't in any way prepare children (or ourselves) for its reality. — A.L.

Is Brandt saying that meaning is always in some sense an illusion? I wouldn't use the word illusion *here. A construct, perhaps, but not an illusion.* — A.L.

asked one father what he had done about his kids' religious education and he said, "Nothing whatsoever." Well, I went on, how did he answer their questions about God and things like that? He didn't remember there being any. And even if there are questions, a parent can say, "Go ask your mother" or "I'm no expert on that" or simply "I don't know," and let it go at that. Western culture is so secularized that parents can evade or dismiss "religious" questions without feeling that they're merely getting themselves off the hook. No one is surprised anymore by this kind of religious indifference.

Surprised? No. But what are the consequences? — J.R.

For believers, too, the problem doesn't exist. Secure in their own faith, they can confidently answer the questions of a child.

How can he be so sure? Don't all people—believers or not—have doubts? — J.G.R.

Another mother and father, not so secure in their faith, say it was actually their children who brought them back to religion. They had both been raised Roman Catholic; each had children from a previous marriage; both had lapsed from the church. But they were sending their kids to a Protestant Sunday school. One night at dinner the oldest child said, "Don't you think we should pray for this food?" This was something of a shock. It was even more so when the child said, in prayer, "And thank you, God, for bringing our whole family together." The following Sunday the parents went to church. They have been actively involved (in a Protestant congregation) ever since. "Children come up with some really interesting questions," the mother told me, "and we still have to do a lot of explaining. But we have faith. We don't feel that we're alone with these questions."

This isn't at all clear to me. Faith in what? And how does this faith have to do with not "being alone" with these questions? — A.L.

For those of us without faith it's not so easy. Do we send our kids to Sunday school when we ourselves never go to church? Do we have them baptized even though we have no intention of raising them to be religious? I argued against having my son baptized. It's a meaningless ritual, I said. I didn't think he had been "born in sin," so why wash him free of it, even symbolically? Why bow to conven-

The author seems earnest. Why do I feel uneasy as a reader? — J.R.

tion simply for convention's sake? I gave in, but only to keep peace in the family.

For me religious education raised the issue of honesty. I thought it would be hypocritical to make my kids attend Sunday school when I not only didn't go to church but also didn't have any religious beliefs. My parents had sent me to Sunday school when neither of them was in the least religious, and under the circumstances I came to think Sunday school was a joke. I learned a few Bible stories, but that was all. I believed I should spare my children that kind of charade. My wife took them to church from time to time, but only once or twice did they attend a Sunday school class.

Are there reasons for sending children to Sunday school that go beyond religious beliefs? — A.L.

I'm still wondering whether we did the right thing. In *Childhood and Society* the renowned psychoanalyst Erik Erikson makes the unsettling remark that "many are proud to be without religion whose children cannot afford their being without it." Children may not need a religious upbringing, but, says Erikson, they do need a sense of "basic trust," a feeling not only that their fundamental bodily needs will be met and that their parents love them and will take care of them, but also that they have not been abandoned to the empty haphazardness of existence.

Children can be taught moral values and courage without religion. — J.G.R.

I can't see offhand why religion is the only thing that could fulfill this need not to feel abandoned. — A.L.

Erikson relates this sense of trust to the psychosocial origins of religious life. "The parental faith which supports the trust emerging in the newborn," he writes, "has throughout history sought its institutional safeguard . . . in organized religion." The trust of the infant in the parents, in other words, finds its parallel—and takes its mature form—in the parents' trust in God. The implication is that if trust has no institutional reinforcement, it will tend to wither. Basic trust will become basic mistrust, and there will be more work for mental health experts such as Erikson.

The institutional form that trust has taken in America has historically remained within the Judeo-Christian tradition, and the decision to deny that tradition to a child ought at the very least to be well thought out. Children will become aware of

Brandt equates religion with objects and symbols, not beliefs and moral choices. I'm disappointed that all he's worried about is that his children won't fit into a Judeo-Christian culture. — J.R.

the tradition with or without parental teaching; they'll bring it home from school or the playground, wanting to know why their friend Jimmy says they'll go to hell if they don't go to church, or why Alice is getting a beautiful white confirmation dress and they're not. A psychoanalyst, Ana-Marie Rizzuto, once pointed out that no matter what parents teach their children, "religious symbols and language are so widely present in this society that virtually no child reaches school age without having constructed—with or without religious instruction—an image or images of God."

I broached the subject with one couple who have a three-year-old daughter. The father, Pete, was raised in a fundamentalist family and rebelled against it; religion holds a kind of perverse fascination for him, but he is not what you would call a believer. His wife, Valerie, has no religious beliefs to speak of. Yet they both want their daughter to go to Sunday school. "I don't want her to grow up in a religious vacuum," says Pete. He thinks that if they don't give her a religious background they will be depriving her of a choice later on. If she has the background, she can always reject it when she gets older, he says; if she doesn't, there will be nothing to reject but nothing to affirm, either. He doesn't think she would be likely to come to that crossroads on her own. Valerie agrees with this reasoning: "I want her to know the Bible stories, the mythology," she says. "It's a major part of our culture. And I want her to have a sense of mystery, of awe." A sense, says Pete, that in our society has largely been lost.

If this approach seems paradoxical coming from parents who are not themselves believers, it also makes a certain amount of sense. No matter what we believe in, our society's Judeo-Christian tradition retains a good deal of its power. I reject organized religion, yet I cannot listen to Mozart's *Requiem Mass* without being moved. Perhaps nonpracticing Jews feel the same when they hear Hebrew prayers sung. Much of Western culture springs from religious feeling; we are secular but our heritage is not, and there is no true identifica-

What he wants for his children is "religious appreciation," not religion. No hard choices here—religion as art.
— J.R.

Why does religious instruction have to come from a church?
— J.G.R.

How typical of our times to regard "values" as universal and belief as contingent. We'd better hope there is no God! — J.R.

tion with a culture without some feel for its past. To raise children in a culture without at least exposing them to its religious traditions, even if you yourself have abandoned the beliefs on which they are based, may be doing them a disservice. The children will be exposed to those traditions in any case, so why not give them some real instruction?

Pete and Valerie are not alone; among the nonbelieving parents I talked to, theirs was a common rationale for sending their children to Sunday school, and the most common solution to the problem. Several other parents, however, admitted to qualms. "Kids pick up on your real feelings about things pretty fast," one father said. "If you're making them do something you yourself don't believe in, they're going to figure it out." And a mother told me, "I think you can transmit values to your kids, but belief is different. Values—respect for other people, respect for life, not taking what doesn't belong to you, things like that—they're universal, they're everywhere. But belief is a special thing. You have to come to it on your own; nobody can impose it on you."

Too, it is impossible to predict with any confidence what effect a religious education will have on children. It can be more than a little uncomfortable when your children take religious teaching more seriously than you do. It is unsettling to think that they might need religion when you have decided you do not. Do kids in fact need religion? They need "basic trust," as Erikson says, but beyond that, nobody has conclusive answers. We used to think that without religious beliefs, social behavior would come unglued. "If God is dead," wrote Dostoyevski, "then everything is permitted." It hasn't happened.

Morality can survive without religion, it appears; children can be taught the importance of right versus wrong without benefit of religious training. Jean Piaget and Lawrence Kohlberg* have shown that

There's a big difference between introducing children to the religious traditions of our culture (which are quite diverse) and training them into one set of religious beliefs as absolutely the truth and the one way.
— A.L.

Well, yes, or any other training, for that matter. Some of the most horrible characters in our history, for instance, were thoroughly trained in religions and/or other traditions.
— A.L.

All of Brandt's sources are psychologists. What's his own background?
— J.G.R.

Jean Piaget (1896–1980) and Lawrence Kohlberg (1927–87): psychologists who studied the mental and moral development of children and young adults

*Wrong. What—
besides racism and
sexism—is
regarded as sinful
these days? Adul-
tery? Pornogra-
phy? Idolatry?
Abortion? Cov-
etousness?*
    — J.R.

moral understanding is acquired in stages, that it is a developmental process that unfolds, to some extent, as naturally as intelligence itself.

My daughter, now age 27, who was exposed to little more than my own deep skepticism, is studying Buddhism. As I write, in fact, she is in Tibet, on a journey that I'm sure is at least partly spiritual. I have made spiritual journeys during my adult life, all of them outside the sphere of Christianity that I was raised in. I continue to distrust and dislike organized religion but find it hard, as I grow older, to live with only my vague faith that life must have some kind of meaning, even if I don't know what it is.

To believe is to be connected, and those of us who don't believe cannot help but miss the feelings that come with belonging to something larger than ourselves. I hope my children find a straighter road than I've found. "I very much wish I had had some religion, for my kids' sake," one father told me. "My son's into tarot cards now. There's not much comfort in tarot cards."

*This is an inter-
esting definition of
belief—"to be
connected." I'll
have to think
about this; I'm
not sure I agree.*
    — A.L.

The longing for meaning is something we all share, parent and child alike. But it may be that this is an area where a parent can't help a child much. Meaning may be something all of us have to find in our own way. I don't know. I am loath to give ad-vice. Robert Coles* quotes a black woman who worked as a servant for a wealthy white Southern family: "My momma told me: Remember that you're put here only for a few seconds of God's time, and he's testing you. He doesn't want an-swers, though. He wants you to know how to ask the right questions." Teaching our kids how to ask the right questions may be the best we can do.

*This is a safe and
predictable conclu-
sion. No strong
position is taken.
I'm disappointed.*
    — J.R.

*I end up wonder-
ing where Brandt
stands on his orig-
inal question. I'll
need to reread this
to decide whether
his answer is yes,
no, or maybe.*
    — A.L.

Afterwords

I agree that human beings seek meaning, that we yearn for meaning so strongly that we will make meaning(s) at all cost. Further, I consider this yearning to be a function related to our being inside a world of languages—which is why the

---

Robert Coles: an educational psychologist (b. 1929) whose work on the ethical life of chil-dren has been widely influential

philosopher Kenneth Burke defines people as "symbol-using, symbol-abusing animals." Language allows us to assign meaning, and if this capacity is by definition human, then it makes perfect sense that we would need to assign meaning, demand to make meaning.

That said, I'm willing to follow in Brandt's steps as he explores the central question of his essay, which I would rephrase as "Will religion help kids make or find meaning?" Put this way, my answer would be conditional: organized religion can help people make meaning, and it can do so largely by way of its own language, its symbolicity. But I'd also say that organized religion won't automatically help kids or anyone else find meaning.

Brandt claims not to have religion, but rather "spirituality." What seems to give meaning to him and his life is his connection to others, particularly his family, and his commitment to intellectual inquiry, to continued probing of important issues, including those of religion and meaning. In this regard, I am most sympathetic to him. I find meaning in my own life in relationship to someone else, either in person (as with my friends, my family, and especially my students) or in words (with persons I know only through books). Meaning, it strikes me, isn't ever in us or indeed in any one thing; rather, meaning arises out of connections and relations. For me, these are the pathways to spirituality, ones I'd like to share with "kids" of all ages. — A.L.

One reason I am not now particularly religious is that I am unmoved by "soft" notions of religion such as put forth by Brandt and to some extent by A.L. Raised in a strict Catholic tradition, I take little solace or intellectual satisfaction in faith represented chiefly as a quest for meaning or selfhood. Religion makes more sense to me if it also deals with timeless, if evolving, truths.

To offer religion to children as an alternative to harsh reality—as a way of explaining to a ten-year-old why her best friends died in a fire, to use Brandt's example—turns religion into a booster club. That a nonbelieving parent like Brandt might expose his children to organized religion because he wants them to know the tradition behind Mozart's Requiem *is to treat faith with secular contempt, rendering it as worthless as sunshine patriotism. Religion is about hard choices, not easy ones; about truths, not feelings. Questions of faith compel individuals to face the abyss and to confront the responsibility we have for our own souls. Religion defines meaning not in terms of historical and cultural artifacts, but in terms of a higher power. At some point, this faith requires a difficult, uncompromising, and final* credo.

I am not able to speak that word yet, but when and if I do, I don't expect my life to be any easier. — J.R.

As an agnostic parent, I looked forward to reading this piece. After reading it, I feel let down, mostly because it seems long on questions and short on answers.

I wanted guidance, but instead I got descriptions of wishy-washy parents relying on religious institutions they have no faith in to give their children moral security and structure. How hypocritical! I expected a spectrum of authoritative opinions, but Brandt relies solely on psychiatrists.

Because this issue is so critical to me, I may have wanted too much from Brandt. In raising my son, Luke, I can relate to some of Brandt's experiences. But I feel I might be setting Luke up for a spiritual fall if I were to raise him in a religion I have no faith in myself. He might ultimately lose faith in me as well as in religion. Apparently, what I want no writer can objectively give: answers to an eternal enigma.   — J.G.R.

QUESTIONING THE TEXT

1. Brandt quotes a psychoanalyst as saying "religious symbols and language are so widely present in this society that virtually no child reaches school age without having constructed . . . an image or images of God." Does your experience bear out this claim? If so, how did you construct such an image or images? What are your friends' experiences? Do you know some who have *not* constructed an image of God? If so, how did they avoid doing so?
2. What is Brandt's answer to his title question, "Do kids need religion?" What in the essay most clearly tells you what the answer is? If you keep a reading log, answer these questions there.
3. Look at the questions A.L., J.R., and J.G.R. pose in their marginal commentary on this piece. Choose several of their questions and decide what functions each question serves. Can you see any differences in the kinds of questions each reader tends to ask?

MAKING CONNECTIONS

4. Judging from his selection in this chapter (p. 154), what advice would Martin Luther King Jr. likely give Brandt about children and religion? What advice might Andrea Lee, author of the next selection, give? Imagine that you are either King or Lee, and write a letter to Brandt offering such advice.
5. In what ways might Brandt's spiritual quest be compared to that depicted in Kathleen Norris's "Little Girls in Church" (p. 223)? How do Brandt and Norris differ in their relationship to belief or faith?
6. Is Brandt's attitude toward faith chiefly secular? After reading Stephen L. Carter's "The Culture of Disbelief," write your own analysis of the role Brandt would have religion play in society.

JOINING THE CONVERSATION

7. Like other authors in this chapter, Brandt seems to distinguish between spirituality or spiritual quest and religion. Try your hand at comparing and contrasting these terms in writing, and bring your definitions to class for discussion.

8. Working with two or three classmates, answer Brandt's question, "Do kids need religion?" Then together draw up a list of reasons, examples, or other evidence to support your answer. Finally, on your own, draft a one-page position paper, beginning either with "Kids need religion" or "Kids don't need religion."

ANDREA LEE
New African

*P*ART OF GROWING UP *inevitably involves coming to terms with relationships, including those with parents, siblings, partners, and institutions. If all of us are in some sense writing the story of our lives, the story of who we are, then part of that story has to consider how we are connected to others. Andrea Lee (b. 1953) focuses on the relationship her character Sarah has with the religion of her family and her tradition, particularly as it is represented by the New African Baptist Church. Sarah struggles with the "call to Jesus" both her church and her family expect her to answer and puzzles on the ways in which her resistance seems deeply connected to being able to define herself, to find her own identity separate but not isolated from these traditions.*

If you are as intrigued as I have been with Sarah's description of the spiritual road she chooses, you may want to follow her adventures throughout Lee's novel Sarah Phillips *(1984), as she leaves the United States after her father's death and her own graduation from college, settles in Paris, and eventually comes to a greater understanding of herself, the traditions of "New African," and her own southern African American heritage. I chose this selection from the novel because it asks all readers to examine, and then re-examine, the choices of faith they make.* — A.L.

On a hot Sunday morning in the summer of 1963, I was sitting restlessly with my mother, my brother Matthew, and my aunts Lily, Emma, and May in a central pew of the New African Baptist Church. It was mid-August, and the hum of the big electric fans at the back of the church was almost enough to muffle my father's voice from the pulpit; behind me I could hear Mrs. Gordon, a stout, feeble old woman who always complained of dizziness, remark sharply to her daughter that at the rate the air-conditioning fund was growing, it might as well be for the next century. Facing the congregation, my father—who was Reverend Phillips to the rest of the world—seemed hot himself; he mopped his brow with a handkerchief and drank several glasses of ice water from the heavy pitcher on the table by the pulpit. I looked at him critically. He's still reading the text, I thought. Then he'll do the sermon, then the baptism, and it will be an hour, maybe two.

I rubbed my chin and then idly began to snap the elastic band that held my red straw hat in place. What I would really like to do, I decided, would be to go home, put on my shorts, and climb up into the tree house I had set up the day before with Matthew. We'd nailed an old bushel basket up in the branches of the big maple that stretched above the sidewalk in front of the house; it made a sort of crow's nest where you could sit comfortably, except for a few splinters, and read, or peer through the dusty leaves at the cars that passed down the quiet suburban road. There was shade and wind and a feeling of high adventure up in the treetop, where the air seemed to vibrate with the dry rhythms of the cicadas; it was as different as possible from church, where the packed congregation sat in a near-visible miasma of emotion and cologne, and trolleys passing in the city street outside set the stained-glass windows rattling.

I slouched between Mama and Aunt Lily and felt myself going limp with lassitude and boredom, as if the heat had melted my bones; the only thing about me with any character seemed to be my firmly starched eyelet dress. Below the scalloped hem, my legs were skinny and wiry, the legs of a ten-year-old amazon, scarred from violent adventures with bicycles and skates. A fingernail tapped my wrist; it was Aunt Emma, reaching across Aunt Lily to press a piece of butterscotch into my hand. When I slipped the candy into my mouth, it tasted faintly of Arpège; my mother and her three sisters were monumental women, ample of bust and slim of ankle, with a weakness for elegant footwear and French perfume. As they leaned back and forth to exchange discreet tidbits of gossip, they fanned themselves and me with fans from the Byron J. Wiggins Funeral Parlor. The fans, which were fluttering throughout the church, bore a depiction of the Good Shepherd: a hollow-eyed blond Christ holding three fat pink-cheeked children. This Christ resembled the Christ who stood among apostles on the stained-glass windows of the church. Deacon Wiggins, a thoughtful man, had also provided New African with a few dozen fans bearing the picture of a black child praying, but I rarely saw those in use.

There was little that was new or very African about the New African Baptist Church. The original congregation had been formed in 1813 by three young men from Philadelphia's large community of free blacks, and before many generations had passed, it had become spiritual home to a collection of prosperous, conservative, generally light-skinned parishioners. The church was a gray Gothic structure, set on the corner of a run-down street in South Philadelphia a dozen blocks below Rittenhouse Square and a few blocks west of the spare, clannish Italian neighborhoods that produced Frankie Avalon and Frank Rizzo. At the turn of the century, the neighborhood had been a tidy collection of brick houses with scrubbed marble steps—the homes of a group of solid citizens whom Booker T. Washington, in a centennial address to the church, described as "the ablest Negro businessmen of our generation." Here my father had grown up aspiring to preach to the congregation of New African—an ambition encouraged by my grandmother Phillips, a formidable churchwoman. Here, too, my mother and her sisters had walked with linked arms to Sunday services, exchanging affected little catchphrases of French and Latin they had learned at Girls' High.

In the 1950s many of the parishioners, seized by the national urge to-   5
ward the suburbs, moved to newly integrated towns outside the city, leaving

the streets around New African to fill with bottles and papers and loungers. The big church stood suddenly isolated. It had not been abandoned—on Sundays the front steps overflowed with members who had driven in—but there was a tentative feeling in the atmosphere of those Sunday mornings, as if through the muddle of social change, the future of New African had become unclear. Matthew and I, suburban children, felt a mixture of pride and animosity toward the church. On the one hand, it was a marvelous private domain, a richly decorated and infinitely suggestive playground where we were petted by a congregation that adored our father; on the other hand, it seemed a bit like a dreadful old relative in the city, one who forced us into tedious visits and who linked us to a past that came to seem embarrassingly primitive as we grew older.

I slid down in my seat, let my head roll back, and looked up at the blue arches of the church ceiling. Lower than these, in back of the altar, was an enormous gilded cross. Still lower, in a semicircle near the pulpit, sat the choir, flanked by two tall golden files of organ pipes, and below the choir was a somber crescent of dark-suited deacons. In front, at the center of everything, his bald head gleaming under the lights, was Daddy. On summer Sundays he wore white robes, and when he raised his arms, the heavy material fell in curving folds like the ridged petals of an Easter lily. Usually when I came through the crowd to kiss him after the service, his cheek against my lips felt wet and gravelly with sweat and a new growth of beard sprouted since morning. Today, however, was a baptismal Sunday, and I wouldn't have a chance to kiss him until he was freshly shaven and cool from the shower he took after the ceremony. The baptismal pool was in an alcove to the left of the altar; it had mirrored walls and red velvet curtains, and above it, swaying on a string, hung a stuffed white dove.

Daddy paused in the invocation and asked the congregation to pray. The choir began to sing softly:

> Blessed assurance,
> Jesus is mine!
> Oh what a foretaste
> Of glory divine!

In the middle of the hymn, I edged my head around my mother's cool, muscular arm (she swam every day of the summer) and peered at Matthew. He was sitting bolt upright holding a hymnal and a pencil, his long legs inside his navy-blue summer suit planted neatly in front of him, his freckled thirteen-year-old face that was so like my father's wearing not the demonic grin it bore when we played alone but a maddeningly composed, attentive expression. "Two hours!" I mouthed at him, and pulled back at a warning pressure from my mother. Then I joined in the singing, feeling disappointed: Matthew had returned me a glance of scorn. Just lately he had started acting very superior and tolerant about tedious Sunday mornings. A month before, he'd been baptized, marching up to the pool in a line of white-robed children as the congregation murmured happily about Reverend Phillips's son. Afterward Mrs. Pinkston, a tiny, yellow-skinned old woman with a blind left eye, had come up to me and given me a painful hug, whispering that she was praying night and day for the pastor's daughter to hear the call as well.

I bit my fingernails whenever I thought about baptism; the subject brought out a deep-rooted balkiness in me. Ever since I could remember, Matthew and I had made a game of dispelling the mysteries of worship with a gleeful secular eye: we knew how the bread and wine were prepared for Communion, and where Daddy bought his robes (Ekhardt Brothers, in North Philadelphia, makers also of robes for choirs, academicians, and judges). Yet there was an unassailable magic about an act as public and dramatic as baptism. I felt toward it the slightly exasperated awe a stagehand might feel on realizing that although he can identify with professional exactitude the minutest components of a show, there is still something indefinable in the power that makes it a cohesive whole. Though I could not have put it into words, I believed that the decision to make a frightening and embarrassing backward plunge into a pool of sanctified water meant that one had received a summons to Christianity as unmistakable as the blare of an automobile horn. I believed this with the same fervor with which, already, I believed in the power of romance, especially in the miraculous efficacy of a lover's first kiss. I had never been kissed by a lover, nor had I heard the call to baptism.

For a Baptist minister and his wife, my father and mother were unusu-   10 ally relaxed about religion; Matthew and I had never been required to read the Bible, and my father's sermons had been criticized by some older church members for omitting the word "sin." Mama and Daddy never tried to push me toward baptism, but a number of other people did. Often on holidays, when I had retreated from the noise of the family dinner table and sat trying to read in my favorite place (the window seat in Matthew's room, with the curtains drawn to form a tent), Aunt Lily would come and find me. Aunt Lily was the youngest of my mother's sisters, a kindergarten teacher with the fatally overdeveloped air of quaintness that is the infallible mark of an old maid. Aunt Lily hoped and hoped again with various suitors, but even I knew she would never find a husband. I respected her because she gave me wonderful books of fairy tales, inscribed in her neat, loopy hand; when she talked about religion, however, she assumed an anxious, flirtatious air that made me cringe. "Well, Miss Sarah, what are you scared of?" she would ask, tugging gently on one of my braids and bringing her plump face so close to mine that I could see her powder, which was, in accordance with the custom of fashionable colored ladies, several shades lighter than her olive skin. "God isn't anyone to be afraid of!" she'd continue as I looked at her with my best deadpan expression. "He's someone nice, just as nice as your daddy"—I had always suspected Aunt Lily of having a crush on my father—"and he loves you, in the same way your daddy does!"

"You would make us all so happy!" I was told at different times by Aunt Lily, Aunt Emma, and Aunt May. The only people who said nothing at all were Mama and Daddy, but I sensed in them a thoughtful, suppressed wistfulness that maddened me.

After the hymn, Daddy read aloud a few verses from the third chapter of Luke, verses I recognized in the almost instinctive way in which I was familiar with all of the well-traveled parts of the Old and New Testaments. "Prepare the way of the Lord, make his paths straight," read my father in a mild voice. "Every valley shall be filled, and every mountain and hill shall be brought low, and the crooked shall be made straight, and the rough paths made smooth, and all flesh shall see the salvation of God."

He had a habit of pausing to fix his gaze on part of the congregation as he read, and that Sunday he seemed to be talking to a small group of strangers who sat in the front row. These visitors were young white men and women, students from Philadelphia colleges, who for the past year had been coming to hear him talk. It was hard to tell them apart: all the men seemed to have beards, and the women wore their hair long and straight. Their informal clothes stood out in that elaborate assembly, and church members whispered angrily that the young women didn't wear hats. I found the students appealing and rather romantic, with their earnest eyes and timid air of being perpetually sorry about something. It was clear that they had good intentions, and I couldn't understand why so many of the adults in the congregation seemed to dislike them so much. After services, they would hover around Daddy. "Never a more beautiful civil rights sermon!" they would say in low, fervent voices. Sometimes they seemed to have tears in their eyes.

I wasn't impressed by their praise of my father; it was only what everyone said. People called him a champion of civil rights; he gave speeches on the radio, and occasionally he appeared on television. (The first time I'd seen him on Channel 5, I'd been gravely disappointed by the way he looked: the bright lights exaggerated the furrows that ran between his nose and mouth, and his narrow eyes gave him a sinister air; he looked like an Oriental villain in a Saturday afternoon thriller.) During the past year he had organized a boycott that integrated the staff of a huge frozen-food plant in Philadelphia, and he'd been away several times to attend marches and meetings in the South. I was privately embarrassed to have a parent who freely admitted going to jail in Alabama, but the students who visited New African seemed to think it almost miraculous. Their conversations with my father were peppered with references to places I had never seen, towns I imagined as being swathed in a mist of darkness visible: Selma, Macon, Birmingham, Biloxi.

Matthew and I had long ago observed that what Daddy generally did in his sermons was to speak very softly and then surprise everyone with a shout. Of course, I knew that there was more to it than that; even in those days I recognized a genius of personality in my father. He loved crowds, handling them with the expert good humor of a man entirely in his element. At church banquets, at the vast annual picnic that was held beside a lake in New Jersey, or at any gathering in the backyards and living rooms of the town where we lived, the sound I heard most often was the booming of my father's voice followed by shouts of laughter from the people around him. He had a passion for oratory; at home, he infuriated Matthew and me by staging absurd debates at the dinner table, verbal melees that he won quite selfishly, with a loud crow of delight at his own virtuosity. "Is a fruit a vegetable?" he would demand. "Is a zipper a machine?" Matthew and I would plead with him to be quiet as we strained to get our own points across, but it was no use. When the last word had resounded and we sat looking at him in irritated silence, he would clear his throat, settle his collar, and resume eating, his face still glowing with an irrepressible glee.

When he preached, he showed the same private delight. A look of rapt pleasure seemed to broaden and brighten the contours of his angular face until it actually appeared to give off light as he spoke. He could preach in two very different ways. One was the delicate, sonorous idiom of formal oratory, with which he must have won the prizes he held from his seminary days. The second was a hectoring, insinuating, incantatory tone, full of the rhythms of the South he had never lived in, linking him to generations of thunderous Baptist preachers. When he used this tone, as he was doing now, affectionate laughter rippled through the pews.

"I know," he said, looking out over the congregation and blinking his eyes rapidly, "that there are certain people in this room—oh, I don't have to name names or point a finger—who have ignored that small true voice, the voice that is the voice of Jesus calling out in the shadowy depths of the soul. And while you all are looking around and wondering just who those 'certain people' are, I want to tell you all a secret: they are you and me, and your brother-in-law, and every man, woman, and child in this room this morning. All of us listen to our bellies when they tell us it is time to eat, we pay attention to our eyes when they grow heavy from wanting sleep, but when it comes to the sacred knowledge our hearts can offer, we are deaf, dumb, blind, and senseless. Throw away that blindness, that deafness, that sulky indifference. When all the world lies to you, Jesus will tell you what is right. Listen to him. Call on him. In these times of confusion, when there are a dozen different ways to turn, and Mama and Papa can't help you, trust Jesus to set you straight. Listen to him. The Son of God has the answers. Call on him. Call on him. Call on him."

The sermon was punctuated with an occasional loud "Amen!" from Miss Middleton, an excitable old lady whose eyes flashed defiantly at the reproving faces of those around her. New African was not the kind of Baptist church where shouting was a normal part of the service; I occasionally heard my father mock the staid congregation by calling it Saint African. Whenever Miss Middleton loosed her tongue (sometimes she went off into fits of rapturous shrieks and had to be helped out of the service by the church nurse), my mother and aunts exchanged grimaces and shrugged, as if confronted by incomprehensibly barbarous behavior.

When Daddy had spoken the final words of the sermon, he drank a glass of water and vanished through a set of red velvet curtains to the right of the altar. At the same time, the choir began to sing what was described in the church bulletin as a "selection." These selections were always arenas for the running dispute between the choirmaster and the choir. Jordan Grimes, the choirmaster, was a Curtis graduate who was partial to Handel, but the choir preferred artistic spirituals performed in the lush, heroic style of Paul Robeson. Grimes had triumphed that Sunday. As the choir gave a spirited but unwilling rendition of Agnus Dei, I watched old Deacon West smile in approval. A Spanish-American War veteran, he admitted to being ninety-four but was said to be older; his round yellowish face, otherwise unwrinkled, bore three deep, deliberate-looking horizontal creases on the brow, like carvings on a scarab. "That old man is as flirtatious as a boy of twenty!" my mother often said, watching his stiff, courtly movements among the ladies of the church. Sometimes he gave me a dry kiss and a piece of peppermint candy after the service; I liked his crackling white collars and smell of bay rum.

The selection ended; Jordan Grimes struck two deep chords on the   20
organ, and the lights in the church went low. A subtle stir ran through the congregation, and I moved closer to my mother. This was the moment that fascinated and disturbed me more than anything else at church: the prelude to the ceremony of baptism. Deacon West rose and drew open the draperies that had been closed around the baptismal pool, and there stood my father in water to his waist. The choir began to sing:

> We're marching to Zion,
> Beautiful, beautiful Zion,
> We're marching upward to Zion,
> The beautiful city of God!

Down the aisle, guided by two church mothers, came a procession of eight children and adolescents. They wore white robes, the girls with white ribbons in their hair, and they all had solemn expressions of terror on their faces. I knew each one of them. There was Billy Price, a big, slow-moving boy of thirteen, the son of Deacon Price. There were the Duckery twins. There was Caroline Piggee, whom I hated because of her long, soft black curls, her dimpled pink face, and her lisp that ravished grown-ups. There was Georgie Battis and Sue Anne Ivory, and Wendell and Mabel Cullen.

My mother gave me a nudge. "Run up to the side of the pool!" she whispered. It was the custom of unbaptized children to watch the ceremony from the front of the church. They sat on the knees of the deacons and church mothers, and it was not unusual for a child to volunteer then and there for next month's baptism. I made my way quickly down the dark aisle, feeling the carpet slip under the smooth soles of my patent-leather shoes.

When I reached the side of the pool, I sat down in the bony lap of Bessie Gray, an old woman who often took care of Matthew and me when our parents were away; we called her Aunt Bessie. She was a fanatically devout Christian whose strict ideas on child-rearing had evolved over decades of domestic service to a rich white family in Delaware. The link between us, a mixture of hostility and grudging affection, had been forged in hours of pitched battles over bedtimes and proper behavior. Her worshipful respect for my father, whom she called "the Rev," was exceeded only by her pride—the malice-tinged pride of an omniscient family servant—in her "white children," to whom she often unflatteringly compared Matthew and me. It was easy to see why my mother and her circle of fashionable matrons described Bessie Gray as "archaic"—one had only to look at her black straw hat attached with three enormous old-fashioned pins to her knot of frizzy white hair. Her lean, brown-skinned face was dominated by a hawk nose inherited from some Indian ancestor and punctuated by a big black mole; her eyes were small, shrewd, and baleful. She talked in ways that were already passing into history and parody, and she wore a thick orange face powder that smelled like dead leaves.

I leaned against her spare bosom and watched the other children clustered near the pool, their bonnets and hair ribbons and round heads outlined in the dim light. For a minute it was very still. Somewhere in the hot, darkened church a baby gave a fretful murmur; from outside came the sound of cars passing in the street. The candidates for baptism, looking stiff and self-conscious, stood lined up on the short stairway leading to the pool. Sue Anne Ivory fiddled with her sleeve and then put her fingers in her mouth.

Daddy spoke the opening phrases of the ceremony: "In the Baptist Church, we do not baptize infants, but believe that a person must choose salvation for himself."

I didn't listen to the words; what I noted was the music of the whole—how the big voice darkened and lightened in tone, and how the grand architecture of the Biblical sentences ennobled the voice. The story, of course, was about Jesus and John the Baptist. One phrase struck me newly each time: "This is my beloved son, in whom I am well pleased!" Daddy sang out these words in a clear, triumphant tone, and the choir echoed him. Ever since I could understand it, this phrase had made me feel melancholy; it seemed to expose a hard knot of disobedience that had always lain inside me. When I heard it, I thought enviously of Matthew, for whom life seemed to be a sedate and ordered affair: he, not I, was a child in whom a father could be well pleased.

Daddy beckoned to Billy Price, the first baptismal candidate in line, and Billy, ungainly in his white robe, descended the steps into the pool. In soft, slow voices the choir began to sing:

Wade in the water,
Wade in the water, children,
Wade in the water,
God gonna trouble
The water.

In spite of Jordan Grimes's efforts, the choir swayed like a gospel chorus as it sang this spiritual; the result was to add an eerie jazz beat to the minor chords. The music gave me gooseflesh. Daddy had told me that this was the same song that the slaves had sung long ago in the South, when they gathered to be baptized in rivers and streams. Although I cared little about history, and found it hard to picture the slaves as being any ancestors of mine, I could clearly imagine them coming together beside a broad muddy river that wound away between trees drooping with strange vegetation. They walked silently in lines, their faces very black against their white clothes, leading their children. The whole scene was bathed in the heavy golden light that meant age and solemnity, the same light that seemed to weigh down the Israelites in illustrated volumes of Bible stories, and that shone now from the baptismal pool, giving the ceremony the air of a spectacle staged in a dream.

All attention in the darkened auditorium was now focused on the pool, where between the red curtains my father stood holding Billy Price by the shoulders. Daddy stared into Billy's face, and the boy stared back, his lips set and trembling. "And now, by the power invested in me," said Daddy, "I baptize you in the name of the Father, the Son, and the Holy Ghost." As he pronounced these words, he conveyed a tenderness as efficient and impersonal as a physician's professional manner; beneath it, however, I could see a strong private gladness, the same delight that transformed his face when he preached a sermon. He paused to flick a drop of water off his forehead, and then, with a single smooth, powerful motion of his arms, he laid Billy Price back into the water as if he were putting an infant to bed. I caught my breath as the boy went backward. When he came up, sputtering, two church mothers helped him out of the pool and through a doorway into a room where he would be dried and dressed. Daddy shook the water from his hands and gave a slight smile as another child entered the pool.

One by one, the baptismal candidates descended the steps. Sue Anne   30
Ivory began to cry and had to be comforted. Caroline Piggee blushed and looked up at my father with such a coquettish air that I jealously wondered how he could stand it. After a few baptisms my attention wandered, and I began to gnaw the edge of my thumb and to peer at the pale faces of the visiting college students. Then I thought about Matthew, who had punched me in the arm that morning and had shouted, "No punchbacks!" I thought as well about a collection of horse chestnuts I meant to assemble in the fall, and about two books, one whose subject was adults and divorces, and another, by E. Nesbit, that continued the adventures of the Bastable children.

After Wendell Cullen had left the water (glancing uneasily back at the wet robe trailing behind him), Daddy stood alone among the curtains and the mirrors. The moving reflections from the pool made the stuffed dove hanging over him seem to flutter on its string. "Dear Lord," said Daddy, as Jordan Grimes struck a chord, "bless these children who have chosen to be baptized in accordance with your teaching, and who have been reborn to carry out your work. In each of them, surely, you are well pleased." He paused, staring out into the darkened auditorium. "And if there is anyone out there—man, woman, child—who wishes to be baptized next month, let him come forward now." He glanced around eagerly. "Oh, do come forward and give Christ your heart and give me your hand!"

Just then Aunt Bessie gave me a little shake and whispered sharply, "Go on up and accept Jesus!"

I stiffened and dug my bitten fingernails into my palms. The last clash of wills I had had with Aunt Bessie had been when she, crazily set in her old southern attitudes, had tried to make me wear an enormous straw hat, as her "white children" did, when I played outside in the sun. The old woman had driven me to madness, and I had ended up spanked and sullen, crouching moodily under the dining-room table. But this was different, outrageous, none of her business, I thought. I shook my head violently and she took advantage of the darkness of the church to seize both of my shoulders and jounce me with considerable roughness, whispering, "Now, listen, young lady! Your daddy up there is calling you to Christ. Your big brother has already offered his soul to the Lord. Now Daddy wants his little girl to step forward."

"No, he doesn't." I glanced at the baptismal pool, where my father was clasping the hand of a strange man who had come up to him. I hoped that this would distract Aunt Bessie, but she was tireless.

"Your mama and your aunt Lily and your aunt May all want you to answer the call. You're hurting them when you say no to Jesus."

"No, I'm not!" I spoke out loud and I saw the people nearby turn to look at me. At the sound of my voice, Daddy, who was a few yards away, faltered for a minute in what he was saying and glanced over in my direction.

Aunt Bessie seemed to lose her head. She stood up abruptly, pulling me with her, and, while I was still frozen in a dreadful paralysis, tried to drag me down the aisle toward my father. The two of us began a brief struggle that could not have lasted for more than a few seconds but that seemed an endless mortal conflict—my slippery patent-leather shoes braced against the floor, my straw hat sliding cockeyed and lodging against one ear, my right arm twisting and twisting in the iron circle of the old woman's grip, my nostrils full of the dead-leaf smell of her powder and black skirts. In an instant I had wrenched my arm free and darted up the aisle toward Mama, my aunts, and Matthew. As I slipped past the pews in the darkness, I imagined that I could feel eyes fixed on me and hear whispers. "What'd you do, dummy?" whispered Matthew, tugging on my sash as I reached our pew, but I pushed past him without answering. Although it was hot in the church, my teeth were chattering: it was the first time I had won a battle with a grownup, and the earth seemed to be about to cave in beneath me. I squeezed in between Mama and Aunt Lily just as the lights came back on in the church. In the baptismal pool, Daddy raised his arms for the last time. "The Lord bless you and keep you," came his big voice. "The Lord be gracious unto you, and give you peace."

What was curious was how uncannily subdued my parents were when they heard of my skirmish with Aunt Bessie. Normally they were swift to punish Matthew and me for misbehavior in church and for breaches in politeness toward adults; this episode combined the two, and smacked of sacrilege besides. Yet once I had made an unwilling apology to the old woman (as I kissed her she shot me such a vengeful glare that I realized that forever after it was to be war to the death between the two of us), I was permitted, once we had driven home, to climb up into the green shade of the big maple tree I had dreamed of throughout the service. In those days, more than now, I fell away into a remote dimension whenever I opened a book; that afternoon, as I sat with rings of sunlight and shadow moving over my arms and legs, and winged yellow seeds plopping down on the pages of *The Story of the Treasure Seekers,* I felt a vague uneasiness floating in the back of my mind—a sense of having misplaced something, of being myself misplaced. I was holding myself quite aloof from considering what had happened, as I did with most serious events, but through the adventures of the Bastables I kept remembering the way my father had looked when he'd heard what had happened. He hadn't looked severe or angry, but merely puzzled, and he had regarded me with the same puzzled expression, as if he'd just discovered that I existed and didn't know what to do with me. "What happened, Sairy?" he asked, using an old baby nickname, and I said, "I didn't want to go up there." I hadn't cried at all, and that was another curious thing.

After that Sunday, through some adjustment in the adult spheres beyond my perception, all pressure on me to accept baptism ceased. I turned twelve, fifteen, then eighteen without being baptized, a fact that scandalized some of the congregation; however, my parents, who openly discussed everything else, never said a word to me. The issue, and the episode that had illuminated it, was surrounded by a clear ring of silence that, for our garrulous family, was something close to supernatural. I continued to go to New African—in fact, continued after Matthew, who dropped out abruptly during his freshman year in college; the ambiguousness in my relations with the old church gave me at times an inflated sense of privilege (I saw myself as a romantically isolated religious heroine, a sort of self-made Baptist martyr) and at other times a feeling of loss that I was too proud ever to acknowledge. I never went up to take my father's hand, and he never commented upon that fact to me. It was an odd pact, one that I could never consider in the light of day; I stored it in the subchambers of my heart and mind. It was only much later, after he died, and I left New African forever, that I began to examine the peculiar gift of freedom my father—whose entire soul was in the church, and in his exuberant, bewitching tongue—had granted me through his silence.

QUESTIONING THE TEXT

1. Freewrite for 15 or 20 minutes on Lee's use of religious symbols in this story. Before beginning, quickly reread the story, noting such images as the stuffed dove, the gilded cross, the robes, the red curtain, the representations of Christ and the apostles, and so on.
2. At one point in the story, Sarah's father refers to her using her "baby nickname" of "Sairy." What is the effect of his using this nickname? Who was Sarah in the Bible? Does the biblical Sarah suggest anything about why her parents might have chosen this name for their "Sairy"?
3. Respond to A.L.'s suggestion in the introduction that "All of us are in some sense writing the story of our lives. . . ." Do you agree? Why, or why not?

MAKING CONNECTIONS

4. Lee's story might be read as an implicit response to Anthony Brandt's question "Do Kids Need Religion?" How do you think Lee would answer this question explicitly, and what reasons might she offer for her answer?
5. Read Kathleen Norris's poem "Little Girls in Church" (p. 223), and then compare the picture that emerges with the "little girl in church" in Lee's story about Sarah. Try your hand at writing a poem, perhaps called "Little Girls in the New African Baptist Church," from Sarah's point of view.

JOINING THE CONVERSATION

6. How does Lee's story suggest that the New African Baptist Church views children? Talk with several members of your class about ways to answer this question. Then use your discussion as a springboard for investigating how a religion or place of worship you are familiar with views or represents children. Write a brief essay summarizing your findings and exploring your own responses to this representation of children.
7. Toward the end of "New African," Sarah runs from the baptismal pool at the front of the church, her teeth chattering even in the hot church as she realizes she has just won her first "battle with a grownup." Freewrite for a few minutes about any memories you may have of a significant "battle with a grownup." Then write a brief essay in which you explain what lessons you may have learned about yourself from that struggle.

JOHN PAUL II
A Minority by the Year 2000

THE AUTHOR OF a best-selling book and Time *magazine's man-of-the-year in 1994 was not a politician, rock star, or sports hero, but an aging and ailing Pole who had led the Roman Catholic Church for almost twenty years, John Paul II (b. 1920). The editors of* Time *chose to acknowledge the confidence of the pope's moral vision in an era of shifting values and relativistic principles. Some of that confidence is evident in the following selection from his book* Crossing the Threshold of Hope *(1995), in which John Paul responds to a question about the future of the church posed to him by the interviewer Vittorio Messori. I chose this selection less because of the position John Paul stakes out than because of the evangelical voice we hear.*

The religious tradition over which John Paul presides as the 263rd pope in a line stretching back to Saint Peter recognizes him as the vicar of Christ, his words carrying authority that Americans today invest perhaps only in portions of the Constitution and the Declaration of Independence. The pope speaks decisively in this short selection, but not in imperatives; his examination of the status of the church in the world today is both philosophical and pastoral, and we encounter the convictions of a moral tradition passed down from pope to council to faithful for almost two millennia. Religion here is more than awe in the presence of a swelling choir or feelings of solidarity with planetary auras; it is relentless struggle to understand and then act on the imperatives of God, partly revealed and partly mysterious: "Always and everywhere the Gospel will be a challenge to human weakness." — J.R.

[Vittorio Messori:] Pardon me, Your Holiness, but my role (which gives me great honor but also a certain responsibility) is also that of a respectful "provocateur" with regard to questions—even troubling ones—which are also present among Catholics.

I will continue, then, by observing how you have frequently recalled—with an awareness of the symbolic importance of the event—the approach of the third millennium of the Redemption. According to statistical projections, by the year 2000, for the first time in history, Muslims will outnumber Catholics.* Already Hindus alone are more numerous than Protestants and Orthodox Greeks and Slavs combined. In your pastoral journeys around the

---

Muslims will outnumber Catholics: For another perspective on these statistics, see Diana L. Eck, "In the Name of Religions," p. 212.

world, you have often visited places where believers in Christ, and Catholics in particular, are a small and even shrinking minority.

How do you feel when faced with this reality, after twenty centuries of evangelization? What divine plan do you see at work here?

[John Paul II:] I think that such a view of the problem arises from a somewhat simplistic interpretation of the matter. In reality, the essence goes far deeper, as I have already tried to explain in my response to the preceding question. Here statistics are not useful—we are speaking of *values which are not quantifiable.*

To tell the truth, the sociology of religion—although useful in other areas—does not help much here. As a basis for assessment, the criteria for measurement which it provides do not help when considering people's interior attitude. *No statistic* aiming at a quantitative measurement of faith (for example, the number of people who participate in religious ceremonies) will get to the heart of the matter. *Here numbers alone are not enough.*

The question you ask—albeit "provocatively," as you say—amounts to this: let us count the number of Muslims in the world, or the number of Hindus, *let us count the number of Catholics,* or Christians in general, and we can determine which religion is in the majority, *which has a future ahead of it,* and which instead seems to belong only to the past, or is undergoing a systematic process of decomposition and decline.

From the point of view of the Gospel the issue is completely different. Christ says: *"Do not be afraid any longer, little flock,* for your Father is pleased to give you the kingdom" (Lk 12:32). I think that in these words Christ best responds to this problem that some find troubling and that is raised in your question. Jesus goes even further when He asks: "When the Son of Man comes, will he find faith on earth?" (cf. Lk 18:8).

Both this question and the earlier saying about the little flock indicate the profound realism which inspired Jesus in dealing with His apostles. *He did not prepare them for easy success.* He spoke clearly, He spoke of the persecutions that awaited those who would believe in Him. At the same time, *He established a solid foundation for the faith.* "The Father was pleased to give the Kingdom" to those twelve men from Galilee, and through them to all humanity. He forewarned them that the mission He sent them on would involve opposition and persecution because He Himself had been persecuted: "If they persecuted me, they will also persecute you." But He hastened to add: "If they kept my word, they will also keep yours" (cf. Jn 15:20).

Since my youth I have felt that the heart of the Gospel is contained in these words. *The Gospel is not a promise of easy success.* It does not promise a comfortable life to anyone. It makes demands and, at the same time, it is *a great promise*—the promise of eternal life for man, who is subject to the law of death, and the promise of victory through faith for man, who is subject to many trials and setbacks.

The Gospel contains a *fundamental paradox:* to find life, one must lose   10
life; to be born, one must die; to save oneself, one must take up the cross. This is the essential truth of the Gospel, which always and everywhere is bound to meet with man's protest.

Always and everywhere the Gospel will be a challenge to human weakness. But precisely in this challenge lies all its power. Man, perhaps, subconsciously waits for such a challenge; *indeed, man feels the inner need to transcend himself.* Only in transcending himself does man become fully human (cf. Blaise Pascal, *Pensées,* ęd. Brunschvicg, 434: "Apprenez que l'homme passe infiniment l'homme").

This is the most profound truth about man. *Christ is the first to know this truth.* He truly knows "that which is in every man" (cf. Jn 2:25). With His Gospel He has touched the intimate truth of man. He has touched it first of all with His Cross. Pilate, who, pointing to the Nazarene crowned with thorns after His scourging, said, "Behold, the man!" (Jn 19:5), did not realize that he was proclaiming an essential truth, expressing that which always and everywhere remains the heart of evangelization.

QUESTIONING THE TEXT

1. After reading "A Minority by the Year 2000," brainstorm three additional questions you would ask the pope if you were doing the interview.
2. In the introduction to "A Minority by the Year 2000," J.R. asserts that religion is more than "awe in the presence of a swelling choir." Who might J.R. be referring to in such an implied criticism? Review the introduction and speculate.

MAKING CONNECTIONS

3. How does the attitude toward faith in "A Minority by the Year 2000" compare with that expressed in Kathleen Norris's "Little Girls in Church" (p. 223)? Write a paragraph exploring any differences, but also look for commonalities.
4. Does the confidence of John Paul II in "A Minority by the Year 2000" or of Martin Luther King Jr. in "Our God Is Able" (p. 154) strengthen the appeal of their arguments or hinder their ability to communicate with people who hold different views of the world? You might com-

pare the ways these men teach with the way a moral lesson is presented in Yaffa Eliach's "Good Morning, Herr Müller" (p. 218) or Andrea Lee's "New African" (p. 196).

JOINING THE CONVERSATION

5. John Paul underscores this line in his text: *The Gospel is not a promise of easy success.* What sorts of difficulties do people of faith either encounter or cause in the world as you experience it? Write a short essay exploring the issue.
6. Spend some time in the library reading about the history and character of the papacy. Generate a series of questions about the role of the papacy in the modern world. Then interview several Catholic friends and acquaintances, using your questions to explore their attitudes toward the pope. Write your findings in a short report to your classmates, explaining how you gathered your information and qualifying your conclusions appropriately according to the size and representativeness of your sample.

DIANA L. ECK
In the Name of Religions

DIANA L. ECK (b. 1945), in this selection from her essay "In the Name of Religions," suggests that Americans today need new ways of thinking about their surging and often contentious religious diversity. In 1893, when the first World Parliament of Religions met in Chicago, the United States thought of itself as a Protestant nation with a significant Catholic minority and a much smaller community of Jews. Other religious groups, when they registered on the national consciousness at all, probably seemed either eccentric or heathen. So representatives of the Buddhist, Hindu, or Muslim faiths who attended the Chicago conference must surely have felt that they had entered an alien world on the shores of Lake Michigan. Still, the intellectual mood of the times was buoyant and forward looking, expressed in the concept of "universalism," a belief that under the skin, all religions shared core values and that people of goodwill would work toward harmony and understanding.

One hundred difficult years later, when a second Chicago World Congress of Religions met in 1993, much had changed in the United States and the world, including its ethnic and religious landscapes and allegiances. Eck's essay surveys some of those remarkable shifts. The most religious of Western nations is no longer exclusively Western in its orientation. Universalism has all but been forgotten in the United States and elsewhere, rejected both by fundamentalists who seek to preserve the uniqueness of their belief and by pluralists who seek paths to harmony mindful of individual religious differences. The world map of faith is clearly more complex than ever and more challenging.

Diana L. Eck is a professor of comparative religion at Harvard and the author of Encountering God: A Spiritual Journey from Bozeman to Banaras *(1993). Her full essay appeared in the* Wilson Quarterly *(Autumn 1993).* – J.R.

The religious demography of the West has changed radically during the past century, and especially the past quarter century, making the questions of the World's Parliament of 1893 increasingly the questions of every city council in 1993. When the delegates from Asia came to the Parliament, they traveled halfway around the world by boat. Vivekananda, coming from Calcutta, arrived in Chicago too early for the Parliament, ran out of money after 10 days, and by chance met a woman from Boston who put up the young Hindu at her farm in the Boston area for several weeks. He quickly became the toast of the North Shore, where scarcely anyone had met a Hindu before. In 1893, one could have counted the number of Hindus in this country on the fingers of one hand. One hundred years ago, Buddhists, Hindus, Sikhs, and Jains lived in Asia; Muslims, in the wide stretch of the Islamic world from Indonesia to Morocco.

Today, however, the religious landscape of the United states alone displays the diversity of traditions that were present at the World's Parliament. Had Vivekananda come to this year's centennial celebration of the Parliament, he would have been welcomed by a Hindu host committee in the Chicago area (a group that organized a fund-raising dinner that netted $45,000 for the centennial gathering). Had he traveled to Boston he would have found tens of thousands of Indian immigrants—engineers, doctors, and businesspeople—and he would have been greeted at Bengali picnics, Tamil festivals, and Hindu summer family camps. He would have visited the Sri Lakshmi temple in Boston, consecrated in 1991 with the waters of the Ganges mingled with the waters of the Mississippi and the Missouri.

At the time of the Parliament, the Statue of Liberty raised her torch-bearing arm of refuge in New York harbor, facing the Atlantic. In San Francisco, however, at least after the railways were built by using cheap Chinese labor, the language of welcome for the tired and the poor was replaced by the language of exclusion. The first Chinese Exclusion Act was passed in 1882 and revised regularly for several decades, gradually dilating to include other Asians. In 1923, the U.S. Supreme Court ruled that Bhagat Thind, a Sikh who had settled in California and married an American woman, could be stripped of his naturalized U.S. citizenship because he was a Hindu, by which the court meant his race, not his religion. Such was the disposition of America toward Asia. At the Parliament, a Buddhist delegate from Japan called attention to the "No Japanese" signs posted at establishments on the West Coast. "If such be Christian ethics," he declared, "we are perfectly satisfied to remain heathen."

Since the Immigration Act of 1965, however, immigrants from throughout the world have entered the United States in greater numbers than ever before. According to the 1990 census, the "Asian and Pacific Islander" population is by far the fastest growing, having increased more than sevenfold since 1965. This group includes Hindus, Muslims, Jains, and Sikhs from South Asia, Christians and Muslims from the Philippines, and Buddhists and Christians from Southeast and East Asia. From refugees to voluntary immigrants, from unskilled workers to highly trained professionals, these newcomers have changed the cultural and religious landscape of the United States.

A century ago, the monks in the Japanese temple of Engaku-ji tried to 5 dissuade their leader, Soyen Shaku, from attending the Parliament, arguing that it would not be fitting for a Zen monk to set foot in such an uncivilized land as America. He insisted, however. (The young monk who drafted his letter of acceptance in English was D. T. Suzuki, later to become the greatest translator of the Zen tradition to the West.) Were Soyen Shaku to arrive in San Francisco today, he would find headquartered in a multistory office building the Buddhist Churches of America. He would find not only immigrant Buddhist communities from Japan, China, and Vietnam but a multitude of Euro-American Buddhists, including *roshis,* or teachers, initiated by Asian mentors. He would find American Buddhist newspapers and magazines, feminist Zen sitting groups, and a Zen AIDS Hospice Project.

In 1893, the Sultan of Turkey declined to send delegates from the Muslim world to Chicago. Today, the United States is part of the Muslim world. Even if a conservative estimate of three to five million is used, Muslims outnumber Episcopalians in the United States. Within a short time there will surely be more Muslims than Jews. In June 1991, Imam Siraj Wahaj of Brooklyn opened a session of the U.S. Congress with Islamic prayers, the first imam ever to do so. On Labor Day weekend each year, more than 5,000 American Muslims attend the annual convention of the Islamic Society of North America. There they discuss American public schools and American politics. The youth network organizes summer camps and Islamic leadership workshops. The Islamic Medical Association discusses ethical issues in medical practice.

The symbolic diversity of the 1893 Parliament has today become the reality of its host city. Chicago's yellow pages list dozens of entries under the headings "Churches: Buddhist" and "Churches: Islamic." The Muslims of Chicago say there are more than 70 mosques in the metropolitan area and nearly half a million Muslims. The suburbs of Lemont and Aurora boast two impressive Hindu temples—both built from the ground up by Hindu temple architects cooperating with American engineers and contractors. There are 50 Buddhist temples in the Midwest Buddhist Association. There are Jain temples and Sikh *gurudwaras,* a Zoroastrian temple, and a Bahai temple. The Council for a Parliament of the World's Religions, the local Chicago planning team for the centennial, is more representative of the diversity and complexity of the world's religions than the Parliament itself was.

The interreligious encounter that was engineered by visionaries in Chicago in 1893 is today an American main street affair. A parliament of sorts could be duplicated in almost every major American city. There are five mosques in Oklahoma City (none, incidentally, with a sign saying it is a mosque) along with four Hindu temples, one Sikh *gurudwara,* two Vietnamese Buddhist temples, and one Thai Buddhist temple. And Oklahoma City is far from unusual. Denver has 11 Buddhist temples serving its immigrant Asian population, including an older Japanese Jodo Shinshu temple, and more recently Thai, Cambodian, Korean, and Laotian temples have been established as well as six Vietnamese Buddhist temples. Denver also has three mosques, two Sikh *gurudwaras,* two Hindu temples, and a Taoist temple. All of this new diversity burgeoned in the years between 1970 and 1990.

These changes are not unique to the United States. Today's unprecedented economic and political migration of peoples—the United Nations has recently estimated that two percent of the world's population now lives outside its country of origin—has changed the map of the world. Hindus live in Leicester, Buddhists in Boston, and Muslims in Heidelberg. The new immigration has produced a spate of neonativist movements in North America and Europe, but it has also produced a whole range of new religious, cultural, and intellectual encounters. It has brought interfaith relations from the international to the local scene. It has drawn attention to the stereotypes which, for many, constitute the extent of their knowledge of other religious traditions. And it has heightened the significance of religious literacy as a basic component of education.

The interaction of peoples and traditions in the 20th century has produced much that is new—distinctively Balinese or south Indian forms of Christianity, distinctively North American Hindu communities, marriages between Christians and Muslims, Jews for Jesus, neopagan environmentalist movements, and many forms of religious syncretism. The wide variety of religious life in the 20th century seems, to some, to threaten and blur the boundaries of identity—which is one reason for the resurgence of religious exclusivism and fundamentalism.

10

The universalism so dominant 100 years ago is now challenged by fundamentalists and pluralists alike, though for different reasons. For the fundamentalist, the very idea that all religions have a common kernel and core undermines the particularity of one's own faith and reduces those well-defended boundaries to mere husks. For the pluralist, universalism poses a more covert problem. As the Parliament so clearly demonstrated, and as the early phases of the comparative study of religion confirmed, the universal is usually somebody's particular writ large. Pluralism, however, is a distinctively different perspective. The pluralist does not expect or desire the emergence of a universal religion, a kind of religious Esperanto. Nor does the pluralist seek a common essence in all religions, though much that is common may be discovered. The commitment of the pluralist is rather to engage the diversity, in the mutually transformative process of understanding, rather than to obliterate it.

Benedict Anderson, in *Imagined Communities* (1983), investigates the ways in which nations envision themselves. Even when citizens do not know one another, "in the minds of each lives the image of their communion." The imagined community of religious traditions is even more deeply rooted than that of the nation-state. Religious communalism, both national and international, is a powerful force in today's world, but one might suggest that religious exclusivism or chauvinism that depends for its survival upon the isolation of one people from another is bound, finally, to fail. In the late 20th century, the old imagined communities are in the process of tumultuous change. East and West are no more. We speak of the "former Soviet Union" and the "former Yugoslavia." "Christendom" and "the Islamic world" have no identifiable geographical borders. There are Sikh mayors in Britain and Muslim mayors in Texas. The Buddha would smile at the collapse of our reifications.

Recently, Harvard political scientist Samuel Huntington spoke of the new geopolitical reality of "the West and the rest" and proposed that "civilizational identity" will have a major role in the coming political realignment. He contends that the Confucian, Islamic, and Hindu worlds will be forces to reckon with. But where exactly are these worlds? With mosques in every major Western city and a thriving panoply of Asian-American subcultures, it is difficult to know what he means. It is precisely the interpenetration and proximity of ancient civilizations and cultures that is the hallmark of the late 20th century.

Finding new forms of imagined communities—national and international, religious and interreligious—is one of the more challenging tasks of our time. The worlds of technology, business, and communications have put concerted effort into the imagining of transnational networks of activity and loyalty, for better or for worse. Even the political and military implications of our global situation have received attention. Yet the careful construction of forms of interreligious communication and cooperation that might be considered part of the basic infrastructure of the world of the 20th century lags behind. And in academia, the comparative study of religion, still in its infancy in many parts of the world, is just beginning to develop the dynamic and dialogical models adequate to the interpretive task. The centennial of the World's Parliament of Religions, however, gives evidence of a radically new multireligious social reality—in Chicago and throughout the world. The move in the past century from idealized Protestant universalism to the difficult dialogue of real pluralism is a step in the right direction.

QUESTIONING THE TEXT

1. What is the most surprising fact you discovered in reading "In the Name of Religions"? Explore that fact or observation, teasing out its implications.
2. Do you understand the differences between universalism, fundamentalism, and pluralism as Eck uses these terms in her essay? Working in a group—preferably one that includes members from several different faiths—explore the terms as they relate to differences among religious communities.

3. Characterize the tone of the introduction to "In the Name of Religions." What attitudes—if any—does the introduction convey toward Eck's essay?

MAKING CONNECTIONS

4. Review Stephen L. Carter's "The Culture of Disbelief" (p. 175), and then write an essay explaining the difficulties that mainstream American groups—including the legal community and the news media—might have dealing with the beliefs of religious groups relatively new to the United States.
5. Read Eck's essay alongside Pope John Paul II's "A Minority by the Year 2000." How do you think individual religious communities are apt to react to the need for what Eck describes as "interreligious communication and cooperation"?

JOINING THE CONVERSATION

6. Eck suggests that religious literacy ought to be a basic part of education. In a group, discuss the problem of religious literacy; then write a proposal outlining a possible college-level course in religious literacy.
7. Use the phone book or local World Wide Web sites to explore the religious diversity of your own community. Write a report detailing your discoveries.
8. Use the library to write a brief essay about a religious community, tradition, belief, or practice with which you are only remotely familiar. If possible, have a member of the faith about which you are writing read your essay in draft stage. Narrow the scope of your essay to a specific tradition or practice; don't try to explain Buddhism in three pages.

YAFFA ELIACH
Good Morning, Herr Müller

THE HASIDIC TALE is a product of a Jewish religious movement called Ha-sidism that arose in eastern Europe in the eighteenth century, spreading a mes-sage of piety, optimism, and humanity among various religious communities. The earliest tales were heavy with folklore elements, but they soon developed into a literary genre themselves, examining the spirit of religion in the lives of common folk and their zaddiks. The zaddik was an exemplar of piety and faith, what Christians might describe as a saint.

In this century, Hasidic tales, always concerned with good and evil, con-fronted a new and horrible reality—the devastating persecution of the Jewish people in Europe under the Nazi terror we now call the Holocaust. From the raw material of oral histories and interviews, Yaffa Eliach, a Polish-born profes-sor of history and literature at Brooklyn College, gathered Holocaust memories circulating among Hasidic communities in Hasidic Tales of the Holocaust *(1982). I chose "Good Morning, Herr Müller" from Eliach's book because the simple decency of the rabbi in the story embodies one powerful aspect of the reli-gious life. The story also explores, in its own way, the presence of others.* —J.R.

Near the city of Danzig lived a well-to-do Hasidic rabbi, scion of prominent Hasidic dynasties. Dressed in a tailored black suit, wearing a top hat, and carrying a silver walking cane, the rabbi would take his daily morn-ing stroll, accompanied by his tall, handsome son-in-law. During his morning walk it was the rabbi's custom to greet every man, woman, and child whom he met on his way with a warm smile and a cordial "Good morning." Over the years the rabbi became acquainted with many of his fellow townspeople this way and would always greet them by their proper title and name.

Near the outskirts of town, in the fields, he would exchange greetings with Herr Müller, a Polish *Volksdeutsche* (ethnic German). "Good morning, Herr Müller!" the rabbi would hasten to greet the man who worked in the fields. "Good morning, Herr Rabbiner!" would come the response with a good-natured smile.

Then the war began. The rabbi's strolls stopped abruptly. Herr Müller donned an S.S. uniform and disappeared from the fields.[1] The fate of the

---

[1]After the German occupation of Poland, many *Volksdeutschen* were eager to serve the Nazi cause. They joined the Nazis and took revenge upon their Polish neighbors in reprisal for the alleged anti-*Volksdeutschen* pogroms that took place in Poland in the late 1930s. See Hans Schadeaaldt, comp., *Polish Acts of Atrocity against the German Minority in Poland: Documenting Evi-dence,* published for the German Foreign Office (Berlin/New York, 1940).

rabbi was like that of much of the rest of Polish Jewry. He lost his family in the death camp of Treblinka and, after great suffering, was deported to Auschwitz.

One day, during a selection at Auschwitz, the rabbi stood on line with hundreds of other Jews awaiting the moment when their fates would be decided, for life or death. Dressed in a striped camp uniform, head and beard shaven and eyes feverish from starvation and disease, the rabbi looked like a walking skeleton. "Right! Left, left, left!" The voice in the distance drew nearer. Suddenly the rabbi had a great urge to see the face of the man with the snow-white gloves, small baton, and steely voice who played God and decided who should live and who should die. He lifted his eyes and heard his own voice speaking:

"Good morning, Herr Müller!"   5

"Good morning, Herr Rabbiner!" responded a human voice beneath the S.S. cap adorned with skull and bones. "What are you doing here?" A faint smile appeared on the rabbi's lips. The baton moved to the right—to life. The following day, the rabbi was transferred to a safer camp.

The rabbi, now in his eighties, told me in his gentle voice, "This is the power of a good-morning greeting. A man must always greet his fellow man."

QUESTIONING THE TEXT

1. How might you explain the emphasis the story puts on the fact that the rabbi greets everyone by "their proper title and name"? Who is Herr Müller at the beginning of the tale, and what has he become when the rabbi greets him at Auschwitz?
2. The rabbi draws one clear lesson from his encounter with Herr Müller at Auschwitz: "A man must always greet his fellow man." Working with several classmates, make a list of additional lessons the story might teach.
3. How might your reading of "Good Morning, Herr Müller" have been different without the information in the introduction on Hasidic tales?

MAKING CONNECTIONS

4. Review Stephen L. Carter's "The Culture of Disbelief" (p. 175), and then explore this question: Would it be appropriate for students in public schools to read Hasidic tales like "Good Morning, Herr Müller"? Defend your opinion in a paragraph.
5. Both "Good Morning, Herr Müller" and Andrea Lee's "New African" (p. 196) are religious stories. But they also differ significantly in tone, purpose, and even length. Write a brief analysis of the two stories, exploring the different ways they try to move you to think about moral experiences.

JOINING THE CONVERSATION

6. In a group, share moral tales you may recall from times past—they need not be religious in character. Then try your hand at writing a tale structured like "Good Morning, Herr Müller."
7. Use the library to find out more about the way the history of the Holocaust has been recorded and told. Write a research report on one aspect of this important story.

THE QUR'AN
Prayer

PRAYERS FORM A VERY IMPORTANT PART *of the Qur'an, the holy text that records the revelations of God to Muhammad and guides the many millions of people who follow Islam. The Arabic word* Qur'an *can be translated as "recitation," reflecting the divine commandment to Muhammad to go forward and "recite" the wisdom of God. Indeed, recitation is a key practice for faithful Muslims, who commit the Qur'an to memory—in its original and beautiful Arabic. My friend Lahoucine Ouzgane, who grew up with the Qur'an, says that hearing the text recited by a gifted reader is an "unforgettably powerful experience." This is one text, Ouzgane says, that really "must be heard."*

Among the most important of Muslim duties are confessing faith by reciting the shahada *("There is no other god but God, and Muhammad is the Prophet of God"); praying—at dawn, at noon, in the afternoon, at dusk, and at night; fasting during Ramadan (the ninth month of the Islamic year); giving to the needy; and, if possible, making a pilgrimage to the holy city of Mecca. Given the importance of prayer, it seems particularly appropriate that the first of the Qur'an's 114 chapters is itself a brief prayer, which follows. Readers familiar with the Christian Lord's Prayer may recognize some resonances between these two important religious texts.*

Census Bureau figures tell us that, of the large number of faiths practiced in the United States today, Islam is strong and growing. For this reason, and because I have long been fascinated by the many similar stories that seem to occur across religious texts, I include a passage from the Qur'an here. – A.L.

In the name of God, the merciful, the compassionate.
Praise be to God, Lord of the worlds,
The merciful, the compassionate,
Master of the day of judgment.
You alone we serve; to You alone we cry for help.   5
Guide us in the straight path,
The path of those You have blessed;
Not of those who have incurred Your anger,
Nor of those who go astray.

QUESTIONING THE TEXT

1. The Qur'an has been translated into scores of languages, including English. Although people who know it in Arabic say that the translations fail to capture the original's richness, beauty, and unique flavor, the English text has its own sense of directness, of deep longings rendered in simple language. What strikes you as the most powerful line in this translation of the Islamic prayer? Why have you chosen this line?
2. How do you know this is a prayer? What characteristics lead you to that conclusion? Make a list of these characteristics and bring them to class for discussion.
3. What words or phrases are repeated most often in this prayer? What effect do these repetitions have?
4. Why do you think A.L. quotes her "friend, Lahoucine Ouzgane" in the introduction?

MAKING CONNECTIONS

5. Read this prayer and then look back at the sermon by Martin Luther King Jr. (p. 154). What similarities do you find between the "Gods" that appear in each?
6. For which, if any, of the other pieces in this chapter would this prayer be an appropriate part? Write a brief explanation of your choice.

JOINING THE CONVERSATION

7. Write a "prayer" of your own, one that sums up your own wishes and needs—and those of others you care for—in the most eloquent way possible.
8. Working with several classmates, do some research on the history and teachings of the Qur'an. Assign a classmate to get a copy of the entire text and, if possible, another copy in Arabic so that you can see what the original looks like. Ask another classmate to look up some commentary on or interpretations of the text. And assign a third classmate to interview someone from the religious studies department, someone who teaches courses in philosophy of religion, or someone on your faculty who attends a local mosque and knows the Qur'an to gather additional information about this religious text. Pool your findings and, together, prepare a 20-minute presentation for your class on "Introducing the Qur'an."

KATHLEEN NORRIS
Little Girls in Church

KATHLEEN NORRIS (b. 1947) has published many works since graduating from Bennington College in 1969. In addition to Little Girls in Church, *from which the following poem is taken, Norris has published five poetry chapbooks and two other full-length books of poetry,* Falling Off *(1971), and* The Middle of the World *(1981). Although she lives in western South Dakota with her husband, the poet David Dwyer, she has written two compelling nonfiction books while living in monasteries, including* Dakota: A Spiritual Geography *(1993). In* Cloister Walk *(1996), a second book of nonfiction, she continues her exploration of spiritual places and spaces. Her favorite piece in this latest book, Norris says, is one that describes and reflects on the wide-ranging responses that Benedictine nuns gave to her question of why they do or do not wear habits.*

Norris's poem "Little Girls in Church" also records a wide range of responses to the question of faith and its relationship to institutionalized religion. For me, the poem calls up the many Sundays I spent in my grandmother's Baptist church and in my parents' Presbyterian one, days that run together in my memory of Bible-school stories (I still vividly recall Joseph and his Coat of Many Colors), covered-dish suppers, prayer meetings, and songs—lots and lots of songs. I wonder what memories Norris's words may evoke for you. — A.L.

I

I've made friends
with a five-year-old
Presbyterian. She tugs at her lace collar,
I sympathize. We're both bored.
I give her a pencil;   5
she draws the moon,
grass, stars, and
I name them for her,
printing in large letters.
The church bulletin   10
begins to fill.
Carefully, she prints her name
on it, *KATHY*, and hands it back.

Just last week,
in New York City, the Orthodox liturgy   15
was typically intimate,
casual. An old woman greeted the icons
one by one
and fell asleep
during the Great Litany.   20
People went in and out,
to smoke cigarettes and chat on the steps.

A girl with long brown braids
was led to the icons
by her mother. They kissed each one,   25
and the girl made a confession
to the youngest priest. I longed to hear it,
to know her name.

II

I worry for the girls.
I once had braids,   30
and wore lace that made me suffer.
I had not yet done the things
that would need forgiving.

Church was for singing, and so I sang.
I received a Bible, stars   35
for all the verses;
I turned and ran.

The music brought me back
from time to time,
singing hymns   40
in the great breathing body
of a congregation.
And once in Paris, as
I stepped into Notre Dame
to get out of the rain,   45
the organist began to play:
I stood rooted to the spot,
looked up, and believed.

It didn't last.
Dear girls, my friends,   50
may you find great love
within you, starlike
and wild, as wide as grass,
solemn as the moon.
I will pray for you, if I can.   55

IN RESPONSE

1. Norris's narrator talks about the songs and hymns of the church she attended. What songs or lullabies do you remember from your childhood? Choose one, and jot down what you remember of its words and
   what you liked (or disliked) about it. Bring your notes to class for discussion.
2. Think for a while about your own spiritual and/or religious beliefs—or
   about your secular beliefs. Then try your hand at writing a brief poem
   that would capture the essence of those beliefs. Bring your poem to
   class to share with others.
3. What in Norris's poem helps readers understand why she "worr[ies] for
   the girls"?

OTHER READINGS

Coughlin, John J. "Religion, Education and the First Amendment." *America* 15 May 1993: 12. Argues that the First Amendment was never intended to keep religion out of public life or schools.

Norris, Kathleen. *Dakota: A Spiritual Geography.* New York: Ticknor, 1993. A memoir about place and spirituality.

Remnick, David. "The Devil Problem." *New Yorker* 3 April 1995: 54–65. An article concerning Elaine Pagels, author of "The Gnostic Gospels" and *What Is Satan.*

Schoenberger, Chana. "Getting to Know about You and Me." *Newsweek* 20 Sept. 1993: 8. Looks at religious prejudice and ignorance in American high schools.

Winter, Miriam Therese. "The Women-Church Movement." *Christian Century* 8 Mar. 1989: 258–60. Describes an interdenominational movement of women seeking freedom from the limits of traditional church structures.

ELECTRONIC RESOURCES

Catholic Information Center on Internet (CICI):
    hhtp://www.catholic.net/
    Lists Web sites with information about Catholicism.

Christian Internet Directory:
    http://www.bakerbooks.com/ccc/cid/
    Provides a listing of Christian sites.

Islamic Resources:
    http://latif.com/welcome.html
    Lists Web sites with information about Islam.

Judaism and Jewish Resources:
    http://shamash.org/trb/judaism.html
    Lists Web sites with information about Judaism.

The Official Internet Site of the Church of Jesus Christ of Latter-Day Saints:
    http://www.lds.org/
    Lists Web sites with information about the Church of Jesus Christ of Latter-Day Saints.

The World Wide Web Virtual Library: Religion:
    http://sunfly.ub.uni-freiburg.de/religion/
    Lists Web sites covering a wide range of world religions.

Science:
O Brave New World

Look closely at this page taken from a NASA Web site. What seems to be the major purpose of this page? How is the visual text organized, and what effect does that organization have on your ability to "read" it? What details are included and emphasized? What other details might have been included—and why do you think they may have been omitted? How do the words add to or affect the way the images work to create meaning? What does this image suggest to you about the values, status, and general aims of late twentieth-century science?

Learn from me . . . how dangerous is the acquirement of knowledge and how much happier that man is who believes his native town to be the world, than he who aspires to become greater than his nature will allow.

MARY SHELLEY, *Frankenstein*

Should we stop short of learning about some things, for fear of what we, or someone, will do with the knowledge?

LEWIS THOMAS, *The Hazards of Science*

A lot of Neo-Luddites and techno-resisters today, I think, have made bad choices by saying that they can use the tools of the masters in order to free the slaves. I don't think this is possible.

KEVIN KELLY, *Interview with the Luddite*

Resistance to science is born of fear. Fear, in turn, is bred by ignorance. And it is ignorance that is our deepest malady.

J. MICHAEL BISHOP, *Enemies of Promise*

The portrait of the body conveyed most often and most vividly in the mass media shows it as a defended nation-state, organized around a hierarchy of gender, race, and class.

EMILY MARTIN, *The Body at War*

The leader of the electronic tribe would not be the person who knew most, but the one who could execute the broadest range of technical functions. What, I hesitate to ask, would become of the already anti-quated notion of wisdom?

SVEN BIRKERTS, *Perseus Unbound*

Unlike snowflakes, there are only three types of raindrops.

MATTHEW ROHRER, *Found in the Museum of Old Science*

Introduction

TIME AND AGAIN in the twentieth century, we have found our industrial society—like the hero of Mary Shelley's *Frankenstein* (1818)—creating and using technologies that drive it beyond the limits of moral, legal, and ethical precedents. Indeed, there seem to be no boundaries to what the human imagination can first contemplate and then achieve. Scientists have already mapped out the genes that control life, performed surgery in the womb, extracted the secrets of the atom, and planned colonies in outer space. Occasionally, experiments escape our control and we watch them poison our landscapes or explode before our eyes. But the quest for knowledge continues.

Julius Caesar, a military genius and a shrewd politician, observed once that "it is better to have expanded the frontiers of the mind than to have pushed back the boundaries of the empire." As Caesar doubtless understood, the two are often the same thing, the powers of mind enabling one people or nation to dominate others, to cast itself in the role of a god and its neighbors as servants or slaves.

This chapter is designed to explore the resonances of *Frankenstein*, the many questions it raises, and the ways it makes us think about science, progress, and alienation. In our mythologies, ancient and modern, we show a fondness for rebels like Victor Frankenstein, who would steal the fire of the gods and, with their new knowledge, shake the foundations of empires. Yet we cannot entirely identify with such figures either. They remain a threat to us too, a reminder that humanity finally lacks the wisdom to play God.

Your own thinking about these issues may be stimulated by considering the following questions:

- Why do contemporary readers (and moviegoers) continue to find *Frankenstein* fascinating?

- What makes the intellectual dreamer or rebel an attractive figure?

- Why does a society usually react with suspicion toward people who, like Victor Frankenstein's monster, seem different? How do we define the outsider? How does the outsider act as a result?

- What motivates people to explore what is unknown and possibly dangerous?

- Does scientific progress always entail some loss or disruptive change? You might want to discuss this issue with a group of classmates.

• • •

MARY SHELLEY
Frankenstein

WITH FRANKENSTEIN, Mary Shelley (1797–1851) created a myth as pow-
erful, complex, and frightening as the monster in the novel itself. The book in-
trigues us today as a narrative with many dimensions and interpretations. It
works as the story of a scientist whose ambitions exceed his understanding, as an
account of a scientific project that begins with great promise but leads to disaster,
as the lament of an alien creature spurned by his maker, as the tract of an out-
sider besieged by his sense of difference, as the protest of a rebel striking out
against a conventional and restrictive society.

The daughter of early feminist Mary Wollstonecraft and political theorist
William Godwin and the wife of Percy Bysshe Shelley, Mary Shelley began
Frankenstein; or, The Modern Prometheus, *to use its full title, in the*
summer of 1816 after the poet Byron invited his friends at a lake resort in
Switzerland to "each write a ghost story." The short piece she composed even-
tually grew through several revisions (1818, 1823, 1831) into the novel we
know today.

The protagonist of her work, Victor Frankenstein, is an ambitious young
scholar who discovers how to bestow "animation upon lifeless matter." He uses
this knowledge to assemble a grotesque manlike creature, and then, horrified by
what he has done, abandons it the moment he brings it to life. The following
selection from the novel is Victor's account of those events. – J.R.

I see by your eagerness, and the wonder and hope which your eyes express, my friend, that you expect to be informed of the secret with which I
am acquainted; that cannot be: listen patiently until the end of my story, and
you will easily perceive why I am reserved upon that subject. I will not lead
you on, unguarded and ardent as I then was, to your destruction and infallible
misery. Learn from me, if not by my precepts, at least by my example, how
dangerous is the acquirement of knowledge, and how much happier that man
is who believes his native town to be the world, than he who aspires to become greater than his nature will allow.

When I found so astonishing a power placed within my hands, I hesitated a long time concerning the manner in which I should employ it. Although I possessed the capacity of bestowing animation, yet to prepare a
frame for the reception of it, with all its intricacies of fibers, muscles, and
veins, still remained a work of inconceivable difficulty and labour. I doubted
at first whether I should attempt the creation of a being like myself, or one of
simpler organization; but my imagination was too much exalted by my first

success to permit me to doubt of my ability to give life to an animal as complex and wonderful as man. The materials at present within my command hardly appeared adequate to so arduous an undertaking; but I doubted not that I should ultimately succeed. I prepared myself for a multitude of reverses; my operations might be incessantly baffled, and at last my work be imperfect: yet, when I considered the improvement which every day takes place in science and mechanics, I was encouraged to hope my present attempts would at least lay the foundations of future success. Nor could I consider the magnitude and complexity of my plan as any argument of its impracticability. It was with these feelings that I began the creation of a human being. As the minuteness of the parts formed a great hindrance to my speed, I resolved, contrary to my first intention, to make the being of a gigantic stature; that is to say, about eight feet in height, and proportionably large. After having formed this determination, and having spent some months in successfully collecting and arranging my materials, I began.

No one can conceive the variety of feelings which bore me onwards, like a hurricane, in the first enthusiasm of success. Life and death appeared to me ideal bounds, which I should first break through, and pour a torrent of light into our dark world. A new species would bless me as its creator and source; many happy and excellent natures would owe their being to me. No father could claim the gratitude of his child so completely as I should deserve theirs. Pursuing these reflections, I thought, that if I could bestow animation upon lifeless matter, I might in process of time (although I now found it impossible) renew life where death had apparently devoted the body to corruption.

These thoughts supported my spirits, while I pursued my undertaking with unremitting ardour. My cheek had grown pale with study, and my person had become emaciated with confinement. Sometimes, on the very brink of certainty, I failed; yet still I clung to the hope which the next day or the next hour might realize. One secret which I alone possessed was the hope to which I had dedicated myself; and the moon gazed on my midnight labors, while, with unrelaxed and breathless eagerness, I pursued nature to her hiding-places. Who shall conceive the horrors of my secret toil, as I dabbled among the unhallowed damps of the grave, or tortured the living animal to animate the lifeless clay? My limbs now tremble, and my eyes swim with the remembrance; but then a resistless, and almost frantic, impulse, urged me forward; I seemed to have lost all soul or sensation but for this one pursuit. It was indeed but a passing trance, that only made me feel with renewed acuteness so soon as, the unnatural stimulus ceasing to operate, I had returned to my old habits. I collected bones from charnel-houses; and disturbed, with profane fingers, the tremendous secrets of the human frame. In a solitary chamber, or rather cell, at the top of the house, and separated from all the other apartments by a gallery and staircase, I kept my workshop of filthy creation: my eye-balls were starting from their sockets in attending to the details of my employment. The dissecting room and the slaughter-house furnished many of my materials; and often did my human nature turn with loathing from my occupation, whilst, still urged on by an eagerness which perpetually increased, I brought my work near to a conclusion.

The summer months passed while I was thus engaged, heart and soul, in one pursuit. It was a most beautiful season; never did the fields bestow a more plentiful harvest, or the vines yield a more luxuriant vintage: but my eyes were insensible to the charms of nature. And the same feelings which made me neglect the scenes around me caused me also to forget those friends who were so many miles absent, and whom I had not seen for so long a time. I knew my silence disquieted them; and I well remembered the words of my father: "I know that while you are pleased with yourself, you will think of us with affection, and we shall hear regularly from you. You must pardon me if I regard any interruption in your correspondence as a proof that your other duties are equally neglected."

I knew well therefore what would be my father's feelings; but I could not tear my thoughts from my employment, loathsome in itself, but which had taken an irresistible hold of my imagination. I wished, as it were, to procrastinate all that related to my feelings of affection until the great object, which swallowed up every habit of my nature, should be completed.

I then thought that my father would be unjust if he ascribed my neglect to vice, or faultiness on my part; but I am now convinced that he was justified in conceiving that I should not be altogether free from blame. A human being in perfection ought always to preserve a calm and peaceful mind, and never to allow passion or a transitory desire to disturb his tranquility. I do not think that the pursuit of knowledge is an exception to this rule. If the study to which you apply yourself has a tendency to weaken your affections, and to destroy your taste for those simple pleasures in which no alloy can possibly mix, then that study is certainly unlawful, that is to say, not befitting the human mind. If this rule were always observed; if no man allowed any pursuit whatsoever to interfere with the tranquility of his domestic affections, Greece had not been enslaved; Caesar would have spared his country; America would have been discovered more gradually; and the empires of Mexico and Peru had not been destroyed.

But I forgot that I am moralizing in the most interesting part of my tale; and your looks remind me to proceed.

My father made no reproach in his letters, and only took notice of my silence by enquiring into my occupations more particularly than before. Winter, spring, and summer passed away during my labors; but I did not watch the blossom or the expanding leaves—sights which before always yielded me supreme delight—so deeply was I engrossed in my occupation. The leaves of that year had withered before my work drew near to a close; and now every day showed me more plainly how well I had succeeded. But my enthusiasm was checked by my anxiety, and I appeared rather like one doomed by slavery to toil in the mines, or any other unwholesome trade, than an artist occupied by his favorite employment. Every night I was oppressed by a slow fever, and I became nervous to a most painful degree; the fall of a leaf startled me, and I shunned my fellow-creatures as if I had been guilty of a crime. Sometimes I grew alarmed at the wreck I perceived that I had become; the energy of my purpose alone sustained me: my labors would soon end, and I believed that exercise and amusement would then drive away incipient disease; and I promised myself both of these when my creation should be complete.

It was on a dreary night of November, that I beheld the accomplishment of my toils. With an anxiety that almost amounted to agony, I collected the instruments of life around me, that I might infuse a spark of being into the lifeless thing that lay at my feet. It was already one in the morning; the rain pattered dismally against the panes, and my candle was nearly burnt out, when, by the glimmer of the half-extinguished light, I saw the dull yellow eye of the creature open; it breathed hard, and a convulsive motion agitated its limbs.

How can I describe my emotions at this catastrophe, or how delineate the wretch whom with such infinite pains and care I had endeavored to form? His limbs were in proportion, and I had selected his features as beautiful. Beautiful!—Great God! His yellow skin scarcely covered the work of muscles and arteries beneath; his hair was of lustrous black, and flowing; his teeth of a pearly whiteness; but these luxuriances only formed a more horrid contrast with his watery eyes, that seemed almost of the same colour as the dun white sockets in which they were set, his shriveled complexion and straight black lips.

The different accidents of life are not so changeable as the feelings of human nature. I had worked hard for nearly two years, for the sole purpose of infusing life into an inanimate body. For this I had deprived myself of rest and health. I had desired it with an ardor that far exceeded moderation; but now that I had finished, the beauty of the dream vanished, and breathless horror and disgust filled my heart. Unable to endure the aspect of the being I had created, I rushed out of the room, and continued a long time traversing my bedchamber, unable to compose my mind to sleep. At length lassitude succeeded to the tumult I had before endured; and I threw myself on the bed in my clothes, endeavoring to seek a few moments of forgetfulness. But it was in vain; I slept, indeed, but I was disturbed by the wildest dreams. I thought I saw Elizabeth,* in the bloom of health, walking in the streets of Ingolstadt. Delighted and surprised, I embraced her; but as I imprinted the first kiss on her lips, they became livid with the hue of death; her features appeared to change, and I thought that I held the corpse of my dead mother in my arms; a shroud enveloped her form, and I saw the graveworms crawling in the folds of the flannel. I started from my sleep with horror; a cold dew covered my

---

Elizabeth: adopted sister of Victor Frankenstein

forehead, my teeth chattered, and every limb became convulsed; when, by the dim and yellow light of the moon, as it forced its way through the window shutters, I beheld the wretch—the miserable monster whom I had created. He held up the curtain of the bed; and his eyes, if eyes they may be called, were fixed on me. His jaws opened, and he muttered some inarticulate sounds, while a grin wrinkled his cheeks. He might have spoken, but I did not hear; one hand was stretched out, seemingly to detain me, but I escaped, and rushed down stairs. I took refuge in the courtyard belonging to the house which I inhabited; where I remained during the rest of the night, walking up and down in the greatest agitation, listening attentively, catching and fearing each sound as if it were to announce the approach of the demoniacal corpse to which I had so miserably given life.

Oh! no mortal could support the horror of that countenance. A mummy again endued with animation could not be so hideous as that wretch. I had gazed on him while unfinished; he was ugly then; but when those muscles and joints were rendered capable of motion, it became a thing such as even Dante* could not have conceived.

I passed the night wretchedly. Sometimes my pulse beat so quickly and hardly, that I felt the palpitation of every artery; at others I nearly sank to the ground through langur and extreme weakness. Mingled with this horror, I felt the bitterness of disappointment; dreams that had been my food and pleasant rest for so long a space were now become a hell to me; and the change was so rapid, the overthrow so complete!

Morning, dismal and wet, at length dawned, and discovered to my sleepless and aching eyes the church of Ingolstadt, its white steeple and clock, which indicated the sixth hour. The porter opened the gates of the court, which had that night been my asylum, and I issued into the streets, pacing them with quick steps, as if I sought to avoid the wretch whom I feared every turning of the street would present to my view. I did not dare return to the apartment which I inhabited, but felt impelled to hurry on, although drenched by the rain which poured from a black and comfortless sky.   15

QUESTIONING THE TEXT

1. How does Victor Frankenstein explain his drive to work hard to bring a nonliving entity to life? Annotate the margins of the *Frankenstein* selection to highlight places where Frankenstein explains his motives. Do you think any of these motives account for the continuing development of science and technology today? Explore this issue with classmates.

Dante (1265–1321): Italian poet, author of *Divine Comedy*

2. To create his monster, what does Victor Frankenstein have to do to himself and to other creatures? Have you ever been so single-minded in the pursuit of a goal or passion?
3. What precisely about the creature disappoints Frankenstein? In a group, discuss Frankenstein's rejection of his monster, exploring its meanings and implications.
4. The introduction suggests that the Frankenstein story has become a modern myth. How many versions of Shelley's tale can you think of? List them.

MAKING CONNECTIONS

5. At one point in the selection, Victor Frankenstein warns that knowledge is dangerous: "how much happier that man is who believes his native town to be the world, than he who aspires to become greater than his nature will allow" (p. 230). Freewrite on this idea, taking into account the essays in this chapter by Lewis Thomas (p. 236) and J. Michael Bishop (p. 255). Is it likely that men and women will ever live contentedly in their native towns?
6. Can you think of ways in which the anthologized passage from the novel differs from film versions of the Frankenstein tale you may have seen? Brainstorm a list of differences and jot them down.

JOINING THE CONVERSATION

7. Write a parody of this selection from *Frankenstein*, perhaps detailing the creation and consequences of some similar but more recent "monster," understanding that term broadly or metaphorically. You might even read Dave Barry's "Guys vs. Men" (p. 343) in chapter 6 for a perspective on the peculiarly male desire to build "neat stuff."
8. Working with a group, discuss the monster as a creature who is similar to, but also different from, a human being. Can you compare his situation to that of other individuals or groups considered "different" in society? Write a brief position paper about Frankenstein's monster as a symbol of what it means to be different. Is the comparison convincing? Why, or why not?
9. Some critics suggest that *Frankenstein* reflects an early view of industrialization as a monstrous creation out of control. Use the library to learn what changes the industrial revolution was imposing on the landscape of England during the nineteenth century. Try also to determine how favorably people regarded changes such as the building of factories, industrial plants, and railroads. This subject is complex enough to support a full-scale research paper. Give it a try.

LEWIS THOMAS
The Hazards of Science

*A*FTER GRADUATING *from Princeton University and Harvard Medical School, Lewis Thomas (1913–93) served on the staff of many important hospitals and medical schools, as dean of medicine at Newfoundland University, and as president of the Sloane-Kettering Cancer Institute in New York City. At the invitation of a journal editor, he began writing the essays for a wide-ranging audience that have been collected in* Lives of a Cell, *winner of a National Book Award, and several other volumes, including* The Medusa and the Snail; Etcetera, Etcetera; *and* The Youngest Science. *In the following essay, Thomas opens by considering the question of hubris, that overreaching pride that leads humans to start "doing things reserved for the gods." This pride is, of course, central to Victor Frankenstein's quest—and to his fall. Thomas puts a different spin on the word* hubris, *however, and in doing so offers a complex answer to the question "are there some kinds of information . . . human beings are really better off not having?"*

I chose Thomas's piece because he raises the specter of Frankensteinian destruction in the opening paragraph, because his argument is clear and succinct, and because he allows us to challenge and question science without rejecting it. Most of all, I admire the way Thomas makes his work accessible to nonscientists like me—and thus allows me in on some of the conversations animating science today. – A.L.

The code word for criticism of science and scientists these days is "hubris." Once you've said that word, you've said it all; it sums up, in a word, all of today's apprehensions and misgivings in the public mind—not just about what is perceived as the insufferable attitude of the scientists themselves but, enclosed in the same word, what science and technology are perceived to be doing to make this century, this near to its ending, turn out so wrong.

"Hubris" is a powerful word, containing layers of powerful meaning, derived from a very old world, but with a new life of its own, growing way beyond the limits of its original meaning. Today, it is strong enough to carry the full weight of disapproval for the cast of mind that thought up atomic fusion and fission as ways of first blowing up and later heating cities as well as the attitudes which led to strip-mining, offshore oil wells, Kepone, food additives, SSTs, and the tiny spherical particles of plastic recently discovered clogging the waters of the Sargasso Sea.

The biomedical sciences are now caught up with physical science and technology in the same kind of critical judgment, with the same pejorative word. Hubris is responsible, it is said, for the whole biological revolution. It is hubris that has given us the prospects of behavior control, psychosurgery, fetal research, heart transplants, the cloning of prominent politicians from bits of their own eminent tissue, iatrogenic disease, overpopulation, and recombinant DNA. This last, the new technology that permits the stitching of one creature's genes into the DNA of another, to make hybrids, is currently cited as the ultimate example of hubris. It is hubris for man to manufacture a hybrid on his own.

So now we are back to the first word again, from "hybrid" to "hubris," and the hidden meaning of two beings joined unnaturally together by man is somehow retained. Today's joining is straight out of Greek mythology: it is the combining of man's capacity with the special prerogative of the gods, and it is really in this sense of outrage that the word "hubris" is being used today. That is what the word has grown into, a warning, a code word, a shorthand signal from the language itself: if man starts doing things reserved for the gods, deifying himself, the outcome will be something worse for him, symbolically, than the litters of wild boars and domestic sows were for the ancient Romans.

To be charged with hubris is therefore an extremely serious matter, and   5
not to be dealt with murmuring things about antiscience and antiintellectualism, which is what many of us engaged in science tend to do these days. The doubts about our enterprise have their origin in the most profound kind of human anxiety. If we are right and the critics are wrong, then it has to be that the word "hubris" is being mistakenly employed, that this is not what we are up to, that there is, for the time being anyway, a fundamental misunderstanding of science.

I suppose there is one central question to be dealt with, and I am not at all sure how to deal with it, although I am quite certain about my own answer to it. It is this: are there some kinds of information leading to some sorts of knowledge that human beings are really better off not having? Is there a limit to scientific inquiry not set by what is knowable but by what we *ought* to be knowing? Should we stop short of learning about some things, for fear of what we, or someone, will do with the knowledge? My own answer is a flat no, but I must confess that this is an intuitive response and I am neither inclined nor trained to reason my way through it.

There has been some effort, in and out of scientific quarters, to make recombinant DNA into the issue on which to settle this argument. Proponents of this line of research are accused of pure hubris, of assuming the rights of gods, of arrogance and outrage; what is more, they confess themselves to be in the business of making live hybrids with their own hands. The mayor of Cambridge and the attorney general of New York have both been advised to put a stop to it, forthwith.

It is not quite the same sort of argument, however, as the one about limiting knowledge, although this is surely part of it. The knowledge is already here, and the rage of the argument is about its application in technology. Should DNA for making certain useful or interesting proteins be incorporated into *E. coli* plasmids or not? Is there a risk of inserting the wrong sort of toxins or hazardous viruses, and then having the new hybrid organisms spread beyond the laboratory? Is this a technology for creating new varieties of pathogens, and should it be stopped because of this?

If the argument is held to this level, I can see no reason why it cannot be settled, by reasonable people. We have learned a great deal about the handling of dangerous microbes in the last century, although I must say that the opponents of recombinant-DNA research tend to downgrade this huge body of information. At one time or another, agents as hazardous as those of rabies, psittacosis, plague, and typhus have been dealt with by investigators in secure laboratories, with only rare instances of self-infection of the investigators themselves, and no instances at all of epidemics. It takes some high imagining to postulate the creation of brand-new pathogens so wild and voracious as to spread from equally secure laboratories to endanger human life at large, as some of the arguers are now maintaining.

But this is precisely the trouble with the recombinant-DNA problem: it   10
has become an emotional issue, with too many irretrievably lost tempers on both sides. It has lost the sound of a discussion of technological safety, and begins now to sound like something else, almost like a religious controversy, and here it is moving toward the central issue: are there some things in science we should not be learning about?

There is an inevitably long list of hard questions to follow this one, beginning with the one which asks whether the mayor of Cambridge should be the one to decide, first off.

Maybe we'd be wiser, all of us, to back off before the recombinant-DNA issue becomes too large to cope with. If we're going to have a fight about it, let it be confined to the immediate issue of safety and security, of the recombinants now under consideration, and let us by all means have regulations and guidelines to assure the public safety wherever these are indicated or even suggested. But if it is possible let us stay off that question about limiting human knowledge. It is too loaded, and we'll simply not be able to cope with it.

By this time it will have become clear that I have already taken sides in the matter, and my point of view is entirely prejudiced. This is true, but with a qualification. I am not so much in favor of recombinant-DNA research as I am opposed to the opposition to this line of inquiry. As a longtime student of infectious-disease agents I do not take kindly the declarations that we do not know how to keep from catching things in laboratories, much less how to keep them from spreading beyond the laboratory walls. I believe we learned a lot about this sort of thing, long ago. Moreover, I regard it as a form of hubris-in-reverse to claim that man can make deadly pathogenic microorganisms so easily. In my view, it takes a long time and a great deal of interliving before a microbe can become a successful pathogen. Pathogenicity is, in a sense, a highly skilled trade, and only a tiny minority of all the numberless tons of microbes on the earth has ever been involved itself in it; most bacteria are busy with their own business, browsing and recycling the rest of life. Indeed, pathogenicity often seems to me a sort of biological accident in which signals are misdirected by the microbe or misinterpreted by the host, as in the case of endotoxin, or in which the intimacy between host and microbe is of such long standing that a form of molecular mimicry becomes possible, as in the case of diphtheria toxin. I do not believe that by simply putting together new combinations of genes one can create creatures as highly skilled and adapted for dependence as a pathogen must be, any more than I have ever believed that microbial life from the moon or Mars could possibly make a living on this planet.

But, as I said, I'm not at all sure this is what the argument is really about. Behind it is that other discussion, which I wish we would not have to become enmeshed in.

I cannot speak for the physical sciences, which have moved an immense distance in this century by any standard, but it does seem to me that in the biological and medical sciences we are still far too ignorant to begin making judgments about what sorts of things we should be learning or not learning. To the contrary, we ought to be grateful for whatever snatches we can get hold of, and we ought to be out there on a much larger scale than today's, looking for more. 15

We should be very careful with that word "hubris," and make sure it is not used when not warranted. There is a great danger in applying it to the search for knowledge. The application of knowledge is another matter, and there is hubris in plenty of our technology, but I do not believe that looking for new information about nature, at whatever level, can possibly be called unnatural. Indeed, if there is any single attribute of human beings, apart from language, which distinguishes them from all other creatures on earth, it is their insatiable, uncontrollable drive to learn things and then to exchange the information with others of the species. Learning is what we do, when you think about it. I cannot think of a human impulse more difficult to govern.

But I can imagine lots of reasons for trying to govern it. New information about nature is very likely, at the outset, to be upsetting to someone or other. The recombinant-DNA line of research is already upsetting, not because of the dangers now being argued about but because it is disturbing, in a fundamental way, to face the fact that the genetic machinery in control of the planet's life can be fooled around with so easily. We do not like the idea that anything so fixed and stable as a species line can be changed. The notion that genes can be taken out of one genome and inserted in another is unnerving. Classical mythology is peopled with mixed beings—part man, part animal or plant—and most of them are associated with tragic stories. Recombinant DNA is a reminder of bad dreams.

The easiest decision for society to make in matters of this kind is to appoint an agency, or a commission, or a subcommittee within an agency to look into the problem and provide advice. And the easiest course for a committee to take, when confronted by any process that appears to be disturbing people or making them uncomfortable, is to recommend that it be stopped, at least for the time being.

I can easily imagine such a committee, composed of unimpeachable public figures, arriving at the decision that the time is not quite ripe for further exploration of the transplantation of genes, that we should put this off for a while, maybe until next century, and get on with other affairs that make us less discomfited. Why not do science on something more popular, say, how to get solar energy more cheaply? Or mental health?

The trouble is, it would be very hard to stop once this line was begun. There are, after all, all sorts of scientific inquiry that are not much liked by one constituency or another, and we might soon find ourselves with crowded rosters, panels, standing committees, set up in Washington for the appraisal, and then the regulation, of research. Not on grounds of the possible value and usefulness of the new knowledge, mind you, but for guarding society against scientific hubris, against the kinds of knowledge we're better off without.

It would be absolutely irresistible as a way of spending time, and people would form long queues for membership. Almost anything would be fair game, certainly anything to do with genetics, anything relating to population control, or, on the other side, research on aging. Very few fields would get by, except perhaps for some, like mental health, in which nobody really expects anything much to happen, surely nothing new or disturbing.

The research areas in the greatest trouble would be those already containing a sense of bewilderment and surprise, with discernible prospects of upheaving present dogmas.

It is hard to predict how science is going to turn out, and if it is really good science it is impossible to predict. This is in the nature of the enterprise. If the things to be found are actually new, they are by definition unknown in advance, and there is no way of telling in advance where a really new line of inquiry will lead. You cannot make choices in this matter, selecting things you think you're going to like and shutting off the lines that make for discomfort. You either have science or you don't, and if you have it you are obliged to accept the surprising and disturbing pieces of information, even the overwhelming and upheaving ones, along with the neat and promptly useful bits. It is like that.

The only solid piece of scientific truth about which I feel totally confident is that we are profoundly ignorant about nature. Indeed, I regard this as the major discovery of the past hundred years of biology. It is, in its way, an illuminating piece of news. It would have amazed the brightest minds of the eighteenth-century Enligtenment to be told by any of us how little we know, and how bewildering seems the way ahead. It is this sudden confrontation with the depth and scope of ignorance that represents the most significant contribution of twentieth-century science to the human intellect. We are, at last, facing up to it. In earlier times, we either pretended to understand how things worked or ignored the problem, or simply made up stories to fill the gaps. Now that we have begun exploring in earnest, doing serious science, we are getting glimpses of how huge the questions are, and how far from being answered. Because of this, these are hard times for the human intellect, and it is no wonder that we are depressed. It is not so bad being ignorant if you are totally ignorant; the hard thing is knowing in some detail the reality of ignorance, the worst spots and here and there the not-so-bad spots, but no true light at the end of any tunnel nor even any tunnels that can yet be trusted. Hard times, indeed.

But we are making a beginning, and there ought to be some satisfac-   25
tion, even exhilaration, in that.* The method works. There are probably no questions we can think up that can't be answered, sooner or later, including even the matter of consciousness. To be sure, there may well be questions we can't think up, ever, and therefore limits to the reach of human intellect which we will never know about, but that is another matter. Within our limits, we should be able to work our way through to all our answers, if we keep at it long enough, and pay attention.

I am putting it this way, with all the presumption and confidence that I can summon, in order to raise another, last question. Is this hubris? Is there something fundamentally unnatural, or intrinsically wrong, or hazardous for the species in the ambition that drives us all to reach a comprehensive understanding of nature, including ourselves? I cannot believe it. It would seem to me a more unnatural thing, and more of an offense against nature, for us to come on the same scene endowed as we are with curiosity, filled to overbrimming as we are with questions, and naturally talented as we are for the asking of clear questions, and then for us to do nothing about it or, worse, to try to suppress the questions. This is the greater danger for our species, to try to pretend that we are another kind of animal, that we do not need to satisfy our curiosity, that we can get along somehow without inquiry and exploration and experimentation, and that the human mind can rise above its ignorance by simply asserting that there are things it has no need to know. This, to my way of thinking, is the real hubris, and it carries danger for us all.

QUESTIONING THE TEXT

1. What is hubris? Why does Thomas begin his essay with a discussion of that term?
2. Thomas suggests that the question of what to do with certain kinds of scientific knowledge—about recombinant DNA, for example—should

---

But we are making a beginning . . . in that: For differing views on the kinds of beginnings that science now confronts, see Kevin Kelly's "Interview with the Luddite" (p. 243).

not be treated as "an emotional issue" or "a religious controversy." Do you agree? Why, or why not?

3. What is A.L.'s attitude toward Thomas and his argument? What words, phrases, or sentences in the introduction to this essay reveal her attitude to you?

MAKING CONNECTIONS

4. If Thomas were charged with the task of writing an evaluation of Victor Frankenstein's work, what do you think he would say? Try your hand at such an evaluation.

5. "New information about nature," Thomas says, "is very likely, at the outset, to be upsetting to someone or other." Would Kevin Kelly, author of "Interview with the Luddite," agree? Why, or why not?

JOINING THE CONVERSATION

6. With two or three classmates, brainstorm about and then discuss what Thomas identifies as "the central question" of his essay: "are there some kinds of information leading to some sorts of knowledge that human beings are really better off not having?" If you keep a reading log, answer this question there.

7. Thomas defends scientific inquiry by noting, "I do not believe that looking for new information about nature, at whatever level, can possibly be called unnatural. Indeed, if there is any single attribute of human beings, apart from language, which distinguishes them above all other creatures on earth, it is their insatiable, uncontrollable drive to learn things and then to exchange the information with others of the species." Do you agree? Write a brief position paper in which you argue for or against the accuracy of Thomas's claim.

KEVIN KELLY
Interview with the Luddite

KEVIN KELLY *(b. 1952) is one of the reasons more and more people have been reading* Wired *lately. This popular print and online magazine, with its Day-Glo glitz and its fragmented, jittery format, has swept the country in the last couple of years, outstripping even its own wildest imaginings of success. I have gone so far as to subscribe to* Wired, *although I am not entirely enamored of the views it projects. It tends to report in sound bytes, for example, lacking any in-depth discussion of even the most problematic issues surrounding digital culture. And it usually ignores anything by or about women in the cyberspace world. (Indeed, for a look at how masculine-identified the entire computer industry is, just flip through any issue, noting the advertisements in particular.)*

Still, I subscribe, and one reason I do so is that I enjoy the interviews, usually a feature of each issue. Perhaps it is the sense of hearing someone talking face to face. Perhaps it is the breezy, irreverent, feisty manner of most interviewers. Perhaps it is the complex and often contradictory picture of those interviewed that inevitably emerges. For whatever reasons, I like the Wired *interviews. And the one from the June 1995 issue of* Wired *with Kirkpatrick Sale, which you are about to read, is no exception. Sale, a leader of contemporary Neo-Luddites and author of* Rebels against the Future: The Luddites and Their War on the Industrial Revolution—Lessons for the Computer Age *(1995), takes his work seriously—but not too seriously, interweaving his radical critique of technology with jokes at his own, and sometimes his interviewer's, expense. His interviewer, Kevin Kelly, author of* Out of Control: The Rise of Neo-biological Civilization *(1994), who has his own take on the future of technology, holds an almost diametrically opposed position on technology, arguing that Sale is "stuck on an old language of technology" when Kelly and others like him are "creating a new one" that is "improved, smarter, wiser, more organic." Read on and then take your own position: where do you stand on the question of technology's usefulness to society?* – A.L.

KEVIN KELLY: *Other than arson and a lot of vandalism, what did the Luddites* accomplish in the long run?*

KIRKPATRICK SALE: The Luddites raised what was called at the time "the machinery question," and they raised it in such a forceful way that it could not ever go away: Whether machinery was simply to be for greater

---

* *Luddite:* a word derived from the name of Ned Ludd, a leader of nineteenth-century workers who sabotaged machinery in textile mills as a means of protesting the mechanization of labor and resulting unemployment

production by the industrialists, regardless of its consequences, or whether the people who were affected by these machines had some say in the matter of how they were to be used. The Luddites also established themselves as the symbol of those who resist the new technologies and demand a voice in how they are to be used.

KK: *Were they able in any way to alter the course of the Industrial Revolution?*

KS: To some extent they were able to delay the adoption of machines in some of the textile branches. Although there were some regional effects of the Luddites, in general they failed to make any real impact on the rush of technology and industrialism.

KK: *Do you consider yourself a modern-day Luddite?*   5

KS: I do, in the sense that we modern-day Luddites are not, or at least not yet, taking up the sledgehammer and the torch and gun to resist the new machinery, but rather taking up the book and the lecture and organizing people to raise these issues. Most of the people who would today call themselves Luddites confine their resistance, so far at any rate, to a kind of intellectual and political resistance.

KK: *Yet you did smash a computer recently, right?*

KS: I did.

KK: *I hope it made you feel better.*

KS: It was astonishing how good it made me feel! I cannot explain it to   10
you. I was on the stage of New York City's Town Hall with an audience of 1,500 people. I was behind a lectern, and in front of the lectern was this computer. And I gave a very short, minute-and-a-half description of what was wrong with the technosphere, how it was destroying the biosphere. And then I walked over and I got this very powerful sledgehammer and smashed the screen with one blow and smashed the keyboard with another blow. It felt wonderful. The sound it made, the spewing of the undoubtedly poisonous insides into the spotlight, the dust that hung in the air . . . some in the audience applauded. I bowed and returned to my chair.

KK: *So, what did you accomplish?*

KS: It was a statement. At other forums, I attempt to discuss the importance of understanding new technologies and what they are doing to us. But at that moment, when I had only four minutes to talk, I thought this was a statement better than anything else I could possibly say.

KK: *Violence is very powerful, isn't it?*

KS: And remarkably satisfying when it is injurious to property, not people.

KK: *I find it instructive that most of this Neo-Luddite sentiment is arising not   15 from people who are out of jobs because of computers, but from over-educated academic or author types. I don't detect much dissatisfaction among the unemployed regarding computers, per se.*

KS: You're quite right that in these last 20 or 25 years, the immense efforts of automation on the labor force have not been met by resistance other than the most trivial kind. What happened was that unions caved in and accepted strategies of the corporations to give workers lifetime pay in return for having their jobs automated. However, the luxury of lifetime pay is now no longer being offered, so we have an estimated 6 million people who have lost their jobs to automation, or to overseas shops, since 1988. These 6 million people have not ventured forth with sledgehammers, but some of them are turning to crime, for sure, and some of them are part of that dissatisfied, white male constituency that voted for the Republicans last fall. So, instead of going to the sledgehammer, they've gone to the ballot box, though I don't think that's going to achieve what they think it will.

KK: *But it's also leading them to study computers and to learn how to get a job with computers. You mentioned 6 million jobs lost to computers, but the number of jobs created by computers and technology is really more sizable. Where, for instance, do you think the hundreds of millions of jobs in America in the last 100 years have come from? They certainly didn't come from farming or handicrafts. These jobs were made by industry.*

KS: There is no question that jobs are created, so long as an economy can keep growing. But it's not the technology, or it's only indirectly and accidentally the technology, that creates them. It's warfare, empire, government expansion, resources exploitation, ecological exhaustion, consumption, and the manufacture of needs. Today, in the second Industrial Revolution, it's just as it was back in the first. The technology itself simply does put people out of jobs. And anyway, the idea that the whole end of life is jobs and job creation is just pathological. The question is, What do those jobs achieve and at what expense? A job in itself is not a virtue.

KK: *That's exactly right. Quality of jobs is vital. The Luddite cottagers thought it was inhuman to be put out of work by machines. But what's really inhuman is to have cloth made by human labor at all. Cloth should be made by machines, because machines make much better cloth than humans. Making cloth is not a good job for humans, unless they want to make a few pieces for art.*

KS: Well, *they* didn't think so. Nor do I: nothing is superior to handi-   20
crafts.

KK: *One of the most revealing claims in your book is when you say, "The idea that technology creates jobs is* hogwash.*" That statement is nonsense itself. Where did your own job come from, if it didn't come from the printing press?*

KS: To begin with, I don't have a job. And my work would be the same—writing about the perils of our civilization—no matter what technologies were at hand. But the real point about technology's impact over the last, say, 200 years is that it puts people out of jobs when it's introduced, and that's *why* it's introduced. *The point of a new technology is to save on labor costs and all the attendant costs with actual people.*

KK: *No, the point of technology is to make higher-quality and more diverse products than we can make by hand.*

KS: No, quantity, quantity. We have a mass society, a mass market, and mass production. Mass quantity is why we have computers.

KK: *We have technology not just to make mass things but to make new things*   25
we could not make other ways.

KS: I regard that as trivial.

KK: *OK, then you tell me. What was the effect of printing technology? Did the*
invention of printing just allow us to make more books? Or did it allow new and differ-
ent kinds of books to be written? What did it do? It did both.

KS: That wasn't mass society back then, but what it eventually achieved
was a vast increase in the number of books produced; and it vastly reduced
forests in Europe so as to produce them.

KK: *I don't think so. The forests of Europe were not cut down to create books for*
Europe. Printing allowed several things. It increased literacy. And it allowed more vari-
eties of books to be written—and faster. It allowed better communication.

KS: Literacy does go hand in hand with industrialism, but at the same   30
time, it destroys orality. No oral traditions and no oral abilities.

KK: *There's no doubt that technology obsoletes many things.*

KS: Right. So, let's not simply say how wonderful is literacy, without
saying what the price is for this literacy, without asking what is it that we are
now reading with all of this fancy literacy. The truth is that we are reading little of merit.

KK: *I would say that in oral traditions, there was very little of merit said. There*
is this tendency to think that the old things, the old times, the oral traditions, the tribal
traditions, were somehow more lofty, that people of those times used things more judi-
ciously, that they didn't gossip, that they didn't use good things for trash. This is com-
plete nonsense.

KS: Sure, people gossiped, and sure, people said nasty things. At the
same time, these oral traditions were what kept these societies together for
eons. If we lose oral tradition and all that goes with it, we lose a due regard
for nature and the preservation of nature. The successive empires that have
driven civilizations for the last 6,000 years have had, almost uniformly, no regard for nature. That's why they were as short-lived as they were: in addition
to having very little regard for the majority of their own population, they had
no regard for the rest of the living world. That is essential to the peril we're in
today.

KK: *Do you see civilization as a catastrophe?*   35

KS: Yes.

KK: *All civilizations?*

KS: Yes. There are some presumed benefits, but civilizations as such are
all catastrophic, which is why they all end by destroying themselves and the
natural environment around them.

KK: *Your are quick to talk about the downsides of technological civilizations and*
the upsides of tribal life. But you pay zero attention to the downsides of tribal life or the
upsides of civilizations. For instance, the downsides of tribal life are infanticide, tribal
warfare, intertribal rape, slavery, sexism. Not to mention a very short life span, perpet-
ual head lice, and diseases that are easily cured by five cents' worth of medicine now.

This is what you get when you have tribal life with no civilization. This is what you want?

KS: Tribal life does not have these mythical downsides that you describe.   40
What you are describing are tribal societies that have become pathological because of the invasion of some outside force or other. In the case of the American Indians and of Africa, it's the Europeans. Tribes have long-established practices to keep themselves harmonious and stable, including the practice of birth control so as not to exceed the carrying capacity of the places where they live. You can call it infanticide if you like; they would understand it as birth control, appropriate to their regard for nature.

KK: *Yeah. I'm very glad not be living in a tribal society.*

KS: Don't dismiss the virtues of that society. I think the sense of sodality and comradeship and inner peace and harmony that we know happens in these traditional societies is not to be lightly dismissed; even *you* might welcome it.

KK: *Well, whatever romantic glories it may have, it all comes at a price. You keep forgetting it comes at a price. And the price of tribal life is no pianos, no violins, no paint, no telescope. No Mozart, no van Gogh. If a Beethoven is born, he can only be a genius at finding tubers. That's the price of that society.*

KS: Well, if your clan thought that the violin was a useful and nonharmful tool, you could choose to invent that.

KK: *You can't have a violin without civilization. Look, what you get with a*   45
nontechnological tribal society is a very constrained society. OK, the people in a tribe adjust to those constraints and they adapt. But the advantages of civilization are options and diversity. You have increasing opportunities for people to be creative in new ways that you don't have in those tribal societies.

KS: The way I like to come at this is with this quotation from Herbert Read: "Only a people serving an apprenticeship to nature can be trusted with machines. Only such people will so contrive and control those machines that their products are an enhancement of biological needs, and not a denial of them."

KK: *I agree with the ideas of making technology more biological and making it express the organic. The more we make our technology lifelike, the better that technology will be. You're critiquing industrial technology just as industrial technology is becoming outmoded. The qualities you assign to technology—centralization, order, uniformity, regularity, linearity, passivity—wonderfully described technology in the 1950s. But the reason you're wrong about technology is that this kind of technology is being superseded. As we import biological principles into technology, we are generating technology that's decentralized, that plays on differences, that's irregular on demand, that's nonlinear, and that's very interactive. If we were stuck with having to make technology that was centralized and stupid and brute, we would be looking forward to a dismal future. But we don't have to make technology that way.*

KS: I don't buy your statement. It *is* true that within the larger construct of contemporary computer technology there is room for decentralization, some irregularity, and some of what you suggest; but that's not what the overarching character of this technology is about. It is designed precisely to create a uniformity of production, consumption, distribution—distribution of money or ideas or so-called information. If within it you can find these nuggets of the contrary, that doesn't change the overall nature of the industrial mechanism or the industrial civilization behind it.

KK: *I don't think you should close your mind to the possibility that these nuggets will become the predominant form of technology. As humans, we crave differences and diversity, as well as uniformity and reliability. And we have a model out there, which you're familiar with, that does both of these things. Nature has a very regular, dependable aspect to it that we count on. At the same time, it has a surprising and unpredictable nature. Both uniformity of production and diversity of production happen in nature and can happen with technology.*

KS: I cannot get my mind even *close* to what you're saying. This is simply an attempt to use science and its technologies to manipulate nature. This is an attempt to make nature technological, so that humans can determine everything about nature.   50

KK: *You're right in the sense that civilization is anthropocentric. All societies say a human life is worth more than a flea's life. And because of our consciousness, we can and do modify our surroundings, including nature, to our benefit and to make new things.*

KS: Case closed.

KK: *Right. And so, the question is, When we have the choice, which way will people go? Will they retreat back to this utopian idea of undoing civilization somehow? I really don't think people will do that.*

KS: Given the culture of our current society, I would agree there is no chance of going back. But there is also no chance for people to even raise the question. I ask not that we devise some kind of utopia and work toward it, but rather that there be some kind of power of the citizenry, regular and often, to raise questions about, to assess, and to determine whether they want the technologies that are there before them.

KK: *And in the end, people will choose technology and civilization. The Luddites will be left behind.*   55

KS: Those of us who oppose may be easily accommodated by this society, since society has no fear that we're going to have the effect that we desire to have. But it is possible for individuals to act out, either alone or with colleagues and neighbors, their opposition to certain technologies. This has been done in many instances—from nuclear power to the Dalkon shield. We can as individuals say, This technology is wrong and harmful and we ought to act against it. That technology over there seems at the moment not to be wrong and harmful, so we can either use it or not as we wish. I urge people to take a clear-headed look at what is in front of them, and not to feel guilty if they reject something, and to be able to say, with a rational explanation, This is wrong, I will not myself buy into it, and I would urge others not to buy into it for the following reasons.

KK: *As you know, there's a huge difference between rejecting specific technological implementations and rejecting technology as a whole, as you have been doing. The Amish do this well, this selective adoption of technology, without rejecting civilization as a whole.*

KS: The Amish have said there are limits: There are certain things that we like, that seem to enhance our lives, and that do not do danger to our sense of family and community, and therefore we can use them; and there are others, quite clearly, that do harm. This is intelligent decision making. The Luddites were the same. The Luddites all worked with machinery, some with fairly complicated weaving machines in their cottages. They were not against machinery, but against "machinery hurtful to commonality," as one of their statements put it. They were not by any means against all technologies. In fact, something like the spinning jenny had come along in the 18th century and had been rather readily adopted.

KK: *I have a different take. The only reason the Luddites are known, and the reason we don't call antitechnologists "Amishites," is that Luddites resisted it in a violent way, and that makes very good TV. This guy with the sledgehammer breaking weaving frames late at night makes a memorable image. If the Luddites had just resisted it, Amish-like, and said in a very nonviolent way, Sorry, we're simply not going to adopt larger weaving frames, I believe they would have had more impact in the long run, but they wouldn't be famous. But while we are quick to honor the Amish, most admirers forget that the Amish refusal of certain technologies directly stems from an old-fashioned spiritual stance: their sureness of the reality of God and sin. Are you suggesting that people can go back to those old-time values?*

KS: I would absolutely say that morality is an essential part of one's world view. By *moral judgment* I mean the capacity to decide that a thing is right when it enhances the integrity, stability, and beauty of nature and is wrong when it does otherwise.

KK: *You have to remember that the basis of the Amish belief is not the worship of nature. Their moral distinction is the worship of God, and the reason they reject certain technologies is that they see them as worldly, as sinful, as evil. You keep using words like* moral viewpoint, taboo, *and* worship. *When it comes right down to it, we're talking about a spiritual orientation, a religion that holds technology as evil. So tell me, what does your religion say about the morality of computers?*

KS: Quite apart from the environmental and medical evils associated with them being produced and used, there are two moral judgments against computers. One is that computerization enables the large forces of our civilization to operate more swiftly and efficiently in their pernicious goals of making money and producing things. And, however much individuals may feel that there are industrial benefits in their lives from the use of the computer (that is to say, things are easier, swifter), these are industrial virtues that may not be virtues in another morality. And secondly, in the course of using these, these forces are destroying nature with more speed and efficiency than ever before.

KK: *And how do you, as a Neo-Luddite, resist or refuse computers?*

KS: I don't have a computer.

KK: *You don't think you have a computer.*   65

KS: I take your point about that. I mean the computer is indeed pervasive. If I have a credit card, as I do, then I am in that sense wired.

KK: *Do you use the phone and the computer embedded in its lines?*

KS: On those occasions when I am forced to. It is, I have to tell you, a
kind of painful accommodation to the world for me to have to do this. I find
talking on the phone a physical pain, as well as a mental anguish. But, there it
is. And one makes accommodations, unless one wants to try to live alone, in
the woods. So anybody who wants to stay engaged in the world will have to
make some accommodations. The question, I think, becomes, Which ones
do you make? A lot of Neo-Luddites and techno-resisters today, I think, have
made bad choices by saying that they can use the tools of the masters in order
to free the slaves. And I don't think this is possible.

KK: *But you're doing that, right? You're using techno stuff, right?*

KS: If I could find a publisher that didn't use word processing in a com-   70
puter, I would.

KK: *What about printing presses?*

KS: These are the kinds of accommodations that I felt I've had to make.
Given the persuasiveness of the computer, I don't think that there's any way
to stay engaged and to escape it. But that means that you might decide that
you're not going to own a computer, you're not going to have a word
processor, you're not going to fly on jet planes, you're not going to use a car.

KK: *But you use a car at your country place.*

KS: I will sometimes use a car. I'm not trying to say that there's a way to
purity here. But what I'm trying to say is that one is conscious of one's
choices.

KK: *But you're not giving up electricity. Environmentally, using electricity has*   75
far more consequences than using a computer. You're not giving up an automobile,
which again, in terms of the number of deaths caused by it, has far more impact on our
surroundings than does the manufacturing of a computer. You're basically giving up
only technologies that are convenient for you to give up. You use computers, but not one
on your desk.

KS: I choose not to enter into that technology so intimately as to have a
computer confronting me that way. If I can keep the computer distant the
way the Amish can keep the telephone distant, I choose to do so.

KK: *But only because it is a convenient choice.*

KS: I don't in truth have *any* choice about a publisher that will produce
and market my book without a computer. Look at how pernicious is the use
of the computer. For example, if I may quote an outfit that is as celebratory of
the technological world as any, *Newsweek* magazine's recent issue on techno-
mania says: "The revolution is only just begun. It's already starting to overwhelm us, outstripping our capacity to cope, antiquating our laws, transform-

ing our mores, reshuffling our economy, reordering our priorities, redefining our workplaces, putting our Constitution to the fire, shifting our concept of reality." I think that anything that is doing that to us is something that ought to be resisted.

KK: *I feel otherwise. I'm not at all wedded to the past. I'm not wedded to this idea that somehow or other in the past everything was OK, and that it's all been downhill since then, that, basically, civilization is a catastrophe that's getting worse. I think that is the idea to resist, with all possible force.*

KS: And what gives you the confidence that the same technologies that   80
have worked to destroy the Earth are going save the Earth? We still have the same mind-set. Until we change our minds, how are we going to change our technologies?

KK: *Technology is a language. Technology is a language of artifacts. And when you have a bad thought, when you have a stupid thought, the answer to that is not to be silent. The response to a stupid thought is a wiser thought. Since technology is a language of artifacts, the response to "this technology is stupid" is to make smarter technology, not to withdraw from it.*

KS: But suppose you have nothing in your language that will allow a smarter thought. All you have to choose from are dumb thoughts because your language limits you. In the language of technology, you are not able to use certain words because they don't exist in that language. It might be possible for you in the language of technology to come up with something faster, but you can't come up with something smarter, because you don't have that in your language bank.

KK: *That's where I think you are fundamentally wrong. Because you are stuck on an old language of technology, and we are creating a new one. It is possible to make an improved, smarter, wiser, more organic technology that can serve us better.*

KS: Right! That is to say, using up the world's resources at a faster rate!

KK: *No. It doesn't have to. We don't have to continue to use more matter to*   85
make more technology. That's why instead of violently smashing a computer because it seems dumb now, my response is to make the computer so that is uses less matter, so that is has less impact on nature. And we can do that technologically.

KS: But then how are we going [to] use the computer?! What do you use that technology for?! Here's how: it's going to be used for the dominance and exploitation of nature for our benefit.

KK: *We dominate nature at first so that we can survive, but beyond survival I believe the focus of technology, culture and civilization is on human creativity, to allow humans to be creative, to allow every human born to have a chance to create, to write a book, to make a film, to make music, to love, to understand the universe. I think that's what technology is for. I think that's why we're here. It's not to worship nature.*

KS: I'm not asking you to worship nature. I'm asking for a regard for nature.

KK: *So why are we here? What are humans here for?*

KS: [Pauses.] To exist.   90

KK: *That's very interesting. So, what would be a measure of a successful human culture?*

KS: That it's able to exist in harmony with the rest of nature.

KK: *I totally reject that. It's not enough.*

KS: Not enough?!

KK: *Yes. Naked existence is for animals. That's basically all animals do: they   95 exist in harmony with their surroundings.*

KS: And what's wrong with that?

KK: *Plenty. We left that phase eons ago.*

KS: If you think that somehow now we are able to have a different mind-set that will suddenly transform us into being a due-regarding useful creature on the planet, I'd say that it is you who are talking utopian pipe dreams.

KK: *You're right. I have a vision of where we'd like to go, and this is more than just being an animal on Earth.*

KS: But, can't you see that if you come from a culture that is based upon   100 the destruction of nature, your image that technology will prevent us from destroying nature is ill-founded?

KK: *No, it's not ill-founded: already we have reduced pollution, when we wanted to.*

KS: Your optimism is contrary to all history up to the present, which suggests that given the values and norms of our particular civilization, we will perfect technology to the task of exploitation and destruction of nature. My optimism, such as it is, argues that because we know of previous societies that existed on every continent, and that existed far longer than Western civilization, and that have judged their technologies on other grounds than Western civilization, that it is possible to recover such societies in the future.

KK: *Even though we have no evidence of us ever retreating into the past and undoing technologies?*

KS: History is full of civilizations that have collapsed, followed by people who have had other ways of living. My optimism is based on the certainty that this civilization will collapse.

KK: *You get very specific in the closing pages of your book, where you say that if   105 industrial civilization does not crumble because of the resistance from, say, Neo-Luddites or others, then it will crumble of its own accumulative excesses, specifically "within not more than a few decades." Now, if somebody two decades hence wanted to decide inarguably if you were right or wrong about that forecast, what would be the evidence of that? How would someone know whether you were right?*

KS: I would say that you can measure it in three ways. The first would be an economic collapse. The dollar would be worthless, the yen would be worthless, the mark would be worthless—the dislocation we saw in the Depression of 1930, magnified many times over. A second would be the distention *within* various societies of the rich and the poor, in which the poor, who comprise, let's say, a fifth of society, are no longer content to be bought off with alcohol and television and drugs, and rises up in rebellion. And at the same time, there would be the same kind of distention *within* nations, in which the poor nations are no longer content to take the crumbs from our table, and rise up in either a military or some other form against the richer societies. And then the third is accumulating environmental problems, such that Australia, for example, becomes unlivable because of the ozone hole there, and Africa, from the Sahara to South Africa, becomes unlivable because of new diseases that have been uncovered through deforestation. At any rate, environmental catastrophes on a significant scale.

KK: *So you have multinational global currency collapse, social friction and warfare both between the rich and the poor and within nations, and you have continent-wide environmental disasters causing death and great migrations of people. All by the year 2020, yes? How certain are you about all this, what you call your optimism?*

KS: Well, I have spent the last 20 years looking into these problems, and I have suggested to my daughters, who are in their 20s, that it would be a mistake to have children.

KK: *Would you be willing to bet on your view?*

KS: Sure.

KK: *OK. [Pulls out a check.] Here's a check for a thousand dollars, made out to Bill Patrick, our mutual book editor. I bet you US $1,000 that in the year 2020, we're not even close to the kind of disaster you describe—a convergence of three disasters: global currency collapse, significant warfare between rich and poor, and environmental disasters of some significant size. We won't even be close. I'll bet on my optimism.*

KS: [Pauses. Then smiles.] OK. [Sale reaches over to checkbook on his desk and writes out a check. They shake hands.]

KK: *Oh, boy, this is easy money! But you know, besides the money, I really hope I am right.*

KS: I hope you are right, too.

110

QUESTIONING THE TEXT

1. Sale argues that technology's impact is always to put people out of jobs. In fact, he says that putting people out of jobs is the "point of a new technology"—to "save on labor costs and all the attendant costs with actual people." What evidence does Sale offer to support this claim? In what way does Kelly counter the claim?

2. Reread the interview, noting places where you agree with Sale and/or with Kelly. Which voice is most convincing to you? What specific places in the interview led you to that decision?

3. Take a look at the adjectives A.L. uses in describing *Wired* in her introduction. What effect do these adjectives have on your impression of the magazine?

MAKING CONNECTIONS

4. Might Sven Birkerts (p. 279) be called a Neo-Luddite? Why, or why not? List briefly the points where Sale and Birkerts might be likely to agree.
5. Look carefully at the images and metaphors used throughout the interview. What view of technology do they create? Are the images and metaphors that Sale uses different from those that Kelly uses? What might Emily Martin (p. 264) say to Sale and Kelly about the metaphors each uses?

JOINING THE CONVERSATION

6. New technologies are often seen as both exciting and threatening. With one or two classmates, discuss your own attraction to and/or fear of specific new technologies. Then, if you keep a reading log, record your ideas and feelings there.
7. Choose a technology that has been instrumental in improving your quality of life. Then write an essay in which you describe and explain the ways this technology has affected your daily life. You may begin by recounting what life was like before, or imagining what life would be like without, this technology.

J. MICHAEL BISHOP
Enemies of Promise

NOT LONG AGO *I discovered that the onboard diagnostic system of my new truck will let me know via a "Check Engine" light when I haven't screwed the gas cap on tight enough to prevent fumes from polluting the atmosphere. The computer in the truck discovers the problem not by monitoring a crude switch on the gas cap itself but by checking the entire combustion process and searching for irregularities. Anomalies—even momentary ones—detected this way are stored in the computer's memory so a technician can fix them later. The technology in my truck is almost as wondrous as that of the Internet, which enables me to converse with people anywhere in the world; or consider the science that recently produced a new asthma medication that means I can now play racquetball without carrying an inhaler. As you might suspect, I'm not in the camp of those who denigrate science or criticize technological change.*

I do understand the fears of the Luddites, who yearn for a world less chemically reprocessed and technologically demanding. But I also think that many who criticize science today have either short memories or little historical sense.

If you aren't moved by what science has done over the decades to reduce infant mortality or extend the human life span, consider a more immediate example: your teeth. You're likely to enjoy them all your life, intact and cavity-free, a benefit previous generations couldn't take for granted. Thank fluoride in toothpaste and drinking water for your pearly whites.

Sure, science can cause problems in our lives or environment. Many of us might prefer a world without synthetic fibers or nuclear fission. But that is no excuse for misconstruing the role of science or being ignorant of what scientists can and cannot do.

To counter a little of that ignorance, I wanted to share "Enemies of Promise" by J. Michael Bishop (b. 1936), a professor of microbiology at the University of California, San Francisco, and winner of the Nobel Prize. He warns that the misperceptions many people have about science could have serious consequences for all Americans. The piece is also a fine example of an expert writing clearly to an audience of non-specialists—something scientists will have to do more often if faith in science is to be restored.

"Enemies of Promise" appeared originally in my favorite magazine, the Wilson Quarterly *(Summer 1995), a publication of the Woodrow Wilson International Center for Scholars.* — J.R.

We live in an age of scientific triumph. Science has solved many of nature's puzzles and greatly enlarged human knowledge. And the fruits of scientific inquiry have vastly improved human welfare. Yet despite these proud achievements, science today is increasingly mistrusted and under attack.

Some of the opposition to science comes from familiar sources, including religious zealots who relentlessly press for the mandatory teaching of creationism in the public schools. It is discouraging to think that more than a century after the publication of Charles Darwin's *Origin of Species* (1859), and seventy years after the Scopes trial dramatized the issue, the same battles must still be fought. But fight them we must.

Other antagonists of science are less familiar. Strange though it may seem, there is within academe a school of thought that considers science to be wholly fraudulent as a way of knowing. According to these "postmodernists," the supposedly objective truths of science are in reality all "socially constructed fictions," no more than "useful myths," and science itself is "politics by other means." Anyone with a working knowledge of science, anyone who looks at the natural world with an honest eye, should recognize all of this for what it is: arrant nonsense.

Science, of course, is not the exclusive source of knowledge about human existence. Literature, art, philosophy, history, and religion all have their insights to offer into the human condition. To deny that is scientism—the belief that the methods of the natural sciences are the only means of obtaining knowledge. And to the extent that scientists have at times indulged in that belief, they must shoulder some of the blame for the misapprehensions that some people have about science.

But science does have something inimitable to offer humankind: it is, in   5
the words of physician-author Lewis Thomas,* "the best way to learn how the world works." A postmodernist poet of my acquaintance complains that it is in the nature of science to break things apart, thereby destroying the "mysterious whole." But we scientists take things apart in order to understand the whole, to solve the mystery—an enterprise that we regard as one of the great, ennobling tasks of humankind.

In the academic medical center where I work, the efficacy and benefits of science are a daily reality. So when I first encountered the postmodernist view of science some years ago, I dismissed it as either a strategy for advancement in parochial precincts of the academy or a display of ignorance. But now I am alarmed because the postmodernist cry has been joined, outside the academy, by other strong voices raised against science.

Consider these lines from Václav Havel, the widely admired Czech writer and statesman, who has vigorously expressed his disenchantment with

---

Lewis Thomas: See Thomas's "The Hazards of Science" on p. 236

the ethos of science: "Modern rationalism and modern science . . . now systematically leave [the natural world] behind, deny it, degrade and defame it—and, of course, at the same time, colonize it."

Those are angry words, even if their precise meaning is elusive. And anger is evident, too, in Havel's main conclusion: "This era [of science and rationalism] has reached the end of its potential, the point beyond which the abyss begins."

Even some influential men who know science well and who have been good friends to it in the past have joined in the chorus of criticism and doubt. Thanks in part to Havel's ruminations, Representative George E. Brown, Jr. (D.-Calif.), who was trained as a physicist, reports that his faith in science has been shaken. He complains of what he calls a "knowledge paradox": an expansion of fundamental knowledge accompanied by an increase in social problems. He implies that it shouldn't be that way, that as science progresses, the problems of society should diminish. And he suggests that Congress and the "consumers" of scientific research may have to take more of a hand in determining how science is conducted, in what research gets funded.

A similar critique has been made by former Colorado governor Richard   10
Lamm. He claims no longer to believe that biomedical research contributes to the improvement of human health—a truly astonishing stance. To validate his skepticism, he presents the example of the University of Colorado Medical Center. It has done "little or nothing," he complains, about increasing primary care, expanding medical coverage to the uninsured, dealing with various addictions and dietary excesses, and controlling violence. As if biomedical research, or even academic medical centers, had either the resources or the capabilities to do what Lamm desires!

The source of these dissatisfactions appears to be an exaggerated view of what science can do. For example, agitation within Congress may induce the National Science Foundation to establish a center for research on violence, but only the naive would expect a quick fix for that momentous problem. Three-quarters of a century after the death of the great German sociologist Max Weber (1864–1920), the social and behavioral sciences have yet to produce an antidote for even one of the common social pathologies. The genesis of human behavior entails complexities that still lie beyond the grasp of human reason.

Critics such as Brown and Lamm blame science for what are actually the failures of individuals or society to use the knowledge that science has provided. The blame is misplaced. Science has produced the vaccines required to control many childhood infections in the United States, but our nation has failed to deploy properly those vaccines. Science has sounded the alarm about acid rain and its principal origins in automobile emissions, but our society has not found the political will to bridle the internal combustion engine. Science has documented the medical risks of addiction to tobacco, yet our federal government still spends large amounts of money subsidizing the tobacco industry.

These critics also fail to understand that success in science cannot be dictated. The progress of science is ultimately driven by feasibility. Science is the art of the possible, of the soluble, to recall a phrase from the late British immunologist and Nobel laureate Sir Peter Medawar. We seldom can force nature's hand; usually, she must tip it for us.

Nor is it possible, especially in the early stages of research, to anticipate what benefits are likely to result. My own experience is a case in point. In 1911, Peyton Rous at the Rockefeller Institute in New York City discovered a virus that causes cancer in chickens, a seemingly obscure observation. Yet 65 years later, that chicken virus was the vehicle by which Harold Varmus and I, and our colleagues, were able to uncover genes that are involved in the genesis of human cancer. The lesson of history is clear: the lines of inquiry that may prove most fruitful to science are generally unpredictable.

Biologist John Tyler Bonner has whimsically recalled an exchange he   15 had some decades ago with the National Science Foundation, which had given him a grant for a research project. "After the first year, I wrote that things had not worked out very well—had tried this, that, and the other thing, and nothing had really happened. [The foundation] wrote back, saying, 'Don't worry about it—that is the way research goes sometimes. Maybe next

"In layman's terms? I'm afraid I don't know any layman's terms."
(© 1992 by Nick Downes)

year you will have better luck." Alas, no scientist today would think of writing such a report, and no scientist today could imagine receiving such a reply.

The great successes of science have helped to create the exaggerated expectations about what science can accomplish. Why has malaria not been eradicated by now? Why is a there still no cure for AIDS? Why is there not a more effective vaccine for influenza? When will there be a final remedy for the common cold? When will we be able to produce energy without waste? When will alchemy at last convert quartz to gold?

When scientists fail to meet unrealistic expectations, they are condemned by critics who do not recognize the limits of science. Thus, playwright and AIDS activist Larry Kramer bitterly complains that science has yet to produce a remedy for AIDS, placing much of the blame on the National Institutes of Health (NIH)—"a research system that by law demands compromise, rewards mediocrity and actually punishes initiative and originality."

I cannot imagine what law Kramer has in mind, and I cannot agree with his description of what the NIH expects from its sponsored research. I have assisted the NIH with peer review for more than twenty years. Its standards have always been the same: it seeks work of the highest originality and demands rigor as well. I, for one, have never knowingly punished initiative or originality, and I have never seen the agencies of the NIH do so. I realize with sorrow that Mr. Kramer is unlikely to believe me.

Biomedical research is one of the great triumphs of human endeavor. It has unearthed usable knowledge at a remarkable rate. It has brought us international leadership in the battle against disease and the search for understanding. I wonder how all this could have been accomplished if we scientists did business in the way that Kramer and critics like him claim that we do.

The bitter outcry from AIDS activists over the past decade was echoed in   20
the 1992 film *Lorenzo's Oil,* which portrays medical scientists as insensitive, close-minded, and self-serving, and dismisses controlled studies of potential remedies as a waste of precious time. The film is based on a true story, the case of Lorenzo Odone, a child who suffers from a rare hereditary disease that cripples many neurological functions and leads at an agonizing pace to death.

Offered no hope by conventional medical science, Lorenzo's desperate parents scoured the medical literature and turned up a possible remedy: the administration of two natural oils known as erucic and oleic acid. In the face of the skepticism of physicians and research specialists, Lorenzo was given the oils and, in the estimation of his parents, ceased to decline—perhaps even improved marginally. It was a courageous, determined, and even reasoned effort by the parents. (Mr. Odone has since received an honorary degree from at least one university.) Whether it was effective is another matter.

The movie portrays the treatment of Lorenzo as a success, with the heroic parents triumphant over the obstructionism of medical scientists. The film ends with a collage of parents testifying that the oils had been used successfully to treat Lorenzo's disease in their children. But it fails to present any of the parents who have tried the oils with bitter disappointment. And, of course, all of this is only anecdotal information. Properly controlled studies are still in progress. To date, they have not given much cause for hope.

Meanwhile, as if on cue, medical scientists have since succeeded in isolating the damaged gene responsible for the rare disease. Thus, the stage is set for the development of decisive clinical testing and effective therapy (although the latter may be long in coming).

If misapprehensions abound about what science can and cannot do, so do misplaced fears of its hazards. For more than five years now, my employer, the University of California, San Francisco, has waged a costly battle for the right to perform biomedical research in a residential area. For all intents and purposes, the university has lost. The opponents were our neighbors, who argued that we are dangerous beyond tolerance; that we exude toxic wastes, infectious pathogens, and radioactivity; that we put at risk the lives and limbs of all who come within reach—our own lives and limbs included, I suppose, a nuance that seems lost on the opposition. One agitated citizen suggested in a public forum that the manipulation of recombinant DNA at the university had engendered the AIDS virus; another declared on television her outrage that "those people are bringing DNA into my neighborhood."

Resistance to science is born of fear. Fear, in turn, is bred by ignorance. 25 And it is ignorance that is our deepest malady. The late literary critic Lionel Trilling described the difficulty well, in words that are even more apposite now than when he wrote them: "Science in our day lies beyond the intellectual grasp of most [people] . . . This exclusion . . . from the mode of thought which is habitually said to be the characteristic achievement of the modern age . . . is a wound . . . to our intellectual self-esteem . . . a diminution of national possibility . . . a lessening of the social hope."

The mass ignorance of science confronts us daily. In recent international testing, U.S. high school students finished ninth in physics among the top twelve nations, eleventh in chemistry, and dead last in biology. Science is poorly taught in most of our elementary and secondary schools, when it is taught at all. Surveys of adult Americans indicate that only a minority accepts evolution as an explanation for the origin of the human species. Many do not even know that the Earth circles the Sun. In a recent committee hearing, a prominent member of Congress betrayed his ignorance of how the prostate gland differs from the testes. Accountants, laborers, lawyers, poets, politicians, and even many physicians look upon science with bewilderment.

Do even we scientists understand one another? A few years ago, I read of a Russian satellite that gathers solar light to provide constant illumination of large areas of Siberia. "They are taking away the night," I thought. "They are taking away the last moments of mystery. Is nothing sacred?" But then I wondered what physicists must think of biologists' hopes to decipher the entire human genome and perhaps recraft it, ostensibly for the better.

Writing an article about cancer genes for *Scientific American* some years ago, I labored mightily to make the text universally accessible. I consulted students, journalists, laity of every stripe. When these consultants all had approved, I sent the manuscript to a solid-state physicist of considerable merit. A week later, the manuscript came back with this comment: "I have read your paper and shown it around the staff here. No one understands much of it. What exactly is a gene?"

Robert M. Hazen and James Trefil, authors of *The Sciences: An Integrated Approach* (1994), tell of twenty-three geophysicists who could not distinguish between DNA and RNA, and of a Nobel Prize–winning chemist who had never heard of plate tectonics. I have encountered biologists who thought string theory had something to do with pasta. We may be amused by these examples; we should also be troubled. If science is no longer a common culture, what can we rightfully expect of the laity by way of understanding?

Lionel Trilling knew where the problem lay in his time: "No successful   30
method of instruction has been found . . . which can give a comprehension of sciences . . . to those students who are not professionally committed to its mastery and especially endowed to achieve it." And there the problem lies today: perplexing to our educators, ignored by all but the most public-minded of scientists, bewildering and vaguely disquieting to the general public.

We scientists can no longer leave the problem to others. Indeed, it has always been ours to solve, and all of society is now paying for our neglect. As physicist and historian of science Gerald Holton has said, modern men and women "who do not know the basic facts that determine their very existence, functioning, and surroundings are living in a dream world . . . are, in a very real sense, not sane. We [scientists] . . . should do what we can, or we shall be pushed out of the common culture. The lab remains our workplace, but it must not become our hiding place."

The enterprise of science embodies a great adventure: the quest for understanding in a universe that the mathematician Freeman Dyson once characterized as "infinite in all directions, not only above us in the large but also below us in the small." We of science have begun the quest well, by building a method of ever-increasing power, a method that can illuminate all that is in the natural world. In consequence, we are admired but also feared, mistrusted, even despised. We offer hope for the future but also moral conflict and ambiguous choice. The price of science seems large, but to reject science is to deny the future.

QUESTIONING THE TEXT

1. Have you ever encountered the attitude toward science that Bishop describes as *postmodern?* If so, explain this notion of science as a set of "socially constructed fictions." If not, explore the concept of science as what Lewis Thomas describes as "the best way to learn how the world works." Share your work with classmates, and explore the difference between science as a useful fiction and science as an ennobling fact.

2. Are there any words, concepts, or examples in "Enemies of Promise" that you don't understand? Based on his text, how would you characterize Bishop's intended readership?

3. What is J.R.'s attitude toward scientific progress as demonstrated in his introduction? How does the introduction influence your reading of Bishop's "Enemies of Promise" ?

MAKING CONNECTIONS

4. On the Internet, explore a Usenet group or listserv that discusses scientific issues. Follow a discussion or controversy for several days, and then write a paragraph reporting on it.

5. Victor Frankenstein, in Mary Shelley's selection from *Frankenstein* (p. 230), describes this way the rejection of the monster that he created: "I felt the bitterness of disappointment; dreams that had been my food and pleasant rest for so long a space were now become a hell to me; and the change was so rapid, the overthrow so complete!" Does the rejection of science in our time as described by Bishop reflect disappointment and bitterness that we have not created the technological Utopia that once seemed just over the horizon? Freewrite on this subject, and then write a position paper on this question: Has science today become Dr. Frankenstein's monster?

6. Write an imaginary dialogue between J. Michael Bishop and a Luddite similar to the dialogue presented in Kevin Kelly's "Interview with the Luddite." Fashion it as an argument that explores several sides of the issue and searches for areas of agreement.

JOINING THE CONVERSATION

7. Write a 200-word summary or abstract of "Enemies of Promise" for readers who might not have time to study the entire piece.

8. Choose an example of a scientific or technological change that has occurred in the last 100 years; read about it in the library, using at least three different sources; and then write an evaluation of that change.

9. Examine a technology that you believe has caused more problems than it has solved, and write an essay in which you propose a solution to at least some of those problems. Trace the cause of the problem in the technology—is it a problem in the science, in social attitudes, in politics, and so on?

EMILY MARTIN
The Body at War: Media Views of the Immune System

WRITING SOME FORTY YEARS AGO about "Roots for a New Rhetoric" that could foster global understanding, Father Daniel Fogarty called language our "most significant invention." "Out of language," he continued, we "have fashioned the exquisite sensitivity of Hamlet, the instruments of psychotherapy, and that sizable but sensible dream that became the United Nations." Fogarty's statements stress the power of language to shape the reality we perceive. Chief among the powers of language is that of metaphor, the very basis of language symbols. In "Metaphors We Live By," for instance, the linguists George Lakoff and Mark Johnson demonstrate the ways in which metaphors underlie and reinforce not only the values we hold but the reasons we give for holding them.

We have all seen these insights enacted on television: think, for example, of the toothpaste commercials you have seen featuring chemical creatures fighting plaque or tooth decay in the service of sales, or consider the number of songs that depend on the metaphor of a broken heart to sell their particular sentiments. And powerful metaphors inform our desktops well: think how different the "product" might be if we had not "Microsoft office" as a guiding metaphor but, say, "Microsoft kitchen."

Building on these insights about language and metaphor, the cultural critic Emily Martin (b. 1944), Mary Garrett Professor of Anthropology at the Johns Hopkins University, traces the metaphoric representation of the human immune system from its first widespread dissemination as a topic of interest in 1957 to the present. Martin's analysis reveals that the most powerful metaphors associated with the immune system are those of war and battle, and she reflects on the ways in which these war scenes are populated by identities that are gendered, raced, and classed. Using vivid examples drawn from books, songs, paintings, cartoons, and advertising, Martin shows how saturated our culture is with the image of "the body at war" and asks us to think about the full implications of viewing our bodies in this way.

Having studied the history and theory of rhetoric, of how we persuade and understand one another, for most of my adult life, I am particularly interested in the questions Martin asks: What difference does it make how we represent or image ourselves in words? How does our manner of talking about things inevitably shape how we can know (and not know) those things? I believe that examining the work of science with these questions in mind will not detract from the importance of the scientific enterprise but rather enrich and strengthen it. Read this chapter from Martin's book Flexible Bodies: Tracking Immunity in American Culture—From the Days of Polio to the Age of AIDS *(1994) and think about the power of metaphor in your own life. − A.L.*

But the thing that sticks to my mind more than anything else is, do you remember the movie *The Fantastic Voyage?* Where they shoved people down inside the body? Do you remember the scene when they had to go outside the ship to fix the cell, and the little antibodies were coming all around them and everything like that? I think that's where I get a lot of my ideas from, you know? That was probably the first real exposure I had to the human body and the immune system, because I was young, I was still in elementary school.

CHARLES KINGSLEY

When Mack Drury found out that his lover had tested positive for HIV, he told us, he faced the difficult task of getting himself tested. At the clinic he visited, Mack and the others in the waiting room watched a film about AIDS that illustrated graphically how HIV will destroy the cells in your immune system. He said that he fled from the clinc, disturbed because the images and language in the film were so upsetting, and afraid that his health would be affected by them.

Mack's conviction that his health would be harmed by the images in the film made me want to explore in some detail media coverage of the immune system. I include here audio, print, and other visual media that are usually available to a mass audience. . . .

Perhaps the notion of an immune "system" was first widely disseminated to the reading public through an article condensed in the *Reader's Digest* in 1957 (Brecher and Brecher 1957). Accompanying a small but steady rate of publications about the immune system in mass market magazines throughout the 1960s and 1970s, two major film productions featured the immune system.[1] *The Fantastic Voyage*, starring Raquel Welch, first appeared in 1966, and several people we interviewed mentioned that they remembered it vividly. (It is now available in local video stores.) Several main components of the immune system (antibodies, macrophages, lymph nodes) had a role to play in the film, which involved miniaturizing a submarine for travel through the arteries and veins of a Russian scientist who had defected from the Soviet Union. The scientist had been so severely injured that conventional surgery would have been no use. The goal of the crew was to remove a blood clot caused by his injury so the Russian could recover consciousness and divulge Soviet secrets to the Americans. The team of medical specialists and army personnel inside the submarine tried to travel through the Russian's body to reach the site of his injury, which they attempted to repair with a laser. Along the way, caught while wearing a diving suit outside the submarine, Raquel Welch was attacked by antibodies. These were depicted as flickering shapes that adhered tightly to her chest and nearly suffocated her, until, just in the nick of time, the male members of the team managed (more than slightly lasciviously) to pull them off with their hands. In the end, the villain of the drama (a double

---

[1]According to *Magazine Index,* there were about thirty articles on some aspect of immunity or the immune system published per year from 1960 to 1980.

agent) was horribly killed, suffocated by the billowing white mass of a macrophage as the ship passed through a lymph node.

In the early 1970s, a television program called "The Immortal" featured a hero who had a "supercharged immune system that made him impervious to the diseases and the gradual wearing down the flesh is heir to. Traumas like a bullet to the heart could kill the guy, but if he survived, his wounds would heal within hours" (Laliberte 1992:56; see also Terrace 1985–86:215).

Riding the crest of the huge wave of media interest in the immune sys-   5
tem that began in the early 1980s, science writers such as Peter Jaret published major articles on the immune system and embellished them with electron micrographs of immune system cells and their interactions. According to the readers' survey carried out by the National Geographic Society, Jaret's 1986 photographic essay garnered the most commendations of any article published that year and prompted a large number of requests of reprints. [2]

Jaret's essay in the *National Geographic* apparently inspired writers for several other mass media periodicals, which shortly thereafter featured cover stories on the immune system (see fig. 1): *Time* (Jaroff 1988), *U.S. News and World Report* (Brownlee 1990), and *Awake!* (November 1990).[3] The *Reader's Digest* once again presented a major article on the immune system, this time a condensation of Jaret's article (Jaret 1987).

At the same time, the syndrome that we now call AIDS was beginning to be understood as an immune system dysfunction, enormously increasing both scientific and public interest in how the immune system works or fails to work. Beginning in the early 1980s, there was an explosion of interest in periodicals on the immune system, whether measured in absolute numbers or as a percentage of all articles in periodicals.[4] Apart from periodicals, other print media on the immune system mushroomed. Here I can give only the slightest indication of the quantity of this material by indicating its range. There are books that combine science education with practical guidelines for a healthy immune system (e.g., Dwyer 1988; Fox and Fox 1990; Pearsall 1987; Potts and Morra 1986). There are books that appeal to methods of strengthening the immune system that are intended to be different from those of biomedicine (e.g., Chopra 1989; DeSchepper 1989; Michaud and Feinstein 1989; Muramoto 1988; Serinus 1987). There is also a special genre of children's books on the immune system (e.g, Benziger 1989, 1990; Galland 1988; Gelman 1992).

As one would expect given the flourishing of books and magazines, there are many audiotapes devoted to the health of the immune system, subliminal and otherwise (e.g., Sutphen 1988; Mars 1992; Achterberg and Lawlis 1992). There are also high school and college science teaching films galore

---

[2]Peter Jaret, interview, December 1992. The details were kindly provided by the National Geographic Society.

[3]This magazine is translated into sixteen languages.

[4]According to a count produced by *Magazine Index*, by 1981–85 there were over 150 articles a year, by 1986–90 over 300 per year, and in 1992 alone over 450.

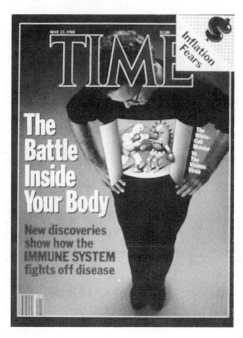

Fig. 1. The body's immune system (the white-cell wonder) shown in a boxing match with the vicious virus. From *Time*, **23 May 1988. © 1988 Time Inc. Reprinted by permission.**

(*The Human Immune System: The Fighting Edge, Immune System Disorders, Lupus,* and *Internal Defenses* are examples from one catalog),[5] science films for grade school and middle school students (*The Immune System: Your Magic Doctor, The Immune System: Our Internal Defender*),[6] seminars for health professionals of all sorts,[7] and seminars for continuing adult education.[8]

The portrait of the body conveyed most often and most vividly in the mass media shows it as a defended nation-state, organized around a hierarchy of gender, race, and class.[9] In this picutre, the boundary between the body

---

[5]Films for the Humanities and Sciences, *1992–93 Health Education Video Catalogue* (Princeton, N.J.).

[6]For descriptions, see Copeland (1992) and Rubin (1989).

[7]Mind Matters Seminars (Stanford, Calif.) ran three seminars on "The Immune System: Minding the Body, Embodying the Mind" in the Baltimore area in the fall of 1992.

[8]The Johns Hopkins School of Continuing Studies ran a course on psychoneuroimmunology in the fall of 1991 that was oversubscribed; the course was offered again the following year.

[9]Haraway (1989:14) terms this the "hierarchical, localized organic body." In her work, Haraway eloquently stresses the displacement of the hierarchical, localized body by new parameters: "a highly mobile field of strategic differences . . . a semiotic system, a complex meaning-producing field"(p. 15). No one could improve on her characterization of these new elements; I would add only that there may be strategic reasons why a remnant of the old body is carried forward with the new.

("self") and the external world ("nonself") is rigid and absolute: "At the heart of the immune system is the ability to distinguish between self and nonself. Virtually every body cell carries distinctive molecules that identify it as self" (Schindler 1988:1). These molecules are class 1 MHC proteins, present on every nucleated cell in an individual's body and different from every other individual's. One popular book calls these our "trademark" (Dwyer 1988:37). The maintenance of the purity of self within the borders of the body is seen as tantamount to the maintenance of the self: a chapter called "The Body under Siege," in the popular book on the immune system *In Self Defense,* begins with an epigraph, from Shakespeare: "To be or not to be, that is the question" (Mizel and Jaret 1985:1).[10]

The notion that the immune system maintains a clear boundary between self and nonself is often accompanied by a conception of the nonself world as foreign and hostile.[11] Our bodies are faced with masses of cells bent on our destruction: "To fend off the threatening horde, the body has devised astonishingly intricate defenses" (Schindler 1988:13). As a measure of the extent of this threat, popular publications depict the body as the scene of total war between ruthless invaders and determined defenders:[12] "Besieged by a vast array of invisible enemies, the human body enlists a remarkably complex corps of internal bodyguards to battle the invaders" (Jaret 1986:702). A site of injury is "transformed into a battle field on which the body's armed forces, hurling themselves repeatedly at the encroaching microorganisms, crush and annihilate them" (Nilsson 1985:20).

Small white blood cells called *granulocytes* are "kept permanently at the ready for a blitzkrieg against microorganisms" and constitute the "infantry" of the immune system. "Multitudes fall in battle, and together with their vanquished foes, they form the pus which collects in wounds." Larger macrophages are another type of white blood cell that is depicted as the "armored unit" of the defense system. "These roll forth through the tissues . . . devouring everything that has no useful role to play there." Another part of the immune system, the complement system, can "perforate hostile organisms so that their lives trickle to a halt." These function as "'magnetic mines.' They are sucked toward the bacterium and perforate it, causing it to explode" (Nilsson 1985:24, 25, 24, 72). When complement "comes together in the right sequence, it detonates like a bomb, blasting through the invader's cell membrane" (Jaret 1986:720). The *killer cells,* the technical scientific name of a type of T lymphocyte, are the "immune system's special combat units in the

---

[10]This may relate to what Petchesky (1981:208) calls the ideology of "privatism."

[11]For lack of space, I cannot deal with the subtleties of how this "old body discourse" appears in interviews. Suffice it to say that military metaphors are extremely widespread.

[12]These include mass media magazines such as *Time* and *Newsweek* as well as the *National Geographic.* They also include more expensive items such as Lennert Nilsson's popular coffee table book *The Body Victorious* (1985).

war against cancer." Killer cells "strike," "attack," and "assault" (Nilsson 1985:96, 98, 100). "The killer T cells are relentless. Docking with infected cells, they shoot lethal proteins at the cell membrane. Holes form where the protein molecules hit, and the cell, dying, leaks out its insides" (Jaroff 1988:59).

To understand the immune system, we are to think of it "as a disciplined and effective army that posts soldiers and scouts on permanent duty throughout your body" (Laliberte 1992:56). These warriors identify a threat, attack and destroy our enemies so quickly that we often do not know that we were threatened: the immune system never takes prisoners." The story of the human immune system "reads like a war novel": our lymph nodes are major centers for the breeding of "attack dogs," called antibodies (Gates 1989:16). In sum, the body "has devised a series of defenses so intricate they make war games look like child's play" (National Institute of Allergy and Infectious Diseases 1985:5).

Although the metaphor of warfare against an external enemy dominates these accounts, another metaphor plays nearly as large a role: the body as police state.[13] Every body cell is equipped with "'proof of identity'—a special arrangement of protein molecules on the exterior . . . these constitute the cell's identity papers, protecting it against the body's own police force, the immune system. . . . The human body's police corps is programmed to distinguish between bona fide residents and illegal aliens—an ability fundamental to the body's power of self-defense" (Nilsson 1985:21). What identifies a resident is likened to speaking a national language: "An immune cell bumps into a bacterial cell and says, 'Hey, this guy isn't speaking our language, he's an intruder.' That's defense" (Levy, quoted in Jaret 1986:733). "T cells are able to 'remember for decades' the identity of foreign antigens: the intruders' descriptions are stored in the vast criminal records of the immune system. When a substance matching one of the stored descriptions makes a new appearance, the memory cells see to the swift manufacture of antibodies to combat it. The invasion is defeated before it can make us ill. We are *immune*" (Nilsson 1985:28).

What happens to these illegal aliens when they are detected? They are "executed" in a "death cell," the digestive cavity inside a feeding cell (Nilsson 1985:25, 31, 76, 81). "When the walls have closed around the enemy, the execution—phagocytosis—takes place. The prisoner is showered with hydrogen peroxide or other deadly toxins. Digestive enzymes are sent into the death chamber to dissolve the bacterium" (Nilsson 1985:81).

---

[13]At times the "police" become more like antiterrorist squads, as befits the task of finding enemies within who are bent on destruction. Paula Treichler points out that the AIDS virus is a "spy's spy, capable of any deception . . . a terrorist's terrorist, an Abu Nidal of viruses" (1987:282).

Not surprisingly, identities involving gender, race, and class are present   15
in this war scene. Compare two categories of immune system cells,
macrophages, which surround and digest foreign organisms, on the one hand,
and T cells, which kill by transferring toxin to them, on the other. The
macrophages are a lower form of cell; they are called a "primeval tank corps"
(Michaud and Feinstein 1989:4), "a nightmare lurching to life" (Page
1981:115). T cells are more advanced, evolutionary, and have higher functions, such as memory (Jaroff 1988:60). It is only these advanced cells who
"attend the technical colleges of the immune system" (Nilsson 1985:26).

There is clearly a hierarchical division of labor here, one that is to some
extent overlaid with gender categories familiar in European and American
culture. Specifically, one might wonder about the female associations with the
engulfing and surrounding that macrophages do and the male associations
with the penetrating or injecting that killer T cells do. In addition, many
scholars have pointed out the frequent association of the female, symbolically,
with lower functions, especially with the lack or lesser degree of mental functions.

Beyond this, macrophages are the cells that are the "housekeepers" (Jaret
1986) of the body, cleaning up the dirt and debris, including "dead bodies,"
both themselves and foreign cells. (One immunologist called them "little
drudges.")[14] "The first defenders to arrive would be the phagocytes [a category
of 'eating' cells that includes macrophages]—the scavengers of the system.
Phagocytes constantly scour the territories of our bodies, alert to anything that
seems out of place. What they find, they engulf and consume. Phagocytes are
not choosy. They will eat anything suspicious that they find in the bloodstream,
tissues, or lymphatic system" (Jaret 1986:715). Given their uncultivated origins,
it should not be surprising that, after eating, a macrophage "burps": "After it fin-
ishes its meal, it burps out pieces of the enemy and puts them out on its surface"
(Michaud and Feinstein 1989:6). As macrophages feed, they may be described
as "angry," in a "feeding fury," or "insatiable" (Page 1981:104), combining in
one image uncontrolled emotions and an obliterating, engulfing presence, both
common cultural ascriptions of females.

Gender might not be the only overlay on the division of labor in our
cells. Racial overtones may be there as well, although I have less convincing
evidence for them. Macrophages are the cells that actually eat other cells belonging to the category *self* and so engage in "a kind of small-scale cannibalism" (Nilsson 1985:25). Cannibalism is often associated with the attribution
of a lower, animal nature to those who engage in it (Arens 1979). In media
coverage of the immune system, macrophages are seen as feminized in some
ways but as simply "uncivilized" in others. These "cannibals" are indiscrimi-

---

[14]Overheard by Paula Treichler, personal communication.

nate eaters, barbaric and savage in their willingness to eat any manner of thing at all. Sometimes macrophages are feminized "housekeepers," and sometimes they seem to be marked by race, class, or a combination of the two, as when they are described as "big, primitive garbage collectors" (Jaret 1986:733), "roving garbage collectors" (Brownlee 1990:50), a "'cleanup' crew" (Pearsall 1987:41), or "roving scavengers" (Jaroff 1988:58).

To explore further the popular media imagery of the hierarchy of cells, we need to look at another immune system cell, the B cell. B cells are clearly ranked far above the lowly macrophage. They are not educated in the college of the thymus, but they are "educated" in the bone marrow (Dwyer 1988:47), and they have enormous specificity. They rank below the T cell, however, which is consistently termed the *orchestrator* of the immune response and which activates B cells. In one popular book, this is called giving the B cell "permission" (Dwyer 1988:47) to attack invading organisms. B cells exist in two stages, immature and mature B cells. Mature B cells are the cells that, having been stimulated by antigens of the right specificity, and with T cell "permission," rapidly produce antibodies against invading antigens. In a children's book about the immune system, all the immune system cells are given names and identities. The B cell, called "Bubbles" (see fig. 2), bulged "big and bright" as she began to make antibodies. When "Major D," a type of T cell, gives the order, "Bubbles danced about as she emptied bag after bag into the blood" (Benziger 1990:20).

This suggests that B cells are sometimes feminized but rank much higher in the hierarchy than the lowly macrophage.[15] This means that in the B cell we may have a kind of upper-class female, a suitable partner for the top-ranked T cell. These two types of cells together have been termed "the mind of the immune system" (Galland 1988:10). In illustrations of these cells in *Peak Immunity* (see fig. 3), each of them is depicted with a drawing of a human brain (DeSchepper 1989:16). Far below them in terms of class and race we would find the macrophage, angry and engulfing, or scavenging and cleaning up.

In this system, gendered distinctions are not limited to male and female; they also encompass the distinction between heterosexual and homosexual. T cells convey aspects of male potency, cast as heterosexual potency. They are the virile heroes of the immune system, highly trained commandos who are selected for and then educated in the technical college of the thymus gland. T cells are referred to as the "commander in chief of the immune system" (Jaret 1986:708) or the "battle manager" (Jaroff 1988:58). Some T cells, killer cells, are masculine in the old-fashioned mold of a brawny, brutal he-man: in a mail advertisement from *Prevention* magazine for a book (i.e., Michaud and

20

---

[15]B cells are not always feminized: Michaud and Feinstein (1989:13, 7, respectively) depict them as admirals and supermen.

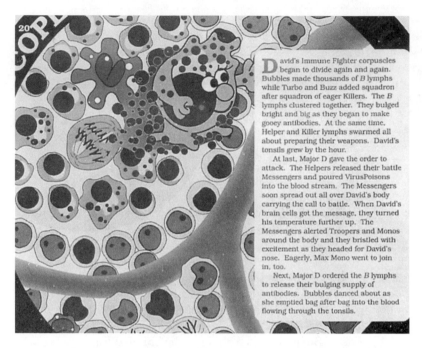

David's Immune Fighter corpuscles began to divide again and again. Bubbles made thousands of *B* lymphs while Turbo and Buzz added squadron after squadron of eager Killers. The *B* lymphs clustered together. They bulged bright and big as they began to make gooey antibodies. At the same time, Helper and Killer lymphs swarmed all about preparing their weapons. David's tonsils grew by the hour.

At last, Major D gave the order to attack. The Helpers released their battle Messengers and poured VirusPoisons into the blood stream. The Messengers soon spread out all over David's body carrying the call to battle. When David's brain cells got the message, they turned his temperature further up. The Messengers alerted Troopers and Monos around the body and they bristled with excitement as they headed for David's nose. Eagerly, Max Mono went to join in, too.

Next, Major D ordered the *B* lymphs to release their bulging supply of antibodies. Bubbles danced about as she emptied bag after bag into the blood flowing through the tonsils.

Fig. 2. A depiction of a B cell as "Bubbles," who is dancing about as she empties antibodies into the blood. From J. Benziger, *The Corpuscles: Adventure in InnerSpace* ([1989]:20)/Corpuscles Intergalactica, 40 Johnson Heights, Waterville, ME 04901.
(Copyright © 1989 by John Benziger, Reprinted with permission of the author.)

Feinstein 1989) on the immune system, we are told, "You owe your life to this little guy, the Rambo of your body's immune system." A comic book produced for AIDS education depicts T cells as a squad of Mister Ts (see fig. 4), the muscular hero from the television show "The A Team."

Other T cells, T 4 cells, have a masculinity composed of intellect, strategic planning ability, and a propensity for corporate team participation, powers well suited for the world of global corporations.[16] The T 4 cell is often called *the quarterback of the immune system* because he orchestrates everything else and because he is the brains and memory of the team. As one source puts it, "Besides killer T cells . . . there are also helper [T 4] and suppressor T cells. *Somebody* has to make strategic decisions." This popular manual on the

---

[16]For a lengthy discussion of why teamwork and group cooperation are required in the economic world, see Kash (1989).

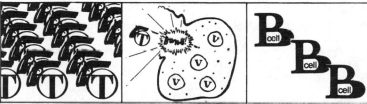

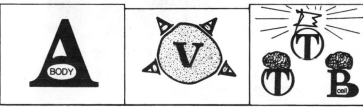

Fig. 3. Star wars of the immune system, showing T cells and B cells with brains and memory.

(From L. DeSchepper, *Peak Immunity* (1989:15–16). Reprinted with permission of the author and Beacon Press.)

Fig. 4. A squad of Mister T cells attempts to do in HIV but is defeated.
(From D. Cherry, "AIDS Virus," in *Risky Business* (1988:5). Reprinted with permission of the publisher. Reprinted by permission of the San Francisco AIDS Foundation.)

immune system, called *Fighting Disease*, clinches the heterosexuality of the T cell: "In order to slip inside a cell, a virus has to remove its protein coat, which it leaves outside on the cell membrane. The viral coat hanging outside signals the passing T cell that viral hanky panky is going on inside. Like the jealous husband who spots a strange jacket in the hall closet and *knows* what's going on in the upstairs bedroom, the T cell takes swift action. It bumps against the body cell with the virus inside and perforates it" (Michaud and Feinstein 1989:10, 8).

However they are marked by gender, sexuality, race, or class, all these cells of the immune system belong to "self" and have the primary function of defending the self against the nonself. When the nonself is a disease-causing microbe, the model works quite logically. But when the nonself is a fetus growing inside a woman's body, the model quickly runs into difficulty. As the popular media explain it, since the fetus is a graft of foreign tissue inside the mother, why does she not "mount an attack against the fetus as she would against any other allograft [a graft from a genetically different member of the same species]?" (Kimball 1986:433). The lack of an attack is even more mysterious given that pregnant women have antibodies to certain antigens expressed by the fetus. The reduction in the woman's normal immune response, which would be to destroy the fetal "nonself," whatever the mechanism, is called *tolerance*. From an immunological point of view, the fetus is a "tumor" that the woman's body should try furiously to attack (Dwyer 1988:60). But the mother's immune system "tolerates" her fetus; all our immune systems "tolerate" our own tissues, unless we suffer from autoimmune disease.

Immunologists have yet fully to answer the question of how the body achieves tolerance; in the meantime, it is interesting to wonder whether other images of the body less reliant on hard boundaries and strict distinctions might produce another set of questions altogether. Work in feminist theory suggests that there is a masculinist bias to views that divide the world into sharply opposed, hostile categories, such that the options are to conquer, be conquered, or magnanimously tolerate the other. The stance is one from which nature can be dominated and a separation from the world maintained (Keller 1985:124).[17] Many mothers and fathers might find the notion of a baby in utero as a tumor that the mother's body tries its best to destroy so counterintuitive as to warrant searching for a different set of organizing images altogether.[18]

Another set of images coexists in the popular media with these scenes of battle and is also imbued with hierarchies involving gender and class. This other set of images coexists uneasily with the first, is subdued by taking up far less space in printed descriptions, and is able to generate far fewer visual images to express itself. It depicts the body as a "regulatory-communications network" (Schindler 1988:1). As Haraway's work emphasizes, the body is seen as "an engineered communications system, ordered by a fluid and dispersed command-control-

[17]Keller (1992:116–17) illustrates how easily the language of evolutionary biology slips from descriptions of nature as neutrally indifferent to descriptions of nature as callous and hostile.

[18]Elsewhere, I am developing an account of fetus-mother interaction in an immunological environment in which blurry self-nonself discrimination is assumed. After all, babies are born, tissue can be grafted, and many bacteria live (to the benefit of our health) in our gut.

intelligence network" (1989:14). Hierarchy is replaced by dispersed control; rigidly prescribed roles are replaced by rapid change and flexible adaptation. The emphasis shifts from the various roles played by the parts of the immune system to "the most remarkable feature of the immune system . . . the system itself—the functioning of diverse elements as an efficient, effective whole" (National Jewish Center for Immunology and Respiratory Medicine 1989:2). As an example, consider a pamphlet on the immune system that is available from the National Cancer Institute.[19] In the midst of elaborate military metaphors—"defense against foreign invaders," "stockpiling a tremendous arsenal," "intricate defenses to fend of the threatening horde"—a very different set of images appears: The immune system is described as "an incredibly elaborate and dynamic regulatory-communications network. Millions and millions of cells, organized into sets and subsets, pass information back and forth like clouds of bees swarming around a hive. The result is a sensitive system of checks and balances that produces an immune response that is prompt, appropriate, effective, and self-limiting" (Schindler 1988:1). This is an image of a complex system held together by communication and feedback, not divided by category and hierarchy. Often, in this mode, accounts stress how rapidly the system can be poised to change in response to its environment. Description of that process can easily slip back into the military analogy: "By storing just a few cells specific for each potential invader, it [the immune system] has room for the entire array. When an antigen appears, these few specifically matched cells are stimulated to multiply into a full-scale army. Later, to prevent this army from overexpanding wildly, like a cancer, powerful suppresser mechanisms come into play" (National Institute of Allergy and Infectious Diseases 1985:3). One way in which a few accounts diminish the tension between these two images is specifically to stress the changed character of contemporary warfare: the great variety of different "weapons" is a product of evolutionary adaptation to changing defense needs: "Just as modern arsenals are ever changing as the weaponry of a potential enemy becomes more sophisticated, so our immune system has adapted itself many times to counter survival moves made by the microbial world to protect itself" (Dwyer 1988:28).

In sum, for the most part, the media coverage of the immune system operates largely in terms of the image of the body at war. Even when the problem is not an external enemy like a microbe but an internal part of "self," the military imagery is extended to notions of "mutiny," "self-destruction," and so on.[20] In one television show, autoimmunity was described

---

[19]This pamphlet can be obtained by calling 1-800-4CANCER or through Info-quest (CD-ROM) in many public libraries.

[20]A Toronto newspaper reported that "Vancouver psychologist Andrew Feldmar offers an intriguing explanation for the adult onset of autoimmune disease: 'It strikes people who in their childhood were inhibited from differentiating who is their enemy, who is their friend'" (Maté 1993:16).

as "we have met the enemy and the enemy is us."[21] A book on AIDS written by a physiologist for a general audience repeatedly refers to autoimmunity as "the immunological equivalent of civil war" (Root-Bernstein 1993:87).[22]

Powerful as the impact of media images may be, we would be terribly misled if we took their content as the only sign of what is being understood in the wider culture. Many studies assume that the content of mass media products gives transparent evidence of "cultural ideas." Some further assert that the mass media do not allow any meaningful response from the public: they are "opposed to mediation"; they "fabricate noncommunication" (Baudrillard 1985).[23] Ethnographic exploration will quickly show us that the reality is far more complex. In the end, we will see that media images, rich as they seem, are impoverished in comparison to the living collage of ideas produced by people—scientists and nonscientists.

QUESTIONING THE TEXT

1. Martin's chapter presents a very large number of sources in support of her thesis. Look back through her chapter to identify the major areas these sources come from. How do these examples support her argument? How credible are they to you?

2. In addition to the image of immune system as a battleground, Martin sketches in another set of images that depict the body as a "regulatory-communications network." In your experience, which set of images is most prevalent? List as many examples as you can think of that add to either category. What other images can you think of that are associated with the body or the body's immune system?

3. What is A.L.'s view of language? How does she reveal this view in her introduction?

---

[21]Reported to me by Ariane van der Straten.

[22]David Napier explores the implications of using a metaphor of self-destruction to describe illness. He suggest that, despite the disorientation that might be produced, telling someone who is suffering that her body is at war with itself can be a helpful thing to do: "People often do feel better when they can salvage a 'self' from a ravaged body; we learn to deal with illness by setting it up as something against which we can define (even through dissociation) a better condition of selfhood" (1992:187).

[23]For a detailed discussion of Baudrillard's views of the media, see Connor (1989). I have found Mah (1991) useful in considering the pitfalls of thinking that any text can be treated as a transparent window into culture. Recent ethnographic media studies have allowed the "reading" of media messages to take into account what people in the culture say (e.g., Morley 1992). For some of the rich variety of current studies of culture through the media, see Gitlin (1987), Fiske (1987), and Robbins (1993).

MAKING CONNECTIONS

4. In "Enemies of Promise" (p. 256), J. Michael Bishop offers a definition (one that seems particularly limited, even a caricature) of "postmodernist" views of science. How might Emily Martin respond to Bishop's definition and discussion of these "postmodernist" views? In what ways might her analysis support Bishop's claims for science?

5. In "Perseus Unbound" (p. 279), Sven Birkerts distinguishes between two kinds of knowledge and study. Which kind of knowledge does Martin's chapter discuss? What in her text allows you to make that decision? What cautions might she add to those raised at the end of Birkerts's chapter?

JOINING THE CONVERSATION

6. Imagine that you, Thomas (the monster from Mary Shelley's *Frankenstein*, p. 230), Birkerts, and Martin are all on a talk show. The host asks each of you to define *science*. Write your own definition of the term, and then try to define science from the perspective of the other guests on the show. Compare your definitions with those of your classmates. What areas of agreement and disagreement do you find?

7. Choose a subject you are particularly interested in, and conduct an investigation of the ways that topic is represented in images and words. You might, for example, look at the ways mothers are represented in popular advertisements, songs, cartoons, or stories, or at how teenagers are depicted in several major newspapers and on television shows. Gather as many examples of the images as you can, and then examine them for their metaphoric power: What do they suggest about the topic you are investigating? What values do they attach to it? This investigation could easily lead to a full-scale research report. If you undertake one, try tracking your topic on the Internet.

8. With one or two classmates, try to corroborate or challenge Martin's findings. Look through contemporary magazines and newspapers, especially those that deal with scientific subjects, and review relevant television programs, movies, or songs. Bring your evidence to class for discussion.

SVEN BIRKERTS
Perseus Unbound

THE HOOPLA OVER *the release of* Windows 95 *made one point clear: America is wired. Businesses and schools use computers in great numbers already, and more and more families every day rely on silicon chips for word processing, tax computing, and entertainment. The long-promised networking of America via the electronic superhighway is accelerating thanks to the seductiveness of the World Wide Web (WWW), an easy path onto the Internet that accommodates words, pictures, sounds, even movies. People trade cool Web sites now, and e-mail addresses are almost as common as phone numbers. What a change, and how quickly it has occurred!*

Is everyone happy with this new electronic world? It's hard to tell. I love the speed and power of the new information technologies, the capability of moving, for example, from my university library to the Library of Congress via a keyboard and monitor. I enjoy answering student queries via e-mail and browsing newsgroups and Web sites. Yet I know, too, that swift change can catch people off guard like a powerful wave, leaving them little time to reflect or to ask, "What are the consequences and costs of these developments?" That's why I thought that a cautionary note about computers and technology, like that in Sven Birkerts's "Perseus Unbound," from The Gutenberg Elegies: The Fate of Reading in an Electronic Age *(1994), might be appropriate for this chapter. Birkerts is a writer and critic—and a bit of a curmudgeon (by his own admission) when it comes to the electronic millennium.* – J.R.

Birkerts's title is a clear allusion to the Promethean myth of the fire-bringer whose gift is also a great burden. Will Birkerts be making the same claim about technology?
— A.L.

Like it or not, interactive video technologies have muscled their way into the formerly textbound precincts of education. The videodisc has mated with the microcomputer to produce a juggernaut: a flexible and encompassing teaching tool that threatens to overwhelm the linearity of print with an array of option-rich multimedia packages. And although we are only in the early stages of implementation—institutions are by nature conservative—an educational revolution seems inevitable.

Several years ago in *Harvard Magazine*, writer Craig Lambert sampled some of the innovative ways in which these technologies have already been applied at Harvard. Interactive video programs at the Law

The ominous terms—"muscled," "juggernaut," "threaten," "overwhelm"—confirm my opinion. All imply that we'll learn something very negative about interactive technologies. — A.L.

279

School allow students to view simulated police busts or actual courtroom procedures. With a tap of a digit they can freeze images, call up case citations, and quickly zero-in on the relevant fine points of precedent. Medical simulations, offering the immediacy of video images and instant access to the mountains of data necessary for diagnostic assessment, can have the student all but performing surgery. And language classes now allow the learner to make an end run around tedious drill repetitions and engage in proto-conversations with video partners.

The hot news in the classics world, meanwhile, is Perseus 1.0, an interactive database developed and edited by Harvard associate professor Gregory Crane. Published on CD-ROM and videodisc, the program holds, according to its publicists, "the equivalent of 25 volumes of ancient Greek literature by ten authors (1 million Greek words), roughly 4,000 glosses in the on-line classical encyclopedia, and a 35,000-word on-line Greek lexicon." Also included are an enormous photographic database (six thousand images), a short video with narration, and "hundreds of descriptions and drawings of art and archeological objects." The package is affordable, too: Perseus software can be purchased for about $350. Plugged in, the student can call up a text, read it side by side with its translation, and analyze any word using the Liddell–Scott lexicon; he can read a thumbnail sketch on any mythic figure cited in the text, or call up images from an atlas, or zoom in on color Landsat photos; he can even study a particular vase through innumerable angles of vantage. The dusty library stacks have never looked dustier.

Although skepticism abounds, most of it is institutional, bound up with established procedures and the proprietorship of scholarly bailiwicks. But there are grounds for other, more philosophic sorts of debate, and we can expect to see flare-ups of controversy for some time to come. For more than any other development in recent memory these interactive technologies throw into relief the fundamental questions about knowledge and learning. Not only what are its ends, but what are its means? And how might the means be changing the ends?

Perseus is remarkable, and extremely helpful for someone like me who has a great interest in the texts but little facility with ancient Greek. I don't see the down side here. — A.L.

These features hardly seem threatening, to students or instructors. — J.R.

As a student growing up during this shift in technology, I am interested in where this point will lead. — T.E.

From the threshold, I think, we need to distinguish between kinds of knowledge and kinds of study. Pertinent here is German philosopher Wilhelm Dilthey's distinction between the natural sciences (*Naturwissenschaften*), which seek to explain physical events by subsuming them under causal laws, and the so-called sciences of culture (*Geisteswissenschaften*), which can only understand events in terms of the intentions and meanings that individuals attach to them.

To the former, it would seem, belong the areas of study more hospitable to the new video and computer procedures. Expanded databases and interactive programs can be viewed as tools, pure and simple. They give access to more information, foster cross-referentiality, and by reducing time and labor allow for greater focus on the essentials of a problem. Indeed, any discipline where knowledge is sought for its application rather than for itself could only profit from the implementation of these technologies. To the natural sciences one might add the fields of language study and law.

The distinction he tries to make in the next 3 paragraphs isn't clear to me. My friends in the natural and physical sciences would not see themselves as seeking "knowledge for its application rather than for itself." Birkerts sets up a false dichotomy. There are those in both the natural sciences and humanities who seek knowledge for its own sake and for "understanding" and who seek knowledge in order to apply it.
— A.L.

But there is a danger with these sexy new options—and the rapture with which believers speak warrants the adjective—that we will simply assume that their uses and potentials extend across the educational spectrum into realms where different kinds of knowledge, and hence learning, are at issue. The realms, that is, of *Geisteswissenschaften,* which have at their center the humanities.

In the humanities, knowledge is a means, yes, but it is a means less to instrumental application than to something more nebulous: understanding. We study history or literature or classics in order to compose and refine a narrative, or a set of narratives about what the human world used to be like, about how the world came to be as it is, and about what we have been—and are—like as psychological or spiritual creatures. The data—the facts, connections, the texts themselves—matter insofar as they help us to deepen and extend that narrative. In these disciplines the *process* of study may be as vital to the understanding as are the materials studied.

I resist surrendering electronic technologies to the hard sciences and consigning the humanities to dusty libraries. — J.R.

Given the great excitement generated by Perseus, it is easy to imagine that in the near future a whole range of innovative electronic-based learning packages will be available and, in many places, in use. These will surely include the manifold variations on the electronic book. Special new software texts are already being developed to bring us into the world of, say, Shakespeare, not only glossing the literature, but bathing the user in multimedia supplements. The would-be historian will step into an environment rich in choices, be they visual detailing, explanatory graphs, or suggested connections and sideroads. And so on. Moreover, once the price is right, who will be the curmudgeons who would deny their students access to the state-of-the-art?

When trying to read a work via an electronic source, I often find the cross-references distracting. — T.E.

Being a curmudgeon is a dirty job, but somebody has to do it. Someone has to hoist the warning flags and raise some issues that the fast-track proselytizers might overlook. Here are a few reservations worth pondering.

Here loaded terms—"dirty job," "warning flags," "fast-track proselytizers"— set Birkerts up as the good guy, white hat firmly in place, riding in to save us from the techno-baddies. — A.L.

1. Knowledge, certainly in the humanities, is not a straightforward matter of access, of conquest via the ingestion of data. Part of any essential understanding of the world is that it is opaque, obdurate. To me, Wittgenstein's famous axiom, "The world is everything that is the case," translates into a recognition of otherness. The past is as much about the disappearance of things through time as it is about the recovery of traces and the reconstruction of vistas. Say what you will about books, they not only mark the backward trail, but they also encode this sense of obstacle, of otherness. The look of the printed page changes as we regress in time; under the orthographic changes are the changes in the language itself. Old-style textual research may feel like an unnecessarily slow burrowing, but it is itself an instruction: It confirms that time is a force as implacable as gravity.

Right. We need to be critical about embracing technologies that radically change our relationship to information. It's easy to lose perspective. — J.R.

Yet the multimedia packages would master this gravity. For opacity they substitute transparency, promoting the illusion of access. All that has been said, known, and done will yield to the dance of the fingertips on the terminal keys. Space becomes

How is this an entirely bad phenomenon? — T.E.

hyperspace, and time, hypertime ("hyper-" being the fashionable new prefix that invokes the nonlinear and nonsequential "space" made possible by computer technologies). One gathers the data of otherness, but through a medium which seems to level the feel—the truth—of that otherness. The field of knowledge is rendered as a lateral and synchronic enterprise susceptible to collage, not as a depth phenomenon. And if our media restructure our perceptions, as McLuhan* and others have argued, then we may start producing generations who know a great deal of "information" about the past but who have no purchase on pastness itself.

Described in this way, the effects of interactive programs on users sound a good deal like the symptoms of postmodernism. And indeed, this recent cultural aesthetic, distinguished by its flat, bright, and often affectless assemblages of materials may be a consequence of a larger transformation of sensibility by information-processing technologies. After all, our arts do tend to mirror who we are and anticipate what we might be becoming. Changes of this magnitude are of course systemic, and their direction is not easily dictated. Whether the postmodern "vision" can be endorsed as a pedagogic platform, however, is another question.

2. Humanistic knowledge, as I suggested earlier, differs from the more instrumental kinds of knowledge in that it ultimately seeks to fashion a comprehensible narrative. It is, in other words, about the creation and expansion of meaningful contexts. Interactive media technologies are, at least in one sense, anticontextual. They open the field to new widths, constantly expanding relevance and reference, and they equip their user with a powerful grazing tool. One moves at great rates across subject terrains, crossing borders that were once closely guarded. The multimedia approach tends ineluctably to multidisciplinarianism. The positive effect, of course, is the creation of new levels of

There's merit in his objection. Web sites in particular do have the flat, bright faces Birkerts bemoans. The "interfaces" of electronic technologies might change and perhaps homogenize the reading experience.   — J.R.

Personal limits will be set as to where an individual travels on electronic media. Birkerts seems afraid of too much information.— T.E.

He is right to say that electronic technologies allow for nonlinearity and nonsequential ways of reading and knowing. Scholars have been pointing this out for at least fifteen years. We must investigate all the implications of these new possibilities, but I was expecting more concrete discussion or advice from Birkerts about how to do it.   — A.L.

Who will create these "grazing tools"? Who or what will provide the links we need to make sense of so much information?   — A.L.

McLuhan: Marshall McLuhan, theorist of contemporary culture. For more on McLuhan, see Neil Postman's "The Word Weavers / The World Makers," p. 133.

This seems a bit far-fetched.
— T.E.

connection and integration; more and more variables are brought into the equation.

But the danger should be obvious: The horizon, the limit that gave definition to the parts of the narrative, will disappear. The equation itself will become nonsensical through the accumulation of variables. The context will widen until it becomes, in effect, everything. On the model of Chaos science, wherein the butterfly flapping its wings in China is seen to affect the weather system over Oklahoma, all data will impinge upon all other data. The technology may be able to handle it, but will the user? Will our narratives—historical, literary, classical—be able to withstand the data explosion? If they cannot, then what will be the new face of understanding? Or will the knowledge of the world become, perforce, a map as large and intricate as the world itself?

A specific example would help here. If electronic texts encourage unexpected connections and links, they also tend to be hierarchically structured at deeper levels—providing a creative tension in the way we experience them.
— J.R.

3. We might question, too, whether there is not in learning as in physical science a principle of energy conservation. Does a gain in one area depend upon a loss in another? My guess would be that every lateral attainment is purchased with a sacrifice of depth. The student may, through a program on Shakespeare, learn an immense amount about Elizabethan politics, the construction of the Globe theater, the origins of certain plays in the writings of Plutarch,* the etymology of key terms, and so on, but will this dazzled student find the concentration, the will, to live with the often burred and prickly language of the plays themselves? The play's the thing—but will it be? Wouldn't the sustained exposure to a souped-up cognitive collage not begin to affect the attention span, the ability if not willingness to sit with one text for extended periods, butting up against its cruxes, trying to excavate meaning from the original rhythms and syntax? The gurus of interaction love to say that the student learns best by doing, but let's not forget that *reading* a work is also a kind of doing.

Most Shakespearean plays I have read contained this information in forewords or afterwords. I fail to see how what Birkerts is referring to could be much different.
— T.E.

This change has already taken place under the influence of TV. If we want people to have longer attention spans, we are certainly going to have to teach to this goal. — A.L.

4. As a final reservation, what about the long-

Plutarch (CE 46?–120?): Greek writer, author of *Parallel Lives*, a source for several of Shakespeare's plays

I'm not sure read-
ers will have to
process information
more rapidly be-
cause of electronic
technologies.
They'll just have
easier access to in-
formation. Isn't
the time and en-
ergy wasted in li-
braries locating
books or searching
indexes better
spent reading the
materials that on-
line or hypertex-
tual sources pro-
vide so readily?
— J.R.

Humans use only
a fraction of their
brain capacity.
Why not stretch
that? — T.E.

Electronic infor-
mation in essence
is not much differ-
ent from books;
we can look up al-
most anything
now in texts.
Birkerts is being
petty. — T.E.

term cognitive effects of these new processes of data absorption? Isn't it possible that more may be less, and that the neural networks have one speed for taking in—a speed that can be increased—and quite another rate for retention? Again, it may be that our technologies will exceed us. They will make it not only possible but irresistible to consume data at what must strike people of the book as very high rates. But what then? What will happen as our neural systems, evolved through millennia to certain capacities, modify themselves to hold ever-expanding loads? Will we simply become smarter, able to hold and process more? Or do we have to reckon with some other gain/loss formula? One possible cognitive response—call it the "S.A.T. cram-course model"—might be an expansion of the short-term memory banks and a correlative atrophying of long-term memory.

But here our technology may well assume a new role. Once it dawns on us, as it must, that our software will hold all the information we need at ready access, we may very well let it. That is, we may choose to become the technicians of our auxiliary brains, mastering not the information but the retrieval and referencing functions. At a certain point, then, we could become the evolutionary opposites of our forebears, who, lacking external technology, committed everything to memory. If this were to happen, what would be the status of knowing, of being educated? The leader of the electronic tribe would not be the person who knew most, but the one who could execute the broadest range of technical functions. What, I hesitate to ask, would become of the already antiquated notion of wisdom?

I recently watched a public television special on the history of the computer. One of the many experts and enthusiasts interviewed took up the knowledge question. He explained how the formerly two-dimensional process of book-based learning is rapidly becoming three-dimensional. The day will come, he opined, when interactive and virtual technologies will allow us to more or less dispense with our reliance on the sequence-

History teaches us
that our technolo-
gies always exceed
us, that we always
lag behind in
terms of under-
standing the ethi-
cal and moral,
perhaps even the
pedagogical, im-
pact of technolo-
gies. The technol-
ogy of the book
provides a perfect
example. — A.L.

No doubt the sta-
tus of knowledge
is changing and in
the next century
we will value dif-
ferent things as
"knowledge." But
this too has been
the way of the
world. — A.L.

I sometimes shudder too. But then I remember the charges brought against early Greek poetry and drama: that it wasn't "real," not the "old hard world" but only an imitation. The more things change, the more they stay the same! — A.L.

based print paradigm. Whatever the object of our study, our equipment will be able to get us there directly: inside the volcano or the violin-maker's studio, right up on the stage. I was enthralled, but I shuddered too, for it struck me that when our technologies are all in place—when all databases have been refined and integrated—that will be the day when we stop living in the old hard world and take up residence in some bright new hyperworld, a kind of Disneyland of information. I have to wonder if this is what Perseus and its kindred programs might not be edging us toward. That program got its name, we learn from the brochure, from the Greek mythological hero Perseus, who was the explorer of the limits of the known world. I confess that I can't think of Perseus without also thinking of Icarus, heedless son of Daedalus, who allowed his wings to carry him over the invisible line that was inscribed across the skyway.

Oh, dear. Has Birkerts seen the World Wide Web? It is already this Disneyland of information he fears. —J.R.

Afterwords

I appreciate but do not entirely share the reservations that Sven Birkerts expresses about the place of electronic technology in the humanities. No doubt, there are differences in our experiences of meeting an idea in a book and on the screen. By coincidence, I read Birkerts's "Perseus Unbound" on the very day that I gained network access to the English Poetry Full-Text Database, a huge and searchable database that can summon 165,000 poems to my computer screen via the World Wide Web. Using a powerful search function, I type in the word bicycle *and, moments later, discover that it occurs in only five of those many poems—the labor of months accomplished in mere seconds. But when I call up one of those works to my screen—"A Bird of Night" by Gerald Massey—it appears in plain script against a gray screen, an unappealing scrawl of words unprotected by the comforting textures of a book. "A Bird of Night," I discover, is a forgettable poem I'd likely never have encountered but for this experiment. Still, I wonder: Would a greater poem—"Tintern Abbey," for example—seem diminished if viewed coldly on a screen? Only a few keystrokes bring Wordsworth's masterpiece, a poem I haven't read in years, to my computer. Yet as I scroll through its 160 familiar lines, the poet's reflections on nature seem as rewarding as ever and I am somehow relieved. Wordsworth needs no parchment to touch the heart. And so perhaps Shakespeare will prove a prophet yet again: There is magic in the Web!* — J.R.

I had heard quite a bit about Birkerts's book, and I knew it had been well re-viewed, so I approached it full of expectations. But I came away disappointed, for many of the reasons I try to point out in my annotations. Like J.R., I "do not entirely share the reservations" Birkerts "expresses about the place of electronic technology in the humanities." While I am a devoted fan of books, not to mention a lifelong avid reader, and while I have an aesthetic feel for books as Birkerts does, those are, in my opinion, acquired habits. After all, when I pause to think about it, books are fairly flat items themselves, bound and regimented in the many ways that print culture has dictated: black on white; repetitive and standard type size; controlled margins, everything nice and neat. Long gone are the luxuriant illuminated manuscripts of old, the eccentric and colorful hand-made documents that broke all the rules, creating their own sense of aesthetics as they went along. So I am not particularly nostalgic about books, especially in their present largely regimented forms. Electronic textuality, as I see it, offers a way to recapture some of the playfulness and joie de vivre *of very early books: with hypertext, interactive fiction, multimedia capabilities of all kinds, writers have aesthetic options that print text does not easily allow. (I often think that James Joyce would be in writerly heaven with the new technologies, since his novels call out for just the kinds of capabilities electronic textuality now offers.) And electronic technology brings books as well as myriad other materials to my desk at a keystroke, as it did just recently when I called up* Moby-Dick *to search for a particular passage, or when I needed to find the spot in* Beowulf *where the hero talks about his "word horde."*

These are benefits I would not want to give up. But am I a total fan of the new technology? I am not, although my concerns seem different from those of Birkerts. Rather than fret over cognitive effects, or the loss of print books, I worry about other things. Most of all, I worry about who will have access to this wide world of information and who will not. I worry about the teacher from South Africa who told me last year, "We don't even have books and paper yet, never mind computers or the Internet." And I worry that people controlling the architecture and hardware of our technology will work not for freedom of information and expression but for the almighty dollar alone. These are the concerns I hope my students will help me explore as we move beyond the Gutenberg Elegies *and into the twenty-first century.* — A.L.

This article brings to light very important questions, such as the impact that easy access to information will have on the learning process. However, I feel that Birkerts's assumptions come across as products of an overactive imagination colored by panic. But we must be realistic. It remains unlikely that electronic sources will wipe out written texts: too many people enjoy sitting down and digging through books; it would be inconvenient and difficult to take an electronic novel on a car trip.

It is also unlikely that electronic aids will cause students to focus more on the electronic dazzle than on content. Electronic tools can be used as supple-

ments. If educators are tuned in to the advantages of both media of learning, students will be able to absorb the benefits of both without feeling overwhelmed by the sheer mass of information available. The issue need not turn into an either/ or debate, nor is it likely that we will ever be forced to choose between written text and electronic sources. — T.E.

QUESTIONING THE TEXT

1. Birkerts acknowledges that video technology in the classroom raises fundamental questions: "Not only what are its ends, but what are its means? And how might the means be changing the ends?" Try asking these questions in different and perhaps more familiar contexts. Working in a group, think of additional examples of technology changing not only how something happens but what in fact is accomplished. For example, did the introduction of jet aircraft change more than just the speed of travel?
2. Birkerts argues that interactive video "books" and familiar technologies may be better suited to teaching factually based subjects like the sciences and the law than culturally based subjects like the humanities. Choose a subject from the course catalog at your school and design an interactive video to support it, using words, sound, images, and various linked texts. Then compare your "products" with those invented by classmates and discuss the issue that Birkerts raises: Might video books be better suited to some subjects than to others?
3. In the last paragraph of his essay, Birkerts explains how the Perseus database got its name. To what does Birkerts's title "Perseus Unbound" allude?
4. In his introduction, J.R. expresses the fear that technological change may be occurring too quickly for many people to grasp. Reflect upon this concern. Have you been influenced by rapid change?

MAKING CONNECTIONS

5. From what you have observed, do humans have a grasp on the changes occurring as a result of electronic networks and computers, or is change out of control—like Frankenstein's monster? Freewrite on this idea, and then develop a position paper on the subject.
6. Compare Birkerts's skepticism about computer technology with Kirkpatrick Sale's Luddite views in Kevin Kelly's "Interview with the Luddite" (p. 243). With whom do you agree more: Birkerts, Sale, or the interviewer Kevin Kelly?

7. In "The Word Weavers / The World Makers" in chapter 3 (p. 133), Neil Postman suggests that students need to be educated about the uses and impacts of technology. Review Postman's essay in light of Birkerts's "Perseus Unbound." Do you think the kind of education in technology that Postman proposes addresses the concerns Birkerts has about electronic books?

JOINING THE CONVERSATION

8. Birkerts argues that newer "hypertextual" ways of organizing information flatten our perspectives on knowledge by reducing the effort we put into reading. Analyze Birkerts's essay, thinking particularly of any electronic resources you have used, and then write a critical response to "Perseus Unbound."

9. Birkerts agrees to take on the role of curmudgeon, criticizing a technology that everyone else seems to embrace. In a short essay, play the curmudgeon yourself, daring to question a concept, technology, proposal, or organization that almost everyone else seems unwilling to doubt.

MATTHEW ROHRER
Found in the Museum of Old Science

THE FORERUNNERS OF true scientific texts, such as Pliny's Natural History *(77 C.E.), a catalog of "the contents of the entire world," can seem to readers today like eccentric collections of lore gleefully conflating sober fact and robust fiction. In his thirty-seven-volume encyclopedia, Pliny, an indefatigable scholar and advisor to the emperor Vespasian, offered both perceptive truths, especially about botany and agriculture, and outrageous fallacies, some still believed—for example, that people's ears ring when others are talking about them. Early museums of science were just as eccentric and unsystematic as the old texts, more like the overstuffed drawers of hyperactive twelve-year-olds than the serious institutions we visit today. But these ancient treasure troves gathered from all corners of the globe surely fired the imagination of thinkers.*

When he wrote "Found in the Museum of Old Science," Matthew Rohrer (b. 1970) was working in the Van Allen Astronomy Building at the University of Iowa and thinking about ancient books and cosmology: "I liked the styles of the old texts I was reading—they weren't very fluid; they were like haphazard jottings by someone who wanted to be sure they didn't forget to record every detail." It was also a summer of disastrous floods in the Midwest, so that Rohrer would ponder raindrops is not surprising.

"Found in the Museum of Old Science" is from Rohrer's A Hummock in the Malookas *(1995), winner of the 1994 National Poetry Series.*

Beyond the sky is a great river, along whose banks grow spectacular
plants: the celestial peach, the moon rose, the lily-of-the-void. When the
flowers fall into the river and sink to the bottom, the river overflows and a
drop of water is forced out of the bottom into the sky. Finding itself all
alone up there, it falls.   5

Unlike snowflakes, there are only three types of raindrops.

A raindrop crowded out by a celestial peach blossom is the largest and
falls the fastest. A raindrop crowded out by a moon rose falls at an angle
and is nearly impossible to catch on the tongue. A raindrop crowded out
by the lily can fall through the eye of a needle, if you hold it just right.   10

Unlike a tear, a raindrop has no parents. A raindrop has no idea why it has
been born, and sadly, no one to ask. So one does not hear raindrops
complain when they fall onto the clear roof of a greenhouse.

As a raindrop falls it reflects the whole world. A raindrop falling over
Oklahoma seems evenly divided by roads. A raindrop falling onto a grove   15
of aspens in a pine forest seems to have left its lights on. A raindrop
falling on one city holds a knife; on another, a tiny black pistol. A raindrop
falling into your eye thinks it's you, watching a raindrop fall into its eye.

Famous Raindrops:

Obviously, the first one to fall.   20
The lucky raindrop who fell down the neck of Helen's dress.
The drop that tried to save the library at Alexandria.
The first raindrop to land on the Ark, on the nose of the figurehead
that was Noah's wife.
Edison's favorite raindrop; the one he kept in a test tube.   25
The last drop Beethoven ever heard.

IN RESPONSE

1. Can you explain how raindrops—or other natural phenomena such as
   lightning, tornadoes, waves, photosynthesis—work? With two or three
   classmates, choose several natural phenomena and then write paragraphs
   explaining them as clearly and technically as you can to an imagined audience of fourth and fifth graders. How good is your working knowledge of the natural world?
2. Choosing one of the phenomena you worked with in question 1, write
   an imaginative response to it similar to Rohrer's treatment of raindrops
   in "Found in the Museum of Old Science."
3. Read "Found in the Museum of Old Science" alongside "The Creation" (p. 166). In what ways might creation stories be like old scientific
   texts?
4. Try adding several items to the poem's roster of "Famous Raindrops,"
   or choose a similar category (famous lightning bolts, flames, gusts of
   wind) and compose your own list.

OTHER READINGS

Bolter, Jay David, *Writing Space: The Computer, Hypertext, and the History of Writing*. Hillsdale, NJ: Lawrence Erlbaum, 1991. Considers the shape of writing in the computer age.

Florman, Samuel C. *Blaming Technology: The Irrational Search for Scapegoats*. New York: St. Martin's, 1981. Argues the importance of not turning away from technological change.

Griffin, Susan. *Woman and Nature: The Roaring Inside Her*. New York: Harper, 1978. Juxtaposes patriarchal views of nature and women as inferior to men and shows the importance of passion in dealing with ecological issues.

Gross, Paul R., and Norman Levitt. *Higher Superstition: The Academic Left and Its Quarrels with Science*. Baltimore: Johns Hopkins UP, 1994. Debunks the assumptions of feminist, African American, and other leftist critiques of science.

Holton, Gerald. "What Place for Science in Our Culture at the 'End of the Modern Era'?" *Einstein, History, and Other Passions*. New York: American Institute of Physics Press, 1994. Argues that attacks on objectivity represent an attempt to delegitimize science.

Johnson, George. *Fire in the Mind: Science, Faith, and the Search for Order*. New York: Knopf, 1995. Focuses on Los Alamos to explore the human drive for order as expressed in different cultural traditions.

Weinberg, Steven. "The Methods of Science . . . And Those by Which We Live." *Academic Questions* Spring 1995: 7–13. Defends scientific method.

ELECTRONIC RESOURCES

Latest Hubble Space Telescope Pictures:
http://www.stsci.edu/EPA/Latest.html
Furnishes the latest pictures from the Hubble Space Telescope.

The NASA Homepage:
http://www.gsfc.nasa.gov/NASA_homepage.html
Provides information about the National Aeronautics and Space Administration.

Skeptic Magazine:
http://www.rtd.com/~lippard/skeptic/ss-skeptic.html
Provides access to a journal that explores scientific and pseudoscientific phenomena.

The Smithsonian Institution Home Page:
http://www.si.edu/
Provides access to information about the many Smithsonian museums.

6

Gender:
Women . . . and Men

SHE'S VERY CHARLIE.

Charlie

REVLON

Look carefully at this perfume advertisement. Why did the advertising team compose as they have, in terms of what the eye is drawn to, what is foregrounded or emphasized, and so on? Given that the ad intends to sell perfume, what appeals does it make to prospective buyers? Who is the targeted audience for this advertisement —a certain age group? a certain socioeconomic class? a certain gender? What values does this ad implicitly hold and recommend? What details project those values? What statements does this ad make about gender?

And the rib, which the LORD God had taken from man, made he a woman, and brought her unto the man.

Genesis, 1–3

If the first woman God ever made was strong enough to turn the world upside down all alone, these women together ought to be able to turn it back. . . .

SOJOURNER TRUTH, *Ain't I a Woman?*

Growing up homosexual was to grow up normally but displaced; to experience romantic love, but with the wrong person; to entertain grand ambitions, but of the unacceptable sort; to seek a gradual self-awakening, but in secret, not in public.

ANDREW SULLIVAN, *What Are Homosexuals For?*

She obeyed him; she always did as she was told.

MAXINE HONG KINGSTON, *No Name Woman*

There is indeed a national "hysteria" over [the] new forceful feminism—but it's *male* hysteria.

SUSAN FALUDI, *Whose Hype?*

Believing that women are virtually under siege, the "gender feminists" naturally seek recruits to their side of the gender war. They seek support. They seek vindication. They seek ammunition.

CHRISTINA HOFF SOMMERS, *Figuring Out Feminism*

. . . I suspect that it is better to accept that boys are not, on the whole, docile creatures who wish to live in harmony with one another, but are, instead, highly competitive, physically energetic creatures who hunt in packs.

DAVID THOMAS, *The Mind of Man*

. . . if God did not want us to make gender-based generalizations, She would not have given us genders.

DAVE BARRY, *Guys vs. Men*

Into any new world we enter, let us take this man.

SHARON OLDS, *Son*

Introduction

IN CHOOSING THE SELECTIONS for this chapter, we found ourselves talking about the old nursery rhyme:

> What are little girls made of?
> What are little girls made of?
> Sugar and spice and everything nice,
> That's what little girls are made of.

> What are little boys made of?
> What are little boys made of?
> Snips and snails and puppy dog tails,
> That's what little boys are made of.

The readings in this chapter ask you to give serious attention to the
question this old rhyme asks. What *are* the differences between girls and
boys, between men and women? Are such differences solely genetic/
biological? Or are the differences due more to culture and to our life experiences? Are they some of both "nature" and "nurture"?

In thinking about these questions, you may want to consider a
distinction many people make between sex and gender. Researchers
often define *sex* as the chromosomal patterns that identify humans as
male or female and *gender* as those psychological patterns that give humans a sense of being male or female. According to this distinction, we
are born one sex or the other—but we develop gender identities
through social and cultural practices. Another way to think about this
distinction is to see sex as a bipolar set, either male or female, but gender as a range of roles people may adopt—from the intensely "feminine" at one extreme to the intensely "masculine" at the other, but
with limitless degrees of variation in between.

We have realized during our discussion of readings in this chapter
that, although we have many things in common (we are about the same
age, come from the same racial group, went to graduate school together,
and even got our Ph.D.'s on the same day), we are also very different people. And we have puzzled and argued over how our differences may be related to our differing sexes. As you turn to the readings, you may wish to
think about the ways in which being either male or female has affected
your life—the choices you have made, the ways you have related to other
people, and the way others have related to you. Each of the readings addresses this central concern or some of its implications. Following are
some questions to start you thinking about gender:

- List ten things—jokes, foods, sports, attitudes—you think of as
  characteristic of women and ten you consider characteristic of

men. Then compare the two lists. What do they reveal about your assumptions regarding gender?

- Do men and/or women need to be liberated, and if so, from what? Why, or why not?
- How have feminists improved—or failed to improve—the lot of women today?
- Do you know of examples or have personal experience of sexual harassment on the job?
- Can you remember a time when you were treated in a special way or treated unfairly because of your sex or gender? You might want to meet with a group of classmates to exchange stories about these experiences.

• • •

Genesis 1–3

EVERY CULTURE WE KNOW OF has a story of creation, one that chronicles the origins of the world and, often enough, the making of the first man and/or woman. The ancient Greek culture, for example, told the story of Gaia, the Earth, who sprang out of chaos and created Uranus, the Heavens, with whom she then mated to produce the Titans. A Native American culture describes Raven, a powerful mythological creature, as discovering the first people in a large clamshell. One very familiar account of the creation appears in chapters 1 through 3 of the book of Genesis in the Bible: God creates man in the image of God, gives man dominion over all things on earth, and then creates woman to be a helper to man. After she is tempted by the serpent, the couple fall out of a perfect existence and into self-consciousness and knowledge of evil.

This familiar story, of which the best-known English translation, the King James Version of 1611, is printed below, raises a number of questions about men and women. Are the two sexes equal creations of God—or is woman subordinate to man? Who is responsible for the temptation and fall? Most important for the discussion taking place in this chapter, how does this passage from Genesis represent the sexes—and how does this representation affirm or contradict your own views of the relationship between them? — A.L.

CHAPTER 1

26   And God said, Let us make man in our image, after our likeness: and let them have dominion over the fish of the sea, and over the fowl of the air, and over the cattle, and over all the earth, and over every creeping thing that creepeth upon the earth. . . .

CHAPTER 2

18   And the LORD God said, *It is* not good that the man should be alone; I will make him an help meet for him.

19   And out of the ground the LORD God formed every beast of the field, and every fowl of the air; and brought *them* unto Adam to see what he would call them: and whatsoever Adam called every living creature, that *was* the name thereof.

20   And Adam gave names to all cattle, and to the fowl of the air, and to every beast of the field; but for Adam there was not found an help meet for him.

21   And the LORD God caused a deep sleep to fall upon Adam, and he slept: and he took one of his ribs, and closed up the flesh instead thereof;

22   And the rib, which the LORD God had taken from man, made he a woman, and brought her unto the man.

CHAPTER 3

Now the serpent was more subtil than any beast of the field which the LORD God had made. And he said unto the woman, Yea, hath God said, Ye shall not eat of every tree of the garden?

2   And the woman said unto the serpent, We may eat of the fruit of the trees of the garden:

3   But of the fruit of the tree which *is* in the midst of the garden, God hath said, Ye shall not eat of it, neither shall ye touch it, lest ye shall die.

4   And the serpent said unto the woman, Ye shall not surely die:

5   For God doth know that in the day ye eat thereof, then your eyes shall be opened, and ye shall be as gods, knowing good and evil.*

6   And when the woman saw that the tree *was* good for food, and that it *was* pleasant to the eyes, and a tree to be desired to make *one* wise, she took of the fruit thereof, and did eat, and gave also unto her husband with her; and he did eat.

7   And the eyes of them both were opened, and they knew that they *were* naked; and they sewed fig leaves together, and made themselves aprons.

QUESTIONING THE TEXT

1. Look up *dominion* in the dictionary and find out its derivation—where the word comes from. What does it mean to have "dominion" over all things on earth? Write two or three sentences to explain this passage.

2. After eating the forbidden fruit, man and woman become suddenly aware of their nakedness. Why is this awareness a result of eating from the tree of knowledge of good and evil? Why were they unaware of their nakedness before?

3. Examine Genesis, chapters 1–3, in their entirety. Then look at A.L.'s excerpts from these chapters. Are there passages in those chapters you would have included? Why might A.L. have omitted them?

---

ye shall be as gods . . . good and evil: For an exploration of the idea that modern science represents a human effort to "be as gods," see "The Hazards of Science," by Lewis Thomas (p. 236).

MAKING CONNECTIONS

4. In "The Mind of Man" (p. 337), David Thomas quotes an "old calypso song" that states "Man smart, Woman smarter." How might the writers of Genesis respond to this song? What evidence in the passage from Genesis might be used to support—or refute—this statement?
5. In what ways might the serpent's interaction with the woman be interpreted as a form of victimization? Consider the arguments made by Susan Faludi (p. 324).

JOINING THE CONVERSATION

6. Write your own brief (a page or so) version of the creation story, one that might come from your own culture or another culture you know about. In it, put your own "spin" on how the first people were created.
7. Work with three or four classmates to conduct an informal survey of students or of some children you know, trying for a total of thirty to forty and for an equal number of males and females. Ask them to list the three most important differences between men and women and the three most important similarities. Then make a brief report to your class summing up your findings. Did men and women tend to answer your questions in different ways?

SOJOURNER TRUTH
Ain't I a Woman?

SOJOURNER TRUTH (1797–1883) took her name from mystical visions that urged her, after her escape from slavery, to sojourn and speak the truth. Although she never learned to write on paper, the words of her speeches often wrote on her listeners' souls. The following speech, one of her most famous, was originally written down by Elizabeth Cady Stanton, an early proponent of women's rights, and printed in The History of Woman Suffrage. *Truth delivered it at the Women's Rights Convention in Akron, Ohio, in 1851. On that occasion she spoke to an almost all-white audience, since African Americans were, ironically, not welcome at such events. In "Ain't I a Woman?" Truth speaks not just for women but for many who are oppressed, combining her devotion to abolitionism and to women's suffrage. With vigor and humor, she argues for basic human rights for "all God's children."*

This brief speech always reminds me of the power of the spoken word—and of the difference one voice can sometimes make. I love Truth's use of some of the colloquialisms I grew up with (like "out of kilter"), her familiar references to those in her audience as "honey" and "children," and other aspects of her speaking style that help me feel as though she is right here in front of me talking. I chose this speech for these reasons and because Truth counters perfectly all those voices down through the ages that have dismissed people such as her as "just" women. To hear her rebuttal, and to get at some of this speech's rhythmic power, try reading it aloud. – A.L.

Well, children, where there is so much racket there must be something out of kilter. I think that 'twixt the negroes of the South and the women of the North, all talking about rights, the white men will be in a fix pretty soon. But what's all this here talking about?

That man over there says that women need to be helped into carriages, and lifted over ditches, and to have the best place everywhere. Nobody ever helps me into carriages, or over mud-puddles, or gives me any best place! And ain't I a woman? Look at me! Look at my arm! I have ploughed and planted, and gathered into barns, and no man could head me! And ain't I a woman? I could work as much and eat as much as a man—when I could get it—and bear the lash as well! And ain't I a woman? I have borne thirteen children, and seen them most all sold off to slavery, and when I cried out with my mother's grief, none but Jesus heard me! And ain't I a woman?

Then they talk about this thing in the head; what's this they call it? [Intellect, someone whispers.] That's it, honey. What's that got to do with women's rights or negro's rights? If my cup won't hold but a pint, and yours holds a quart, wouldn't you be mean not to let me have my little half-measure full?

Then that little man in black there, he says women can't have as much rights as men, 'cause Christ wasn't a woman! Where did your Christ come from? Where did your Christ come from? From God and a woman! Man had nothing to do with Him.

If the first woman God ever made was strong enough to turn the world 5 upside down all alone, these women together ought to be able to turn it back, and get it right side up again! And now they is asking to do it, the men better let them.

Obliged to you for hearing me, and now old Sojourner ain't got nothing more to say.

QUESTIONING THE TEXT

1. Truth punctuates her speech with a rhetorical question—"And ain't I a woman?" What effect does the repetition of this question have on you as a reader? What answer does Truth invoke?
2. Her introduction reveals that A.L. is obviously a fan of Sojourner Truth. What criticisms *could* she have leveled at Truth's argument?

MAKING CONNECTIONS

3. Christina Hoff Sommers (p. 328) argues that what she calls "gender feminists" believe that "the oppression of women, sustained from generation to generation, is a structural feature of our society." How might Truth respond? Would she agree with Sommers that such claims are exaggerated and wrong-headed? Why, or why not?
4. Truth says that the first woman God made was "strong enough to turn the world upside down." Is this similar to the view of woman in the reading from Genesis—or not?

JOINING THE CONVERSATION

5. List as many reasons as you can to support the belief that men and women should or should not have the same rights and responsibilities. Explain from your own experiences *why* you believe as you do.

ANDREW SULLIVAN
What Are Homosexuals For?

ANDREW SULLIVAN's argument in favor of "normalizing" homosexuality in America—understood as legalizing homosexual marriage and permitting gay men and women to serve in the military—speaks quietly and eloquently to the entire political spectrum. In Virtually Normal *(1995) Sullivan (b. 1963), former editor of the* New Republic *and homosexual himself, systematically examines arguments on all sides of a thorny issue to hammer out a compromise "politics of homosexuality." He places himself squarely in the middle, clearing ground for tolerance by seeming tolerant himself, acknowledging, for example, that conservative critics of homosexuality may be expressing "sincerely held moral beliefs." Yet he also bravely questions those who might be logical allies. About the radical activities of* ACT UP, *for example, Sullivan observes: "A politics which seeks only to show and not to persuade will only be as successful as its latest theatrical escapade, and will be as susceptible to the fashion of audiences as any other fad."*

Reviewed favorably in many periodicals, Virtually Normal *caused a minor ripple when it debuted, Sullivan himself playing the TV talk show circuit. But a book so sober and rational can change public opinion only one reader at a time. The more immediate accomplishment of* Virtually Normal *may be to set a standard for civil argument at precisely the moment when America's public square has become a tough, bellicose place. Our selection is from the epilogue of* Virtually Normal, *a personal part of Sullivan's book, and one that conveys the honesty and lucidity that make the entire work worth reading.* — J.R.

> Reason has so many shapes we don't know what to seize hold of; experience has just as many. What we infer from the similarity of events is uncertain, because they are always dissimilar: there is no quality so universal here as difference.
>
> — MICHEL DE MONTAIGNE

The discovery of one's homosexuality is for many people the same experience as acting upon it. For me, alas, this was not the case. Maybe, in some respects, this was intellectually salutary: I was able, from an early age, to distinguish, as my Church taught, the condition of homosexuality from its practice. But in life, nothing is as easily distinguished. Even disavowing homosexuality is a response to it; and the response slowly, subtly alters who you are. The sublimation of sexual longing can create a particular form of alienated person: a more ferocious perfectionist, a cranky individual, an extremely brittle emotionalist, an ideological fanatic. This may lead to some brilliant lives: witty, urbane, subtle, passionate. But it also leads to some devastating loneliness. The abandonment of intimacy and the rejection of one's emotional core are, I have come to believe, alloyed evils. All too often, they preserve the persona at the expense of the person.

I remember a man, a university figure, who knew everyone in a distant avuncular fashion. I suppose we all understood that somewhere he was a homosexual; he had few women friends, and no emotional or sexual life to speak of. He lived in a carefully constructed world of university gossip, intellectual argument, and intense, platonic relationships with proteges and students. He was immensely fat. One day, he told me, in his mid-forties, he woke up in a room at the Harvard Club in New York and couldn't move. He stayed there immobile for the morning and much of the afternoon. He realized at that moment that there was no honesty at the core of his life, and no love at its center. The recognition of this emptiness literally paralyzed him. He was the lucky one. He set about re-ordering his life; in his late middle age, he began to have adolescent affairs; he declared his sexuality loudly and somewhat crudely to anyone who could hear; he unloaded himself to his friends and loved ones. In one of those ultimately unintelligible tragedies, he died of a swift and deadly cancer three years later. But at his funeral, I couldn't help but reflect that he had at least tasted a few years of life. He had regained himself before he lost himself forever.

Others never experience such dreadful epiphanies. There was a time when I felt that the closeted homosexual was a useful social creature, and possibly happier than those immersed in what sometimes seems like a merciless and shallow subculture. But the etiolation of the heart which this self-abnegation requires is enormous. For many of us, a shared love is elusive anyway, a goal we rarely achieve and, when we do, find extremely hard to maintain. But to make the lack of such an achievement a condition of one's existence is to remove from a human life much that might propel it forward. Which is why I cannot forget the image of that man in a bed. He could not move. For him, there was no forward, no future to move into.

This is how the world can seem to many adolescent homosexuals; and I was no exception. Heterosexual marriage is perceived as the primary emotional goal for your peers; and yet you know this cannot be your fate. It terrifies and alarms you. While its form comforts, its content appalls. It requires a systematic dishonesty; and this dishonesty either is programmed into your soul and so warps your integrity, or is rejected in favor of—what? You scan your mind for an alternative. You dream grandiose dreams, construct a fantasy of a future, pour your energies into some massive distraction, pursue a consuming career to cover up the lie at the center of your existence. You are caught between escape and the constant daily wrench of self-denial. It is a vise from which many teenagers and young adults never emerge.

I was lucky. I found an escape, an escape into a world of ideas, into a   5
career, and into another country. America provided an excuse for a new beginning, as it had done for millions of immigrants before me. I often wonder,
had I stayed in the place which reminded me so much of where I was from,
whether I would have found a way to construct a measurably honest life. I
don't know. But I do know that in this as well I was not alone. So many homosexuals find it essential to move away from where they are before they can
regain themselves. Go to any major city and you'll find thousands of exiles
from the heartland, making long-distance phone calls which echo with the
same euphemisms of adolescence, the same awkward pauses, the same banal
banter. These city limits are the equivalent of the adolescent's bedroom door:
a barrier where two lives can be maintained with some hope of success and a
minimal amount of mutual embarrassment.

It was in the safety of this exile that I could come home. I remember
my first kiss with another man, the first embrace, the first love affair. Many
metaphors have been used to describe this delayed homecoming—I was
twenty-three—but to me, it was like being in a black-and-white movie that
suddenly converted to color. The richness of experience seemed possible for
the first time; the abstractions of dogma, of morality, of society, dissolved into
the sheer, mysterious pleasure of being human. Perhaps this is a homosexual
privilege: for many heterosexuals, the pleasures of intimacy and sexuality are
stumbled upon gradually when young; for many homosexuals, the entire experience can come at once, when an adult, eclipsing everything, humiliating
the developed person's sense of equilibrium, infantilizing and liberating at the
same time. Sometimes I wonder whether some homosexuals' addiction to
constant romance, to the thrill of the new lover, to the revelation of a new
and obliviating desire, is in fact an attempt to relive this experience, again and
again.

What followed over the years was not without its stupidity, excess, and
hurt. But it was far realler than anything I had experienced before. I was
never really "in the closet" in this sense. Until my early twenties, I was essentially heterosexual in public disclosure and emotionless in private life. Within
a year, I was both privately and publicly someone who attempted little disguise of his emotional orientation. In this, I was convinced I was entering finally into normal life. I was the equal of heterosexuals, deserving of exactly
the same respect, attempting to construct in the necessarily contrived world of
the gay subculture the mirror image of the happy heterosexuality I imagined
around me. Like many in my generation, I flattered myself that this was a
first: a form of pioneering equality, an insistence on one's interchangeability
with the dominant culture, on one's radical similarity with the heterosexual
majority.

And in a fundamental sense, as I have tried to explain, this was true.
The homosexual's emotional longings, his development, his dreams are
human phenomena. They are, I think, instantly recognizable to any hetero-

sexual, in their form if not their content. The humanity of homosexuals is clear everywhere. Perhaps nothing has illustrated this more clearly than the AIDS epidemic. Gay people have to confront grief and shock and mortality like anybody else. They die like all people die.

Except, of course, that they don't. Homosexuals in contemporary America tend to die young; they sometimes die estranged from their families; they die among friends who have become their new families; they die surrounded by young death, and by the arch symbols of cultural otherness. Growing up homosexual was to grow up normally but displaced; to experience romantic love, but with the wrong person; to entertain grand ambitions, but of the unacceptable sort; to seek a gradual self-awakening, but in secret, not in public.

But to live as an adult homosexual is to experience something else   10 again. By the simple fact of one's increasing cultural separation, the human personality begins to develop differently. As an adolescent and child, you are surrounded by the majority culture: so your concerns and habits and thoughts become embedded in the familiar and communicable. But slowly, and gradually, in adulthood, your friends and acquaintances become increasingly gay or lesbian. Lesbian women can find themselves slowly distanced from the company of men; gay men can find themselves slowly disentangled from women. One day, I glanced at my log of telephone calls: the ratio of men to women, once roughly even, had become six-to-one male. The women I knew and cared about had dwindled to a small but intimate group of confidantes and friends, women who were able to share my homosexual life and understand it. The straight men, too, had fallen in number. And both these groups tended to come from people I had met *before* I had fully developed an openly gay life.

These trends reinforced each other. Of course, like most gay people, I worked in a largely heterosexual environment and still maintained close links with my heterosexual family. But the environmental incentives upon me were clearly in another direction. I naturally gravitated toward people who were similar. Especially in your twenties, when romantic entanglement assumes a dominant role in life, you naturally socialize with prospective partners. Before you know where you are, certain patterns develop. Familiarity breeds familiarity; and, by no conscious process, your inculturation is subtly and powerfully different than that of your heterosexual peers.

In the world of emotional and sexual life, there were no clear patterns to follow: homosexual culture offered a gamut of possibilities, from anonymous sex to bourgeois coupling. But its ease with sexual activity, its male facility with sexual candor, its surprising lack of formal, moral stricture—all these made my life subtly and slowly more different than my straight male (let alone my straight female) peers'. In my late twenties, the difference became particularly acute. My heterosexual male friends became married; soon, my straight peers were having children. Weddings, babies, career couples, en-

gagements: the calendar began to become crowded with the clatter of heterosexual bonding. And yet in my gay life, something somewhat different was
occurring.

I remember vividly one Labor Day weekend. I had two engagements to
attend. The first was a gay friend's thirtieth birthday party. It was held in the
Deep South, in his family's seaside home. He had told his family he was gay
the previous winter; he had told them he had AIDS that Memorial Day. His
best friends had come to meet the family for the first time—two straight
women, his boyfriend, his ex-boyfriend, and me. That year, we had all been
through the trauma of his illness, and he was visibly thinner now than he had
been even a month before. Although we attended to the typical family functions—dinners, beach trips, photo ops—there was a strained air of irony and
sadness about the place. How could we explain what it was like to live in
one's twenties and thirties with such a short horizon, to face mortality and
sickness and death, to attend funerals when others were attending weddings?
And yet, somehow the communication was possible. He was their son, after
all. And after they had acclimatized to our mutual affection, and humor, and
occasional diffidence, there was something of an understanding. His father
took me aside toward the end of the trip to thank me for taking care of his
son. I found it hard to speak any words of reply.

I flew directly from that event to another family gathering of another
thirty-year-old friend of mine. This one was heterosexual; and he and his fi-
ancee were getting married surrounded by a bevy of beaming acquaintances
and family. In the Jewish ceremony, there was an unspoken, comforting
rhythm of rebirth and life. The event was not untouched by tragedy: my
friend's father had died earlier that year. But the wedding was almost an in-
stinctive response to that sadness, a reaffirmation that the cycles and structures
that had made sense of most of the lives there would be making sense of another two in the years ahead. I did not begrudge it at all; it is hard not to be
moved by the sight of a new life beginning. But I could not help also feeling
deeply, powerfully estranged.

AIDS has intensified a difference that I think is inherent between homo-   15
sexual and heterosexual adults. The latter group is committed to the procreation of a new generation. The former simply isn't. Yes, there are major qualifications to this—gay men and lesbians are often biological fathers and
mothers—but no two lesbians and no two homosexual men can be parents in
the way that a heterosexual man and a heterosexual woman with a biological
son or daughter can be. And yes, many heterosexuals neither marry nor have
children and many have adopted children. But in general, the difference
holds. The timeless, necessary, procreative unity of a man and a woman is inherently denied homosexuals; and the way in which fatherhood transforms
heterosexual men, and motherhood transforms heterosexual women, and
parenthood transforms their relationship, is far less common among homosexuals than among heterosexuals.

AIDS has only added a bitter twist to this state of affairs. My straight peers in their early thirties are engaged in the business of births; I am largely engaged in the business of deaths. Both experiences alter people profoundly. The very patterns of life of mothers and fathers with young children are vastly different than those who have none; and the perspectives of those who have stared death in the face in their twenties are bound to be different than those who have stared into cribs. Last year, I saw my first nephew come into the world, the first new life in my life to whom I felt physically, emotionally connected. I wondered which was the deeper feeling: the sense of excrutiating pain seeing a member of my acquired family die, or the excruciating joy of seeing a member of my given family born. I am at a loss to decide; but I am not at a loss to know that they are different experiences: equally human, but radically different.

In a society more and more aware of its manifold cultures and subcultures, we have been educated to be familiar and comfortable with what has been called "diversity": the diversity of perspective, culture, meaning. And this diversity is usually associated with what are described as cultural constructs: race, gender, sexuality, and so on. But as the obsession with diversity intensifies, the possibility of real difference alarms and terrifies all the more. The notion of collective characteristics—of attributes more associated with blacks than with whites, with Asians than with Latinos, with gay men than with straight men, with men than with women—has become anathema. They are marginalized as "stereotypes." The acceptance of diversity has come to mean the acceptance of the essential sameness of all types of people, and the danger of generalizing among them at all. In fact, it has become virtually a definition of "racist" to make any substantive generalizations about a particular ethnicity, and a definition of "homophobic" to make any generalizations about homosexuals.

What follows, then, is likely to be understood as "homophobic." But I think it's true that certain necessary features of homosexual life lead to certain unavoidable features of homosexual character. This is not to say that they define any random homosexual: they do not. As with any group or way of life, there are many, many exceptions. Nor is it to say that they define the homosexual life: it should be clear by now that I believe the needs and feelings of homosexual children and adolescents are largely interchangeable with those of their heterosexual peers. But there are certain generalizations that can be made about adult homosexuals and lesbians that have the ring of truth.

Of course, in a culture where homosexuals remain hidden and wrapped in self-contempt, in which their emotional development is often stunted and late, in which the closet protects all sorts of self-destructive behavior that a more open society would not, it is still very hard to tell what is inherent in a homosexual life that makes it different, and what is simply imposed upon it. Nevertheless, it seems to me that even in the most tolerant societies, some of the differences that I have just described would inhere.

The experience of growing up profoundly different in emotional and   20
psychological makeup inevitably alters a person's self-perception, tends to
make him or her more wary and distant, more attuned to appearance and its
foibles, more self-conscious and perhaps more reflective. The presence of homosexuals in the arts, in literature, in architecture, in design, in fashion could
be understood, as some have, as a simple response to oppression. Homosexuals have created safe professions within which to hide and protect each other.
But why these professions? Maybe it's also that these are professions of appearance. Many homosexual children, feeling distant from their peers, become experts at trying to figure out how to disguise their inner feelings, to
"pass." They notice the signs and signals of social interaction, because they do
not come instinctively. They develop skills early on that help them notice the
inflections of a voice, the quirks of a particular movement, and the ways in
which meaning can be conveyed in code. They have an ear for irony and for
double meanings. Sometimes, by virtue of having to suppress their natural
emotions, they find formal outlets to express themselves: music, theater, art.
And so their lives become set on a trajectory which reinforces these trends.

As a child, I remember, as I suppressed the natural emotions of an adolescent, how I naturally turned in on myself—writing, painting, and participating in amateur drama. Or I devised fantasies of future exploits—war leader,
parliamentarian, famous actor—that could absorb those emotions that were
being diverted from meeting other boys and developing natural emotional relationships with them. And I developed mannerisms, small ways in which I
could express myself, tiny revolts of personal space—a speech affectation, a
ridiculous piece of clothing—that were, in retrospect, attempts to communicate something in code which could not be communicated in language. In
this homosexual archness there was, of course, much pain. And it came as no
surprise that once I had become more open about my homosexuality, these
mannerisms declined. Once I found the strength to be myself, I had no need
to act myself. So my clothes became progressively more regular and slovenly;
I lost interest in drama; my writing moved from fiction to journalism; my
speech actually became less affected.

This, of course, is not a universal homosexual experience. Many homosexuals never become more open, and the skills required to survive the closet
remain skills by which to earn a living. And many homosexuals, even once
they no longer need those skills, retain them. My point is simply that the universal experience of self-conscious difference in childhood and adolescence—
common, but not exclusive, to homosexuals—develops identifiable skills.
They are the skills of mimesis; and one of the goods that homosexuals bring
to society is undoubtedly a more highly developed sense of form, of style.
Even in the most open of societies, I think, this will continue to be the case.
It is not something genetically homosexual; it is something environmentally
homosexual. And it begins young.

Closely connected to this is a sense of irony. Like Jews who have developed ways to resist,* subvert, and adopt a majority culture, so homosexuals have found themselves ironizing their difference. Because, in many cases, they have survived acute periods of emotion, they are more likely to appreciate—even willfully celebrate—its more overwrought and melodramatic depictions. They have learned to see the funny side of etiolation. This, perhaps, is the true origin of camp. It is the ability to see agony and enjoy its form while ignoring its content, the ability to watch emotional trauma and not see its essence but its appearance. It is the aestheticization of pain.

This role in the aestheticization of the culture is perhaps enhanced by another unavoidable fact about most homosexuals and lesbians: their childlessness. This generates two related qualities: the relative freedom to procreate in a broader, structural sense, and to experiment with human relationships that can be instructive for the society as a whole.

The lack of children is something some homosexuals regard as a curse;   25 and it is the thing which many heterosexuals most pity (and some envy) about their homosexual acquaintances. But it is also an opportunity. Childless men and women have many things to offer a society. They can transfer their absent parental instincts into broader parental roles: they can be extraordinary teachers and mentors, nurses and doctors, priests, rabbis, and nuns; they can throw themselves into charity work, helping the needy and the lonely; they can care for the young who have been abandoned by others, through adoption. Or they can use all their spare time to forge an excellence in their field of work that is sometimes unavailable to the harried mother or burdened father. They can stay late in the office, be the most loyal staffer in an election campaign, work round the clock in a journalistic production, be the lawyer most able and willing to meet the emerging deadline.

One of their critical roles in society has also often been in the military. Here is an institution which requires dedication beyond the calling to the biological, nuclear family, that needs people prepared to give all their time to the common endeavor, that requires men and women able to subsume their personal needs into the formal demands of military discipline. Of all institutions in our society, the military is perhaps the most naturally homosexual, which is part of the reason, of course, why it is so hostile to their visible presence. The displacement of family affection onto a broader community also makes the homosexual an ideal person to devote him- or herself to a social institution: the university, the school, the little league, the Boy Scouts, the church, the sports team. Scratch most of these institutions and you'll find a homosexual or two sustaining many of its vital functions.

Like Jews who have developed ways to resist: For example, see "Good Morning, Herr Müller," p. 218.

But the homosexual's contribution can be more than nourishing the society's aesthetic and institutional life. It has become a truism that in the field of emotional development, homosexuals have much to learn from the heterosexual culture. The values of commitment, of monogamy, of marriage, of stability are all posited as models for homosexual existence. And, indeed, of course, they are. Without an architectonic institution like that of marriage, it is difficult to create the conditions for nurturing such virtues, but that doesn't belie their importance.

It is also true, however, that homosexual relationships, even in their current, somewhat eclectic form, may contain features that could nourish the broader society as well. Precisely because there is no institutional model, gay relationships are often sustained more powerfully by genuine commitment. The mutual nurturing and sexual expressiveness of many lesbian relationships, the solidity and space of many adult gay male relationships, are qualities sometimes lacking in more rote, heterosexual couplings. Same-sex unions often incorporate the virtues of friendship more effectively than traditional marriages; and at times, among gay male relationships, the openness of the contract makes it more likely to survive than many heterosexual bonds. Some of this is unavailable to the male–female union: there is more likely to be greater understanding of the need for extramarital outlets between two men than between a man and a woman; and again, the lack of children gives gay couples greater freedom. Their failures entail fewer consequences for others. But something of the gay relationship's necessary honesty, its flexibility, and its equality could undoubtedly help strengthen and inform many heterosexual bonds.

In my own sometimes comic, sometimes passionate attempts to construct relationships, I learned something of the foibles of a simple heterosexual model. I saw how the network of gay friendships was often as good an emotional nourishment as a single relationship, that sexual candor was not always the same as sexual license, that the kind of supportive community that bolsters many gay relationships is something many isolated straight marriages could benefit from. I also learned how the subcultural fact of gay life rendered it remarkably democratic; in gay bars, there was far less socioeconomic stratification than in heterosexual bars. The shared experience of same-sex desire cut through class and race; it provided a humbling experience, which allowed many of us to risk our hearts and our friendships with people we otherwise might never have met. It loosened us up, and gave us a keener sense, perhaps, that people were often difficult to understand, let alone judge, from appearances. My heterosexual peers, through no fault of their own, were often denied these experiences. But they might gain from understanding them a little better, and not simply from a position of condescension.

As I've just argued, I believe strongly that marriage should be made 30 available to everyone, in a politics of strict public neutrality. But within this model, there is plenty of scope for cultural difference. There is something baleful about the attempt of some gay conservatives to educate homosexuals and lesbians into an uncritical acceptance of a stifling model of heterosexual normality. The truth is, homosexuals are not entirely normal; and to flatten their varied and complicated lives into a single, moralistic model is to miss what is essential and exhilarating about their otherness.

This need not mean, as some have historically claimed, that homosexuals have no stake in the sustenance of a society, but rather that their role is somewhat different; they may be involved in procreation in a less literal sense: in a society's cultural regeneration, its entrepreneurial or intellectual rejuvenation, its religious ministry, or its professional education. Unencumbered by children, they may be able to press the limits of the culture or the business infrastructure, or the boundaries of intellectual life, in a way that heterosexuals, by dint of a different type of calling, cannot. Of course, many heterosexuals perform similar roles; and many homosexuals prefer domesticity to public performance; but the inevitable way of life of the homosexual provides an opportunity that many intuitively seem to grasp and understand.

Or perhaps their role is to have no role at all. Perhaps it is the experience of rebellion that prompts homosexual culture to be peculiarly resistant to attempts to guide it to be useful or instructive or productive. Go to any march for gay rights and you will see the impossibility of organizing it into a coherent lobby: such attempts are always undermined by irony, or exhibitionism, or irresponsibility. It is as if homosexuals have learned something about life that makes them immune to the puritanical and flattening demands of modern politics. It is as if they have learned that life is fickle; that there are parts of it that cannot be understood, let alone solved; that some things lead nowhere and mean nothing; that the ultimate exercise of freedom is not a programmatic journey but a spontaneous one. Perhaps it requires seeing one's life as the end of a biological chain, or seeing one's deepest emotions as the object of detestation, that provides this insight. But the seeds of homosexual wisdom are the seeds of human wisdom. They contain the truth that order is in fact a euphemism for disorder; that problems are often more sanely enjoyed than solved; that there is reason in mystery; that there is beauty in the wild flowers that grow randomly among our wheat.

QUESTIONING THE TEXT

1. Sullivan begins by discussing how the cultural dominance of heterosexual marriage shapes the outlook of young homosexuals. Consider the power of this social institution, whatever one's sexual orientation or expectations in life. What does it mean when our culture defines "normal" through the prism of heterosexual marriage? If you keep a reading log, answer this question there.

2. Sullivan presents the rituals and routines of heterosexual life through the eyes of a gay male who feels like an outsider. Describe an experience you have had as an outsider, looking in. Is this the experience of women peering in at male institutions? of men watching women socializing? of poor looking at rich? of the physically challenged considering the fully able? of conservative students in liberal classrooms?

3. The introduction to Sullivan's "What Are Homosexuals For?" praises the piece as an example of "civil argument." Do you find the essay as balanced and reasonable as the introduction promises? Use examples from the essay to support your answer.

MAKING CONNECTIONS

4. Maxine Hong Kingston's "No Name Woman" describes a woman whose life is destroyed because society cannot accept her out-of-wedlock pregnancy. Homosexuals, too, Sullivan argues, are culturally marginalized for their sexual behavior. In a group, discuss both the constraints society puts on sexuality and the reasons for them. Are there legitimate differences, for example, among *constraints, taboos,* and *prejudices?* Then write a short essay about one way society manages sexual behavior in your community—religious, social, or political.

5. Read Dave Barry's "Guys vs. Men" (p. 343) from the point of view that Sullivan offers. Does Barry's world of "guys" have room for homosexuals? Why, or why not? Write a paragraph or two on the subject.

JOINING THE CONVERSATION

6. Not many years ago, a common journal or essay assignment in college was to write about a first date or first love. With the selection by Sullivan in mind, write an essay exploring the appropriateness of such an assignment.

7. Sullivan argues that the way homosexuals are raised and the defenses they use to survive make them "more wary and distant, more attuned to appearance and its foibles, more self-conscious and perhaps more selective." He also admits that such assertions come dangerously close to homophobic generalizations. Can people talk about the behavior of particular groups—whether gay men, lesbians, heterosexual women, or even "guys"—without engaging in harmful stereotypes? Explore this question by writing a dialogue. (See Kevin Kelly's "Interview with the Luddite," p. 243, for an example.)

MAXINE HONG KINGSTON
No Name Woman

Maxine Hong Kingston was born (in 1940) and raised in California, but her roots grow deep in Chinese soil and culture, as is evidenced in two highly acclaimed books, The Woman Warrior *(1970) and* China Men *(1980). In these and other works, Kingston explores the effects of Chinese legend and custom on her own experiences as a woman and as a Chinese American.*

In "No Name Woman," an excerpt from The Woman Warrior, *Kingston examines one difference between women and men—the fact that women bear children—and she explores the consequences of that difference. Many readers of this text may be able to identify a shadowy relative in their own pasts—an absent parent, a grandparent much discussed but seldom seen, a mysterious uncle or aunt or cousin about whom older family members whispered. Few of us are likely to have written so powerfully about such a figure, however, or to have evoked in such a short space what it would be like to be "No Name Woman." I chose this selection precisely for its power. It has stayed vividly with me ever since I first read it—so vividly, in fact, that "No Name Woman" seems like someone I know personally. To me, she tells not only her own story but the story of all those whose lives are destroyed by narrow and rigid beliefs. —* A.L.

"You must not tell anyone," my mother said, "what I am about to tell you. In China your father had a sister who killed herself. She jumped into the family well. We say that your father has all brothers because it is as if she had never been born.

"In 1924 just a few days after our village celebrated seventeen hurry-up weddings—to make sure that every young man who went 'out on the road' would responsibly come home—your father and his brothers and your grandfather and his brothers and your aunt's new husband sailed for America, the Gold Mountain. It was your grandfather's last trip. Those lucky enough to get contracts waved good-bye from the decks. They fed and guarded the stowaways and helped them off in Cuba, New York, Bali, Hawaii. 'We'll meet in California next year,' they said. All of them sent money home.

"I remember looking at your aunt one day when she and I were dressing; I had not noticed before that she had such a protruding melon of a stomach. But I did not think, 'She's pregnant,' until she began to look like other pregnant women, her shirt pulling and the white tops of her black pants showing. She could not have been pregnant, you see, because her husband had been gone for years. No one said anything. We did not discuss it. In early summer she was ready to have the child, long after the time when it could have been possible.

"The village had also been counting. On the night the baby was to be born the villagers raided our house. Some were crying. Like a great saw, teeth strung with lights, files of people walked zigzag across our land, tearing the rice. Their lanterns doubled in the disturbed black water, which drained away through the broken bunds. As the villagers closed in, we could see that some of them, probably men and women we knew well, wore white masks. The people with long hair hung it over their faces. Women with short hair made it stand up on end. Some had tied white bands around their foreheads, arms, and legs.

"At first they threw mud and rocks at the house. Then they threw eggs 5 and began slaughtering our stock. We could hear the animals scream their deaths—the roosters, the pigs, a last great roar from the ox. Familiar wild heads flared in our night windows; the villagers encircled us. Some of the faces stopped to peer at us, their eyes rushing like searchlights. The hands flattened against the panes, framed heads, and left red prints.

"The villagers broke in the front and the back doors at the same time, even though we had not locked the doors against them. Their knives dripped with the blood of our animals. They smeared blood on the doors and walls. One woman swung a chicken, whose throat she had slit, splattering blood in red arcs about her. We stood together in the middle of our house, in the family hall with the pictures and tables of the ancestors around us, and looked straight ahead.

"At that time the house had only two wings. When the men came back, we would build two more to enclose our courtyard and a third one to begin a second courtyard. The villagers pushed through both wings, even your grandparents' rooms, to find your aunt's, which was also mine until the men returned. From this room a new wing for one of the younger families would grow. They ripped up her clothes and shoes and broke her combs, grinding them underfoot. They tore her work from the loom. They scattered the cooking fire and rolled the new weaving in it. We could hear them in the kitchen breaking our bowls and banging the pots. They overturned the great waist-high earthenware jugs; duck eggs, pickled fruits, vegetables burst out and mixed in acrid torrents. The old woman from the next field swept a broom through the air and loosed the spirits-of-the-broom over our heads. 'Pig.' 'Ghost.' 'Pig,' they sobbed and scolded while they ruined our house.

"When they left, they took sugar and oranges to bless themselves. They cut pieces from the dead animals. Some of them took bowls that were not broken and clothes that were not torn. Afterward we swept up the rice and sewed it back up into sacks. But the smells from the spilled preserves lasted. Your aunt gave birth in the pigsty that night. The next morning when I went up for the water, I found her and the baby plugging up the family well.

"Don't let your father know that I told you. He denies her. Now that you have started to menstruate, what happened to her could happen to you. Don't humiliate us. You wouldn't like to be forgotten as if you had never been born. The villagers are watchful."

Whenever she had to warn us about life, my mother told stories that ran   10 like this one, a story to grow up on. She tested our strength to establish realities. Those in the emigrant generations who could not reassert brute survival died young and far from home. Those of us in the first American generations have had to figure out how the invisible world the emigrants built around our childhoods fit in solid America.

The emigrants confused the gods by diverting their curses, misleading them with crooked streets and false names. They must try to confuse their offspring as well, who, I suppose, threaten them in similar ways—always trying to get things straight, always trying to name the unspeakable. The Chinese I know hide their names; sojourners take new names when their lives change and guard their real names with silence.

Chinese-Americans, when you try to understand what things in you are Chinese, how do you separate what is peculiar to childhood, to poverty, insanities, one family, your mother who marked your growing with stories, from what is Chinese? What is Chinese tradition and what is the movies?

If I want to learn what clothes my aunt wore, whether flashy or ordinary, I would have to begin, "Remember Father's drowned-in-the-well sister?" I cannot ask that. My mother has told me once and for all the useful parts. She will add nothing unless powered by Necessity, a riverbank that guides her life. She plants vegetable gardens rather than lawns; she carries the odd-shaped tomatoes home from the fields and eats food left for the gods.

Whenever we did frivolous things, we used up energy; we flew high kites. We children came up off the ground over the melting cones our parents brought home from work and the American movie on New Year's Day— *Oh, You Beautiful Doll* with Betty Grable one year, and *She Wore a Yellow Ribbon* with John Wayne another year. After the one carnival ride each, we paid in guilt; our tired father counted his change on the dark walk home.

Adultery is extravagance. Could people who hatch their own chicks and   15 eat the embryos and the heads for delicacies and boil the feet in vinegar for party food, leaving only the gravel, eating even the gizzard lining—could such people engender a prodigal aunt? To be a woman, to have a daughter in starvation time was a waste enough. My aunt could not have been the lone romantic who gave up everything for sex. Women in the old China did not choose. Some man had commanded her to lie with him and be his secret evil. I wonder whether he masked himself when he joined the raid on her family.

Perhaps she encountered him in the fields or on the mountain where the daughters-in-law collected fuel. Or perhaps he first noticed her in the marketplace. He was not a stranger because the village housed no strangers. She had to have dealings with him other than sex. Perhaps he worked an adjoining field, or he sold her the cloth for the dress she sewed and wore. His demand must have surprised, then terrified her. She obeyed him; she always did as she was told.

When the family found a young man in the next village to be her husband, she stood tractably beside the best rooster, his proxy, and promised before they met that she would be his forever. She was lucky that he was her age and she would be the first wife, an advantage secure now. The night she first saw him, he had sex with her. Then he left for America. She had almost forgotten what he looked like. When she tried to envision him, she only saw the black and white face in the group photograph the men had taken before leaving.

The other man was not, after all, much different from her husband. They both gave orders: she followed. "If you tell your family, I'll beat you. I'll kill you. Be here again next week." No one talked sex, ever. And she might have separated the rapes from the rest of living if only she did not have to buy her oil from him or gather wood in the same forest. I want her fear to have lasted just as long as rape lasted so that the fear could have been contained. No drawn-out fear. But women at sex hazarded birth and hence lifetimes. The fear did not stop but permeated everywhere. She told the man, "I think I'm pregnant." He organized the raid against her.

On nights when my mother and father talked about their life back home, sometimes they mentioned an "outcast table" whose business they still seemed to be settling, their voices tight. In a commensal tradition, where food is precious, the powerful older people made wrongdoers eat alone. Instead of letting them start separate new lives like the Japanese, who could become samurais and geishas, the Chinese family, faces averted but eyes glowering sideways, hung on to the offenders and fed them leftovers. My aunt must have lived in the same house as my parents and eaten at an outcast table. My mother spoke about the raid as if she had seen it, when she and my aunt, a daughter-in-law to a different household, should not have been living together at all. Daughters-in-law lived with their husbands' parents, not their own; a synonym for marriage in Chinese is "taking a daughter-in-law." Her husband's parents could have sold her, mortgaged her, stoned her. But they had sent her back to her own mother and father, a mysterious act hinting at disgraces not told me. Perhaps they had thrown her out to deflect the avengers.

She was the only daughter; her four brothers went with her father, husband, and uncles "out on the road" and for some years became western men. When the goods were divided among the family, three of the brothers took land, and the youngest, my father, chose an education. After my grandparents gave their daughter away to her husband's family, they had dispensed all the adventure and all the property. They expected her alone to keep the traditional ways, which her brothers, now among the barbarians, could fumble without detection. The heavy, deep-rooted women were to maintain the past   20 against the flood, safe for returning. But the rare urge west had fixed upon our family, and so my aunt crossed boundaries not delineated in space.

The work of preservation demands that the feelings playing about in one's guts not be turned into action. Just watch their passing like cherry blossoms. But perhaps my aunt, my forerunner, caught in a slow life, let dreams grow and fade and after some months or years went toward what persisted. Fear at the enormities of the forbidden kept her desires delicate, wire and bone. She looked at a man because she liked the way the hair was tucked behind his ears, or she liked the question-mark line of a long torso curving at the shoulder and straight at the hip. For warm eyes or a soft voice or a slow walk—that's all—a few hairs, a line, a brightness, a sound, a pace, she gave up family. She offered us up for a charm that vanished with tiredness, a pigtail that didn't toss when the wind died. Why, the wrong lighting could erase the dearest thing about him.

It could very well have been, however, that my aunt did not take subtle enjoyment of her friend, but, a wild woman, kept rollicking company. Imagining her free with sex doesn't fit, though. I don't know any women like that, or men either. Unless I see her life branching into mine, she gives me no ancestral help.

To sustain her being in love, she often worked at herself in the mirror, guessing at the colors and shapes that would interest him, changing them frequently in order to hit on the right combination. She wanted him to look back.

On a farm near the sea, a woman who tended her appearance reaped a reputation for eccentricity. All the married women blunt-cut their hair in flaps about their ears or pulled it back in tight buns. No nonsense. Neither style blew easily into heart-catching tangles. And at their weddings they displayed themselves in their long hair for the last time. "It brushed the backs of my knees," my mother tells me. "It was braided, and even so, it brushed the backs of my knees."

At the mirror my aunt combed individuality into her bob. A bun could have been contrived to escape into black streamers blowing in the wind or in quiet wisps about her face, but only the older women in our picture album wear buns. She brushed her hair back from her forehead, tucking the flaps behind her ears. She looped a piece of thread, knotted into a circle between her index fingers and thumbs, and ran the double strand across her forehead. When she closed her fingers as if she were making a pair of shadow geese bite, the string twisted together catching the little hairs. Then she pulled the thread away from her skin, ripping the hairs out neatly, her eyes watering from the needles of pain. Opening her fingers, she cleaned the thread, then rolled it along her hairline and the tops of her eyebrows. My mother did the same to me and my sisters and herself. I used to believe that the expression "caught by the short hairs" meant a captive held with a depilatory string. It especially hurt at the temples, but my mother said we were lucky we didn't

²⁵

have to have our feet bound when we were seven. Sisters used to sit on their beds and cry together, she said, as their mothers or their slave removed the bandages for a few minutes each night and let the blood gush back into their veins. I hope that the man my aunt loved appreciated a smooth brow, that he wasn't just a tits-and-ass man.

Once my aunt found a freckle on her chin, at a spot that the almanac said predestined her for unhappiness. She dug it out with a hot needle and washed the wound with peroxide.

More attention to her looks than these pullings of hairs and pickings at spots would have caused gossip among the villagers. They owned work clothes and good clothes, and they wore good clothes for feasting the new seasons. But since a woman combing her hair hexes beginnings, my aunt rarely found an occasion to look her best. Women looked like great sea snails—the corded wood, babies, and laundry they carried were the whorls on their backs. The Chinese did not admire a bent back; goddesses and warriors stood straight. Still there must have been a marvelous freeing of beauty when a worker laid down her burden and stretched and arched.

Such commonplace loveliness, however, was not enough for my aunt. She dreamed of a lover for the fifteen days of New Year's, the time for families to exchange visits, money, and food. She plied her secret comb. And sure enough she cursed the year, the family, the village, and herself.

Even as her hair lured her imminent lover, many other men looked at her. Uncles, cousins, nephews, brothers would have looked, too, had they been home between journeys. Perhaps they had already been restraining their curiosity, and they left, fearful that their glances, like a field of nesting birds, might be startled and caught. Poverty hurt, and that was their first reason for leaving. But another, final reason for leaving the crowded house was the never-said.

She may have been unusually beloved, the precious only daughter, 30 spoiled and mirror-gazing because of the affection the family lavished on her. When her husband left, they welcomed the chance to take her back from the in-laws; she could live like the little daughter for just a while longer. There are stories that my grandfather was different from other people, "crazy ever since the little Jap bayoneted him in the head." He used to put his naked penis on the dinner table, laughing. And one day he brought home a baby girl, wrapped up inside his brown western-style greatcoat. He had traded one of his sons, probably my father, the youngest, for her. My grandmother made him trade back. When he finally got a daughter of his own, he doted on her. They must have all loved her, except perhaps my father, the only brother who never went back to China, having once been traded for a girl.

Brothers and sisters, newly men and women, had to efface their sexual color and present plain miens. Disturbing hair and eyes, a smile like no other, threatened the ideal of five generations living under one roof. To focus blurs, people shouted face to face and yelled from room to room. The immigrants I know have loud voices, unmodulated to American tones even after years away from the village where they called their friendships out across the fields. I have not been able to stop my mother's screams in public libraries or over telephones. Walking erect (knees straight, toes pointed forward, not pigeon-toed, which is Chinese-feminine) and speaking in an inaudible voice, I have tried to turn myself American-feminine. Chinese communication was loud, public. Only sick people had to whisper. But at the dinner table, where the family members came nearest one another, no one could talk, not the outcasts nor any eaters. Every word that falls from the mouth is a coin lost. Silently they gave and accepted food with both hands. A preoccupied child who took his bowl with one hand got a sideways glare. A complete moment of total attention is due everyone alike. Children and lovers have no singularity here, but my aunt used a secret voice, a separate attentiveness.

She kept the man's name to herself throughout her labor and dying; she did not accuse him that he be punished with her. To save her inseminator's name she gave silent birth.

He may have been somebody in her own household, but intercourse with a man outside the family would have been no less abhorrent. All the village were kinsmen, and the titles shouted in loud country voices never let kinship be forgotten. Any man within visiting distance would have been neutralized as a lover—"brother," "younger brother," "older brother"—115 relationship titles. Parents researched birth charts probably not so much to assure good fortune as to circumvent incest in a population that has but one hundred surnames. Everybody has eight million relatives. How useless then sexual mannerisms, how dangerous.

As if it came from an atavism deeper than fear, I used to add "brother" silently to boys' names. It hexed the boys, who would or would not ask me to dance, and made them less scary and as familiar and deserving of benevolence as girls.

But, of course, I hexed myself also—no dates. I should have stood up, both arms waving, and shouted out across libraries, "Hey, you! Love me back." I had no idea, though, how to make attraction selective, how to control its direction and magnitude. If I made myself American-pretty so that the five or six Chinese boys in the class fell in love with me, everyone else—the Caucasian, Negro, and Japanese boys—would too. Sisterliness, dignified and honorable, made much more sense.

Attraction eludes control so stubbornly that whole societies designed to organize relationships among people cannot keep order, not even when they bind people to one another from childhood and raise them together. Among the very poor and the wealthy, brothers married their adopted sisters, like doves. Our family allowed some romance, paying adult brides' prices and providing dowries so that their sons and daughters could marry strangers. Marriage promises to turn strangers into friendly relatives—a nation of siblings.

35

In the village structure, spirits shimmered among the live creatures, balanced and held in equilibrium by time and land. But one human being flaring up into violence could open up a black hole, a maelstrom that pulled in the sky. The frightened villagers, who depended on one another to maintain the real, went to my aunt to show her a personal, physical representation of the break she made in the "roundness." Misallying couples snapped off the future, which was to be embodied in true offspring. The villagers punished her for acting as if she could have a private life, secret and apart from them.

If my aunt had betrayed the family at a time of large grain yields and peace, when many boys were born, and wings were being built on many houses, perhaps she might have escaped such severe punishment. But the men—hungry, greedy, tired of planting in dry soil, cuckolded—had been forced to leave the village in order to send food-money home. There were ghost plagues, bandit plagues, wars with the Japanese, floods. My Chinese brother and sister had died of an unknown sickness. Adultery, perhaps only a mistake during good times, became a crime when the village needed food.

The round moon cakes and round doorways, the round tables of graduated size that fit one roundness inside another, round windows and rice bowls—these talismans had lost their power to warn this family of the law: a family must be whole, faithfully keeping the descent line by having sons to feed the old and the dead who in turn look after the family. The villagers came to show my aunt and lover-in-hiding a broken house. The villagers were speeding up the circling of events because she was too shortsighted to see that her infidelity had already harmed the village, that waves of consequences would return unpredictably, sometimes in disguise, as now, to hurt her. This roundness had to be made coin-sized so that she would see its circumference: punish her at the birth of her baby. Awaken her to the inexorable. People who refused fatalism because they could invent small resources insisted on culpability. Deny accidents and wrest fault from the stars.

After the villagers left, their lanterns now scattering in various directions   40
toward home, the family broke their silence and cursed her. "Aiaa, we're going to die. Death is coming. Death is coming. Look what you've done. You've killed us. Ghost! Dead Ghost! Ghost! You've never been born." She ran out into the fields, far enough from the house so that she could no longer hear their voices, and pressed herself against the earth, her own land no more. When she felt the birth coming, she thought that she had been hurt. Her body seized together. "They've hurt me too much," she thought. "This is gall, and it will kill me." With forehead and knees against the earth, her body convulsed and then relaxed. She turned on her back, lay on the ground. The black well of sky and stars went out and out forever; her body and her complexity seemed to disappear. She was one of the stars, a bright dot in blackness, without home, without a companion, in eternal cold and silence. An agoraphobia rose in her, speeding higher and higher, bigger and bigger; she would not be able to contain it; there would be no end to fear.

Flayed, unprotected against space, she felt pain return, focusing her body. This pain chilled her—a cold, steady kind of surface pain. Inside, spasmodically, the other pain, the pain of the child, heated her. For hours she lay on the ground, alternately body and space. Sometimes a vision of normal comfort obliterated reality: she saw the family in the evening gambling at the dinner table, the young people massaging their elders' backs. She saw them congratulating one another, high joy on the mornings the rice shoots came up. When these pictures burst, the stars drew yet further apart. Black space opened.

She got to her feet to fight better and remembered that old-fashioned women gave birth in their pigsties to fool the jealous, pain-dealing gods, who do not snatch piglets. Before the next spasms could stop her, she ran to the pigsty, each step a rushing out into emptiness. She climbed over the fence and knelt in the dirt. It was good to have a fence enclosing her, a tribal person alone.

Laboring, this woman who had carried her child as a foreign growth that sickened her every day, expelled it at last. She reached down to touch the hot, wet, moving mass, surely smaller than anything human, and could feel that it was human after all—fingers, toes, nails, nose. She pulled it up on to her belly, and it lay curled there, butt in the air, feet precisely tucked one under the other. She opened her loose shirt and buttoned the child inside. After resting, it squirmed and thrashed and she pushed it up to her breast. It turned its head this way and that until it found her nipple. There, it made little snuffling noises. She clenched her teeth at its preciousness, lovely as a young calf, a piglet, a little dog.

She may have gone to the pigsty as a last act of responsibility: she would protect this child as she had protected its father. It would look after her soul, leaving supplies on her grave. But how would this tiny child without family find her grave when there would be no marker for her anywhere, neither in the earth nor the family hall? No one would give her a family hall name. She had taken the child with her into the wastes. At its birth the two of them had felt the same raw pain of separation, a wound that only the family pressing tight could close. A child with no descent line would not soften her life but only trail after her, ghostlike, begging her to give it purpose. At dawn the villagers on their way to the fields would stand around the fence and look.

Full of milk, the little ghost slept. When it awoke, she hardened her   45
breasts against the milk that crying loosens. Toward morning she picked up the baby and walked to the well.

Carrying the baby to the well shows loving. Otherwise abandon it. Turn its face into the mud. Mothers who love their children take them along. It was probably a girl; there is some hope of forgiveness for boys.

"Don't tell anyone you had an aunt. Your father does not want to hear her name. She has never been born." I have believed that sex was unspeakable and words so strong and fathers so frail that "aunt" would do my father mysterious harm. I have thought that my family, having settled among immigrants who had also been their neighbors in the ancestral land, needed to clean their name, and a wrong word would incite the kinspeople even here. But there is more to this silence: they want me to participate in her punishment. And I have.

In the twenty years since I heard this story I have not asked for details nor said my aunt's name; I do not know it. People who comfort the dead can also chase after them to hurt them further—a reverse ancestor worship. The real punishment was not the raid swiftly inflicted by the villagers, but the family's deliberately forgetting her. Her betrayal so maddened them, they saw to it that she would suffer forever, even after death. Always hungry, always needing, she would have to beg food from other ghosts, snatch and steal it from those whose living descendants give them gifts. She would have to fight the ghosts massed at crossroads for the buns a few thoughtful citizens leave to decoy her away from village and home so that the ancestral spirits could feast unharassed. At peace, they could act like gods, not ghosts, their descent lines providing them with paper suits and dresses, spirit money, paper houses, paper automobiles, chicken, meat, and rice into eternity—essences delivered up in smoke and flames, steam and incense rising from each rice bowl. In an attempt to make the Chinese care for people outside the family, Chairman Mao encourages us now to give our paper replicas to the spirits of outstanding soldiers and workers, no matter whose ancestors they may be. My aunt remains forever hungry. Goods are not distributed evenly among the dead.

My aunt haunts me—her ghost drawn to me because now, after fifty years of neglect, I alone devote pages of paper to her, though not origamied into houses and clothes. I do not think she always means me well. I am telling on her, and she was a spite suicide, drowning herself in the drinking water. The Chinese are always very frightened of the drowned one, whose weeping ghost, wet hair hanging and skin bloated, waits silently by the water to pull down a substitute.

QUESTIONING THE TEXT

1. The narrator of "No Name Woman" tells several different versions of her aunt's life. Which do you find most likely to be accurate, and why?

2. What is the narrator's attitude toward the villagers? What in the text reveals her attitude—and how does it compare with your own attitude toward them?

3. A.L.'s introduction sympathizes with No Name Woman. If one of the villagers had written the introduction, how might it differ from A.L.'s?

MAKING CONNECTIONS

4. The serpent in the Genesis reading (p. 297) tells the woman that eating the fruit will open her eyes so that thenceforth she will know good and evil. What of good and evil does No Name Woman learn after tasting her society's "forbidden fruit"?

5. Andrew Sullivan's discussion in "What Are Homosexuals For?" is very different from Kingston's story of No Name Woman. But Sullivan does explore, sometimes implicitly, the reasons homosexuals might choose to keep secrets as well as the complications if they choose to tell. After rereading these pieces, freewrite for 10 to 15 minutes on some secrets in our society that people are never supposed to tell.

JOINING THE CONVERSATION

6. Interview—or spend an hour or so talking with—one of your parents, grandparents, aunts, or uncles, or another older person you know fairly well. Ask your interviewee to describe the attitudes that governed female sexual behavior in his or her day. How were "good girls" supposed to act? What counted as *bad* behavior—and what were the subtle or overt social punishments for that behavior? Write a brief report of your findings, comparing the older person's description of attitudes at an earlier time with those you hold today.

7. Try rewriting one of Kingston's versions of No Name Woman's story from the point of view of the man. How might he see things differently? After you have written this man's version, jot down a few things about him. What does he value? What does he think of women? What is his relationship to women? Finally, bring your version to class to compare with those of two classmates. After studying each version, work together to make a list of what the three versions have in common and a list of how they differ.

SUSAN FALUDI
Whose Hype?

*SUSAN FALUDI (b. 1959) is no stranger to controversy. From high school ar-
ticles about the unconstitutionality of fundamentalist Christian gatherings held
at school, to a college story about sexual harassment at Harvard, to a Pulitzer
Prize–winning article on the devastating impact of Safeway's leveraged buyout
on individual people's lives, she has never hesitated to take a stand. Alarmed
by a 1986 study of marriage that was widely reported and repeated even
though it was shown to be based on a flawed study and suspect conclusions,
Faludi began tracking what she later came to call* Backlash: The Undeclared
War Against American Women *(1991). In this book, Faludi examines
many taken-for-granted claims about women—and finds that they rest on no
firm empirical basis. Faludi herself presents a vast array of information to
illustrate the "backlash" against women, much of it drawn from newspapers, magazines, television and movies, the fashion industry, and the political
forum.*

Faludi's Backlash *led to a backlash of its own, including the work of
Christina Hoff Sommers, whose essay appears on p. 328. Like many others
who speak as critics of feminism, Sommers tends to set up easy dichotomies that
are, ultimately, false ones. Either there is an epidemic of anorexia or none to
worry about; either women have made tremendous gains in the workplace or
men have held them back. Faludi can also be guilty of such either/or thinking,
but at her best she shows the ways in which "both/and" is a more productive
pairing for understanding the positions of women, and of men as well.*

In the following essay, which appeared in a 1995 Newsweek *column,
Faludi takes on those who claim that the concern over the rising number of reported rapes in the United States is just a matter of hype. Suggesting that those
who make such an argument interview women who have actually been raped,
and praising the "stand-tall" feminist groups who use wit (not whining) to
make their points, Faludi draws public attention to the dangers and injustices
facing many women in our society. As a teacher on a very large university campus, I know firsthand about some of these dangers, including rape. And I know
something of what these dangers evoke in the lives of my students. I wanted to
include this essay to suggest that all of us—men and women alike—need to be
vigilant about violence against women.*

*Whether or not you agree with Faludi, you won't be lulled to sleep by her
arguments. She says she is currently at work on a new book—on the "crisis in
masculinity." Watch for it!* — A.L.

Did you get the same irksome feeling of *déjà vu* as I did reading about Katie Roiphe's book, "The Morning After,"* that much ballyhooed attack on so-called victim feminism? You're not imagining things. You may have read an excerpt from the book "Rape Hype Betrays Feminism," in the June 13 *New York Times Magazine,* or you may remember Roiphe's "Date Rape Hysteria" on the *Times*'s op-ed page of Nov. 20, 1991. Or maybe you saw a reprint of her op-ed piece—in *Playboy.* Strange times we live in when *Playboy* finds its best misogynist fare in the pages of the *Times.*

Or maybe you didn't enter the Roiphe echo chamber but just read one of the many recent features that deem acquaintance rape a nonproblem and paint feminists as "neo-Victorian" prudes terrorizing gals with rape tall tales. What you probably missed was the coverage that viewed acquaintance rape as legitimate. Not your fault; it went by in a flash. When the media discover a feminist concern, it gets less than five minutes of serious consideration; then comes a five-year attack. Most stories have raised a doubting eyebrow: "Crying Rape" or "Date Rape, Part 2: The Making of a Crisis" (complete with cartoons).

Roiphe and others "prove" their case by recycling the same anecdotes of false accusations; they all quote the same "expert" who disparages reports of high rape rates. And they never interview any real rape victims. They advise us that a feeling of victimization is no longer a reasonable response to sexual violence; it's a hallucinatory state of mind induced by witchy feminists who cast a spell on impressionable coeds. These date-rape revisionists claim to be liberating young women from the victim mind-set. But is women's sexual victimization just a mind trip—or a reality?

Roiphe's book says the feminist assertion that one in four women is a victim of rape or attempted rape can't be right because, "If 25 percent of my women friends were being raped—wouldn't I know it?" Roiphe must've skipped Statistics 101: one's friends don't constitute a scientific sample. She then bases her entire argument on the "findings" of University of California professor Neil Gilbert. Gilbert has actually never done any research on rape, but he's denounced feminist scholarship on rape in such conservative periodicals as The Public Interest. And he's not a neutral academic; he successfully campaigned to cancel a California school sex abuse prevention program and is now crusading against federal funds for rape prevention. He argues that the one-in-four rape/attempted rape figure is based on a "radical feminist" study that labeled anything from "the slightest pressure" to "sweet talk" as rape. The real number, he says, is one in 1,000.

Katie Roiphe: . . . *The Morning After: Sex, Fear and Feminism on Campus* (1993). Discusses feminism and education, and issues of sexual harassment on colleges campuses.

Gilbert gets this figure from the National Crime Survey (NCS), a poll   5
that even its own researchers fault for undercounting rape. Until recently, the
NCS asked the people polled if they had experienced just about every crime
but rape; victims had to volunteer it on their own. The survey uses an old definition of rape that doesn't fit current laws; for instance, the NCS doesn't
term forced oral or anal sex as rape. And the one-in-1,000 figure is based on
rapes and attempted rapes in a six-month period; the one-in-four figure reflects how many occurred since a college-age woman turned 14.

Despite Gilbert's claim, the one-in-four figure does not include women
who felt sweet-talked into sex. It's true the survey (funded not by a feminist
cabal but by the National Institute of Mental Health) asked women if they
ever felt pressured into sex, but that data was not included in the final count.
Numerous other studies bear these figures out. The bottom line: the number
of sexual assaults in the FBI files has risen four times as fast as the total crime
rate in the last decade.

The date-rape revisionists claim a feminist-provoked rape hysteria is
causing young women to "wallow in victimhood." According to a Senate report, at least 84 percent of rapes go unreported. So where exactly have these
chroniclers of "rape hype" spied hordes of victim-emoting gals anyway?
Maybe in Hollywood films or on TV where "women in jep" clot the screen.
Maybe in the fashion ads featuring wan, cowering waifs. But not in feminist
circles where the most striking recent development has been a massive influx
not of hanky-clutching neo-Victorians but of such stand-tall feminist groups
as Riot GRRRL, Guerrilla Girls, WHAM, YELL, and, my personal favorite, Random Pissed Off Women. These new feminists use wit, not whining, mega-
phones, not moping, to deliver their point.

There is indeed a national "hysteria" over this new forceful feminism—
but it's *male* hysteria. The real cultural fear is not that women are becoming
too Victorian but that they're becoming too damn aggressive—in and out of
bed. Let's recall where this victimhood argument first surfaced: in conservative journal articles by men. Nearly two years before the *Times* printed
Roiphe's "Rape Hype," *Commentary* published Norman Podhoretz's seven-
page denial of date rape. This "brazen campaign" by feminists, he warned,
will deny men their privilege of "normal seduction" and "male initiative."
"The number of 'wimps' . . . will multiply apace," as will—drum roll—"the
incidence of male impotence."

Now I ask you, just who's spouting hype?

QUESTIONING THE TEXT

1. What does Faludi mean by a "victim mind-set"? According to her view,
   who holds such a mind-set, and how does she respond to them?

2. Faludi disputes the claims of Roiphe and others about a "date rape hysteria" that exaggerates the national statistics on rape. What figures does Faludi introduce as a corrective to the "hysteria" thesis? Which of her sources seems most credible to you, and why?

3. A.L. says that Faludi "can be guilty of either-or thinking" but that at her best she shows that "both/and" may be a better way to understand the position women are in. Find examples in Faludi's essay of both these kinds of thinking at work.

MAKING CONNECTIONS

4. Faludi remarks on the strength of feminists who "use wit, not whining," to make their points. Sojourner Truth used her wit in powerful ways, refusing to see herself as a victim, and certainly never whining. What other points of comparison can you draw between the arguments Truth and Faludi make? Bring your answers to class for discussion.

5. Sharon Olds's poem "Son" (p. 355) might have a companion piece called "Daughter." If Susan Faludi were writing such a poem, how might it go? Try your hand at writing this poem, and bring it to class to compare with those of others.

JOINING THE CONVERSATION

6. Imagine that Faludi decided to follow Dave Barry's example (p. 343) and write a new book called *Susan Faludi's Complete Guide to Gals* (note that "gals" is a word she uses twice in her essay). How might Faludi differentiate between "women" and "gals" in such a book? Try writing an introduction to the book that would make such a distinction.

7. Working with two or three classmates, do some research on violence against women on your own campus. Determine whether your campus has a policy on sexual harassment—and get a copy if it does. Then talk with relevant people on campus: staff at a rape crisis center, for example, or at student services, student health campus safety, or those involved with student organizations. Continue by examining the campus newspaper for the last several years to locate all articles on campus violence against women. Then pool your resources and write a brief report of your findings. End it with your own conclusions about the incidence of violence against women on campus.

CHRISTINA HOFF SOMMERS
Figuring Out Feminism

A RULE OF THUMB among political conservatives warns that any figures the mainstream liberal media (ABC, CBS, NBC, CNN) offer to define a crisis (homelessness, kidnapped children, youngsters deprived of lunch by GOP budget cuts) will, when researched, prove roughly ten times higher than the actual number. No doubt the political left feels the same way about statistics reeled off by Newt Gingrich. Sad to say, we live in an era defined by frightening figures, usually too big to comprehend and often preceded by dollar signs.

When statistics bear on human behavior, perhaps we should more routinely ask "Just where did those numbers come from?" Christina Hoff Sommers (b. 1950), philosophy professor at Clark University, poses that question over and over in the following article from National Review, *a piece that appeared later as the preface to* Who Stole Feminism?: How Women Have Betrayed Women *(1994). Sommers is a persistent critic of gender feminists such as Susan Faludi who attempt to blame most of the world's problems on male-dominated social and political structures. Her arguments in the book are wide ranging and complex (not either/or pronouncements as Faludi's tend to be), but I'm interested in this selection chiefly for how clearly it exposes numbers juggled to shape public attitudes. Whether or not you agree with Sommers politically, you'll find that she offers an important lesson in critical reading and thinking.*

— J.R.

In *Revolution from Within,* Gloria Steinem informs her readers that "in this country alone . . . about 150,000 females die of anorexia each year." That is more than three times the annual number of fatalities from car accidents for the total population. Miss Steinem refers readers to Naomi Wolf's *The Beauty Myth,* where one again finds the statistic, along with the author's outrage. "How," she asks, "would America react to the mass self-immolation by hunger of its favorite sons?" Although "nothing justifies comparison with the Holocaust," she cannot refrain from making one anyway. "When confronted with a vast number of emaciated bodies starved not by nature but by men, one must notice a certain resemblance."

Where did Miss Wolf get her figures? Her source is *Fasting Girls: The Emergence of Anorexia Nervosa as a Modern Disease* by Joan Brumberg, a historian and former director of women's studies at Cornell University. She, too, is fully aware of the political significance of the startling statistic. She points out that the women who study eating problems "seek to demonstrate that these disorders are an inevitable consequence of a misogynistic society that demeans women . . . by objectifying their bodies." Professor Brumberg, in turn, attributes the figure to the American Anorexia and Bulimia Association.

I called the American Anorexia and Bulimia Association and spoke to Dr. Diane Mickley, its president. "We were misquoted," she said. In a 1985 newsletter the association had referred to 150,000 to 200,000 *sufferers* (not *fatalities*) of anorexia nervosa. What is the correct morbidity rate? Most experts are reluctant to give exact figures. One clinician told me that of 1,400 patients she had treated in ten years, 4 had died—all through suicide. The National Center for Health Statistics reported 101 deaths from anorexia nervosa in 1983 and 67 deaths in 1988. Thomas Dunn of the Division of Vital Statistics at the National Center for Health Statistics reports that in 1991 there were 54 deaths from anorexia nervosa and no deaths from bulimia. The deaths of these young women are a tragedy, certainly, but in a country of one hundred million adult females, such numbers are hardly evidence of a "holocaust."

Yet now the false figure, supporting the view that our "sexist society" demeans women by objectifying their bodies, is widely accepted as true. Ann Landers repeated it in her syndicated column in April 1992: "Every year, 150,000 American women die from complications associated with anorexia and bulimia."

Will Miss Steinem advise her readers of the egregious statistical error?   5
Will Mrs. Landers? Will it even matter? By now, the 150,000 figure has made it into college textbooks. A recent women's studies text, aptly titled *The Knowledge Explosion,* contains the erroneous figure in its preface.

NEXT CRISIS, PLEASE

The anorexia "crisis" is only one example of the kind of provocative but inaccurate information being purveyed by women about "women's issues" these days. On November 4, 1992, Deborah Louis, president of the National Women's Studies Association, sent a message to the Women's Studies Electronic Bulletin Board: "According to [the] last March of Dimes report, domestic violence (vs. pregnant women) is now responsible for more birth defects than all other causes combined. Personally [this] strikes me as the most disgusting piece of data I've seen in a long while." This was, indeed, unsettling news. But it seemed implausible. I asked my neighbor, a pediatric neurologist at Boston's Children's Hospital, about the report. He told me that although severe battery may occasionally cause miscarriage, he had never heard of battery as a significant cause of birth defects.

I called the March of Dimes to get a copy of the report. Maureen Corry, director of the March's Education and Health Promotion Program, denied any knowledge of it. "We have never seen this research before," she said. I did a search and found that—study or no study—journalists around the country were citing it.

"Domestic violence is the leading cause of birth defects, more than all other medical causes combined, according to a March of Dimes study." (*Boston Globe,* September 2, 1991.)

"Especially grotesque is the brutality reserved for pregnant women: the March of Dimes has concluded that the battering of women during pregnancy causes more birth defects than all the diseases put together for which children are usually immunized." (*Time* magazine, January 18, 1993.)

"The March of Dimes has concluded that the battering of women during   10 pregnancy causes more birth defects than all the diseases put together for which children are usually immunized." (*Dallas Morning News,* February 7, 1993.)

I called the March of Dimes again. Andrea Ziltzer of their media-relations department told me that the rumor was spinning out of control. Governors' offices, state health departments, and Washington politicians had flooded the office with phone calls. Even the office of Senator Edward Kennedy had requested a copy of the "report."

When I finally reached Jeanne McDowell, who had written the *Time* article, the first thing she said was, "That was an error." She sounded genuinely sorry and embarrassed. She explained that she is always careful about checking sources, but this time, for some reason, she had not. *Time* has since called the March of Dimes to apologize. An official retraction finally appeared in the magazine on December 6, 1993, under the heading "Inaccurate Information."

I asked Miss McDowell about her source. She had relied on information given her by the San Francisco Family Violence Prevention Fund, which had obtained it from Sarah Buel, a founder of the domestic-violence advocacy project at Harvard Law School. She in turn had obtained it from Caroline Whitehead, a maternal nurse and child-care specialist in Raleigh, North Caroline. I called Miss Whitehead.

"It blows my mind. *It is not true,*" she said. The whole mixup began, she explained, when she introduced Sarah Buel as a speaker at a 1989 conference for nurses and social workers. In presenting her, Miss Whitehead mentioned that according to some March of Dimes research she had seen, more women are screened for birth defects than are ever screened for domestic battery. Miss Whitehead had said nothing at all about battery *causing* birth defects. "Sarah misunderstood me," she said. Miss Buel went on to put the erroneous information into a manuscript which was then circulated among family-violence professionals. They saw no reason to doubt its authority.

I called Sarah Buel and told her that it seemed she had misheard Caro-   15 line Whitehead. She was surprised. "Oh, I must have misunderstood her. I'll have to give her a call. She is my source." She thanked me for having informed her of the error, pointing out that she had been about to repeat it yet again in a new article.

WHERE WERE THE SKEPTICS?

Why was everybody so credulous? Battery responsible for more birth defects than *all* other causes combined? More than genetic disorders such as spina bifida, Down syndrome, Tay-Sachs, sickle-cell anemia? More than congenital heart disorders? More than alcohol, crack, or AIDS—more than all these things *combined?* Where were the fact-checkers, the editors, the skeptical journalists?

To that question we must add another: Why are certain feminists so eager to put men in a bad light? I shall try to answer both these questions.

American feminism is currently dominated by a group of women who seek to persuade the public that American women are not the free creatures we think we are. The leaders and theorists of the women's movement believe that our society is best described as a patriarchy, a "male hegemony," a "sex/gender system" in which the dominant gender works to keep women cowering and submissive. The feminists who hold this divisive view of our social and political reality believe that all our institutions, from the state to the family to the grade schools, perpetuate male dominance. Believing that women are virtually under siege, the "gender feminists" naturally seek recruits to their side of the gender war. They seek support. They seek vindication. They seek ammunition.

Not everyone, including many women who consider themselves feminists, is convinced that contemporary American women live in an oppressive "male hegemony." To confound the skeptics and persuade the undecided, the gender feminists are constantly on the lookout for the smoking gun, the telling fact that will drive home how profoundly the system is rigged against women. It is not enough to remind us that many brutal and selfish men harm women. They must persuade us that the system itself sanctions male brutality. They must convince us that the oppression of women, sustained from generation to generation, is a structural feature of our society.

Thus gender-feminist ideology holds that physical menace toward   20
women is the norm. Gloria Steinem's portrait of male–female intimacy under patriarchy is typical: "Patriarchy *requires* violence or the subliminal threat of violence in order to maintain itself. . . . The most dangerous situation for a woman is not an unknown man in the street, or even the enemy in wartime, but a husband or lover in the isolation of their own home."

Miss Steinem's description of the dangers women face in their own home is reminiscent of the Super Bowl hoax of January 1993. Here is the chronology:

Thursday, January 27. A news conference was called in Pasadena, California, the site of the forthcoming Super Bowl game, by a coalition of women's groups. At the news conference, reporters were informed that Super Bowl Sunday is "the biggest day of the year for violence against women." Forty per cent more women would be battered on that day. In support of the

40 per cent figure, Sheila Kuehl of the California Women's Law Center cited a study done at Virginia's Old Dominion University three years before. The presence of Linda Mitchell, a representative of a media "watchdog" group called Fairness and Accuracy in Reporting (FAIR), lent credibility to the claim.

At about the same time a very large media mailing was sent by Dobisky Associates, FAIR's publicists, warning at-risk women: "Don't remain at home with him during the game." The idea that sports fans are prone to attack their wives or girlfriends on that climactic day persuaded many men as well: Robert Lipsyte of the *New York Times* would soon be referring to the "Abuse Bowl."

Friday, January 28. Lenore Walker, a Denver psychologist and author of *The Battered Woman,* appeared on *Good Morning America* claiming to have compiled a ten-year record showing a sharp increase in violent incidents against women on Super Bowl Sundays.

Here, again, a representative from FAIR, Laura Flanders, was present to   25
lend credibility to the claim.

Saturday, January 29. A story in the *Boston Globe* written by Lynda Gorov reported that women's shelters and hotlines are "flooded with more calls from victims [on Super Bowl Sunday] than on any other day of the year." Miss Gorov cited "one study of women's shelters out West" that "showed a 40 per cent climb in calls, a pattern advocates said is repeated nationwide, including in Massachusetts."

In this roiling sea of media credulity was a lone island of professional integrity. Ken Ringle, a *Washington Post* staff writer, took the time to call around. When he asked Janet Katz—professor of sociology and criminal justice at Old Dominion, and one of the principal authors of the study cited by Miss Kuehl—about the connection between violence and football games, she said: "That's not what we found at all." Instead, she told him, they had found that an increase in emergency-room admissions "was not associated with the occurrence of football games in general."

Mr. Ringle checked with Lynda Gorov, who told him she had never seen the study she cited but had been told of it by FAIR. Linda Mitchell of FAIR told Mr. Ringle that the authority for the 40 per cent figure was Lenore Walker. Miss Walker's office, in turn, referred calls on the subject to Michael Lindsey, a Denver psychologist and an authority on battered women. Pressed by Mr. Ringle, Mr. Lindsey admitted he could find no basis for the report. "I haven't been any more successful than you in tracking down any of this," he said. "You think maybe we have one of these myth things here?"

Later, other reporters pressed Miss Walker to detail her findings. She said they were not available. "We don't use them for public consumption," she explained, "we used them to guide us in advocacy projects."

It would have been more honest for the feminists who initiated the   30
campaign to admit that there was no basis for saying that football fans are

MIKE SHAPIRO

" REMEMBER, IT'S NOT REALLY A LIE IF IT'S
    BASED ON THE FACTS. "

(Mike Shapiro, Cartoonists & Writers Syndicate)

more brutal to women than are chess players or Democrats nor any basis for saying that there was a significant rise in domestic violence on Super Bowl Sunday.

Ken Ringle's unraveling of the "myth thing" was published on the front page of the *Washington Post* on January 31. On February 2, *Boston Globe* staff writer Bob Hohler published what amounted to a retraction of Miss Gorov's story. Mr. Hohler had done some more digging and had gotten FAIR's Steven Rendell to back off from the organization's earlier support of the claim. "It should not have gone out in FAIR materials," said Mr. Rendell.

Linda Mitchell would later acknowledge that she was aware during the original news conference that Miss Kuehl was misrepresenting the Old Dominion study. Mr. Ringle asked her whether she did not feel obligated to challenge her colleague. "I wouldn't do that in front of the media," Miss Mitchell said. "She has a right to report it as she wants."

The shelters and hot lines, which monitored the Sunday of the 27th Super Bowl with special care, reported no variation in the number of calls for help that day, not even in Buffalo, whose team (and fans) had suffered a crushing defeat.

But despite Ken Ringle's exposé, the Super Bowl "statistic" will be with us for a while, doing its divisive work of generating fear and resentment. In the book *How to Make the World a Better Place for Women in Five Minutes a Day,* a comment under the heading "Did You Know?" informs readers that "Super Bowl Sunday is the most violent day of the year, with the highest reported number of domestic battering cases." How a belief in that misandrist canard can make the world a better place for women is not explained.

Female Gains or Male Backlash?

How a feminist reacts to data about gender gaps in salaries and eco-   35
nomic opportunities is an excellent indication of the kind of feminist she is.
In general, the equity feminist points with pride to the many gains women
have made toward achieving parity in the workplace. By contrast, the gender
feminist makes it a point to disparage these gains and to speak of backlash. It
disturbs her that the public may be lulled into thinking that women are doing
well and that men are allowing it. The gender feminist insists that any so-
called progress is illusory.

By most measures, the Eighties were a time of rather spectacular gains
by American women—in education, in wages, and in such traditionally male
professions as business, law, and medicine. The gender feminist will have
none of this. According to Susan Faludi, in her much ballyhooed book, the
Eighties were the backlash decade, in which men successfully retracted many
of the gains wrested from them in preceding decades. And since any criticism
of Miss Faludi's claim is apt to be construed as just more backlashing, one
must be grateful to the editors of the *New York Times* business section for
braving the wrath of feminist ideologues by presenting an objective account
of the economic picture as it affects women.

Surveying several reports by women economists on women's gains in
the 1980s, *New York Times* business writer Sylvia Nasar rejected Susan Faludi's
thesis. She pointed to masses of empirical data showing that "Far from losing
ground, women gained more in the 1980s than in the entire postwar era before that. And almost as much as between 1890 and 1980."

The *Times* reports that the proportion women earn of each dollar of men's
wages rose to a record 72 cents by 1990. But the *Times* points out that even this
figure is misleadingly pessimistic, because it includes older women who are only
marginally in the work force, such as "the mother who graduated from high
school, left the work force at twenty, and returned to a minimum wage at a local
store." Younger women, says the *Times,* "now earn 80 cents for every dollar
earned by men of the same age, up from 69 cents in 1980."

None of these facts has made the slightest impression on the backlash
mongers. For years, feminist activists have been wearing buttons claiming
women earn "59 cents to a man's dollar." Some journalists have questioned
this figure. Miss Faludi calls them "spokesmen" for the backlash and says: "By
1988, women with a college diploma could still wear the famous 59-cent buttons. They were still making 59 cents to their male counterparts' dollar. In
fact, the pay gap for them was now a bit worse than five years earlier."

The sources Miss Faludi cites do not sustain her figure. The actual fig-   40
ure for 1988 is 68 cents, both for all women and for women with a college
diploma. This is substantially higher, not lower, than it was five years earlier.
The most recent figures, for 1992, are considerably higher yet: 71 cents for all
women and 73 cents for women with a college diploma.

What of the remaining gap between male and female earnings? For the gender feminists, the answer is simple: the wage gap is the result of discrimination against women. But in fact, serious economic scholars who are trained to interpret these data (including many eminent female economists) point out that most of the differences in earnings reflect such prosaic matters as shorter work weeks. For example, the average work week for full-time, year-round female workers is shorter than for comparable male workers. When economists compare men's and women's *hourly* earnings instead of their *yearly* earnings, the wage gap narrows even more.

Economists differ on exactly how much, if any, of the remaining gap is discrimination. Most economists agree that much of it simply represents the fact that, on average, women have accrued less workplace experience than men of the same age. One recent scholarly estimate shows that as of 1987, females who were currently working full-time and year-round had, on average, one-quarter year less of work experience than comparable males.

These data are important in understanding the oft-cited claim of a "glass ceiling" for women. Promotion in high-powered professional jobs often goes to those who have put in long hours in evenings and on weekends. Husbands may be more likely to do so than wives, for a variety of reasons, including unequal division of responsibilities at home, in which case the source of the difficulty is at home, not in the marketplace.

Obviously, the experience gap also reflects the fact that many women choose to move into and out of the work force during child-bearing and child-rearing years. This reduces the amount of experience they acquire in the workplace and naturally results in lower earnings, quite apart from any possible discrimination. Some evidence of this is provided by data on childless workers, for whom the experience gap should be much narrower, resulting in a narrower earnings gap. This, in fact, is the case: as of 1987, among childless white workers aged 20 to 44, females' hourly earnings were between 86 to 91 per cent of males' hourly earnings.

Robert Reich, the U.S. secretary of labor, wrote a blurb for *Backlash* describing it as "spellbinding and frightening . . . a wake-up call to the men as well as the women who are struggling to build a gender-respectful society." One can only hope that Mr. Reich was too spellbound to have read *Backlash* with a discriminating mind. What is more alarming than anything Miss Faludi has to say about an undeclared war against American women is the credulity it has met in high public officials on whose judgment we ought to be able to rely.   45

QUESTIONING THE TEXT

1. Sommers repeatedly refutes one set of numbers by citing what she claims are more accurate figures. What techniques does she employ to

undermine the original numbers? What grounds does she offer for the reliability of her own statistics? Annotate her essay critically.

2. Locate Sommers's definition of "gender feminists." How can you tell that Sommers disapproves of gender feminists?

3. If you had only J.R.'s introduction to Sommers's "Figuring Out Feminism" and A.L.'s introduction to Faludi's "Whose Hype?" what could you tell about their political disagreements in the area of gender politics?

MAKING CONNECTIONS

4. Read Sommers's essay alongside that of Susan Faludi. Then write a letter addressed to both women suggesting ways they might find common ground.

5. In "Enemies of Promise" in chapter 5, J. Michael Bishop complains of a widespread public misunderstanding of science. What does Sommers's piece suggest about the ability of an educated public to understand statistics? In your reading log, comment on the attention your education has paid to interpreting numbers and statistics.

JOINING THE CONVERSATION

6. Some of the people Sommers "corrects" seem grateful to have their errors pointed out. But how can professional people believe statistics that seem so overwhelmingly at odds with reality—for example, 150,000 women dying of anorexia each year? In a personal narrative, explore your own reaction to statistics, especially to those that confirm what you already believe. Have you ever been willingly misled by numbers?

7. Why might "gender feminists" wish to target the National Football League's annual Super Bowl as an event that provokes spousal abuse? Write a short report describing cultural and gender roles enacted in and around the Super Bowl. How do men and women stereotypically behave during Super Bowl weekend? Are the stereotypes based on fact?

DAVID THOMAS
The Mind of Man

MOST STUDIES THAT COMPARE the academic performances of boys and girls focus on the one or two areas where males routinely outperform females, usually in mathematics and in the perception of spatial relationships. We are advised, as a result of such revelations, that society needs to do more to close the gaps between male and female accomplishment. All but ignored in press accounts and accompanying editorials are the other halves of those studies, the realms of achievement where young women decisively outperform young men, as if male deficiencies—for example, in verbal skills—were natural and beyond remediation.

So it's a crisis requiring immediate attention (and funding) when Sam does better than Suzie in geometry; but it seems not to matter that she reads and writes better than he and probably possesses better study skills and more positive attitudes toward learning.

Even at the college level, researchers in rhetoric and composition rarely address the writing difficulties of young men, problems that women as a group seem not to have. This persistent male/female difference intrigues scholars much less than do more politically fashionable issues—such as why men supposedly dominate class discussions, including those on computer networks. Even in college, getting boys to behave seems to concern some academics more than teaching them something.

Am I making this up? Read the following essay by David Thomas (b. 1959) from his book Not Guilty *(1993). You'll discover that boys have trouble getting fair treatment in schools not only in the United States but also in Britain, where single-sex education—one potential solution to disparities experienced by both sexes in educational achievement—has been more common than it has been here. David Thomas is a writer and journalist who served for a time (1989–92) as editor of the famous English periodical* Punch. *– J.R.*

An old calypso song states that "Man Smart, Woman Smarter," but it is generally agreed by most researchers than men and women are indivisible in terms of their average overall intelligence. In *A Question of Sex,* Dr. John Nicholson summarizes the history of research into intelligence, much of which had presumed the intellectual superiority of men. He concludes with a sentence from which there has been little subsequent dissent: "The most important fact is that men are not more intelligent than women—the average man's IQ score is indistinguishable from that of the average woman." Yet, as Dr. Nicholson points out with the aid of a few simple experiments, the sexes do differ in the types of mental tasks at which they excel.

In the words of a *Time* magazine cover story, published in January 1992, "Psychology tests consistently support the notion that men and women perceive the world in subtly different ways. Males excel at rotating three-dimensional objects in their head. Females prove better at reading the emotions of people in photographs. A growing number of scientists believe the discrepancies reflect functional differences in the brains of men and women . . . some misunderstandings between the sexes may have more to do with crossed wiring than cross-purposes."

Women are also better at verbal tasks. If given two minutes in which to come up with as many synonyms as possible for a series of words, they will, on the whole, score better than men. In both of these tests, however, some individuals will do much better or worse than their sex suggests that they "ought" to.

Do we, however, make the best of what nature has provided when the time comes to educate our young? Over the last few years, nationwide school exam results have shown an increasing gap between the performances of girls and boys, in the girls' favor. Many more boys than girls leave school without any form of qualification. And amongst those who do pass GCSE and A-Level exams, girls are getting the higher grades. The introduction of course work into the GCSE syllabus appears to favor girls, who tend to be diligent and less rebellious. Boys appear to prefer the one-off competition of the examination hall. These preferences may be due, in part, to differences in the male and female brain, which will be discussed anon. However, since white working-class boys now score more poorly in England and Wales than almost any other racial or sexual grouping, and since highly privileged public schoolboys can be coached and coaxed into achieving astonishingly high marks, the possibility must be considered that there are social forces at work.

Much has been written in the past about the difficulties girls face in mixed classrooms. It has always been assumed that boys tend to speak up more forcefully than girls, and tend to be spoken to more frequently by teachers. If so, this reflects life in society as a whole. In both Britain and America, researchers have found that a woman who speaks as much as a man in a conversation, class or meeting will be thought, by both male and female observers, to have been hectoring and domineering: we are, quite simply, used to men taking the lion's share of conversation.

Recently, however, suggestions have been made that question this view of the classroom. At kindergarten and primary-school level, in which little girls out-perform the boys, the vast majority of teachers are female. Surveys by the now-defunct Inner London Education Authority showed that women teachers consistently praised girls more than boys, and equally consistently criticized the boys' behavior, often regarding it as a serious problem requiring remedial treatment. In the words of Tony Mooney, a secondary-school head-master, writing in the *Independent on Sunday:* "Women teachers find boys too noisy, too aggressive, too boisterous. Unconsciously or not, they consistently reinforce and reward more 'feminine' behavior. If all this is true, it is under-standable that boys should not be as advanced as girls in the hands of women junior school teachers. There is a direct relationship between a child's aca-demic achievement and a favorable response from the teacher."

Mooney was first alerted to this possibility by the behavior of his own son, whose performance and self-confidence at school altered markedly when he was taught by a woman, rather than a man. When the boy's mother asked him why this should be so, he replied, "Because the men teachers never shout at me as much as the women teachers."

Research evidence, from an experiment at the University of California, Los Angeles, appeared to support Mooney's anecdotal experience: "Seventy-two boys and sixty girls at kindergarten . . . learned reading with a self-teaching machine. There were no differences between the sexes in their reac-tions to the mechanical gadgetry. Yet when the girls were tested on their reading progress they scored lower than the boys. Then the children were placed under the normal classroom instruction of women teachers. The chil-dren were tested again on the words they had been taught by the teacher. This time the boys' scores were inferior to the girls'."

Mooney noted that boys' exam results at secondary-school were declin-ing just as the number of women secondary-school teachers was increasing. Boys, however, continued to out-perform girls in scientific and technical sub-jects where teaching was still dominated by men. The issue here is not just the favoritism that teachers may show to pupils of their own sex, but the in-stinctive understanding that an adult will enjoy with a child who is going through a process which he or she went through too.

The notion that boys might in some way be disadvantaged was too   10
shocking for at least one reader of Mooney's article. As far as Christine Cosker—a correspondent to the *Independent on Sunday's* letters page was concerned, it was partly the fault of the boys themselves. "If girls achieve higher standards than boys," she wrote, "it is not the result of sympathetic fe-male teachers: it is that boys fail to be motivated because of their attitude to women. Boys' early experience is almost entirely one of a society which re-gards women's traditional roles as trivial, dull and second-rate and dismisses their opinions. If girls have a positive role model in the female teacher, they will do better than boys. But if boys, unencumbered by society's prejudices, valued their female teachers, then their progress would match that of girls."

It is worth examining some of the prejudices revealed by this letter in some detail, because I suspect that they would be shared by a broad swathe of supposedly progressive opinion.

In the first place, note that she has found it impossible to accept that female teachers could, in any way, be responsible for the situation. It has to be the fault of males and an anti-female social order. Specifically, boys are to be blamed for their own disadvantages.

Secondly, she has misinterpreted the article. Mr. Mooney indicated that his son's problem was not that he did not value his teacher, but that she did not value him. He was frightened of her because she shouted at him.

Thirdly, although it is extremely important to primary-school-aged boys not to be seen to act in any way that might be interpreted as cissy or girly, that is not necessarily to say that they regard women's traditional roles as "trivial, dull and second-rate." The most traditional role that women have is to be a mother. And the mother of a small boy is still one of the two most important people in his life. In the experience of most "traditional" housewives I know, it is other, career-minded women who hold them in the greatest contempt. Their children value them above all else.

Finally, observe the double standard applied to girls and boys. Cosker 15 maintains, and few would disagree, that girls benefit from a "positive role model." There is, however, no need for boys to be given the same benefit. Instead, they must pull their socks up and change their attitudes. Heaven forbid that they should be given any consideration or compassion. Heaven forbid that the prejudices of the new age should be challenged. If you ever doubted that feminists have taken over from apoplectic old colonels as the great reactionaries of society, just read this letter.

Alternatively, look at the facts. One of the few generally accepted differences between boys and girls is that boys are, across all cultures, much more boisterous and overtly competitive than girls. Boys enjoy games of rough and tumble. They play with guns, real or imaginary. They seek out physical competition, whether through sport or informal bouts of playground warfare. This makes them harder to control than girls, particularly if, as is the case in the majority of state primary schools in this country, they are being taught in an open-plan classroom. Janet Daley, writing in the *Independent,* has observed that "Anyone who visits an open-plan infant-school classroom, where the children organize much of their own time, will notice a pattern. Groups of little girls will be absorbed in quite orderly work or play . . . requiring little supervision. A few of the boys will be engrossed in solitary creative or constructive activity. A large number of children will be noisily participating in some loosely directed project which needs guidance and some of those will be boys who are persistently disruptive and out of control."

Daley ascribes this behavior to the fact that the neurological development of boys is slower than that of girls, and thus boys are "physically and mentally unstable for much of their childhood and adolescence." Are they?

Or does Ms. Daley share a prejudice—unintended, no doubt—with the boys' teachers, who are trained to define the relative maturity of their charges by their ability to sit quietly and be attentive? By those standards, boys may appear backward, troublesome and even threatening. All that has happened, however, is that we are criticizing boys for their failure to be more like girls.

It has for some time been recognized that girls do better in single-sex education, where their particular needs can be catered for exclusively. Having spent ten years in single-sex boarding-school education, I have mixed feelings about its benefits for boys, but I am absolutely certain that there are great social benefits to be had from recognizing that boys may need specially tailored treatment to at least as great an extent as their sisters (a point with which Janet Daley concurs).

In the years before puberty, boys are, I suspect, perfectly happy to be left to themselves. At the age of eleven or twelve, I doubt whether I would have been at all pleased to see girls getting in the way of my games of football, or intruding in the serious business of building huts and encampments in the woods behind the school. By my teens, however, I was painfully aware of the distorting effect that an all-male institution was having on my own emotional development and that of my classmates.

Despite that, however, I was taught in a system that was designed to bring the best out of boys, intellectually, creatively and on the sports field. It was certainly a world away from the non-achieving atmosphere that has been prevalent throughout much of English state education over the last twenty years. Of course, the boys with whom I was educated came from privileged backgrounds. But one of the mistakes made by critics of the public-school system is to underestimate the efficiency, not to say ruthlessness, with which its pupils are programmed to perform to the best of their ability. We were constantly tested, constantly ranked and constantly urged to do better. And, on reflection, I suspect that it is better to accept that boys are not, on the whole, docile creatures who wish to live in harmony with one another, but are, instead, highly competitive, physically energetic creatures who hunt in packs.

Some boys will suffer in that sort of environment, and they need to be respected and protected. I can remember all too well what it is like to be on the receiving end of bullying and oppression. But I also know that there is no point in deciding that, since traditional male behavior is politically unacceptable, boys must somehow be conditioned to behave in ways that are not natural to them. That process leads only to disaster.

Boys whose lives are led without structure and discipline do not find themselves liberated. Instead they become bored, frustrated and maladaptive. They fight. They misbehave and they perform badly, both at school and thereafter. However much it might want boys to change, any society that wants to limit the antisocial behavior of young men should start by accepting the way they are. Then it should do everything possible to make sure that their energies are directed towards good, rather than evil. When Yoda sat on his rock in *The Empire Strikes Back* and told Luke Skywalker that he had to choose between the dark force and the light, he knew what he was talking about.

QUESTIONING THE TEXT

1. Men and women differ, according to Thomas, in "the mental tasks at which they excel." Research this claim to determine the nature and quality of these differences—or whether they exist at all. Then discuss your reaction to the situation, focusing on the consequences any difference might have for educational policy.
2. Annotate places in Thomas's text where you notice a difference between the British educational system that he describes and the educational system that you know. How do the differences affect the way you ought to regard his claims?
3. Have you read claims like those discussed in J.R.'s introduction that girls are not treated equally in school? Have you ever read reports on the problems boys have getting fair treatment?

MAKING CONNECTIONS

4. Keeping in mind that most elementary and secondary school teachers in the United States are women, read Thomas's essay side by side with Sharon Olds's poem "Son" (p. 355). Then, if you keep a reading log, record your reaction.
5. Does the situation of young males in the educational system Thomas describes in any way resemble that of young females as described by Adrienne Rich (p. 44)? Freewrite on this subject; don't hesitate to explore differences as well.

JOINING THE CONVERSATION

6. In a group of men and women, discuss single-sex education. Then write a report that weighs the advantages and disadvantages of segregating boys and girls at the elementary, secondary, or college level.
7. Write a narrative about an incident in your school experience that revealed differences in the way teachers treated girls and boys.

DAVE BARRY
Guys vs. Men

ONE OF THE FIRST WORDS *I ever spoke was* truck, *and now, forty-five years later, I finally drive one, a fully skid-plated 4 × 4 Yukon tall enough to scrape the garage roof and designed to roll me safely over the treacherous ravines and gullies . . . between home and work. Well, I'm man enough to admit that gas-guzzling Big Blue makes as much sense today as a drawbridge, but the guy in me wonders: How would it look with brush guards and a Superwinch?*

Dave Barry (b. 1947) is a smart guy. Unlike every other piece in this anthology, "Guys vs. Men" is absolutely, positively right about everything. So take notes as you read. The guys in class will need to borrow them for the quiz tomorrow.

"Guys vs. Men" is the preface to Dave Barry's Complete Guide to Guys: A Fairly Short Book *(1995). —* J.R.

This is a book about guys. It's *not* a book about men. There are already way too many books about men, and most of them are *way* too serious.

Men itself is a serious word, not to mention *manhood* and *manly.* Such words make being male sound like a very important activity, as opposed to what it primarily consists of, namely, possessing a set of minor and frequently unreliable organs.

Could a woman get away with such a trivialization of womanhood? The fact that a man can (and so successfully at that) is evidence in itself for Barry's argument. — J.G.R.

But men tend to attach great significance to Manhood. This results in certain characteristically masculine, by which I mean stupid, behavioral patterns that can produce unfortunate results such as violent crime, war, spitting, and ice hockey. These things have given males a bad name.[1] And the "Men's Movement," which is supposed to bring out the more positive aspects of Manliness, seems to be densely populated with loons and goobers.

So I'm saying that there's another way to look at males: not as aggressive macho dominators; not as sensitive, liberated, hugging drummers; but as *guys.*

And what, exactly, do I mean by "guys"? I don't know. I haven't thought that much about it. One

Who might write "Gals vs. Women"? Whoopi Goldberg? Madonna? Hillary Rodham Clinton? Maybe Terry McMillan? — A.L.

---

[1] Specifically, "asshole."

of the major characteristics of guyhood is that we guys don't spend a lot of time pondering our deep innermost feelings. There is a serious question in my mind about whether guys actually *have* deep innermost feelings, unless you count, for example, loyalty to the Detroit Tigers, or fear of bridal showers.

But although I can't define exactly what it means to be a guy, I can describe certain guy characteristics, such as:

GUYS LIKE NEAT STUFF

By "neat," I mean "mechanical and unnecessarily complex." I'll give you an example. Right now I'm typing these words on an *extremely* powerful computer. It's the latest in a line of maybe ten computers I've owned, each one more powerful than the last. My computer is chock full of RAM and ROM and bytes and megahertzes and various other items that enable a computer to kick data-processing butt. It is probably capable of supervising the entire U.S. air-defense apparatus while simultaneously processing the tax return of every resident of Ohio. I use it mainly to write a newspaper column. This is an activity wherein I sit and stare at the screen for maybe ten minutes, then, using only my forefingers, slowly type something like:

Henry Kissinger* looks like a big wart.

I stare at this for another ten minutes, have an inspiration, then amplify the original thought as follows:

Henry Kissinger looks like a big fat wart.

Then I stare at that for another ten minutes, pondering whether I should try to work in the concept of "hairy."

This is absurdly simple work for my computer. It sits there, humming impatiently, bored to death, passing the time between keystrokes via brain-teaser activities such as developing a Unified Field Theory

He is counting on powerful stereotypes here, and with this one he seems right on target. Boys love toys maybe? — A.L.

Aha! Barry's first slip—completely neglecting the computer's all-important functions of Solitaire and Hearts. How would we play these without a computer? — J.G.R.

Henry Kissinger (b. 1923): foreign policy advisor to President Nixon and U.S. Secretary of State 1973–77

of the universe and translating the complete works of Shakespeare into rap.[2]

In other words, this computer is absurdly overqualified to work for me, and yet soon, I guarantee, I will buy an *even more powerful* one. I won't be able to stop myself. I'm a guy.

Probably the ultimate example of the fundamental guy drive to have neat stuff is the Space Shuttle. Granted, the guys in charge of this program *claim* it has a Higher Scientific Purpose, namely to see how humans function in space. But of course we have known for years how humans function in space: They float around and say things like: "Looks real good, Houston!"

No, the real reason for the existence of the Space Shuttle is that it is one humongous and spectacularly gizmo-intensive item of hardware. Guys can tinker with it practically forever, and occasionally even get it to work, and use it to place *other* complex mechanical items into orbit, where they almost immediately break, which provides a great excuse to send the Space Shuttle up *again*. It's Guy Heaven.

Other results of the guy need to have stuff are Star Wars, the recreational boating industry, monorails, nuclear weapons, and wristwatches that indicate the phase of the moon. I am not saying that women haven't been involved in the development or use of this stuff. I'm saying that, without guys, this stuff probably would not exist; just as, without women, virtually every piece of furniture in the world would still be in its original position. Guys do not have a basic need to rearrange furniture. Whereas a woman who could cheerfully use the same computer for fifty-three years will rearrange her furniture on almost a weekly basis, sometimes in the dead of night. She'll be sound asleep in bed, and suddenly, at 2 A.M., she'll be awakened by the urgent thought: *The blue-green sofa needs to go perpendicular to the wall instead of parallel, and it needs to go there RIGHT NOW.* So she'll get up and move it,

---

Probably the most tell-tale line of this piece.   —J.G.R.

Little boys don't have to be taught to want toy cars or video games.   J.R.

How about dividing Shakespeare's characters into guys or men? Falstaff—now, there was a guy. — A.L.

Less than amusing—especially in light of the Space Shuttle disaster. Is he implying that guys aren't interested in basic ethical questions like what results their gizmos have on people's lives? — A.L.

---

[2]To be or not? I got to *know*.
Might kill myself by the end of the *show*.

which of course necessitates moving other furniture, and soon she has rearranged her entire living room, shifting great big heavy pieces that ordinarily would require several burly men to lift, because there are few forces in Nature more powerful than a woman who needs to rearrange furniture. Every so often a guy will wake up to discover that, because of his wife's overnight efforts, he now lives in an entirely different house.

Another stereotype neatly deployed. And he counts on our not minding that he lumps all women into one category—it's part of what he has to do to make such portraits "funny."
— A.L.

(I realize that I'm making gender-based generalizations here, but my feeling is that if God did not want us to make gender-based generalizations, She would not have given us genders.)

A tongue-in-cheek nod at the politically correct. Nice.
— J.G.R.

GUYS LIKE A REALLY POINTLESS CHALLENGE

Not long ago I was sitting in my office at the *Miami Herald*'s Sunday magazine, *Tropic,* reading my fan mail,[3] when I heard several of my guy coworkers in the hallway talking about how fast they could run the forty-yard dash. These are guys in their thirties and forties who work in journalism, where the most demanding physical requirement is the ability to digest vending-machine food. In other words, these guys have absolutely no need to run the forty-yard dash.

But one of them, Mike Wilson, was writing a story about a star high-school football player who could run it in 4.38 seconds. Now if Mike had written a story about, say, a star high-school poet, none of my guy coworkers would have suddenly decided to find out how well they could write sonnets. But when Mike turned in his story, they became *deeply* concerned about how fast they could run the forty-yard dash. They were so concerned that the magazine editor, Tom Shroder, decided that they should get a stopwatch and go out to a nearby park and find out. Which they did, a bunch of guys taking off their shoes and running around barefoot in a public park on company time.

OK. Now I know I am not and never can be a "guy." This is the last thing I would do in response to a story about 40-yard dash times.
— A.L.

---

[3]Typical fan letter: "Who cuts your hair? Beavers?"

This is what I heard them talking about, out in the hall. I heard Tom, who was thirty-eight years old, saying that his time in the forty had been 5.75 seconds. And I thought to myself: This is ridiculous. These are middle-aged guys, supposedly adults, and they're out there *bragging* about their performance in this stupid juvenile footrace. Finally I couldn't stand it anymore.

"Hey!" I shouted. "*I* could beat 5.75 seconds."

So we went out to the park and measured off forty yards, and the guys told me that I had three chances to make my best time. On the first try my time was 5.78 seconds, just three-hundredths of a second slower than Tom's, even though, at forty-five, I was seven years older than he. So I just *knew* I'd beat him on the second attempt if I ran really, really hard, which I did for a solid ten yards, at which point my left hamstring muscle, which had not yet shifted into Spring Mode from Mail-Reading Mode, went, and I quote, "pop."

I may expire on the racquetball court some day. But I'll go happy—so long as I'm winning.
— J.R.

I had to be helped off the field. I was in considerable pain, and I was obviously not going to be able to walk right for weeks. The other guys were very sympathetic, especially Tom, who took the time to call me at home, where I was sitting with an ice pack on my leg and twenty-three Advil in my bloodstream, so he could express his concern.

Any guy who has ever competed in an "eat-'til-you-puke" contest with 49-cent tacos can relate to this.
— J.G.R.

"Just remember," he said, "*you didn't beat my time.*"

Or "Last one to the moon has to eat the Berlin Wall." (It took them over 20 years to pay up for this one.)
—J.G.R.

There are countless other examples of guys rising to meet pointless challenges. Virtually all sports fall into this category, as well as a large part of U.S. foreign policy. ("I'll bet you can't capture Manuel Noriega!"* "Oh YEAH??")

Who is it that proposed cutting out all militaries the world over and resolving all foreign policy crises by sending out squads to play some game? I can just imagine Barry describing such scenes. — A.L.

GUYS DO NOT HAVE A RIGID AND WELL-DEFINED MORAL CODE

This is not the same as saying that guys are bad. Guys *are* capable of doing bad things, but this generally happens when they try to be Men and start

---

Manuel Noriega (b. 1934): Panamanian dictator removed from power by armed U.S. intervention in 1989

becoming manly and aggressive and stupid. When they're being just plain guys, they aren't so much actively *evil* as they are *lost*. Because guys have never really grasped the Basic Human Moral Code, which I believe was invented by women millions of years ago when all the guys were out engaging in some other activity, such as seeing who could burp the loudest. When they came back, there were certain rules that they were expected to follow unless they wanted to get into Big Trouble, and they have been trying to follow these rules ever since, with extremely irregular results. Because guys have never *internalized* these rules. Guys are similar to my small auxiliary backup dog, Zippy, a guy dog[4] who has been told numerous times that he is *not* supposed to (1) get into the kitchen garbage or (2) poop on the floor. He knows that these are the rules, but he has never really understood *why,* and sometimes he gets to thinking: Sure, I am *ordinarily* not supposed to get into the garbage, but obviously this rule is not meant to apply when there are certain extenuating[5] circumstances, such as (1) somebody just threw away some perfectly good seven-week-old Kung Pao Chicken, and (2) I am home alone.

And so when the humans come home, the kitchen floor has been transformed into Garbage-Fest USA, and Zippy, who usually comes rushing up, is off in a corner disguised in a wig and sunglasses, hoping to get into the Federal Bad Dog Relocation Program before the humans discover the scene of the crime.

Guys do care about rules when it comes to their machines or games, the more complicated the better. Only guys could have invented f-stops or the infield fly rule.

— J.R.

When I yell at him, he frequently becomes so upset that he poops on the floor.

Morally, most guys are just like Zippy, only taller and usually less hairy. Guys are *aware* of the rules of moral behavior, but they have trouble keeping these rules in the forefronts of their minds at certain times, especially the present. This is especially true in the area of faithfulness to one's mate. I

---

[4]I also have a female dog, Earnest, who *never* breaks the rules.

[5]I am taking some liberties here with Zippy's vocabulary. More likely, in his mind, he uses the term *mitigating.*

realize, of course, that there are countless examples of guys being faithful to their mates until they die, usually as a result of being eaten by their mates immediately following copulation. Guys outside of the spider community, however, do not have a terrific record of faithfulness.

I'm not saying guys are scum. I'm saying that many guys who consider themselves to be committed to their marriages will stray if they are confronted with overwhelming temptation, defined as "virtually any temptation."

Okay, so maybe I *am* saying guys are scum. But they're not *mean-spirited* scum. And few of them— even when they are out of town on business trips, far from their wives, and have a clear-cut opportunity—will poop on the floor.

Wonder if his wife read this? — J.G.R.

Well, that's a relief—considering that they will readily foul up their marriages. — A.L.

GUYS ARE NOT GREAT
AT COMMUNICATING THEIR
INTIMATE FEELINGS, ASSUMING
THEY HAVE ANY

This is an aspect of guyhood that is very frustrating to women. A guy will be reading the newspaper, and the phone will ring; he'll answer it, listen for ten minutes, hang up, and resume reading. Finally his wife will say: "Who was that?"

And he'll say: "Phil Wonkerman's mom."

(Phil is an old friend they haven't heard from in seventeen years.)

And the wife will say, "Well?"

And the guy will say, "Well what?"

And the wife will say, "What did she *say?*"

And the guy will say, "She said Phil is fine," making it clear by his tone of voice that, although he does not wish to be rude, he is trying to read the newspaper, and he happens to be right in the middle of an important panel of "Calvin and Hobbes."

But the wife, ignoring this, will say, "That's *all* she said?"

And she will not let up. She will continue to ask district-attorney-style questions, forcing the guy to recount the conversation until she's satisfied that she has the entire story, which is that Phil just got out of prison after serving a sentence for a murder he committed when he became a drug addict because of the guilt he felt when his wife died in a freak submarine accident while Phil was having an affair with a nun, but now he's all straightened out and has a good job as a trapeze artist and is almost through with the surgical part of his sex change and recently became happily engaged to marry a prominent member of the Grateful Dead, so in other words he is fine, which is *exactly* what the guy told her in the first place, but is that enough? No. She wants to hear *every single detail*.

Or let's say two couples get together after a long separation. The two women will have a conversation, lasting several days, during which they discuss virtually every significant event that has occurred in their lives and the lives of those they care about, sharing their innermost thoughts, analyzing and probing, inevitably coming to a deeper understanding of each other, and a strengthening of a cherished friendship. Whereas the guys will watch the play-offs.

This is not to say the guys won't share their feelings. Sometimes they'll get quite emotional.

"That's not a FOUL??" they'll say.

Or: "YOU'RE TELLING ME THAT'S NOT A *FOUL*???"

I have a good friend, Gene, and one time, when he was going through a major medical development in his life, we spent a weekend together. During this time Gene and I talked a lot and enjoyed each other's company immensely, but—this is true—the most intimate personal statement he made to me is that he has reached Level 24 of a video game called "Arkanoid." He had even seen the Evil Presence, although he refused to tell me what it looks like. We're very close, but there is a limit.

You may think that my friends and I are Neanderthals, and that a lot of guys are different. This is true. A lot of guys don't use words at *all*. They communicate entirely by nonverbal methods, such as sharing bait.

Are you starting to see what I mean by "guyness"? I'm basically talking about the part of the male psyche that is less serious and/or aggressive than the Manly

This section on "communication," especially this communication between men and women, is the subject of several books by Deborah Tannen, whose studies might suggest that Barry is not far off the mark here.
— A.L.

I am glad to say I know some men who really are different, especially in the way they communicate their feelings.   — A.L.

Manhood part, but still essentially very male. My feeling is that the world would be a much better[6] place if more males would stop trying so hard to be Men and instead settle for being Guys. Think of the historical problems that could have been avoided if more males had been able to keep their genderhood in its proper perspective, both in themselves and in others. ("Hey, Adolf, just because you happen to possess a set of minor and frequently unreliable organs, that is no reason to invade Poland.") And think how much happier women would be if, instead of endlessly fretting about what the males in their lives are thinking, they could relax, secure in the knowledge that the correct answer is: *very little.*

Yes, what we need, on the part of both genders, is more understanding of guyness. And that is why I wrote this book. I intend to explore in detail every major facet of guyhood, including the historical facet, the sociological facet, the physiological facet, the psychosexual facet, and the facet of how come guys spit so much. Every statement of fact you will read in this book is either based on actual laboratory tests, or else I made it up. But you can trust me. I'm a guy.

All kidding aside, I do think women need a better understanding of the way guys think, if that's the right verb for the process. — J.R.

C'mon, Dave . . . even you had to do some thinking to come up with this book. — A.L.

Example Chart

Men	Guys
Vince Lombardi	Joe Namath
Oliver North	Gilligan
Hemingway	Gary Larson
Columbus	Whichever astronaut hit the first golf ball on the Moon
Superman	Bart Simpson
Doberman pinschers	Labrador retrievers
Abbott	Costello
Captain Ahab	Captain Kangaroo
Satan	Snidely Whiplash
The pope	Willard Scott
Germany	Italy
Geraldo	Katie Couric

---

[6]As measured by total sales of [my] book.

Stimulus-Response Comparison Chart:
Women vs. Men vs. Guys

Stimulus	Typical *Woman* Response	Typical *Man* Response	Typical *Guy* Response
An untamed river in the wilderness.	Contemplate its beauty.	Build a dam.	See who can pee the farthest off the dam.
A child who is sent home from school for being disruptive in class.	Talk to the child in an effort to determine the cause.	Threaten to send the child to a military academy.	Teach the child how to make armpit farts.
Human mortality	Religious faith	The pyramids	Bungee-jumping

A f t e r w o r d s

While reading "Guys vs. Men," most males and a great many women will likely discover a bit of the guy within themselves. The kernels of truth residing within Barry's stereotypes are what make this essay funny and oddly provocative. When Barry observes that "Guys like neat stuff," he's acknowledging the inventiveness and curiosity that have driven human beings from chariots to Stealth bombers in a couple thousand years. We owe a debt to all the geeks and tinkerers who began a sentence "Wouldn't it be neat if . . . ?" and then followed through. Sometimes in their mania, guys land on the moon and sometimes they blow themselves up. I guess it's the responsibility of more proper "men" and "women" to make sure that the former happens more often than the latter. —J.R.

What can I say? Some of my best friends are "guys"? I even know women who are "guys"? I wish I knew more real "guys"? Not likely. I admire Barry's way with words, and especially the way he can poke fun at himself. And I laughed out loud at some of the early parts of this essay. But in my serious moments, I worry about the need to "blow things up" and to outperform everyone at everything at every minute of the day and night. I worry about what the "culture of guyhood" has done (is doing?) to us all, and to men in particular. Squeezing infinitely varied males into the little square space allowed to "guys" can't be all that much fun. Can it? —A.L.

Dave Barry hits the nail on the head with this piece—or to be more precise, the galvanized, flat-head 5 1/4" nail with a stainless steel, all-metal, lifetime-guaranteed hammer. Barry is right on with the simplicity of "guyness." Not even a man could complicate it, but for some reason I bet that women won't understand. — J.G.R.

QUESTIONING THE TEXT

1. Barry's humor obviously plays off of gross stereotypes about men. Underscore or annotate all the stereotypes you can find in the essay.
2. Barry employs a lengthy analogy featuring his dog Zippy to explore the moral behavior of guys (see p. 348). In a group, discuss this analogy, focusing on the observations that seem especially apt.
3. How do you react to J.R.'s claim in the introduction that Barry is "absolutely, positively right about everything"? What tells you that J.R. is overstating the case?

MAKING CONNECTIONS

4. Compare Dave Barry's relatively mild mannered humor in "Guys vs. Men" to P. J. O'Rourke's take-no-prisoners invective in "Review of *Guidelines for Bias-Free Writing*" (p. 424). As precisely as possible, explain the differences in purpose, intended audience, and style between the two comic articles.
5. Barry comically suggests that the Space Shuttle is the ultimate guy thing—a complicated gizmo that men can tinker with forever. Examine Barry's comic observations side by side with any of the readings in chapter 5 on science. Then, if you keep a reading log, write a serious response there to Barry's humorous observation. Is science a male obsession with how things work?

JOINING THE CONVERSATION

6. "Guys vs. Men" is almost a textbook exercise in writing an extended definition. Annotate the different techniques Barry uses to craft his definition (definition by contrast; class/characteristics; definition by exam-

ple; negative definition). Then write a similar definitional piece—
humorous if you like—contrasting two terms that might at first glance
seem similar: Gals vs. Women; Cops vs. Police Officers; Freshmen vs.
First-Year Students.

7. Barry illustrates the competitiveness of men with a short anecdote about
the forty-yard dash. Choose another stereotypical trait of either men or
women (insensitivity, bad driving, excessive concern with appearance),
and write an anecdote from your own experience that illustrates the
trait. Try some of the techniques Barry uses to make his story funny:
understatement, exaggeration, irony, self-deprecation, dialogue.

SHARON OLDS
Son

Sharon Olds, born in 1942 in San Francisco and educated at Stanford and Columbia (where she received a Ph.D.), is one of our country's most distinguished poets. For her six volumes of poetry, Olds has earned many awards, including the 1985 National Book Critics Circle Award for The Dead and the Living, *in which "Son" appears.*

Olds is also one of my personal favorites, for she has a way of creating word images that have stayed with me for decades. Who, for instance, has not stood looking at a small child sleeping, all innocence and powerful promise? Yet who has been able to capture such a picture more vividly than Olds does in the following poem? Of her work, I find myself agreeing with one critic who says that while her poems are sometimes "unexpected," or even "jarring," they are also "always loving and deeply rewarding." Read this one and draw your own conclusions. — A.L.

Coming home from the women-only bar,
I go into my son's room.
He sleeps—fine, freckled face
thrown back, the scarlet lining of his mouth
shadowy and fragrant, his small teeth   5
glowing dull and milky in the dark,
opal eyelids quivering
like insect wings, his hands closed
in the middle of the night.

                Let there be enough   10
room for this life: the head, lips,
throat, wrists, hips, cock,
knees, feet. Let no part go
unpraised. Into any new world we enter, let us
take this man.   15

IN RESPONSE

1. The second part of Olds's poem is like a prayer, asking for "room" and "praise" for the sleeping boy. Freewrite a response to this prayer: What **355**

would you most hope for your own children? How are your hopes like
or unlike those Olds expresses?

2. In "On Going Home," (p. 493), Joan Didion talks of her wishes and
hopes for her daughter. How do you think Olds might write a similar
prayerlike invocation—but for a daughter rather than a son? What
would she be likely to hope or wish for a daughter?

OTHER READINGS

Belenky, Mary Field, et al. *Women's Ways of Knowing: The Development of Self, Voice, and Mind.* New York: Basic, 1986. A study based on interviews with 135 women.

Crichton, Sarah. "Sexual Correctness: Has It Gone Too Far?" *Newsweek* 25 Oct. 1993: 52–56. Examines whether feminist politics has gone too far.

Cruikshank, Margaret, ed. *The Lesbian Path: 37 Lesbian Writers Share Their Personal Experiences, Viewpoints, Traumas, and Joys.* Monterey: Angel, 1980. Personal narratives by gay women.

Ferguson, Andrew. "America's New Man." *American Spectator* Jan. 1992: 26–33. Examines a men's movement convention in Texas.

Gilder, George. "Still Seeking a Glass slipper." *National Review* 14 Dec. 1992: 38–41. Argues that the "glass ceiling" for women in American business is a myth.

Gilligan, Carol. *In a Different Voice: Psychological Theory and Women's Development.* Cambridge: Harvard UP, 1982. Considers the ways in which women's moral development differs from men's.

Goldberg, Steven. *Why Men Rule: A Theory of Male Dominance.* Chicago: Open Court, 1993. Examines the roots of male dominance.

Morrison, Toni, ed. *Race-ing Justice, En-gendering Power: Essays on Anita Hill, Clarence Thomas, and the Construction of Social Reality.* New York: Pantheon, 1992. Explores the implications of the Hill-Thomas hearings in essays by a group of distinguished writers.

ELECTRONIC RESOURCES

The Dave Barry Page:
   http://www.sjmercury.com/living/dbarry/
   Lists sites related to Dave Barry, his columns, and his other work.

Feminist Internet Gateway:
   http://www.feminist.org/gateway/1_gatway.html
   Provides access to a variety of sites concerned with women's issues.

Men's Issues Page:
   http://www.vix.com/men/index.html
   Provides a comprehensive list of sites concerned with men's issues.

National Organization for Women:
   http://now.org/now/home.html
   Provides information about the feminist group NOW.

7

Difference:
E Pluribus Unum?

Look carefully at this photograph of a crowd. Where was the photographer
likely situated in order to take this shot? What story or message does
this photograph tell? Where is your eye drawn first, and how do you
proceed to "read" the photo? In choosing this photograph to open this
chapter, what might the editors be saying about the subject of difference?

We have no princes, for whom we toil, starve, and bleed: we are the most perfect society now existing in the world.
                        HECTOR ST. JEAN DE CRÈVECOEUR, *What Is an American?*

I have no separate feeling about being an American citizen and colored. I am merely a fragment of the Great Soul that surges within the boundaries. My country, right or wrong.
                        ZORA NEALE HURSTON, *How It Feels to Be Colored Me*

The whole point is that while multiculturalism is in some instances what it sounds like it should be, a fuller realization of American pluralism, it is for the most part a code word for something that . . . is not multi, or cultural, or even an ism.
                        RICHARD BERNSTEIN, *Dérapage*

Say to the young man sitting by your brother's side, / "I'm his brother." / Try not to be shocked when the young man says, / "I'm his lover. Thanks for coming."
                        MICHAEL LASSELL, *How to Watch Your Brother Die*

Of the students who drop my class after the first meeting, there may be some who find the idea of a blind professor ludicrous, aggravating, or frightening. But I will never know.
                        GEORGINA KLEEGE, *Call It Blindness*

In this case of blonde on black . . . and the ugly punctuation marks of two bloody victims in a high-rent district, we are forced to examine almost everything that crosses the T's of American lives.
                        STANLEY CROUCH, *Another Long Drink of the Blues*

The son of a Mexican American doctor or lawyer is treated as if he suffered the same disadvantage as the child of a Mexican farm worker.
                        LINDA CHAVEZ, *Toward a New Politics of Hispanic Assimilation*

. . . *Guidelines for Bias-Free Language* is a product of the pointy-headed wowsers at the American Association of University Presses who, in 1987 established a "Task Force on Bias-Free Writing" filled with cranks, pokenoses, blow-hards, four-flushers, and pettifogs.
                        P. J. O'ROURKE, *Review of* Guidelines for Bias-Free Writing

I guess being colored doesn't make me not like
the same things other folks like who are other races.
So will my page be colored that I write?
Being me, it will not be white.
                        LANGSTON HUGHES, *Theme for English B*

Introduction

MORE THAN TWO CENTURIES AGO, Hector St. Jean De Crèvecoeur posed the daunting question "What Is an American?" Perhaps the query can never be answered fully, as the face of the nation will continue to evolve and change. Currently, however, many in the United States seem to be pledging allegiance not to a nation, which once celebrated its role as a melting pot of peoples, but to various interest groups. Citizens who trace their roots to Africa, Asia, or the North American continent itself routinely challenge the domination of U.S. history, literature, and political institutions by descendants of Europeans. While many citizens interpret the American saga as one of progress, development, growth, and inclusion, others read it as a story of oppression, alienation, violence, and betrayal. Indeed, the latter interpretation is often seen, albeit derisively, as the "politically correct" view.

Some would assert that racial, ethnic, sexual, and class fractures in our national unity have always been present, but deliberately hidden by those who stood to benefit from unequal distributions of wealth, power, or influence. Others invert the argument, claiming that interest groups today exaggerate the ills they have suffered in order to gain a slice of the national pie. These issues are debated daily in the courts and legislatures, in businesses, and on college campuses.

To put these issues into more concrete terms, close your eyes and try to picture all the people in one of your classes. At a glance, in what ways are these people alike—and like you? In what ways do you differ? In this simple experiment lies a key question the readings in this chapter will address: How can we best honor and respect human commonalities while also honoring and respecting human differences? Can we in some sense be *both* together and separate from one another? In short, can we have at the center of our national life both "difference" and *"e pluribus unum"*?

Here are some questions to consider as you read this chapter:

- In what ways is cultural diversity and public attention to it an advantage or a disadvantage to a society?
- In what ways does prejudice show itself?
- Are the prejudices of the powerful and privileged more damaging than those of other groups? Why, or why not?
- Is a fear of difference part of human nature?
- Can you think of times when you judged someone on the basis of a stereotype that later turned out to be inaccurate or unfair? of times when you yourself were unfairly stereotyped?

•   •   •

HECTOR ST. JEAN DE CRÈVECOEUR
What Is an American?

HECTOR ST. JEAN DE CRÈVECOEUR's letter "What Is an American?" is a classic statement of the virtues of integration and harmony, one of the defining documents of the American vision of the melting pot. Crèvecoeur (1735–1813) was himself something of an outsider when he wrote about life in the colonial United States. A native of France who worked for a time for the British government in Canada, he eventually became a farmer in New York until the American Revolution disrupted his peaceful life and his political loyalties. Fleeing to Europe, he spent his time there finishing an account of life in America, Letters from an American Farmer, *that would earn him fame and high regard after its publication in 1782.*

While aware of the plight of slaves and Native Americans, Crèvecoeur argued nonetheless that the spacious American territories were breeding a new and happier species of European. To him, the typical American was an immigrant free of aristocratic assumptions who had set aside the Old World's potent national and religious prejudices to construct new communities on principles of liberty and individual merit.

"What Is an American?" may strike some readers today as a rustic fantasy or as testament to a dream betrayed. But we shouldn't be disappointed when a writer of an earlier era fails to anticipate our contemporary concerns. The pioneering Americans Crèvecoeur describes were more inclusive, democratic, and visionary than their forebears in Europe. Great changes were occurring in a green and pleasant land. Indeed, I'd be inclined to argue that the hardy farmers whose lives Crèvecoeur describes have proven to be more consequential revolutionaries than the sans-culottes of Paris, the Bolsheviks of Red Square, or the free-speechers of Berkeley. — J.R.

I wish I could be acquainted with the feelings and thoughts which must agitate the heart and present themselves to the mind of an enlightened Englishman, when he first lands on this continent. He must greatly rejoice that he lived at a time to see this fair country discovered and settled; he must necessarily feel a share of national pride, when he views the chain of settlements which embellishes these extended shores. When he says to himself, this is the work of my countrymen, who, when convulsed by factions, afflicted by a variety of miseries and wants, restless and impatient, took refuge here. They brought along with them their national genius, to which they principally owe what liberty they enjoy, and what substance they possess. Here he sees the industry of his native country displayed in a new manner, and traces in their works the embryos of all the arts, sciences, and ingenuity which flourish in Europe. Here he beholds fair cities, substantial villages, extensive fields, an immense country filled with decent houses, good roads, orchards, meadows, and bridges, where an hundred years ago all was wild, woody, and unculti-vated! What a train of pleasing ideas this fair spectacle must suggest; it is a prospect which must inspire a good citizen with the most heartfelt pleasure. The difficulty consists in the manner of viewing so extensive a scene. He is arrived on a new continent; a modern society offers itself to his contempla-tion, different from what he had hitherto seen. It is not composed, as in Eu-rope, of great lords who possess everything, and of a herd of people who have nothing. Here are no aristocratical families, no courts, no kings, no bishops, no ecclesiastical dominion, no invisible power giving to a few a very visible one; no great manufacturers employing thousands, no great refinements of luxury. The rich and the poor are not so far removed from each other as they are in Europe. Some few towns excepted, we are all tillers of the earth, from Nova Scotia to West Florida. We are a people of cultivators, scattered over an immense territory, communicating with each other by means of goods roads and navigable rivers, united by the silken bands of mild government, all re-specting the laws, without dreading their power, because they are equitable. We are all animated with the spirit of an industry which is unfettered and un-restrained, because each person works for himself. If he travels through our rural districts he views not the hostile castle, and the haughty mansion, con-trasted with the clay-built hut and miserable cabin, where cattle and men help to keep each other warm, and dwell in meanness, smoke, and indigence. A pleasing uniformity of decent competence appears throughout our habita-tions. The meanest of our log-houses is a dry and comfortable habitation. Lawyer or merchant are the fairest titles our towns afford; that of a farmer is the only appellation of the rural inhabitants of our country. It must take some time ere he can reconcile himself to our dictionary, which is but short in words of dignity, and names of honor. There, on a Sunday, he sees a congre-gation of respectable farmers and their wives, all clad in neat homespun, well mounted, or riding in their own humble wagons. There is not among them an esquire, saving the unlettered magistrate. There he sees a parson as simple as his flock, a farmer who does not riot on the labor of others. We have no princes, for whom we toil, starve, and bleed: we are the most perfect society now existing in the world. Here man is free as he ought to be; nor is this pleasing equality so transitory as many others are. Many ages will not see the shores of our great lakes replenished with inland nations, nor the unknown bounds of North America entirely peopled. Who can tell how far it extends? Who can tell the millions of men whom it will feed and contain? for no Eu-ropean foot has as yet traveled half the extent of this mighty continent!

The next wish of this traveler will be to know whence came all these people? They are a mixture of English, Scotch, Irish, French, Dutch, Ger-mans, and Swedes. From this promiscuous breed, that race now called Americans have arisen. The eastern provinces* must indeed be excepted, as being the unmixed descendants of Englishmen. I have heard many wish that they had been more intermixed also: for my part, I am no wisher, and think it much better as it has happened. They exhibit a most conspicuous figure in this great and variegated picture; they too enter for a great share in the pleasing perspective displayed in these thirteen provinces. I know it is fashionable to reflect on them, but respect them for what they have done; for the accuracy and wisdom with which they have settled their territory; for the decency of their manners; for their early love of letters; their ancient college,* the first in this hemisphere; for their industry, which to me who am but a farmer is the criterion of everything. There never was a people, situated as they are, who with so ungrateful a soil have done more in so short a time. Do you think that the monarchical ingredients which are more prevalent in other governments have purged them from all foul stains? Their histories assert the contrary.

In this great American asylum, the poor of Europe have by some means met together, and in consequence of various causes; to what purpose should they ask one another what countrymen they are? Alas, two thirds of them had no country. Can a wretch who wanders about, who works and starves, whose life is a continual scene of sore affliction or pinching penury, can that man call England or any other kingdom his country? A country that had no bread for him, whose fields procured him no harvest, who met with nothing but the frowns of the rich, the severity of the laws, with jails and punishments; who owned not a single foot of the extensive surface of this planet? No! Urged by a variety of motives, here they came. Everything has tended to regenerate them; new laws, a new mode of living, a new social system; here they are become men: in Europe they were as so many useless plants, wanting vegetative mold and refreshing showers; they withered, and were mowed down by want, hunger, and war; but now by the power of transplantation, like all other plants they have taken root and flourished! Formerly they were not numbered in any civil lists of their country, except in those of the poor; here they rank as citizens. By what invisible power has this surprising metamorphosis been performed? By that of the laws and that of their industry. The laws, the indulgent laws, protect them as they arrive, stamping on them the symbol of adoption; they receive ample rewards for their labors; these accumulated rewards procure them lands; those lands confer on them the title of freemen, and to that title every benefit is affixed which men can possibly require. This is the great operation daily performed by our laws. From whence proceed these laws? From our government. Whence the government? It is derived from the original genius and strong desire of the people ratified and confirmed by the crown. This is the great chain which links

---

eastern provinces: the area known as New England today
ancient college: Harvard, founded in 1636

us all, this is the picture which every province exhibits, Nova Scotia excepted. There the crown has done all; either there were no people who had genius, or it was not much attended to: the consequence is that the province is very thinly inhabited indeed; the power of the crown in conjunction with the mosquitoes has prevented men from settling there. Yet some parts of it flourished once, and it contained a mild, harmless set of people. But for the fault of a few leaders, the whole were banished.* The greatest political error the crown ever committed in America was to cut off men from a country which wanted nothing but men!

What attachment can a poor European emigrant have for a country where he had nothing? The knowledge of the language, the love of a few kindred as poor as himself, were the only cords that tied him: his country is now that which gives him land, bread, protection, and consequence: *Ubi panis ibi patria** is the motto of all emigrants. What then is the American, this new man? He is either a European, or the descendant of a European, hence that strange mixture of blood, which you will find in no other country. I could point out to you a family whose grandfather was an Englishman, whose wife was Dutch, whose son married a French woman, and whose present four sons have now four wives of different nations. *He* is an American, who, leaving behind him all his ancient prejudices and manners, receives new ones from the new mode of life he has embraced, the new government he obeys, and the new rank he holds. He becomes an American by being received in the broad lap of our great *Alma Mater.** Here individuals of all nations are melted into a new race of men, whose labors and posterity will one day cause great changes in the world. Americans are the western pilgrims, who are carrying along with them that great mass of arts, sciences, vigor, and industry which began long since in the east; they will finish the great circle. The Americans were once scattered all over Europe; here they are incorporated into one of the finest systems of population which has ever appeared, and which will hereafter become distinct by the power of the different climates they inhabit. The American ought therefore to love this country much better than that wherein either he or his forefathers were born.* Here the rewards of his industry follow with equal steps the progress of his labor; his labor is founded on the basis of nature, *self-interest;* can it want a stronger allurement? Wives and children, who before in vain demanded of him a morsel of bread, now, fat and frolicsome, gladly help their father to clear those fields whence exuberant crops are to arise to feed and to clothe them all; without any part being

---

the whole were banished: The British government expelled the French-speaking Acadians from Nova Scotia during the French and Indian War (1755–63), when they were suspected of disloyalty.

Ubi panis ibi patria: Latin for "where one's bread is, there is one's native country"

Alma Mater: Latin for "Nourishing Mother"

The American . . . born: For a longer argument in favor of assimilation rather than separatism on the part of immigrants, see the reading by Linda Chavez, "Toward a New Politics of Hispanic Assimilation" (p. 415).

claimed, either by a despotic prince, a rich abbot, or a mighty lord. Here religion demands but little of him; a small voluntary salary to the minister, and gratitude to God; can he refuse these? The American is a new man, who acts upon new principles; he must therefore entertain new ideas, and form new opinions. From involuntary idleness, servile dependence, penury, and useless labor, he has passed to toils of a very different nature, rewarded by ample subsistence.—This is an American.

QUESTIONING THE TEXT

1. What specific accomplishments does the Frenchman Crèvecoeur grant to the "unmixed descendants of Englishmen" who populate what is now New England? How are the descendants of these people sometimes regarded by other ethnic groups today?
2. According to Crèvecoeur, what do the poor gain in America that they never had in their native lands?
3. What is Crèvecoeur's attitude toward nature? Might he find contemporary attempts to preserve wilderness areas peculiar? If you keep a reading log, answer these questions there.
4. Do you agree or disagree with the assertion in J.R.'s introduction that pioneering American farmers were more important revolutionaries than those responsible for the French and Russian revolutions?

MAKING CONNECTIONS

5. How does the American that Crèvecoeur imagines compare with that depicted by Richard Bernstein (p. 372)? Make a list of questions Crèvecoeur might have for Bernstein.
6. Crèvecoeur uses the image of "individuals of all nations" being "melted into a new race of men." Compare that image with the one of the "bag of miscellany" in the last paragraph of the next reading, by Zora Neale Hurston. Which image of Americans appeals to you more—and why? Write an essay explaining your answer.

JOINING THE CONVERSATION

7. On the board, list all the national and ethnic ties represented by the people in your writing class. With that information fresh in mind, write a paragraph defining "American."
8. The America that Crèvecoeur describes is "the most perfect society now existing in the world." Write an essay arguing that such is or is not the case today, either by the standards Crèvecoeur uses or by your own standards for a perfect society.

ZORA NEALE HURSTON
How It Feels to Be Colored Me

Zora Neale Hurston (1891–1960), born and raised in the first all-black town in the United States to be incorporated and self-governing (Eatonville, Florida), packed an astonishing number of jobs and careers into her sixty-nine years. She was a "wardrobe girl" for traveling entertainers, a manicurist, an anthropologist and folklorist, a college professor, a drama coach, an editor, and— above all—a writer of great distinction. Author of numerous articles, essays, and stories as well as folklore collections, plays, and an autobiography, Hurston is today probably best known for her novels: Their Eyes Were Watching God, Jonah's Gourd Vine, *and* Moses, Man of the Mountain.*

    Hurston studied anthropology at Barnard College, where she was the only African American student, and gained a strong reputation for her academic work on folklore. But by the 1930s, she was being criticized for what were said to be caricatures of blacks, especially in her "minstrel" novels. Her growing conservatism led to further attacks from writers such as Richard Wright, and by 1950, her reputation gone, she was working in Florida as a maid. Evicted from her home in 1956, she suffered a stroke in 1959 and died, penniless, the next year. In recent years, Alice Walker sought out her unmarked grave in Fort Pierce, Florida, and erected a marker in memory of Hurston and her work, which is, today, widely read and influential.

    The essay that follows, published in 1928, makes an intriguing companion piece to the passage from Crèvecoeur, particularly to his description of Americans as "united by the silken bands of mild government, all respecting the laws, without dreading their power, because they are equitable." His portrait of the "perfect society," where "man is free as he ought to be," would have come as a surprise to many African Americans in 1782. Hurston is deeply aware of such ironies and of the bitter struggles obscured by the happy image of the melting pot. But she is not cast down or resentful; she has no time to waste on negativity. I chose "How It Feels to Be Colored Me" for its irrepressible spirit in the face of what are clear inequalities in America, for its ironic self-representation, and for the sheer delight it gives me to think that Hurston has triumphed after all. − A.L.

    I am colored but I offer nothing in the way of extenuating circumstances except the fact that I am the only Negro in the United States whose grandfather on the mother's side was *not* an Indian chief.

    I remember the very day that I became colored. Up to my thirteenth year I lived in the little Negro town of Eatonville, Florida. It is exclusively a colored town. The only white people I knew passed through the town going to or coming from Orlando. The native whites rode dusty horses, the Northern tourists chugged down the sandy village road in automobiles. The town knew the Southerners and never stopped cane chewing* when they passed. But the Northerners were something else again. They were peered at cautiously from behind curtains by the timid. The more venturesome would come out on the porch to watch them go past and got just as much pleasure out of the tourists as the tourists got out of the village.

The front porch might seem a daring place for the rest of the town, but it was a gallery seat for me. My favorite place was atop the gate-post. Proscenium box for a born first-nighter. Not only did I enjoy the show, but I didn't mind the actors knowing that I liked it. I usually spoke to them in passing. I'd wave at them and when they returned my salute, I would say something like this: "Howdy-do-well-I-thank-you-where-you-goin'?" Usually automobile or the horse paused at this, and after a queer exchange of compliments, I would probably "go a piece of the way" with them, as we say in farthest Florida. If one of my family happened to come to the front in time to see me, of course negotiations would be rudely broken off. But even so, it is clear that I was the first "welcome-to-our-state" Floridian, and I hope the Miami Chamber of Commerce will please take notice.

During this period, white people differed from colored to me only in that they rode through town and never lived there. They liked to hear me "speak pieces" and sing and wanted to see me dance the parse-me-la, and gave me generously of their small silver for doing these things, which seemed strange to me for I wanted to do them so much that I needed bribing to stop. Only they didn't know it. The colored people gave no dimes. They deplored any joyful tendencies in me, but I was their Zora nevertheless. I belonged to them, to the nearby hotels, to the country—everybody's Zora.

But changes came in the family when I was thirteen, and I was sent to   5
school in Jacksonville. I left Eatonville, the town of the oleanders, as Zora. When I disembarked from the river-boat at Jacksonville, she was no more. It seemed that I had suffered a sea change. I was not Zora of Orange County any more. I was now a little colored girl. I found it out in certain ways. In my heart as well as in the mirror, I became a fast brown—warranted not to rub nor run.

But I am not tragically colored. There is no great sorrow dammed up in my soul, nor lurking behind my eyes. I do not mind at all. I do not belong to the sobbing school of Negrohood who hold that nature somehow has given them a lowdown dirty deal and whose feelings are all hurt about it. Even in the helter-skelter skirmish that is my life, I have seen that the world is to the

---

cane chewing: chewing sugar-cane stalks

strong* regardless of a little pigmentation more or less. No, I do not weep at the world—I am too busy sharpening my oyster knife.*

Someone is always at my elbow reminding me that I am the grand-daughter of slaves. It fails to register depression with me. Slavery is sixty years in the past. The operation was successful and the patient is doing well, thank you. The terrible struggle* that made me an American out of a potential slave said "On the line!" The Reconstruction said "Get set!"; and the generation before said "Go!" I am off to a flying start and I must not halt in the stretch to look behind and weep. Slavery is the price I paid for civilization, and the choice was not with me. It is a bully adventure and worth all that I have paid through my ancestors for it. No one on earth ever had a greater chance for glory. The world to be won and nothing to be lost. It is thrilling to think—to know that for any act of mine, I shall get twice as much praise or twice as much blame. It is quite exciting to hold the center of the national stage, with the spectators not knowing whether to laugh or to weep.

The position of my white neighbor is much more difficult. No brown specter pulls up a chair beside me when I sit down to eat. No dark ghost thrusts its leg against mine in bed. The game of keeping what one has is never so exciting as the game of getting.

I do not always feel colored. Even now I often achieve the unconscious Zora of Eatonville before the Hegira. I feel most colored when I am thrown against a sharp white background.

For instance at Barnard. "Beside the waters of the Hudson"* I feel my   10
race. Among the thousand white persons, I am a dark rock surged upon, and overswept, but through it all, I remain myself. When covered by the waters, I am; and the ebb but reveals me again.

Sometimes it is the other way around. A white person is set down in our midst, but the contrast is just as sharp for me. For instance, when I sit in the drafty basement that is The New World Cabaret with a white person, my color comes. We enter chatting about any little nothing that we have in common and are seated by the jazz waiters. In the abrupt way that jazz orchestras have, this one plunges into a number. It loses no time in circumlocutions, but gets right down to business. It constricts the thorax and splits the heart with its tempo and narcotic harmonies. This orchestra grows rambunctious, rears on its hind legs and attacks the tonal veil with primitive fury, rending it, claw-

---

the world is to the strong: an allusion to the biblical passage (in Ecclesiastes 11) that reads "The race is not to the swift, nor the battle to the strong"

sharpening my oyster knife: an allusion to the saying "The world is my oyster," which appears in Shakespeare's The Merry Wives of Windsor

the terrible struggle: the Civil War

"Beside the waters of the Hudson": Barnard College is near the Hudson River in New York City. For another account of how it felt to be a black student at Columbia University in the early twentieth century, see the poem by Langston Hughes "Theme for English B" (p. 432).

ing it until it breaks through to the jungle beyond. I follow those heathen—follow them exultingly. I dance wildly inside myself; I yell within, I whoop; I shake my assegai above my head, I hurl it true to the mark *yeeeeoouw!* I am in the jungle and living in the jungle way. My face is painted red and yellow and my body is painted blue. My pulse is throbbing like a war drum. I want to slaughter something—give pain, give death to what, I do not know. But the piece ends. The men of the orchestra wipe their lips and rest their fingers. I creep back slowly to the veneer we call civilization with the last tone and find the white friend sitting motionless in his seat, smoking calmly.

"Good music they have here," he remarks, drumming the table with his fingertips.

Music. The great blobs of purple and red emotion have not touched him. He has only heard what I felt. He is far away and I see him but dimly across the ocean and the continent that have fallen between us. He is so pale with his whiteness then and I am *so* colored.

At certain times I have no race, I am *me.* When I set my hat at a certain angle and saunter down Seventh Avenue, Harlem City, feeling as snooty as the lions in front of the Forty-Second Street Library,* for instance. So far as my feelings are concerned, Peggy Hopkins Joyce* on the Boule Mich* with her gorgeous raiment, stately carriage, knees knocking together in a most aristocratic manner, has nothing on me. The cosmic Zora emerges. I belong to no race nor time. I am the eternal feminine with its string of beads.

I have no separate feeling about being an American citizen and colored.   15
I am merely a fragment of the Great Soul that surges within the boundaries. My country, right or wrong.

Sometimes, I feel discriminated against, but it does not make me angry. It merely astonishes me. How *can* any deny themselves the pleasure of my company? It's beyond me.

But in the main, I feel like a brown bag of miscellany propped against a wall. Against a wall in company with other bags, white, red and yellow. Pour out the contents, and there is discovered a jumble of small things priceless and worthless. A first-water diamond, an empty spool, bits of broken glass, lengths of string, a key to a door long since crumbled away, a rusty knife-blade, old shoes saved for a road that never was and never will be, a nail bent under the weight of things too heavy for any nail, a dried flower or two still a little fragrant. In your hand is the brown bag. On the ground before you is the jumble it held—so much like the jumble in the bags, could they be emptied, that all might be dumped in a single heap and the bags refilled without altering the content of any greatly. A bit of colored glass more or less would not

---

the lions in front of the Forty-Second Street Library: two statutes of lions that stand in front of the main building of the New York Public Library, on Fifth Avenue at 42nd Street

Peggy Hopkins Joyce: a famous beauty who set fashions in the 1920s

the Boule Mich: the Boulevard Saint-Michel, a street in Paris

matter. Perhaps that is how the Great Stuffer of Bags filled them in the first place—who knows?

QUESTIONING THE TEXT

1. Color is a central theme in this brief essay. Jot down as many of the ways color appears as you can remember. Then go back and check the text. Complete your list and compare it with the lists of others in your class. What are the different things color is attributed to?
2. In her introduction to this essay, A.L. makes absolutely clear how much she admires Hurston. How did her praise affect your evaluation of the essay?
3. Hurston exemplifies the *differences* among people in her vivid descriptions of her experience of jazz. First, try to describe your experience with the kind of music that most engages and moves you. What do you find in common with or different from Hurston's experience? Does what you have discovered lead you to see "sharp" contrasts, as Hurston does, or commonalities? What do such contrasts and commonalities have to do with your race?

MAKING CONNECTIONS

4. Read Hurston's piece along with Langston Hughes's "Theme for English B" (p. 432). Do these writers hold different—or similar—views on commonalities among all people? Explain your answer in an informal statement (about a page or two) addressed to your class.
5. Hurston dwells in this essay on color, using it metaphorically to evoke her experiences and literally to evoke her own—and others'—colors. Color, of course, depends largely on sight, on vision. What would happen to the world Hurston describes if vision were *not* so important? Write a brief dialogue that Georgina Kleege (p. 390) and Hurston might have on this question.
6. What does *assimilate* mean to you? After jotting down your definition, look up the word and compare your own and the dictionary definitions with the way Linda Chavez uses the word (p. 415). Is Hurston an assimilationist? Why, or why not?

JOINING THE CONVERSATION

7. Hurston concludes with a simile about bags. First, consider what simile or metaphor you might use to describe your own race or ethnicity and

its relationship to others. Begin perhaps by completing the sentence "But in the main, I feel like. . . ." Then write an extended description of your simile or metaphor and bring it to class for discussion.

8. Working with two or three classmates, draft a composite description of the metaphors you came up with. What do these metaphors have in common? How do they differ?

RICHARD BERNSTEIN
Dérapage

WITHIN THE LAST DECADE, *multiculturalism has become the professional creed of a vast number of U.S. educators and scholars. Textbooks, conferences, and course curricula have been designed to orient students and instructors to the diversity of American life, its rich tapestry of ethnic and cultural experiences. But because of this emphasis on groups formerly marginalized in history, politics, and literature, some complain that a student today is more likely to know about the Iroquois Convention than the Constitutional Convention, about Phillis Wheatley than Thomas Jefferson, about Rosie the Riveter than General Eisenhower. Multiculturalism touches on politics and business too, providing a rationale for affirmative action programs, racial and gender set-asides in government grants, enhanced immigrant rights, and racial gerrymandering of congressional districts.*

Multiculturalism has sparked strong opposition, in part because it challenges core American beliefs. Are individuals responsible for their own actions or are they to be judged as members of a group, liable for that group's failings or historical deprivations? Is the United States a melting pot, one people from many lands sharing a common language and Constitution? Or is even the English language a tool of imperialistic white males?

Richard Bernstein (b. 1944), a book critic for the New York Times *and a journalist who has written for* Time *magazine, addresses many issues related to multiculturalism in his book* Dictatorship of Virtue: Multiculturalism and the Battle for America's Future *(1994).*

The following selection is the prologue to Bernstein's volume, where he outlines his case against multiculturalism, defines several crucial terms, and invites readers on all sides of the question to enter the debate. In urging you to consider Bernstein's work, I must acknowledge my own interest. In a chapter later in the book, "The Battle of Texas," Bernstein chronicles a multicultural dispute in which I participated; his analysis supports my side of the argument. — J.R.

> Loyalty to petrified opinion never yet broke a chain or freed a human soul.
>
> — MARK TWAIN

There is a school of French historians that uses the word *dérapage* to describe the fateful moment when the Great Revolution of 1789, the first monumental effort to break the chain, skidded from the enlightened universalism of the Declaration of

Explaining dérapage puts multiculturalism in a deliberately dramatic historical context. —J.R.

Drop the big historical analogy and get to the point.
— J.G.R.

the Rights of Man* and Citizen into the rule of the Committee of Public Safety* and the Terror. *Dérapage,* which literally means a "skid" or a "slide," refers to the way fanaticism and dogmatism swept the great upheaval from constitutionalism to dictatorship, from eighteenth-century rationalism, inspired by the thinkers of the Enlightenment, to a dramatic foreshadowing of twentieth-century totalitarianism, urged on by grim, prim Robespierrean despots with a gift for demagogy who believed they were serving the cause of Liberty, Equality, and Fraternity.

In 1794 Robespierre told the elected parliamentary assembly known as the Convention that the Revolution aimed at such good things—"to substitute morality for egotism, probity for honor . . . the empire of reason for the tyranny of fashions"—that nothing, not even reason, could stand in its way. Robespierre* was an elegant maker of speeches, an aristocrat of words. "Terror," he told the Jacobin* assembly, justifying the ferreting out of enemies real and imagined, "is naught but prompt, severe, inflexible justice; it is therefore an emanation of virtue."

I don't want to be melodramatic here. We are not reexperiencing the French Revolution, and we are not in danger of the guillotine or rule by a national-level Committee of Public Safety (though I think subsequent pages show the existence of rather smaller versions of that committee). But we are threatened by a narrow orthodoxy—and the occasional outright atrocity—imposed, or committed, in the name of the very values that are supposed to define a pluralist society. That is why that word *dérapage* has stuck in my mind as I have studied a movement gathering force in the United States during the past decade or so, aimed supposedly at a

Wow—look at the negatively charged words piled up here: fateful, skid, fanaticism, dogmatism, dictatorship, totalitarianism, despots, demagogy. Bernstein is setting up an analogy of some kind, preparing to say that just as the ideals of the French Revolution descended into all these negatives, so too has . . . what?
— A.L.

Clearly he does want to be melodramatic. Otherwise, why all the hyperbole?
— A.L.

Declaration of the Rights of Man: adopted by the French Constituent Assembly in August 1789 as a general statement of revolutionary principles

Committee of Public Safety: a war dictatorship set up in France in 1793 to save the republic, but responsible for the Reign of Terror during which thousands were killed to eliminate opposition to the revolution

Robespierre (1758–94): French revolutionary leader associated with the Reign of Terror

Jacobin: member of a radical French revolutionary party

greater inclusiveness of all of the country's diverse component parts, that has somehow slipped from its moorings and turned into a new petrified opinion of the sort it was supposed to transcend.

Now he's got the ball rolling. I'm more interested.
— J.G.R.

I am speaking of multiculturalism, which is the term that has emerged to encompass a host of activities, a number of different ways of seeing things, a set of goals that ranges from teaching first-graders in Oregon about the achievements of sub-Saharan African civilization to racial set-asides and quotas at newspapers on the East Coast. Certain other words are being used as well, most common among them "inclusion" and "diversity," and these too are rhetorical crystallizations of the, as it were, diverse tendencies arising from the multiculturalist sensibility. A search of NEXIS, the electronic data bank with the complete texts of most of the major American newspapers, reveals that the words "multiculturalism" and "multicultural" appeared in forty articles in 1981. In 1992, the number had risen to more than two thousand, a fiftyfold increase in just eleven years.

Because multi-culturalism is in the subtitle of his book, I suspected that this might be the key term I was being set up for. So now I have to find out how multiculturalism is "fanaticism," "totalitarianism," and so on.
— A.L.

Presumably, American society did not suddenly become fifty times as multicultural as it was before, so the increase in the use of the word "multiculturalism" suggests less an actual change than a discovery of something, perhaps a wish for it or, just as likely, a new trope used not so much to describe things the way they are but to try to make them conform with the way they should be. Certainly, the term is imprecise. It is used for everything from multicultural curricula to what one newspaper, referring to African motifs in the fashion business, called "multiculturally-aware wear."

Definitions play a critical role here. He is carefully setting down the terms of his argument. J.R.

What exactly is it?

I remember a scholar of China talking years ago about the Great Proletarian Cultural Revolution,* which raged in that country in the late 1960s and early 1970s. Certainly, he said, the term referred to something momentous happening in China, but whatever it was, it was not Great, it was not Prole-

---

Cultural Revolution: a movement of radical students (1966–69) led by Communist Party chair Mao Zedong to revitalize his revolution by overturning all vestiges of prerevolutionary thinking

tarian, it had nothing to do with Culture, and it was certainly not a Revolution. Similarly with multiculturalism. It does not have the kind of consistent or coherent set of ideas behind it to make it an ism exactly. That prefix "multi" is, yes, applicable in theory, but in practice it is often a mask for what would more accurately be called "mono." Most important, multiculturalism has no more to do with culture than the Cultural Revolution did.

Its most common usage seems to relate to things that happen at our schools and universities where offices of multicultural education and mandatory training in the "multicultural realities" of America are becoming nearly universal. Multiculturalism, and its rhetorical sidekicks, diversity and inclusion, represent, at least in theory, a sensibility of openness to the enormous cultural difference that has always existed in American life, but whose fullness has been suppressed by the might of the dominant European culture. The logical corollary of this is that the domination that white men have enjoyed needs to end in order to allow for full pride of place to other identities, especially those of women and people of color, who have been excluded or marginalized in the past.

In other words multiculturalism is good, unobjectionable, virtuous. It is like Liberty, Equality, Fraternity,* like economic justice for the working class and an end to exploitation. It is a way of saying, "Let's be truly diverse, tolerant of difference. Let's give everybody in the gorgeous mosaic an equal shot at racial, ethnic, religious, or sexual pride and through that pride a genuinely equal chance at success." Multiculturalism in this sense would seem to be the logical extension of the civil rights movement of the 1960s, when the relative invisibility of people of color and women became, at least in theory, unacceptable to the political majority. And to be sure, in my travels I have certainly seen much that is rich and wonderful in the work of scholars, writers, artists, and journalists to bring to light previously neglected identities.

Liberty, Equality, Fraternity: the catch phrase of the French Revolution

Bang. Down it goes. — A.L.

This is only non-specific, anecdotal evidence. Who are these people whose "lack of curiosity" confirms his views? Who are these "tremulous" multiculturalists? He never says. — A.L.

Again, whose experience is he talking about here? Not mine. — A.L.

But is multiculturalism ordinarily, mostly, in the main, the logical extension of the civil rights movement? Or is it actually a cloak for a late-twentieth-century American *dérapage*?

There are clues to these questions among the self-proclaimed multiculturalists themselves. They rarely, at least as I have gotten to know them, know much about culture at all and even more rarely about somebody else's culture. There are interesting and worthy and certainly very well-intentioned people within the ranks of what I will call the ideological multiculturalists. And yet their lack of curiosity about the real cultural richness of the world, or their reduction of that richness to a few rhapsodic clichés, seems to confirm that culture is not really what is at issue in multiculturalism. At best, the ideological multiculturalists reiterate a few obsessively sincere phrases about the holistic spirit of Native American cultures or about how things are done in what they call the Asian culture or in the African-American culture. The Asian culture, it happens, is something I know a bit about, having spent five years at Harvard striving for a Ph.D. in a joint program called History and East Asian Languages and, after that, living either as a student (for one year) or a journalist (for six years) in China and Southeast Asia. At least I know enough to know that there is no such thing as the "Asian culture." There are dozens of cultures that exist in that vast geographical domain called Asia. When the multiculturalists speak, tremulous with respect, of the "Asian culture," it is out of goodness of heart, but not much actual knowledge.

My experience leads me to believe that insofar as culture is involved in multiculturalism, it is not so much for me to be required to learn about other cultures as for me to be able to celebrate myself and for you to be required to celebrate me, and, along the way, to support my demand for more respect, more pride of place, more jobs, more foundation support, more money, more programs, more books, more prizes, more people like me in high places, a higher degree of attention.

The paradox is that the power of culture is utterly contrary to the most fervently held beliefs and

His either/or proposition here again simplifies the issue dramatically. But his notion of dérapage *provides an important challenge to the purportedly benign multiculturalism peddled by academics and others. — J.R.*

An important qualification. — J.R.

values of the advocates of multiculturalism. Multiculturalism is a movement of the left, emerging from the counterculture of the 1960s. But culture is powerfully conservative. Culture is what enforces obedience to authority, the authority of parents, of history, of custom, of superstition. Deep attachment to culture is one of the things that prevents different people from understanding one another. It is what pushes groups into compliance with practices that can be good or bad, depending on one's point of view. Suttee (the practice, eradicated by British colonialism, in which Indian widows were burned alive on the funeral pyres of their husbands) and female circumcision, as well as the spirit of rational inquiry and a belief in the sanctity of each human life, are products of cultural attachments of different kinds. Those who practiced suttee, or who believe that women who commit adultery should be stoned to death, do not believe there is anything bad about these practices, any more than those who practice rational inquiry under conditions of freedom think there is anything wrong with that.

Here is an intriguing (and perhaps clever) shift from multicultural to culture. But I've seen the shift and am not going to be easily persuaded, especially if he continues to rely on simple assertions rather than evidence or proof.
— A.L.

The reality of culture is something that the ideological multiculturalists would despise, if they knew what it was. The power of culture, especially the culture rooted in ancient traditions, is anathema to the actual goals and ideology of multiculturalism, which does not seek an appreciation of other cultures but operates out of the wishful assumption that the unknown, obscure, neglected, subaltern cultures of the world are actually manifestations of a leftist ideology born out of the particular culture of American and European universities and existing practically no place else.

A lot of ideas for one sentence.
— J.G.R.

The point is that while multiculturalism is in some instances what it sounds like it should be, a fuller realization of American pluralism, it is for the most part a code word for something that, again, is not multi, or cultural, or even an ism. It is a code word for a political ambition, a yearning for more power, combined with a genuine, earnest, zealous, self-righteous craving for social improvement that is characteristic of the mentality of the post-1960s era in American life. The 1960s were the rebellion

Bingo! A key paragraph to appreciating Bernstein's critique. Multiculturalism may not be what it seems to be.
— J.R.

Ironically, multiculturalism is clearly a code word for Bernstein himself—for all that he finds wrong.
— A.L.

years. A new consciousness emerged, involving ir-
reverence for standard beliefs and a sudden illumination of how our traditions were not the results of
some irrefutable logic but rather servants of the
holders of power, how our unexamined habits of
mind perpetuated an unjust status quo. Out of the
burning wish for betterment grew what has now
become a kind of bureaucracy of the good, fighting
battles that have already been won, demanding ever
greater commitments of virtue from a recalcitrant
population. This bureaucracy, made up of people
who, like Robespierre, are convinced that they are
waging the good fight on behalf of virtue, is the instrument of ideological multiculturalism whose effectiveness lies precisely in its ability to appear to be
the opposite of what it actually is. It is an ardently
advocated, veritably messianic political program,
and, like most political programs that have suc-
cumbed to the utopian temptation, it does not take
kindly to true difference.

*What does he
mean by "true dif-
ference"? He has
worked himself up
to quite a state
here!* — A.L.

Multiculturalism, in short, cannot be taken at
face value, and that is what makes it so tricky. Nobody wants to appear to be against multiculturalism.
Hence, the irresistible temptation of the post–1960s,
radical-left inhabitants of a political dreamland to
use the term "multiculturalism" as a defense against
exposure or criticism and to bring into service a vocabulary to which multiculturalism has an almost
salacious attraction, words like "racist," "sexist,"
"homophobic." To put matters bluntly: the multiculturalist rhetoric has the rest of us on the run, unable to respond for fear of being branded unicul-
tural, or racist, or (to get into the trendy academic
lingo) complicit in the structures of hegemony imposed by the Eurocentric patriarchy and its strategies of domination.

*Nobody but our
hero, Mr. Bern-
stein!* — A.L.

*Debate can be sti-
fled by controlling
beforehand what
may be said. In-
terestingly, campus
controversies over
"political correct-
ness" often inter-
sect with efforts to
impose multicul-
tural agendas.*
— J.R.

*Here Bernstein re-
leases all his anger
against what he
sees as multicul-
turalism, bringing
a charge that he
has offered no con-
crete evidence to
support.* — A.L.

In such a way does multiculturalism limit discussion; it makes people afraid to say what they think
and feel; it presents dubious and cranky interpretations and analyses as self-evident, indisputable
truths. It often operates, not through the usual
means of civil discourse and persuasion, but via intimidation and intellectual decree. It rewrites history. It sanctions a cultivation of aggrievement, a

*The victims and
whiners seem to
have inherited the
earth.* — J.G.R.

*If this were the
case, we wouldn't
have seen a bar-
rage of attacks
pretty much like
Bernstein's over
the last decade. A
glance at almost
any newspaper or*

constant claim of victimization, an excessive, fussy, self-pitying sort of wariness that induces others to spout pieties. And that, in turn, covers the public discussion of crucial issues with a layer of fear, so that we can no longer speak forthrightly and honestly about such matters as crime, race, poverty, AIDS, the failure of schools, single-parenthood, affirmative action, racial preferences, welfare, college admissions, merit, the breakup of the family, and the disintegration of urban life.

magazine will demonstrate that this statement is not accurate. — A.L.

Multiculturalism, in short, has reached the point of *dérapage*. It is a universe of ambitious good intentions that has veered off the high road of respect for difference and plunged into a foggy chasm of dogmatic assertions, wishful thinking, and pseudoscientific pronouncements about race and sex. At its worst, it is what my title suggests. It draws on the old Puritan notion of America as the city on the hill, a new moral universe, to impose a certain vision of rectitude. And, in this, the idealistic and good-hearted movement of inclusion and greater justice veers toward a dictatorship of virtue.

Here is the climax of his argument and a return to the opening analogy. But he hasn't argued cogently enough to convince me. — A.L.

Again, he links multiculturalists with repressive authoritarians, in this case the Puritans. — J.R.

It is not easy to say these things, in part because one does not want to lose sight of all that there is to be admired in the sensibility that gave rise to the multiculturalist challenge in the first place. I am part of the broad liberal consensus that assumes the correctness of the values and practices that emerged from the civil rights movement of the 1960s, one of the most profound and truly liberating social upheavals of all of history, comparable, and indeed linked to, the great events of 1789 in Paris. But the movement known as multiculturalism is no longer that. Indeed, a single-sentence summation of my theme would be this: multiculturalism as it is commonly formulated and practiced is the *dérapage* of the civil rights movement.

A timely concession here, acknowledging the good intentions of many people— teachers and students among them—swept up in multiculturalism's divisive crusades. — J.R.

I'd like to believe this linking to the ideals of the civil rights movement, but it doesn't ring quite true to me after all he's said. — A.L.

Multiculturalism as it is defined by Bernstein is the dérapage of the civil rights movement. But on the (little) evidence provided here, I don't see why I should accept his definition. — A.L.

As I have said, the guillotine does not await us at the other end of the *dérapage*. The dangers that do lurk on the dark side of the multiculturalist revolution are less than that, but they are nonetheless serious enough. Some writers before me have dwelled on one particular consequence of the multiculturalist impulse, deriving from its tendency to make a religion of "difference" and to exalt race, ethnicity, and sex as the sole components of identity. This, as the essayist Charles Krauthammer has said, is shoving us toward a "new tribalism," a splintering of the national culture and an intensification of our conflicts. After all, these writers have noted, we have arrayed before us in the pages of our newspapers the tragedies being played out elsewhere among people who have stressed their differences rather than their commonalities. There is the nightmare in the former Yugoslavia, for example. There are wars between Hutu and Tutsi in Burundi and Rwanda, and between Zulu and Xhosa in South Africa, between Armenians and Azerbaijani, Protestants and Catholics in Northern Ireland, Arabs and Jews in the Middle East, Abkhazians and Georgians in the former Soviet republic of Georgia, and a dozen other conflicts involving, not usually race, but an aggressive ethnicity demonstrating that human beings are just as likely to live in conditions of group animosity as in some harmonious ethnic salad. My own sense is that we are more likely to end up in a simmering sort of mutual dislike on the level of everyday unpleasantness than we are in full-scale Balkan warfare. But that is bad enough.

Familiar scare tactics. But is either/or helpful? Must we either be all alike, or nightmarishly splintered into tribes? I fervently hope not. — A.L

Those who uncritically embrace diversity as an ideal rarely mention these instances of national and ethnic strife. Emphasizing difference can encourage fear and conflict. — J.R.

More alarming perhaps than the prospect of disunion is the possibility that multicultural doctrine will turn out to be a false promise to those members of our society who can least endure yet another false promise. After all, the pattern of assimilation, so easily dismissed by the champions of sweeping change, worked pretty well for millions of people and continues to work well for the many new arrivals who flock, legally and otherwise, to our shores every year. Now a certain racial militancy and small-group affiliation are encouraged by the multiculturalist missionaries on the grounds that these attitudes will help to break the vicious cycles of poverty and violence that are keeping millions of American citizens down.

You can either sit on the bottom of the ladder of success complaining, waiting for the top to come to you, or you can climb its rungs to the top yourself. — J.G.R.

Multiculturalism in this sense is a code word for an expanded concept of moral and cultural rela-

This is the code word Bernstein *assigns—and it is not one that all critics would agree to.* — A.L.

tivism. Originally, relativism deflated the imperial arrogance of Western civilization. By now, the *dérapage* has pushed us to the point where we are fearful of upholding any aspect of the Western way of doing things as better than other ways. It was perhaps inevitable in the liberal American culture that multiculturalism got conflated with an expanded version of a phenomenon that Daniel Patrick Moynihan* has called "defining down deviancy." Moynihan was talking about the way our tolerant and forgiving liberal culture removes more and more bad behavior from the category of the delinquent, so that it can no longer be punished. My own belief is that the multiculturalist rhetoric has the effect of defining down many other forms of bad behavior. Teenage pregnancy is transformed from a cause of shame into one of many "diverse forms of the family." Violence in schools is not an offense but the teachers' ignorance of the "cultures" of a "diverse student population." Their pupils fail to learn, not because they do not study hard enough but because they have "different ways of knowing" or because they do not see themselves "reflected" in the curriculum. Anti-male, anti-white, and anti-Semitic bigotry at institutions of higher learning is coddled in the belief that it is the natural expression of the rage of the culturally dispossessed.

How has he moved from the ideals of multiculturalism to teen pregnancy, violence in schools, bigotry, and fraud? In his view, whatever he means by multiculturalism, and it is clearly bad, is responsible for many of our social problems. — A.L.

Multiculturalists aren't to blame for all these problems, but he's on target in suggesting that multiculturalism must be understood as part of an overall leftist political agenda. Its patrons are neither bipartisan nor disinterested. —J.R.

But what if this relativism turns out to be a fraud, perpetrated by mostly middle-class intellectuals, all of whom have jobs? What if the ideas coded in multiculturalism do not so much prepare people for real life as foster illusions about it, or, worse, provide a pretext for repudiating the values and behaviors that have traditionally led to success, such as objectivity and achievement, on the grounds that they are the values of the despised Eurocentrist group?

One of my own underlying theses is that, like it or not, there are certain cultural norms, certain things to know and do, a mastery of a certain discourse, that is most likely to get people on the great engine of upward social mobility in the United

---

Daniel Patrick Moynihan (b. 1927): sociologist and U.S. Senator from New York

States. The multiculturalists contend that there are many different avenues to the same result. They promise, as we will see, that different "learning styles," these things vaguely tied to race and gender, will lead to success, which can no longer be defined in the masculine, Eurocentric way. They promise that the enforcement of a certain rhetorical code will address the real problems of inequality and prejudice that have bedeviled American society from the beginning of its history. And, in this, they would impose a certain conformity to their ideas, one originating in the concept of virtue and that puts the vast and ever-growing multiculturalist bureaucracy into the tradition of Robespierre.

Now multiculturalism is guilty of destroying learning itself. Methinks the gentleman doth protest too much. — A.L.

Joseph Conrad* wrote in *Under Western Eyes* that "in a real revolution the best characters do not come to the front. . . . The scrupulous and the just, the noble, humane and devoted natures, the unselfish and the intelligent may begin a movement— but it passes away from them." This, I believe, is true of multiculturalism, a humane and humanizing idea that has, somehow, gone wrong. It is nobility perverted. And those who are perverting it, not the scrupulous and the just, but the zealots and the tyrants, belong to a burgeoning bureaucracy that, like all bureaucracies, finds ways to perpetuate and aggrandize itself. Its members may not deliver on their promise to the victimized of our society. They will, nonetheless, not lose their jobs.

Who are these "perverted" "zealots" and "tyrants"? — A.L.

The plain and inescapable fact is that the derived Western European culture of American life produced the highest degree of prosperity in the conditions of the greatest freedom ever known on planet Earth. The rich and the advantaged of our society will survive even if they are taught to believe something different. But to teach the poor and the disadvantaged that they can ignore the standards and modes of behavior that have always made for success in American life is more than mere silliness. It is a lie.

A great point— can Eurocentric ways be so bad when the product of those ideas has been the freest society the world has ever known? — J.G.R.

Apparently he believes that multiculturalism is teaching the poor to ignore the "standards and modes of behavior" that make for success in America. I don't think so. — A.L.

Joseph Conrad (1857–1924): Polish-born English novelist

Afterwords

The line that resonates most powerfully with my own experience is Bernstein's assertion that multiculturalism "is a code word for political ambition." Some of the glitter falls from multiculturalism when one realizes that its policies and programs are motivated less by intellectual ideals than by an intention to acquire wealth and power for its numerous constituencies. That's what partisanship is all about—as Bernstein suggests—and there's certainly nothing odd about bare-knuckled politics in America. The problem with multiculturalism is that it often masquerades as a benign intellectual and cultural movement meant to benefit everyone, although its opponents are inevitably called "mean spirited." Crafted as celebrations of diverse cultures, multicultural programs seem quite unobjectionable. But more accurately labeled as programs, courses, or seminars in leftist or progressive politics, multicultural requirements take on a wholly different cast.

Of course, multiculturalists will argue that existing programs and structures are political, too, set in place to serve the interests of groups currently in power. Fine, I say, then make the arguments for multiculturalism on political grounds. Don't pretend that multicultural projects are loftier in their ambitions than other political platforms or more open to difference *or* inclusiveness. *From what I have seen—up close and personal—multiculturalism is designed to funnel public or corporate money into the hands of the political left to advance a familiar agenda. There's nothing especially wrong with that, but there's nothing noble about it either. And I'm tired of sanctimony.*

Next time you encounter a multicultural proposal on your campus, ask the ancient question: Cui bono? *Who benefits? Then follow the money trail.* —J.R.

J.R. asks a good question, one we should all ask of those who would persuade us: "Who benefits?" Thinking about this question will lead us not only to the outward trappings of power (the money trail) but to more subtle and often hidden benefits like who has access to education, to jobs, to upward mobility in our society, to personal and spiritual fulfillment. When I ask "who benefits" if we accept Bernstein's reading of multiculturalism, the answer I get is "those already in power" or "the status quo"—that is, folks pretty much like Bernstein himself.

This kind of analysis is always enlightening. But it isn't what is most important to me about this essay. Instead, I want to talk about the struggle for control of language going on here. The Russian theorist Mikhail Bakhtin wrote eloquently about this struggle, saying that key words are always contested in society and that the way these key terms are eventually defined reveals a great deal about the society's values, aspirations, and goals. I think it is this kind of struggle or contestation that is going on over the term multicultural *today. If it comes to mean what Bernstein says (or what J.R. defines as a "code word for political ambition"), I believe our society will be greatly diminished and our values revealed as small and even mean spirited. I want to call into being another understanding of* multicultural, *one that only hovers on the margins of Bern-*

stein's essay. In this sense, multicultural *is descriptive of the rich—and multiple—linguistic and cultural heritages of the United States; it is inclusive rather than divisive; it signals respect, openness, and reciprocity; it reflects the poet Walt Whitman's description of himself: "I am large," Whitman says; "I contain multitudes." So do we all.* — A.L.

The civil rights movement has twisted itself 180 degrees since Dr. Martin Luther King Jr. so eloquently longed for a society that judged its members by the "content of their character" instead of their skin color. Supporters of multiculturism and affirmative action are as much the enemy of a color-blind society as are white supremacists and racists in general. I have been affected by racism and sexism, refused admission to a university because of my gender and the color of my skin. In the 1960s such institutional bias was considered an outrage. Now, it is not only seen as morally correct, but intellectually justified. However, I refuse to accept such a position.

Americans have more opportunity to succeed than any people of any nation in history. But instead of being thankful for these opportunities and aggressively pursuing them, too many Americans waste energy finding excuses for their failures. They point to statistics that say they will never succeed. But statistics are just numbers—no more. And they no more apply to a particular individual than that individual allows them to apply to himself.

Consider the implications of multiculturalism. Would you have your children grow up believing that they are granted or denied certain privileges because of their ethnicity, race, or gender? Or would you rather they grow up in a color-blind society believing that success is a result of their own effort and determination? — J.G.R.

QUESTIONING THE TEXT

1. Keep a record of all the times *multiculturalism* as a term or concept comes up at your school or workplace. When you have accumulated five or six such references, consider them in light of Bernstein's criticism of multiculturalism. Is the concept as politicized as he suggests, or is it being used in other ways?
2. "Nobody wants to appear to be against multiculturalism," says Bernstein. Choose another important term in our society that, like *multiculturalism,* seems beyond easy criticism, such as *family values, motherhood,* or *self-reliance.* Then explore it critically, the way Bernstein deconstructs some meanings of multiculturalism.
3. J.R. acknowledges in his introduction that he is mentioned in Bernstein's book (in a chapter not reprinted in this volume). How does that information affect your response to J.R.'s introduction or to Bernstein's article?

MAKING CONNECTIONS

4. After reading or reviewing what Neil Postman says about definitions in "The Word Weavers/The World Makers" (p. 133), write a paragraph on the way Bernstein uses the word *dérapage* to organize his argument. You might want to begin by annotating every occurrence of *dérapage* in the essay.

JOINING THE CONVERSATION

5. Bernstein is concerned that multiculturalism may increase ethnic divisions in the United States. Reflect on your own experience with multicultural education, then write a position paper addressing Bernstein's concern—supporting him, refuting him, or offering a different perspective.

MICHAEL LASSELL
How to Watch Your Brother Die

MICHAEL LASSELL (b. 1947), a former editor of a national gay and lesbian news magazine, The Advocate, *is the author of several collections of poetry, including* Poems for Lost and Un-Lost Boys *(1985) and* Decade Dance *(1990).*

"How to Watch Your Brother Die," first published in 1985, is often reprinted, for it was one of the most powerful early poems attempting to respond to AIDS. In this brief and highly accessible work, the narrator evokes the confusing mass of emotions he feels during the death of a brother who happens to be gay. In doing so, he asks us to think about our own brothers, both literal siblings and all those for whom we feel brother- (or sister-)hood. In particular, the poem suggests to me that watching a brother die is in some ways also watching yourself die.

I chose this poem because human experience encompasses a diverse range of sexuality, in spite of our society's traditional and persistent focus only on heterosexuality. Lassell's poem challenges that focus and in doing so speaks for many, many gay people whose voices have been muted, ignored, or silenced. Finally, I chose this poem for a personal reason as well, for I watched my own brother, who lived with cancer for eight long years, die. — A.L.

When the call comes, be calm.
Say to your wife, "My brother is dying. I have to fly
to California."
Try not to be shocked that he already looks like
a cadaver.   5
Say to the young man sitting by your brother's side,
"I'm his brother."
Try not to be shocked when the young man says,
"I'm his lover. Thanks for coming."

Listen to the doctor with a steel face on.   10
Sign the necessary forms.
Tell the doctor you will take care of everything.
Wonder why doctors are so remote.

Watch the lover's eyes as they stare into
your brother's eyes as they stare into   15
space.
Wonder what they see there.

Remember the time he was jealous and
opened your eyebrow with a sharp stick.
Forgive him out loud   20
even if he can't
understand you.
Realize the scar will be
all that's left of him.
                                                                25

Over coffee in the hospital cafeteria
say to the lover, "You're an extremely good-looking
young man."
Hear him say,
"I never thought I was good enough looking to
deserve your brother."   30

Watch the tears well up in his eyes. Say,
"I'm sorry. I don't know what it means to be
the lover of another man."
Hear him say,
"It's just like a wife, only the commitment is   35
deeper because the odds against you are so much
greater."
Say nothing, but
take his hand like a brother's.
                                                                40

Drive to Mexico for unproven drugs that might
help him live longer.
Explain what they are to the border guard.
Fill with rage when he informs you,
"You can't bring those across."
Begin to grow loud.   45
Feel the lover's hand on your arm
restraining you. See in the guard's eye
how much a man can hate another man.
Say to the lover, "How can you stand it?"
Hear him say, "You get used to it."   50
Think of one of your children getting used to
another man's hatred.

Call your wife on the telephone. Tell her,
"He hasn't much time.
I'll be home soon." Before you hang up say,   55
"How could anyone's commitment be deeper than

a husband and wife?" Hear her say,
"Please. I don't want to know all the details."

When he slips into an irrevocable coma,
hold his lover in your arms while he sobs,   60
no longer strong. Wonder how much longer
you will be able to be strong.
Feel how it feels to hold a man in your arms
whose arms are used to holding men.
Offer God anything to bring your brother back.   65
Know you have nothing God could possibly want.
Curse God, but do not
abandon Him.

Stare at the face of the funeral director
when he tells you he will not   70
embalm the body for fear of
contamination. Let him see in your eyes
how much a man can hate another man.

Stand beside a casket covered in flowers,
white flowers. Say,   75
"Thank you for coming," to each of several hundred men
who file past in tears, some of them
holding hands. Know that your brother's life
was not what you imagined. Overhear two
mourners say, "I wonder who'll be next?" and   80
"I don't care anymore,
as long as it isn't you."

Arrange to take an early flight home.
His lover will drive you to the airport.
When your flight is announced say,   85
awkwardly, "If I can do anything, please
let me know." Do not flinch when he says,
"Forgive yourself for not wanting to know him
after he told you. He did."
Stop and let it soak in. Say,   90
"He forgave me, or he knew himself?"
"Both," the lover will say, not knowing what else
to do. Hold him like a brother while he
kisses you on the cheek. Think that
you haven't been kissed by a man since   95

your father died. Think,
"This is no moment not to be strong."

Fly first class and drink Scotch. Stroke
your split eyebrow with a finger and
think of your brother alive. Smile   100
at the memory and think
how your children will feel in your arms,
warm and friendly and without challenge.

QUESTIONING THE TEXT

1. The word *forgive* appears a number of times in the poem. Who needs to forgive and/or to be forgiven, and why?

MAKING CONNECTIONS

2. In Langston Hughes's "Theme for English B" (p. 432), the narrator says "I like to eat, sleep, drink, and be in love." What might the narrator of this poem list as his wishes—what he would most like?
3. At the end of "Call It Blindness" (p. 390), Georgina Kleege describes a scene in which a bus passenger stops the bus so that a disabled person can board. Then, Kleege says, they all ride along contemplating their "shared humanity and mutual acceptance" and knowing that when someone else needs help, these passengers will be able to "sense what's needed." How does Kleege's essay respond implicitly to the issues of "shared humanity and mutual acceptance" raised by Lassell's poem?

JOINING THE CONVERSATION

4. Write a page or two responding to this poem—how it made you feel, what it made you think of, ways in which it puzzled or troubled or comforted you.

GEORGINA KLEEGE
Call It Blindness

ON MY FORTY-FIFTH BIRTHDAY, I had a sudden shock: I could no longer read the condensed version of the Oxford English Dictionary *without using the handy magnifying glass that accompanies that two-volume work. I merely had presbyopia, my doctor informed me, and I was certainly not unique: at about my age, almost everyone could count on failing vision. Luckily, I could also count on glasses to help me out, a luxury that our ancestors did not have and one that provides precious little help for those who are "legally blind."*

Now meet Georgina Kleege (b. 1956), whose own experiences with blindness and sight are both extensive and intensive. Pronounced "legally blind" when she was eleven, Kleege's loss of vision was so gradual that she has "no memory of losing" it. Indeed, she long "passed" as sighted and only gradually came to "see" the myriad and destructive ways in which our society equates sight with goodness and blindness with evil. The difference of blindness evokes fear more than any other emotion, however, a fear as "ancient as the fear of darkness." In moving and meticulously crafted prose, Kleege challenges this fear, challenges each of us to examine our own dependence on sight and to assess just how well and how much we can really "see."

Currently living in Columbus, Ohio, and teaching at Ohio State University, Kleege grew up in New York City, attending Grace Church School. Since graduating from Yale in 1979, she has written two books of fiction, Home for the Summer *(1989) and* Judgment Calls *(forthcoming), and is now at work on a collection of creative nonfiction essays titled* Sight Unseen.

"Call It Blindness" was named one of the Best American Essays of 1995. My students were unanimous in urging that it be included in the second edition of The Presence of Others. *I couldn't agree more.* – A.L.

I tell the class, "I am legally blind." There is a pause, a collective intake of breath. I feel them look away uncertainly and then look back. After all, I just said I couldn't see. Or did I? I had managed to get there on my own—no cane, no dog, none of the usual trappings of blindness. Eyeing me askance now, they might detect that my gaze is not quite focused. My eyes are aimed in the right direction but the gaze seems to stop short of touching anything. But other people do this, sighted people, normal people, especially in an awkward situation like this one, the first day of class. An actress who delivers an aside to the audience, breaking the "fourth wall" of the proscenium, will aim her gaze somewhere above any particular pair of eyes. If I hadn't said anything, my audience might understand my gaze to be like that, a part of the performance. In these few seconds between sentences, their gaze becomes intent. They watch me glance down, or toward the door where someone's coming in late. I'm just like anyone else. Then what did I actually mean by "legally blind"? They wait. I go on, "Some people would call me 'visually challenged.'" There is a ripple of laughter, an exhalation of relief. I'm making a joke about it. I'm poking fun at something they too find aggravating, the current mania to stick a verbal smiley-face on any human condition which deviates from the status quo. Differently abled. Handicapable. If I ask, I'm sure some of them can tell jokes about it: "Don't say 'bald,' say 'follicularly challenged.'" "He's not dead, he's metabolically stable." Knowing they are at least thinking of these things, I conclude, "These are just silly ways of saying I don't see very well."

I probably shouldn't make these jokes. In fact the term *legally blind* is not a new, politically correct euphemism. Nor is the adverb interchangeable with *half, partially,* or *nearly*. Someone is legally blind whose visual acuity is 20/200 or less, or whose visual field is 20 degrees or less, in the better eye, with corrective lenses. The term seems to have been coined by the American Medical Association in 1934, then adopted by the federal government in the Social Security Act of 1935, as a standard measure to determine eligibility for new federal programs for the blind. The definition has been controversial since it was instituted. It turns on only two aspects of sight, and does not measure how well or poorly an individual uses residual sight. There are many who would like to abandon the definition, enlarge it, contract it, or create new categories. I could tell my students this, a tidbit of medical and social history. I could also explain that the legally blind often "see" something, and often use visual experience to understand the world, and thus "appear" sighted. I could hand out diagrams of the human eye, photographs simulating various types of "legal blindness." But I do not.

Instead I detail how my condition will affect them. Someone will have to read me their papers and exams. Or else they will have to tape their written work, which can be time-consuming. When I look at them I cannot tell if their eyes are focused with interest or glazed over with confusion, boredom, or fatigue. In other words, I cannot "read" the class as effectively as other teachers. I cannot ask for a show of hands, or if I do someone else must count them. If they want to make a comment they must break the cardinal rule of classroom decorum drummed in since the first grade and interrupt me. It may take the entire term for me to match each of them, whatever it is I see of them, to a name.

Most of this may not matter to them at all. Perhaps they have other instructors with comparable foibles. Perhaps there's no need even to mention it. They can tell I don't see well just by watching me read, holding the page an inch from my eyes, squinting through coke-bottle lenses. But I must talk about it, as a way to dispel possible confusion or discomfort. I bring it up so the student in the back row with his hand in the air can drop it and say, "Excuse me, I have a question" and not "What's the matter, can't you see?"

In other public speaking situations I never mention my blindness. I used   5
to give educational and fund-raising talks about domestic violence, sexual assault, and other issues. I spoke from memory, never using notes. I shifted my
focus here and there in the way all the literature about public speaking advises. I learned to direct my eyes at any sound, to raise them to the ceiling or
lower them to the floor, as if searching for the right words. Perhaps I came off
as stagy, phony, insincere, but certainly not blind. The only risky moments
during any of these occasions were the question-and-answer periods. But
usually there was a host—the chair of the meeting, the teacher of the class—
who pointed to the raised hands. Though I could not make eye contact (I do
not really know what eye contact feels like or does), I doubt my audiences
ever really noticed. Often the subject matter made them drop their eyes and
stare at their shoes. Or else they so identified with the topic, they became dis-
tracted by memories, blinded by tears. If I had introduced myself as blind, it
would have detracted from my topic. They might have felt compelled to
watch out for my safety. I might be about to knock something over or fall off
the stage. Or else they might have suspected me of fraud, a rather clumsy deception meant to milk their sympathy. As with my students, I could have
taken the time to educate them, to explain that blindness does not equal ineptitude. It does not even mean an absolute lack of sight. But I had more important things to say. My blindness was an irrelevant fact they did not need to
know about me, like my religion or political affiliation.

In social situations I never announce my blindness. And as long as I'm
not obliged to read anything, or identify a person or a plate of food, people
tend not to notice. I pass as sighted. I have many acquaintances, people who
know me slightly, or only by sight, who would be shocked to learn that my
vision is not normal. The fact that I do not look people in the eye they may
chalk up to shyness, reserve, or boredom.

Some blind people introduce their disability when they shake hands.
They feel it's best to get it out of the way in the first moments of acquaintance. I have never mastered the technique. If I have to explain why I don't
drive, for instance, the discomfort of the sighted people is debilitating. Tension solidifies around us. Their voices become softer, even hushed with a so-
licitous piety. They become self-conscious about language, hesitant to say "I
see what you mean" or "See you later." I feel them glance around for whoever brought me, whoever is responsible for me. Sometimes there's a degree
of desperation in this, an anxiety to turn me back over to the person in
charge, as if this disaster only just occurred in the second it took to speak the
word. I've learned to speed-skate around it, to feign gaiety, to babble my way
into another topic, but equilibrium is hard to recover.

Once, at a party, a man I was speaking to was almost reduced to tears to
learn I was a blind writer. There was a tremor in his voice. He kept saying
something about "the word fading." I tried to tell him that since my condition is stable, the word has already faded as much as it ever will, unless some

other condition develops. And as far as these things go, a writer is not a bad thing to be if you can't see. There are other ways to write, other ways to read. It is easier for a writer to compensate for sight loss than a visual artist, a race car driver, an astronomer. I might have even mentioned Homer, Milton, and Joyce, the sight-impaired literary luminaries most often invoked at such times. But he had already receded from me, become preoccupied with a new, reductive view of me and my restricted future.

Of course, it's the word *blind* which causes all the problems. To most people, blindness means total, absolute darkness, a complete absence of any visual experience. Though only about ten per cent of the legally blind have this degree of impairment, people think the word should be reserved to designate this minority. For the rest of us, with our varying degrees of sight, a modifier becomes necessary. We're encouraged to indicate that we're not quite "that bad." Better to speak of a visual impairment, a sight deficit, low vision. Better still to accentuate the positive and call it "partially sighted."

Sometimes I use these other terms, but I find them no more precise or   10 pleasing. The word *impairment* implies impermanence, an encumbrance which could disappear, and my condition has no cure or treatment. The term *low vision* reminds me too much of *short eyes,* a prison term for child molesters. And anyway, I crave the simplicity of a single, unmodified adjective. Blind. Perhaps I could speak in relative terms, say I am blinder than some, less blind than others.

"But," people object, "you are not really blind," attaching yet another adverb to separate me from the absolutely sightless. The modern, legal definition is arbitrary, a convention based on notions of what visual skills are necessary for an adult to be gainfully employed or a child traditionally educated. The definition has more to do with the ability to read print or drive a car than with the ability to perceive color, light, motion, or form. If I lived in a different culture or a different age, no one would define me as blind. I could transport myself on foot or horseback. I could grow or gather my own food, relying on other senses to detect ripeness, pests, soil quality. I would have trouble hunting. The protective coloration of most animals and birds is always good enough to deceive me. But I might learn to devise cunning traps, and I could fish. I could become adept at crafts—certain kinds of weaving or pottery— which require as much manual dexterity and digital sensitivity as visual acuity. If I looked at people strangely it might be accepted as a personality flaw. Or else it might be a culture where a too-direct gaze is considered impolite. In any case, I could live independently, with enough sight to perform routine tasks without aid. If I had a sense that others' eyes were stronger or more discerning than mine, I still would not define myself as blind. Especially if it was the sort of culture which put the blind to death.

Though in the here and now execution is unlikely, a stigma exists. So why should I want to label myself in that way? Isn't the use of the word at all, even with one of the imprecise modifiers, a form of self-dramatization, a demand for attention and pity better bestowed elsewhere? Isn't it a dishonest claim of marginal status, now that marginality is fashionable?

In fact, it is only recently that I have started using the word. I was pronounced "legally blind" when I was eleven, though my condition probably developed a year or two earlier. I have no memory of losing my sight. I imagine it took place so gradually I was unaware of what I was not seeing. The only outward sign was that I began to read with the book very close to my eyes. Everyone assumed I was simply nearsighted, but tests did not show this. My cornea and lenses refracted normally. Remarkably, my doctor did not pursue the matter, even though the early signs of retinal damage should have been revealed in a standard eye exam. Apparently it was not what he was looking for. Instead, he jumped to the conclusion that I was faking, even though I was not the sort of child who would do that. My parents and teachers were advised to nag me into holding the book away from my face. For a while I complied, keeping the book at the prescribed distance, turning pages at appropriate intervals. Then, when no one was looking, I would flip back and press my nose to the page. Eventually it became clear to everyone that this was not a phase I was going to outgrow. Additional tests were performed. When it was all over, my doctor named my disorder "macular degeneration," defined my level of impairment as legally blind, and told me there was no treatment or cure, and no chance of improvement. And that was all. Like many ophthalmologists then and perhaps still, he did not feel it was his responsibility to recommend special education or training. He did not send me to an optometrist for whatever magnification devices might have been available then. This was in the mid-sixties, so the boom in high-tech "low vision" aids had not yet begun. He said that as long as I continued to perform well at school, there was no point in burdening me with cumbersome gadgetry or segregating me from my classmates. He did not tell me I was eligible to receive recorded materials for the blind. He did not even explain legal blindness, much less the specifics of my condition. I did not find out what my macula was for several years. He said nothing about adaptation, did not speculate about what my brain had already learned to do to compensate for the incomplete images my eyes were sending to it. This was not his job. Since then I have heard accounts of other doctors faced with the dilemma of telling patients there is no cure for their condition. They admit they sometimes see these patients as embarrassments, things they'd rather sweep under the carpet, out of public view. As a child of eleven I did not understand his dilemma. I assumed his failure to give me more information was a measure of the insignificance of my problem. I was confused and scared, but also disappointed not to receive the glasses I expected him to prescribe. I left with no glasses, no advice, no explanations, nothing but the words *macular degeneration,* which I did not understand, and more significantly, the word *blind,* which I understood only too well.

But I did not use the word. I was not blind. Blind people saw nothing, only darkness. *Blind* meant the man in the subway station, standing for hours near the token booth, tin cup in hand, a mangy German shepherd lying on a bit of blanket at his feet. That was not how I saw myself. Surely there was some sort of mistake. Or else it was a lie, and as long as I did not repeat it, refrained from speaking the hateful word and claiming identity with the beggar in the subway, I could keep the lie from becoming a reality. Because if I were blind, or going blind, surely someone would do something about it. I'd read about Helen Keller. I knew what went on. Shouldn't someone be teaching me braille? At school they didn't use the word either. They moved me to the front row, stopped telling me to hold the book away from my face, and kept an eye on me. From this I understood not only that the word should not be spoken, but also that I shouldn't ask for special favors, shouldn't draw undue attention to my disability (a word I didn't use either), shouldn't make a spectacle of myself. I learned to read the blackboard from the motion of the teacher's writing. If I suspected I would have to read aloud in class, I'd memorize pages of text, predicting with reasonable accuracy which paragraph would fall to me. The routines of my teachers saved me. Also, by the sixth grade, reading aloud in class was usually only required in French, and then only a few sentences at a time. Outside of school, if other kids said, "Look at that!" I determined from the tone of voice whether they saw something ugly, strange, or cute, and would adjust my response accordingly. On the bus I counted streets to know my stop. In elevators I counted buttons.

The most I would admit to was "a problem with my eyes," sometimes   15
adding, "and They won't give me glasses," indicating that it was not me but the willfully obstructionist medical establishment which was to blame for my failure to see as I should.

Once, in Paris, I met a banker who announced to me as he shook my hand that he had "un problème" with his eyes. He explained that this was why he couldn't look me straight in the eye. I understood that a person in his profession had to say something. For him, as for a used-car dealer or clergyman, failure to maintain a direct gaze would affect his business. I noted, too, that he did not use the word *aveugle,* any medical term, nor any other phrase I could translate into one of the current American ones to designate impaired sight. The imprecision of his phrase allowed for the possibility that the problem might be only temporary, a side-effect of medication, an adjustment to new glasses. But the tension in his tone gave him away. He was a French banker of the old school. His suit was that particular shade of navy. His repertoire of elegant pleasantries was extensive. Everything about him was calculated to affirm, in the most reassuring way, that he could dispatch even the most distasteful or compromising financial matter with discretion so deft it would seem effortless. But his own phrase, "un problème avec mes yeux," tripped him up. In his rehearsed delivery, his haste to move the conversation along, I recognized the uncomfortable anticipation of the usual responses, the hushed surprise, the "So sorry for your loss."

Reluctance to use the word *blind,* even in modified form, is as common as the desire to keep one's visual problems a secret. Many people conceal their sight loss for years, even from people close to them and certainly from strangers. Looking sighted is not so hard. For one thing, the sighted are not all that observant. And most blind people are better at appearing sighted than the sighted are at appearing blind. We compose our faces in expressions of preoccupation. We walk fast, purposefully. We do not ask directions. Forced to read something, we pat our pockets for reading glasses we do not own. When we make mistakes, we feign absentmindedness, slapping our foreheads, blinking our eyes.

An astonishing amount of the literature on the "training" and "rehabilitation" of the blind deals with appearance, the visible manifestations of blindness. Eliminate "blindisms," the experts say, the physical traits the blind are allegedly prone to—the wobbly neck, uneven posture, shuffling gait, unblinking gaze. Discolored or bulging eyes should be covered with patches or dark glasses, empty sockets filled with prostheses. But the books and pamphlets go further. They also urge that the blind, or their sighted keepers, be extra attentive to personal grooming, choose clothes which are stylish and color-coordinated. Having nice clothes and clean fingernails may contribute to a person's self-esteem whether they can see these things or not. And certainly hints about labeling socks or applying makeup can be useful. But the advice of the experts has another message. Blindness is unsightly, a real eyesore. No one wants to look at that.

So the blind, of all levels of impairment and all stages of sight loss, find themselves encouraged to sham sight. And even if there is no overt encouragement from well-meaning family members or social workers, we know, or sense instinctively, that our charade of sight is easier than the consequences of speaking the single word *blind*. Because the word bears such a burden of negative connotations and dreaded associations it can hardly be said to have any neutral, merely descriptive meaning at all. *Blind* means darkness, dependence, destitution, despair. *Blind* means the beggar in the subway station. Look at him slouching there, unkempt, head bowed, stationary among the rushing crowd. Intermittently, an involuntary twitch jerks his arm upward, making the coin or two in his cup clink. Otherwise he is silent, apparently speechless. A sign hung around his neck reads: "I'm blind. Please help." Because *blind* means "needs help," and also "needs charity." But the people rushing by barely oblige. They barely see him. They certainly don't stop to stare. And they certainly do not expand their vision to allow for any other image of blindness. Told that there are blind people in all walks of life—medicine, law, social work, education, the arts—they are not impressed. They see those successes as flukes, exceptions, while the beggar in the subway is the rule. Those people went blind late in life, after the habits of their professions were formed, and probably, if you looked closely, after their major accomplishments were already achieved. Or else they're not "really" blind. They have just enough sight to get by. Besides, they probably had special help. If, behind every great man there is a woman, in front of every accomplished blind person that is a sighted helper, spouse, child, or parent, leading the way. Helen Keller had Annie Sullivan. Milton had daughters.

The blind beggar stands alone. As long as we can manage, we keep our   20 distance, both because he makes such a displeasing spectacle of himself and because we know the consequences of claiming identity with him. Note how few coins there are in his cup. He might be faking. If he greets the token clerk changing shifts, his take will plummet. Every visually impaired, partially sighted, hard-of-seeing person knows the suspicion. And we know the story of the cop beating the man with his nightstick for the crime of carrying both a white cane and a newspaper. "My mother is really blind," the cop shouts. The blind man says nothing. No chance to explain how his particular condition leaves him enough sight to read but not the right kind to get around. Too late for him to say he was bringing the paper home for someone to read aloud to him. The cop's mother sits in the dark, wishing someone would read the paper to her. The rest of us compose our faces, fake it as best we can, and scuttle toward the exit. We bite our tongues, dare not speak the word aloud, like the true name of God.

The word *blind* has always meant more than merely the inability to see. The Anglo-Saxon translators of the Gospels made the metaphoric leap from literal sightlessness to spiritual or cognitive incapacity. Of course they were only following an ancient lead. Throughout the history of the language and in common usage today, the word connotes lack of understanding or discernment, willful disregard or obliviousness, a thing meant to conceal or deceive. In fact, when you stop to listen, the word is far more commonly used in its figurative than its literal sense. And it comes up so often: blind faith, blind devotion, blind luck, blind lust, blind trust, blind chance, blind rage, blind alley, blind curve, blind-nail flooring, blind date (more dangerous than you think), duck blind, window blind, micro-mini blind (when open, they're hard to see), blind taste test, double blind study, flying blind, following blind, blind leading the blind, blind landing, color-blind (in the racial sense, a good thing), blind summit, blind side, blind spot, blindfold, blindman's buff, three blind mice (have you ever seen such a sight in your life?). Pick up any book or magazine and you will find dozens of similes and metaphors connecting blindness and blind people with ignorance, confusion, indifference, ineptitude. An image of a blind man stumbling around an unfamiliar and presumably overfurnished room is used to depict someone grappling with a difficult moral problem. A woman flails blindly (not only sightless but feeble) at an assailant, blinded by hatred and rage. Other disabilities are used similarly, but not as often. A politician may be deaf to the concerns of his constituents and lame in his responses, but first and foremost he is blind to their needs. Writers and speakers seem so attached to these meanings for *blind* they don't even find them clichéd. Deny them the use of the word and they feel gagged, stymied. If you want to talk about stupidity, prejudice, weakness, narrow-mindedness, no other word will do.

To express the opposite of blindness, however, we need at least two words. Generally, we use the words *sight* and *vision* interchangeably, though recently, some eye specialists make a distinction, using *sight* to refer to the functioning of the eye itself, and *vision* to refer to the functioning of the eye and brain together. Originally *vision* was used to mean spiritual or metaphysical perception. Later it became synonymous with sight. In common usage positive connotations predominate. Seeing, after all, is believing. We speak of vision as a virtue. Hindsight is always 20/20. We want our leaders to be at least clear-sighted, if not possessed of "that vision thing." We hold dear our views, outlooks, perspectives. We know a picture is worth a thousand words. We want to see eye to eye.

Of course people who are blind use language the same way. Though the joke "'I see,' says the blind man" can always get a laugh out of children and perhaps adults as well, blind people are as likely to say "I see what you mean" or "Let me look at that" as anyone else, and without excessive self-consciousness or irony.

The absolute equation of sight with good and blindness with evil breaks down from time to time. Seeing may be believing, but sometimes you cannot (should not) believe your eyes. When we say "Love is blind," it cuts both ways. Love makes us oblivious to the beloved's flaws, putting us at risk of exploitation, abuse, deception. But it also causes us to overlook the superficial defects and shortcomings of physical appearance, financial condition, social status, which others may see as obstacles to happiness. Myth and folklore abound with complex portrayals of the interplay between love and sight. Willful deities divert themselves by temporarily or permanently blinding mortals for the sole purpose of watching them fall in love with inappropriate partners. Sight restored, there's always a joke on someone, human or divine. Psyche finds herself united to a man she cannot see. When she finally lights the lamp and looks at Love, his beauty so startles her, she drops hot oil on him and he flees. The message: look too closely at the beloved and someone will get burned.

It's no accident that the eyes are the most often mentioned feature in all   25
love poetry. Beautiful themselves for their gemlike color and liquid sheen, eyes are not only windows into the soul but can also send elaborate messages of love. They glow with affection, smoulder with passion, dilate with emotion. When we gaze into the eyes of the beloved and see a reflection of ourselves contained there, our narcissistic tendencies are gratified. Now, as in the past, women spend more time and money accentuating, highlighting, lining, defining, emphasizing their eyes than any other feature. Small wonder that women and men losing their sight often report anxiety about their sexuality. Women fear that without sight, their eyes will no longer be alluring. No more bedroom eyes, come-hither looks. Men seldom make passes at girls who wear glasses. If the girl is blind, she will be that much more unattractive, or that much less able to control her own sexuality. Blind girls have been sold

into prostitution. Presumably they were expected to service men other women would find repulsive to look at. Or else a blind woman provides an extra level of voyeuristic titillation, the additional level of excitement Peeping Toms seek: to observe the unseeing. For men the loss of sight is devastating in a different way. The male gaze is supposed to project messages of intention and desire. But the act of seeing also plays a large part in male sexual arousal. This is an argument often made to defend pornography. If voracious and deviant males can get their jollies looking at dirty pictures, they'll keep their lecherous looks (and hands) to themselves. Oedipus tears out his eyes even if another organ might seem more appropriate, given his crime. His act not only symbolizes castration, but makes it unnecessary. What you can't see, you can't want. And don't forget: masturbation will make you blind.

Look at Justice. Observe that she is not blind but blindfolded. True, it's difficult to depict blindness in painting or sculpture without representing some unsightly deformity, unless the blindfold is actually a bandage hiding a gruesome wound. But it seems more likely that she has willingly renounced sight. She makes herself blind to extenuating circumstances, even to the fact that one of the litigants may be a family member or friend. Presumably when Justice is off duty she can see. The blindfold could even slip. She could lift an edge of it and peek if her hands weren't full. In one hand she holds a book, presumably of law, which she cannot read blindfolded. Perhaps it's there as a reminder that she could at any moment rip off the rag and look up the relevant statute. In the other hand she holds a scale to weigh evidence. But she cannot see the balance or lack of balance which is achieved. Perhaps she can feel it with the heightened sensitivity blind people are supposed to have.

Despite this apparent reverence for the impartiality of the blind, still, in some states, the legally blind are automatically exempt from jury duty. Though Justice is blind, the jury should be sighted. Jurors may have to examine evidence, respond to the ocular proof of a bloodstain or fingerprint. Attorneys coach witnesses not only on what to say, but how to look saying it. "Look at the defendant," the lawyer urges, "are those the eyes of a murderer?" True, looks can be deceiving, but in a court of law they still count for a great deal.

My husband was once dismissed from a jury pool because of my blindness. A doctor had allegedly misdiagnosed a patient's symptoms as psychosomatic, and failed to treat her for the brain tumor which caused her to go blind. The jurors were asked if the fact that the patient had ended up blind, as opposed to disabled in some other way, would have any bearing on their ability to arrive at an equitable settlement. Both attorneys viewed Nick's close association with blindness as an impairment of his vision, his ability to make a clear-sighted judgment. He might even upset the balance in the minds of other jurors with irrelevant details of the exact nature of this disability.

Law, love, language—the peculiar, double-edged sword of sight never leaves us alone. It's fear, of course, Americans' fear of blindness is second only to their fear of cancer, and as ancient as the fear of darkness. So these constant references to blindness, equating it with stupidity, narrow-mindedness, or evil, are a verbal game of chicken. Taunt the fates. Name the demon you fear and insult it. It's a way perpetually to reanimate the fear, keep the sense of dread alive. This is why the clichés seem always fresh. At the same time, calling justice and love blind is a dire warning. There's more here than meets the eye, but what meets the eye is still what matters most. Look deeper. Watch carefully. Don't blink. Use it or lose it.

The fear of blindness leads naturally to the fear of the blind. The competent and independent blind pose a particular threat to the sighted, and they can't refrain from comment. Every blind person is familiar with the praise. "You manage so well," the sighted coo. They go into raptures over the simplest tasks: our ability to recognize them from their voices, to eat spaghetti, to unlock a door. They are so utterly convinced of the absolute necessity of sight, and the absolute helplessness of the blind, that any display of independence makes them wonder how well they would fare. "I'd never guess you were blind," they say, a slight edge of resentment coming into their tone now. They label us exceptional and secretly suspect some unseen force prompting our response, guiding our hands. Since they can see with their own eyes that there are no strings, no mirrors, they are compelled to reinvent the ancient myths about compensatory powers, supersensory perception. The sixth sense, second sight. We are supposed to have both extra-accurate hearing and perfect pitch, more numerous and more acute taste buds, a finer touch, a bloodhound's sense of smell. We allegedly possess an unfair advantage, which we could use against the sighted, hearing the secrets in their sighs, smelling their fear. We are either supernatural or subhuman, alien or animal. We are not only different but dangerous. But when we express any of this, they scoff: "Don't be silly. I can see you as you really are. You don't scare me. You're just being oversensitive." 30

It's so much simpler to deal with the blind beggar in the subway. The sighted can pity him and fear becoming like him. Specifically, they fear the absolute dependence he represents, dependence on his dog, on family, educators, social workers, public and private charities, strangers. This dread may be particularly pronounced in Americans, driven as we are by ideals of individual freedom and self-determination. Being blind is un-American. Our national anthem asks a question the blind can only answer in the negative. "No. I cannot see it. The dawn's early light is too feeble. The rocket's red glare was too fleeting to prove anything to me." The National Federation of the Blind, the organization most concerned with the civil rights and political status of the blind, schedules its annual convention to coincide with Independence Day. To the tune of "The Battle Hymn of the Republic" they sing: "Blind eyes have seen the vision / Of the Federalist way. . . ." When the National Library Service began to offer recorded books for the blind in the 1930s, the first offerings included not only the Bible and some works of Shakespeare, but the

American Constitution and Declaration of Independence, perhaps in an effort to educate and patriate a population already at the farthest periphery of the American scene.

A major part of the American fear of blindness has to do with driving. "It's not just your car; it's your freedom," one car ad proclaimed recently. Thus, if you can't drive, your freedom, your enjoyment of the great American open road, will be seriously restricted. Growing up in New York City, I was spared awareness of this aspect of my disability until I was an adult. I could get wherever I wanted to go on public transportation or on foot, as all my peers did. In other parts of the country, teenagers who, because of impaired sight or other conditions, cannot join in the automotive rites of passage of driver's ed classes and road tests, experience shame and an increased sense of isolation. Since most American cities and towns today sprawl outward from abandoned downtowns, the inability to drive is not only a handicap but an oddity that demands explanation. Public transit and special transportation for the disabled are haphazard at best. Even in places where there is decent public transit, most of the riders are people who do not own or cannot drive a car. A fellow transplanted New Yorker expressed her surprise about riding the bus in Columbus, Ohio. "It's not like New York, where everybody rides the bus. Here, everybody on the bus is . . ." she paused, searching for an inoffensive phrase. "People who ride the bus here are not. . . ." She stopped again, conscious suddenly that the word she wanted was "normal." Because in America today, *normal* means not only to see, to hear, to walk, to talk, to possess an average IQ and income, but also to drive.

But the fear of blindness is international, and goes beyond a fear of the inconveniences of personal transport. In the simplest terms, the fear is linked to the fear of old age and death. Since blindness equals darkness in most people's eyes, and darkness equals death, the final equation seems to follow as inevitably as the ones linking sight and light and life. In this view, blindness is as good as death. When I was eleven, after my condition was diagnosed, I wrote a poem about death. Memory has kindly erased all but the bouncy lines: "I've just been told, I'm getting old. / I don't want to die." But I do remember knowing what I was really writing about was blindness. My fear, only barely acknowledged, was that, like Bette Davis in *Dark Victory,* my lost sight was simply a sign of imminent death. The belief that human experience, both physical and mental, is essentially visual, and any other type of experience is necessarily second-rate, leads to the conclusion that not to see is not to experience, not to live, not to be. At best, the sighted imagine blindness as a state between life and death, an existence encased in darkness, an invisible coffin.

As overextended as this logic may be, the fact remains that the most common causes of blindness tend to occur late in life, thus close to death. Two-thirds of the legally blind in America are over age fifty-five. Cells atrophy. Irregular blood pressure does damage. Even a relatively minor stroke can affect the vision centers of the brain. Macular degeneration affects ten percent of Americans over seventy. Twenty-five percent develop cataracts. And this is not counting glaucoma, diabetes, nor accidents—projectiles, chemical spills, gunshot wounds. Of course some of these conditions can be corrected surgically, arrested in early stages, or controlled with drugs, and medical science continues to come up with new techniques, treatments, and cures. But there is no guarantee that vision disorders can only occur one at a time. Live long enough and, chances are, you'll go blind too.

You won't be alone. As more and more people live longer, the ranks of   35 the blind will swell. For the currently blind this is cause for, if not celebration, at least optimism. We imagine the blind becoming a more and more significant force, demanding services and rights, changing the image of blindness.

But this optimism is countered by the fact that we seem to be becoming more and more visually dependent. Television has replaced newspapers as the primary source of information. Movies replace novels. Image is everything. But as society becomes increasingly visual, it becomes more audio as well. The telephone and voice mail replace the letter. Technology will also increase the ease with which large print, braille, and recorded materials are made available. Multimedia databases which allow subscribers to access texts combined with images and sound will spawn technologies for blind-friendly talking computers and other appliances. Increased demand will drive down costs. As the desire to preserve the environment continues to grow, public transportation will become more fashionable, efficient, and widespread. If you have to go blind, you've chosen a good time to do it.

All this should be reassuring, or at least no more frightening than any reminder of mortality. And it's true that the elderly who lose their sight may have a harder time than the younger blind, because their loss may be complicated by other problems—lost hearing, lost agility, lost memory, lost financial security. But the possibility of blindness still summons a particular kind of fear. The currently sighted don't want to talk about it. They are unnaturally squeamish about the whole subject. They recoil from any mention of their eyes, their parts or functions. They're far more comfortable discussing comparatively cruder organs: the heart, the bowels, the genitals. They pick up scraps of information and use them as a shield. "Don't they have an operation to fix that?" they say. "Don't they use lasers or something?" Though they may know someone who had a cataract operation, they have a less than perfect understanding either of the condition or the procedure, and certainly don't want to hear it described in detail. If the patient had some trouble adjusting to the intra-ocular implants, or the retina detached and the laser repair only restored partial vision, they shrug and say, "Better than nothing. He's retired. How much does he have to see anyway?" They cross their fingers, knock on wood, ward off the evil eye. When it happens to them, they hope, the techniques will be perfected and the surgeons will be more careful.

The funny thing is, of all the things people fear—cancer, murder, rape, torture, loss of limb, loss of loved ones—blindness is the one anyone can simulate. Simply close your eyes. If you are so afraid of future dependence, why not break this absolute dependence you have on your eyesight? "But," you object, "real blindness is worse than that. With my eyes shut I can still perceive light." True. But given the degrees of blindness you are most likely to experience, you will probably see more than you do with your lids lowered. So go ahead. Close your eyes. It is not an unfamiliar condition for you. You experience it every time you blink. You are the same person with your eyes closed. You can still think, remember, feel. See? It's not so bad. You discover not that you hear better, but that you are better able to make sense of sounds. You hear children playing across the street. After only a minute or two you find you can distinguish their different voices, and follow their game from their words. An acorn falls on the roof of the garage next door. You know, without looking, that it is neither a pebble nor a pellet of hail. A branch rustles, and you know that a squirrel is running across it, jumping to another branch then down the trunk and away. You create a mental picture of this and it pleases you.

Now challenge yourself a little. Drop your pen on the floor. Even if the floor is carpeted you hear where it falls, you can reach down and find it. It may take you a couple of tries, but each time your aim improves. Gravity acts on objects the same way even when your eyes are closed.

Get up and move around the room. Don't be afraid. You know the arrangement of the furniture. Chances are, you arranged it yourself. You have a mental map of the room and use it to navigate. After only a few minor bumps and scrapes your mental map becomes more detailed and precise. You begin to move with assurance. You discover you do not lose your balance or become disoriented. You can reach out and touch a chair or the wall, or feel the breeze through the window, or hear sounds in other rooms. The mental map in your head is in motion. You move more rapidly now. Perhaps you run, skip. It occurs to you it might help if you were neater, if you weren't forever leaving things lying about where you might step on them. Or else you use your memory in new ways. You discover you can find your shoes because you re-create the moment when you took them off. In fact you always take them off there. You are more a creature of habit than you thought.

Go to your closet. Clothes you thought you could identify only by color and cut you find readily recognizable from their texture. And you can dress yourself with your eyes closed. You have lost none of the manual dexterity required to button buttons, zip zippers. Finding socks to match may be tricky, except you may be someone who arranges your socks in some ordered sequence. Certainly you can imagine doing so. With a minimal amount of help and practice, you could do this.

40

In fact you discover you can accomplish most of your routine daily tasks with your eyes closed. That may be how you define them as routine. You can bathe, fix your hair. You find you don't really need to look at yourself in the mirror when you brush your teeth. A few tasks may require more thought: shaving, makeup, manicure. But your brain isn't impaired. You will come up with something.

And you can feed yourself with ease. You may be surprised by how easily the spoon finds your mouth, the cup your lip. You've been putting things in your mouth for many years now. Feeding yourself was one of your earliest feats of coordination and one which has long since ceased to be amazing, even to your parents.

This really isn't as terrible as you were always led to believe. You can make a list of the things which are impossible to do with your eyes closed, but the list is not very long. And with a little more thought and perhaps some organizational tricks, you can take care of yourself and even others—pets, children. Your problem-solving capacities are as sharp as ever. You are already figuring out clever ways to arrange food in the refrigerator, sort the laundry, wash the windows.

You turn on the TV. You have probably already observed that it is not   45
really necessary to watch the TV. TV is aimed at people who are not as smart as you. You know what's going on even with your eyes closed.

But maybe you're more in the mood for music. Perhaps you already keep records, tapes, and CDs in chronological, alphabetical, or some other order. Perhaps you wish you did and now have an incentive to do so. Or perhaps you enjoy randomness, a trial-and-error selection. And there's always the radio. You can tune the dial to find something you like. You may even feel like dancing. Go ahead.

You have cause to celebrate. You have faced one of your more debilitating fears and seen it for what it is. This is not to say that the loss of sight will not be traumatic, nor that there are things about the visible world which you will miss. But blindness does not in itself constitute helplessness. You will be as resourceful, capable, and intelligent as you ever were.

But suddenly you're not dancing anymore. The fear creeps back and overtakes you. It occurs to you slowly that you will not be alone in this. Your blindness will affect other people—family, friends, co-workers, strangers— and you are afraid they will not adapt as well as you. You worry that well-meaning loved ones will start doing everything for you, that they will refer to your condition as tragic, use hushed tones when they think you can't hear, display exaggerated cheerfulness when you can. If you're in school you worry that "special" classes will not provide you with the education you need. You have the nagging suspicion that teachers and counselors will want to guide your choices in ways that do not fully acknowledge your aptitudes, but only your limitations. You wonder if your employers value you enough to purchase equipment or hire staff to assist you, if they will do so grudgingly and only because the law obliges them. If you quit a job will someone else hire you? You're afraid that people on the street will stare at you or offer help when you don't need it. And when you need help, you're afraid people will mislead you, take unfair advantage, rob you blind.

Face it. What you fear is not your inability to adapt to the loss of sight, it is the inability of people around you to see you the same way. It's not you, it's them. And it's not because you have an unduly malevolent view of human nature. Nor are you guiltily acknowledging this prejudice in yourself. You may not see it as prejudice. Pity and solicitude are not the same as prejudice, you assert. The disabled should be a little more gracious. But the words stick in your throat. You know that's not the only response people have to the disabled.

Once Nick and I took a flight from Paris to Dallas. A man carried a   50
young woman on board and placed her in the seat in front of us. Then he returned with her wheelchair, which she dismantled and arranged in a nearby closet. Then the man left. After take-off, the flight crew discovered that the woman was traveling alone, which was against regulations. The gate agent should have prevented her from boarding. There was a great deal of debate and bustle, complicated by the fact that the woman spoke no English and only one or two crew members spoke French. They questioned her at length. Why had no one stopped her? They briefed her on the airline's responsibilities, the safety of other passengers which her presence on board impaired. What had she been thinking? They did not adopt any of the obvious solutions. They did not move her to an empty seat in first class, where a less-burdened crew member could serve her without imperiling the comfort of others. Instead, they opted for what is too often the first response of the able-bodied to the disabled: they ignored her. Throughout the long flight they rushed past her, greeting her requests for help, when they heard them at all, with surly admonitions about the needs of other passengers and their busy schedule. After a while she started to cry. She cried so hard she made herself sick. We and some other passengers tried to pitch in, but the shock of witnessing this cruelty made us ashamed and somewhat inept. But the woman had astonishing fortitude and cheered up. She was a swimmer, on her way to the Special Olympics. She had never been to America before, and her treatment on this airplane made her understandably apprehensive. We discussed the treatment of the disabled in our respective countries. She said her sense was that Americans tended to warehouse and conceal their disabled. Her exact sentence was: "Les handicappés sont moins visible aux Etas-Unis." One's patriotism flares at odd moments. I began to point out that I had never observed excessive concern for people's disabilities in Paris. High curbs and cobbled streets would be hazards to wheelchairs and crutches. I'd never noticed ramps in public buildings, kneeling buses, braille buttons in elevators. Once I tried to buy a large-print dictionary, a request met with the highest degree of Gallic stupefaction in every bookshop I tried. Was it possible that

anyone could not read regular print? But the swimmer was from Bordeaux, where conditions might be better. And I knew that any claims I might make about facilities and services in the United States would seem ludicrous to her after the mistreatment she'd experienced.

And I did not tell her that the airlines have been a battleground for the blind for the last two decades. As the blind, like other Americans, began to fly more and more, the airlines and the Federal Aviation Administration adopted regulations to deal with them. Blind activists have been forcibly removed from airplanes for refusing to give up their white canes. The airlines saw the canes as a hazard to other passengers. "You might poke out someone's eye." In fact, there is a well-documented case of an emergency crash landing where a blind man was the first passenger to find and open an exit door. Accustomed as he was to navigating without eyesight, a little smoke and darkness were no obstacle to him. Today, the FAA has amended its policies, though individual airlines and flight crews sometimes still discriminate.

At the end of the flight, the crew reassembled around the French swimmer, ready to whisk her through immigration and into the hands of whoever was in charge, presumably with more reprimands and warnings. They were profuse in their thanks and praise to Nick and me and the other passengers who had helped her or, as they saw it, helped them. As we approached solid ground again, they felt a need to reestablish the us/them divide, and so efface any error or atrocity on their part. They wanted us to know they understood the ordeal we'd been through, thrown together with such a person. We, after all, like them, were normal. She was the aberration. Because my disability was invisible to them, I squeaked by undetected. Now, I am ashamed I didn't announce myself. At the time, I was too disturbed, too depressed, too frightened. I doubt it would have made them revise their views.

If the mistreatment of people with disabilities were limited to overzealous solicitude and an insensitive use of language, one could be more gracious. But everyone has witnessed the reality. Special treatment leads to resentment, which prompts ridicule, which barely conceals hate, and in extreme cases, suggests annihilation. Don't forget that in Hitler's vision of a perfect world there was no place for the blind, the deaf, the crippled, the mentally deficient. These views are still held, if, for now, only in secret. "Don't stare," parents warn a child watching a blind person with a cane, a deaf person speaking sign language, a person in a wheelchair. Don't stare. Don't look at that. Close your eyes and it will go away. Out of sight, out of mind. The child receives two messages: first, that people with disabilities should be ignored, pushed to the periphery of society, if not over the edge. And the parent reinforces yet again the idea of the preeminence of sight, the Almighty Eye which controls both consciousness and the world outside. What you can't see can't hurt you, can't matter, doesn't exist.

Which is why I call it blindness. When I identify myself in this way on the first day of class, it is perhaps presumptuous, an assertion of solidarity I have not earned because I see too much. But I hope by using the word I can help my students redefine it and, in some small way, correct their vision of the world. Of the students who drop my class after the first meeting, there may be some who find the idea of a blind professor ludicrous, aggravating, or frightening. But I will never know. The ones who stay adapt. They stand in my office doorway and identify themselves by name. They describe what's going on outside the window. They read me the slogans on their T-shirts. These gestures become natural to them. I tell them if they commit a crime in my presence I would not be able to pick them out of a police lineup. They indulge me with laughter. I have a conversation with one student about being a blind writer. He wants to know how I can describe things I cannot see. I explain how I question the sighted people I know about what they can see from what distance. We laugh. We talk about memory, how I can still recall what things look like from before I lost my sight, and how I use memory and imagination in the same way any writer does. He is a psychology major. We discuss visual perception. He tells me he knows a blind painter and describes how he manages. We are comfortable. We exchange these ideas with matter-of-fact ease. His question is not condescending or prying, not the "How ever do you possibly manage?" of the ignorant and insensitive. Another student talks about an anecdote I told in class, one of those extended narratives any teacher uses to make an obscure point. The anecdote made sense to him, he tells me, then adds, "And while you were talking, I looked around the room and everybody was just staring. They were all really into it." And for a moment I see this, creating the mental picture which goes with the words. The student sees me do this, but adds no embellishment. His subtle, unadorned generosity moves me.

This is how it's supposed to be, the whole point about integration,   55
mainstreaming, inclusion. They accept me and forget I ever used the ugly word. And perhaps later, the word will cease to seem so ugly.

Perhaps it doesn't matter what words you use as long as you know what you mean. On the bus recently a man stopped the driver, saying, "Yo! There's a little handicap' brother wants to get on." The word *handicap* is in disfavor, despite the fact that in horse racing or golf, it is the most skillful competitor who carries the heaviest handicap. Still, *disabled* and *challenged* are more in vogue. But there on the bus no one challenged the man's use of the word. He was a big man, over six feet tall. His voice boomed out of his chest and had more than a hint of a threat in it. Besides, we all knew what he meant. It was early in the afternoon, an hour when everyone on the bus is challenged in some way: physically, developmentally, financially, chronologically. Simply by being on the bus we announce our difference, our specialness, our handicap.

The bus knelt. The handicapped brother got on. He was not in a wheelchair. He was about three and a half feet tall. His whole body rocked from side to side as he propelled himself forward. He belly-flopped into a seat, flipped, and sat. I could not see him well enough to give a name to his condition. The man who had stopped the bus made no move to assist him further. But he waited, watching him, and said, "I saved it for you, brother." His voice was full of defiance, the bravado that comes from a bond of shared identity. In his words was a challenge to anyone who dared come between them.

The man who spoke was African-American. The handicapped brother was not. The bond between them, between us all at that moment, was the bus.

The handicapped brother said "Thank you" with the deft graciousness of someone who regularly accepts assistance from strangers. The other man found a seat. The driver pulled the bus into traffic. The rest of us settled into a comfortable contemplation of our shared humanity and mutual acceptance. Those of us who could gazed through the window, looking down at the un-challenged in their cars, complacent in their independence, their unobstructed door-to-door mobility. Someday some of them will join us on the bus—sooner rather than later, given the way some of them drive. When it happens, we will do what we can for them. We'll give up our seat. We'll announce their stop, reach for the button to ring the bell, take an extra moment to explain. We've been riding the bus long enough to sense what's needed. The bus lurched and stalled in a snarl of traffic. Someone groaned. Someone laughed. We were not fooled. The bus is no more perfect than the world outside. But that day it felt right to us. It was where we all belonged. And eventually, with a shudder, another lurch, we moved forward, and, unsteadily at first but picking up speed, we bounced along together.

QUESTIONING THE TEXT

1. Kleege gives examples of the positive connotations associated with vi-sion and sight ("seeing is believing," "that vision thing," "a picture is worth a thousand words," "seeing eye to eye") and the negative conno-tations associated with blindness ("blind alley," "blind rage," "blind leading the blind," "blind to their needs"). Brainstorm other words and phrases to add to these lists and bring them to class for discussion. How do these words and phrases suggest that society values sight and blind-ness?

2. The word *fear* reverberates like a drumbeat throughout this essay. Reread the essay, noting all the uses of *fear* and related words. What ex-actly is it that people fear? Write one or two paragraphs in response to this question and bring them to class for discussion.

3. Why do you think A.L. opens her introduction with a personal anec-dote? What effect(s) might she hope to create by doing so?

MAKING CONNECTIONS

4. Read P. J. O'Rourke's "Review of *Guidelines for Bias-Free Writing*" (p. 424). Do you find any use of metaphors of vision/sight or blindness/darkness that Georgina Kleege has mentioned? Make a list and bring them to class.

5. At the end of her essay, after describing a scene in one of her classes, Kleege says, "This is how it's supposed to be, the whole point about integration, mainstreaming, inclusion. They accept me and forget I ever used the ugly word. And perhaps later, the word will cease to seem so ugly." Using this statement as a starting point, write a letter to P. J. O'Rourke or Richard Bernstein in which you try to explain Kleege's point to him.

JOINING THE CONVERSATION

6. Take up the challenge that Kleege issues on pp. 403–404. Close your eyes and carry out the tasks she describes. Then write a description of your experience, ending with a discussion of Kleege's claim that "You can make a list of the things which are impossible to do with your eyes closed, but the list is not very long." Bring your description to class to compare with those of classmates.

STANLEY CROUCH

Another Long Drink of the Blues: The Race Card in the Simpson Case

ANDREA AND I initially resisted including a piece on the O. J. Simpson trial in this book. The legal and judicial spectacle that ended with Simpson's acquittal of the murders of his former wife Nicole Brown and Ronald Goldman disturbed and dispirited many people—perhaps because the 1995 trial ultimately had so little to do with truth and justice. But precisely because the event touched the national psyche so deeply, its questions of race, wealth, and abuse of power roiling in a torrent of media hype, Americans cannot ignore its consequences if they are ever to deal with issues now so clearly separating them, black and white. Although we walk the same streets, we cannot say we live in the same cities governed by the same laws.

Perhaps we shouldn't have been surprised by the outcome. Well before the trial began, Stanley Crouch (b. 1945), former critic for the Village Voice *and one of the nation's most influential commentators on jazz, published a piece in the* Los Angeles Times *predicting a defense strategy that would portray Simpson as the victim of yet another "high-tech lynching" by a white power structure. Crouch foresaw, too, how black jurists might react to a police investigation that featured an officer as controversial as Mark Fuhrman. He anticipated that something more than a former running back for the Buffalo Bills would be on trial in Los Angeles. Crouch's prescient essay follows, reprinted from his provocative book* The All-American Skin Game *(1995). − J.R.*

> This was published in the *Los Angeles Times* on July 31, 1994, long before the formal murder trial began and long before sustained media involvement had made the case parallel in attention to the Vietnam War or the Watergate hearings. I include it here because this was the first piece that looked at the Simpson case in light of the many things about our society that it brought into view. The all-American reality of the context, which stretched out in so many directions, was made clear in this short essay. For perhaps the first time in my career, all of the predictions came true, regardless of the many twists that were beyond not only my imagination but everyone's.

With the O.J. Simpson case, we are allowed another chance to recognize how fallacious is the idea that black Americans are some perpetually excluded group forced to watch the parade of the society from behind a barbed wire fence. If anything, the Simpson story is further proof of the fact that black Americans are at the center of our national tale, functioning both as flesh and blood movers and metaphors in the ongoing democratic debate that redefines our policies and our attitudes toward our political, professional, and intimate lives.

The impact of Afro-American culture and the Civil Rights Movement has touched us everywhere, from the dance floor to the senatorial debate. In professional athletics, Curt Flood was the martyr who led the way to the presently acceptable idea of free agentry, destroying his career in the process. Army sergeant Perry Watkins was the first homosexual that I became aware of who was openly willing to take on the military. Now, because of the Simpson case, the ravages of domestic violence have risen into high media view, just as deep questions of sexual harassment came with the charges Anita Hill laid on Clarence Thomas.

So it is impossible to discuss issues of freedom and fair play with any seriousness and not recognize the ways in which black Americans have indelibly influenced our attitudes and policies. It is also impossible to pretend that victimization has not become a growth industry. We make most-favored-victim laws, we hire separatist boneheads onto our university faculties, we tailor our history to self-flagellating theories, experience the national Peeping Tom craze for geeks on talk television, and slip through our problems on the snake oil of recovery experts.

That is why the Simpson case is so loaded. It is fused to a complexity that will play itself out in everything from eloquence to lunacy, high-mindedness to opportunism, as the trial progresses. The charges against him, and what we think we now know about his world, put us smack dab in the middle of our schizophrenic suspicion of privilege and our "wish for kings," as Lewis Lapham calls it. Simpson's American dream wealth was made possible by the gold rush aspect of our society that we most often see in the worlds of popular entertainment and drug dealing.

Though he had an objective talent that separated him from the stars of   5
pop music and movies, Simpson moved from the back of the bus to the wheel by playing a boy's game, which meant that he excelled in the excessively celebrated adolescent world of sports. His generosity as an athlete was displayed when he brought the offensive line that blocked for him to his locker room interviews, clarifying the importance of the team to his achievements. He was the strong, nearly silent type, low-keyed and marvelous at his game.

With the blood-encrusted gore of the murders and the inevitable snooping into the darker sides of his intimate life, Simpson joined the long line of figures whose private lives have a dissonant relationship to their public images. Though race wasn't discussed at first, there was always a media code. The murdered ex-wife was endlessly referred to as "the beautiful, blonde Nicole," while he was never described as "the handsome, brown, wooly-headed O.J."

Some dismiss her description as typical mass media sexism of the sort re-served for blondes and redheads. They are partially correct because the blonde has had an unnaturally high position in our erotic iconography since the per-oxide explosion of the thirties. But it is also true that her color was underlined in code because she was half of an interracial couple living in a world whisper-close to those deep-dipped in the decadence and melodrama of upper-class soap operas. Finally, there must be, in the wake of so many black brutes in the popular work of writers like Alice Walker* and Toni Morrison,* the question of whether this is what any woman should be pre-pared for from one of *them,* rich or poor, famous nor nameless.

In a court of law, none of these things should matter. It would be pretty to think so, but once it is possible to play the race trump in a city that has the recent history of Los Angeles, one shouldn't be surprised to hear the card loudly smack the media table. Still, the ways in which race, class, sex, and ideas about racial allegiance can influence potential jurors, law enforcement, and the legal process itself are much more complicated than their surfaces would suggest.

Because of affirmative action, whites seem more bothered when execu-tive positions are held by mediocre or incompetent black people than by their white parallels; the sustained, murderous barbarism of black street crime strains past tolerance to simmering hostility within the most exasperated; and the flippant hedonism of the worst upper-class black party animals instigates envy and resentment, even in certain police officers.

That is why the dirt on Detective Mark Fuhrman won't be taken   10
lightly. His alleged hostility toward Mexicans and "niggers" in 1983, his sup-posed membership in a group presently opposed to female police officers, the whispered allegations of sexual harassment, and his imperious bending of the Fourth Amendment by scaling the wall of Simpson's estate, rerun all of the vilest stereotypes of the Los Angeles Police Department. This makes the possibility of his planting the bloody glove plausible among those most wary of white men with badges and guns.

Such elements give unfortunate weight to the racial admonishments put on District Attorney Garcetti by defense lawyer Johnnie Cochran and the Los Angeles civil rights establishment. A grand irony is that if Garcetti submits to the pressure and pushes for an integrated jury, black women could as easily be wild cards as not, given the resentment a large number feel toward successful black men who marry white women, thereby reducing the already limited pool available to them.

The television interview with Nicole Simpson's therapist in which the therapist said that the murdered woman told her that she enjoyed sparking her

---

Alice Walker (b. 1944): American novelist, author of *The Color Purple* (1982)
Toni Morrison (b. 1931): American novelist and winner of the Nobel Prize in Literature (1993). Author of *The Bluest Eye* (1969) and *Beloved* (1987).

ex-husband's jealousy could make some men think she was cruelly toying with the green-eyed monster in her hot black man and paid the consequences. It is possible, with Johnnie Cochran now on the defense team, that intimations of what Clarence Thomas called "a high-tech lynching" will maintain the constant and incantational undertone of a mantra. That will make it the prosecution's slippery job to prove otherwise.

So we end up in a big, fat, peculiarly American mess, the kind that allows us to understand why one writer said she would choose a good case of murder if her intent was to ascertain the broadest identity of a culture. In this case of blonde on black, omnipresent media magnification, wife-beating, sudden wealth, workout partners, golf courses, the disco life, Bentleys rolling into McDonald's, rumors of drug-spiced promiscuity, and the ugly punctuation marks of two bloody victims in a high-rent district, we are forced to examine almost everything that crosses the T's of our American lives. What we will finally learn, however, is the smell and the taste of another long drink of the blues.

QUESTIONING THE TEXT

1. Do any portions of Crouch's essay make you uneasy? Annotate those sentences and, if you keep a reading log, write about them there, explicating the nature of your discomfort.
2. How do you understand the term "the race card" as Crouch uses it and as other media commentators have employed it with respect to the Simpson trial?
3. Should A.L. and J.R. have followed their initial impulse—described in the introduction to this essay—not to include an essay on the Simpson trial? Why or why not?

MAKING CONNECTIONS

4. Read Zora Neale Hurston's essay (p. 366) alongside Crouch's essay, especially his final line: "What we will finally learn, however, is the smell and the taste of another long drink of the blues." Freewrite for 10 minutes on this juxtaposition, and then share your thoughts with a classmate.
5. In "Toward a New Politics of Hispanic Assimilation," Linda Chavez urges policies that would move Hispanics closer to what she regards as the mainstream of American life. In "Another Long Drink of the Blues," Crouch claims that African Americans "are at the center of our national tale, functioning both as flesh and blood movers and metaphors in the ongoing democratic debate." Are Chavez and Crouch talking

about the same sort of participation for minority groups in the United States? What goals might Chavez set for Hispanics? What role does Crouch foresee for African Americans? In a short essay, explore these questions.

JOINING THE CONVERSATION

6. In a letter to a friend teaching English in a remote foreign town (away from Western news sources), briefly explain the Simpson trial as you saw it.
7. Write a research report focusing on the media attention paid to another noteworthy American trial of this century. How did the media react to the trial and its outcome? Did the case provoke divided feelings among the general public? Were biases obvious in the news coverage? Did coverage intrude into the trial itself?

LINDA CHAVEZ
Toward a New Politics of Hispanic Assimilation

HISPANIC IS A TERM *adopted by federal bureaucrats to describe people in the United States who speak Spanish but who often have little else in common. Falling under the Hispanic rubric are Puerto Ricans, heavily concentrated in the Northeast; Cuban Americans, predominantly in Florida; immigrant Mexicans in Texas and California; people of Mexican and Spanish ancestry native to all portions of the Southwest; refugees from El Salvador and Nicaragua; and immigrants from other Latin American countries. Although it obscures significant cultural and political differences, the Hispanic (some prefer "Latino") label confers political clout on this group as a sizable minority in the United States, second in number only to African Americans.*

In "Toward a New Politics of Hispanic Assimilation," the last chapter of her book Out of the Barrio *(1991), Linda Chavez describes the reluctance of various Hispanic leaders to champion the path of assimilation followed by immigrants to the United States from Germany, Ireland, Poland, China, and elsewhere. Unlike their leaders, however, most Hispanics are eager to enter the American mainstream, Chavez claims, and they are succeeding in great numbers.*

Chavez (b. 1947) is a senior fellow of the Manhattan Institute for Policy Research and a former member of the U.S. Commission on Civil Rights. In 1986, she ran as a Republican for a U.S. Senate seat from Maryland. I chose to include this reading because Chavez provides an alternative to the mainstream view of minorities as people struggling without hope within a hostile system. She suggests that the political and social destinies of Hispanics are, like those of other minority groups who shaped this country, in their own hands— an empowering and radical notion these days. – J.R.

Assimilation has become a dirty word in American politics. It invokes images of people, cultures, and traditions forged into a colorless alloy in an indifferent melting pot. But, in fact, assimilation, as it has taken place in the United States, is a far more gentle process, by which people from outside the community gradually become part of the community itself. Descendants of the German, Irish, Italian, Polish, Greek, and other immigrants who came to the United States bear little resemblance to the descendants of the countrymen their forebears left behind. America changed its immigrant groups—and was changed by them. Some groups were accepted more reluctantly than

415

others—the Chinese, for example—and some with great struggle. Blacks, whose ancestors were forced to come here, have only lately won their legal right to full participation in this society; and even then civil rights gains have not been sufficiently translated into economic gains. Until quite recently, however, there was no question but that each group desired admittance to the mainstream. No more. Now ethnic leaders demand that their groups remain separate, that their native culture and language be preserved intact, and that whatever accommodation takes place be on the part of the receiving society.

Hispanic leaders have been among the most demanding, insisting that Hispanic children be taught in Spanish; that Hispanic adults be allowed to cast ballots in their native language and that they have the right to vote in districts in which Hispanics make up the majority of voters; that their ethnicity entitle them to a certain percentage of jobs and college admissions; that immigrants from Latin America be granted many of these same benefits, even if they are in the country illegally. But while Hispanic leaders have been pressing these claims, the rank and file have been moving quietly and steadily into the American mainstream. Like the children and grandchildren of millions of ethnic immigrants before them, virtually all native-born Hispanics speak English—many speak only English. The great majority finish high school, and growing numbers attend college. Their earnings and occupational status have been rising along with their education. But evidence of the success of native-born Hispanics is drowned in the flood of new Latin immigrants—more than five million—who have come in the last two decades, hoping to climb the ladder as well. For all of these people, assimilation represents the opportunity to succeed in America. Whatever the sacrifices it entails—and there are some—most believe that the payoff is worth it. Yet the elites who create and influence public policy seem convinced that the process must be stopped or, where this has already occurred, reversed.

From 1820 to 1924 the United States successfully incorporated a population more ethnically diverse and varied than any other in the world. We could not have done so if today's politics of ethnicity had been the prevailing ethos. Once again, we are experiencing record immigration, principally from Latin America and Asia. The millions of Latin immigrants who are joining the already large native-born Hispanic population will severely strain our capacity to absorb them, unless we can revive a consensus for assimilation. But the new politics of Hispanic assimilation need not include the worst features of the Americanization era. Children should not be forced to sink or swim in classes in which they don't understand the language of instruction. The model of Anglo conformity would seem ridiculous today in a country in which 150 million persons are descended from people who did not come here from the British Isles. We should not be tempted to shut our doors because we fear the newcomers are too different from us ever to become truly "American." Nonetheless, Hispanics will be obliged to make some adjustments if they are to accomplish what other ethnic groups have.

LANGUAGE AND CULTURE

Most Hispanics accept the fact that the United States is an English-speaking country; they even embrace the idea. A *Houston Chronicle* poll in 1990 found that 87 percent of all Hispanics believed that it was their "duty to learn English" and that a majority believed English should be adopted as an official language.[1] Similar results have been obtained in polls taken in California, Colorado, and elsewhere. But Hispanics, especially more recent arrivals, also feel it is important to preserve their own language. Nearly half the Hispanics in the *Houston Chronicle* poll thought that people coming from other countries should preserve their language and teach it to their children. There is nothing inconsistent in these findings, nor are the sentiments expressed unique to Hispanics. Every immigrant group has struggled to retain its language, customs, traditions. Some groups have been more successful than others. A majority of Greek Americans, for example, still speak Greek in their homes at least occasionally.[2] The debate is not about whether Hispanics, or any other group, have the right to retain their native language but about whose responsibility it is to ensure that they do so.

The government should not be obliged to preserve any group's distinctive language or culture. Public schools should make sure that all children can speak, read, and write English well. When teaching children from non–English-speaking backgrounds, they should use methods that will achieve English proficiency quickly and should not allow political pressure to interfere with meeting the academic needs of students. No children in an American school are helped by being held back in their native language when they could be learning the language that will enable them to get a decent job or pursue higher education. More than twenty years of experience with native-language instruction fails to show that children in these programs learn English more quickly or perform better academically than children in programs that emphasize English acquisition.

If Hispanic parents want their children to be able to speak Spanish and know about their distinctive culture, they must take the responsibility to teach their children these things. Government simply cannot—and should not—be charged with this responsibility. Government bureaucracies given the authority to create bicultural teaching materials homogenize the myths, customs, and history of the Hispanic peoples of this hemisphere, who, after all, are not a single group but many groups. It is only in the United States that "Hispanics" exist; a Cakchiquel Indian in Guatemala would find it remarkable

[1]Jo Ann Zuniga, "87% in Poll See Duty to Learn English," *Houston Chronicle,* July 12, 1990.

[2]Commission on Civil Rights, *The Economic Status of Americans of Southern and Eastern European Ancestry* (Washington, D.C.: GPO, 1986), 45.

that anyone could consider his culture to be the same as a Spanish Argentinean's. The best way for Hispanics to learn about their native culture is in their own communities. Chinese, Jewish, Greek, and other ethnic communities have long established after-school and weekend programs to teach language and culture to children from these groups. Nothing stops Hispanic organizations from doing the same things. And, indeed, many Hispanic community groups around the country promote cultural programs. In Washington, D.C., groups from El Salvador, Guatemala, Colombia, and elsewhere sponsor soccer teams, fiestas, parades throughout the year, and a two-day celebration in a Latin neighborhood that draws crowds in the hundreds of thousands.[3] The Washington Spanish Festival is a lively, vibrant affair that makes the federal government's effort to enforce Hispanic Heritage Month in all of its agencies and departments each September seem pathetic by comparison. The sight and sound of mariachis strolling through the cavernous halls of the Department of Labor as indifferent federal workers try to work above the din is not only ridiculous; it will not do anything to preserve Mexican culture in the United States.

Hispanics should be interested not just in maintaining their own, distinctive culture but in helping Latin immigrants adjust to their American environment and culture as well. Too few Hispanic organizations promote English or civics classes, although the number has increased dramatically since the federal government began dispensing funds for such programs under the provisions of the Immigration Reform and Control Act, which gives amnesty to illegal aliens on the condition that they take English and civics classes.[4] But why shouldn't the Hispanic community itself take some responsibility to help new immigrants learn the language and history of their new country, even without government assistance? The settlement houses of the early century thrived without government funds. The project by the National Association

---

[3]In May 1991, a riot broke out in a Latino neighborhood in Washington, D.C., where many new immigrants live (many of them illegal aliens). Both the local and national media described the two nights of arson and looting in political terms, as an expression of the alienation of the Hispanic community. In fact, fewer than half of the people arrested during the incident were Hispanic; most were young black males from a nearby neighborhood. There were few injuries and no deaths, and much criticism was directed at the police by local residents for standing by while young men looted stores, many of which were owned by Latinos. The Washington, D.C., metropolitan area is home to nearly a quarter of a million Hispanics, more than 80 percent of whom live in the suburbs of the city, far from the neighborhood where this incident occurred. Nonetheless, national Hispanic leaders, including members of the Hispanic Congressional delegation, flocked to the scene of the violence to portray as typical of the area's Latino population the problems which occurred in the few blocks of this urban settlement of recent immigrants.

[4]For fiscal year 1989 the federal government distributed nearly $200 million in grants to state and local governments to assist in providing English and civics classes for adults and other services for those eligible for amnesty.

of Latino Elected and Appointed Officials (NALEO) to encourage Latin immigrants to become U.S. citizens is the exception among Hispanic organizations; it should become the rule.

POLITICAL PARTICIPATION

The real barriers to Hispanic political power are apathy and alienage. Too few native-born Hispanics register and vote; too few Hispanic immigrants become citizens. The way to increase real political power is not to gerrymander districts to create safe seats for Hispanic elected officials or treat illegal aliens and other immigrants as if their status were unimportant to their political representation; yet those are precisely the tactics Hispanic organizations have urged lately. Ethnic politics is an old and honored tradition in the United States. No one should be surprised that Hispanics are playing the game now, but the rules have been changed significantly since the early century. One analyst has noted, "In the past, ethnic leaders were obliged to translate raw numbers into organizational muscle in the factories or at the polls. . . . In the affirmative-action state, Hispanic leaders do not require voters, or even protestors—only bodies."[5] This is not healthy, for Hispanics or the country.

Politics has traditionally been a great equalizer. One person's vote was as good as another's, regardless of whether the one was rich and the other poor. But politics requires that people participate. The great civil rights struggles of the 1960s were fought in large part to guarantee the right to vote. Hispanic leaders demand representation but do not insist that individual Hispanics participate in the process. The emphasis is always on rights, never on obligations. Hispanic voter organizations devote most of their efforts toward making the process easier—election law reform, postcard registration, election materials in Spanish—to little avail; voter turnout is still lower among Hispanics than among blacks or whites. Spanish posters urge Hispanics to vote because it will mean more and better jobs and social programs, but I've never seen one that mentions good citizenship. Hispanics (and others) need to be reminded that if they want the freedom and opportunity democracy offers, the least they can do is take the time to register and vote. These are the lessons with which earlier immigrants were imbued, and they bear reviving.

Ethnic politics was for many groups a stepping-stone into the mainstream. Irish, Italian, and Jewish politicians established political machines that drew their support from ethnic neighborhoods; and the machines, in turn, provided jobs and other forms of political patronage to those who helped elect them. But eventually, candidates from these ethnic groups went beyond

10

---

[5]Peter Skerry, "Keeping Immigrants in the Political Sweatshops," *Wall Street Journal,* Nov. 6, 1989.

ethnic politics. Governor Mario Cuomo (D) and Senator Alfonse D'Amato (R) are both Italian American politicians from New York, but they represent quite different political constituencies, neither of which is primarily ethnically based. Candidates for statewide office—at least successful ones—cannot afford to be seen merely as ethnic representatives. Ethnic politics may be useful at the local level, but if Hispanic candidates wish to gain major political offices, they will have to appeal beyond their ethnic base. Those Hispanics who have already been elected as governors and U.S. senators (eight, so far) have managed to do so.

EDUCATION

Education has been chiefly responsible for the remarkable advancements most immigrant groups have made in this society. European immigrants from the early century came at a time when the education levels of the entire population were rising rapidly, and they benefited even more than the population of native stock, because they started from a much lower base. More than one-quarter of the immigrants who came during the years from 1899 to 1910 could neither read nor write.[6] Yet the grandchildren of those immigrants today are indistinguishable from other Americans in educational attainment; about one-quarter have obtained college degrees. Second- and third-generation Hispanics, especially those who entered high school after 1960, have begun to close the education gap as well. But the proportion of those who go on to college is smaller among native-born Hispanics than among other Americans, and this percentage has remained relatively constant across generations, at about 10–13 percent for Mexican Americans. If Hispanics hope to repeat the successful experience of generations of previous immigrant groups, they must continue to increase their educational attainment, and they are not doing so fast enough. Italians, Jews, Greeks, and others took dramatic strides in this realm, with the biggest gains in college enrollment made after World War II.[7] Despite more than two decades of affirmative action programs and federal student aid, college graduation rates among native-born Hispanics, not to mention immigrants, remain significantly below those among non-Hispanics.

The government can do only so much in promoting higher education for Hispanics or any group. It is substantially easier today for a Hispanic stu-

---

[6]Richard A. Easterlin, "Immigration: Economic and Social Characteristics," in Stephan Thernstrom, ed., *Harvard Encyclopedia of American Ethnic Groups* (Cambridge: Harvard University Press, 1981), 478.

[7]See Richard Alba, *Ethnic Identity: The Transformation of White America* (New Haven: Yale University Press, 1990), 7. Both men and women born after 1930 showed large gains, although the gains were higher for men, probably reflecting the increase in college attendance by veterans under the G.I. Bill.

dent to go to college than it was even twenty or thirty years ago, yet the proportion of Mexican Americans who are graduating from college today is unchanged from what it was forty years ago. When the former secretary of education Lauro Cavazos, the first Hispanic ever to serve in the Cabinet, criticized Hispanic parents for the low educational attainment of their children, he was roundly attacked for blaming the victim. But Cavazos's point was that Hispanic parents must encourage their children's educational aspirations and that, too often, they don't. Those groups that have made the most spectacular socioeconomic gains—Jews and Chinese, for example—have done so because their families placed great emphasis on education.

Hispanics cannot have it both ways. If they want to earn as much as non-Hispanic whites, they have to invest the same number of years in schooling as these do. The earnings gap will not close until the education gap does. Native-born Hispanics are already enjoying earnings comparable to those of non-Hispanic whites, once educational differences are factored in. If they want to earn more, they must become better educated. But education requires sacrifices, especially for persons from lower-income families. Poverty, which was both more pervasive and severe earlier in this century, did not prevent Jews or Chinese from helping their children get a better education. These families were willing to forgo immediate pleasures, even necessities, in order to send their children to school. Hispanics must be willing to do the same—or else be satisfied with lower socioeconomic status. The status of second- and third-generation Hispanics will probably continue to rise even without big gains in college graduation; but the rise will be slow. Only a substantial commitment to the education of their children on the part of this generation of Hispanic parents will increase the speed with which Hispanics improve their social and economic status.

ENTITLEMENTS

The idea of personal sacrifice is an anomaly in this age of entitlements. The rhetoric is all about rights. And the rights being demanded go far beyond the right to equality under the law. Hispanics have been trained in the politics of affirmative action, believing that jobs, advancement, and even political power should be apportioned on the basis of ethnicity. But the rationale for treating all Hispanics like a permanently disadvantaged group is fast disappearing. What's more, there is no ground for giving preference in jobs or promotions to persons who have endured no history of discrimination in this country—namely, recent immigrants. Even within Hispanic groups, there are great differences between the historical discrimination faced by Mexican Americans and Puerto Ricans and that faced by, say, Cubans. Most Hispanic leaders, though, are willing to have everyone included in order to increase the population eligible for the programs and, therefore, the proportion of jobs and academic placements that can be claimed. But these alliances are beginning to fray at the edges. Recently, a group of Mexican American firemen in San Francisco challenged the right of two Spanish Americans to participate in a department affirmative action program, claiming that the latter's European roots made them unlikely to have suffered discrimination comparable to that of other Hispanics. The group recommended establishing a panel of twelve Hispanics to certify who is and who is not Hispanic.[8] But that is hardly the answer.

Affirmative action politics treats race and ethnicity as if they were syn-   15
onymous with disadvantage. The son of a Mexican American doctor or lawyer is treated as if he suffered the same disadvantage as the child of a Mexican farm worker; and both are given preference over poor, non-Hispanic whites in admission to most colleges or affirmative action employment programs. Most people think this is unfair, especially white ethnics whose own parents and grandparents also faced discrimination in this society but never became eligible for the entitlements of the civil rights era. It is inherently patronizing to assume that all Hispanics are deprived and grossly unjust to give those who aren't preference on the basis of disadvantages they don't experience. Whether stated or not, the essence of affirmative action is the belief that Hispanics—or any of the other eligible groups—are not capable of measuring up to the standards applied to whites. This is a pernicious idea.

Ultimately, entitlements based on their status as "victims" rob Hispanics of real power. The history of American ethnic groups is one of overcoming disadvantage, of competing with those who were already here and proving themselves as competent as any who came before. Their fight was always to be treated the same as other Americans, never to be treated as special, certainly not to turn the temporary disadvantages they suffered into the basis for permanent entitlement. Anyone who thinks this fight was easier in the early part of this century when it was waged by other ethnic groups does not know history. Hispanics have not always had an easy time of it in the United States. Even though discrimination against Mexican Americans and Puerto Ricans was not as severe as it was against blacks, acceptance has come only with struggle, and some prejudices still exist.

Discrimination against Hispanics, or any other group, should be fought, and there are laws and a massive administrative apparatus to do so. But the way to eliminate such discrimination is not to classify all Hispanics as victims and treat them as if they could not succeed by their own efforts. Hispanics can and will prosper in the United States by following the example of the millions before them.

---

[8]"Spanish Progeny Are Not Hispanic, S. F. Group Insists," *San Diego Union,* Nov. 24, 1990. Ironically, both Spanish American firemen would have been promoted in the department even without benefit of affirmative action; they received the third- and sixth-highest scores on exams administered to sixty-eight persons for twenty promotion slots.

QUESTIONING THE TEXT

1. According to Chavez, what process statistically obscures the success of Hispanic assimilation into the United States?
2. What in Chavez's views might have made her so controversial that she was "disinvited" from speaking on several college campuses during the years (1983–85) she served on the U.S. Commission on Civil Rights? Who might have a vested interest in silencing her views?
3. Does J.R.'s introduction provide you with sufficient information about Chavez? What other information might you have liked to have?

MAKING CONNECTIONS

4. Compare the attitudes toward immigrant assimilation described or implied in Crèvecoeur's (p. 361) and Chavez's essays.
5. Read Langston Hughes's poem on p. 432. How does the poem speak to Chavez's comments about education for Hispanics? If you keep a reading log, answer this question there.

JOINING THE CONVERSION

6. Chavez argues that real economic progress for Hispanics will be stifled until their families place a greater emphasis on education. Is she just reciting a pious platitude, or can education make a difference? Write a narrative about the role education has played in your own life or that of your family. Then form a group with two or three classmates and compare your stories.
7. In class, discuss the implications of Chavez's assertion that "The government should not be obliged to preserve any group's distinctive language or culture." Then write a short position paper on the issue.

P. J. O'ROURKE
Review of Guidelines for Bias-Free Writing

*I*T'S TOUGH BEING A SENSITIVE GUY—*I mean person—these days. Choose the wrong pronoun (as in "God and his creation") and all the gals—I mean ladies— I mean women—start whining—I mean complaining. Try to be more gender sensitive (as in "Satan and her works") and those same dames—I mean persons of the superior sex—get royally p.o.'ed—I mean angry. And it gets worse when you try to talk about those dolts who can't program their VCRs.*

Imagine Christ preaching in this helpful and caring decade: Blessed are the poor for they shall receive earned income credits. Blessed are the meek for they shall get prompt assertiveness training. Blessed are they who suffer persecution for justice's sake for they shall receive whopping cash settlements!

As you see, I'm not as good at humor as P. J. O'Rourke (b. 1947), author, humorist, and frequent contributor to both Rolling Stone *and the* American Spectator. *In the following selection, originally published in the* American Spectator *in August 1995, O'Rourke prods the sacred cattle of academia with jolts of near-Shakespearean contumely. I chose to include O'Rourke's searing, sneering review to showcase invective as a literary form. O'Rourke's target is a guide to politically proper English published by the association of American University Presses entitled* Guidelines for Bias-Free Writing. *I think you'll find, in his review, O'Rourke lets fly the most splattering shots of ridicule since Falstaff's "you dried neat's tongue, you bull's pizzle, you stock-fish . . . you vile standing tuck." Honest, healthy—dare I say* manly?—*invective of a rip-roaring kind is all too rare these days; we'll need more of it if we're ever to clear the decks for discussing difference and diversity. So don't get mad at P. J., even if you're from Indiana University or in the trenches with the Task Force on Bias-Free Language—it's all in fun—if you have a sense of humor.* – J.R.

Says the press release that arrived with this volume, "Anyone who spends even a few minutes with the book will be a better writer." And, indeed, I feel a spate of better writing coming on. The pharisaical, malefic, and incogitant *Guidelines for Bias-Free Writing* is a product of the pointy-headed wowsers at the Association of American University Presses, who in 1987 established a "Task Force on Bias-Free Language" filled with cranks, pokenoses, blow-hards, four-flushers, and pettifogs. The foolish and contemptible product of this seven years wasted in mining the shafts of indignation has been published by that cow-besieged, basketball-sotted sleep-away

424

camp for hick bourgeois offspring, Indiana University, under the aegis of its University Press—a traditional dumping ground for academic deadwood so bereft of talent, intelligence, and endeavor as to be useless even in the dull precincts of Midwestern state college classrooms.

But perhaps I'm biased. What, after all, is wrong with a project of this ilk? Academic language is, I guess, supposed to be exact and neutral, a sort of mathematics of ideas, with information recorded in a complete and explicit manner, the record formulated into theories, and attempts made to prove those formulae valid or not. The preface to *Guidelines* says, "Our aim is simply to encourage sensitivity to usages that may be imprecise, misleading, and needlessly offensive." And few scholars would care to have their usages so viewed, myself excluded.

The principal author of the text, Ms. Schwartz . . . (I apologize. In the first chapter of *Guidelines,* titled "Gender," it says, in Section 1.41, lines 4–5: "Scholars normally refer to individuals solely by their full or their last names, omitting courtesy titles.")

The principal author of the text, Schwartz . . . (No, I'm afraid that won't do. Vid. Section 1.41, lines 23–25: "Because African-American women have had to struggle for the use of traditional courtesy titles, some prefer *Mrs.* or *Miss,*" and it would be biased to assume that Schwartz is a white name.)

Mrs. or Miss Marilyn Schwartz . . . (Gee, I'm sorry. Section 1.41, lines 1–2: "Most guidelines for nonsexist usage urge writers to avoid gratuitous references to the marital status of women.")   5

Anyway, as I was saying, Ms. Schwartz . . . (Excuse me. Lines 7–9: "*Ms.* may seem anachronistic or ironic if used for a woman who lived prior to the second U.S. feminist movement of the 1960s," and the head of the Task Force on Bias-Free Language may be, for all we know, old as the hills.)

So, Marilyn . . . (Oops. Section 1.42, lines 1–3: "Careful writers normally avoid referring to a woman by her first name alone because of the trivializing or condescending effect.")

And *that's* what's wrong with a project of this ilk.

Nonetheless, the principal author—What's-Her-Face—has crafted a smooth, good-tempered, even ingratiating tract. The more ridiculous neologisms and euphemistic expressions are shunned. Thieves are not "differently ethiced," women isn't spelled with any *y*'s, and men aren't "ovum-deprived reproductivity aids—optional equipment only." A tone of mollifying suggestion is used: "The following recommendations are not intended as prescriptive . . ." (Though in a project this bossy it is impossible for the imperative mood to completely disappear: "Writers must resort to gender-neutral alternatives where the common gender form has become strongly marked as masculine." Therefore, if the Fire Department's standards of strength and fitness are changed to allow sexual parity in hiring, I shall be careful to say that the person who was too weak and small to carry me down the ladder was a *fire fighter,* not a *fireman.*)

And pains are taken to extend linguistic sensitivity beyond the realms of   10
the fashionably oppressed to Christians ("Terms may be pejorative rather than descriptive in some contexts—*born again, cult, evangelical, fundamentalist, sect . . .*"), teenagers, and adolescents ("these terms may carry unwanted connotations because of their frequent occurrence in phrases referring to social and behavioral problems"), and even Republicans ("some married women . . . deplore *Ms.* because of its feminist connotations"). Levity is attempted. Once. This unattributed example of textbook prose is given to show just how funny a lack of feminism can be:

> Man, like other mammals, breast feeds his young.

A *mea culpa* turn is performed at the end of the preface:

> Finally, we realize—lest there be any misunderstanding about this—that there is no such thing as truly bias-free language and that our advice is inevitably shaped by our own point of view—that of white, North American (specifically U.S.), feminist publishing professionals.

And there is even an endearing little lapse on page 36:

> A judicious use of ellipses or bracketed interpolations may enable the author to *skirt the problem* [italics, let this interpolation note, are my own].

Why then do the laudable goals claimed and the reasonable tone taken in *Guidelines for Bias-Free Writing* provoke a no less laudable fury and a completely reasonable loathing in its reader? First, there is the overweening vanity of twenty-one obscure and unrenowned members of the Task Force on Bias-Free Language presuming to tell whole universities full of learned people what is and what is not an "unwarranted bias." No doubt in the future the Task Force will sit down and use feminist theory to map the genes in human DNA.

Then there is *petitio principii,* begging the question, the logical fallacy of assuming as true that which is to be proven. This book, a purported device to assist in truth-finding, instead announces what truths are to be found: "Sensitive writers seek to avoid terms and statements implying or assuming that heterosexuality is the norm for sexual attraction." Which is why the earth is populated by only a few dozen people, all wearing Mardi Gras costumes.

Fallacious disregard for the truth is habitual in *Guidelines.* We are told that "sexist characterizations of animal traits and behaviors are inappropriate" (thereby depriving high-school biology students of a classroom giggle over the praying mantis eating her mate after coitus). We are warned against considering animals in "gender-stereotyped human terms," and are given, as an admonitory example, the sentence, "A stallion guards his brood of mares," though the stallion will do it no matter how many task forces are appointed by the Association of American University Presses. We hear that it is permitted to use "traditional technical terms, such as *feminine rhyme,*" but are told to "avoid introducing gender stereotypes—e.g. 'weak' rhymes." Never mind that a feminine rhyme, with its extra unaccented syllable, is, in fact, lame. Note the effect on this children's classic by Clement Clarke Moore.

> 'Twas the night before Christmas, when
>   all through the housing
> Not a creature was stirring—not
>   even a mousing;
> The stockings were hung by the
>   chimney with caring,
> In hopes that St. Nicholas soon
>   would be thereing.

We are scolded for using "illegal alien" when "*undocumented resident* or *undocumented worker* is generally preferred as less pejorative." What, they *aren't* illegal? And *Guidelines* goes so far as to urge utter dishonesty upon translators, saying they should make up their own sanctimonious minds about "whether gender-biased characteristics of the original warrant replication in English."

When the book is not lying or creating reasons to do so, it is engaging in the most tiresome sort of feminist scholasticism. Thirteen pages are devoted to wrestling with alternatives to the generic "he." A central thesis of *Guidelines* is thereby nearly disproven. If they need thirteen pages to discuss a pronoun, maybe women *are* inferior.

Why doesn't the Task Force just combine "she" and "it" and pronounce the thing accordingly? This would be no worse than the rest of the violence the book does to the language. Use of the obnoxious singular "they" is extolled. Shakespeare is cited by way of justification, and let me cite *Taming of the Shrew* as grounds for my critique. Dwarfism is described as a medical condition "resulting in severe short stature." Gosh, that was a strict midget. And the word "man," meaning humanity, is to be discarded, replaced by "people" or "person."   15

What a piece of work is person!

No, not even the members of the Task Force on Bias-Free Language are this tin-eared. They admit "these terms cannot always substitute for generic *man*" and suggest that "other revisions may be preferable." For instance, the sentence can be recast so that the first person plural is used.

What a piece of work we are!

Much of *Guidelines* is simply mealy-mouthed, touting the Mrs. Grundyisms (she lived before the second U.S. feminist movement) that pompous nonentities have always favored: "*Congenital disability* . . . is preferable to *birth defect*" and "manifestations of epilepsy are termed *seizures* not *fits*."

But on some pages, pretension progresses to delusion, e.g., "Terms such as *mentally deranged, mentally unbalanced, mentally diseased, insane, deviant, demented,* and *crazy* are not appropriate." Which statement is—how else to put it?—mentally deranged, mentally unbalanced, mentally diseased, insane, deviant, demented, and crazy.

The members of the Task Force on Bias-Free Language should be exiled to former Yugoslavia and made to teach bias-free Serbo-Croatian to Serbs and Croats for the rest of their natural lives, that is to say until their pupils tear them limb from limb. But this is just for the book's minor sins. Bad as *Guidelines* is so far, it gets worse.   20

The text assaults free will:

> Most people do not consider their sexuality a matter of choice.

Oh, oh. Left my zipper down and there goes Mr. Happy. Who knows what he'll do? Better lock up your daughters. Also, of course, your sons. And, since "Writers are enjoined to avoid gratuitous reference to age," better lock up granny, too.

The authors deprecate common-sense standards of good:

> Designating countries as *undeveloped* or *underdeveloped* implies an evolutionary hierarchy of nations based on wealth, type of economy, and degree of industrialization.

Of course it does, you feebleminded idiots.

> Labels such as *feebleminded, idiot, imbecile, mentally defective, mentally deficient, moron,* and *retard* are considered offensive.

I mean, you possessors of "a condition in which a person has significantly below-average general intellectual functioning."

Morals are attacked. We are told that "many stereotypical terms that are still found in writing about American Indians" are "highly offensive." One of them being "*massacre* (to refer to a successful American Indian raid or battle victory against white colonizers and invaders)." Ugh, Chief. Log cabins all burn. Heap many scalps. And U.N. High Commissioner for Refugees got-em all women and children.

And even the idea of normal is condemned:

> The term *normal* may legitimately refer to a statistical norm for human ability ("Normal vision is 20/20") but should usually be avoided in other context as . . . invidious.

Thus deprived of all tools of independent judgment and means of private action, the gender-neutral, age-non-specific, amoral, abnormal *person* is rendered helpless. Or, as *Guidelines* puts it, "The term *able-bodied* obscures [a] continuum of ability and may perpetuate an invidious distinction between persons so designated and those with disabilities."   25

We're all crippled. And we're all minorities, too, because "a 'minority' may be defined not on the basis of population size, color or ethnicity (e.g., women and people with disabilities are sometimes described as minorities), but in terms of power in a particular society."

Guidelines then goes about treating these overwhelming minorities with absurd "sensitivity." We are warned off "the many common English expressions that originate in a disparaging characterization of a particular group or people." "*Siamese twins,*" "*get one's Irish up,*" and even "*to shanghai*" are cited. Nonwhite is "objectionable in some contexts because it makes white the standard by which individuals are classified." Far East is "Eurocentric, East Asia is now preferred." "The expression *ghetto blaster* for a portable stereo (or, more colloquially, a 'boom box') is offensive as a stereotype [the pun goes unremarked in the text] of African American culture." Objection is made to the designation Latin American "because not all persons referred to as Latin American speak a Latin-based language." We are told that "some long accepted common names for botanical species—Niggerhead Cactus, Digger Pine (from a derogatory name for California native people who used the nuts from the *Pinus sabiniana*)—are offensive and are now undergoing revision in the scientific community." Artwork, also, must be carefully reviewed. "Graphic devices and clip art used by production and marketing staff can be generic and misleading . . . a traditional Zuni design gracing chapter openings in a book about the Iroquois; an illustration of a geisha advertising a press's books on Japan." Law enforcement, too. "Mafia" is held to be "Discriminatory against Italian Americans unless used in the correct historical sense; not interchangeable with *organized crime.*" And we mustn't say anything good about minorities either. "Gratuitous characterizations of individuals, such as *well-dressed, intelligent, articulate,* and *qualified* . . . may be unacceptably patronizing in some contexts, as are positive stereotypes—the polite, hard-working Japanese person or the silver-tongued Irish person."

What's going on here? Is the Task Force just going to bizarre lengths to avoid hurt feelings? Or is it trying to make those feelings hurt as much as possible? Has the Association of American University Presses crossed the line between petting minorities and giving them—as it were—a Dutch rub? So we're all pathetic members of oppressed minority factions, and the whole world—now wildly annoyed by reading *Guidelines for Bias-Free Writing*—hates our guts. And everything, everything, right down to the grammar itself, is terribly unfair. Oh, what will become of us? Whatever shall we do?

Some enormous power for good is needed. Government will hardly answer, since *Guidelines* has shown that even such well-meaning political entities as Sweden and Canada are no better than Cambodia or Zaire. Perhaps there is a religious solution. But when we encounter the word "heathen" in *Guidelines* we are told that "uncivilized or irreligious" is a "pejorative connotation." So God is out. And, anyway, He is notorious for His bias in favor of certain minorities and for the gross inequities of His creation. Really we have only one place to turn—the Association of American University Presses and, specifically, the members of its Task Force on Bias-Free Language. Who has been more fair than they? Who more sensitive? Who more inclusive? Who more just?

Sure, the Task Force seems to be nothing but a rat bag of shoddy peda-   30
gogues, athletes of the tongue, professional pick-nits filling the stupid hours of their pointless days with nagging the yellow-bellied editors of University Presses which print volume after volume of bound bum-wad fated to sit unread in college library stacks until the sun expires. But nothing could be further from the truth. The very Association of American University Presses says so in the position statement adopted by the AAUP Board of Directors in November 1992:

> Books that are on the cutting edge of scholarship should also be at the forefront in recognizing how language encodes prejudice. They should be agents for change and the redress of past mistakes.

And that is exactly what *Guidelines for Bias-Free Writing* means to do. If its suggestions are followed diligently by the acknowledged cultural vanguard, everything will change, all ills will be rectified, and redemption will be available to us all.

The Task Force on Bias-Free Language shall be our salvation, truth, and light. If you close your eyes, if you open your heart, if you empty your mind—especially if you empty your mind—you can see the Task Force members. There they are in a stuffy seminar room in some inconvenient corner of the campus, with unwashed hair, in Wal-Mart blue jeans, batik print tent dresses, and off-brand running shoes, the synthetic fibers from their fake Aran Island sweaters pilling at the elbows while they give each other high fives.

"Yes! Tremble at our inclusiveness! Bow down before our sensitivity! Culturalism in all its multi-ness is ours! No more shall the pejorative go to and fro in the Earth! Woe to the invidious! Behold *Guidelines for Bias-Free Writing,* ye Eurocentric, male-dominated power structure, and despair!"

The nurse (either a man or a woman since it is no longer proper to use the word as a "gender-marked" term) is coming from the university infirmary with their medications.

QUESTIONING THE TEXT

1. Does O'Rourke go over the top in his criticism of *Guidelines for Bias-Free Writing?* What, for example, does he gain and lose by immediately describing the authors of the book he is reviewing as "pointy-headed

wowsers"? In a group, discuss the way O'Rourke presents himself in the piece.

2. Does J.R.'s introduction offend you? Would a more neutral introduction prepare you better to read O'Rourke's biting review?

MAKING CONNECTIONS

3. Georgina Kleege (p. 390) describes the awkwardness many people feel in dealing with blind people. Does her discussion of blindness undercut O'Rourke's assault on those who wish to have words used sensitively? Or does Kleege's frank acceptance of her situation suggest that O'Rourke's frankness might not offend those the Task Force on Bias-Free Language is eager to protect?

4. Crèvecoeur (p. 361) characterizes Americans as independent and unfettered, "as free" as they ought to be. Consider both O'Rourke's essay and the work of the Task Force on Bias-Free Language in terms of Crèvecoeur's essay. Do O'Rourke and the Task Force express attitudes new to the scene, or do they both have deeper roots in American tradition?

JOINING THE CONVERSATION

5. O'Rourke mocks the Task Force on Bias–Free Language when he rewrites a famous line from *Hamlet:* "What a piece of work is man!" becomes "What a piece of work is person!" Does O'Rourke make a legitimate point, or do you agree more with the Task Force—that generic *man* should be avoided? Discuss this issue in class, and then write a position paper about this controversial matter of usage.

6. Can O'Rourke's essay be considered an argument in any serious sense? What is his thesis? Does he present evidence to support that thesis? Write a critical response to the review as an argument.

LANGSTON HUGHES
Theme for English B

LANGSTON HUGHES *(1902–67), as a young man in Joplin, Missouri, worked as an assistant cook, a launderer, and a busboy—jobs similar to ones you may have held—before leaving to attend Columbia University in New York City. (He eventually graduated in 1929 from Lincoln University in Pennsylvania.) A prolific writer and part of the great artistic movement of the 1920s and 1930s known as the Harlem Renaissance, Hughes worked in many genres—novels, short stories, plays, essays, and poems. From his early collection of poems,* The Weary Blues *(1926), to his posthumous volume of essays,* Black Misery *(1969), he explored numerous themes touching on the lives of African Americans, including that of higher education.*

The poem that follows, from 1926, describes one event in the speaker's college career and raises questions about relationships between instructors and students, between those "inside" the university and those "outside." It is one of my favorite poems, one of the few special ones I carry around with me and, in fact, now find that I know "by heart." With every new class I teach, I think of Hughes's "Theme for English B," for it speaks volumes to me about the necessity of respecting individual differences while at the same time valuing those bonds that link us to one another. – A.L.

The instructor said,

    Go home and write
    a page tonight.
    And let that page come out of you—
    Then, it will be true.   5

I wonder if it's that simple?

I am twenty-two, colored, born in Winston-Salem.
I went to school there, then Durham, then here
to this college on the hill above Harlem.
I am the only colored student in my class.   10
The steps from the hill lead down to Harlem,
through a park, then I cross St. Nicholas,
Eighth Avenue, Seventh, and I come to the Y,
the Harlem Branch Y, where I take the elevator
up to my room, sit down, and write this page: 15

It's not easy to know what is true for you or me
at twenty-two, my age. But I guess I'm what

I feel and see and hear. Harlem, I hear you:
hear you, hear me—we two—you, me talk on this page.
(I hear New York, too.) Me—who?   20

Well, I like to eat, sleep, drink, and be in love.
I like to work, read, learn, and understand life.
I like a pipe for a Christmas present,
or records—Bessie,* bop, or Bach.

I guess being colored doesn't make me not like   25
the same things other folks like who are other races.
So will my page be colored that I write?
Being me, it will not be white.
But it will be
a part of you, instructor.   30
You are white—
yet a part of me, as I am a part of you.
That's American.

Sometimes perhaps you don't want to be a part of me.
Nor do I often want to be a part of you.   35
But we are, that's true!
As I learn from you,
I guess you learn from me—
although you're older—and white—
and somewhat more free.   40

This is my page for English B.

IN RESPONSE

1. Near the end of the poem, the speaker says, addressing his instructor, "You are white—yet a part of me, as I am a part of you. That's American." What do you think Hughes means by "American"?
2. The speaker of this poem notes that given who he is, his theme will not be "white," but he goes on to say that it will still be "a part of you, instructor." What do you think he means? Can you describe a time when you've had a similar experience?

Bessie: Bessie Smith (1898?–1937), a famous blues singer

3. Shelby Steele (p. 63) writes at length of the myth of inferiority among African American youths. What, if any, evidence of a myth of inferiority do you find in Hughes's poem? How might Hughes respond to Steele's essay?

4. Would Hughes—or his teacher—likely be found in John Henry Newman's ideal university (p. 39)? Why, or why not?

5. Consider what effects your own gender, race, class, or family background has had on your success in school. Then write a brief (one- or two-page) essay explaining those effects.

6. Brainstorm with two or three classmates about whether it is important for students to identify with their teachers, to have a number of things in common with them. Come to an agreement among yourselves on how to answer this question, and then write one page explaining why you answered it as you did.

OTHER READINGS

Bland, Alisa. "I Am a Waif." *Glamour* Nov. 1994: 118. Argues that not all thin women suffer from eating disorders.

D'Souza, Dinesh. *The End of Racism.* New York: Free, 1995. Explores the role that racism has played in American society and suggests how racial problems might be resolved.

Funderburg, Lise. *Black, White, Other: Biracial Americans Talk about Race and Identity.* New York: Morrow, 1994. Incorporates (with commentary) the voices of many biracial people talking about a variety of subjects.

Hill, Patrick J. "Multi-Culturalism: The Crucial Philosophical and Organizational Issues." *Change* July–Aug. 1991: 38–47. Examines the debates about multiculturalism in higher education.

Lapham, Lewis H. "Who and What Is American?" *Harper's* Jan. 1992: 43–49. Argues that politicians promote false constructions of American identity.

Meyerson, Adam. "Nixon's Ghost: Racial Quotas—May They Rest in Peace." *Policy Review* Summer 1995: 4–5. Argues against affirmative action programs.

Sacks, David O., and Peter Thiel. *The Diversity Myth: "Multiculturalism" and the Politics of Intolerance at Stanford.* Oakland: Independent Institute, 1995. Examines the influence of multiculturalism on admissions policies, curricula, and campus life at Stanford University.

Sowell, Thomas. "Crusades of the Anointed." *The Vision of the Anointed: Self-Congratulation as a Belief for Social Policy.* New York: Basic, 1995. Shows how the crusade of interest groups is manipulated for political gain.

Yamato, Gloria. "Something About the Subject Makes It Hard to Name." *Making Face, Making Soul = Haciendo Caras: Creative and Critical Perspectives by Women of Color.* Ed. Gloria Anzaldúa. San Francisco: Aunt Lute Foundation Books, 1990. Analyzes racism.

ELECTRONIC RESOURCES

ACLU Freedom Network.
    http://www.aclu.org/
    Provides information about the American Civil Liberties Union.

Queer Resources Directory:
    http://www.qrd.org/QRD/
    Lists Web sites related to gay and lesbian issues and concerns.

Young America's Foundation:
    http://www.townhall.com/yaf/
    Provides information about a student-oriented group critical of American universities.

8

Legends:
Larger Than Life

Look carefully at this photograph of a so-called legend, Kurt Cobain. What overall impression of Cobain do you think the photographer intends—and what details about the image create that impression? Is that impression a positive or a negative one, or is it in any way ambiguous? If so, what creates the ambiguity? Is anything in the photograph "supernormal," idealized, or exaggerated—and to what effect? What ideals or values does this visual text express? What does this photograph suggest about the place of "legends" in our society?

"The winnah, and still heavyweight champeen of the world . . . Joe
Louis."

> MAYA ANGELOU, *Champion of the World*

The creator originates. The parasite borrows. The creator faces nature
alone. The parasite faces nature through an intermediary.

> AYN RAND, *The Soul of the Individualist*

I believe we all should have people we look up to as examples.

> ROSA PARKS, *Role Models*

Clinton loves America at her best. But Reagan loved America, period.

> PEGGY NOONAN, *Why We Already Miss the Gipper*

This is a woman who could describe the genesis of one of her most
well-known paintings—the "Cow's Skull: Red, White, and Blue"
owned by the Metropolitan—as an act of quite deliberate and derisive
orneriness.

> JOAN DIDION, *Georgia O'Keeffe*

The papal chair is now occupied by a man who, alone among his contemporaries, has the international stature associated with the generation
of Churchill and de Gaulle.

> GEORGE SIM JOHNSTON, *Pope Culture*

There is no question that inside the world of computers, Bill Gates has
assumed dimensions that far exceed human scale. "It's like walking the
Vatican with the pope. . . ."

> STEVEN LEVY, *Bill's New Vision*

She became all human sorrow. And she called the heart of the nation
home.

> STANLEY CROUCH, *Blues for Jackie*

Well, there were days when Mickey Mantle was so darn good that we
kids would bet that even God would want his autograph.

> BOB COSTAS, *Eulogy for Mickey Mantle*

prophets were ambushed as they spoke
and from their holes black eagles flew
screaming through the streets

> LUCILLE CLIFTON, *malcolm*

Introduction

"I WANT A HERO," says the English poet Lord Byron (1788–1824) in the introduction to *Don Juan,* his satiric epic about the legendary lover. In fact, every country, every culture, every people that we know of shares at least one thing in common: they all tell stories, stories that are often about the legends who reflect a society's deepest values and goals. In the United States, many legends tell varying narratives of America and Americans— legends based on real people like George Washington, Pocahontas, or Malcolm X or on mythical figures like Paul Bunyan, Br'er Rabbit, or White Buffalo Woman. In addition to these cultural legends, many smaller, more intimate groups (such as families) tell legends that pass on traditions from generation to generation. You may indeed have such legends in your family or in some other group you belong to.

Where do such legends come from? How are they created? Who in our own society, for instance, can become "hero material"—and who cannot? What values and attitudes do we find reflected in the legends characteristic of American cultures? And finally, in what ways may such values clash with one another? In short, under what circumstances may one person's hero be another person's villain, one person's powerful legend another person's meaningless tale? These are questions central to this chapter's conversation, for each of the readings in it treats a legendary person or character and, in doing so, implicitly explores what it means to be "a legend" as well as what functions legends fulfill in our personal and public lives.

As we made the difficult choices necessary to come up with final selections for this chapter, we noted with interest that our choice of who is a legend varies a good bit: A.L. chose, for example, Rosa Parks while J.R. chose Ronald Reagan. Why not begin this chapter by making your own list of your most significant legends? As you do so, you may benefit from considering any or all of the following questions:

- How would you define a legend? a hero/heroine? How do the definitions differ?

- Make a list of the legends that have been or are most important in your own life. What do such legends represent to you? Get together with two or three classmates to compare your lists, noting the differences in your choices.

- How do you think legends get made? What characteristics are necessary for someone (or something) to become a legend?

- Does your family have any legends or stories that are passed down from generation to generation? What are they?

- Are your legends the same as those of your parents? Why, or why not?

• • •

MAYA ANGELOU
Champion of the World

Maya Angelou, born in St. Louis in 1928, spent her youth in Arkansas and California, a period described evocatively in her autobiographical I Know Why the Caged Bird Sings *(1970), the volume from which the following excerpt is taken. She has written four more books about her eventful life, which among other things has included jobs as a Creole cook, a cocktail waitress, a dancer, a singer, a streetcar conductor, and a coordinator for the Southern Christian Leadership Conference. She has also published six volumes of poetry and was invited by Bill Clinton to compose a poem to read during his 1993 inauguration as president of the United States. Currently a professor of American studies at Wake Forest University, Angelou says that she quite simply loves writing, loves "the sense of achievement" when she's "almost got the sentence right."*

In the chapter that follows, Angelou has gotten many such sentences right. In them, she tells about her childhood memories of her grandmother and uncle's store, a center of activity for the black people in their small Arkansas community, on the night that Joe Louis, the boxer who symbolized the ideals and hopes of African Americans, was to defend his title as world heavyweight champion against a white contender. This brief chapter exemplifies the way in which a sport and a particular athlete can take on the symbolic hopes and fears of an entire group. For the people gathered around the radio on this evening in the 1930s, Joe Louis was a hero fighting not only for the title but also for dignity and justice for black people everywhere.

I chose this chapter from Angelou's book because she is herself a hero and legend to me, even as she writes about another legend, Joe Louis. In addition, I have always particularly liked this chapter because I, too, can remember sitting around a radio as a very small child, feeling warm and happy in the circle of my grandmother and other family members and friends. — A.L.

The last inch of space was filled, yet people continued to wedge themselves along the walls of the Store. Uncle Willie had turned the radio up to its last notch so that youngsters on the porch wouldn't miss a word. Women sat on kitchen chairs, dining-room chairs, stools, and upturned wooden boxes. Small children and babies perched on every lap available and men leaned on the shelves or on each other.

The apprehensive mood was shot through with shafts of gaiety, as a black sky is streaked with lightning.

"I ain't worried 'bout this fight. Joe's gonna whip that cracker like it's open season."

"He gone whip him till that white boy call him Momma."

At last the talking finished and the string-along songs about razor blades   5
were over and the fight began.

"A quick jab to the head." In the Store the crowd grunted. "A left to
the head and a right and another left." One of the listeners cackled like a hen
and was quieted.

"They're in a clinch, Louis is trying to fight his way out."

Some bitter comedian on the porch said, "That white man don't mind
hugging that niggah now, I betcha."

"The referee is moving in to break them up, but Louis finally pushed
the contender away and it's an uppercut to the chin. The contender is hanging on, now he's backing away. Louis catches him with a short left to the
jaw."

A tide of murmuring assent poured out the door and into the yard.   10

"Another left and another left. Louis is saving that mighty right . . ."
The mutter in the Store had grown into a baby roar and it was pierced by the
clang of a bell and the announcer's "That's the bell for round three, ladies and
gentlemen."

As I pushed my way into the Store I wondered if the announcer gave
any thought to the fact that he was addressing as "ladies and gentlemen" all
the Negroes around the world who sat sweating and praying, glued to their
"master's voice."*

There were only a few calls for RC Colas, Dr. Peppers, and Hires root
beer. The real festivities would begin after the fight. Then even the old
Christian ladies who taught their children and tried themselves to practice
turning the other cheek would buy soft drinks, and if the Brown Bomber's
victory was a particularly bloody one they would order peanut patties and
Baby Ruths also.

Bailey and I laid the coins on top of the cash register. Uncle Willie
didn't allow us to ring up sales during a fight. It was too noisy and might
shake up the atmosphere. When the gong rang for the next round we pushed
through the near-sacred quiet to the herd of children outside.

"He's got Louis against the ropes and now it's a left to the body and a right   15
to the ribs. Another right to the body, it looks like it was low . . . Yes, ladies and
gentlemen, the referee is signaling but the contender keeps raining the blows on
Louis. It's another to the body, and it looks like Louis is going down."

My race groaned. It was our people falling. It was another lynching, yet
another Black man hanging on a tree. One more woman ambushed and
raped. A Black boy whipped and maimed. It was hounds on the trail of a man
running through slimy swamps. It was a white woman slapping her maid for
being forgetful.

---

their "master's voice": a reference to a long-standing symbol of RCA Victor recordings,
which features a dog apparently listening to an old-fashioned phonograph with the caption "His
Master's Voice"

The men in the Store stood away from the walls and at attention. Women greedily clutched the babes on their laps while on the porch the shufflings and smiles, flirtings and pinching of a few minutes before were gone. This might be the end of the world. If Joe lost we were back in slavery and beyond help. It would all be true, the accusations that we were lower types of human beings. Only a little higher than apes. True that we were stupid and ugly and lazy and dirty and, unlucky and worst of all, that God Himself hated us and ordained us to be hewers of wood and drawers of water,* forever and ever, world without end.

We didn't breathe. We didn't hope. We waited.

"He's off the ropes, ladies and gentlemen. He's moving towards the center of the ring." There was no time to be relieved. The worst might still happen.

"And now it looks like Joe is mad. He's caught Carnera* with a left   20 hook to the head and a right to the head. It's a left jab to the body and another left to the head. There's a left cross and a right to the head. The contender's right eye is bleeding and he can't seem to keep his block up. Louis is penetrating every block. The referee is moving in, but Louis sends a left to the body and it's an uppercut to the chin and the contender is dropping. He's on the canvas, ladies and gentlemen."

Babies slid to the floor as women stood up and men leaned toward the radio.

"Here's the referee. He's young. One, two, three, four, five, six, seven . . . Is the contender trying to get up again?"

All the men in the Store shouted, "NO."

"—eight, nine, ten." There were a few sounds from the audience, but they seemed to be holding themselves in against tremendous pressure.

"The fight is all over, ladies and gentlemen. Let's get the microphone   25 over the referee . . . Here he is. He's got the Brown Bomber's hand, he's holding it up . . . Here he is . . ."

Then the voice, husky and familiar, came to wash over us—"The winnah, and still heavyweight champeen of the world . . . Joe Louis."

Champion of the world. A Black boy. Some Black mother's son. He was the strongest man in the world. People drank Coca-Colas like ambrosia and ate candy bars like Christmas. Some of the men went behind the Store and poured white lightning in their soft-drink bottles, and a few of the bigger boys followed them. Those who were not chased away came back blowing their breath in front of themselves like proud smokers.

---

hewers . . . water: a reference to the biblical verse Joshua 9:23, which in the King James Version reads "Let them live; but let them be hewers of wood and drawers of water unto all the congregation." The verse, referring to the Gibeonites after their surrender to Joshua's forces, was often cited by those arguing that blacks were naturally or divinely destined to perform menial physical labor.

Carnera: an apparent error by Angelou. Primo Carnera fought Louis only once, in 1935, two years before Louis became world heavyweight champion, so the fight she recalls must have involved a different contender.

It would take an hour or more before the people would leave the Store and head for home. Those who lived too far had made arrangements to stay in town. It wouldn't do for a Black man and his family to be caught on a lonely country road on a night when Joe Louis had proved that we were the strongest people in the world.

QUESTIONING THE TEXT

1. What is the attitude toward Louis of the crowd gathered at the store? Point out places in the text that allow you to identify this attitude. Is Angelou's attitude the same as that of the other listeners she describes? What supports your answer to this question?
2. Why does Angelou put quotation marks around "master's voice"? List all the reasons you can think of.
3. Read this story aloud, noting those places where the language sounds "spoken" instead of "written." What effect does the use of the sounds and rhythms of spoken English have on the story?
4. Why do you think A.L., as she says in her introduction to the reading, sees Angelou herself as a hero and a legend?

MAKING CONNECTIONS

5. What elements does Angelou draw on to establish Joe Louis's status as a legend and role model? How do they compare with the "individualist" described by Ayn Rand (p. 443)? If you keep a reading log, answer these questions there.
6. Compare the scene of joy that Angelou paints after Louis's victory with the scene that Lucille Clifton paints in "malcolm" (p. 488). Spend some time writing about how legendary status may call for great triumph *and* great sacrifice or even failure.

JOINING THE CONVERSATION

7. Jot down what you know or have heard about Joe Louis. Then do a little research on him and prepare a brief summary of his career for your class. In what ways does what you find out about Louis agree or disagree with what Angelou says about him?
8. Working with two classmates, devise a new "national game" that would be the "perfect" game for the United States. Give it a name, decide on its rules, and create a "legend" who would epitomize its appeal and its characteristics. Come to class ready to describe the game and its legendary hero to your classmates.

AYN RAND
The Soul of the Individualist

BOTH THE OBJECTIVIST PHILOSOPHER *Ayn Rand (1905–82) and the hero
she created for her novel* The Fountainhead *(1943), Howard Roark, are legends. Roark embodies the principles of extreme individualism and self-
determination that Rand championed for decades in books, novels, and plays.
In a letter to the architect Frank Lloyd Wright, Rand describes Roark as "my
conception of man as god, of the absolute human ideal." In the novel, Roark
destroys a government housing project he designed rather than see his vision ruined by lesser men. The speech in the following selection is his defense of that
action at his trial. As you'll see, in many respects Roark is the antithesis of the
title of this volume; the* presence of others *matters to him not at all. For the
contrast Roark represents to many prevailing values, I think it worthwhile to
consider him as a kind of legend.*

*I also wanted to include a selection by Ayn Rand in this anthology as a
nod to her special status among U.S. students.* The Fountainhead *was an
unexpected best-seller in 1943 and was made into a movie starring Gary
Cooper as Howard Roark in 1949. I'm amazed by the enduring popularity of*
The Fountainhead *almost two generations after its publication and by the
continuing vitality and presence of objectivist groups on campuses—even though
Rand is largely ignored by the academic community. Objectivists believe that
happiness in life results from the application of reason to human activity; they
privilege freedom and individuality and champion unfettered capitalism.*

*Many serious students have an objectivist period, a peculiar and waggish
moment of rebellion usually sparked by reading one of Rand's novels. As a junior in high school, I fell briefly under the spell of* The Fountainhead—*with
its glorification of selfishness and contempt for altruism—shortly before a religious retreat, where I must have seemed the most recalcitrant Catholic since
Luther; a friend of mine recalls spending a full week under the spell of objectivism—until he was hit by a bus.* − J.R.

> *This is the speech that Howard Roark makes in his own
> defense, while on trial for having dynamited a government
> housing project under construction; he had designed the
> project for another architect, Peter Keating, on the agree-
> ment that it would be built exactly as he designed it; the
> agreement was broken by the government agency; the two
> architects had no recourse to law, not being permitted to
> sue the government.*

"Thousands of years ago, the first man discovered how to make fire. He was probably burned at the stake he had taught his brothers to light. He was considered an evildoer who had dealt with a demon mankind dreaded. But thereafter men had fire to keep them warm, to cook their food, to light their caves. He had left them a gift they had not conceived and he had lifted darkness off the earth. Centuries later, the first man invented the wheel. He was probably torn on the rack he had taught his brothers to build. He was considered a transgressor who ventured into forbidden territory. But thereafter, men could travel past any horizon. He had left them a gift they had not conceived and he had opened the roads of the world.

"That man, the unsubmissive and first, stands in the opening chapter of every legend mankind has recorded about its beginning. Prometheus was chained to a rock and torn by vultures—because he had stolen the fire of the gods. Adam was condemned to suffer—because he had eaten the fruit of the tree of knowledge. Whatever the legend, somewhere in the shadows of its memory mankind knew that its glory began with one and that that one paid for his courage.

"Throughout the centuries there were men who took first steps down new roads armed with nothing but their own vision. Their goals differed, but they all had this in common: that the step was first, the road new, the vision unborrowed, and the response they received—hatred. The great creators—the thinkers, the artists, the scientists, the inventors—stood alone against the men of their time. Every great new thought was opposed. Every great new invention was denounced. The first motor was considered foolish. The airplane was considered impossible. The power loom was considered vicious. Anesthesia was considered sinful. But the men of unborrowed vision went ahead. They fought, they suffered and they paid. But they won.

"No creator was prompted by a desire to serve his brothers, for his brothers rejected the gift he offered and that gift destroyed the slothful routine of their lives. His truth was his only motive. His own

---

Roark is on trial, so we should grant him some rhetorical leeway. But wasn't it the god Jupiter who punished Prometheus for stealing fire for mankind? And Adam never struck me as courageous—just disobedient and dumb. — J.R.

Does Roark fancy himself one of these great names? I am skeptical of his argument almost before it begins. — T.E.

We admire those who had courage to stand up for causes, ideas, or innovations, people as different as Socrates, Joan of Arc, Galileo, Robert E. Lee, Sitting Bull, and Rosa Parks. Yet they had allies, too, and their "creations" routinely touched many other people. — J.R.

Not compelling to me. The greatest human achievements inevitably grow out of a whole complex of forces and efforts of many people. Rand insists, as have many others, that great creations or achievements can always be attributed to a solitary creator. Our society has liked (and needed?) to tell the story this way for some 300 years, but it is only one way of telling the story, and to me it is increasingly unsatisfying. — A.L.

I am put off by the overwhelming assumption that these individual creators are all men, acting with and against other men. — A.L.

The use of every makes me uncomfortable. Surely some people appreciated new inventions for the important aid they offered. — T.E.

truth, and his own work to achieve it in his own way. A symphony, a book, an engine, a philosophy, an airplane or a building—that was his goal and his life. Not those who heard, read, operated, believed, flew or inhabited the thing he had created. The creation, not its users. The creation, not the benefits others derived from it. The creation which gave form to his truth. He held his truth above all things and against all men.

"His vision, his strength, his courage came from his own spirit. A man's spirit, however, is his self. That entity which is his consciousness. To think, to feel, to judge, to act are functions of the ego.

"The creators were not selfless. It is the whole secret of their power—that it was self-sufficient, self-motivated, self-generated. A first cause, a fount of energy, a life force, a Prime Mover. The creator served nothing and no one. He lived for himself.

"And only by living for himself was he able to achieve the things which are the glory of mankind. Such is the nature of achievement.

"Man cannot survive except through his mind. He comes on earth unarmed. His brain is his only weapon. Animals obtain food by force. Man has no claws, no fangs, no horns, no great strength of muscle. He must plant his food or hunt it. To plant, he needs a process of thought. To hunt, he needs weapons, and to make weapons—a process of thought. From this simplest necessity to the highest religious abstraction, from the wheel to the skyscraper, everything we are and everything we have comes from a single attribute of man—the function of his reasoning mind.

"But the mind is an attribute of the individual. There is no such thing as a collective brain. There is no such thing as a collective thought. An agreement reached by a group of men is only a compromise or an average drawn upon many individual thoughts. It is a secondary consequence. The primary act—the process of reason—must be performed by each man alone. We can divide a meal among many men. We cannot digest it in a collective stomach. No man can use his lungs to breathe for another man. No man can use his brain to think for another. All the functions of body and spirit are private. They cannot be shared or transferred.

"We inherit the products of the thought of other men. We inherit the wheel. We make a cart. The cart becomes an automobile. The automobile becomes an airplane. But all through the process what we receive from others is only the end product of their thinking. The moving force is the creative faculty which takes this product as material, uses it and originates the next step. This creative faculty cannot be given or received, shared or borrowed. It belongs to single, individual men. That which it creates is the property of the creator. Men learn from one another. But all learning is only the exchange of material. No man can give another the capacity to think. Yet that capacity is our only means of survival.

"Nothing is given to man on earth. Everything he needs has to be produced. And here man faces his basic alternative: he can survive in only one of two ways—by the independent work of his own mind or as a parasite fed by the minds of others. The creator originates. The parasite borrows. The creator faces nature alone. The parasite faces nature through an intermediary.

"The creator's concern is the conquest of nature. The parasite's concern is the conquest of men.

"The creator lives for his work. He needs no other men. His primary goal is within himself. The parasite lives secondhand. He needs others. Others become his prime motive.

"The basic need of the creator is independence. The reasoning mind cannot work under any form of compulsion. It cannot be curbed, sacrificed or subordinated to any consideration whatsoever. It demands total independence in function and in motive. To a creator, all relations with men are secondary.

"The basic need of the second-hander is to secure his ties with men in order to be fed. He places relations first. He declares that man exists in order to serve others. He preaches altruism.

"Altruism is the doctrine which demands that man live for others and place others above self.

So is it bad to take advantage of another's inventions? — T.E.

His praise of the creator seems extreme—in part because we've become a society that cultivates dependency. Everyone is a victim now. For once, I'm reading Roark sympathetically. — J.R.

He's generalizing again. — T.E.

When reading The Fountainhead *in high school, I was stunned by Roark's attack on altruism. I felt I'd*

He oversimplifies. The creativity of individuals may lead to important changes, but their insights take root usually after others till the soil. — J.R.

I agree with Rand up to this point in the paragraph, but I can't stick with her here. Creativity is vast and unpredictable, but nothing is created in a vacuum. If we ignore or devalue the roles others play in creation, that says more about us than it does about the act of creation. — A.L.

Here is that odd either/or again: either a man is a creator or a parasite. No mixture possible, no recognition that such labels act to stereotype and reduce men to one dimension only. (Women need not apply!) — A.L.

"No man can live for another. He cannot share his spirit just as he cannot share his body. But the second-hander has used altruism as a weapon of exploitation and reversed the base of mankind's moral principles. Men have been taught every precept that destroys the creator. Men have been taught dependence as a virtue.

"The man who attempts to live for others is a dependent. He is a parasite in motive and makes parasites of those he serves. The relationship produces nothing but mutual corruption. It is impossible in concept. The nearest approach to it in reality—the man who lives to serve others—is the slave. If physical slavery is repulsive, how much more repulsive is the concept of servility of the spirit? The conquered slave has a vestige of honor. He has the merit of having resisted and of considering his condition evil. But the man who enslaves himself voluntarily in the name of love is the basest of creatures. He degrades the dignity of man and he degrades the conception of love. But this is the essence of altruism.

"Men have been taught that the highest virtue is not to achieve, but to give. Yet one cannot give that which has not been created. Creation comes before distribution—or there will be nothing to distribute. The need of the creator comes before the need of any possible beneficiary. Yet we are taught to admire the second-hander who dispenses gifts he has not produced above the man who made the gifts possible. We praise an act of charity. We shrug at an act of achievement.

"Men have been taught that their first concern is to relieve the suffering of others. But suffering is a disease. Should one come upon it, one tries to give relief and assistance. To make that the highest test of virtue is to make suffering the most important part of life. Then man must wish to see others suffer—in order that he may be virtuous. Such is the nature of altruism. The creator is not concerned with disease, but with life. Yet the work of the creators has eliminated one form of disease after another, in man's body and spirit, and brought more relief from suffering than any altruist could ever conceive.

"Men have been taught that it is a virtue to agree with others. But the creator is the man who disagrees. Men have been taught that it is a virtue to swim with the current. But the creator is the man who goes against the current. Men have been taught that it is a virtue to stand together. But the creator is the man who stands alone.

"Men have been taught that the ego is the synonym of evil, and selflessness the ideal of virtue. But the creator is the egoist in the absolute sense, and the selfless man is the one who does not think, feel, judge or act. These are functions of the self.

"Here the basic reversal is most deadly. The issue has been perverted and man has been left no alternative—and no freedom. As poles of good and evil, he was offered two conceptions: egoism and altruism. Egoism was held to mean the sacrifice of others to self. Altruism—the sacrifice of self to others. This tied man irrevocably to other men and left him nothing but a choice of pain: his own pain borne for the sake of others or pain inflicted upon others for the sake of self. When it was added that man must find joy in self-immolation, the trap was closed. Man was forced to accept masochism as his ideal—under the threat that sadism was his only alternative. This was the greatest fraud ever perpetrated on mankind.

"This was the device by which dependence and suffering were perpetuated as fundamentals of life.

"The choice is not self-sacrifice or domination. The choice is independence or dependence. The code of the creator or the code of the second-hander. This is the basic issue. It rests upon the alternative of life or death. The code of the creator is built on the needs of the reasoning mind which allows man to survive. The code of the second-hander is built on the needs of a mind incapable of survival. All that which proceeds from man's independent ego is good. All that which proceeds from man's dependence upon men is evil.

"The egoist in the absolute sense is not the man who sacrifices others. He is the man who stands above the need of using others in any manner. He does not function through them. He is not concerned with them in any primary matter. Not in his aim, not in his motive, not in his thinking, not in his desires, not in the source of his energy. He does not exist for any other man—and he asks no other man to exist for him. This is the only form of brotherhood and mutual respect possible between men.

Afterwords

Certainly Roark's vision of a society of robust creators joined in a brotherhood of genius has romantic appeal. But where does that leave the rest of us? One might argue that it would serve the interests of ordinary people to keep Ayn Rand's potent "creators" in check or to appropriate what they've created for more general use. And therein lies a problem with unbridled selfishness; it turns humanity into a den of vipers. Yet there's a glint of truth in Roark's vision—in his resistance to those who would prefer a world wholly level in its distribution of talent, wealth, and enterprise. We know from experience now that societies organized that way don't work; some people are always more "equal" than others.

Roark and Rand go off track, I believe, in reading love out of human interactions—or perhaps they are ignoring what James Q. Wilson calls "the moral sense." Roark and Rand can't seem to imagine that the natural affection we acquire for members of our families, tribes, and local communities might reasonably motivate us to act for the good of all humankind. We are nurtured in our home communities, and that care later feeds the springs of the altruism Roark despises. It may take an intellectual act to extend the devotion we feel for those closest to us—our children, parents, siblings, neighbors, and colleagues— to more distant communities; but such extensions of self don't diminish one's self-respect or heroism. They make civil society possible. – J.R.

J.R. and I seem to be reading along remarkably similar lines here. Certainly I reject Roark's and Rand's notion of radical individualism, one that depends on the vision of creators as heroic figures working in utter isolation and that rejects the possibility that human love and compassion are anything other than disguised self-interest. Evidence from every field of endeavor—from art to zoology—demonstrates that creativity loves company, that creativity engenders more creativity, and that the greatest geniuses we have ever known drew extensively on the ideas and works of others, as well as on all those around them.

I am also not ready to give up on the possibility for human love and compassion. Well over two thousand years ago, Plato described one kind of love, that focusing on the good, the well-being, of the other, which Socrates explores in several of Plato's dialogues. I have experienced such uninterested "love" on at least a few occasions in my life, primarily from teachers or mentors who have helped me try to be all that I can be, as well as from members of my small extended family. As we try to extend such caring to others, we join in an ever-widening circle that has the potential for reaching those very, very far removed from us and for bringing them into the circle of care as well—even Howard Roark. – A.L.

All inventors take substantial risks. Venturing into uncharted territory is always dangerous, and no one knows quite how new technology will be treated. Consider Birkerts's view of electronic information in "Perseus Unbound" (p. 279); he clearly believes these advances could be detrimental to the fate of education. However, we must remember that not everyone views it as such. Therein lies the flaw in Roark's argument. He claims that all inventors create for their own personal gain. Perhaps in the most elemental sense this is true. However, no one can create an object or idea without considering the repercussions that will echo throughout society.

Every invention, from the wheel to the supercomputer, has changed life as we know it. Of course, skeptics exist everywhere who will attack any new idea, some for the pure joy of criticizing others. However, there will always be those who realize the true genius behind incredible inventions. Roark denies the existence of this compassion and understanding. He claims that all innovators walk a lonely path to discovery, fighting criticism all the way. How can this be? In a world with many differing opinions, it seems inconceivable that someone should face anything completely alone.

In addition, to view all of humankind as the parasite or the creator seems too cut and dried. We advance as a culture by building on each other's ideas and working together. True, group decisions consist of a series of compromises. However, we must look at these compromises as the invention of an entire group, for the discoveries and decisions would not have been the same had one person created the product.

Perhaps even the creator, according to Roark's argument, can be considered a parasite. The inventor of the computer could not have accomplished what he did without earlier advancements in electronics. He undoubtedly worked in a room with artificial light, reflecting his dependence on Thomas Edison, the inventor of the light bulb. Edison owes some credit to the one who discovered how to produce and mold glass. Every invention owes something to an innovation from an earlier time. For this reason, we are all parasites, under Roark's definition. – T.E.

QUESTIONING THE TEXT

1. What kinds of actions, according to Roark, make a person a legend or creator? What type of reaction does the creator get from the masses of people? After reading Roark's account, compare his description of the

legend with your own. Do the people you regard as legendary fit Roark's definition?

2. Roark argues that the person who lives to help others makes suffering "the most important part of life." Examine this claim by examining people you know whom Roark might consider altruistic.

3. Does J.R.'s brief account in the introduction of his own and a friend's experiences with objectivism taint your view of the philosophy espoused by Howard Roark? Why or why not?

MAKING CONNECTIONS

4. Could a Howard Roark understand the heroism that Bob Costas describes in his eulogy for Mickey Mantle (p. 483) or that Maya Angelou finds in Joe Louis? In other words, could a sports figure be a legend or creator in Roark's vision of the world? Write a paragraph exploring the issue.

5. According to Hannah Arendt, who provides the title for this anthology, "For excellence, the presence of others is always required." According to Ayn Rand's character Howard Roark, "The creator lives for his work. He needs no other men." Who do you think is right? Discuss this question with classmates or, if you keep a reading log, answer this question there.

6. Roark concludes that only people who do not exist for anyone else are capable of "mutual respect" and "brotherhood." Do you find this attitude in any other figure in this chapter? Explain your view in a paragraph.

JOINING THE CONVERSATION

7. Roark complains that "Men have been taught dependence as a virtue" and then compares altruism to slavery. Assess Roark's claim by considering your own civic, moral, and/or religious training. Then write an essay, imagining how the world might be different if more people agreed with Howard Roark.

8. In a group, list and discuss any film or television heroes who might fit Howard Roark's profile of the creator or legend. Then write a paragraph or short essay about one of those figures, assessing his or her impact on popular culture.

ROSA PARKS
Role Models

ROSA PARKS (b. 1913) BOARDED A BUS in Montgomery, Alabama, on December 1, 1955. She ended her ride by making history, becoming a legend in her own time by refusing to give up her seat to a white passenger. This act may seem simple and uncontroversial now, but it was not so in 1955. At that time, schools and other institutions in the South were still largely segregated by race, as were public facilities such as buses, where African Americans were expected to "step to the back of the bus." Rosa Parks chose to resist this system, and although she was jailed for her transgression, it resulted in a massive boycott of the Montgomery bus system that, led by the young clergyman Martin Luther King Jr., ended segregation on the city's buses and launched King's career as a civil rights leader.

In the following chapter from Quiet Strength: The Faith, the Hope, and the Heart of a Woman Who Changed a Nation, *Parks reflects on the special people who served as role models in her life: her husband, her mother, her grandmother, and two ministers—the Reverends Martin Luther King Jr. and Jesse Jackson. Published in 1995 to celebrate the fortieth anniversary of Parks's courageous act, the reflections in this book demonstrate her humility, her steadfast faith, and her commitment to young people everywhere. "I want to be remembered as a person who stood up to injustice, who wanted a better world for young people," she says—and her Rosa and Raymond Parks Institute for Self-Development is devoted to those goals. Awarded the Nonviolent Peace Prize in 1980 and an honorary degree from Mount Holyoke College in 1981, and honored at the White House on many occasions, Parks seems unconcerned with such accolades, returning repeatedly to her central concerns—to care for those around her and to make "whatever contribution I can make." She lives today in Detroit, Michigan, and she represents to me, and to millions of others, the difference just one person can make. −* A.L.

I believe we all should have people we look up to as examples. I list my husband, Raymond Parks, among the persons I admired most. He was a good man, full of courage and inner strength. Before meeting him, I had never really talked about racial issues with another African-American, outside of my family. And Raymond—"Parks," as I called him—was keenly interested in changing the current racial conditions. Although he had almost no formal schooling, he was very intelligent and read widely.

One thing that really impressed me about Parks was that he refused to be intimidated by white people—unlike many blacks, who figured they had no choice but to stay under "Mr. Charlie's" heel. ("Mr. Charlie" was our name for white men in general.) Parks would have none of it, and he became active in NAACP and in civil rights issues.

Parks worked courageously for the release of the Scottsboro Boys, a group of nine young black men who were wrongly accused of raping two white women in 1931. They were found guilty and condemned to die for a crime they did not commit. They did not die, thanks to the efforts of many. Anyone who supported them had to meet in secret. To do anything openly for this cause could mean death. And yet Parks, along with the NAACP, fearlessly pursued justice for these men. That is why I later decided to name my legacy after Raymond so that people would know how devoted he was to civil rights and the uplifting of blacks.

My mother, Leona McCauley, helped me to grow up feeling proud of myself and other black people, even while living under racist conditions. She taught me not to judge people by the amount of money they had or the kind of house they lived in or the clothes they wore. People should be judged, she told me, by the respect they have for themselves and others. Her advice helped me to do the hard things that I had to do later in life.

Mother was a woman of determination who believed in reading the   5
Bible for guidance. She also believed in the value of education and saw it as a way to better yourself. She was a schoolteacher and had a teaching certificate, but she did not go to college. Back then black teachers got paid less than white teachers, but the money was better than what housekeepers got. One of the reasons I cofounded, with Elaine Steele, the Rosa and Raymond Parks Institute for Self-Development was because I wanted to carry on what my mother so strongly believed in: the education of our people.

My grandmother, Grandma Rose, was also dear to me. She helped raise me to be a strong woman. She set an example of caring and love for her children and grandchildren. She was very strong-willed and believed in discipline. I so enjoyed reading the Bible with her. It always made me feel good. I guess that is why it seemed natural for me to read the Bible to her when her eyesight failed. She died when I was sixteen years old. She was calm-spirited and not easily excited. My great-grandmother, Grandma Jane, on the other hand, was excitable and feisty, and Grandpappy would calm her spirit.

My family, and the values they taught me, gave me a sense of who I am. I remember my grandfather, Sylvester Edwards. Because he had very light skin and looked white, he would shake hands with white people and call them by their first names. These acts were extremely risky for a black person to do in those days and could lead to being manhandled or lynched.

Although he looked white, my grandfather was hostile toward whites. He was not a hateful man; he had simply been cruelly treated by white people all of his life. As a boy he had been beaten, forbidden to have shoes, and starved by the overseer of the plantation he lived on. Too many years of humiliation had given him a belligerent attitude toward white people.

His memory will always be with me. While I do not think I inherited his hostility, my mother and I both learned not to let anyone mistreat us. It was passed down almost in our genes.

Martin Luther King Jr. set a profound example for me in day-to-day   10
living. He was such a young man—just twenty-six years old—when I first met him at the beginning of the bus boycott. I was forty-two.

I'll always remember the way Dr. King would respond to violence. He would use the same words that Jesus said on the cross: "Father, forgive them, for they know not what they do." Brutality was to be received with love, he would say. Though I knew we needed to strive for nonviolence, when I saw the brutal treatment some of us got, I had trouble believing it was always the best thing to do.

Dr. King was a true leader. I never sensed fear in him. I just felt as though he knew what had to be done and took the leading role without regard to consequences. I knew he was destined to do great things. He had an elegance about him and a speaking style that let you know where you stood and inspired you to do the best you could. He truly is a role model for us all. The sacrifice of his life should never be forgotten, and his dream must live on.

During the civil rights movement, another young man came forth to help black people fight the unjust treatment they were receiving. His name was Malcolm X. He was twenty-seven years old. When I look back, this strong-willed man reminded me somewhat of my grandfather. He was full of conviction and pride in his race. The last time I saw him, he was speaking in Detroit, and he signed a program for me.

I admired the way he had changed his position from one of distrust toward whites to one of tolerance and building self-respect among blacks. His ideas were different than what many of us heard publicly, but his strong conviction of self-determination and pride energized blacks in economic development. The way he stood up and voiced himself showed that he was a man to be respected.

During the time that the Reverend Jesse Jackson was running for presi-   15
dent, he carried the banner for our people very well. If he continues, I believe he will one day be president. I believe that Reverend Jackson is someone black people can depend on for leadership. I welcomed him as a presidential candidate, and I'll welcome him again if he decides to run. Reverend Jackson made all of us proud during his campaign, and he is continuing to do so today.

QUESTIONING THE TEXT

1. Commenting on the woman who portrayed her in a film, Parks said that "she was good. Very quiet, she didn't get excited or use any extra words." In what way does this description seem characteristic of the Parks we meet in "Role Models"?
2. Look at the words and phrases A.L. uses in her introduction to describe Parks and her actions. How do they lead you to see Parks?
3. Read this selection again, and make a list of the characteristics that Rosa Parks's role models have in common. Are they characteristics we ordinarily associate with legends? Why, or why not?

MAKING CONNECTIONS

4. Imagine a conversation between Ayn Rand and Rosa Parks on the subject of role models. On what points would they be most likely to disagree? Write a brief essay in which you support one or the other view of what a role model should be.
5. Look back at the conclusion of Maya Angelou's essay (p. 442). In what ways does Rosa Parks's discussion of her role models illuminate Angelou's claim that "we were the strongest people in the world"?

JOINING THE CONVERSATION

6. Working with two or three classmates, conduct some additional research on Rosa Parks. You might look up the *New York Times* stories about the Montgomery bus boycott; contemporary reports in *Time*, *Newsweek*, or *Life*; and reports in the Montgomery newspaper or your own local newspapers. Examine other materials published by and about Parks, and consider interviewing people who remember the bus boycott well and ask them to share those memories with you. On the basis of the information you gather, prepare a presentation for the class on "Rosa Parks: Legend in Her Own Time."
7. Parks says, "I believe we all should have people we look up to as examples." Write an essay in which you describe those people you most look up to. Conclude by analyzing the characteristics most representative of your own role models.

PEGGY NOONAN
Why We Already Miss the Gipper

REMOVED FROM THE PUBLIC EYE *by his affliction with Alzheimer's disease, Ronald Reagan (b.1911) remains a potent symbolic force in U.S. politics, perhaps the only president since Franklin Roosevelt to change the way large numbers of people think about their relationship to government. He did so less by force of intellect than by clarity of vision. He was—to use current political jargon—on message for all eight years of his presidency with his tales of government waste and abuse, although he rarely seemed as brash as the legislators and governors who now claim to be his heirs. With a twinkle in the eye and a nod of his chin, Reagan reassured Americans that he always had their best interests at heart.*

More than that, he brought dignity and good cheer to the White House, with the ease of an actor playing a part written especially for him. Yet he took a bullet in stride (famously joking with his doctors) and stared down a Soviet empire he wasn't shy about calling "evil" at a time when more learned political commentators couldn't have imagined being so honest. Like Franklin Roosevelt, Ronald Reagan will probably outlive his critics to become the American who defines his era, a figure almost large enough for Mount Rushmore.

Peggy Noonan, author of the Newsweek *story I've selected for this chapter, served as a speech writer for both Ronald Reagan and his successor, George Bush. She is credited with preparing Reagan's moving eulogy for the astronauts killed in the* Challenger *explosion and with writing Bush's famous line about a "kinder, gentler America." She is also the author of* Life, Liberty, and the Pursuit of Happiness *(1994), a memoir about her political career. Her essay originally appeared in* Newsweek *(October 2, 1995) following a story about Reagan's declining health.* – J.R.

When Steve Forbes announced for president last week, he said Republicans have an "empty feeling" about the '96 race, and it's true. They're poised for victory, it's a Republican year, they've already won the Congress, and yet . . . they're frustrated. . . .

There is an absence, a lack, this presidential year. Will Newt run? Will Colin Powell? Some say the general's qualities are Reaganesque, but more and more of us see him as our favorite moderate Democrat. There *is* one Republican out there who unites the party; who has the respect and affection of both its elders and collegiate Dittoheads; and who, in a party riven somewhat by class, is happily claimed as One of Us by Greenwich millionaires, Chillicothe Christians and Little Rock auto mechanics; who soothes the chafing

456

tensions between pro- and anti-gun, pro- and anti-abortion. And he even comes from California.

He is, of course, Ronald Reagan, more than ever the party's undiminished hero. Seven years out of office, no one has quite taken his place. That's what the empty feeling is—his big absence.

The feeling is not confined to his party. He is old now and ill, and for the nation, he is a poignant presence. He is in a kind of twilight; we cannot mourn him, but we can miss him, and we do.

Which is not to say his critics have ever stopped trying to tear down his record. But it doesn't seem to have worked. Almost two years ago, I wrote to him and asked how he felt about it. "I'm not the sort to lose sleep over what a few revisionists say," the president wrote back. "Let history decide; it usually does."

Other presidents have loomed large. Nixon loomed, but like a shadow. Reagan looms like a sun, lighting the stage on which the year's contenders stand. But his light is so bright they squint in the glare and seem paler, washed out.

Part of this is inevitable. We appreciate presidents more than we appreciate candidates. When a man becomes president, we suddenly discover virtues of which we—and they—had been unaware. If he is elected, Dole's wit will be called not mean but trenchant and deep, a gallant mask for pain; Gramm's stark and prickly conservatism will become a no-frills tribute to authenticity.

And it's good to remember we didn't always love Reagan. In 1980 he was called an aging nuclear cowboy who'd throw Grandma into the snow, a washed-up grade-B former-actor former-governor who'd run twice and lost and whose hands were clasped in victory over a pompadour people said was dyed.

The media and academe saw him not as a statesman but as a joke. And there were failures: he never really cut the size and scope of government, and the deficit grew. There were irritating excesses (glitz, glamour), insensitivities and derelictions.

But for all that, he is missed and admired, still the man you see when you hear the phrase The American President. Why? Because of a combination of qualities in the man and in his presidency.

He set out to make big change. Only a few times a century do you find a president who really changed things. Most presidents, one way or another, have no serious grievance with the status quo. Ford, Carter, Kennedy, Eisenhower, Bush—they made progress or mischief at the margins. But Reagan changed things as much as Franklin Roosevelt—only in the opposite direction. He changed the way we look at the role of government in America. In the 50 years preceding his presidency it was generally agreed (though not generally stated) that the government created wealth and should supervise its distribution. But Reagan said no—it does *not* create wealth, it is an impediment to prosperity, and it should not be distributing your money, you should. Like it or not, that was change.

He knew what he thought and why he thought it. He had thought it through, was a conservative for serious philosophical reasons, had read his Hayek and his Friedman, knew exactly why "that government governs best that governs least." And he became a conservative at some cost, in the early '60s, when the country was beginning to turn left and the community in which he lived and earned his living, Hollywood, was turning lefter still.

He didn't hold views to be popular, he held them because he thought they were right. The men around him sometimes used polls to divine which issues to hit hard. That's not how he used polls. He used them to see if what he was saying was what people were hearing, and to cheer himself up when he was blue. He liked it when the pollsters could tell him 82 percent of the people thought he was doing a good job. He'd breathe the numbers in, stick out his chest and wade back into the fray. But his positions were not poll driven, and the people could tell. So even when they disagreed with him, they still respected him.

He meant it. His beliefs were sincerely held. And because he was sincere, the people cut him some slack where they wouldn't cut it for others. Reagan raised taxes in '82 and won by a landslide in '84. When George Bush raised taxes, they sent him to Elba.

He was right. He said the Soviet Union was evil and an empire, and it   15 was; he said history would consign it to the ash heap, and it did. Thirty-one years ago in The Speech, the one he gave a week before the '64 election and which put him on the political map, he said: high taxes are bad, heavy regulation is bad, bureaucracies cause more ills than they cure and government is not necessarily your friend. It could have been given by half the congressional candidates of 1994—and was.

He had the presidential style. He knew how to act the part. In this he was like FDR and JFK, who also understood the role. He intuited that a certain detachment produces mystery, and mystery enhances power. He was not on television every night. It would have lowered his currency, made him common. He wasn't Ron-is-the-caller-there-Reagan, and wouldn't have understood a president who is. He thought it boorish to be in the nation's face all the time.

He would not have talked about his underwear on TV—they would never have asked him—and he not only wouldn't feel your pain, he barely agreed to feel *his* pain. He had dignity. Clinton has the baby boomer's discomfort with dignity: they equate it with formality and formality with phoniness, and what could be worse than that?

He loved America. He really *loved* it. His eyes went misty when he spoke of her. It was personal, emotional, protective and trusting. He was an American exceptionalist—we weren't like other countries, God put us in a special place with a special job, to lead the forces of good, to be the city on a hill

John Winthrop saw and hoped for. Clinton grows misty-eyed, too, but over abstractions: justice, harmony. Clinton loves America at her best. But Reagan loved America, period.

It worked. If, when he ran for president in 1980, a little angel had whispered in your ear, "If Reagan wins, by the time he leaves Soviet communism will be dead, the Dow will have passed 2000, taxes will be cut and we'll all have a more spirited sense of the historical possibilities," would you have voted for him? Of course you would have.

He won by 10 points that year, but if we'd known what was coming he   20
would have won by 30. The fact is he was a big man who did big things, and that is why we already miss him.

QUESTIONING THE TEXT

1. Explore the allusions in Noonan's phrase suggesting that Reagan appealed equally to "Greenwich millionaires, Chillicothe Christians and Little Rock auto mechanics" (p. 456). What would she have lost (or gained) by suggesting more simply that Reagan was popular with "all sorts of people"?

2. Noonan structures her argument around a simple list of reasons why Reagan is missed. Do you find this way of organizing the article effective? Why, or why not?

3. Look at the words and phrases J.R. uses in his introduction to make it clear he admires Ronald Reagan. How does this clear expression of a political opinion shape your reading of Noonan's piece?

MAKING CONNECTIONS

4. Of Reagan, Noonan writes: "He didn't hold views to be popular, he held them because he thought they were right." Through the character of Howard Roark, Ayn Rand similarly suggests that the creator is a man who acts independently of public opinion. Review Roark's speech from *The Fountainhead* (p. 444), and then consider whether Reagan, as Noonan draws him, fits the mold of hero that Ayn Rand fashions. Write a paragraph explaining your opinion.

JOINING THE CONVERSATION

5. Choose a public figure you admire and list the qualities you respect most, the way Noonan does of Reagan. Add particular examples to

your list of qualities and then turn this prewriting exercise into a full essay.

6. Interview a range of people from different walks of life and of different ages. Prepare a series of questions that require more than yes/no answers, and ask their assessment of Reagan or another influential public figure of the recent past. Then use your findings to write a short essay on the figure you have chosen.

JOAN DIDION
Georgia O'Keeffe

WHEN I BEGAN THINKING about the second edition of The Presence of Others, my first-year students suggested that I concentrate in this chapter on legends rather than heroes. "Heroes," they said, "are personal; they can be anyone—your mom or dad, even a pet. Legends, on the other hand, are people everyone knows, kind of larger than life. And not always good." I thought these students made an excellent point, and so I began thinking not so much about my personal heroes (I soon realized that they included my grandmother as well as Rosa Parks) but about figures who have gained legendary status.

In the art world, Georgia O'Keeffe (1887–1986) certainly stands out as a legend: a fiercely independent woman determined to follow her own lights no matter what the outcome and no matter whether anyone ever recognized her work. Born and raised in Wisconsin, O'Keeffe seems to have wanted to be an artist forever, and to have known what kind of painting she wanted to do. After studying at the Art Institute of Chicago and the Art Students League in New York City, O'Keeffe struck out on her own, developing her own unique style. Although they seemed odd, even bizarre and ugly, to some of her contemporaries, many of her paintings have impressed themselves on the national psyche: the enormous, powerful flowers; the cow's sun-bleached skull; the stark southwestern landscapes.

In the following essay, the novelist and essayist Joan Didion (b. 1934) aims to capture the spirit of O'Keeffe's work—and of O'Keeffe herself. In the opening paragraph, Didion alludes to a famous photograph of O'Keeffe taken by Alfred Stieglitz, to whom O'Keeffe was married in 1924. Although Didion doesn't say so, what follows is her own photograph of this legendary artist.

— A.L.

"Where I was born and where and how I have lived is unimportant," Georgia O'Keeffe told us in the book of paintings and words published in her ninetieth year on earth. She seemed to be advising us to forget the beautiful face in the Stieglitz photographs. She appeared to be dismissing the rather condescending romance that had attached to her by then, the romance of extreme good looks and advanced age and deliberate isolation. "It is what I have done with where I have been that should be of interest." I recall an August afternoon in Chicago in 1973 when I took my daughter, then seven, to see what Georgia O'Keeffe had done with where she had been. One of the vast O'Keeffe "Sky Above Clouds" canvases floated over the back stairs in the Chicago Art Institute that day, dominating what seemed to be several stories

461

of empty light, and my daughter looked at it once, ran to the landing, and kept on looking. "Who drew it," she whispered after a while. I told her. "I need to talk to her," she said finally.

My daughter was making, that day in Chicago, an entirely unconscious but quite basic assumption about people and the work they do. She was assuming that the glory she saw in the work reflected a glory in its maker, that the painting was the painter as the poem is the poet, that every choice one made alone—every word chosen or rejected, every brush stroke laid or not laid down—betrayed one's character. *Style is character.* It seemed to me that afternoon that I had rarely seen so instinctive an application of this familiar principle, and I recall being pleased not only that my daughter responded to style as character but that it was Georgia O'Keeffe's particular style to which she responded: this was a hard woman who had imposed her 192 square feet of clouds on Chicago.

"Hardness" has not been in our century a quality much admired in women, nor in the past twenty years has it even been in official favor for men. When hardness surfaces in the very old we tend to transform it into "crustiness" or eccentricity, some tonic pepperiness to be indulged at a distance. On the evidence of her work and what she has said about it, Georgia O'Keeffe is neither "crusty" nor eccentric. She is simply hard, a straight shooter, a woman clean of received wisdom and open to what she sees. This is a woman who could early on dismiss most of her contemporaries as "dreamy," and would later single out one she liked as "a very poor painter." (And then add, apparently by way of softening the judgment: "I guess he wasn't a painter at all. He had no courage and I believe that to create one's own world in any of the arts takes courage.") This is a woman who in 1939 could advise her admirers that they were missing her point, that their appreciation of her famous flowers was merely sentimental. "When I paint a red hill," she observed coolly in the catalogue for an exhibition that year, "you say it is too bad that I don't always paint flowers. A flower touches almost everyone's heart. A red hill doesn't touch everyone's heart." This is a woman who could describe the genesis of one of her most well-known paintings— the "Cow's Skull: Red, White and Blue" owned by the Metropolitan—as an act of quite deliberate and derisive orneriness. "I thought of the city men I had been seeing in the East," she wrote. "They talked so often of writing the Great American Novel—the Great American Play—the Great American Poetry. . . . So as I was painting my cow's head on blue I thought to myself, 'I'll make it an American painting. They will not think it great with the red stripes down the sides—Red, White, and Blue—but they will notice it.'"

The city men. The men. They. The words crop up again and again as this astonishingly aggressive woman tells us what was on her mind when she was making her astonishingly aggressive paintings. It was those city men who stood accused of sentimentalizing her flowers: "I made you take time to look at what I saw and when you took time to really notice my flower you hung all your associations with flowers on my flower and you write about my flower as if I think and see what you think and see—and I don't." *And I don't.* Imagine those words spoken, and the sound you hear is *don't tread on me.* "The men" believed it impossible to paint New York, so Georgia O'Keeffe painted New York. "The men" didn't think much of her bright color, so she made it brighter. The men yearned toward Europe so she went to Texas, and then New Mexico. The men talked about Cézanne, "long involved remarks about the 'plastic quality' of his form and color," and took one another's long involved remarks, in the view of this angelic rattlesnake in their midst, altogether too seriously. "I can paint one of those dismal-colored paintings like the men," the woman who regarded herself always as an outsider remembers thinking one day in 1922, and she did: a painting of a shed "all low-toned and dreary with the tree beside the door." She called this act of rancor "The Shanty" and hung it in her next show. "The men seemed to approve of it," she reported fifty-four years later, her contempt undimmed. "They seemed to think that maybe I was beginning to paint. That was my only low-toned dismal-colored painting."

Some women fight and others do not. Like so many successful guerrillas   5
in the war between the sexes, Georgia O'Keeffe seems to have been equipped early with an immutable sense of who she was and a fairly clear understanding that she would be required to prove it. On the surface her upbringing was conventional. She was a child on the Wisconsin prairie who played with china dolls and painted watercolors with cloudy skies because sunlight was too hard to paint and, with her brother and sisters, listened every night to her mother read stories of the Wild West, of Texas, of Kit Carson and Billy the Kid. She told adults that she wanted to be an artist and was embarrassed when they asked what kind of artist she wanted to be: she had no idea "what kind." She had no idea what artists did. She had never seen a picture that interested her, other than a pen-and-ink Maid of Athens in one of her mother's books, some Mother Goose illustrations printed on cloth, a tablet cover that showed a little girl with pink roses, and the painting of Arabs on horseback that hung in her grandmother's parlor. At thirteen, in a Dominican convent, she was mortified when the sister corrected her drawing. At Chatham Episcopal Institute in Virginia she painted lilacs and sneaked time alone to walk out to where she could see the line of the Blue Ridge Mountains on the horizon. At the Art Institute in Chicago she was shocked by the presence of live models and wanted to abandon anatomy lessons. At the Art Students League in New York one of her fellow students advised her that, since he would be a great painter and she would end up teaching painting in a girls' school, any work of hers was less important than modeling for him. Another painted over her work to show her how the Impressionists did trees. She had not before heard how the Impressionists did trees and she did not much care.

At twenty-four she left all those opinions behind and went for the first time to live in Texas, where there were no trees to paint and no one to tell her how not to paint them. In Texas there was only the horizon she craved. In Texas she had her sister Claudia with her for a while, and in the late afternoons they would walk away from town and toward the horizon and watch the evening star come out. "That evening star fascinated me," she wrote. "It was in some way very exciting to me. My sister had a gun, and as we walked she would throw bottles into the air and shoot as many as she could before they hit the ground. I had nothing but to walk into nowhere and the wide sunset space with the star. Ten watercolors were made from that star." In a way one's interest is compelled as much by the sister Claudia with the gun as by the painter Georgia with the star, but only the painter left us this shining record. Ten watercolors were made from that star.

QUESTIONING THE TEXT

1. Didion uses quotation marks not only to mark off quotations but also to call attention to certain words such as "hardness." What effect does this use of quotation marks have on the portrait of O'Keeffe that emerges? Why do you think Didion uses quotation marks in this way? Take some notes toward an answer to these questions and bring them to class for discussion.

2. What is Didion's attitude toward O'Keeffe? What in the text alerts you to this attitude? How does Didion's attitude toward her subject affect the way you respond to O'Keeffe? If you keep a reading log, answer these questions there.

3. Look back at what A.L. says in the introduction about a distinction between heroes and legends. How would you define the two terms, and what differences do you perceive between the two?

MAKING CONNECTIONS

4. O'Keeffe says that "Where I was born and where and how I have lived is unimportant." Would Ayn Rand's character Howard Roark (p. 444) make the same comment about himself? Why, or why not?

5. Peggy Noonan and Joan Didion clearly admire the people they are writing about (Ronald Reagan and Georgia O'Keeffe). Reread the two essays together, taking notes on what each author finds admirable (the traits may be implicit as well as explicit in the essays). Do the two authors agree on some or many of these admirable traits? Do you find one or the other more convincing? Write a brief (one- or two-page) analysis of one of the essays, explaining the basis of the author's admiration and adding your own response.

JOINING THE CONVERSATION

6. Choose a legendary figure not explored in this chapter and do some research, finding out all you can about him or her. Then, using Didion's "Georgia O'Keeffe" as a general guide, write a brief essay in which you attempt to capture the life, personality, and importance of the legend you have chosen to study.

7. In paragraph 4, Didion refers repeatedly to those who didn't understand or appreciate O'Keeffe's work as "the men," never giving them individual names. Working with a classmate, interview a member of the art department on your campus to get some ideas about who those "men" might be. With the information you glean, go to the library and investigate the male artists. Then get together and write another version of paragraph 4 of Didion's essay from the point of view, perhaps, of "the men."

GEORGE SIM JOHNSTON
Pope Culture

POPE JOHN PAUL II (b. 1920), *the spiritual leader of a billion Catholics worldwide, rose to the throne of Peter in troubled times, a Polish prelate who had endured the Nazi occupation of his homeland while young and then watched as his highly religious country was devoured by atheistic communism. Yet at his election in 1978, his first words to a stunned crowd in Saint Peter's Square accustomed to Italian pontiffs were "Be not afraid," a message of hope that the former Karol Wojtyla has continued to spread to the church worldwide, especially in Africa and Asia.*

More conservative on doctrine and teaching than many Americans would like, John Paul has been a beacon of faith to others, a pope in the Polish style who reveres the Virgin Mary and relishes the miraculous. Yet he is a shrewd politician as well, maneuvering behind the scenes throughout the 1980s, for example, to strengthen the Polish union Solidarity and to challenge the grip of Soviet totalitarianism on Eastern Europe. Returning to his homeland as pontiff, John Paul proved that, contrary to Stalin's belief, the pope indeed had many legions willing to stand up for their beliefs, far more than Karl Marx could muster. Later shot in Vatican City by a man possibly working as an agent of the KGB, John Paul survived to watch the empire of Stalin crumble and to see freedom restored to his homeland for the first time in his adult life.

In the following essay from the American Spectator *(July 1995), a conservative journal, writer George Sim Johnston (b. 1951) assesses the impact that John Paul has had not only on Europe but on the United States, where the pope's uncompromising views on abortion and sexuality have drawn considerable fire. Johnston makes few apologies for John Paul; indeed, he suggests that the West in particular badly needs a stern messenger to turn it away from "the death culture" to a nobler ideal of human nature.* − J.R.

Last autumn a senior writer at *Time* was advised to put the final touches on the obituary of Pope John Paul II. The pope's health seemed to be failing, and like the rest of the media, *Time* was getting ready to wrap up his pontificate. Since then, however, he has, if anything, been moving even faster. John Paul has resumed his punishing world travels, drawing four million people in Manila—the largest crowd to assemble in history. He has stepped up his literary output, feeding a sudden public appetite for papal books and documents. And he is talking about the year 2000 as though he fully expects to be there, having announced plans for a meeting of the great monotheistic faiths at the foot of Mount Sinai.

Enlightened opinion long ago wrote off the papacy as a quaint relic of the Middle Ages. When Pius IX barricaded the Church against all forms of liberalism a century and a half ago, it was widely held that the papacy was slated for a long slide into oblivion. But the papal chair is now occupied by a man who, alone among his contemporaries, has the international stature associated with the generation of Churchill and de Gaulle. And John Paul could not be more "modern"—he is a survivor of two totalitarian regimes, a disciple of Scheler and Husserl, and an underground playwright and actor whose delivery on television John Gielgud once called "perfect."

That in a dreary decade of Clinton and Yeltsin the pope has a monopoly on public gravitas may partly explain the attention he now commands. But something deeper is going on here, a historical reversal whose drift is sensed even by the religiously tone-deaf media. After the European wars of religion centuries ago, faith was banished to the realm of private opinion. Thinkers like Spinoza, who was agnostic, maintained that we had to give up on the idea of religion as a bond between people; man-made philosophy would have to do the job instead. This of course was the project of the Enlightenment. It was in many respects successful, although its prophets did not appreciate the extent to which the modern state would have to draw on the reserves of Judeo-Christianity in order to survive and prosper.

John Paul II is not alone in thinking that the West is close to depleting its religious account. As Nietzsche said to the West: You have killed off God, but it will take a century for you to start behaving as though it were really true. This is the "culture of death" about which John Paul is so eloquent. And he is attempting a dramatic reversal. He is trying to put God back into the public discourse of the West, not as private opinion or under the sectarian banner of Catholicism, but as normative reality. No other antidote exists for the skepticism and moral relativism eating away at our democracies.

John Paul is urging on the West a Christian humanism that can be   5
grasped by all but the most obdurate materialist. The United States and Western Europe are the only credible political and economic models left, but their cultures are another matter. A kind of soft nihilism has settled on the West, one that, in John Paul's view, does not differ radically from the hard nihilism of Marxism. Both treat man as a thing or, at best, a clever ape. Both deny to man mystery and transcendence. The pope, who is a great admirer of the West, believes that we can do better and that if we don't, we are headed the way of the late classical Greek and Roman cultures.

Born in 1920 as Karol Wojtyla, he came to maturity just in time for the Nazi occupation of Poland.[1] During the early war years, he worked in a

---

[1]Tad Szulc's new book, *Pope John Paul II: The Biography* (Charles Scribner's Sons, 542 pages, $27.50), gives a surprisingly good account of the pope's life.

chemical factory and a stone quarry. He was placed on the Gestapo blacklist for helping Jewish families escape from Cracow, just a short distance from Auschwitz. After Hitler came Yalta, where, as the Poles say, they lost World War II a second time. Wojtyla was ordained a priest in 1946 after training in an underground seminary, and soon became an adversary of the Communist regime. The main lesson he drew from the Stalinist decades was that a political order based on a radical misreading of the human person will fail for reasons not purely technical or economic. Far from producing the New Socialist Man, the militant atheism of Marxism-Leninism created instead a hunger for religion that is now playing itself out in remarkable ways.

As pope, Wojtyla was a key player in the endgame of the Cold War. He and Ronald Reagan were the two forces that hastened the end of the Soviet empire. Western journalists and academics have not given either man proper credit. (Nor have they grasped the role that Christianity played in the Revolution of 1989. Those crucifixes and Madonnas in the Gdansk shipyard made our pundits uneasy, when they noticed them at all.) But it is premature to talk of a dramatic spiritual revival in the former Soviet bloc. Those countries are too busy playing catch-up with Western materialism. The pope has been very vocal about their new pursuit of consumerism. In his view, the Central European countries are simply trading one faulty anthropology for another.

John Paul's criticisms of the Western democracies have been widely misrepresented in such places as the *New York Times,* which is always quick to run a headline like "Papal Encyclical Urges Capitalism to Shed Injustices." The pope is actually a strong advocate of private property and individual initiative. In *Centesimus Annus* (1991), which marked a watershed in Catholic social thinking, he not only excoriated the modern welfare state but also closed the door on the so-called "third way," that non-existent compromise between collectivism and capitalism so dear to left-wing Catholics. (As a Czech minister once snapped, the third way leads to the Third World.) But what concerns John Paul is not so much specific economic mechanisms as the cultural norms that support them. And this is where he is warning the East to keep a tactful distance from its new mentors.

First and foremost, he points to the West's loss of "the truth about man." For those who don't mind the Bible, the best way to get at John Paul's thinking is to read his meditations on the opening of Genesis in books like *The Original Unity of Man and Woman.* Like St. Augustine, he draws from it lessons that make the most cutting-edge Sartrean existentialism seem mildly quaint. He focuses on the second chapter, which depicts the original solitude of Adam and his finding himself in relation to Eve. This account, which obviously has metaphorical elements, points to the difference between man and beast: Man is a creature defined by interiority and inwardness—and by the need to make a gift of self to another being. This, if anything, is what it means to be created in the image of God.

After making the case for the inviolable dignity of man, the pope makes   10
a second point: Man, however noble, is not his own creator. This self-evident
fact tortured the young Marx until he discovered Darwin. But even unaided
reason, according to John Paul, does not support the idea of man as self-
created and thus free of norms and obligations.

Above all, the pope objects to the notion of the individual conscience as
a little god, a supreme tribunal making categorical decisions about right and
wrong. Along with a new generation of Catholic intellectuals, he is suggesting that the modern world either rediscover the principles of natural law,
found in documents ranging from the Declaration of Independence to Martin
Luther King's letter from the Birmingham Jail, or prepare itself for an increasingly fragmented and unhappy existence.

The idea of natural law, an antecedent moral sense implanted in man
and written into the nature of things, was last broached in public during the
confirmation hearings of Clarence Thomas. Educated in Catholic schools,
Thomas was skewered by the Senate Judiciary Committee because he had
once given a speech agreeing with Abraham Lincoln about the natural-law
basis of the Constitution. Thomas did not help matters by backing away from
the questions. He ought to have asked the senators where else one can find a
basis for morality. The alternative is a legal positivism which keeps manufacturing "rights" with no reference to duties or obligations. The result is a
splintered and demoralized social order. If God has created an objective moral
order, it is beyond whim and manipulation. On the other hand, if there is no
God, and man is the result of a blind, material process, there is no basis for
constructing any moral order whatsoever. Sartre, modernity's Village Atheist,
understood this quite clearly. He was merely being consistent when he criticized the Nazi war-crime trials at Nuremberg, since "crimes against humanity" must be deduced from a natural law decreed by a Creator.

There is a certain irony in a Polish pope suggesting that a democracy go
back and read its founding documents. Fifty years ago, Catholic thinkers such
as Jacques Maritain expressed delight and amazement that the most powerful
nation on earth should believe in limited, constitutional government based on
natural law. The legal forms of this country worked because of the unwritten
consensus that produced them. (Read Tocqueville, another insightful
Catholic.) But that consensus has been replaced by a radical pluralism that
obliges people to respect all views and honor no truths. Instead of values, frail
humanity now has "options" and opinions to guide it.

John Paul has repeatedly warned, most recently in *Evangelium Vitae*
("The Gospel of Life"), that the kind of pluralism now espoused in the West
is a thinly disguised tyranny. Our liberal champions of pluralism do not want
society to be truly pluralistic. That would leave too much room for people
who believe in moral absolutes. What they want is that each person be a
walking container of pluralism, so that religious values have no chance of

reaching the public square. The new ground rules are odd by any historical standard: an unborn child is not sacrosanct, for example, but a plurality of views about the child's worth is.

This absolutizing of the relative produces rich contradictions in the be-   15
havior of liberals. The English medical journal *Lancet* recently published an article which claimed that the unborn child, or whatever you wish to call it, experiences extreme pain during an abortion and so ought to be given anesthetic (we have yet to hear from the animal rights crowd). Similarly, in overturning the state of Washington's assisted suicide law, federal judge Barbara Rothstein wrote that each individual has the right to define his or her own "concept of existence, meaning, and the universe." If that is so, and Judge Rothstein inhabits a different universe from the rest of us, how does she come to be handing down legal opinions?

In *Evangelium Vitae,* John Paul makes the reasonable suggestion that we "call things by their proper name." The advocates of abortion and euthanasia operate on a classic Orwellian principle: before engineering a social reality, you must first engineer the language. Phrases such as "reproductive health" and "safe motherhood" hardly do justice to what happens in a second-trimester abortion.

Fifty years ago, euthanasia was a Nazi war crime; now it is a desideratum of progressive opinion. Hidden in the Clinton administration's health-care bill was a shocking money-saving device that got little attention. Medical care was to be denied to older persons who no longer enjoyed "quality of life." This utilitarian approach to life has already been adopted in Holland, where many elderly are terrified of entering a hospital even for routine tests.

The main battle ground of John Paul's war against this "culture of death" has been the population conferences sponsored by the United Nations. These forums have been going on for decades, but it took the Clinton administration to make them dangerous. The one constant theme discernible in the twists and turns of the Clinton White House is support for abortion on demand—at any stage of pregnancy—and population control abroad. Led by Under Secretary of State Tim Wirth, the Clinton team wants to spend billions of dollars to spread its sexual philosophy to every corner of the globe.

The track record of the zero-population lobby that runs these forums is remarkable—a perfect score of being wrong in their apocalyptic forecasts. First there was Paul Ehrlich's 1968 book *The Population Bomb,* which forecast worldwide famines in the seventies; then the 1974 Club of Rome report, whose prediction of imminent scarcities of basic resources was laughably off the mark. Such Malthusian scenarios take no account of man's ingenuity in using the earth's resources. Since World War II the food output of the world has tripled while its population has doubled. The earth's present population of six billion occupies less than two percent of the earth's land mass; if everyone of them moved to Texas, each would have the living space of the average American.

John Paul recognizes that there are places where demographics are a   20
problem and the prudential spacing of children is in order. But he should
make even clearer an obvious fact: wars and famines today are caused by ethnic feuding and socialism, not by population pressures. Birth rates in Europe,
America, and even China are now below replacement level. Germany is offering cash rewards to married couples who have babies, since there are not
enough children to fill the schools. At some point in the next millennium,
every Italian will fit comfortably in a medium suburb of Rome. This "birth
dearth," in Ben Wattenberg's phrase, is *the* geo-political story of the end of
the century; if history is any guide, the coming decline of numbers in the
West promises to be a devastating phenomenon.

"The evil nature" of the population control movement, writes Charles
Rice of Notre Dame, "is one of the best kept secrets in the world." This perhaps explains why the Vatican gets such bad press for its skirmishes against the
radical feminists and eugenicists who are drafting documents for the U.N.
Conference on Women in Peking in September. (China's policy of forced
abortions was apparently not a negative in the choice of venue.) High on the
radical agenda is a proposal to expand the number of "genders" to five.

Sex, of course, is the engine that drives much of the hostility to the
Catholic Church. In 1959, Wojtyla wrote a wise and densely philosophical
book on the subject, *Love and Responsibility.* It influenced Paul VI's arguments
against birth control in *Humanae Vitae,* a document that does not look as retrograde now as it did in the early days of the sexual revolution. (Suffice it to say
that the divorce rate among couples who use contraceptives is way above the
national average.) John Paul is anything but a puritan. But he does insist that
having sex is not the same thing as shaking hands; it has consequences. Now that
our society has become a hothouse of divorce, illegitimacy, and sexually trans-
mitted diseases, it may be worth pondering his contention that the "trivialization of sexuality" is opposed to the truth about man. The Catholic Church does
not assert that certain behavior is evil simply because it has bad consequences,
but it does suggest that acts which violate objective norms inevitably have such
results.

Mention of sex leads us to the situation of the Catholic Church in
America. The whining and gnashing of teeth the pope has to contend with
in this country stems from a widespread frustration at not finding loopholes in
the Sixth and Ninth Commandments. Cardinal Ratzinger once dismissed
American Catholic dissent as the expression of a "bourgeois" Christianity that
seeks to make religion as undemanding as possible. He suggested that this
Catholicism Lite does not have much of a future. He is right about that; but
in the meantime, it is very popular in Catholic seminaries and universities,
and its adherents make no secret of their impatience for a new pope, who,
they presume, will canonize all their whims.

Still, a healthy populism has sprung up among Catholics in the United
States; it communicates on the Internet, tunes in to Mother Angelica's cable

network, buys the Pope's books and audio tapes, and reads the new Catechism, a volume that the official Catholic apparatus in Washington did not exactly welcome, since it makes crystal clear that the Second Vatican Council did not abolish *any* of the traditional teachings of the Church. This Catholic populism has connections with the new political populism; both are going to bring down cultural fiefdoms which have ruled since the sixties.

It is hard to convey what this pope means to orthodox Catholics who   25
for decades have suffered a catalogue of stupidities—ranging from the new churches that look like auto-parts distribution warehouses to liturgical abuses whose purpose seems to be the inflation of the collective ego of the congregation. Apart from his forceful articulation of Catholic doctrine, this pope has an effect on people which Mikhail Gorbachev, who reportedly still visits John Paul when in Rome, calls "extraordinary." The French journalist André Frossard probably expressed it best:

> That October day when he appeared for the first time on the steps of St. Peter's, with a big crucifix planted in front of him like a two-handed sword, and his first words, *Non abbiate paura!* ("Be not afraid"), echoing over the square, everyone realized then and there that something had happened in heaven: after the man of good will who had opened the Council, after the deeply spiritual man who had closed it and after an interlude as gentle and fleeting as the flight of a dove, God was sending us a witness.

The political sideshows ought not to distract us from the person and message of a pope who some day may be the third in his line to be called "the Great." The West has come to a parting of ways. On the one hand there is an understanding of man that has sustained Christendom, however imperfectly, for two millennia; on the other, the way summed up by Pascal: Man without a Creator either becomes a deity and goes mad, or becomes a beast. The pope is a great friend of the West, and his warning ought to be regarded as coming from one who wants to see it stand for something beyond a morally vacuous "freedom of choice."

Apart from a great man with a message, the same message of two thousand years ago, what does Catholicism have to offer the sole remaining superpower? Richard Rodriguez once observed that Mexico is Catholic and tragic, and everyone there is cheerful; the United States is Protestant and optimistic, and everyone is depressed. With the Cold War over, however, even our optimism seems to have faded a bit. The promised end of history, in which man, tired of ideologies, spends several millennia fine-tuning sophisticated consumer needs, is a dreary prospect.

QUESTIONING THE TEXT

1. Johnston discusses Pope John Paul II's views on natural law at some
   length, noting that they contradict the relativism of most contemporary

thinkers "that obliges people to respect all views and honor no truths." Do some library reading to understand the basic differences between natural law and relativistic perspectives on morality, and take notes. Then come to class prepared to discuss some of the consequences of accepting either of these worldviews.

2. Does Johnston's lengthy digression on the "culture of death" in which he discusses the population dilemma (starting on p. 470) seem germane to the main theme of "Pope Culture"? Why, or why not?

3. In the introduction, J.R. suggests that the pope may be "more conservative on doctrine and teaching than many Americans would like." What are some of the controversial positions to which J.R. is alluding?

MAKING CONNECTIONS

4. Do you see any significance in the fact that both John Paul and Ronald Reagan (see Peggy Noonan's essay on p. 456) were actors earlier in their lives? What might make someone with stage training an especially effective leader today?

5. According to Johnston, John Paul sees human beings as specially created: "Man is a creature defined by interiority and inwardness—and by the need to make a gift of self to another being." Contrast this view of self with that offered by Ayn Rand (p. 443). Which view of humankind do you find more challenging or heroic?

6. Read Johnston's piece side by side with that by Stephen L. Carter (p. 175). How much influence can a spiritual leader like John Paul exercise over the political decisions of a given country? Write an essay describing the role you think religious leaders should or should not play in a democratic society.

JOINING THE CONVERSATION

7. Write a narrative about a leader—spiritual or otherwise—who has made an impact on the way you view the world. Or, if you can think of no figure who has had such an impact, explain whether you think that absence of influence is good or bad. Do we really all need heroes?

STEVEN LEVY
Bill's New Vision

"*BILL'S SO SMART*," says a character in Douglas Coupland's Microserfs. "*Bill is wise. Bill is kind. Bill is benevolent. Bill, Be My Friend . . . Please!*" *Friend or not, William Henry Gates III (b. 1955) is surely the stuff legends are made of. Says Tom Brokaw, no small-fry himself, of a stroll with Gates through the Comdex computer show, "It's like walking the Vatican with the pope." With his twenty-year-old Microsoft, his acquisition of everything from the world's reference texts to the world's archived images, and his new $80 million home on the shores of Seattle's Lake Washington, Gates is the richest man alive—and increasingly one of the most controversial. Is Gates a visionary genius whose company aims at fierce but fair competition? Or is he a shrewd entrepreneur/technocrat, whose ethical principles are shaky at best, as evidenced in Microsoft's drive to dominate world markets as well as access to global information systems—at any cost? As with most either/or questions, the answer to this one is probably "A little bit of both."*

In the review that follows (originally published in Newsweek*), journalist Steven Levy (b. 1951) takes a look at Gates's book-length forecast of the future* The Road Ahead, *comparing Gates's words with his actions. Against the resolutely upbeat view of a future in which there's a personal computer on every desk in every home putting the wonders of the world at our fingertips, Levy juxtaposes the monopolistic tendencies of the software giant Microsoft and its leader, who aims to ensure that every computer in every home runs on Microsoft products and that the information we have access to will be ours only for a fee we will pay to—guess who?*

Whatever the outcome of Bill Gates's next twenty years on the business scene, it is bound to affect much of our lives. That's why I wanted to include an essay about Gates in this book: in some very important ways, as Gates and Microsoft go, so go the rest of us as well. – A.L.

"Who's that guy next to Bill Gates?" the question comes from one of the 200,000 conventioneers at the mammoth Comdex computer show in Las Vegas, and the answer is Tom Brokaw, whose face is not exactly unknown in most of America. But as Brokaw conducts a roving interview past the gleaming booths representing the giants of silicon—Sony, Apple, Hewlett-Packard, IBM and, of course, Microsoft—chipheads abandon their commerce and jerk their heads backward in astonishment, not at the NBC anchorman but at the tousle-haired 40-year-old animatedly conversing with him, seemingly oblivious of the camera crew ahead and a growing procession of gawkers behind, trailing through the carpeted aisles like a human comet's tail. It's him! The King of Comdex, if not the computer industry, if not the future itself. The richest man on the planet, and maybe the smartest: William Henry Gates III.

There is no question that inside the world of computers, Bill Gates has assumed dimensions that far exceed human scale. "It's like walking the Vatican with the pope," Brokaw said to a crew member after the Comdex jaunt. As the chairman, cofounder and CEO of Microsoft, the company that reaps almost half the revenue in PC software worldwide, Gates is indeed regarded as nearly divine—though some competitors view him as satanic. More recently he has become a figure of fascination to the public, as befits a former computer nerd who used digital machismo and hardball business skills to accumulate a net worth of nearly $15 billion, give or take. He is also revered as the person who understands computer technology best, at a time when just about everybody else is still trying to figure out how to get their CD-ROM to play. But to date he has been reluctant to play his powerful celebrity card. While his appearances have been increasingly splashy—the recent rollout of Windows 95 software saw him trading quips with Jay Leno and being picked up like a round ball by Shaquille O'Neal—they have always been strictly in the service of Microsoft business. Aspects of his private life have been closely held, as evidenced by his wedding last year at a privately owned Hawaiian island, where he took the precaution of renting every helicopter in the area to assure no tabloid flybys.

But now Bill Gates is trying something different. Later this month "The Road Ahead" hits the stands, a book that explains how the Information Highway—or whaddever you wanna call it—will change our lives. He believes beyond question that this digital infrastructure will be built, though it may take some time (20 years, perhaps) before the wish list of amazing transformations in his book is converted to everyday reality. Though Gates had the help of two collaborators—Microsoft's vice president Nathan Myhrvold and writer Peter Rinearson—at a certain point, well past the book's original publication date a year ago, the chairman himself took charge, concentrating on the text to make sure the book wound up "sounding like me." In effect, he has adopted the role of a high-tech Disney, guiding us through the way we will live after this new revolution morphs us into wireheads.

To say he is bullish is an understatement. For those of us who suspect that this world presents exciting new opportunities, Gates tells us our hopes will be fulfilled and attempts to outline specifically how our chances for fortune will expand: by doing away with distribution middlemen, he explains, the Internet will allow for "friction-free capitalism" that enables even the most humble business to reach a worldwide audience. For those titillated at the prospect of wonderful new toys, he gives us a delicious rundown of various "information appliances" and their functions (imagine! running a version of "Gone With the Wind" with your face mouthing the words of Scarlett or Rhett). For people who dread the changes that will come from such a major shift, he assures us with Panglossian confidence that though "dislocations" will indeed occur (meaning: you're fired), the net result of these disruptions will be a more empowered, better educated, wealthier populace. "It's a great time to be alive," he says.

Some may disagree, and that's fine with Gates, who hopes the book will   5
generate a useful discussion about how we negotiate the future's uncharted shoals. And there's plenty to talk about. In his predictions about the fate of privacy, for instance, Gates outlines the possibilities of video cameras mounted on every streetlight, or devices capable of capturing every conversation and transaction a human being will ever make, in what he calls "the documented life." Though he professes neutrality on these issues, he does admit that the prospect is "chilling."

And what of Microsoft's role in all this? There is a theory afoot that the Internet revolution Bill Gates describes in "The Road Ahead" is the immovable object that will thwart his company's heretofore perpetual ascendancy. Proponents of this view charge that Gates can thrive only when he controls the field of play, and that in the wide-open competition to commercialize the Internet, Microsoft not only holds no particular advantage but is hobbled by its unwieldy size and the degree of its involvement in the current desktop-computer world. (Last Thursday those theories led a Goldman, Sachs analyst to downgrade his investment rating of Microsoft stock, which promptly dropped $4.125 per share.) Then there is the constant threat of a government antitrust action: Microsoft dodged a bullet in its first settlement with the Justice Department's complaint about abuse in distributing the Windows operating system, but a later ruling thwarted its purchase of Intuit, the creator of Quicken, the country's most popular personal-finance software. As a result, even as Microsoft becomes more powerful, it has become fashionable to predict its decline. *What? Microsoft will sell only 20 million copies of Windows 95 this year, and not 30 million? Write them off!* But Gates's competitors will not be pleased at the climax of his book when he proclaims, seemingly between clenched teeth, "There has never been a leader from one [computer] era who was also a leader in the next. . . . But I want to defy historical tradition." Immovable object, meet irresistible force.

How will Microsoft pull this off? The same way it has earned its dominance to date. The company throws waves of resources at a problem, draws on the talents of very smart people and leverages its current position in the marketplace to accelerate acceptance of its new products, be they operating systems, applications or actual content. Earlier this month, for example, Microsoft hired *über* political pundit Michael Kinsley to edit its upcoming electronic magazine. ("If you can't ship more bits," Gates writes in characteristic techspeak, "an alternative is to have a financial interest in the bits being shipped.") In Gates's keynote speech at Comdex, he outlined how within five years a new generation of his company's applications software (like word processors and spreadsheets) will have built-in features that allow users to take complete advantage of the Information Highway simply by upgrading the current versions of Microsoft's Office suite of tools that are already fixtures on so many of the world's hard-disc drives.

Meanwhile, Microsoft will fight fiercely to whittle down the lead in the "browser" market assumed by Netscape Communications, which currently boasts a 70 percent share of the software used by the millions of World Wide Web cruisers. One small contribution will be the distribution of 800,000 copies of Microsoft's own Web browser, by including it in the CD-ROM that comes with "The Road Ahead." The disc also offers the reader a chance to reread the book on screen, accessing hypertext links to selected terms. For instance, click on Melinda French, the name of Gates's bride, and you see a picture of the happy couple and a list of her accomplishments as a Microsoft marketer.

Of course, there are plenty of potential readers less concerned with the niceties of broadband technology—discussed in a chapter that decodes the difference between ISDN, DSVD and ATM (don't ask)—than with the gossipy truth of what Bill Gates is really like. There is no sloppy self-confession from Bill's inner child here, but sprinkled throughout are a few anecdotes that shed some light on our era's Horatio Alger. He tells of a self-imposed mission he began at the age of 8 to read the entire World Book Encyclopedia, A to Z (the marathon ended at the P's, five years later). Then there is the odd practice of "virtual dating." When conducting a (pre-Melinda, one assumes) long-distance romance, Gates and his lady friend would look for a movie playing in their respective cities at about the same time. Driving to the theater, they would talk to each other on their car cellular phones; on the way home, they would reestablish the connection and hash out the movie. The most personal section of the book comes in a tour of the $80 million house he is building for himself on the shore of Lake Washington, a short hop in the Porsche from Microsoft's headquarters in Redmond, Wash. The house's use of new technology is important to Gates, particularly in the proliferation of display screens that will portray a continually changing set of artistic images, movies and patterns, customized to each resident or guest. Neo-Luddites will find it comforting, however, that the house's most imposing feature is not technological, but natural; massive beams from 500-year-old Douglas fir trees, rescued from a recently demolished Weyerhaeuser lumber mill.

A more subtle revelation in the book is the degree to which Gates   10 seems frustrated at the limitations of time itself. His main complaint about writing a book, in fact, is that it burned up so many days of work. An important goal of the software he is building for the future—complete with "intelligent assistants" to dispatch tasks for you and built-in conferencing equipment to spare you from business trips—is to provide more time for its users and himself. At one point he writes that he would change his negative attitude about casino gambling if it were possible to win not money, but extra hours.

Last Tuesday, for instance, you could sense his impatience as he endured a series of a half-dozen television interviews in a backstage dressing room at Las Vegas's Aladdin Hotel after delivering his Comdex keynote speech. He reeled off sound bites in a makeshift studio with broiling klieg lights, each interviewer providing variations on the same interrogatories, including the query du jour: can Microsoft compete in the wide-open world of the Internet? (Answer: you bet.) Between interviews, he talked to colleagues or sat alone, intensely rocking back and forth in his chair. At one point there was trouble with the audio in the TV satellite connection, and Bill Gates had to keep talking until the sound kicked in. "I can hear you," he said, looking into a bright light, to a stranger somewhere across the country. "Can you hear me? Am I speaking in your ear? Can you read my lips? You don't hear me at all? Not even the vowels? He should hear me. *I* can hear me. Why don't they send my audio the way they send my video?" Then he closed his eyes for a second and sighed very deeply.

Is this what Bill Gates really wants for himself? The answer seems to be yes. He has never presented himself as anything other than a software entrepreneur, passionately devoted to maintaining his company's continued leadership and profits. If submitting to interviews, or writing a book, will help matters, so be it. The road ahead is important to Gates, but what keeps him going is his drive to get there first.

QUESTIONING THE TEXT

1. Levy uses quotations from Gates himself quite sparingly. What effect does his use of quotations create? What picture of Bill Gates emerges in this article from his own quoted words?
2. Look through the article, highlighting any words (or acronyms) that are unfamiliar to you. Can you tell what the words mean from their context? Do these words have anything in common? (Are they technical terms? brand names?) Bring your list of words to class for discussion.
3. What do you think A.L. thinks of Bill Gates? What in her introduction leads you to that conclusion?

MAKING CONNECTIONS

4. If Ayn Rand (p. 443) had been writing in 1995, might she have used Gates as a model for one of her heroes? Imagine, for instance, a conversation between Bill Gates and Rand's character Howard Roark. What might they share in common?
5. Imagine that Bill Gates, Maya Angelou (p. 439), Ronald Reagan (p. 456), and Georgia O'Keeffe (p. 461) are being interviewed by

Barbara Walters. Walters asks each of them to name two significant role models. Choose Bill Gates and one other of these figures, and try your hand at writing their answers to this question.

JOINING THE CONVERSATION

6. How dependent are you on electronic forms of information and on electronic technology in general? Monitor your activities for several days, taking notes on every time you use some form of electronic communication technology. Then write a brief report, intended for your class, on "A Day in My Life—with Technology."

7. With two or three classmates, do some research on Bill Gates. You might start by looking up the issue of *Newsweek* in which Levy's article appeared (November 27, 1995), or by reading and taking notes on a long essay that appeared in the *New York Times Magazine* (November 5, 1995). Track the hoopla surrounding the introduction of Microsoft's Windows 95. You also might read Gates's book *The Road Ahead*. Remember to check Internet sources. After you have pooled your information and compared notes, work together to write a response to Steven Levy's article, perhaps titled "More on Bill's New Vision."

STANLEY CROUCH
Blues for Jackie

THE STYLE AND GRACE with which Jacqueline Kennedy Onassis (1929–94) carried herself during her White House years made her something special—and different from any other first lady in living memory. She was delicate, soft-spoken, vaguely foreign, and wholly apolitical, a woman raised with Old World, old-money manners who should have made elbows-on-the-table Americans uneasy. Instead they cherished her like a rare flower, admiring how perfectly she represented their best instincts and how graciously she smiled.

What social critic Stanley Crouch (b. 1945) depicts memorably in this essay marking Jacqueline Kennedy Onassis's death in 1994 is the moment she moved from the status of admired first lady—territory she might have shared with Betty Ford and Barbara Bush—to haunting American icon. Confirming, as Crouch puts it, "that elegance is a form of courage," Jackie bore the weight of her husband's sudden and brutal death with a courage that inspired a whole nation to endure. Those who lived those hours in 1963 will never forget her; those who can only read about them must learn from writers like Crouch why Jackie shouldn't be soon forgotten.

"Blues for Jackie" appeared in the New York Daily News *and is reprinted from Crouch's collection of essays* The All-American Skin Game, or, The Decoy of Race: The Long and Short of It, 1900–1994 *(1995).* – J.R.

The inaccurate idea of extremely separate realities that make collective experience a sentimental fantasy hadn't set in when Jackie Kennedy and her husband moved into the White House. In that America, for all its segregation, a sense of community was at work and the ideals of the nation were being forced to come alive, like stone monuments of mythological figures, or the weeping statues of the Virgin Mary, even the storybook toys on display when lights are low and the shopowner has gone home.

She appeared as a national presence in a time of turmoil and elegance, when the threats of nuclear missiles and universal destruction were in the air, when extraordinary young people of the sort we rarely see now were surging forward in the Civil Rights Movement, when the idea of a homemade American aristocracy was being taken seriously, when Khrushchev, in one of those terrible suits that then distinguished Russian leadership, ostentatiously slid his chair closer to that smiling Kennedy woman.

The blue-collar Negroes I grew up among took a liking to the Kennedys because they thought the Eisenhowers were dull and that Ike was on the golf course too much when he should have been doing his presidential job. Mamie Eisenhower was the sort of homely white woman Negro females loved to make fun of, from the way they dressed to the way they spoke. Most of those Negroes remembered when the radio voice of FDR had brought the nation through the Depression and World War II. Wanting some more of that, they went with the Kennedys over the Nixons.

The Kennedys had spark and Jack had grown into a handsome man, a male swan rising out of the Billy the Kid version of an Irish duckling he had been when he was a young senator. His lady, whose myth went back to Lafayette's time and whose maiden name was Bouvier and who wore those marvelous Chanel dresses and spoke perfect French, well, she added strut and mustard to the White House. Gatherings of domestic workers in my mother's kitchen would admire her poise and clothes, something they had learned about from working in the homes of the extremely rich but the less than famous.

Because of their positions of service, those domestics knew more about 5 how it really worked at the top than middle and upper middle class white Americans. They knew that neither the blues nor stupidity nor callousness nor any of the maladies of human life fall down before money. So their experience made them high-quality critics of those privileged Americans who would be aristocrats, most of whom, like rock and movie stars, had *only* money—no grace, no manners, no taste—and were forever lost in the praises of those intimidated by their positions.

They thought Jackie Kennedy was the real thing because she had what they were confident all aristocrats, no matter their social stations, had to have—the ability to bring rich human warmth to refinement, which was very different from the flatiron pretension of the professionally repressed. Those domestics also knew that elegance is a form of courage, a way of standing up to the inevitabilities of disillusionment, decay, dissolution, and death.

When she sat in that limousine with Jack Kennedy's brains in her hand, her life crossed a line into blues territory that few of the privileged or the destitute ever know. Her face had the stupor of shock as she stood next to Lyndon Johnson while he was being sworn in on Air Force One. Jacqueline Bouvier Kennedy had reached across a century to take the hand of Mary Todd Lincoln, to experience the gangster politics of murder most foul. She was then put to the televised measure of public mourning, and in the ritual of Jack Kennedy's funeral, Jackie Kennedy's grief took on the majesty associated with Bessie Smith or Mahalia Jackson or Mary staring at the body of her son when he was taken down from the cross. She became all human sorrow. And she called the heart of the nation home.

QUESTIONING THE TEXT

1. From the perspective of what groups of people does Crouch portray Jackie and John Kennedy? From what perspectives do you understand the Kennedy era?

2. Crouch mentions the "majesty associated with Bessie Smith or Mahalia Jackson." Research the life of one of these women and then explain Crouch's allusion more fully.

MAKING CONNECTIONS

3. Both Crouch's remembrance of Jacqueline Kennedy and Bob Costas's remarks in the next selection, on Mickey Mantle, are *eulogies*. Look up both the definition and the etymology of *eulogy,* and then use these selections to describe some of the features of the eulogy genre of writing.
4. Like Peggy Noonan describing Ronald Reagan (p. 456), Crouch clearly admires Jackie Kennedy. Compare the techniques the two writers use to establish each as a legend.

JOINING THE CONVERSATION

5. Use the library to research in detail one aspect of Jacqueline Kennedy Onassis's life, such as her life before marrying Kennedy, her televised White House tour, her experiences when the president was assassinated, or her controversial marriage to Greek shipping magnate Aristotle Onassis. Then write a short report, and be prepared to present your work in class.
6. In class, discuss the different roles that first ladies have played in recent presidential administrations, from Jackie Kennedy to Hillary Rodham Clinton. Then write an essay describing how you believe the role of presidential spouses will develop in the next decade.
7. The Kennedy administration carefully cultivated an association with the legend of Camelot—especially as depicted in a Broadway musical of the same name. Investigate the legend and/or musical, and explain the potential political power of such an association.

BOB COSTAS
Eulogy for Mickey Mantle

I SAW MICKEY MANTLE (1931–95) play baseball in the early 1960s on a Yankee team full of future hall-of-famers—Roger Maris, Whitey Ford, Yogi Berra. Baseball's premier franchise, the Yankees, was then dominating the sport, as it had for more than a generation, appearing in twenty-seven World Series between 1921 and 1964, and counting Babe Ruth, Lou Gehrig, and Joe DiMaggio among its alumni. Yet Mantle was no hero to me—just another of those damned Yankees regularly crushing the team I cared about most, the hapless Cleveland Indians. After a flicker of glory in 1954, the Indians would wander baseball's diamonds pennantless for more years than the Israelites spent in the Sinai desert. Mantle, in contrast, would enjoy twelve World Series during his eighteen-year career. And on the very Sunday that Mickey Mantle died in Texas, a mourning Yankees team beat my Indians yet again, 4–1.

But if the Mick wasn't a personal favorite, I include the moving eulogy that Costas delivered at his funeral because it helps us understand the importance of both legends and sports. Costas (b. 1952), an Emmy-winning sports broadcaster for NBC, observes how Mickey Mantle at the plate displayed an instance of human perfection, a grace that lifted everyone who watched the slugger a little higher. Athletic records are, in some respects, the most ephemeral of human accomplishments; in the grand scheme, what difference does whacking a baseball 565 feet or winning the Super Bowl make? But most people don't live out their lives in grand schemes. They raise families, work hard at their jobs, pay taxes—and dream about the possibility of glory. Costas shows us how Mickey Mantle, despite his many troubles on and off the field, endured to touch the lives of millions with a little glory and then rose to face his death with as much power as he swung a bat.

And don't worry about the Indians. They won the American League pennant in 1995. – J.R.

It occurs to me as we're all sitting here thinking of Mickey, he's probably somewhere getting an earful from Casey Stengel, and no doubt quite confused by now.

One of Mickey's fondest wishes was that he be remembered as a great teammate, to know that the men he played with thought well of him.

But it was more than that. Moose and Whitey and Tony and Yogi and Bobby and Hank, what a remarkable team you were. And the stories of the visits you guys made to Mickey's bedside the last few days were heartbreakingly tender. It meant everything to Mickey, as would the presence of so many baseball figures past and present here today.

I was honored to be asked to speak by the Mantle family today. I am not standing here as a broadcaster. Mel Allen is the eternal voice of the Yankees and that would be his place. And there are others here with a longer and deeper association with Mickey than mine.

But I guess I'm here, not so much to speak for myself as to simply represent the millions of baseball-loving kids who grew up in the '50s and '60s and for whom Mickey Mantle was baseball.

And more than that, he was a presence in our lives—a fragile hero to whom we had an emotional attachment so strong and lasting that it defied logic. Mickey often said he didn't understand it, this enduring connection and affection—for men now in their 40s and 50s, otherwise perfectly sensible, who went dry in the mouth and stammered like schoolboys in the presence of Mickey Mantle.

Maybe Mick was uncomfortable with it, not just because of his basic shyness, but because he was always too honest to regard himself as some kind of deity.

But that was never really the point. In a very different time than today, the first baseball commissioner, Kenesaw Mountain Landis, said every boy builds a shrine to some baseball hero, and before that shrine, a candle always burns.

For a huge portion of my generation, Mickey Mantle was that baseball hero. And for reasons that no statistics, no dry recitation of facts can possibly capture, he was the most compelling baseball hero of our lifetime. And he was our symbol of baseball at a time when the game meant something to us that perhaps it no longer does.

Mickey Mantle had those dual qualities so seldom seen, exuding dynamism and excitement but at the same time touching your heart—flawed, wounded. We knew there was something poignant about Mickey Mantle before we knew what poignant meant.

We didn't just root for him, we felt for him.

Long before many of us ever cracked a serious book, we knew something about mythology as we watched Mickey Mantle run out a home run through the lengthening shadows of a late Sunday afternoon at Yankee Stadium.

There was greatness in him, but vulnerability too.

He was our guy. When he was hot, we felt great. When he slumped or got hurt, we sagged a bit too. We tried to crease our caps like him; kneel in an imaginary on-deck circle like him; run like him heads down, elbows up.

Billy Crystal is here today. Billy says that at his bar mitzvah he spoke in an Oklahoma drawl. Billy's here today because he loved Mickey Mantle, and millions more who felt like him are here today in spirit as well.

It's been said that the truth is never pure and rarely simple.

Mickey Mantle was too humble and honest to believe that the whole truth about him could be found on a Wheaties box or a baseball card. But the emotional truths of childhood have a power to transcend objective fact. They stay with us through all the years, withstanding the ambivalence that so often accompanies the experiences of adults.

That's why we can still recall the immediate tingle in that instant of recognition when a Mickey Mantle popped up in a pack of Topps bubble gum cards—a treasure lodged between an Eli Grba and a Pumpsie Green.

That's why we smile today, recalling those October afternoons when we'd sneak a transistor radio into school to follow Mickey and the Yankees in the World Series.

Or when I think of Mr. Tomasee, a very wise sixth-grade teacher who   20
understood that the World Series was more important, at least for one day, than any school lesson could be. So he brought his black-and-white TV from home, plugged it in and let us watch it right there in school through the flicker and the static. It was richer and more compelling than anything I've seen on a high-resolution, big-screen TV.

Of course, the bad part, Bobby, was that Koufax struck 15 of you guys out that day.

My phone's been ringing the past few weeks as Mickey fought for his life. I've heard from people I hadn't seen or talked to in years—guys I played stickball with, even some guys who took Willie's side in those endless Mantle-Mays arguments. They're grown up now. They have their families. They're not even necessarily big baseball fans anymore. But they felt something hearing about Mickey, and they figured I did too.

In the last year, Mickey Mantle, always so hard on himself, finally came to accept and appreciate that distinction between a role model and a hero. The first he often was not, the second he always will be.

In the end, people got it. And Mickey Mantle got from America something other than misplaced and mindless celebrity worship. He got something far more meaningful. He got love—love for what he had been; love for what he made us feel; love for the humanity and sweetness that was always there mixed in with the flaws and all the pain that wracked his body and his soul.

We wanted to tell him that it was OK, that what he had been was   25
enough. We hoped he felt that Mutt Mantle would have understood and that Merlyn and the boys loved him.

And then in the end, something remarkable happened—the way it does for champions. Mickey Mantle rallied. His heart took over, and he had some innings as fine as any in 1956 or with his buddy, Roger, in 1961.

But this time, he did it in the harsh and trying summer of '95. And what he did was stunning. The sheer grace of that ninth inning—the humility, the sense of humor, the total absence of self pity, the simple eloquence and honesty of his pleas to others to take heed of his mistakes.

All of America watched in admiration. His doctors said he was, in many ways, the most remarkable patient they'd ever seen. His bravery, so stark and real, that even those used to seeing people in dire circumstances were moved by his example.

Because of that example, organ donations are up dramatically all across America. A cautionary tale has been honestly told and perhaps will affect some lives for the better.

And our last memories of Mickey Mantle are as heroic as the first.   30

None of us, Mickey included, would want to be held to account for every moment of our lives. But how many of us could say that our best moments were as magnificent as his?

This is the cartoon from this morning's *Dallas Morning News*. Maybe some of you saw it. It got torn a little bit on the way from the hotel to here. There's a figure here, St. Peter I take it to be, with his arm around Mickey, that broad back and the number 7. He's holding his book of admissions. He says "Kid, that was the most courageous ninth inning I've ever seen."

It brings to mind a story Mickey liked to tell on himself and maybe some of you have heard it. He pictured himself at the pearly gates, met by St. Peter who shook his head and said "Mick, we checked the record. We know some of what went on. Sorry, we can't let you in. But before you go, God wants to know if you'd sign these six dozen baseballs."

Well, there were days when Mickey Mantle was so darn good that we kids would bet that even God would want his autograph. But like the cartoon says, I don't think Mick needed to worry much about the other part.

I just hope God has a place for him where he can run again. Where he   35
can play practical jokes on his teammates and smile that boyish smile, 'cause God knows, no one's perfect. And God knows there's something special about heroes.

So long, Mick. Thanks.

QUESTIONING THE TEXT

1. Annotate Costas's speech carefully to point out particular features that mark it as a spoken text delivered at Mantle's funeral in 1995. What role does the audience play in Costas's remarks?

2. In the introduction, J.R. suggests that while Mickey Mantle wasn't a personal hero, he still regards the Yankee slugger as a legend. Is this a distinction you consider legitimate? Is it a distinction you sometimes make?

MAKING CONNECTIONS

3. Compare Costas's account of Mantle's influence on youngsters with what Maya Angelou has to say about Joe Louis (p. 439). Then write a short essay assessing J.R.'s claim in the introduction: "Athletic records are, in some respects, the most ephemeral of human accomplishments."

4. How does one compare the achievements of Mickey Mantle with those of Pope John Paul II described by George Sim Johnston (p. 466)? Is this an apples and oranges comparison, not worth making? Does our society give too much credit to sports heroes and other celebrities?

JOINING THE CONVERSATION

5. Write a eulogy for a sports or entertainment figure you admired. You might consult sources for biographical facts, but make your speech more than just a life history.
6. Costas acknowledges that Mantle, given to drink and gambling, did not live a flawless life. Write an essay exploring how much of a legend's life the public is entitled to know and judge.
7. In a short article, describe a sports event you have attended that seemed more important than a mere game or competition. Help readers experience the importance of the event.
8. Costas makes a distinction between "a role model and a hero" (p. 485). Write a comparison/contrast essay exploring the differences you see in these two terms.

LUCILLE CLIFTON
malcolm

LUCILLE CLIFTON, born in Depew, New York, in 1936, and educated at the State University of New York at Fredonia and Howard University, is internationally known for her poetry, fiction, and screenplays, which have earned her two nominations for the Pulitzer Prize in poetry as well as an Emmy Award from the American Academy of Television Arts and Sciences.

Clifton often reminds me of Emily Dickinson, another poet whose work I love to read, perhaps because so many of her poems are extremely brief. Like Dickinson, Clifton can encompass vast emotions in very little space. But her poems have a rhythm all her own, perhaps related to the history of jazz and rhythm and blues, perhaps to the cadences of the African American preaching tradition, perhaps to what her own inner ear and heart hear. (See, for example, any of her seven volumes of poetry, including good times, good news about the earth, two-headed woman, *or* quilting: poems 1987–1990.*) In* "malcolm," *from another book of her poems, titled* good woman: poems and a memoir 1969–1980, *Clifton evokes the moment of Malcolm X's assassination in the scope of seven lines. In doing so, she captures Malcolm's charismatic strength and legendary status.* — A.L.

> nobody mentioned war
> but doors were closed
> black women shaved their heads
> black men rustled in the alleys like leaves
> prophets were ambushed as they spoke   5
> and from their holes black eagles flew
> screaming through the streets

IN RESPONSE

1. Does Clifton feel any ambivalence toward Malcolm? What in the poem leads you to answer this question in the way that you do?
2. Write a paragraph or two of response to the images used in this poem: what do they suggest about Malcolm?
3. Write a poem about another legend featured in this chapter, calling it, for example, "Rosa," "Georgia," "John Paul," "Bill," or "Mickey."

OTHER READINGS

Boynton, Robert S. "The Professor of Connection." *New Yorker* 6 Nov. 1995. Profiles writer and music critic Stanley Crouch.

Carlson, Peter. "Carlson's 10 Laws of Celebrity." *Washington Post Magazine* 5 Dec. 1993. Provides a tongue-in-cheek look at the concept of celebrity.

Duncan, David James. "The Mickey Mantle Koan." *Riverteeth.* New York: Doubleday, 1995. A personal narrative about the death of Duncan's brother and the arrival of a baseball, autographed by Mickey Mantle, at the Duncans' home the day after the death.

Gogola, Tom. "Generation Why." *Nation* 2 May 1994: 581. Considers the blame of corporate imagemakers in Kurt Cobain's suicide.

Himmelfarb, Gertrude. "Of Heroes, Villains, and Valets." *Commentary* June 1991: 20–26. Analyzes heroism and history.

King, Florence. "Oh, Sparta." *National Review* 12 Sept. 1994: 96. Laments the passing of the heroic man capable of suffering in silence.

Kramer, Yale. "Day on the Beach." *American Spectator* Aug. 1994: 32–38. Argues that Americans today may lack the resolve of the forces who fought on Normandy beaches.

Marcus, Greil. *Dead Elvis: A Chronicle of a Cultural Obsession.* New York: Doubleday, 1991. Explores the Elvis myth.

Ward, Geoffrey C. *American Originals: The Private Worlds of Some Singular Men and Women.* New York: HarperCollins, 1991. Includes politicians, entertainers, writers, artists, and "bad men and liars."

ELECTRONIC RESOURCES

Objectivism—The Philosophy of Ayn Rand:
    http://www.hypermall.com/~willp/phil/
    Gives information about Ayn Rand, author of *The Fountainhead.*

The Pope Page:
    http://www.catholic.net/RCC/POPE/Pope.html
    Lists sites related to John Paul II.

The Ronald Reagan Home Page:
    http://www.dnaco.net/~bkottman/reagan.html
    Lists sites relating to the life and politics of the former U.S. president.

Bill Gates:
    http://www.microsoft.com/corpinfo/bill-g.htm
    Provides a biography of Microsoft's founder and other information.

9

At Home:
The Places I Come From

Look carefully at this promotional photograph of Roseanne's television
family. What does the placement of various characters tell you about who
or what is most important in this photograph? What do you think is the
main purpose of this photograph—and how effective is it? What values
or ideals does the image suggest, and what details of the photograph
point to or represent those values? What does this photograph
suggest about the nature and status of "home"?

I would like to promise [my daughter] that she will grow up with a sense of her cousins and of rivers and of her great-grandmother's teacups. . . .
JOAN DIDION, *On Going Home*

I remember early morning fogs in Georgia, not so dramatic as California ones, but magical too because out of the Southern fog of memory tramps my dark father, smiling and large, glowing with rootedness, and talking of hound dogs, biscuits, and coons.
ALICE WALKER, *The Place Where I Was Born*

"We will look after you when you are old. You will come and live with us and our children."
JEREMY SEABROOK, *Family Values*

Sometimes I feel like I'm frozen in time, caught in a nightmare of a hot October afternoon when everything changed because my mother stopped living.
BARBARA SMITH, *Home*

Most statistics tell us breast cancer is genetic, hereditary, with rising percentages attached to fatty diets, childlessness, or becoming pregnant after thirty. What they don't say is living in Utah may be the greatest hazard of all.
TERRY TEMPEST WILLIAMS, *The Clan of One-Breasted Women*

As far as the law is concerned, it is safer to have a bastard child than to double-park.
WILLIAM F. BUCKLEY JR., *Should There Be a Law?*

And if shame, cleanliness, and charity are rediscovered, can that other Victorian virtue, chastity, be far behind?
GERTRUDE HIMMELFARB, *The Victorians Get a Bad Rap*

The long-term-care facility . . . I work for is owned by a corporation that owns nursing homes throughout the country. Giving corporations like this control over the quality of medical care is handing over control to the fox.
JILL FRAWLEY, *Inside the Home*

Grandpa's flowers are scattered
down the line of tombstones, decorating
the graves of his wife, his children
ED MADDEN, *Family Cemetery, near Hickory Ridge, Arkansas*

Introduction

CONSIDER FOR A MOMENT some well-known phrases that feature the word *home:* "Home is where the heart is," for example, or "there's no place like home"; home, sweet home"; "the home of the brave"; "you can't go home again." These phrases suggest that "home" is a place of comfort or solace, or at least "where the heart is." They capture what might be described as an American ideal of "home": a place where you can be safe and secure and living among those who care unconditionally for you.

In one of the most famous opening passages in literature, however, Leo Tolstoy complicates such an ideal vision of home: "Happy families are all alike," he says, but "every unhappy family is unhappy in its own way" (*Anna Karenina*). Tolstoy's sentence suggests what most of us know already in our bones: homes can be sites not only of comfort and solace but of pain and bitter unhappiness as well. In addition, one person's happy home is another person's disaster; what may look like a peaceful, loving home from one perspective may look just the opposite from another.

As this chapter will illustrate, in fact, what is "home" to one person may well be a "shelter" or a "long-term–care facility" or a place that exists only in the imagination to another. And whatever your own individual experience has been, you have certainly had some experience with the concept of "home." In fact, you have probably had multiple experiences with homes of various kinds, and some of these experiences may contradict or conflict with one another. This chapter may provide a timely opportunity, then, to consider the various places, people, or concepts you have known as "home" and to explore your own thinking about them. Before beginning it, you might want to consider these questions:

- What places could be categorized as "home" for you?
- What are some of the positive and/or negative qualities you associate with "home"?
- What kind of home would you most like to be part of? What problems might keep you from having the home and family you desire?
- How is "home" represented in the media? How is the word used in music and in the titles of films and TV and radio shows? You may want to brainstorm these questions with two or three classmates and bring your list to class for discussion.

• • •

JOAN DIDION
On Going Home

JOAN DIDION (b. 1934) has been writing for most of her life, from her days in high school and college in California through her years as copywriter and feature editor at Vogue *magazine to her ensuing highly successful career as a novelist and essayist. The essay on home and family that opens this chapter's conversation was written in 1966 and included in one of Didion's best-known collections,* Slouching Towards Bethlehem *(1969). The collection's title alludes to W. B. Yeats's poem "The Second Coming," which ends with the haunting question "And what rough beast, his hour come round at last, slouches towards Bethlehem to be born?"*

In "On Going Home," Didion says that for her "home" is not the place where she lives with her husband and baby daughter, but the one where the family in which she grew up lives. In that home, Didion locates the tension that comes from having had a "happy" home life that in adulthood routinely reduced her to tears after a phone conversation with family members. As she contemplates her baby daughter's birthday, she is certain that her daughter will receive the "ambushes" of family life in her own time. But Didion hopes for more for her daughter, more of a sense of home and family that will endure and sustain her.

This essay seems to me to capture the ambivalence many people feel about home and family. Certainly I can recall ambushes, pains, and fears associated with family life as I knew it, as well as deeply felt connections—particularly with my sisters—that have brought great happiness to me. And I am aware that although I live alone now, I have a very strong sense of the home I have made and the extended family I count as part of that home. I chose this essay, then, to prompt my own reassessment of what home and family mean to me. I hope they will prompt yours as well. – A.L.

I am home for my daughter's first birthday. By "home" I do not mean the house in Los Angeles where my husband and I and the baby live, but the place where my family is, in the Central Valley of California. It is a vital although troublesome distinction. My husband likes my family but is uneasy in their house, because once there I fall into their ways, which are difficult, oblique, deliberately inarticulate, not my husband's ways. We live in dusty houses ("D-U-S-T," he once wrote with his finger on surfaces all over the house, but no one noticed it) filled with mementos quite without value to him (what could the Canton dessert plates mean to him? how could he have known about the assay scales, why should he care if he did know?), and we

493

appear to talk exclusively about people we know who have been committed to mental hospitals, about people we know who have been booked on drunk-driving charges, and about property, particularly about property, land price per acre and C-2 zoning and assessments and freeway access. My brother does not understand my husband's inability to perceive the advantage in the rather common real-estate transaction known as "sale-leaseback," and my husband in turn does not understand why so many of the people he hears about in my father's house have recently been committed to mental hospitals or booked on drunk-driving charges. Nor does he understand that when we talk about sale-leasebacks and right-of-way condemnations we are talking in code about the things we like best, the yellow fields and the cottonwoods and the rivers rising and falling and the mountain roads closing when the heavy snow comes in. We miss each other's points, have another drink and regard the fire. My brother refers to my husband, in his presence, as "Joan's husband." Marriage is the classic betrayal.

Or perhaps it is not any more. Sometimes I think that those of us who are now in our thirties were born into the last generation to carry the burden of "home," to find in family life the source of all tension and drama. I had by all objective accounts a "normal" and a "happy" family situation, and yet I was almost thirty years old before I could talk to my family on the telephone without crying after I had hung up. We did not fight. Nothing was wrong. And yet some nameless anxiety colored the emotional charges between me and the place that I came from. The question of whether or not you could go home again was a very real part of the sentimental and largely literary baggage with which we left home in the fifties; I suspect that it is irrelevant to the children born of the fragmentation after World War II. A few weeks ago in a San Francisco bar I saw a pretty young girl on crystal* take off her clothes and dance for the cash prize in an "amateur-topless" contest. There was no particular sense of moment about this, none of the effect of romantic degradation, of "dark journey," for which my generation strived so assiduously. What sense could that girl possibly make of, say, *Long Day's Journey into Night?** Who is beside the point?

That I am trapped in this particular irrelevancy is never more apparent to me than when I am home. Paralyzed by the neurotic lassitude engendered by meeting one's past at every turn, around every corner, inside every cupboard, I go aimlessly from room to room. I decide to meet it head-on and clean out a drawer, and I spread the contents on the bed. A bathing suit I wore the summer I was seventeen. A letter of rejection from *The Nation,** an aerial photograph of the site for a shopping center my father did not build in 1954. Three teacups hand-painted with cabbage roses and signed "E.M.," my

---

crystal: a stimulant drug

Long Day's Journey into Night: an autobiographical play by Eugene O'Neill (1888–1953) focusing on his early family life

The Nation: a long-standing liberal weekly magazine

grandmother's initials. There is no final solution for letters of rejection from *The Nation* and teacups hand-painted in 1900. Nor is there any answer to snapshots of one's grandfather as a young man on skis, surveying around Donner Pass in the year 1910. I smooth out the snapshot and look into his face, and do and do not see my own. I close the drawer, and have another cup of coffee with my mother. We get along very well, veterans of a guerrilla war we never understood.

Days pass. I see no one. I come to dread my husband's evening call, not only because he is full of news of what by now seems to me our remote life in Los Angeles, people he has seen, letters which require attention, but because he asks what I have been doing, suggests uneasily that I get out, drive to San Francisco or Berkeley. Instead I drive across the river to a family graveyard. It has been vandalized since my last visit and the monuments are broken, overturned in the dry grass. Because I once saw a rattlesnake in the grass I stay in the car and listen to a country-and-Western station. Later I drive with my father to a ranch he has in the foothills. The man who runs his cattle on it asks us to the roundup, a week from Sunday, and although I know that I will be in Los Angeles I say, in the oblique way my family talks, that I will come. Once home I mention the broken monuments in the graveyard. My mother shrugs.

I go to visit my great-aunts. A few of them think now that I am my   5
cousin, or their daughter who died young. We recall an anecdote about a relative last seen in 1948, and they ask if I still like living in New York City. I have lived in Los Angeles for three years, but I say that I do. The baby is offered a horehound drop, and I am slipped a dollar bill "to buy a treat." Questions trail off, answers are abandoned, the baby plays with the dust motes in a shaft of afternoon sun.

It is time for the baby's birthday party: a white cake, strawberry-marshmallow ice cream, a bottle of champagne saved from another party. In the evening, after she has gone to sleep, I kneel beside the crib and touch her face, where it is pressed against the slats, with mine. She is an open and trusting child, unprepared for and unaccustomed to the ambushes of family life, and perhaps it is just as well that I can offer her little of that life. I would like to give her more. I would like to promise her that she will grow up with a sense of her cousins and of rivers and of her great-grandmother's teacups, would like to pledge her a picnic on a river with fried chicken and her hair uncombed, would like to give her *home* for her birthday, but we live differently now and I can promise her nothing like that. I give her a xylophone and a sundress from Madeira, and promise to tell her a funny story.

QUESTIONING THE TEXT

1. What does Didion mean by saying that she and her mother are veterans of a "guerrilla war"? Do the details she gives us in this essay support this statement? Explain.

2. Didion says she thinks that perhaps people in their thirties when this essay was written (1966) are the "last generation to carry the burden of 'home,' to find in family life the source of all tension and drama." Do you think her hunch is accurate? Why, or why not?

3. What, finally, is Didion's attitude toward "home"? What in the text helps you identify her attitude? Summarize this attitude in your own words, and bring your summary to class for discussion.

4. What is the effect (if any) of the last paragraph in A.L.'s introduction on your reading?

MAKING CONNECTIONS

5. How do you think Didion would respond to Barbara Smith's essay (p. 507)? Is her definition of "home" similar to or different from the one Didion offers? Explain these similarities or differences in a paragraph or two.

6. What might one or two other writers in this chapter most wish for their (real or imagined) daughters or sons? How do their wishes compare with Didion's wish for her young daughter? What would you wish for your own daughter or son, and why?

JOINING THE CONVERSATION

7. Take one of the following quotations from Didion's essay and write a response to it, detailing what the sentence(s) makes you think of and feel, whether you identify with it, and providing examples from your own experience to back up your identification or lack of it. (a) "Marriage is the classic betrayal." (b) "We did not fight. Nothing was wrong. And yet some nameless anxiety colored the emotional charges between me and the place that I came from." (c) "I smooth out the snapshot and look into [my grandfather's] face, and do and do not see my own."

8. Working with two classmates, compose a letter to Didion, telling her how you responded to this essay and explaining your reasons. Be sure to include differences of opinion, if you have them, in your letter.

ALICE WALKER
The Place Where I Was Born

ALICE WALKER (b. 1944), perhaps best known for her Pulitzer Prize-winning 1982 novel The Color Purple, *is a writer of distinction in many areas, including other novels (*The Third Life of Grange Copeland, *1970;* The Temple of My Familiar, *1989;* Possessing the Secret of Joy, *1992), poetry (*Revolutionary Petunias, *1973;* Horses Make a Landscape More Beautiful, *1984), short stories (*In Love and Trouble, *1973), and essays (*In Search of Our Mothers' Gardens, *1983,* The Same River Twice, *1996). After attending Spelman College and graduating from Sarah Lawrence in 1965, Walker moved to Mississippi and taught at Jackson State College while working as a civil rights activist during one of the most harrowing times in our nation's history. Her personal courage during those years is reflected in the actions of many of her fictional characters, as is her commitment to celebrating the lives and achievements of African American women.*

In the brief prose poem (the opening of Walker's 1991 volume of poetry, Her Blue Body Everything We Knew*) that follows, Walker, one of eight children of Georgia sharecroppers Willie Lee and Minnie T. Walker, speaks evocatively of the "land of my birth," the "small rounded hills" and "big leaf poplar" and pines of middle Georgia that for her speak of home.*

I debated a long time with myself before choosing this selection, for I was tempted by many other pieces of Alice Walker's writing, particularly her powerful essay "Looking for Zora [Neale Hurston]," which describes another kind of homecoming. In the end, I was drawn to this less well known piece, partly because it mixes the genres of poetry and prose, partly because I too grew up in the South and counted Brer Rabbit a friend, and partly because I hoped it would spark some very fond memories in you. – A.L.

I am a displaced person. I sit here on a swing on the deck of my house in Northern California admiring how the fog has turned the valley below into a lake. For hours nothing will be visible below me except this large expanse of vapor; then slowly, as the sun rises and gains in intensity, the fog will start to curl up and begin its slow rolling drift toward the ocean. People here call it the dragon; and, indeed, a dragon is what it looks like, puffing and coiling, winged, flaring and in places thin and discreet, as it races before the sun, back to its ocean coast den. Mornings I sit here in awe and great peace. The mountains across the valley come and go in the mist; the redwoods and firs, oaks and giant bays appear as clumpish spires, enigmatic shapes of green, like the stone forests one sees in Chinese paintings of Guilin.*

It is incredibly beautiful where I live. Not fancy at all, or exclusive. But from where I sit on my deck I can look down on the backs of hawks, and the wide, satiny wings of turkey vultures glistening in the sun become my present connection to ancient Egyptian Africa. The pond is so still below me that the trees reflected in it seem, from this distance, to be painted in its depths.

All this: the beauty, the quiet, the cleanliness, the peace, is what I love. I realize how lucky I am to have found it here. And yet, there are days when my view of the mountains and redwoods makes me nostalgic for small rounded hills easily walked over, and for the look of big leaf poplar and the scent of pine.

I am nostalgic for the land of my birth, the land I left forever when I was thirteen—moving first to the town of Eatonton,* and then, at seventeen, to the city of Atlanta.

I cried one day as I talked to a friend about a tree I loved as a child. A tree that had sheltered my father on his long cold walk to school each morning: it was midway between his house and the school and because there was a large cavity in its trunk, a fire could be made inside it. During my childhood, in a tiny, overcrowded house in a tiny dell below it, I looked up at it frequently and felt reassured by its age, its generosity despite its years of brutalization (the fires, I knew, had to hurt), and its tall, old-growth pine nobility. When it was struck by lightning and killed, and then was cut down and made into firewood, I grieved as if it had been a person. Secretly. Because who among the members of my family would not have laughed at my grief?

I have felt entirely fortunate to have had this companion, and even today remember it with gratitude. But why the tears? my friend wanted to know. And it suddenly dawned on me that perhaps it *was* sad that it was a tree and not a member of my family to whom I was so emotionally close.

> O, landscape of my birth
> because you were so good to me as I grew
> I could not bear to lose you.
> O, landscape of my birth
> because when I lost you, a part of my soul died.   5
> O, landscape of my birth
> because to save myself I pretended it was *you*
> who died.
> You that now did not exist
> because I could not see you.   10
> But O, landscape of my birth
> now I can confess how I have lied.

Guilin: a city in China (Kweilin or Kueilin) characterized by its mountains
Eatonton: the town in which Walker attended high school

Now I can confess the sorrow
of my heart
   as the tears flow   15
and I see again with memory's bright eye
my dearest companion cut down
and can bear to resee myself
so lonely and so small
there in the sunny meadows   20
and shaded woods
of childhood
where my crushed spirit
and stricken heart
ran in circles   25
looking for a friend.

Soon I will have known fifty summers.
Perhaps that is why
my heart
an imprisoned tree   30
so long clutched tight
inside its core
insists
on shedding
like iron leaves   35
the bars
from its cell.

You flow into me.
And like the Aborigine or Bushperson or Cherokee
who braves everything   40
to stumble home to die
no matter that cowboys
are herding cattle where the ancestors slept
I return to you, my earliest love.
                      45

Weeping in recognition at the first trees
I ever saw, the first hills I ever climbed and rested my
unbearable cares
upon, the first rivers I ever dreamed myself across,
the first pebbles I ever lifted up, warm from the sun, and put
into   50
my mouth.

O landscape of my birth
you have never been far from my heart.
It is *I* who have been far.
   If you will take me back   55
   Know that I
   Am yours.

As a child I assumed I would always have the middle Georgia landscape to live in, as Brer Rabbit,* a native also, and relative, had his brier patch. It was not to be. The pain of racist oppression, and its consequence, economic impoverishment, drove me to the four corners of the earth in search of justice and peace, and work that affirmed my whole being. I have come to rest here, weary from travel, on a deck—not a Southern front porch—overlooking another world.

I am content; and yet, I wonder what my life would have been like if I had been able to stay home?

I remember early morning fogs in Georgia, not so dramatic as California ones, but magical too because out of the Southern fog of memory tramps my dark father, smiling and large, glowing with rootedness, and talking of hound dogs, biscuits and coons. And my equally rooted mother bustles around the corner of our house preparing to start a wash, the fire under the black wash pot extending a circle of warmth in which I, a grave-eyed child, stand. There is my sister Ruth, beautiful to me and dressed elegantly for high school in gray felt skirt and rhinestone brooch, hurrying up the road to catch the yellow school bus which glows like a large glow worm in the early morning fog.

QUESTIONING THE TEXT

1. Walker writes of a tree she "loved as a child." What about this tree is comforting and lovable—and sad? What in the natural world do you love most? Does this element "make up" for something else in any way?
2. Reread Walker's poem. What is the "lie" she has told? Discuss this question with one or two classmates.
3. Note the details of Walker's life A.L. highlights in her introduction. Why do you think A.L. chose these specifics? How does she want readers to view Walker?

MAKING CONNECTIONS

4. Look carefully at the descriptions of "home" included in this essay and in those by Joan Didion (p. 493) and by Terry Tempest Williams (p. 513). In what ways do they reveal similar attitudes toward "home," and in what ways do they differ? Which description of "home" is most compelling to you, and why? If you keep a reading log, answer these questions there.

Brer Rabbit: from African legend, a trickster figure popularized in the Uncle Remus stories by Joel Chandler Harris (1848–1908), also born in the country near Eatonton, Georgia

5. Which other essays in this chapter speak indirectly of "displaced persons"? Are their definitions of "displaced" all the same? Try your hand at writing a definition of this term.

JOINING THE CONVERSATION

6. Working with two or three classmates, prepare an introduction to Alice Walker. Gather biographical information, and perhaps read two or three other works by Walker. You might watch *The Color Purple,* available on video, and check out Walker's more recent writings about the making of that film. Pool your information, and select from it material for a 20-minute class presentation—"Introducing Alice Walker." (You may have gathered enough information for a more intensive research project on Walker. If so, talk with your instructor about pursuing such a project.)
7. Write your own brief essay titled "The Place Where I Was Born." If you wish, include a poem as Walker does in her essay.

JEREMY SEABROOK
Family Values

WHEN A CONCEPT such as "family values" has been the subject of such intense political scrutiny that one hardly knows what it means anymore, observing it from a foreign perspective can sometimes help. Jeremy Seabrook (b. 1940), writing for the British magazine of news and politics, New Statesman and Society *in 1993, does precisely that in telling readers a story about his relationship with a family in India. Although mired in what many Westerners would regard as dire poverty, the athlete Jagat's single-parent family offers a refreshing perspective on friendship, caring, dependency, and love. In the realm of concern and commitment, Seabrook suggests, it may be difficult to separate "advanced" societies from "less fortunate" ones.*

Families, it turns out, represent the kind of Faustian bargain that Neil Postman (p. 133) uses to describe humankind's relationship to technology—for every gain there is a loss; for every winner, a loser. The independence that young Westerners often enjoy from family ties and obligations comes at a price; more and more, they must learn to rely on the tender mercies of a nanny state that substitutes monthly checks for loving care. — J.R.

The first time I met Jagat, I thought he was a hustler. I had been talking to a group of shoeshine boys in Connaught Place, in the center of Delhi. They had all come from Agra, and were earning a living in the tourist area of the capital. Jagat stood apart, watching. As I walked away, he followed me, and we crossed the road at the same time. He said: "You speak Hindi."

I stopped and we talked for a while. I assumed he would tell me he was my best friend and then ask me for money, which is one of the hazards of talking to strangers in that part of the city. But he didn't ask for anything. Perhaps he just wants to practice his English; perhaps he wants me to find him a job in Europe—there were many possibilities, none of them very charitable thoughts on my part.

He was, he told me, 25. He was in the Border Security Force. None of this was especially endearing. He came from the hills, Nainitak, and he had the eyes of a hill-boy, clear brown, with amber skin. He was in the athletics team, and spent his time training for championships. As long as he won most of his races, he would not be required to go on active duty. If he were to lose, he would be off to Kashmir or Punjab. This gives him a powerful incentive to win. He doesn't like fighting.

After an hour or so, he has to return to camp just outside Delhi. Can we meet tomorrow? Why not.

Next evening, I wait for him on the edge of the rotunda. Behind, under 5
the trees, a constant coming and going of the real hustlers—shadows who
whisper as they pass you: "Change money? . . . Smoke? . . . You want girl?"
"You sell something?"

Over the next two or three weeks, we met several times, and I learned
more about him. His mother, after her marriage, went to live with her husband's family, as is the custom, near Almora in the foothills of the Himalayas.
Her husband died when Jagat was two, and his sister five. Their mother was
turned out of the house by her husband's brother. She came down from the
hills with the two children to look for work in Haldwani, which is the first
town of the plains. It is a small, crowded settlement, dominated by the hills, at
certain times of the year indigo with their swirls of cloud, at others sharp as
metal blades against the clear sky. She found work with a landowner close to
the town; fields of maize, soya and rice in the rich soil. She lived in an abandoned shed on the edge of the farm with the two children, and worked as
cook for the farm-owners. When her labor was required in the fields, harvest-
ing and preparing the ground for rice and clearing the remains of the wheat-
fields, she would work, sometimes, 17 or 18 hours a day.

Her daughter helped her, but Jagat, the boy, was privileged. He was allowed to study, while the women waited on him. His task was to provide for
them both in due course; the early years of his life were protected. He was
their most valuable, indeed, only, resource. His would be the responsibility of
looking after his mother.

He was a good runner; and from his early years in school he had won
short-distance races. He went to English-medium college, and got a degree in
commerce—and then to college where he spent a year specializing in physical
training. He joined the Border Security Force as part of the athletics team,
and continued to win medals and cups in all the competitions, both within
the BSF and against outside teams. Technically, he is a policeman—rank of
constable—a curious anomaly for a man so unaggressive.

He asked me if I would like to meet his family. We traveled the eight
hours by bus to Haldwani in the oppressive August heat. Rainstorms had
flooded the road and forced the bus to take diversions. Jagat's mother had
saved some money over the years; enough to buy five bighas of land—a little
less than an acre. She bought the land from her employer; enough ground to
be self-sufficient in rice and wheat, with a little over to sell in the market.
Here, she had begun to build a house for her son, for when he would marry
and bring home his wife. It is a concrete cube with veranda and three rooms,
simply furnished, with a flat roof where she stores fuelwood for the winter.

Her life remains hard; she is up at 5 A.M. to milk the buffaloes and pre- 10
pare the meal. Her employer allows her to take vegetables from the fields; and
she grows pumpkins, chillies and herbs in the immediate vicinity of the
house. Her daughter is at home. She married, and went to stay with her husband's family. He was a drinker, and unkind to her. She had no choice but to

return home; a sad, self-effacing woman, now 31. She, too, is her brother's responsibility.

While I was there, she was taken ill; she had been suffering from stomach pains, had been given drugs and tonics, placebos. It turned out she had a burst appendix. She needed an immediate operation. There was no public hospital doctor in Haldwani who could do it. They needed cash urgently. I gave the 3,500 rupees (about 80 pounds) and the operation was done privately. She survived.

This chance act of charity has been repaid beyond measure. They asked me about my family, and were shocked and disturbed to learn that I was unmarried, that my twin brother and I were estranged and that my mother was living in a nursing home. How can this be? I felt abandoned, deprived, orphaned under their puzzled stare. "What happened?" they asked. Nothing. It is quite usual.

It is strange to see what you take for granted relativized by the practice of others. It is difficult to defend it as evidence of advanced society or a more enlightened dispensation than one in which ties of blood are not replaced by a paid division of labor.

Jagat was due to be married. Being an athlete, he is regarded as a good match. His mother prudently rejected some of the offers from well-to-do farmers in the neighborhood, and settled for a woman from a more modest family with only a little land. She and Jagat liked each other, and were married in May 1992.

The family say that love-marriages cannot last. When a marriage is made by the people who love you best, and to whom your security and well-being is more important than any other consideration, it cannot so easily go wrong as when it is based upon a passing attraction, a momentary inclination. Of course, some terrible things happen in India; brides have been burned because they fail to bring enough dowry; violent antipathies have no easy way out of the bonds tied in this manner. But they know, too, that the west is full of lonely people, of elective relationships that have fallen apart, of what they see as incomprehensible dissolutions and abandonings. They know that psychological loneliness and social isolation are widespread.

Jagat and his wife said to me: "We will look after you when you are old. You will come and live with us and our children. We shall not let you be alone."

And they meant it. The friendship, he assured me, is friendship for life. We don't make friends one day, to cast them off the next. His family have, as it were, adopted me. A mature adult. This has given me a glimpse of the possibility that social security might mean something other than long waits on chained chairs in smoky rooms in order to petition functionaries behind toughened glass for enough money to survive the week.

It is a curious reversal, a poignant and touching variant on the aid, the help, the succor that the west is supposed to bring to the south. There is, surely, a lesson here, some instruction in humility, never really one of the salient features of the west. That we might have lost something, that our bondings, associations and relationships might be suffering in spite of our wealth and power, is usually dismissed as exotic romanticism.

But it isn't true. Whatever the advantages of life in the west—and they are too obvious to require enumeration—there are also deficiencies and absences that we scarcely notice, so accustomed are we to setting the pace for the whole world. I have learned from Jagat and his family a kind of commitment, a form of friendship that is not always available in the west, where we have become cynical and instrumental in so many of our relationships with others.

In the hot afternoon, women are working in the fields around, gather-   20
ing fodder for the cattle, fuel for cooking; they stoop in the tall crops and are lost to sight beneath the soft grass. Jagat's mother and sister stand on the mound that marks the boundary of their little piece of land. We turn round and wave. They stand and watch and wave until we are out of sight.

QUESTIONING THE TEXT

1. Working in a group, make a list of those areas where the view of family life as Seabrook experiences it in India differs markedly from perspectives on family values in the United States. Which differences do you think would be the most difficult for the two cultures to reconcile? If you keep a reading log, answer this question there.

2. Within the Indian family circle, Seabrook notes that "the boy was privileged" in his upbringing compared with his older sister. Would Indian family life be better off if brothers and sisters were treated more equitably?

MAKING CONNECTIONS

3. Try reading Joan Didion's essay (p. 493) from the perspective of Jagat or a member of his family—particularly his mother. How might an Indian describe the relationship that Joan Didion has with parents, aunts, uncles, husband?

4. How do you think a family arrangement like that Seabrook describes might accommodate the kinds of differences narrated in Barbara Smith's (p. 507) or Andrew Sullivan's (p. 302) essay?

JOINING THE CONVERSATION

5. How might the United States be different today if parents chose spouses for young people as Jagat's mother chose a bride for him? Write an essay exploring some of those potential differences.

6. Seabrook becomes an honorary member of Jagat's family when he provides money to save the life of a sister. Keeping in mind recent political
   controversies in the United States over the funding of social programs
   such as Medicare, Medicaid, and Social Security, discuss in a group
   what happens when government takes over family functions and replaces them with what Seabrook describes as "a paid division of labor."
   What is the potential trade-off when a government relieves extended
   families of their responsibilities?

BARBARA SMITH
Home

BARBARA SMITH'S story "Home" presents home not as a specific, physical place but rather as a location in the mind or heart, somewhere outside of time and space that signals rest and, most of all, acceptance. In the story, the narrator thinks about the place she grew up, the house she had to sell when "all the women who'd raised" her were dead. Yet these women and that place exist in her memory, and she yearns to return, to share her history with her aunt and mother and grandmother. Most of all, she wants to introduce them to her partner Leila and to hear her aunt say "Your friend's so nice and down to earth. She's like one of us."

This is a story about love and about loss, about living after the death of the family, and about the need to create new families, even if they can visit "home" only in our memories. Smith (b. 1946) writes out of long-standing exploration of these and similar issues. Cofounder of Kitchen Table: Women of Color Press, she has written Home Girls: A Black Feminist Anthology *(from which we took "Home," 1983);* All the Women Are White, All the Blacks Are Men, but Some of Us Are Brave: Black Women's Studies *(1982); and* Toward a Black Feminist Criticism *(1977). In these and other essays, Smith explores relationships between African American women, exploring the difference that lesbianism makes and calling for inclusion of this and other differences within mainstream African American culture. I included "Home" in this chapter because it speaks directly, and positively, to a need many in our society face: how to create a family and home when the traditional options seem unavailable.* — A.L.

I can't sleep. I am sitting at an open window, staring at the dark sky and the barely visible nighttime gardens. Three days ago we came here to clean and paint this apartment in the new city we're moving to. Each night I wake up, shoulders aching, haunted by unfamiliarity. Come to this window. Let the fresh air and settled look of neighborhood backyards calm me until exhaustion pulls me back to bed.

Just now it was a dream that woke me. One of my dreams.

I am at home with Aunt LaRue and I am getting ready to leave. We are in the bedroom packing. I'm anxious, wonder if she can feel a change in me. It's been so long since I've seen her. She says she has a present for me and starts pulling out dozens of beautiful vests and laying them on the bed. I am ecstatic. I think, "She knows. She knows about me and it's all right." I feel relieved. But then I wake up, forgetting for a minute where I am or what has

507

happened until I smell the heavy air, see Leila asleep beside me. The dream was so alive.

I felt as if I'd been there. Home. The house where I grew up. But it's been years since then. When Aunt LaRue died, I had to sell the house. My mother, my grandmother, all the women who'd raised me were already dead, so I never go back.

I can't explain how it feels sometimes to miss them. My childish desire 5 to see a face that I'm not going to see. The need for certitude that glimpsing a profile, seeing a head bent in some ordinary task would bring. To know that home existed. Of course I know they're gone, that I won't see them again, but there are times when my family is so real to me, at least my missing them is so real and thorough, I feel like I have to do something, I don't know what. Usually I dream.

Since we got here, I think of home even more. Like today when we were working, I found a radio station that played swing. . . .

Every so often one of us sings a few lines of a song. I say, "Imagine. It's 1945, the War's over, you've come back, and we're fixing up our swell new place."

Leila laughs. "You're so crazy. You can bet whoever lived here in 1945 wasn't colored or two women either."

"How do you know? Maybe they got together when their husbands went overseas and then decided they didn't need the boys after all. My aunt was always telling me about living with this friend of hers, Garnet, during the War and how much fun they had and how she was so gorgeous."

Leila raises her eyebrows and says, "Honey, you're hopeless. You didn't 10 have a chance hearing stories like that. You had to grow up funny. But you know my mother is always messing with my mind too, talking about her girlfriends this and her girlfriends that. I think they're all closet cases."

"Probably," I answer. We go on working, the music playing in the background. I keep thinking about Aunt LaRue. In the early fifties she and her husband practically built from scratch the old house they had bought for all of us to live in. She did everything he did. More, actually. When he left a few years later she did "his" work and hers too, not to mention going to her job every day. It took the rest of her life to pay off the mortgage.

I want to talk to her. I imagine picking up the phone.

Hi Aunt LaRue. Ahunh. Leila and I got here on Monday. She's fine. The apartment's a disaster area, but we're getting it together. . . .

Leila is asking me where the hammer is and the conversation in my head stops. I'm here smoothing plaster, inhaling paint. On the radio Nat King Cole is singing "When I Marry Sweet Lorraine." Leila goes into the other room to work. All afternoon I daydream I'm talking with my aunt. This move has filled me up with questions. I want to tell someone who knew me long ago what we're doing. I want her to know where I am.

Every week or so Leila talks to her mother. It's hard to overhear them. I try not to think about it, try to feel neutral and act like it's just a normal occurrence, calling home. After battling for years, Leila and her mother are very close. Once she told me, "Everything I know is about my family." I couldn't say anything, thought, "So what do I know?" Not even the most basic things like, what my father was like and why Aunt Rosa never got married. My family, like most, was great at keeping secrets. But I'd always planned when I got older and they couldn't treat me like a kid to ask questions and find out. Aunt LaRue died suddenly, a year after I'd been out of college and then it was too late to ask a thing.

For lack of information I imagine things about them. One day a few   15
weeks ago when I was packing, going through some of Aunt LaRue's papers, I found a bankbook that belonged to both my mother and Aunt LaRue. They had opened the account in 1946, a few months before I was born and it had been closed ten years later, a few months after my mother died. The pages of figures showed that there had never been more than $200 in it. Seeing their two names together, their signatures side by side in dark ink, I got a rush of longing. My mother touched this, held it in her hands. I have some things that belonged to Aunt LaRue, dishes and stuff that I use around the house, even the letters she wrote to me when I was in college. But Mommy died so long ago, I have almost nothing that belonged to her.

I see them the day they open the account. Two young Black women, one of them pregnant, their shoulders square in forties dresses, walking into the cavernous downtown bank. I wonder what they talk about on the bus ride downtown. Or maybe my mother comes alone on the bus and meets Aunt LaRue at work. How does my mother feel? Maybe she senses me kicking inside her as they wait in line. As they leave she tells my aunt, touching her stomach, "I'm afraid." My aunt takes her hand.

I wonder what they were to each other, specifically. What their voices might have sounded like talking as I played in the next room. I know they loved each other, seemed like friends, but I don't have the details. I could feel my aunt missing my mother all through my childhood. I remember the way her voice sounded whenever she said her name. Sometimes I'd do something that reminded her of my mother and she would laugh, remember a story, and say I was just like Hilda. She never pretended that she didn't miss her. I guess a lot of how they loved each other, my aunt gave to me.

But I wonder how someone can know me if they can't know my family, if there's no current information to tell. Never to say to a friend, a lover, "I talked to my mother yesterday and she said. . . ." Nothing to tell. Just a blank where all that is supposed to be. Sometimes I feel like I'm frozen in time, caught in a nightmare of a hot October afternoon when everything changed because my mother stopped living.

Most of my friends have such passionate, complicated relationships with their mothers. Since they don't get married and dragged off into other families, they don't have to automatically cut their ties, be grown-up heterosexuals. I think their mothers help them to be Lesbians. I'm not saying that their mothers necessarily approve, but that they usually keep on loving their daughters because they're flesh and blood, even if they are "queer." I envy my friends. I'd like to have a woman on my side who brought me here. Yes, I know it's not that simple, that I tend to romanticize, that it can be hell especially about coming out. But I still want what they have, what they take for granted. I always imagine with my aunt, it would have been all right.

Maybe I shouldn't talk about this. Even when Leila says she wants to   20
hear about my family and how it was for me growing up, I think sometimes she really doesn't. At least she doesn't want to hear about the death part. Like everyone, a part of her is terrified of her mother dying. So secretly I think she only wants to know from me that it can be all right, that it's not so bad, that it won't hurt as much. My mother died when I was nine. My father had left long before. My aunt took care of me after that. I can't prove to Leila or anybody that losing them did not shatter my life at the time, that on some level I still don't deal with this daily, that my life remains altered by it. I can only say that I lived through it.

The deaths in your life are very private. Maybe I'm waiting for my friends to catch up, so our conversations aren't so one-sided. I want to talk like equals.

More than anything, I wish Leila and I could go there, home. That I could make the reality of my life now and where I came from touch. If we could go, we would get off the bus that stops a block from the house. Leila and I would cross 130th Street and walk up Abell. At the corner of 132nd I would point to it, the third house from the corner. It would still be white and there would be a border of portulaca gleaming like rice paper along the walk. We would climb the porch steps and Leila would admire the black and gray striped awnings hanging over the up and downstairs porches.

The front door would be open and I would lead the way up the narrow stairs to the second floor. Aunt LaRue would be in the kitchen. Before I would see her, I'd call her name.

She'd be so glad to see me and to meet Leila. At first she'd be a little formal with Leila, shy. But gradually all of us would relax. I'd put a record on the hi-fi and Ella would sing in the background. Aunt LaRue would offer us "a little wine" or some gin and tonics. I'd show Leila the house and Aunt LaRue's flowers in the back. Maybe we'd go around the neighborhood, walk the same sidewalks I did so many years ago. For dinner we'd have rolled roast and end up talking till late at night.

Before we'd go to bed, Aunt LaRue would follow me into the bath-   25
room and tell me again, shyly, "Your friend's so nice and down to earth. She's like one of us." I'd tell Leila what she'd said, and then we'd sleep in the room I slept in all the while I was growing up.

Sometimes with Leila, it's like that. With her it can be like family. Until I knew her, I thought it wasn't possible to have that with another woman, at least not for me. But I think we were raised the same way. To be decent, respectful girls. They taught us to work. And to rebel.

Just after we met, Leila and her roommate were giving a party. That afternoon her roommate left and didn't come back for hours so I ended up helping Leila get things ready. As we cleaned and shopped and cooked, it hit me that almost without talking, we agreed on what needed to be done. After years of having to explain, for instance, why I bothered to own an iron, it felt like a revelation. We had something in common, knew how to live in a house like people, not just to camp.

When we first started living together I would get déjà vu, waves of feelings that I hadn't had since I'd lived in that other place, home. Once Leila was in the bathroom and I glimpsed her through the door bending over the tub, her breasts dropping as she reached to turn off the water. It was familiar. The steady comfort of a woman moving through the house.

I don't want to lose that moving here. This new place is like a cave. The poverty of the people who lived here before is trapped in the very walls. Harder than cleaning and painting is altering that sadness.

Tonight we made love here for the first time. It was almost midnight   30 when we stopped working, showered and fell aching into the makeshift bed. When I started to give Leila a single kiss, her mouth caught mine and held me there. Desire surprised me, but then I realized how much everything in me wanted touch. Sometimes our bodies follow each other without will, with no thought of now I'll put my hand here, my mouth there. Tonight there was no strategy, just need and having. Falling into sleep, holding her, I thought, "Now there is something here I know." It calmed me.

But I have been afraid. Afraid of need, of loving someone who can leave. The fear makes me silent, then gradually it closes my heart. It can take days to get beneath whatever haunts me, my spirit weakening like a candle sputtering in some place without air, underground. And Leila has her own nightmare, her own habits of denial. But we get through. Even when I'm most scared, I knew when I first met her that it would be all right to love her, that whatever happened we would emerge from this not broken. It would not be about betrayal. Loving doesn't terrify me. Loss does. The women I need literally disappearing from the face of the earth. It has already happened.

I am sitting at a table by a window. The sky is almost light. My past has left few signs. It only lives through words inside of me.

I get up and walk down the hall to the bathroom. If I can't get back to sleep, I'll never have the strength to work another fourteen hour day. In the bedroom I take off my robe and lie down beside Leila. She turns in her sleep and reaches toward me. "Where were you?" she asks, eyes still closed.

I answer without thinking, "Home."

QUESTIONING THE TEXT

1. About midway through "Home," the narrator says, "Most of my friends have such passionate, complicated relationships with their mothers." What in the text describes the relationship the narrator has with her own mother? with her Aunt LaRue? In what ways do her relationships with them seem "passionate" and "complicated"?
2. At the end of the story, the narrator says that "Loving doesn't terrify me. Loss does." If you keep a reading log, write a page or two in which you reflect on this statement and your own response to it.
3. In the opening of her introduction, A.L. gives her reading of how Barbara Smith presents "home." Do you agree with A.L.'s statement? Why or why not?

MAKING CONNECTIONS

4. Alice Walker (p. 497) calls herself a "displaced person." Compare Walker's essay with Smith's "Home." In what ways is each writer "displaced" from home? In a brief (one or two pages) essay, reflect on the different ways in which one can be "displaced," using examples from these two selections to support your points.
5. Ed Madden's poem "Family Cemetery" (p. 537) gives readers a scene of "home" after death. Try your hand at writing a brief poem called "Family Cemetery" from Smith's perspective, and people it with members of her family as they are evoked in "Home."

JOINING THE CONVERSATION

6. Freewrite for 15 to 20 minutes, jotting down every association you have with "home." Look through your list, highlighting the most interesting or evocative items. Then freewrite again, starting with the items you highlighted and writing down everything they bring to mind. When you have enough material, write an essay in which you define "home."
7. Imagine a conversation among Barbara Smith, Gertrude Himmelfarb (p. 528), Jeremy Seabrook (p. 502), and Terry Tempest Williams (p. 513) on what an ideal home should be. Working with two or three classmates, write an exchange among these four writers that would compare and contrast their likely views on "home."

TERRY TEMPEST WILLIAMS
The Clan of One-Breasted Women

IT IS CURRENTLY A CLICHÉ to say that we live on a small planet, and per-haps a dying one as well. For all we hear of "Mother Earth," this parent of us all has not fared well at our hands. Witness the destruction of ancient forests; the death of rivers, lakes, even oceans; the filth of much city air; the disappear-ing species. The growing awareness of just how small and crowded—and neces-sary—the earth is may be at least partially responsible for an outpouring of work called "nature writing" or "environmental literature." Rachel Carson ar-guably sounded the alarm first, in the riveting opening of her 1963 classic ex-plication of the effects of pesticides, Silent Spring. Carson has now been joined by dozens of other distinguished writers, from Aldo Leopold to Barry Lopez and Leslie Marmon Silko—and Terry Tempest Williams.

Terry Tempest Williams (b. 1955) was born, raised, and educated in Utah, earning her master's degree in environmental education at the University of Utah. Naturalist-in-residence at the Utah Museum of Natural History, Williams, as the following essay suggests, is also a powerful teller of stories in which she attempts to bring the earth to our attention and to convince us that "there is no separation between our bodies and the body of the earth."

In "The Clan of One-Breasted Women," the epilogue of her 1991 book Refuge: An Unnatural History of Family and Place, she explores the human connection to the earth in relation to the lives of women in her family who have died from or are living with cancer. If we poison Mother Earth, our home, she asks, will our own mothers (and we as well) not also be poisoned? These are poignant questions for me, since my mother and aunt also died of breast cancer. The latest figures from the National Institutes of Health, in fact, tell us that one in seven women in the United States today will contract such a cancer, and though medical researchers have identified some of the genetic bases of breast cancer, they have found no cure. These figures suggest that the issues Williams raises about the "home" represented by the earth and by our own bodies will touch every reader of this book, either directly or indirectly. — A.L.

The title fooled me. On my first reading some years ago, unaware of who Terry Tem-pest Williams was

I belong to a Clan of One-Breasted Women. My mother, my grandmothers, and six aunts have all had mastectomies. Seven are dead. The two who survive have just completed rounds of chemother-apy and radiation.

513

and perhaps influ-
enced subtly by
The Clan of the
Cave Bear, I did
not take the title
literally. The first
page shocked me,
then, into close at-
tention. I am not
from Utah, but
my mother and
aunt, now dead
from breast cancer,
belonged to this
clan, as may I in
my turn. — A.L.

I've had my own problems: two biopsies for breast cancer and a small tumor between my ribs diagnosed as a "borderline malignancy."

This is my family history.

Most statistics tell us breast cancer is genetic, hereditary, with rising percentages attached to fatty diets, childlessness, or becoming pregnant after thirty. What they don't say is living in Utah may be the greatest hazard of all.

We are a Mormon family with roots in Utah since 1847. The "word of wisdom" in my family aligned us with good foods—no coffee, no tea, tobacco, or alcohol. For the most part, our women were finished having their babies by the time they were thirty. And only one faced breast cancer prior to 1960. Traditionally, as a group of people, Mormons have a low rate of cancer.

Is our family a cultural anomaly? The truth is, we didn't think about it. Those who did, usually the men, simply said, "bad genes." The women's attitude was stoic. Cancer was part of life. On February 16, 1971, the eve of my mother's surgery, I accidentally picked up the telephone and overheard her ask my grandmother what she could expect.

"Diane, it is one of the most spiritual experiences you will ever encounter."

I quietly put down the receiver.

Two days later, my father took my brothers and me to the hospital to visit her. She met us in the lobby in a wheelchair. No bandages were visible. I'll never forget her radiance, the way she held herself in a purple velvet robe, and how she gathered us around her.

"Children, I am fine. I want you to know I felt the arms of God around me."

We believed her. My father cried. Our mother, his wife, was thirty-eight years old.

A little over a year after Mother's death, Dad and I were having dinner together. He had just returned from St. George, where the Tempest Company was completing the gas lines that would service southern Utah. He spoke of his love for the country, the sandstoned landscape, bare-boned and beautiful. He had just finished hiking the Kolob trail in Zion Na-

No, these are the
women of your
family's history.
—J.G.R.

The issue of
causality is raised
powerfully here,
making us won-
der: what has
changed to make
Utah so danger-
ous? —J.R.

Williams is build-
ing her credibility,
showing that her
family's lifestyle
did not include the
typical cancer-
causing agents.
But she won't be
able to rely on
such arguments for
long—I doubt
they'd be accepted
in a court of law.
—A.L.

Here is a dramatic
juxtaposition of
life and death. I
wonder how she
will weave these
themes together in
the rest of the
essay—or if she
will. — A.L.

tional Park. We got caught up in reminiscing, recalling with fondness our walk up Angel's Landing on his fiftieth birthday and the years our family had vacationed there.

Over dessert, I shared a recurring dream of mine. I told my father that for years, as long as I could remember, I saw this flash of light in the night in the desert—that this image had so permeated my being that I could not venture south without seeing it again, on the horizon, illuminating buttes and mesas.

"You did see it," he said.

"Saw what?"

"The bomb. The cloud. We were driving home from Riverside, California. You were sitting on Diane's lap. She was pregnant. In fact, I remember the day, September 7, 1957. We had just gotten out of the Service. We were driving north, past Las Vegas. It was an hour or so before dawn, when this explosion went off. We not only heard it, but felt it. I thought the oil tanker in front of us had blown up. We pulled over and suddenly, rising from the desert floor, we saw it, clearly, this golden-stemmed cloud, the mushroom. The sky seemed to vibrate with an eerie pink glow. Within a few minutes, a light ash was raining on the car."

I stared at my father.

"I thought you knew that," he said. "It was a common occurrence in the fifties."

It was at this moment that I realized the deceit I had been living under. Children growing up in the American Southwest, drinking contaminated milk from contaminated cows, even from the contaminated breasts of their mothers, my mother—members, years later, of the Clan of One-Breasted Women.

It is a well-known story in the Desert West, "The Day We Bombed Utah," or more accurately, the years we bombed Utah: above ground atomic testing in Nevada took place from January 27, 1951 through July 11, 1962. Not only were the winds blowing north covering "low-use segments of the population" with fallout and leaving sheep dead in their tracks, but the climate was right. The United

In my memory of the 1950s, the "mushroom cloud" blooms, a source of fear and pride. Like Plato's hemlock, "the bomb" was both poison and cure.
— A.L.

The shift from the "light," the "golden-stemmed cloud," the "pink glow," and "light ash" to "contaminated" land and milk becomes explicitly a "deceit."
— A.L.

What does Williams mean by deceit? Could she, as late as the 1970s, have been unaware of nuclear testing that she claims, in the next paragraph, was a "well-known story"? — J.R.

*Her characteriza-
tion of the 1950s
is grossly simpli-
fied, reducing a
complex and diffi-
cult period to crude
stereotypes.*
—J.R.

States of the 1950s was red, white, and blue. The Korean War was raging. McCarthyism was rampant. Ike was it, and the cold war was hot. If you were against nuclear testing, you were for a communist regime.

Much has been written about this "American nuclear tragedy." Public health was secondary to national security. The Atomic Energy Commissioner, Thomas Murray, said, "Gentlemen, we must not let anything interfere with this series of tests, nothing."

Again and again, the American public was told by its government, in spite of burns, blisters, and nausea, "It has been found that the tests may be conducted with adequate assurance of safety under conditions prevailing at the bombing reservations." Assuaging public fears was simply a matter of public relations. "Your best action," an Atomic Energy Commission booklet read, "is not to be worried about fallout." A news release typical of the times stated, "We find no basis for concluding that harm to any individual has resulted from radioactive fallout."

On August 30, 1979, during Jimmy Carter's presidency, a suit was filed, *Irene Allen v. The United States of America.* Mrs. Allen's case was the first on an alphabetical list of twenty-four test cases, representative of nearly twelve hundred plaintiffs seeking compensation from the United States government for cancers caused by nuclear testing in Nevada.

Irene Allen lived in Hurricane, Utah. She was the mother of five children and had been widowed twice. Her first husband, with their two oldest boys, had watched the tests from the roof of the local high school. He died of leukemia in 1956. Her second husband died of pancreatic cancer in 1978.

In a town meeting conducted by Utah Senator Orrin Hatch, shortly before the suit was filed, Mrs. Allen said, "I am not blaming the government, I want you to know that, Senator Hatch. But I thought if my testimony could help in any way so this wouldn't happen again to any of the generations coming up after us . . . I am happy to be here this day to bear testimony of this."

*Her narrative here
is inadequate too,
using three quota-
tions to speak for
decades of contro-
versy.*   —J.R.

*I do not recall
questioning the
need for nuclear
testing until much
later in the
1960s. Williams
makes me want to
study the times
more carefully and
see if any stories of
"burns, blisters,
nausea" were
being told.*
— A.L.

*The decision not
to blame others
seems an impor-
tant part not only
of Mormon culture
as Williams pre-
sents it but of*

God-fearing people. This is just one story in an anthology of thousands.

On May 10, 1984, Judge Bruce S. Jenkins handed down his opinion. Ten of the plaintiffs were awarded damages. It was the first time a federal court had determined that nuclear tests had been the cause of cancers. For the remaining fourteen test cases, the proof of causation was not sufficient. In spite of the split decision, it was considered a landmark ruling. It was not to remain so for long.

In April 1987, the Tenth Circuit Court of Appeals overturned Judge Jenkins's ruling on the ground that the United States was protected from suit by the legal doctrine of sovereign immunity, a centuries-old idea from England in the days of absolute monarchs.

In January 1988, the Supreme Court refused to review the Appeals Court decision. To our court system it does not matter whether the United States government was irresponsible, whether it lied to its citizens, or even that citizens died from the fallout of nuclear testing. What matters is that our government is immune: "The King can do no wrong."

In Mormon culture, authority is respected, obedience is revered, and independent thinking is not. I was taught as a young girl not to "make waves" or "rock the boat."

"Just let it go," Mother would say. "You know how you feel, that's what counts."

For many years, I have done just that—listened, observed, and quietly formed my own opinions, in a culture that rarely asks questions because it has all the answers. But one by one, I have watched the women in my family die common, heroic deaths. We sat in waiting rooms hoping for good news, but always receiving the bad. I cared for them, bathed their scarred bodies, and kept their secrets. I watched beautiful women become bald as Cytoxan, cisplatin, and Adriamycin were injected into their veins. I held their foreheads as they vomited green-black bile, and I shot them with morphine when the pain became inhuman. In the end, I witnessed their last peaceful breaths, becoming a midwife to the rebirth of their souls.

Williams's own strategy. She has testified before Congress on these issues; I'd like to read that testimony. —A.L.

Her treatment of sovereign immunity—like her discussion of Cold War nuclear terror—seems dismissive. —J.R.

Although this evokes strong feelings in the reader, it seems a little too graphic. —J.G.R.

This section is hardest for me to read. Her descriptions, vivid and hurtful as they are, pale in comparison with real-life experiences with these deaths. —A.L.

The price of obedience has become too high.

The fear and inability to question authority that ultimately killed rural communities in Utah during atmospheric testing of atomic weapons is the same fear I saw in my mother's body. Sheep. Dead sheep. The evidence is buried.

The paragraph would be more powerful without the phrase "But I can't prove they didn't." Citing evidence from her own experience might work better than raising the prickly matter of proving causality.
—J.R.

I cannot prove that my mother, Diane Dixon Tempest, or my grandmothers, Lettie Romney Dixon and Kathryn Blackett Tempest, along with my aunts developed cancer from nuclear fallout in Utah. But I can't prove they didn't.

Exact causation is notoriously difficult to prove in almost any case. Perhaps our legal system needs to admit other kinds of proof? —A.L.

My father's memory was correct. The September blast we drove through in 1957 was part of Operation Plumbbob, one of the most intensive series of bomb tests to be initiated. The flash of light in the night in the desert, which I had always thought was a dream, developed into a family nightmare. It took fourteen years, from 1957 to 1971, for cancer to manifest in my mother—the same time, Howard L. Andrews, an authority in radioactive fallout at the National Institutes of Health, says radiation cancer requires to become evident. The more I learn about what it means to be a "downwinder," the more questions I drown in.

What I do know, however, is that as a Mormon woman of the fifth generation of Latter-day Saints, I must question everything, even if it means losing my faith, even if it means becoming a member of a border tribe among my own people. Tolerating blind obedience in the name of patriotism or religion ultimately takes our lives.

As I recall from the 1950s, religious groups were often in the forefront of "Ban the Bomb" movements. —J.R.

When the Atomic Energy Commission described the country north of the Nevada Test Site as "virtually uninhabited desert terrain," my family and the birds at Great Salt Lake were some of the "virtual uninhabitants."

Where do we draw the line? When can we feel civil disobedience is justified, even demanded? These are questions Williams—like Gandhi, Thoreau, King—asks us to consider. —A.L.

A second "dream" is introduced into the essay. Like the first dream, I wonder if this one is somehow related to a real event. —A.L.

One night, I dreamed women from all over the world circled a blazing fire in the desert. They spoke of change, how they hold the moon in their bellies and wax and wane with its phases. They mocked the presumption of even-tempered beings and made promises that they would never fear the witch inside themselves. The women danced wildly as sparks broke away from the flames and entered the night sky as stars.

And they sang a song given to them by Sho-shone grandmothers:

The little I know of Native American cultures suggests that the reverence for the earth that Williams draws on here is a powerful force. — A.L.

Ah ne nah, nah	Consider the rabbits
nin nah nah—	How gently they walk on the earth—
ah ne nah, nah	Consider the rabbits
nin nah nah—	How gently they walk on the earth—
Nyaga mutzi	We remember them
oh ne nay—	We can walk gently also—
Nyaga mutzi	We remember them
oh ne nay—	We can walk gently also—

I read this section as a dream vision of the sort common among mystical poets imagining alternative worlds. — J.R.

The women danced and drummed and sang for weeks, preparing themselves for what was to come. They would reclaim the desert for the sake of their children, for the sake of the land.

A few miles downwind from the fire circle, bombs were being tested. Rabbits felt the tremors. Their soft leather pads on paws and feet recognized the shaking sands, while the roots of mesquite and sage were smoldering. Rocks were hot from the inside out and dust devils hummed unnaturally. And each time there was another nuclear test, ravens watched the desert heave. Stretch marks appeared. The land was losing its muscle.

Here amid the images of death and destruction is an image of life—the "stretch marks" commonly experienced by women after giving birth. Williams seems to be returning to the earlier juxtaposition of life/death images. — A.L.

The women couldn't bear it any longer. They were mothers. They had suffered labor pains but always under the promise of birth. The red hot pains beneath the desert promised death only, as each bomb became a stillborn. A contract had been made and broken between human beings and the land. A new contract was being drawn by the women, who understood the fate of the earth as their own.

Under the cover of darkness, ten women slipped under a barbed-wire fence and entered the contaminated country. They were trespassing. They walked toward the town of Mercury, in moonlight, taking their cues from coyote, kit fox, antelope squirrel, and quail. They moved quietly and deliberately through the maze of Joshua trees. When a hint of daylight appeared they rested, drinking tea and sharing their rations of food. The women closed their eyes. The time had come to protest with the heart, that to deny one's genealogy with the earth was to commit treason against one's soul.

At dawn, the women draped themselves in mylar, wrapping long streamers of silver plastic around their arms to blow in the breeze. They wore clear masks, that became the faces of humanity. And when they arrived at the edge of Mercury, they carried all the butterflies of a summer day in their wombs. They paused to allow their courage to settle.

The town that forbids pregnant women and children to enter because of radiation risks was asleep. The women moved through the streets as winged messengers, twirling around each other in slow motion, peeking inside homes and watching the easy sleep of men and women. They were astonished by such stillness and periodically would utter a shrill note or low cry just to verify life.

The residents finally awoke to these strange apparitions. Some simply stared. Others called authorities, and in time, the women were apprehended by wary soldiers dressed in desert fatigues. They were taken to a white, square building on the other edge of Mercury. When asked who they were and why they were there, the women replied, "We are mothers and we have come to reclaim the desert for our children."

The soldiers arrested them. As the ten women were blindfolded and handcuffed, they began singing:

> You can't forbid us everything
> You can't forbid us to think—
> You can't forbid our tears to flow
> And you can't stop the songs that we sing.

The women continued to sing louder and louder, until they heard the voices of their sisters moving across the mesa:

> Ah ne nah, nah
> nin nah nah—
> Ah ne nah, nah
> nin nah nah—

Are these the same Mormon women she said didn't drink tea at the beginning of this story? —J.G.R.

It is unclear if this is still a dream or if it really happened. —J.G.R.

*Nyaga mutzi
oh ne nay—
Nyaga mutzi
oh ne nay—*

"Call for reinforcements," one soldier said.

"We have," interrupted one woman, "we have—and you have no idea of our numbers."

Williams exhibits the moral certitude common in the American tradition of civil disobedience, justifying crusades such as the civil rights and right-to-life movements. —J.R.

Williams's pen and paper weapons—can they ever be a match for guns and bombs? In the past, they have proved more than equal. —A.L.

I crossed the line at the Nevada Test Site and was arrested with nine other Utahns for trespassing on military lands. They are still conducting nuclear tests in the desert. Ours was an act of civil disobedience. But as I walked toward the town of Mercury, it was more than a gesture of peace. It was a gesture on behalf of the Clan of One-Breasted Women.

As one officer cinched the handcuffs around my wrists, another frisked my body. She found a pen and a pad of paper tucked inside my left boot.

"And these?" she asked sternly.

"Weapons," I replied.

Our eyes met. I smiled. She pulled the leg of my trousers back over my boot.

"Step forward, please," she said as she took my arm.

We were booked under an afternoon sun and bused to Tonopah, Nevada. It was a two-hour ride. This was familiar country. The Joshua trees standing their ground had been named by my ancestors, who believed they looked like prophets pointing west to the Promised Land. These were the same trees that bloomed each spring, flowers appearing like white flames in the Mojave. And I recalled a full moon in May, when Mother and I had walked among them, flushing out mourning doves and owls.

The bus stopped short of town. We were released.

The officials thought it was a cruel joke to leave us stranded in the desert with no way to get home. What they didn't realize was that we were home, soul-centered and strong, women who recognized the sweet smell of sage as fuel for our spirits.

So here is the actual equivalent of the dream, the point at which Williams answers her own questions about civil disobedience with personal action gesturing toward peace and "on behalf of the Clan of One-Breasted Women." —A.L.

I'm surprised by the positive tone of the conclusion. It suggests that Williams hopes that the land will prevail, and that the "sweet smell of sage" can help women continue to bring forth life. —A.L.

Afterwords

I take Terry Tempest Williams's piece to be operating on at least three levels. First, she is writing out her own grief at the pain and loss suffered by her mother, grandmothers, and six aunts, seven of whom had died of breast cancer at the time of this writing. Second, she is raising serious concerns about specific national policies that may well have left great parts of Utah and other western states toxic and extremely hazardous to human health. And third, she is offering an allegory about personal responsibility and civil disobedience, about the dual nature of scientific "advances," and about the need to protect and to celebrate the earth, our mutual home. Williams is not writing a traditional academic "argument," in which she sets up building blocks of "proof" to support her. Instead, she is weaving several strands and stories here, trying to evoke not assent or capitulation but response—and responsibility—in her readers.

I agree with J.R. that citizens in a democracy will always have to face up to the hard decisions involved in "real-world struggles" such as the threat of the bomb. But I also believe that citizens need—and deserve—information about the hard choices leaders may be making. If we choose to trade a certain number of lives in order to deploy a weapon, let us at least know that we have made the choice. If we choose to damage the earth, and the earth's ability to regenerate itself, in order to pursue nuclear dominance, let us at least know what we are doing—and what the possible as well as the real consequences will be. Let us reject silence, as well as the fear that too much knowing may cause in us. — A.L.

Certainly one appreciates the injury Terry Tempest Williams must feel at the unwillingness of the government to compensate Utah's civilian victims of nuclear testing. But I find her earth-mother visions off-putting and inappropriate. The Cold War that prompted the nuclear tests that likely destroyed much of her family was not a shaman's vision, but a real-world struggle that ultimately liberated a quarter of the world's population. The threat of the bomb, the horrible power that Williams herself witnessed, tempered the ambitions of dictators cruel as Stalin and foolhardy as Mao—and probably spared us all a third world war. Home-front victims of this struggle, the members of Williams's family, obviously deserve remembrance, apology, and whatever compensation may give them slender comfort now. But I don't find any special wisdom in Terry Tempest Williams's essay—only a poetic but unfocused anger. —J.R.

Williams writes with a clear voice of her undeniable pain, suffering, and frustration. Her sincerity gives her story a tough edge. It is so honest that I am uncomfortable reading it.

I have one question, though: what about the men in her family? She never mentions any of the men getting cancer. Although she tells of her father witnessing a number of blasts, he is apparently alive. Are men immune from this radiation? No, since she gives an example of Irene Allen who lost two hus-

bands to cancers supposedly from the effects of nuclear radiation. How can she be sure that the breast cancer is not hereditary, if both Tempest men and women were equally exposed to the explosions, but only the women have a history of cancer, and then of breast cancer only? I do not mean to suggest that her suffering could be any less than it is, but her perspective may be clouded by a severe personal bias. She may be giving the United States government a little too much blame and unlucky genes not enough. — J.G.R.

QUESTIONING THE TEXT

1. Williams says that she "cannot prove that my mother . . . or my grandmother . . . along with my aunts developed cancer from nuclear fallout in Utah. But I can't prove they didn't." What strategies and pieces of evidence does Williams use to support her strong hunch that there is a relationship between the nuclear testing and the rate of cancer-related deaths?

2. Images of birth run alongside those of death in this essay. Reread the essay, highlighting all the images that have to do with birth. Then write an entry in your reading log (if you are keeping one) in which you reflect on how they add to the point Williams wants to make.

3. Why might Williams have decided to include her dream in this essay? How does it relate or speak to the section that immediately follows it?

4. What use does A.L. make of the metaphor "mother" in her introduction? How effective do you find the metaphor?

MAKING CONNECTIONS

5. In some ways, Williams's essay is about "family values." Compare it with Jeremy Seabrook's essay by that title (p. 502). What "family values" would Williams share with Jagat? On what might they differ? Working from your notes, write a one- to two-page statement in which you compare the values in each piece.

6. Both William F. Buckley Jr. and Terry Tempest Williams raise important questions about responsibility: what *is* a citizen's responsibility in the face of the kinds of urgent social and environmental problems they describe? Meet with two or three classmates to discuss this question and how Buckley and Williams might respond to it. Then, working as a group or as individuals, write an essay about what a citizen's responsibility should be on a particular topic: nuclear testing and fallout, the rise in teen pregnancy, or any issue in which you feel citizens, yourself included, have much at stake.

JOINING THE CONVERSATION

7. Look into the environmental history of your city, region, or state, searching for issues of concern about the quality of water or air, for example. Then freewrite for half an hour or so about what most concerns you: what environmental hazards might you have encountered while you were growing up? Or was your region completely safe from contaminants? After you have chosen a topic and determined your stance on it, write a letter to the editor of your hometown newspaper raising the issues that concern you.

8. Williams describes a dream that in some ways turns out to be closely related to a real-life experience. How have your dreams been related to either predream or postdream real-life occurrences? If you keep a reading log, answer this question there, exploring the relationships between "dream life" and "real life."

9. Williams describes an act of civil disobedience in which she and other women took part. Spend some time thinking about your own position on civil disobedience: when it is justified, when you would take such actions, when you would not take them, and so on. You might read about other acts of civil disobedience, such as those of Henry David Thoreau, Mahatma Gandhi, Martin Luther King, or Rosa Parks. Then write a position paper in which you tell where you stand on the issue of civil disobedience and support your position with examples from your own, and others', experiences.

WILLIAM F. BUCKLEY JR.
Should There Be a Law?

Not long ago, political "balance" in an anthology of college readings often meant fifty essays by liberal commentators and one piece by conservative William F. Buckley Jr. (b. 1925). In such company, the founder of National Review *and longtime host of PBS's* Firing Line *would probably smile, confident he would still have the intellectual upper hand. Probably more responsible for the conservative tide in American thinking than any other person—including Barry Goldwater and Ronald Reagan—Buckley is an activist, editor, and writer who has made a difference.*

"Should There Be a Law?" (October 13, 1995) appears in this chapter on home and family not because I necessarily endorse Buckley's views but because I admire the genre of writing he offers—one we need to see more of if we're serious about solving society's problems. Pure and simple, "Should There Be a Law?" is an exploratory essay that poses a question Buckley admits he can't answer on his own: How do we reduce the number of American babies born out of wedlock? *He describes the dilemma as best he can within the confines of his* National Review *column, offers some tentative solutions, suggests their limits, and then opens up his forum to readers. He even provides an address so they can send their ideas. In effect, Buckley says: let's solve this problem together. At a time when many commentators—both left and right— offer sound-bite remedies for near-terminal diseases, Buckley's strategy seems downright revolutionary. —* J.R.

This is an exploratory column, its purpose to encourage thought on a question that badly needs thinking about.

The Problem: The birth every year of one million babies to unwed mothers.

The Consequence: One million children who, on reaching the age of 13, tend to run into difficulties. The statistics tell us that the child raised by a single parent is likelier by a factor of 600 per cent to commit crimes, consume drugs, quit school, and bear, or sire, children out of wedlock. Assume—if only to be hopeful—that the problems diminish after age 19, we are still left with six million teenagers who are a heavy social burden, as also, of course, a burden to themselves.

A Social Deterrent? Since manifestly it is against the interest of society, for reasons moral and material, to encourage the birth of babies to unwed mothers, what might be done to discourage the practice? Only one serious suggestion has been made, and at book length, by Mr. Charles Murray. He believes

525

that welfare payments to unwed mothers serve as inducements and therefore that to eliminate that miscarriage of charity would significantly reduce illegitimacy (which is up, in the last thirty years, from 5 per cent to 18 per cent among whites, from 25 per cent to 63 per cent among blacks). We have seen that Congress has played around with this question, and that the proposal is well on its way to limit payments to two illegitimate births. This approach hardly addresses the problem with appropriate sternness. Among other things, we all know that if the third child were sick or starving, we'd look after it. The effort should focus on preventing the procreative act, rather than on mistreating the child.

A Civil Delinquency? As things now stand, the father (or mother) of a   5 child born out of wedlock runs into no civil resistance of any sort. As far as the law is concerned, it is safer to have a bastard child than to double-park. A couple of years ago Bill Moyers did a documentary on the culture of wanton sex and found himself speaking to a young black stud, about twenty years old if memory serves, who proudly acknowledged fatherhood of three children by three different girls/women, and gaily announced his intention of pursuing his bluebirdism, since he found it amusing. All that Mr. Moyers was able to manage was a gentle sigh for the pieties of yesteryear, which will get you exactly nothing from the people we are talking about.

Are There Other Deterrents? Well yes, there are. To list some such is not necessarily to recommend them. But just as the Pentagon undoubtedly has a file on how to invade Switzerland, here is one on some of the deterrents that might be given a little thought.

—Deny a driving license to the parents for five years. (This side of imprisonment and death by hanging, this is the deepest known deprivation in the American culture.)

—Require the father to perform ten hours of appropriate work every week on whatever project makes sense.

—Require the father to spend three evenings every week sequestered. Including Saturday night.

—Do a vasectomy on the man. A Norplant on the girl.

Now these approaches raise problems, to put it lightly. There is, to begin with, the problem of locating the father. This accomplished, some proceeding or another would need to address the question whether, when the sexual union was done, the parties had agreed somewhere along the line to get married. In Sweden, about one-half the babies are conceived premarriage, but 90 per cent are born to two parents living together. How do you handle the situation: "Henry said he loved me and we'd be married just as soon as he finished high school"?

Is there a constitutional problem? Suppose that Henry says that without a driver's license he will be fired, because he earns his money delivering newspapers? Can the physical detention of the father be done without a judicial proceeding? Are there at hand convenient ways of absolutely identifying the father by DNA? Are vasectomies and Norplants acceptable, under such circumstances, in moral theology?

All these are designed as open questions, to flush out thought. Although commentary can't be acknowledged, I'd welcome having it, directed to me here at NATIONAL REVIEW, 150 East 35th Street, New York, N.Y. 10016.

QUESTIONING THE TEXT

1. Underscore or highlight Buckley's assumptions or premises. Do you find his assumptions valid? If not, which would you modify or quality if you were to revise the piece? If you agree with Buckley, which assumptions do you find most compelling, and why?
2. Buckley raises the issue of children born out of wedlock in a rational, almost clinical, style. In a group, discuss other strategies a writer might employ to heighten public interest in a comparable social or political problem.
3. In the introduction, J.R. notes that the Buckley piece is a clear example of an exploratory essay. Have you read many newspaper columns in this form? What are its advantages? its disadvantages?

MAKING CONNECTIONS

4. Can you imagine the problem Terry Tempest Williams describes in "The Clan of One-Breasted Women" (p. 513) recast in the form of an exploratory essay like Buckley's? Or has Williams moved beyond the realm of exploratory writing?

JOINING THE CONVERSATION

5. Using Buckley's exploratory model, write a piece of similar length studying a local or national problem. Use the same devices Buckley employs to organize and focus his piece, including headings and lists.
6. Respond directly to Buckley's challenge offered in the last paragraph. Remember, though, that the Buckley column originally appeared in syndication in October 1995. If you decide to send him your suggestions, be sure they are current.

GERTRUDE HIMMELFARB
The Victorians Get a Bad Rap

MOST PEOPLE REGARD *the Victorian Age in England as a time of sexual repression and stifling manners, when matters of the flesh were rarely discussed and even piano legs were demurely covered. Children were seen, not heard; boys courted girls according to elaborate rituals; and sex outside of marriage just didn't happen among the right sorts of people. In brief, the Age of Victoria (1819–1901) sometimes seems like the 1950s in the United States, without Ike and Elvis, an unsophisticated and humorless period more interested in decoration than substance, totally out of touch with the human psyche.*

But as out-of-wedlock births in the United States spiral past 30 percent, juvenile violence escalates in schools and on street corners, and latchkey kids become a new species of suburban orphan, it's getting harder to mock an era that apparently knew better how to care for its families. That is Gertrude Himmelfarb's message in "The Victorians Get a Bad Rap," a good example of a research-based essay that urges readers to abandon stereotypes for newer perspectives, in this case about Victorians and orphanages. If we've learned to accept many different configurations of family today, perhaps one of those should include group homes that protect abandoned or abused children from criminal parents and dangerous streets, offering hope, discipline, and moral instruction they can't get from blood, school, or gang ties.

The following selection originally appeared as an op-ed piece in the politically liberal New York Times *(January 9, 1995). Himmelfarb (b. 1922) is a social historian.* – J.R.

Computers all over the country have been programmed to type "Dickensian orphanages" as if with a single stroke of the key. George Stephanopoulos proposed sending copies of *Oliver Twist* to all Republican members of Congress. For journalists, "Victorian" has been the preferred invective. The word "orphanages," *Newsweek* said in its cover story on that subject, "sticks in the craw" and "evokes the moral hypocrisies of the Victorian Age."

When Newt Gingrich first uttered that dreaded word on television, the Democratic Party and the liberal press pounced with glee: "Dickensian orphanages" were the Republicans' solution to the problem of poverty. When Hillary Rodham Clinton denounced any plan to put children of poor, unwed mothers into orphanages as "unbelievable and absurd," Mr. Gingrich suggested that she rent a video of the 1938 Mickey Rooney–Spencer Tracy film about Boys Town, whereupon he was accused of confusing reality with "Hollywood illusion."

By this time, the affair began to recall the Murphy Brown brouhaha precipitated by Dan Quayle, who as Vice President criticized the television serial for glamorizing unwed motherhood and was jeered for taking a sitcom so seriously.

In one respect the two episodes are significantly different. It took a full year for President Clinton to admit publicly that Mr. Quayle had been right about family values. It took only a few weeks for the liberal press (although not yet the President) to concede that there might be something in the orphanage idea.

Even *Newsweek's* cover story admitted that there is much to be said for small-scale, family-type group homes like Boys Town—which, its readers may have been surprised to discover, not only still exists but has been much expanded and improved. The article quoted so respected an authority (a Democrat, to boot) as Senator Daniel Patrick Moynihan, who five years ago predicted that as heroin in the 1960's produced the single-parent family, so crack would soon produce the no-parent child, and with it the need for orphanages.

Elsewhere such reputable scholars as the social scientist James Q. Wilson have analyzed the problem of abandoned and abused children and have concluded that something like orphanages are a necessary alternative to dysfunctional or nonexistent families.

"Compared with what?" is the pertinent question. Mr. Clinton's objection, that "there is no substitute—none—for the loving devotion and equally loving discipline of caring parents," is disingenuous, for it is not such loving, devoted, caring and disciplined parents who would be displaced by orphanages. If an orphanage is not the equivalent of the Ozzie and Harriet model family, it is closer to it than the abusive, alcoholic, drug-addicted, violence-prone family, or non-family, that is the normal habitat of many children.

Orphanages are, to be sure, far more expensive than conventional relief. But the cost is not so excessive when compared with that of prisons, hospitals and asylums in which some of these children might otherwise spend a good part of their adult lives, to say nothing of the cost of the crime, delinquency, illiteracy and other social ills that these children might inflict on society.

Moreover, orphanages are only a small part of any welfare system—an agency of last resort. The aim of any welfare reform is not to institutionalize huge numbers of children but to create the conditions in which fewer children require such care.

The press has regaled us with memoirs of people raised in orphanages— not only in Boys Town but in the homes established by Roman Catholic, Protestant, Jewish and secular philanthropies. Their grateful alumni remind us that these institutions have been quietly saving souls and bodies all this time.

When even so unimpeachable a liberal as the columnist Mary McGrory decided that "an institution is better than a crack house or a life on the street," we clearly reached a new stage in the debate over orphanages. Ms.

McGrory also warned liberals not to repeat the mistake they made when they "cackled and sneered" at Dan Quayle for his Murphy Brown speech. If Mr. Quayle was right then, she suggested, Mr. Gingrich might turn out to be right now.

From gaffe to received wisdom in a few weeks—this is the real measure of the conservative victory.

There is another lesson to be drawn from the Murphy Brown and orphanage episodes. Now that we are ready to reconsider orphanages as well as family values, we may be inspired to rethink other ideas and institutions redolent of "Victorianism."

For starters, we might recognize that Victorian England was not nearly as "Dickensian" as Dickens's novels would have us believe. As John Ruskin, himself something of a socialist, said: "It is Dickens's delight in grotesque and rich exaggeration which has made him, I think, nearly useless in the present day." (Dickens did not confuse reality with fiction. He was an enthusiastic advocate of institutions he satirized in his novels—training colleges in *Hard Times* and "ragged schools" in *Our Mutual Friend*.)

Even the orphanage in *Oliver Twist* housed only 20 or 30 children, not the hundreds one might imagine. And while the real version was often miserable enough, it was not quite as miserable as the fictional one. Long before Dickens's day, reformers had tried to alleviate the situation by farming out infants to nursing mothers in the country.   15

And throughout the Victorian period, private institutions—the National Children's Home, run by the Methodists; the Waifs and Strays homes of the Anglicans; the nondenominational Dr. Barnardo's Homes—were generally more humane than the public ones. Again, these were not nearly as humane as we would like today, or, for that matter, as reformers at the time would have liked. But neither were they as "Dickensian" as we might think. (Like Boys Town, the Barnardo Homes still exist.)

While we are rediscovering orphanages (under such euphemisms as group homes, boarding schools or congregate care), we might rediscover other Victorian ideas—about welfare reform, for example.

Confronted with a growing welfare population, the Victorians (pre-Victorians, actually—this was three years before Queen Victoria ascended the throne) enacted a New Poor Law based upon the principle of "less eligibility." The condition of the "able-bodied pauper" (the principle did not apply to widows, children or the aged) was to be "less eligible"—less desirable—than that of the "independent laborer," thus encouraging the laborer to retain his independence rather than lapse into pauperism.

It is a principle we might keep in mind as we consider the "more eligible" condition of the present welfare recipient, who has every incentive to remain dependent, because relief allowances, food stamps and Medicaid are well above the minimum or even modest wage level.

Or we might rediscover another Victorian principle: charity. Foreigners   20
visiting England in the 19th century commented on the extraordinary variety
of philanthropic organizations, the large sums dispensed by private charities
and the unstinting time and energy contributed by individuals. For the Victorians, charity was more than a means of alleviating poverty and misfortune. It
was a moral obligation and a civic duty, and not only for the upper and middle classes: in 1890, a survey showed half of the "respectable" working classes
making regular charitable contributions.

One was reminded of this when President George Bush's "1,000 Points
of Light" campaign was greeted with disdain by sophisticated journalists—and
more recently when Mr. Gingrich remarked that charity would step in to
help unwed mothers who would no longer receive relief, and his interviewer
sneered at so retrograde an idea. Yet charities thrive in America, without the
imprimatur of pundits.

Or we might rediscover the ideas of cleanliness and orderliness, which
Victorians elevated to the level of virtues. These ideas appear in the recent
reminiscences of American orphans, who recall, not resentfully, the tidy quarters they inhabited, the floors washed and polished, shoes lined up as in military formation, precise timetables for meals, study, chores, recreation.

Or we might rediscover, as *Newsweek* has, the idea of shame. "The Name
of the Game Is Shame" is the title of an article on teen-age pregnancy. The "old
moral relativism" is over, we are told, even if some liberals are reluctant to acknowledge it. "The line between right and wrong" must be drawn sharply, and
one way to draw that line is to make teen-age illegitimacy shameful.

Shame is an idea that the Victorians took over from the Greeks and
combined with the Christian idea of guilt to produce the stigma they attached
to illegitimacy. If shame is about to be revived, perhaps stigma may be as well.
One might even contemplate the possibility that all illegitimacy will come to
be stigmatized as wrong and shameful.

And if shame, cleanliness and charity are rediscovered, can that other   25
Victorian virtue, chastity, be far behind? That, to be sure, is the most far-
fetched idea of all. But the extraordinary success of William Bennett's "Book
of Virtues" may tempt one to believe that a revival of even that virtue is not
outside the realm of possibility—improbable, surely, but not impossible.

It is such fanciful, utterly Victorian ideas that may be provoked by the
debate on orphanages.

QUESTIONING THE TEXT

1. Himmelfarb draws attention several times to the hostile reaction of
   sneering pundits to commonsense notions. Annotate the essay carefully
   to catch all the instances of this technique and then write a paragraph

about this strategy. Examine your own reaction to the media people
Himmelfarb indirectly criticizes.

2. Writing a newspaper column, Himmelfarb cannot provide details about
   her sources. But what signals do you get that she may be an authority
   on the subject of the Victorians? Annotate those places where Himmelfarb suggests that she knows more about her subject than she can show
   in a short piece.

MAKING CONNECTIONS

3. In the preceding selection, William F. Buckley Jr. seeks a solution to
   the growing problem of out-of-wedlock births. Does Himmelfarb's
   proposal for more orphanages respond to Buckley's concerns? Why, or
   why not?
4. Would orphanages have a place within the Indian family structure Jeremy Seabrook describes (p. 502)? If you keep a reading log, answer this
   question there.

JOINING THE CONVERSATION

5. Himmelfarb suggests that it may be time to reattach a stigma to out-of-
   wedlock births. Discuss this issue in class, or use the library to explore it
   in more detail. Then write an op-ed-style piece yourself, responding to
   Himmelfarb. Remember that a response does not require you simply to
   agree or disagree; you may want to explore alternatives.
6. Himmelfarb suggests that we may soon see chastity regarded as a virtue,
   as it was in Victorian times. Examine the popular culture for signals that
   Himmelfarb is right or wrong. Then write an essay assessing Himmelfarb's prediction.

JILL FRAWLEY
Inside the Home

JILL FRAWLEY, a registered nurse and advocate for patients, left the employment of the nursing home described in this article. Originally published in Mother Jones *magazine in 1991, this article demonstrates in graphic detail why she left and, in so doing, exposes the "big lie" told by institutions such as the one she worked for: "long-term care facilities" owned by big corporations care little or nothing for the patients whose money supports them or for the employees who do their bidding.*

I chose this essay because—in spite of the designation "nursing home"—I had never considered the word home *to include such institutions. In fact, asked to list dozens of places that might count as "home," I would have failed to include facilities such as the one Frawley describes. And yet I have friends whose parents are even now in such homes. How, then, to explain my omission? Perhaps, I have reflected since reading Frawley's essay, because my silent neglect of such "homes" is part of the big lie she speaks of. Perhaps by ignoring them I bear some responsibility for the many nursing homes that are insufferable and insupportable.*

Perhaps I should think more carefully about what is and is not designated as a "home." And perhaps I should think more carefully when big corporations call themselves "families." Are they families I want to support or belong to? Are the homes they provide ones I'd want to inhabit? Now read "Inside the Home." — A.L.

I'm just one little nurse, in one little "care facility." Each shift I work, I carry in my soul a very big lie. I leave my job, and there aren't enough showers in the world to wash away my rage, my frustration, my impotence.

The long-term-care facility (nursing home) I work for is owned by a corporation that owns nursing homes throughout the country. Giving corporations like this control over the quality of medical care is handing over control to the fox. Every chicken in the coop knows there is no hope—only the ticking away of a life devoid of dignity or even minimal respect.

I watch the videos they show to new employees during "orientation." Smiling people spout corporate policy and speak of "guest relations." They tell us we are special; we are going to participate in a rewarding job. Elderly people in the video are dressed nicely; they are coherent and grateful for the help the staff member has time to give. We sign the attendance sheet: We saw it; now we know what "guest relations" means. It means to act in front of the families so that they think everything is okay.

The truth is ugly; I confess it in a burst of desperation. The elderly lie in feces and urine because there is only one aide for thirty patients. Eventually, they get changed abruptly—too fast, too harshly. They cry out in confused terror. Doors are closed to "protect their privacy"—but really so no one will see. The covers get flung back. It's evening bed check. The old person is shoved from one side of the bed to the other. He tries to protest; he thinks something bad is happening. Whip out the soiled underpad, wipe him, throw the covers over him . . . on the next body.

No time for mouth care; sometimes no time for showers; never time to hold someone's hand even for a moment. Aides feed the helpless two spoon-fuls of pureed stuff, dripping down chins; not time to wait for them to swal-low. It gets charted: "Resident didn't eat much tonight." She loses weight; she gets more frail as each day passes. The food is so bad I can't begin to de-scribe it. The cook is young and doesn't care much; if I complain, he gets mad. One resident asks me for a cup of hot water so she can use the instant soup in her drawer. She can't eat the cold, badly cooked stuff that is on her tray. Slow starvation is hard to get used to. 5

Why is there only one aide on these halls night after night? Most em-ployees don't stay. They can't stand being flung into jobs that are too hard, too horrid, for too little money. The ones that do stay have given up complaining. They shut their eyes and ears and do the best they can. They have children to support, no education, are caught by life in such a way that quitting would intensify their own suffering and not alleviate anyone else's.

We're always short-staffed. We know it's to save money. One tired aide does a double shift, straining to do a job it takes two people to do correctly. I guess when you make four dollars and something an hour, it takes working double shifts (that's sixteen hours) to make enough to live on. Tired people get impatient, make mistakes, take shortcuts. A nurse calls in sick. That means one nurse does three halls. One nurse to pass out medicines for eighty resi-dents.

Patients are dropped or fall. My coworkers agree that it's a widespread practice to chart this to avoid problems. Every incident report I have ever seen states that the patient or resident was "found on the floor" or appeared to have bruises or skin tears of "unknown" origin. When there's no time to turn the bedridden every two hours, skin breaks down and ulcers develop. The elderly get skin tears and bruises because they are fragile, but also because there is no time to handle them gently. Again, we chart carefully so there is no blame. We let our old ones die for many reasons. Sometimes it is because of sickness; sometimes it is from neglect.

The admissions director is a nice lady. She lives uneasily with her task. She tells anxious families not to worry, that the facility will be like a second home to their relative. She tells them what they want to hear. The families go away determined to believe everything will be fine. Secretly, they are relieved that they won't have to deal with dementia, incontinence, or the total dependency of a senile elder.

The silence is ominous in the evening. Nothing to do; no place to go.   10
The residents sit and wait for death. The staff is ground down in despair and hopelessness. The guys at corporate headquarters must be patting each other on the back about the profits they're making.

It got bad at the place I work. Too many unhappy people; too much barely controlled anger always close to erupting. A corporate spokesperson was sent from headquarters to listen to grievances. He listened, this quiet, intelligent man who had been to our facility before. I asked some of my fellow workers why they weren't going to speak out. "It doesn't do any good," was the response. "He's been coming for three or four years. Nothing changes." I went; I spoke out; they were right. Nothing changes.

The elderly suffer quietly. They are afraid they will be punished if they speak up for themselves. Most of them can't speak for themselves. They just want to escape this hell. I do too. They need a place to stay; I need a job. We're trapped.

I am one little nurse, in one little care facility, living with this terrible secret. If they knew I was telling on them, I wouldn't have a job. What about my rent? What about my needs? But I need to tell. I confess to my participation in these crimes. I can't keep this secret any longer.

If you have an elderly relative in a facility:

1. Visit at odd hours.
2. Visit at mealtime.
3. Don't believe what the staff tells you.
4. Ask questions.
5. Don't worry if small items are missing. Petty theft is not serious. Abuse is.
6. Make sure your relative is clean.
7. Notice if your relative is losing weight.
8. Check your relative's skin for bruises.
9. Let "them" know you are watching.
10. Be polite to staff, but raise hell with the administrator or the director of nursing. Though they are just employees and will tell you what you want to hear, it's worth a try.
11. Contact local ombudsmen if you can't get results. If that doesn't work, contact the state regulatory agency.
12. Complain to headquarters or whoever owns the facility.
13. Don't allow yourself to be blackmailed by veiled threats of being forced to move your relative.
14. Don't give up; wear them down.

QUESTIONING THE TEXT

1. What does Frawley mean by the "big lie"? Write out a brief definition of this "big lie."
2. What is Frawley's attitude toward her employers? toward her patients? toward herself? Point to places in the essay that reveal these attitudes to you.
3. Are the questions A.L. poses at the end of her introduction to this reading rhetorical ones, or does she intend for you to answer them? How do you know?

MAKING CONNECTIONS

4. Review the essays, poems, and chapter opening illustration in this chapter and then list all the places in them that fall under the category of "home." What do all these places have in common? Try to write a definition of "home" that would accommodate all these places.
5. Imagine a dialogue between Frawley and Jeremy Seabrook (p. 502) on the definition and importance of "home." Write out a page or so of that dialogue.

JOINING THE CONVERSATION

6. Think for a while about the work you now do or have done. What about that work made you feel good about what you were doing? Did anything about it seem like a "big lie"? What, if anything, filled you with frustration? Based on your exploration of these questions, write a brief position paper on "how I feel about the work I do (or have done)."
7. Working with several members of your class, do some research on nursing homes in your area. How are they regulated? Who owns them? How much does it cost to stay in them? Who works there, and how are such people licensed or certified? Have each member of your group visit one nursing home, taking notes on the facilities and the atmosphere and talking, if possible, to people who work there, as well as to people who live there. Pool your notes and prepare a report for your class on whether your research does or does not support Frawley's picture of nursing homes.

ED MADDEN
Family Cemetery, near Hickory Ridge, Arkansas

WE FEEL THE TOUCH *of our extended families at important moments of tran-sition: birth, graduation, marriage, death. Anyone with a large clan knows, however, that such occasions can bring out the worst in people. Cousins grown a lanky foot taller in the last year may trade blows (or gossip) at a wedding; at a baptism, aunts from different sides of the family will quarrel over the choice of godparents; and otherwise dutiful children will spend a holiday reunion silently coveting Grandpa's power tools, wondering who will inherit them when the old man finally crosses the bar.*

Yet at such thresholds, we need our families too and look for support from these people who knew us from our birth, who share our rambling gait, conspic-uous nose, and deepest memories.

In the following poem Ed Madden writes about one such family time. Madden (b. 1963) is a poet and an assistant professor at the University of South Carolina. He grew up on a rice and soybean farm in northeast Arkansas. His interests range from theology and feminist theory to pop culture and Elvis Presley, and his poems have appeared in College English, Christianity and Literature, *and elsewhere. —* J.R.

I

Redwing blackbirds shout
themselves hoarse from the oaks
of the cemetery. A crop-duster drones
above a nearby ricefield. The long

caravan of cars that left the church   5
is still arriving, the dust drifting
in waves that coat the dull green rows
of grain sorghum and soybeans, dust

still hanging in air hot
with the smell of Arkansas honeysuckle   10
and vetch and the sweet maroon
ferment of funeral roses.

II

I breathe deeply: the summer
grass rich at the verge of brown,
freshly mown, the musty, almost acrid   15
earth of this sandy hillside,

piled by the grave. These things
must be remembered, like the daffodils
in solemn yellow spurts that marked
my grandma's death, standing in silent   20

clusters of mourning at the cemetery,
dotting her yard like relatives, nodding,
touching, like cousins laughing, flaring
their bright lives against the grey spring wind.

III

Grandpa's flowers are scattered   25
down the line of tombstones, decorating
the graves of his wife, his children;
it seems the office of aunts to gather

the blooms, to drape these odd dots
and splashes, against brown earth, grey stone.   30
We the men, the sons and grandsons,
take the shovels in groups of three,

marking our ties with the thuds that fill
the grave: it is love, it is something
of God. And there must be a word   35
to fill the hole it creates.

IN RESPONSE

1. Read "Family Cemetery" along with Jeremy Seabrook's essay (p. 502), and respond with an entry on your own definition of "family" in your reading log, if you are keeping one.

2. Examine the role that nature plays in "Family Cemetery." In a short analysis, explain your reaction to the sights, sounds, and smells in this poem.
3. In a group, share your experience of a family moment that you might turn into a poem.

OTHER READINGS

Baskina, Ada. "All in the Family." *World Press Review* Apr. 1995: 34. Contrasts American and Russian families.

Ehrenreich, Barbara. "Oh, Those Family Values." *Time* 18 July 1994. Reminds readers of some of the negative aspects of family life.

Harrington, Walt. "A Family Portrait in Black and White." *Literary Journalism: A New Collection of the Best American Nonfiction*. Ed. Norman Sims and Mark Kramer. New York: Ballantine, 1995. 153–75. A white man in an interracial marriage reflects on racism and its effects on his family.

Moynihan, Daniel Patrick. "Defining Deviancy Down." *American Scholar* Winter 1993. Argues that American society is accepting as normal some behaviors previously regarded as unhealthy or inappropriate.

Raspberry, William. "What a Difference Marriage Makes." *Washington Post* 11 Apr. 1994. Argues that marriage brings more benefits than contemporary society acknowledges.

Smolowe, Jill. "When Violence Hits Home." *Time* 18 July 1994: 18–25. Discusses how domestic abuse began to be exposed more after Nicole Simpson's death.

Walker, Alice. "Looking for Zora." *In Search of Our Mothers' Gardens*. San Diego: Harcourt, 1983. 93–116. Walker visits Eatonton, Florida, Hurston's hometown, to learn more about "one of the most significant unread authors in America."

ELECTRONIC RESOURCES

Children's Defense Fund Site:
> http://www.tmn.com/cdf/index.html
> Provides information about a group concerned with the needs of children.

Planned Parenthood On Line: A Guide to Healthy Sexuality:
> http://www.ppca.org/
> Provides information about a liberal group supporting birth control, women's health issues, and abortion services.

The Family Research Council Site:
> http://www.frc.org/
> Provides information about a group promoting profamily issues.

Eagle Forum—Phyllis Schlafly:
> http://www.basenet.net/~eagle/
> Provides information about a conservative group interested in family values.

Work:
As Poor Richard Says . . .

"Yes, and the fact that you've been an outstanding employee for twenty-five years is going to look great on your résumé."

Look carefully at this cartoon, from a 1996 issue of *The New Yorker* magazine. What is the relation of the words in the caption to the picture, and how do they work together to produce an overall effect? How is humor used in this cartoon, and how effectively does it convey its overall message? What does the drawing of the characters suggest about the people represented? What thoughts and emotions does the cartoon evoke in you about the general subject of work?

(Drawing by C. Barsotti; © 1996 The New Yorker Magazine, Inc.)

We are taxed twice as much by our idleness, three times as much by our pride, and four times as much by our folly; and from these taxes the commissioners cannot ease or deliver us by allowing an abatement.

BENJAMIN FRANKLIN, *The Way to Wealth*

My first job was to jump off a burning ship into salt water with dangerous tides. I lived.

MERIDEL LeSUEUR, *Women and Work*

Not only must today's young endure a larger-than-usual share of the uncertainties of starting out, but they must contemplate a future that seems truncated and uncompromising.

PAUL OSTERMAN, *Getting Started*

We want to work. We are trying hard to work. . . . We are worth something even if our ships have come in and set sail again without us.

JULIA CARLISLE and FLORENCE HOFF, *Young, Privileged, and Unemployed*

It's a sign of how widespread awareness of [job insecurity] is that sitcoms are creeping closer to the subject.

CARYN JAMES, *Pop Culture: Extremes but Little Reality*

The rhythm of the Third Wave Information Age will be a bit like rafting down the rapids after we have learned to canoe on a quiet lake.

NEWT GINGRICH, *America and the Third Wave Information Age*

The only thing I ask is that [Clinton] stop acting and talking as if anyone who makes more than $30,000 a year is the enemy. . . .

HENRY SCANLON, *Suddenly, I'm the Bad Guy*

Once a society progresses to the point where most people can afford food, clothing, shelter and other necessities, some people choose to work harder for luxuries, while others opt to enjoy more leisure.

W. MICHAEL COX and RICHARD ALM, *By Our Own Bootstraps*

My life is lived day to day, one line of bug-free code at a time.

DOUGLAS COUPLAND, *Microserfs*

The work of the world is common as mud.

542

MARGE PIERCY, *To Be of Use*

Introduction

THE UNITED STATES OF AMERICA declared its independence from Great Britain in 1776, the same year that the Scottish philosopher Adam Smith (1723–90) published what would become the classic work on capitalism, *The Wealth of Nations*. The conjunction of events proved to be auspicious: nowhere on earth would the principles of free market capitalism be more enthusiastically applied than in the nation assembled from Britain's thirteen rebellious colonies. The revolutionaries in New York, Virginia, and Massachusetts fought not only for political liberty but also for the freedom to buy and sell in competitive world markets. At the time of the War of Independence, American entrepreneurs, schooled in the economic wisdom of Benjamin Franklin's Poor Richard, had already set into motion economic forces that would make the United States affluent and powerful.

The American Revolution also coincided with the dawn of the industrial revolution. Within a century after the shots fired at Lexington and Concord, powerful new machines capable of doing many times the work of manual laborers had transformed the economic structure of the nation. Processes as different as weaving, mining, and reaping would be successfully mechanized, reducing the cost of goods and making them available to more people. And the new industries would generate yet more capital, leading to still more entrepreneurship, investment, and development. It seemed that a formula for enduring prosperity had been discovered.

But the convergence of industrialism and capitalism also brought suffering. Human labor became a commodity measurable by the hour and subject to market forces. People looking for employment abandoned the countryside to crowd into urban slums with high crime and poor sanitation. Disease was rampant. Workers, many of them mere children, faced grueling days in dangerous factories and mines earning meager wages that they then often had to spend in company stores. Mills and foundries brutalized the landscape, darkening the skies and fouling the rivers.

In England, conditions like these moved Karl Marx to write *Das Kapital* (vol. 1, 1867), in which he condemned laissez-faire capitalism, predicted its demise, and imagined a utopian socialist alternative: communism. For more than a century afterward, capitalists and communists struggled worldwide for economic and military supremacy—the United States and western Europe as the major proponents of free markets and entrepreneurship, and the Soviet Union, China, and eastern Europe as the advocates of socialism.

Socialism lost. Today, serious arguments are still being made for Marxist economics only perhaps in China, in Cuba, and in American universities. Overcoming industrialism's initial ills, capitalist countries offered their citizens vastly greater wealth and liberty than authoritarian Marxist regimes could. Labor unions and numerous reform movements in the West, too, had helped quash monopolies and increase membership in the dominant middle class.

Yet the United States, which led the industrial democracies through the Cold War, enters the twenty-first century less confident than one would expect a victor to be. Despite statistical increases in wealth in the country as a whole and remarkable advances in electronic technologies, many citizens find their quality of life declining and their jobs unsatisfying or—worse—insecure. The downsizing that restored the efficiency of U.S. corporations in the 1980s has not opened up as many new jobs and industries as expected, in part because a bloated government deficit keeps interests high and devours capital that might be used to create wealth. In some circles, especially on college campuses, questions are even being raised about the wisdom of continuing to pursue market capitalism, with its inevitably unequal distributions of wealth and opportunity.

In this chapter we explore some of the economic problems and opportunities that Americans face today—a subject both vast and complicated. Some of our selections examine the nature of American economic thinking; others look at the ways Americans actually work in or are excluded from the economic mainstream. At times, we can only point to areas for more reading and exploration. This is one chapter we know will raise many questions and provoke lengthy debates.

Following are some questions that you may want to think about as you read this chapter:

- How do Americans feel about work?
- Have the economic values of Americans changed? What major questions of economics divide people or political parties in the United States?
- What rights do workers have to a job? For what reasons may employers exclude someone from employment?
- Is the United States in decline economically?
- Will electronic technology radically change our ways of working?
- Do we put too much emphasis on work? Do Americans fear leisure?

• • •

BENJAMIN FRANKLIN
The Way to Wealth

THE MAXIMS OR APHORISMS that Benjamin Franklin (1704–90) recorded in Poor Richard's Almanac *(first issue, 1733) have become part of American folk culture. There's probably not an American alive who wasn't introduced in preschool to Franklin's advice on waking early or hoarding change:*

> Early to bed, and early to rise, makes a man healthy, wealthy, and wise.

> A penny saved is a penny earned.

Because such adages are short and amusing, we're apt to dismiss them as childish stuff. Why, then, do they and many other sayings from Franklin's "The Way to Wealth" persist in our memories?

Perhaps common sense and thrift never go out of style. The adages Father Abraham doles out in the essay Franklin wrote to mark the twenty-fifth anniversary of Poor Richard's Almanac *still ring true to many readers eager to get ahead. To his credit, Franklin's advice was as stern and honest in 1758 as it is today: you get rich not by manipulating stock funds or light-footing your way through real estate deals, but by working hard, spending little, saving a lot, and borrowing nothing.*

How deeply embedded in the American psyche are attitudes typified by Poor Richard's *maxims? It is hard to say. Benjamin Franklin's fictional character reveals a disturbing mistrust of leisure. Serious writers have even described Franklin—an aggressive, hard-headed, and penurious genius—as the very embodiment of America's defining Protestant ethic. I think old Ben still makes us feel guilty every time we reach for the MasterCard.*

In "The Way to Wealth," Franklin's persona of Poor Richard is at an auction where he hears Father Abraham repeat the most famous maxims from Poor Richard's Almanac. *This framing device allows Richard (a.k.a. Franklin) to comment on his own wisdom without seeming to praise himself too much. —* J.R.

PREFACE TO POOR RICHARD IMPROVED

Courteous Reader,

I have heard that nothing gives an author so great pleasure, as to find his works respectfully quoted by other learned authors. This pleasure I have seldom enjoyed; for though I have been, if I may say it without vanity, an eminent author of almanacs annually now a full quarter of a century, my brother authors in the same way, for what reason I know not, have ever been very sparing in their applauses, and no other author has taken the least notice of me, so that did not my writings produce me some solid pudding, the great deficiency of praise would have quite discouraged me.

I concluded at length, that the people were the best judges of my merit; for they buy my works; and besides, in my rambles, where I am not personally known, I have frequently heard one or other of my adages repeated, with "as Poor Richard says" at the end on 't; this gave me some satisfaction, as it showed not only that my instructions were regarded, but discovered likewise some respect for my authority; and I own, that to encourage the practice of remembering and repeating those wise sentences, I have sometimes quoted myself with great gravity.

Judge, then, how much I must have been gratified by an incident I am going to relate to you. I stopped my horse lately where a great number of people were collected at a vendue* of merchant goods. The hour of sale not being come, they were conversing on the badness of the times and one of the company called to a plain clean old man, with white locks, "Pray, Father Abraham, what think you of the times? Won't these heavy taxes quite ruin the country? How shall we be ever able to pay them? What would you advise us to?" Father Abraham stood up, and replied, "If you'd have my advice, I'll give it you in short, for a *word to the wise is enough, and many words won't fill a bushel,* as Poor Richard says." They joined in desiring him to speak his mind, and gathering round him, he proceeded as follows:

"Friends," says he, "and neighbors, the taxes are indeed very heavy, and if those laid on by the government were the only ones we had to pay, we might more easily discharge them; but we have many others, and much more grievous to some of us. We are taxed twice as much by our idleness, three times as much by our pride, and four times as much by our folly; and from these taxes the commissioners cannot ease or deliver us by allowing an abatement. However, let us hearken to good advice, and something may be done for us; *God helps them that help themselves,* as Poor Richard says, in his Almanack of 1733.

"It would be thought a hard government that should tax its people one-   5 tenth part of their time, to be employed in its service. But idleness taxes many of us much more, if we reckon all that is spent in absolute sloth, or doing of nothing, with that which is spent in idle employments or amusements, that amount to nothing. Sloth, by bringing on diseases, absolutely shortens life. *Sloth, like rust, consumes faster than labor wears; while the used key is always bright,* as Poor Richard says. *But dost thou love life, then do not squander time, for that's the stuff life is made of,* as Poor Richard says. How much more than is necessary do we spend in sleep, forgetting that *the sleeping fox catches no poultry* and that *there will be sleeping enough in the grave,* as Poor Richard says.

---

vendue: a sale

"*If time be of all things the most precious, wasting time must be,* as Poor Richard says, *the greatest prodigality;* since, as he elsewhere tells us, *lost time is never found again; and what we call time enough, always proves little enough:* let us then up and be doing, and doing to the purpose; so by diligence shall we do more with less perplexity. *Sloth makes all things difficult, but industry all easy,* as Poor Richard says; *and he that riseth late must trot all day, and shall scarce overtake his business at night;* while *laziness travels so slowly, that poverty soon overtakes him,* as we read in Poor Richard, who adds, *drive thy business, let not that drive thee,* and *early to bed, and early to rise, makes a man healthy, wealthy, and wise.*

"So what signifies wishing and hoping for better times. We may make these times better, if we bestir ourselves. *Industry need not wish,* as Poor Richard says, *and he that lives upon hope will die fasting. There are no gains without pains; then help hands, for I have no lands,* or if I have, they are smartly taxed. And, as Poor Richard likewise observes, *he that hath a trade hath an estate; and he that hath a calling, hath an office of profit and honor;* but then the trade must be worked at, and the calling well followed, or neither the estate nor the office will enable us to pay our taxes. If we are industrious, we shall never starve, for, as Poor Richard says, *at the workingman's house hunger looks in, but dares not enter.* Nor will the bailiff or the constable enter, for *industry pays debts, while despair increaseth them,* says Poor Richard. What though you have found no treasure, nor has any rich relation left you a legacy, *diligence is the mother of goodluck,* as Poor Richard says, and *God gives all things to industry. Then plow deep, while sluggards sleep, and you shall have corn to sell and to keep,* says Poor Dick. Work while it is called today, for you know not how much you may be hindered tomorrow, which makes Poor Richard say, *one today is worth two tomorrows,* and farther, *have you somewhat to do tomorrow, do it today.* If you were a servant, would you not be ashamed that a good master should catch you idle? Are you then your own master, *be ashamed to catch yourself idle,* as Poor Dick says. When there is so much to be done for yourself, your family, your country, and your gracious king, be up by peep of day; *let not the sun look down and say, inglorious here he lies.* Handle your tools without mittens; remember that *the cat in gloves catches no mice,* as Poor Richard says. 'Tis true there is much to be done, and perhaps you are weak-handed, but stick to it steadily; and you will see great effects, for *constant dropping wears away stones,* and *by diligence and patience the mouse ate in two the cable;* and *little strokes fell great oaks,* as Poor Richard says in his Almanack, the year I cannot just now remember.

"Methinks I hear some of you say, "must a man afford himself no leisure?" I will tell thee, my friend, what Poor Richard says, *employ thy time well, if thou meanest to gain leisure; and, since thou art not sure of a minute, throw not away an hour.* Leisure is time for doing something useful; this leisure the diligent man will obtain, but the lazy man never; so that, as Poor Richard says *a life of leisure and a life of laziness are two things.* Do you imagine that sloth will afford you more comfort than labor? No, for as Poor Richard says, *trouble springs from idleness, and grievous toil from needless ease. Many without labor, would live by their wits only, but they break for want of stock.* Whereas industry gives comfort, and plenty, and respect: *fly pleasures, and they'll follow you. The diligent spinner has a large shift,* and now I have a sheep and a cow, everybody bids me good morrow;* all which is well said by Poor Richard.

"But with our industry, we must likewise be steady, settled, and careful, and oversee our own affairs with our own eyes, and not trust too much to others; for, as Poor Richard says

> *I never saw an oft-removed tree,*
> *Nor yet an oft-removed family,*
> *That throve so well as those that settled be.*

And again, *three removes* is as bad as a fire;* and again, *keep thy shop, and thy shop will keep thee;* and again, *if you would have your business done, go; if not, send.* And again,

> *He that by the plough would thrive,*
> *Himself must either hold or drive.*

And again, *the eye of a master will do more work than both his hands;* and again, *want of care does us more damage than want of knowledge;* and again, *not to oversee workmen is to leave them your purse open.* Trusting too much to others' care is the ruin of many; for, as the Almanack says, *in the affairs of this world, men are saved, not by faith, but by the want of it;* but a man's own care is profitable; for, saith Poor Dick, *learning is to the studious,* and *riches to the careful,* as well as *power to the bold,* and *heaven to the virtuous,* and farther, *if you would have a faithful servant, and one that you like, serve yourself.* And again, he adviseth to circumspection and care, even in the smallest matters, because sometimes *a little neglect may breed great mischief;* adding, *for want of a nail the shoe was lost; for want of a shoe the horse was lost; and for want of a horse the rider was lost, being overtaken and slain by the enemy; all for want of care about a horseshoe nail.*

"So much for industry, my friends, and attention to one's own business; but to these we must add frugality, if we would make our industry more certainly successful. A man may, if he knows not how to save as he gets, keep his nose all his life to the grindstone, and die not worth a groat* at last. A *fat kitchen makes a lean will,* as Poor Richard says; and

> *Many estates are spent in the getting,*
> *Since women for tea forsook spinning and knitting,*
> *And men for punch forsook hewing and splitting.*

If you would be wealthy, says he, in another Almanack, *think of saving as well as of getting: the Indies have not made Spain rich, because her outgoes are greater than her incomes.*

10

---

a large shift: change of clothing, wardrobe
remove: moves
groat: a coin of small value

"Away then with your expensive follies, and you will not then have so much cause to complain of hard times, heavy taxes, and chargeable families; for, as Poor Dick says,

> *Women and wine, game and deceit,*
> *Make the wealth small and the wants great.*

And farther, *what maintains one vice would bring up two children.* You may think perhaps, that a little tea, or a little punch now and then, diet a little more costly, clothes a little finer, and a little entertainment now and then, can be no great matter; but remember what Poor Richard says, *many a little makes a mickle,** and farther, *Beware of little expenses; a small leak will sink a great ship;* and again, *who dainties love shall beggars prove;* and moreover, *fools make feasts, and wise men eat them.*

"Here you are all got together at this vendue of fineries and knicknacks. You call them goods; but if you do not take care, they will prove evils to some of you. You expect they will be sold cheap, and perhaps they may for less than they cost; but if you have no occasion for them, they must be dear to you. Remember what Poor Richard says; *buy what thou hast no need of, and ere long thou shalt sell thy necessaries.* And again, *at a great pennyworth pause a while:* he means, that perhaps the cheapness is apparent only, and not real; or the bargain, by straightening thee in thy business, may do thee more harm than good. For in another place he says, *many have been ruined by buying good penny-worths.* Again, Poor Richard says, *'tis foolish to lay out money in a purchase of repentance;* and yet this folly is practiced every day at vendues, for want of minding the Almanack. *Wise men,* as Poor Dick says, *learn by others' harms, fools scarcely by their own;* but *felix quem faciunt aliena pericula cautum.** Many a one, for the sake of finery on the back, have gone with a hungry belly, and half-starved their families. *Silks and satins, scarlet and velvets,* as Poor Richard says, *put out the kitchen fire.*

"These are not the necessaries of life; they can scarcely be called the conveniences; and yet only because they look pretty, how many want to have them! The artificial wants of mankind thus become more numerous than the natural; and, as Poor Dick says, *for one poor person, there are an hundred indigent.* By these, and other extravagancies, the genteel are reduced to poverty, and forced to borrow of those whom they formerly despised, but who through industry and frugality have maintained their standing; in which case it appears plainly, that *a plowman on his legs is higher than a gentleman on his knees,* as Poor Richard says. Perhaps they have had a small estate left them, which they knew not the getting of; they think, "'Tis day, and will never be night"; that a little to be spent out of so much is not worth minding; *a child and a fool,* as Poor Richard says, *imagine twenty shillings and twenty years can never be spent*

---

mickle: a great deal
felix . . . cautum: the Latin version of the previous saying

but, *always taking out of the meal-tub, and never putting in, soon comes to the bottom;* as Poor Dick says, *when the well's dry, they know the worth of water.* But this they might have known before, if they had taken his advice; *if you would know the value of money, go and try to borrow some; for, he that goes a-borrowing goes a-sorrowing;* and indeed so does he that lends to such people, when he goes to get it in again. Poor Dick farther advises, and says,

> *Fond pride of dress is sure a very curse;*
> *E'er fancy you consult, consult your purse.*

And again, *pride is as loud a beggar as want, and a great deal more saucy.* When you have bought one fine thing, you must buy ten more, that your appearance may be all of a piece; but Poor Dick says, *'tis easier to suppress the first desire, than to satisfy all that follow it.* And 'tis as truly folly for the poor to ape the rich, as for the frog to swell, in order to equal the ox.

> *Great estates may venture more,*
> *But little boats should keep near shore.*

'Tis, however, a folly soon punished; for *pride that dines on vanity sups on contempt,* as Poor Richard says. And in another place, *pride breakfasted with plenty, dined with poverty, and supped with infamy.* And after all, of what use is this pride of appearance, for which so much is risked so much is suffered? It cannot promote health, or ease pain, it makes no increase of merit in the person, it creates envy, it hastens misfortune.

> *What is a butterfly? At best*
> *He's but a caterpillar dressed*
> *The gaudy fop's his picture just,*

as Poor Richard says.

"But what madness must it be to run in debt for these superfluities! We are offered, by the terms of this vendue, *six months' credit;* and that perhaps has induced some of us to attend it, because we cannot spare the ready money, and hope now to be fine without it. But, ah, think what you do when you run in debt; you give to another power over your liberty. If you cannot pay at the time, you will be ashamed to see your creditor; you will be in fear when you speak to him; you will make poor pitiful sneaking excuses, and by degrees come to lose your veracity, and sink into base downright lying; for, as Poor Richard says, *the second vice is lying, the first is running in debt.* And again, to the same purpose, *lying rides upon debt's back.* Whereas a free-born Englishman ought not to be ashamed or afraid to see or speak to any man living. But poverty often deprives a man of all spirit and virtue: *'tis hard for an empty bag to stand upright,* as Poor Richard truly says.

"What would you think of that prince, or that government, who should issue an edict forbidding you to dress like a gentleman or a gentlewoman, on pain of imprisonment or servitude? Would you not say, that you were free, have a right to dress as you please, and that such an edict would be a breach of

15

your privileges, and such a government tyrannical? And yet you are about to put yourself under that tyranny, when you run in debt for such dress! Your creditor has authority, at his pleasure to deprive you of your liberty, by confining you in gaol* for life, or to sell you for a servant, if you should not be able to pay him! When you have got your bargain, you may, perhaps, think little of payment; but *creditors,* Poor Richard tells us, *have better memories than debtors;* and in another place says, *creditors are a superstitious sect, great observers of set days and times.* The day comes round before you are aware, and the demand is made before you are prepared to satisfy it, or if you bear your debt in mind, the term which at first seemed so long, will, as it lessens, appear extremely short. Time will seem to have added wings to his heels as well as shoulders. *Those have a short Lent,* said Poor Richard, *who owe money to be paid at Easter.* Then since, as he says, *The borrower is a slave to the lender, and the debtor to the creditor,* disdain the chain, preserve your freedom; and maintain your independency: be industrious and free; be frugal and free. At present, perhaps, you may think yourself in thriving circumstances, and that you can bear a little extravagance without injury; but,

> *For age and want, save while you may;*
> *No morning sun lasts a whole day,*

as Poor Richard says. Gain may be temporary and uncertain, but ever while you live, expense is constant and entire; and *'tis easier to build two chimneys than to keep one in fuel,* as Poor Richard says. So, *rather go to bed supperless than rise in debt.*

> *Get what you can, and what you get hold;*
> *'Tis the stone that will turn all your lead into gold,*

as Poor Richard says. And when you have got the philosopher's stone,* sure you will no longer complain of bad times, or the difficulty of paying taxes.

"This doctrine, my friends, is reason and wisdom; but after all, do not depend too much upon your own industry, and frugality, and prudence, though excellent things, for they may all be blasted without the blessing of heaven; and therefore, ask that blessing humbly, and be not uncharitable to those that at present seem to want it, but comfort and help them. Remember, Job* suffered, and was afterwards prosperous.

"And now to conclude, *experience keeps a dear school, but fools will learn in no other, and scarce in that;* for it is true, *we may give advice, but we cannot give conduct,* as Poor Richard says: however, remember this, *they that won't be counseled, can't be helped,* as Poor Richard says: and farther, that, *if you will not hear reason, she'll surely rap your knuckles."*

Thus the old gentleman ended his harangue. The people heard it, and approved the doctrine, and immediately practiced the contrary, just as if it

---

gaol: British spelling of *jail*
philosopher's stone: an alchemical object capable of turning crude metals into gold
Job: a figure in the Old Testament sorely tested by God

had been a common sermon; for the vendue opened, and they began to buy extravagantly, notwithstanding, his cautions and their own fear of taxes. I found the good man had thoroughly studied my almanacs, and digested all I had dropped on these topics during the course of five and twenty years. The frequent mention he made of me must have tired any one else, but my vanity was wonderfully delighted with it, though I was conscious that not a tenth part of the wisdom was my own, which he ascribed to me, but rather the gleanings I had made of the sense of all ages and nations. However, I resolved to be the better for the echo of it; and though I had at first determined to buy stuff for a new coat, I went away resolved to wear my old one a little longer. Reader, if thou wilt do the same, thy profit will be as great as mine. I am, as ever, thine to serve thee,

Richard Saunders
July 7, 1757

QUESTIONING THE TEXT

1. Which of the aphorisms Franklin repeats would you regard as outdated today? Why?
2. Based on this selection, what role do you think Franklin expects government to play in the lives of people? Explain.
3. Do you disagree with any assumptions or assertions in J.R.'s introduction? If so, which and why?

MAKING CONNECTIONS

4. After reading "The Way to Wealth," annotate Henry Scanlon's essay (p. 585) "Suddenly, I'm the Bad Guy" from Poor Richard's point of view. Does Poor Richard's perspective offer any insights on contemporary problems? Why, or why not?
5. Douglas Coupland in "Microserfs" (p. 595) hints that some Americans are so work oriented that they have little personal life. What role do work-oriented aphorisms such as Franklin's play in our lives? How and where are our attitudes toward labor, entrepreneurship, and recreation formed? Write a narrative on this subject based on your job experiences.

JOINING THE CONVERSATION

6. Have American values strayed from the path charted by Franklin's Poor Richard, or are Americans still influenced by the attitudes toward getting and spending described here? Write a short dialogue between Poor

Richard and a contemporary figure—Newt Gingrich (p. 576), Kirk-patrick Sale (p. 243), or Bill Gates (p. 474), for example.

7. What is Poor Richard's attitude toward debt? Would such an attitude today hurt or help the U.S. economy? Explain your answer in a short letter to the editor that quotes Poor Richard at least once.

8. Could a family or individual today live normally and comfortably according to Franklin's philosophy? What problems might arise? In an essay, describe what a life lived according to Poor Richard's advice might be like.

9. Try your hand at writing a few aphorisms that Poor Richard might recommend to Americans in the 1990s.

MERIDEL LESUEUR
Women and Work

*M*ERIDEL *L*E*S*UEUR *(b. 1900) has written all her life in the service of those too-often-invisible Americans who do the work of our world. LeSueur—holder of many jobs, including actress, stuntwoman, and labor organizer—is to me a fascinating figure. Her writings, from her earliest essays in the 1920s to the trilogy she is working on today, offer an unromanticized and vivid picture of twentieth-century work and workers (especially women), and she was well known as an author during the 1930s and 1940s. Her association with labor organizations and with communism, however, brought down the wrath of Senator Joseph McCarthy and his cohorts. Blacklisted in the 1950s, LeSueur had great difficulty publishing her work during the next thirty years, although the last two decades have been kinder to her. LeSueur reported doing the "best writing" of her life at ninety-four and rejoiced at the new audience she has found among the American Indian, Chicano/a, and women's movements.*

LeSueur speaks to all people who know what it is to work, and especially to those who do the work of writing. In the brief autobiographical essay that follows, she reflects on what work has meant in her life, on the work she was allowed (and not allowed) to do, and on the 140 notebooks of writing she still has—one hardworking woman's letter to the world. I chose this selection because LeSueur's work and life demonstrate how one can live through the worst deprivations, the worst economic depressions, and still find meaningful work. I also chose this piece because it's fun to see someone pushing one hundred so full of life and ideas. — A.L.

When I was 10 years old in 1910 I knew my two brothers could be anything they wanted. I knew I could be a wife and mother, a teacher, a nurse or a whore. And without an education, I could not be a nurse or teacher and we were very poor. Women could be china painters, quiltmakers, embroiderers. They often wrote secretly. Even read certain books secretly. My mother tried to go to college and women could not take math or history, only the domestic sciences.

I began to write down what I heard, sitting under the quilting frames. I tried to listen to these imprisoned and silenced women. I had a passion to be witness and recorder of the hidden, submerged, and silent women. I did not want to be a writer; I did not know a woman writer; I did not read a woman writer. It was a thick, heavy silence and I began to take down what I heard.

My Gramma hated my writing. "We have tried to hide what has happened to us," she said, "and now you are going to tell it." "I am. I am going to tell it," I cried, and I began a long howl and cry that finally found its voice in the women's movement, as it is called. A book I wrote in 1930, cruelly criticized by male editors, was not published until 1975. My audience was women, who now wanted to talk, bear witness.

I made my living working in factories, writing for the labor movement. A good thing for a writer to keep close to life, to the happening, and I have lived in the most brutal century of two world wars, millions killed and exploited, and now the atom bomb and the global struggle.

I went to the International Women's Conference in Nairobi at 85 years   5 old to see the thousands of women now bearing their own witness and I read my poem *Solidarity,* which I wrote for the Vietnamese Women's Union, and it was translated at once into Swahili as I read it. A great climax to my life. I believe this is the most enlightened moment I have seen in history and rooted in my life's passion to bear witness to the common struggle, the heroic people rising out of the violence, all becoming visible and alive.

My struggle was never alone, always with others. This makes my life bright with comradeship, marches with banners, tribal courage, and warmth. Remember, I didn't vote 'til I was 19 in 1919. Women only came into the offices after the first World War. Every young man I knew in high school never returned. The fathers and husbands had been killed. A terrible reaction set in after that bloody war to consolidate patriarchal money and power. The twenties were a terrible sinking into the Depression.

My mother, wanting to be an actress, sent me to dramatic school. I tried to fulfill her desires. The theater then was developing actresses who exploited the sexist feminine, and males who had to be John Waynes. The plays were also made for this image of sexism. Coming from the prairies, I played *Lady Windermere's Fan* by Oscar Wilde, learning to walk and use a fan and speak British. I didn't cotton to that at all. I went to Hollywood where again, your career was based on sexism, the female stereotypes. You had to go every morning to the hiring hall and show your legs and teeth and get a job for the day signing a contract that if you were killed or injured the company would not be responsible. Many extras were killed. You were a dime a dozen and the studios were flooded with the beautiful prairie girls from the Midwest. It was a meat market and developed one of the greatest prostitute rings in Los Angeles, San Francisco, Seattle, and Las Vegas.

My first job was to jump off a burning ship into salt water with dangerous tides. I lived. You could make $25 a day, an enormous sum, and I could save it and hole in and write for a few months. So I began to write about the open market on women; cheap labor of women, oppression and silencing and bartering of women. Also, fighting in the unions and housing. In the Depression, women were not on any list. There were no soup kitchens for women.

Also, there was the danger of sterilization. Groups of women were netted and taken to women's prisons and might be sterilized by morning. There was a theory that the only solution to the Depression was sterilization of the workers. It began to be known Hitler had the same idea.

In desperation, I think, I boldly had two children at the beginning of the Depression. You couldn't get any other kind of life, and you might give birth to friends and allies. I had two girls, who all my life, have been just that.

I became a correspondent from the Middle West, reporting on the   10 farmers' struggles, the third party, all that was happening. I wrote for several national magazines and began to have stories in *American Mercury,* and university quarterlies, and writings about my children were sold to the women's magazines. So I began to make a modest living at writing, which was wonderful. I became known as a witness, as I wanted to be. I became well known for two pieces: *Corn Village,* about the small town; and, *I Was Marching,* about the '34 teamsters' strike.

I feel we must be deeply rooted in the tribal family and in the social community. This is becoming a strong and beautiful force now in our societies. Women speaking out boldly, going to jail for peace and sanctuary, defending the children against hunger. We still get half of what men get. But as I saw in Nairobi the struggle of women is now global. My Gramma and mother are not any more silenced and alone. Writing has become with women not a concealment, but an illumination. We are not alone. The hundreds of women writers now who speak for us to a large audience.

This makes me write more than I ever did. I have 140 notebooks, my letter to the world, published some day for a new woman I dreamed of. I have 24 great grandchildren who have freedoms I could only dream of. One granddaughter is raising five children herself. Another has two sons. They are not alone; that's the point. They live in collectives and work in social fields with women and children. They have an independence I never had, a boldness and a communal life and support.

I am writing as I never wrote before. I have three books, besides my notebooks, to "finish." I call it getting in my crop before the frost! It is my best writing, I believe . . . I have learned to bear witness with love and compassion and warm readers to whom I am truthful. And they return my witness, so women rise from the darkness singing together, not the small and tortured chorus of my grandmothers, but millions becoming visible and singing.

QUESTIONING THE TEXT

1. LeSueur speaks of "female stereotypes." Reread the essay, highlighting every example of such stereotypes. How much evidence does LeSueur marshal to illustrate these stereotypes?

2. LeSueur calls Hollywood and the film industry a "meat market." What evidence does she give to support this analogy? Does the analogy still hold today? What evidence could you offer to support or to refute it?

MAKING CONNECTIONS

3. Read LeSueur's essay along with Henry Scanlon's (p. 585). Although LeSueur might not call Scanlon a "bad guy," what issues might she raise with him? Try your hand at writing a letter LeSueur might send to Scanlon.
4. Look through all the selections in this chapter and decide which writer LeSueur has the most in common with—and which writer she would probably disagree with most strongly. If you keep a reading log, explore these agreements or disagreements there, and weigh in with your own ideas as well. Which of these writers do you have most in common with, and why?
5. Try writing a few Poor Richard–like maxims as LeSueur might pen them. Bring them to class for discussion.

JOINING THE CONVERSATION

6. Working with two or three classmates, draw up some questions you would like to ask people who are now in their eighties or nineties about their experiences with work. Start with your own grandparents or great grandparents, or those of your friends. If possible, find three or four additional men and women to interview, perhaps through the American Association of Retired Persons or an assisted-living group in your community. Together, write a brief report for your class on your interviewees' experiences with work.
7. Spend some time thinking about the kind of work you most want to do. Then write an exploration of your knowledge and feelings about such work, including an examination of both positive and negative points. If you keep a reading log, explore this issue there.

PAUL OSTERMAN
Getting Started

PEOPLE ENTERING THE WORKFORCE today for the first time will spend the greater portion of their working lives paying off the benefits their elders accrued during the heydey of the welfare state (1964–80). Yet when these same working youths reach retirement, they'll likely find their own pot of gold empty or (more likely) filled with wooden nickels, the nation's currency grossly inflated to pay off crushing debt. When swindlers set up scams, it's a crime; when government does it, it's politics as usual. But either way, some working stiff gets his pocket picked.

Can't happen here? It already has—and the economic strain is more than evident in soft job markets and a dearth of investment capital to create new positions, industries, and ventures. Still, in a multi-trillion-dollar economy, there will always be employment opportunities for those who are quick witted enough to take advantage of them.

That's the sober message of Paul Osterman in "Getting Started," an essay I picked as an example of solid, straightforward reporting. It appeared originally in Wilson Quarterly (Autumn 1994), a publication of the Woodrow Wilson International Center for Scholars. Osterman (b. 1946) is professor of human resources and management at the Massachusetts Institute of Technology. – J.R.

We live in an age of anxiety about jobs, and perhaps the greatest anxiety is felt by young people searching for their first employment. All the other dangers and discontents of the world of work—from stagnant wages to insecurity bred by corporate "re-engineering"—seem to form a dark ceiling over those who are putting their feet on the lowest rungs of the ladder. Not only must today's young endure a larger-than-usual share of the uncertainties of starting out, but they must contemplate a future that seems truncated and unpromising. The news media have cast them as an "edgy," cynical, and disheartened "Generation X," the first generation in American history, we are constantly told, that cannot look forward to a future better than its parents had. A staple of the Generation X story is the young person who invested in four years of college and yet finds himself in a job well below what he expected, both in terms of what it demands and what it pays. The *Washington Post* tells of college graduates forced to take unpaid internships because real jobs are unavailable. *Time* says it all in a headline: "Bellboys with B.A.'s."

There is a crisis among young people who are trying to get started in life, but it is not quite the crisis that the news media describe and its causes are

not quite what one might expect. The facts simply do not support a terribly gloomy view of the immediate prospects for the middle-class, college-educated kids who are generally labeled Generation X. It is true that wage growth, an important part of the escalator of upward mobility, has slowed or ended, and it is far from certain that the old more-or-less automatic increases will resume. College-educated men aged 25 to 29, for example, earned an average of $28,963 in 1992, roughly the same amount in real dollars as in 1983. (Their female peers, however, improved their earnings by a bit more than 10 percent.) But while average pay may not have increased, college grads still get good jobs, jobs that give them responsibility, decent pay, room for a little creativity, and opportunities for advancement. In the boom years of 1984–86, about 47 percent of newly hired college grads in their twenties landed jobs in top-shelf occupations, as executives, managers, or professionals. The years 1989–91 saw a slight decline, to 45 percent, but this hardly represents a collapse of the job market. And another 40 percent of the 1989–91 crowd landed jobs in other desirable areas: technical work, sales, and administration, including jobs as various as air traffic controller, cashier, stockbroker, and ticket and reservations agent.

Slow economic growth has increased the risks facing college graduates and ratcheted up their anxiety. On university campuses a more somber career-oriented atmosphere prevails, shocking the visiting journalists who came of age in sunnier and, some would say, dreamier days. It takes more time and more effort to get a good job, and often the pay is disappointing. Nonetheless these young people are still in relatively good shape.

Don't cry for today's college graduates. They may sometimes have trouble finding jobs, but they earn about $9,000 more than high school graduates.

(Reprinted courtesy Doug Marlette)

The young people who face true difficulty are those with less education. They are in fact the great majority of young jobseekers. In 1992, only 23 percent of 25 to 29-year-olds had a college degree. Another 48 percent had some college or an associate's degree. Sixteen percent had only a high school diploma, and 13 percent lacked even that. In the past, there was a fairly reliable route that kids without college could follow. After high school and perhaps a year or two of college, they churned through a succession of less-than-desirable jobs before settling down. Instead of learning job skills in school, they went through an extended period of what economists call "labor market adjustment." They might work a string of jobs as retail clerks, construction workers, or unskilled factory hands, punctuated by short spells of more-or-less voluntary unemployment. Then, as now, many twentysomethings were not ready for permanent jobs. They were mainly interested in earning some spending money for an apartment and a car and, perhaps, in having a little fun with their coworkers on the job. Few cared much what kind of job it was.

With age, maturity, and new family responsibilities later in their twen-   5
ties, these people settled down into "adult jobs," but the paths they followed were many and varied. Credentials were less important than personal contacts, and many found their adult jobs through the help of parents, relatives, and friends. The young man who followed his father into a particular factory or mine might not have been typical, but his informal way of getting started was. Uncle Bob might pull some strings for you at the union hall or Mom's best friend might tip you off to an opening in the billing office. This system, if it can be called that, succeeded for most people because jobs were plentiful and because most of the skills workers needed could be learned on the job. Today many young men and women cannot count on either the old routes or the old destinations. The factory likely is silent, the union hall half empty, and the help-wanted ads full of jobs requiring specialized skills. Ready to make the leap into adulthood, these young people find there is no obvious place to land.

The system still works for large numbers of high school graduates; most move gradually from "youth jobs" to "adult jobs." The National Longitudinal Survey of Youth, which followed a group of young people between 1979 and 1988, offers a sharper picture of the problem areas. It found that 44 percent of 16 to 19-year-olds worked in wholesale or retail trade, which offers mostly low-paying and high-turnover positions. But by ages 20 to 31 the fraction employed in this sector was down to only 17 percent. Moreover, the study shows steadily growing work commitment among the young people. Only 3.5 percent of the oldest men in the study and four percent of the oldest women were unemployed at the time of the last interview. All of this suggests that the process of integrating the young into the workplace is going fairly well. Yet one also needs to know whether the jobs are steady and whether people are enjoying long stretches without unemployment. Here the news is more troubling. Among employed 29 to 31-year-old high school graduates

who did not go to college, more than 30 percent had not been in their position for even a year. Another 12 percent had only one year of tenure. The
pattern was much the same for women who had remained in the labor force
for the four years prior to the survey. These are adults who, for a variety of
reasons—a lack of skills, training, or disposition—have not managed to secure
"adult" jobs.

For blacks and Latinos, the malfunctioning of the job market has reached
a critical stage. In 1993, only 50 percent of young blacks between the ages of 16
and 24 who were not in school even had jobs. Among young Latinos the figure
was 59 percent. By contrast, nearly three-quarters of their white counterparts
had jobs. (A college degree significantly narrows but does not close the gaps.
Ninety percent of white college graduates in the age group were employed, as
were 82 percent of the black graduates and 85 percent of the Latinos.)

Young people in many other industrialized countries have a lot more
help getting started. In Germany, virtually all students except the small number bound for universities spend the last three years of high school in an apprenticeship system that combines part-time schooling with training in factories, labs, and offices. For each of some 400 recognized occupations there is a
standardized curriculum that specifies the skills to be taught on the job and
the content of schooling. The system is overseen by committees of representatives from government, business, and unions. After formal examinations at
the end of high school, new graduates are placed in "adult" jobs, often with
the company that trained them.

Not all German apprentices can find employment in their field; the
Germans, a notoriously well-fed people, joke that they always seem somehow
to turn out too many bakers. Yet inculcating the essentials of workplace behavior—be prompt, dress properly, follow instructions—is nearly as important a function of the system as teaching particular skills. The German system
has other drawbacks. Women are still "gender tracked" into fields such as
hairdressing, and the system can be slow to react to technological change in
the workplace. Still the training and placement help German youngsters receive are far superior to what is available to their American peers.

In Japan, the process of launching the young into the world of work is   10
not so highly organized as it is in Germany, but it is still far more structured
than in the United States. Teachers maintain contacts with employers and
play an important role in placing high school graduates. In Japan, as in Germany, the first job is a giant step into the work world. The years of casual,
American-style "job shopping" are virtually unknown in these countries, and
especially in Japan the young are expected to remain with their first employer
for a long time. Yet if the American system is less orderly, it also provides
much more freedom for the individual to experiment and change his or her
mind—highly prized qualities that should not be lost in any attempt at
reform.

A Tale of Two Degrees
(Annual Earnings of Men Aged 25 to 29, by Education, in Constant Dollars)

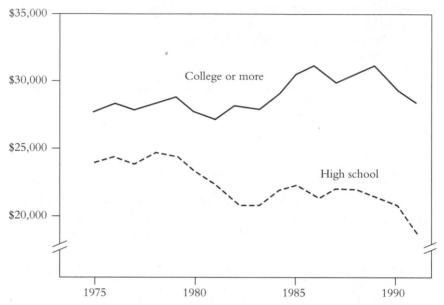

Source: Housing and Household Economic Statistics Division, U.S. Bureau of the Census

Finding a steady job is only half the challenge of getting started. Finding one that pays relatively well is the second, and lately most daunting, hurdle. Pay for college graduates has at least stayed even over the years, but high school graduates and (especially) dropouts have lost a lot of ground. There now exists a huge pay gap between the college educated and their less fortunate peers. Between 1979 and 1991, the real wages of high school dropouts fell more than 20 percent, and the wages of high school graduates without college degrees fell more than 11 percent. People equipped with only a high school degree are finding it increasingly difficult to earn a decent living. According to a recent U.S. Census Bureau report, nearly half of all 18 to 24-year-olds who worked full time in 1992 still had annual incomes below $14,335, the poverty line for a family of four.

The labor market is sending a clear signal. While the American way of moving youngsters from high school to the labor market may be imperfect, the chief problem is that, for many, even getting a job no longer guarantees a decent standard of living. More than ever, getting ahead, or even keeping up, means staying in school longer.

While many things may have contributed to the erosion of wages over the past two decades, including the oft-cited influxes of cheap immigrant labor and cheap imported goods, the new premium on skills explains much of what has happened. When new technologies are combined with new ways of organizing work, such as team production or total quality management programs, the need for various kinds of skills rises. Today, employees are asked to understand and analyze certain kinds of data, to think about ways to improve the processes and products of the workplace, and to work with others to bring improvements about. No longer is it enough to perform rote tasks on an assembly line.

In part, employers are looking for better command of "hard" skills such as math, and the best evidence for this is the fact that they are willing to pay for such hard skills with hard cash. Economists Richard Murnane, John Willett, and Frank Levy recently found that, six years after graduation, members of the high school class of 1986 who had scored in the top third of a standardized math test were earning 16 percent more than those who had scored in the bottom third. In the class of '72, by contrast, top scorers enjoyed an edge of only five percent six years after graduation.

This is a graphic illustration of the growth in demand for relatively sim- 15
ple math skills. And they are "relatively simple." Skills of this sort are not out of reach for most people. The question is whether the schools can do a good job of providing them. The answer is a little more textured than the bitter criticisms of political leaders and employers suggest. In fact, there is little reason to believe that schools are providing worse training than in the past. Scores on the National Assessment of Educational Progress, which declined during the 1970s, generally rose during the 1980s. Kids in most age groups scored slightly higher on most tests at the end of the '80s than they did in the early '70s. High school dropout rates have even improved a bit: In 1972, 16.1 percent of 19 to 20-year-olds lacked a high school diploma and were not enrolled in school. By 1991, that number was down to only 14.3 percent.

The real problem appears to be that jobs (and employers) are requiring ever-higher levels of skill, and that the schools, though moving slowly forward, are failing to keep up. Test scores have not declined, but they are not very impressive either. The National Assessment of Educational Progress, for example, offers the depressing claim that 30 percent of young people lack basic literacy skills (e.g., the ability to collect information from different parts of a document) and that 44 percent of 17-year-olds cannot compute with decimals, fractions, and percentages. And while it is nice that dropout rates are not rising, they are still too high, especially among minority groups: 17 percent of young blacks and 36 percent of Latinos are dropouts.

Employers, moreover, are not simply looking for technical skills. The workplace of the 1990s, with its team-oriented approach and quality programs, requires people who are able to work cooperatively with others. They need good interpersonal skills. The same is true in the service sector—from fast-food restaurants to airlines—where there is a growing emphasis on pleasing the customer. When asked in a survey conducted by the National Association of Manufacturers why they rejected job applicants (more than one reason could be given), 37 percent of employers cited writing skills and 27 percent cited math skills, but 64 percent cited ability to adapt to the workplace.

Thus, despite all the talk of a "deskilled" nation of hamburger flippers, the American labor market is demanding more and more skill. Although unskilled service-sector work has certainly grown, so has the quantity of more demanding work. Indeed, the U.S. Bureau of Labor Statistics projects that between now and 2005 the occupational group with the fastest growth rate will be "professional specialty" jobs—such as engineering, the health-care professions, and teaching—almost all of which require at least some college. Growth in executive, administrative, managerial, and technical occupations will also be faster than average.

It is important for those who would fix the American system to put aside utopian thoughts. Getting started will always be a difficult, anxiety-producing experience. Moreover, young people are and will continue to be marginalized in virtually every labor market in the world. Even Germany does this, albeit subtly, by placing them mostly in apprenticeships at small firms, where long-term career prospects are not good. Young people simply lack the skills and maturity of their elders, and in any event it makes sense to reserve most good jobs for people with adult responsibilities.

Hearkening to the German example, American policymakers have focused on the need to strengthen links between local schools and employers. The Clinton administration's new School to Work Opportunities Act, budgeted at $100 million this year, encourages employers to provide on-the-job training and encourages schools to reformulate their curricula to include real-world examples that can be used both to motivate and to teach. The new "tech-prep" education, unlike the old vocational education, seeks to give teenagers serious instruction in traditional academic disciplines. The hope is that by appealing to a bigger slice of the teenage population, the low-prestige, second-rate taint of old-fashioned vocational education will be avoided. Making all of this work in the highly decentralized American system will be difficult. Individual school systems must be persuaded to rethink how material is taught. Without strong European-style employers' associations, there has to be firm-by-firm recruitment of "good" employers to train students and hire graduates. Still, the effort is well worth making.

Ultimately, however, helping the young find good jobs is more than a matter of tinkering with what happens to teenagers in school and on the job. One of the top requirements in today's job market is schooling beyond high school. This means that increased financial aid to help more youngsters attend college must be a high priority. Likewise, the employment problems of black and Latino youngsters owe much to a daunting array of larger urban ills, from crime to inferior education, for which narrowly focused programs—with the exception of the tiny Job Corps—have been unable to compensate. Overcoming this group's special problems will require large helpings of collective as well as individual ambition and initiative.

QUESTIONING THE TEXT

1. Osterman quotes this headline from *Time* magazine: "Bellboys with B.A.'s." Explore the assumptions about work and education in that pessimistic headline.

2. Osterman suggests that the U.S. job seekers in the most jeopardy today are young people without college degrees. He also shows that employees with relatively basic skills enjoy greater income than those who lack these abilities. How might you persuade high school acquaintances eager to be on their own—with apartments and cars—to wait four or five more years and invest their time and money in college educations?

3. In his introduction, J.R. expresses doubt that Generation Xers will retire with the same benefits seniors enjoy today. Do you share this outlook or feel more confident about your future? Explain your beliefs.

MAKING CONNECTIONS

4. Read Osterman's essay along with the editorial and letter in the next selection. What do the two pieces suggest about success in the job market today? If you keep a reading log, answer this question there.

5. Douglas Coupland (p. 595) describes young people gainfully employed. But do his imaginary Microsoft employees fit the profile of most graduates of two- and four-year schools? Discuss the Osterman and Coupland selections in class, considering your own job prospects.

6. Review John Henry Newman's selection (p. 39) in light of Osterman's report on job markets. Should higher education be conceived primarily as preparation for a slot in our market economy? Can people today afford to treat education any other way?

JOINING THE CONVERSATION

7. Students in two- and four-year colleges are often already job market veterans. If you have work experience, describe it in a short narrative essay. If you don't have work experience, write an essay explaining how (or whether) your academic work is preparing you for a job.

8. Osterman concludes by endorsing the idea of more government involvement in job training and school-to-job transition programs to increase employment. Do these ideas appeal to you? Why, or why not? After researching the issue in the library, write a newspaper column on government intervention in job and skill training.

JULIA CARLISLE and FLORENCE HOFF
Young, Privileged, and Unemployed

WHAT COUNTS AS WORK? Answers to this question vary radically over time and from culture to culture. Some people think of their real work as that which they do when not on the job—as is the case with many serious writers and many "volunteer" workers. Some people think that housework counts as real. Others disagree. And in an age of information, when much of the work that earns a living is sedentary, spent with a keyboard and computer screen, many people think of "working out" as an important, even necessary, form of work.

The issues raised by asking "What counts as work?" are addressed squarely in the following article and letter, published in April 1991 in the New York Times. The first half of this selection is the brief news article in which Julia Carlisle, recently laid off by CBS News, speaks of "life without a job" and of the "absurd" work she and others like her must do while they look for "real" work. In the responding letter to the editor, Florence Hoff, a house-wife, mother, and unemployed clerical worker, scathingly chastises those who have learned too late that "there is no entitlement in life" and points out that the jobs Carlisle labels "absurd" are currently held by a group of people apparently dismissed as unimportant.

I chose these pieces because seldom have I come across an exchange that captured so succinctly what is at stake in our definitions of work. I find myself in sympathy with both writers. How about you? — A.L.

We are young, urban and professional. We are literate, respectable, intelligent and charming. But foremost and above all, we know what it's like to be unemployed.

Forced into dishonesty to survive, we have bounced checks to keep ourselves in oxford shirts and Ann Taylor dresses. But we have no solid ground. Our parents continue to help. Our grandparents send an occasional check. Some of us have trust funds, but the majority do not.

Our parents must wonder, "My child turned 18, then 21, got the right to vote and to drink, graduated from college, found work, then was out of work—and we're still providing the support." And we think the same. "I've done what I had to do, passed my rites of passage and yet, how demeaning, having to go back to my parents for financial support." And that's when we're lucky.

Love, well, there is love. We have loved and lost. We may even have loved and won. But there is little time for love—the kind that comes out with the cherry blossoms—when you're unemployed. Love is a simple life-line, a desperate clinging to a shoulder as we tabulate taxes we cannot pay.

The rent, the car payments and the American Express bill are all figured under the glare of a light bulb, in tears and shouting in rushes of frustration at the only thing we have, the one we "love."

Yes, we read The New York Times and The Wall Street Journal and   5 The Washington Post. We watched "60 Minutes," "Cheers" and the evening news. We read more than we did before—the latest Vintage or Penguin Contemporaries paperbacks.

But the days have been filled with the bureaucracy of life without a job. Unemployment clerks brusquely said that we'd better not risk the full sum of our unemployment checks by earning too much in a part-time job. "Honey," one told us, "Just sit back and draw out those payments."

Shocked, we insisted: "We want to work. We are trying hard to work. We have found a little something that could become permanent." We expect rewards for our efforts and recognition. We are worth something even if our ships have come in and set sail again without us.

We have been confined to our homes more evenings than not. Our spacious studios quickly turned into dorm rooms for two. Still, occasionally, unable to help ourselves, we have gone out to dinner, pretending it's easy and natural. But we wonder if the people around us knew. The $50 bill came, and suddenly we realized that a frozen pizza at home could have caused the same pain.

The work we have to do while "looking" is almost absurd. The television producer became a typist for a home foreclosure agency. The secretary became a baby sitter. The former manager of a lucrative downtown courier service, a man with a new house and boat, went mad caring for his three young children. But, while drinking just a little more often, he gained a new appreciation of his wife who went back to work, trying to sell real estate. The chef became a consultant training waiters and catering birthday parties.

Without a doubt, we are our work. We had it, we made it and we lost   10 it. We worked hard and we feel we deserved something. But we've learned an awful, preposterous truth—that we are expendable. We have been told, in so many ways, that our stature and charm and intelligence are unwanted or are not enough. Our companies' budgets dictated that, talent aside, we were no longer needed. Who could possibly believe it?

To the Editor:

So the young and privileged (Julia Carlisle in the "Voices of the New Generation" series, Op-Ed, April 4) are learning what we of the working classes have always understood too well: there is no entitlement in life.

We have always taken the jobs you label "absurd." Our mothers are the women who clean your mothers' houses, iron the clothes. Our fathers work on the BMW's, on the Lincoln Town Cars. Our sisters type your insurance policies in the factorylike setting of back offices. Our brothers are in the Marine Corps.

We are the polite and patient voice on the 24-hour 800 customer service number when you call to complain that you cannot pay your credit card bill. We are the people who work Sundays at the mall; the people who mind your children while you pursue your meaningful careers.

We do not have meaningful careers. We left school at 17. There was no money for college; we were not among the brilliant few who could win one of the increasingly scarce scholarships. Our parents were on short time themselves.

We are not without our dreams, our longings. We too find eight hours   15
a day seated in a tiny cubicle doing machine transcription demeaning to the human spirit, but we are glad at this time to have a job with a decent company that pays benefits.

We too entered a changed world where well-paying factory jobs had all but disappeared, where the bargaining powers of unions had melted away.

FLORENCE HOFF
San Francisco, April 4, 1991

Afterwords

To the Editor:

I have some sympathy with both Carlisle and Hoff, who write from very different perspectives about changes in the job market and in the nature of work.

Carlisle writes out of her own privileged experience, as one who has learned that work should offer not only challenges but some fulfillment as well. In this sense, work and self-worth are closely linked, as indeed they are for many in a country where strangers typically begin a conversation with "What do you do?" or "What is your work?" Hoff writes out of her experience as well, as one who has not been privileged and who has lived with work not as a means of fulfillment and self-definition but as a means of survival. In this sense, work is what one does in order to be allowed, in other venues, to pursue fulfillment, perhaps in family relations, in religion, in music or sport or art. Both writers, as Hoff says, have "entered a changed world."

But what is the nature of the current "changed world" of work? That is the question that devils me and many of my students. How will work be defined in the twenty-first century? Might work include things we now undervalue (and consequently do not pay much for), such as the work described by Hoff or jobs in elder and child care? Might it include those jobs we now tend to lump under "community service" or "volunteer work"? More to the point, might we need to redefine work in order for there to be enough work—of any kind—to go around? Who will—and who won't—have access to which kinds of work? Even more to the point, as a teacher I wonder how we can best prepare for redefined work and for lives that can be enriched, rather than impoverished, by that work.

These are questions I'd like to hear Carlisle and Hoff—as well as our leaders of government, industry, and community—discuss and then address through action.   — A.L.

To the Editor:

John Henry Newman suggests that among the qualities of mind a liberal education ought to cultivate are "freedom, equitableness, calmness, moderation, and wisdom." Julia Carlisle's education, whatever it entailed, seems to have given her only a sense of entitlement, one that inclines her to imagine happiness in terms of status and objects—oxford shirts and Ann Taylor dresses.

In the long history of humankind, few people have lived lives as comfortable and protected as Ms. Carlisle's, even in her semi-employed state. They haven't had checks to bounce, Vintage paperbacks to read, fifty-dollar dinners to bemoan. They couldn't get out most nights, fall in love at cherry blossom time, or bask in the warmth of paid-in-full American Express accounts. Rather simply, they worked in the sweat of their brows till they returned to the ground. Bummer, hey, Ms. Carlisle, freelance TV and radio news writer?

Florence Hoff, in her response to Ms. Carlisle, demonstrates a calmer and more moderate view of reality—despite her lack of a college education. She understands that people in less-than-glamorous jobs need dreams too, but they must often accept the daily grind Carlisle thinks beneath her for no reason other than that she's been bred to expect better. I only wish for the sake of Hoff and millions of other laborers that our society spoke more often about the dignity of work. We've practically lost our vocabulary for discussing blue-collar jobs. Our popular culture is especially inept when it comes to working people, often depicting them as beer-guzzling, overweight, plaid-shirted rubes. We prefer to celebrate exactly the kind of urban up-and-comers that Carlisle hoped to be. No wonder Julia feels let down and Hoff envious.   — J.R.

To the Editor:

As a college student, I have difficulty ignoring the instability of the "real world." Many of Carlisle's fears lurk in the back of minds of students all over the country. The prospect of succeeding in school and then graduating only to find no opportunities for employment is a real concern for many in colleges and universities today. We have been taught that hard work and dedication to studies are the keys to a bright future, but as Carlisle points out, securing a degree does not always guarantee a job. So many companies have been forced into cutbacks that the jobs simply do not exist anymore. It is also growing increasingly difficult to become an entrepreneur, evident in the number of small hometown businesses that are folding under the market pressure of corporate giants. Where are we supposed to look for encouragement? Carlisle is not alone in her feelings of instability.

Several of Carlisle's described actions may make her audience skeptical of her true level of need. It seems incredible, considering her lack of funds, that Carlisle speaks of bouncing checks to maintain a seemingly extravagant lifestyle.

I was brought up to do without if the money simply was not there, so Carlisle's practices of knowingly going farther into debt seem ridiculous. Going out for dinner when pizza at home was more financially responsible is perhaps Carlisle's way of trying to ignore the pain of unemployment. However, the Florence Hoffs of America cannot afford to take those kinds of risks. Hoff, able to accept what Carlisle refers to as "absurd" positions, possesses a more realistic view of the world. Carlisle needs to realize that those "absurd" jobs provide character-building experiences that would make her (and her contemporaries) more marketable to possible employment opportunities.

It is painful to realize how many others are competing for jobs in your line of business. Earning a degree is not enough anymore: we must now prove that we have what it takes to perform well in any setting; we all have personal dreams and goals that we must sometimes put on the back burner in exchange for more realistic options. No matter how hard we work, sometimes setbacks are unavoidable. We may feel we have "earned" a good place in society, but unfortunately the world does not always respond as we would like it to. The key is persistence and the will not to give in to the pressures and stresses of everyday life. — T.E.

QUESTIONING THE TEXT

1. Look carefully at the concrete language used in both the article and the letter—the "oxford shirts" and "Ann Taylor dresses" mentioned by Carlisle, for example, and the "Lincoln Town Cars" mentioned by Hoff. What do such specific details add to each piece? Do they make one writer more persuasive than the other? Why, or why not?

2. Using the information provided in this selection, write a definition of "work" for each writer. Then write a definition of your own. Bring all three to class to compare with others.

3. Given what she says in her introduction, how do you think A.L. defines "work"?

MAKING CONNECTIONS

4. Read this selection by Carlisle and Hoff along with that by Douglas Coupland (p. 595). What would Hoff be likely to think of the "microserfs" Coupland describes? Write the letter she might send to them. Or try your hand at defining some *Jeopardy!* categories for both Hoff and Carlisle.

5. In his book *To Renew America,* Newt Gingrich says that "the future is going to be very exciting and has the dramatic potential to improve everyone's life" (p. 582). Would either Carlisle or Hoff likely agree with Gingrich? Why, or why not?

JOINING THE CONVERSATION

6. Write your own letter to the editor in response to Julia Carlisle's article. Like Hoff, you may choose to disagree and to criticize her. Or you may write out of agreement and appreciation. Whichever you choose, bring your letter to class for discussion.

7. What experiences, institutions, or other background influences do you think helped create Carlisle's and Hoff's very different attitudes toward work? Choose one of the writers, and freewrite for a while on where you think her attitudes come from. Then turn the spotlight on yourself: Where did you get your attitudes toward and definitions of work? From movies and television? From family? From a place of worship? From school? Bring your reflections to class and discuss them with two or three classmates. Then write an essay for class, perhaps titled "Influences That Have Shaped My View of Work."

CARYN JAMES
Pop Culture: Extremes but Little Reality

CARYN JAMES'S ESSAY, as well as the accompanying "More Than 43 Million Jobs Lost. . . . ," appeared as part of a New York Times *series opener titled "The Price of Jobs Lost: A National Heartache." The weeklong series—"The Downsizing of America," which was published in March 1996—is surely one of the longest ever devoted to one subject by the* Times. *It featured essays that considered the current and future status of the "family company"; the effects that dramatic downsizing has had on families, communities, and young people trying to enter the labor market; the political struggles over how to represent downsizing to the United States public; and the contemporary search for alternatives.*

In "Pop Culture," Caryn James explores the ways in which films, television, and pop music have "begun to play out our worst fears and our fondest hopes about job insecurity." As predicted in the title of her essay, James finds examples at both ends of the spectrum: a nostalgic, rose-colored-glasses view of work as well as the utterly bleak and violent sense of desperation experienced by characters such as those in the film Dead Presidents. *In the illustrated article that appeared with James's piece, the writers (whose names are not given) use graphic illustrations and a series of statistics to underscore the bleak message: 43 million jobs have been "extinguished" in the United States since 1979.*

Taken together, these essays represent one way of looking at the current anxiety over jobs, over who will get them and who will not. I included part of the Times *series because students tell me that—whatever the statistics do or do not prove—they are plenty worried about getting and holding a job. – A.L.*

On the sitcom "News Radio" recently, the owner of a New York radio station decided to sell out to a large company. His small, loyal staff begged him to change his mind. Because they live in a television fantasy, he did. He didn't need any more money, he decided; the friendship of his employees mattered more.

The character of the benevolent boss is unreal enough to seem wacky these days, but the fantasy shouldn't be surprising. Pop culture rarely offers a straight-on reflection of social change. Instead, you can rely on television and movies to provide a fun-house-mirror version. So the scariest of economic changes are now being thrown back at us in exaggerated shapes. Films, television and pop music have begun to play out our worst fears and our fondest hopes about job insecurity.

At one extreme is "News Radio," which wraps unemployment in comforting reassurances. At the other extreme is a film like "Falling Down," in which the white-collar military-industry worker played by Michael Douglas is laid off, becomes enraged at his unemployment (and at the notion of immigrants taking jobs) and reacts by shooting everyone in sight. Such scenarios, with their veiled responses to the fear of layoffs, allow viewers to feel soothed or to vent their rage, vicariously.

This polarization into best- and worst-case scenarios is just the beginning. Pop-culture leaves a huge hole where you'd expect the issue of white collar, middle-aged unemployment to be.

But the blue-collar sitcom families on "Roseanne" and "Grace Under   5
Fire" have been struggling with lost jobs and downsizing for years. (Grace was a crew chief at an oil refinery until she was bumped back to being a regular crew member in a wave of job cuts.)

These television plots resemble common country music songs, expressing economic anxiety. They also resemble the blue-collar folks Bruce Springsteen has been singing about for two decades. On his latest CD, "The Ghost of Tom Joad," he sings about generations of beleaguered factory workers in Youngstown, Ohio. The title song evokes the John Steinbeck character, a scrappy survivor who will never give up.

But such stoic images are giving way to younger, more lackadaisical types.

The most up-to-the-minute response to job insecurity comes from a generation in its 20's and 30's, whose characters are slackers. The term "slacker" became popular after Richard Linklater's 1991 film about young adults in Austin, Tex., who drift through life without ambition. There are no decent jobs out there—or at least none like the ones their white-collar parents had—so why bother looking? In another slacker movie, "Reality Bites," the one young character who wears a suit is regarded with extreme suspicion.

In music, alternative rock is the equivalent of the slacker film. In their song "Long View," the group Green Day proves there is no long view for its generation. The narrator watches television all day and sings: "My mother says to get a job/But she don't like the one she's got." A bleak future—a bad job or no job—is the employment legacy passed on from mom and dad.

And that's the good news. At least it's not violent. In the Hughes   10
Brothers' latest film, "Dead Presidents," the hero is a young black man who loses his job, can't find another, and stages a lethal armored-truck robbery because he is desperate to feed his family. Though the film is set in the 1970's, it clearly alludes to the present. Its rebellious attitude is shared by the group Jr. M.A.F.I.A., with its hit song "Get Money."

In contrast to the drama or hopelessness in movies and music, television provides the ultimate comfort zone, even when it addresses a younger generation's joblessness. On "Friends," the twentysomething middle-class characters have few ambitions, and can afford to be blithe about unemployment. When Monica loses her job as a chef, she borrows rent money from her brother and gets a freelance catering job through her mother. For years, one or another of the thirtysomething characters on "Seinfeld" always seemed to be job hunting. George was finally forced to move in with his parents in Queens, an undignified but funny move. What's revealing is that no one ends up on the

More Than 43 Million Jobs Lost, Reaching Every Walk of Life ...

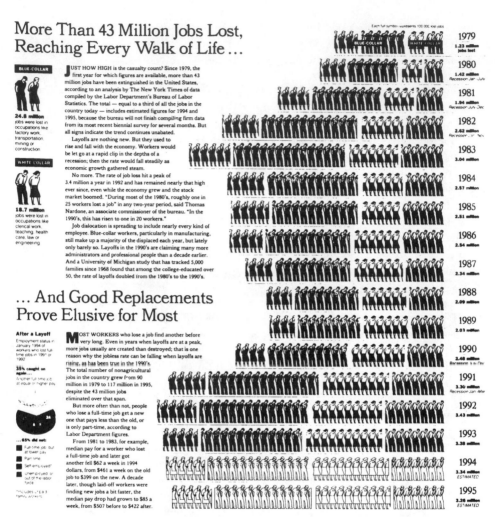

BLUE-COLLAR

24.8 million jobs were lost in occupations like factory work, transportation, mining or construction

WHITE COLLAR

18.7 million jobs were lost in occupations like clerical work, teaching, health care, law or engineering

JUST HOW HIGH is the casualty count? Since 1979, the first year for which figures are available, more than 43 million jobs have been extinguished in the United States, according to an analysis by The New York Times of data compiled by the Labor Department's Bureau of Labor Statistics. The total — equal to a third of all the jobs in the country today — includes estimated figures for 1994 and 1995, because the bureau will not finish compiling firm data from its most recent biennial survey for several months. But all signs indicate the trend continues unabated.

Layoffs are nothing new. But they used to rise and fall with the economy. Workers would be let go at a rapid clip in the depths of a recession; then the rate would fall steadily as economic growth gathered steam.

No more. The rate of job loss hit a peak of 3.4 million a year in 1992 and has remained nearly that high ever since, even while the economy grew and the stock market boomed. "During most of the 1980's, roughly one in 25 workers lost a job" in any two-year period, said Thomas Nardone, an associate commissioner of the bureau. "In the 1990's, this has risen to one in 20 workers."

Job dislocation is spreading to include nearly every kind of employee. Blue-collar workers, particularly in manufacturing, still make up a majority of the displaced each year, but lately only barely so. Layoffs in the 1990's are claiming many more administrators and professional people than a decade earlier. And a University of Michigan study that has tracked 5,000 families since 1968 found that among the college-educated over 50, the rate of layoffs doubled from the 1980's to the 1990's.

... And Good Replacements Prove Elusive for Most

After a Layoff
Employment status in January 1994 of workers who lost full-time jobs in 1991 or 1992

35% caught on again ...
Another full-time job at equal or higher pay

... 65% did not:
- Full-time job but at lower pay
- Part-time
- Self employed'
- Unemployed or out of the labor force

'Includes unpaid family workers

MOST WORKERS who lose a job find another before very long. Even in years when layoffs are at a peak, more jobs usually are created than destroyed; that is one reason why the jobless rate can be falling when layoffs are rising, as has been true in the 1990's. The total number of nonagricultural jobs in the country grew from 90 million in 1979 to 117 million in 1995, despite the 43 million jobs eliminated over that span.

But more often than not, people who lose a full-time job get a new one that pays less than the old, or is only part-time, according to Labor Department figures.

From 1981 to 1983, for example, median pay for a worker who lost a full-time job and later got another fell $62 a week in 1994 dollars, from $461 a week on the old job to $399 on the new. A decade later, though laid-off workers were finding new jobs a bit faster, the median pay drop had grown to $85 a week, from $507 before to $422 after.

Each full symbol represents 100,000 lost jobs

BLUE-COLLAR	WHITE COLLAR	Year	
		1979	1.23 million jobs lost
		1980	1.42 million Recession Jan.-July
		1981	1.94 million Recession Jul.-Dec.
		1982	2.63 million Recession Jan.-Nov.
		1983	3.04 million
		1984	2.57 million
		1985	2.51 million
		1986	2.54 million
		1987	2.34 million
		1988	2.09 million
		1989	2.03 million
		1990	2.48 million Recession Jul.-Dec
		1991	3.30 million Recession Jan.-Mar.
		1992	3.43 million
		1993	3.38 million
		1994	3.34 million ESTIMATED
		1995	3.26 million ESTIMATED

(Copyright © 1996 by The New York Times Co. Reprinted by Permission.)

street. There is always a safety net of family and friends. Pop culture, after all, thrives on entertainment and escapism.

It's a sign of how widespread awareness of this issue is that sitcoms are creeping closer to the subject. The hero of "The Drew Carey Show" works in the personnel office of a department store; the heroine of "Can't Hurry Love" works at an employment agency. These two are employed, but they are surrounded by people who are not. And "Good Company," a sitcom set in an ad agency (to premier tomorrow), promises to deal with layoffs next week.

Even as the most populist art forms play out our employment anxieties, one of the most expensive, least populist forms has responded by looking back to the good old days. Broadway has offered up an elaborate revival or "How to Succeed in Business Without Really Trying." It might help to remember that concept was always a fantasy.

QUESTIONING THE TEXT

1. Does James take a stance toward the seriousness of "downsizing"? What in the essay allows you to identify her attitude? Is A.L.'s attitude toward job insecurity revealed in her introduction? If so, how does it compare with James's?
2. What do James's essay and "More Than 43 Million Jobs Lost" have in common? On what do the essays agree? On what do they disagree?
3. Can you find any good news in "More Than 43 Million Jobs Lost"—information that seems at odds with the bleak picture painted overall? Where is such information placed in the article, and what effect did that placement have on your ability to note or remember it?

MAKING CONNECTIONS

4. How do you think Newt Gingrich (p. 576) would "read" this selection from "The Downsizing of America?" What responses (or solutions) might he give?
5. How do Douglas Coupland's characters (p. 595) demonstrate the anxieties described in these two pieces? If *Microserfs* is itself part of pop culture, how does it fit into James's depiction of the two "extremes" of "our worst fears and our fondest hopes about job insecurity"?

JOINING THE CONVERSATION

6. Working with one or two classmates, do some research to test James's claim that "the scariest of economic changes are now being thrown back at us in exaggerated shapes [in pop culture]." Look at some current television sitcoms, and view several movies that relate to the economy or work. Survey the latest hit music. Pool your information, and use it to write a brief report for your class that supports, denies, or elaborates on James's thesis.
7. Choose an example from pop culture—film, television show, music, video—that best represents your own view of the current job situation in the United States. Then write an essay describing in detail how that example depicts work and the job situation. Explain why this vision is compelling or seems "right" to you.
8. Working with one or two classmates, devise a brief questionnaire asking what students think *downsizing* refers to, what their views on it are, what worries they have about getting and holding a job, and so on. Then survey as many students as you can. Compile your data and report your findings to the class.

NEWT GINGRICH
America and the Third Wave Information Age

NEWT GINGRICH (b. 1943), easily the best-known and probably the least-beloved Speaker of the U.S. House of Representatives in this century, is a cock-eyed optimist about America's future. Where others glom a bleak horizon of diminishing opportunities, Gingrich spies a rising star of economic growth spurred by fast-moving information technologies hostile to traditional institutions (especially big government and unions). The essay included here, from the Speaker's book To Renew America *(1995), suggests that, at least for entrepreneurs and techies, the next century is sure to be as remarkable as the present one, with technological changes giving people more control over their lives and work.*

Gingrich could be right if his federal government can put its own House (and Senate) in order and push the rest of the Washington bureaucracy out of the way. But his real message seems to be that people must learn not to fear change—a hard sell when one's job is threatened or one is asked to learn new skills to earn a paycheck. Ironically, change *was also the 1992 watchword of Gingrich's political nemesis, Bill Clinton. Clearly the two men—both ambitious, self-made, motor-mouthed, and visionary—have more in common than they would care to admit. But visionaries with power can dramatically affect our lives, so it's comforting that Gingrich's economic forecast is dynamic and hopeful.* — J.R.

Just list some of the changes we are living through: laptop computers, cellular telephones, molecular medicine, new discoveries about the dinosaurs, home security systems that talk, composite materials that make cars lighter, microengineering, manufacturing in space, high-definition television, the video store—the list goes on and on. If we were to spend just one week itemizing everything we encounter that our grandparents would not have believed, we would be astonished at the totality of change we are living through.

My aunt Loma gave me a vivid illustration of living through large-scale change when she described her one experience in learning how to drive a car. Aunt Loma was born in 1898 in a mountainous part of Pennsylvania, about forty miles south of State College. Her family worked hard on a poor but comfortable farm. When she married Uncle Cal, she was perfectly content to have him drive. In 1928 he finally convinced her she should try it. "We went out into a large field. I told him I didn't want to drive but he insisted I try. I got behind the wheel and put my foot on the gas. He started yelling something about the brakes but I froze and couldn't do anything. We hit a fence at about fifteen miles an hour. I got out and said, 'There, I have tried.'" And that was that. She lived to age ninety-four, relying on buses and letting others tackle newfangled skills.

People faced with laptop computers, Internet connections, cellular phones, and the possibility of space travel often take Aunt Loma's attitude. If you try to deal with it all, you can get overwhelmed. That was the message of Alvin and Heidi Toffler's first bestseller, *Future Shock,* in which they addressed the pace of change in modern life. If people became overwhelmed with change, said the Tofflers, they could go into a state of dejection and exhaustion.

A decade later, the Tofflers wrote a more sophisticated analysis, which they said could minimize confusion and help people like Aunt Loma understand and adjust to the scale of change we are experiencing. They described our era as the Third Wave of change.

In the Tofflers' view—with which I agree—the transformation we are   5 experiencing is so large and historic that it can be compared with only two other great eras of human history—the Agricultural Revolution and the Industrial Revolution. The Agricultural Revolution—this "First Wave"— occurred when hunting-and-gathering tribes first invented agriculture. Through the earliest part of human history, tribes of twenty to thirty nomads crossed the landscape following game herds (similar to the life of Kalahari Bushmen or Australian Aborigines today). Within a few millennia, these tribes had switched to a densely populated world of six million farmers staying in one place and growing a small number of very productive crops. This First Wave was actually the largest population explosion in human history. The population in Egypt increased three hundred-fold (30,000 percent) during the transition from hunting and gathering to farming. There had never been anything else like it. Suddenly people could accumulate goods over several generations. People became skilled in crafts like carpentry and wagonmaking. Traditions and hierarchies were established. Governments, priesthoods, kingships, armies, and tax collectors appeared.

Imagine trying to tell a hunter-gatherer what the world would be like after the Agricultural Revolution. Imagine trying to tell someone living in a small band that he or she would live in a fixed place surrounded by thousands of people. Imagine telling someone who has hunted over scores of square miles for an occasional large animal that he or she might live among herds of sheep, cows, goat, and camels. It would be difficult if not impossible.

All classic civilizations—Rome, Greece, China, the Indus Valley, Egypt, Babylon, the Inca-Mayan and Aztec civilizations of the Americas—resulted from the Agricultural Revolution. This wave carries us through all of ancient and medieval history. George Washington could have conversed easily with Julius Caesar. Both rode on horseback, relied on sailing ships, and wrote with quill pens. Both relied on ox-drawn carts to supply their armies. Caesar's transport problems in Gaul and Washington's at Valley Forge were essentially the same.

Then, a second wave of change occurred at the start of the eighteenth century. Beginning in Britain and rapidly spreading to Western Europe and America, the development of power-driven industry created another wave of productivity, wealth, and power that transformed people's lives.

In the agricultural era, 97 percent of all workers were engaged in farming. Each produced a tiny surplus. Large systems of government and elites were sustained by gathering together the surpluses from thousands and thousands of small farms. This model remained true everywhere in the agricultural world.

The Second Wave changed all the economic equations. Imagine trying   10
to explain to a resident of Rome or the Middle Ages a world in which only three percent of the work force would be engaged in farming. Imagine further trying to explain that a major side effect would be large agricultural surpluses. Rather than starving to death, people will be overweight and worry about eating too much food. Even under these conditions, farmers will be too productive and every industrial government will have to subsidize them.

When Malthus wrote his dire prediction of overpopulation and mass starvation, the industrial transformation of farming had just begun. At the time, Britain and most other countries were trying to be self-sufficient. Within a few decades, liberalized trade laws allowed Britain to import enormous amounts of food at lower cost. As a result, Great Britain today has a population eleven times the size that Malthus said it could not support.

The Second Wave caused another great discontinuity—only this time at a much more rapid pace. While George Washington could have chatted easily with Julius Caesar, he would have had a difficult time talking with Theodore Roosevelt. While Teddy was President, the mass-produced automobile, the full-length motion picture, and the airplane made their debut—all in one year, 1903. Electric lights were becoming common, streetcars were standard transportation, telephones were more and more available. Roosevelt—who embraced these changes enthusiastically—became the first President to ride in a car and was praised by newspapers for the courage he displayed in doing so.

Now we are entering a third great era of change, the transformation from the Industrial Age to the Information Age. Breakthroughs like computers, worldwide electronic transmissions, satellites, fiber optics, molecular biology, and a host of others are making life vastly different.

One of the great problems people have in entering an era of change is nostalgia for the passing era. People feel a sense of quiet despair in watching an old era end. During the industrial transformation, writers like H. G. Wells and Jules Verne emerged to give the new era an aura of excitement.

One individual in our era who was willing to do the same is Ronald   15
Reagan. He had made a career out of technology, moving from commercial radio (which did not exist when he was born) to movies and television, and then to working for General Electric ("Progress is our most important prod-

uct"). Reagan always saw the potential of new technologies to improve the lives of ordinary people. His favorite line—"You ain't seen nothing yet"—expressed that optimism.

The coming of the Third Wave Information Age brings potential for enormous improvement in the lifestyle choices of most Americans. There is every reason to believe that this new era will see a revolution in goods and services that will empower and enhance most people.

Imagine a morning in just a decade or so. You wake up to a wall-size, high-definition television showing surf off Maui. (This is my favorite island—you can pick your own scene.) You walk or jog or do Stairmaster while catching up on the morning news and beginning to review your day's schedule. Your home office is filled with communications devices, so you can ignore rush-hour traffic. In fact, since most Americans now telecommute, rush hour is dramatically smaller than it used to be. Telecommuting has proved to be the best means of dealing with air pollution.

When you are sick, you sit in your diagnostic chair and communicate with the local health clinic. Sensors take your blood pressure, analyze a blood sample, or do throat cultures. The results are quickly relayed to health aides, who make recommendations and prescribe medicine. The only time you visit a doctor or hospital is when something is seriously wrong. If you need a specialist, a databank at your fingertips gives you a range of choices based on cost, reputation, and outcome patterns. You can choose knowledgeably which risk you want to take and what price you want to pay. If you face some rare or life-threatening disease, information systems will allow you to study the most advanced work around the world—things that even your doctor is unlikely to know. Because information is now so widely available, the guildlike hold of the medical profession has been broken. Health care has become more flexible and convenient—and less expensive.

Your legal problems will work the same way. You can write your own will, file your own adoption papers, form your own partnership or corporation—all with software programs available in your home. Then you e-mail them to the proper authorities. Any disciplined and educated person can now "read the law." Once again, the "legal guild"—so similar to the medieval craft guilds that were scattered by the Industrial Revolution—has been broken. People now bring their own lawsuits, file their own briefs, even represent themselves electronically in court. This democratization of the law—plus the astonishing decline in government regulation—has drastically reduced the demand for professionals. Fortunately, since most lawyers were reasonably smart and well-educated people, they have been able to find other lines of work.

Now imagine you want to learn something new, solve a personal problem, or enter some new profession. Do you have to go to night school or trek twenty-five miles to the nearest college? No, you simply enter the on-line learning system and describe what you need. Say you want to learn batik be-

20

cause a new craft shop has opened at the mall and the owner has told you she will sell some of your work. First, you check in at the "batik station" on the Internet, which gives you a list of recommendations. You can look through dozens of references. The Internet is like a library in which the books are never off the shelves. You may get a list of recommended video or audio tapes that can be delivered to your door the next day by Federal Express. You may prefer a more personal learning system and seek an apprenticeship with the nearest batik master, or you may want to take a traditional course offered at a local college or school. In less than twenty-four hours, you can launch yourself on a new profession. In a society of continuous, lifelong learning, these options will be available to everyone.

Living in a world that is bathed in information—too much information for any one person or company to absorb—your livelihood and security are likely to come from becoming an expert—maybe the world's greatest expert—on one small corner of this vast infosphere. You may become the foremost authority on some obscure medical procedure or accounting principle. You may know more than anyone else about the incorporation laws of Zaire and offer advice to anyone attempting to set up a business in that country. This is the way most professional consultants and small businesses operate now, and the way all businesses are now going. Corporate giants are finding it just doesn't make sense anymore to try to bring all their expertise under one roof. It's much easier to "outsource," relying on small, mobile, independent contractors for information. The world of information these companies must master is exploding.

This means that more and more people are going to be operating *outside* corporate structures and hierarchies in the nooks and crannies that the Information Revolution creates. While the Industrial Revolution herded people into gigantic social institutions—big corporations, big unions, big government—the Information Revolution is breaking up these giants and leading us back to something that is—strangely enough—much more like de Tocqueville's 1830s America.

The rhythm of the Third Wave Information Age will be a bit like rafting down the rapids after we have learned to canoe on a quiet lake. Although rafting may be more difficult or dangerous, the skills and conventions are essentially the same. Once we get adjusted, it can even be exhilarating. There are many more challenges, much more excitement, and our skills are honed to a much finer degree. There will be a lot more challenges in our new world than in the one we grew up in. During the transition, however, people are likely to be uncertain and intimidated.

There will also be enormous advantages for America and Americans if we lead the world in the transition to the Third Wave Information Age. Just as Britain profited enormously by leading the world into the industrial era, so the United States can profit enormously by being the leader in the development of the new goods, services, systems, and standards associated with a technological revolution of this scale.

Bill Loughrey of Scientific Atlanta has developed a good example of the   25
scale of change we are living through. He notes that the advance from the vacuum tube to the transistor to the computer chip has resulted in a million-fold improvement in productivity over the last forty years. The power of computer chips will multiply another million-fold over the next ten years—as big an increase as the productivity improvement of the last forty years. This translates into a one-trillion-fold increase in productivity between 1950 and 2000.

Loughrey then draws a parallel with the failure of improvement in the federal government. If the federal government had improved at the same pace as the computer chip, he notes wryly, it would only have four employees and a total budget of $100,000. While Loughrey is clearly being facetious, there is an enormous truth to this analogy.

Almost every time I make a speech, I pull out a vacuum tube (technically an argon gas electron tube) that is still a key component in our federal air traffic control system. The tube was originally developed in 1895 and represents solid nineteenth-century technology. As the ranking Republican on the House Aviation Subcommittee almost a decade ago, I found that the Federal Aviation Commission was trying to replace this tube with computer chips. You can understand why. A computer chip I show that is almost too small to be seen on camera has the processing power of *three million* vacuum tubes. The United States has even started poking around Eastern Europe for supplies because few companies in the West make them anymore. Yet in the seven years since I first sat on the committee, the FAA has been unable to switch technologies. The United States government is now the largest remaining purchaser of vacuum-type tubes in the Western world.

Why are governments so painfully slow at adjusting to change? Why are their agencies almost always obsolete? The basic reason is that governments are not customer driven. Governments almost always grant monopoly status to their own operations so they won't have to compete. Look at public education. Look at the post office. It's the same story everywhere. Consumers are too often stuck with inefficient service and a poor product because they're not allowed to go anywhere else.

Because government operations don't have to please consumers, they end up catering to employees. That's why most government operations are overstaffed. Unionization has only made things worse. Almost 40 percent of government employees around the country are now members of labor unions. The figure for private industry is only 11 percent.

Change inconveniences employees, and that's why governments end up   30
lagging in technology. Installing computers means employees have to learn new tasks. It's also likely to put a few people out of work—although ulti-

mately it creates more jobs. Private corporations have been vigorous about restructuring and reengineering themselves over the last decade. That's why we've raced to the head of the pack again as the world's most efficient industrial nation. But government lags behind—often by decades, as the vacuum-tube illustration shows. Given the tough choice of restructuring with new technology or adding new employees to the same old tasks, government management will always choose the latter. It's much easier to swallow the costs and raise taxes.

The history of the United States has been a history of encouraging new developments and inventors. From Lewis and Clark's expedition to the Pacific Coast to John Wesley Powell's trip through the Grand Canyon, from Admiral Byrd's expeditions to the poles to Marsh's and Cope's hunts for fossils in the West, Americans have always relished discovery and adventure. At the same time, we were inventing practical solutions to everyday life—the sewing machine, the combine and harvester, barbed wire, and the zipper.

Not only have we been good at making our own discoveries, we have also been energetic and aggressive at developing other countries' ideas. Marconi invented the radio in Italy, but the U.S. Navy put it into practice by encouraging the formation of the Radio Corporation of America (RCA). The internal combustion engine was a German invention, but its use in cars, trucks, and airplanes was pioneered in America. In Europe, inventions often remained the province of the wealthy and the aristocratic. In America, every young man and woman could aspire to participation in the creation of a new world.

The same spirit of democratic entrepreneurialism is alive in America today, but we do far less to encourage it. We have allowed mindless entertainment and liberal social issues to drive entrepreneurialism and invention from popular awareness.

We need to bring back to the center of the popular culture an intense awareness that the future is going to be very exciting and has the dramatic potential to improve everyone's life. We need to develop simple methods for people to participate eagerly and enthusiastically in inventing their own future.

The government needs to look at the changes in taxation, litigation,   35
regulation, education, welfare, and government bureaucracies in order to encourage innovation and discovery. We need a series of commissions made up of entrepreneurs and inventors, plus citizen-customers and practitioners from the industrial-era guilds and professions. What should public safety be like in the Third Wave Information Age? How should a citizen-based health system be structured? What should lifetime learning be like? How could the legal system be simplified and made available to normal citizens without the cost of a lawyer? How could the government be remade to utilize the opportunities of the Information Age? We need a new sense of the opportunities that exist if only we have the courage to open our eyes and minds to them.

We are entering a revolutionary period in telecommunications when the regional "Baby Bells" will be able to compete with long-distance carriers, cable companies will compete with the regional Bells, and the power companies (who have the largest fiber optic network in the United States) may end up competing with everyone. This will be an amazingly complex communications system—a world apart from the black dial telephone of my childhood that was owned by the largest monopoly in the world.

In this world of instant and facile communication, why should schools have a monopoly on learning? Why should doctors and hospitals have a monopoly on practicing medicine? Why should lawyers have a monopoly on the legal profession? And why should all these industrial-era guilds and monopolies have their powers to coerce people protected by the government?

I am not advocating that we take drastic steps tomorrow morning, but I am advocating that we start asking bold and dramatic questions today. When we look around, we are surprised at how many goods and services are legally protected by the government. It is shocking how much protected professionals can charge when people have no choice but to go to them.

In *The Wealth of Nations,* Adam Smith describes brilliantly the impact of the emerging second wave industrial revolution on the medieval guilds. He notes that many groups, like weavers, tried to enlist the power of the state to stop new competitors (the textile mills) from putting them out of business. Smith's classic work became the foundation of modern market economics because he understood the dynamics of his changing era.

The same kind of changes are happening once again today. If we liber-   40
ate entrepreneurs and make it relatively easy for them to discover and invent our new world, we will be rearing a generation that increases our wealth and improves our lives to a degree that we can now barely imagine.

QUESTIONING THE TEXT

1. As Gingrich suggests in his first paragraph, make a list of items and products available today that might not have been part of your grandparents' world when they were your age. Then classify the items on the list. Can you identify areas where changes have been significant? You might also generate a list of things that haven't changed between generations.
2. How would you describe the purpose and audience Gingrich might have in mind in writing "America and the Third Wave Information Age"? Point to specific features and passages in the chapter that support your response.
3. Do you agree with J.R.'s claim in the introduction that Newt Gingrich and Bill Clinton are alike in many ways? How might Gingrich's selection be different if Clinton edited it?

MAKING CONNECTIONS

4. Compare Gingrich's vision of the future with what Steven Levy observes about Bill Gates (p. 474).

5. Gingrich suggests that the future will belong to the nation most readily adapted to technological change. Read Gingrich's argument along with the Neo-Luddite views of Kirkpatrick Sale in Kevin Kelly's interview (p. 243). Do you see any common ground in their positions? In a brief essay, summarize their areas of agreement and disagreement.

JOINING THE CONVERSATION

6. Write a short essay describing your own vision of the future—the next decade or two. You may want to read more on the subject, but don't hesitate to be as freewheeling and wide-ranging as Gingrich.

7. Is it possible to be overwhelmed by too much information or too much change? Describe a situation in which you have felt over-your-head in dealing with technology or with other changes in your life. Write a narrative exploring your feelings and explaining how you dealt with them.

HENRY SCANLON
Suddenly, I'm the Bad Guy

ENVY, REVILED IN THE MIDDLE AGES as a deadly sin, has become a virtue in the language of political representatives eager to pit working Americans against the rich for political gain. You would think such leaders might be embarrassed to suggest that doctors, accountants, shop owners, managers, entrepreneurs, and perhaps even lawyers don't work for a living. But it's part of a rhetorical shell game that counts on Americans coveting their neighbors' goods more than admiring their initiative in acquiring them.

Making a compelling case for the well-to-do is usually difficult because the rewards they enjoy often result from invisible years of study, apprenticeship, and drudgery. The tired resident on the night shift in a hospital emergency room and the small-business owner working sixteen-hour days to get an enterprise off the ground don't play nearly as well to cameras as paid protesters bursting into congressional hearings complaining about nonexistent cuts to their "entitlements." So I admire the powerful case that businessman Henry Scanlon makes for the so-called economic elite in the following essay. In explaining the nature of his work, Scanlon, I think, does a remarkable job establishing a sympathetic personal ethos—the kind that makes readers willing to listen. Although it originally appeared in Newsweek *in 1993, Scanlon's "My Turn" essay raises issues likely to resonate politically and economically for the next decade. — J.R.*

Bill Clinton has me in his cross hairs because I am the enemy. I make more than $100,000 a year. I am, therefore, a member of the "economic elite," a recipient of all the opprobrium my status as a parasite deserves. Yes, I pay taxes, more real dollars than any 10 of my average fellow city-dwellers combined, but I have gotten, nonetheless, a free ride. I deserve scorn and contempt. I deserve to be nailed. I deserve to *not get away with it.*

In short, I'm what's wrong with America.

But I find myself wondering why I'm so confused and dispirited. I find myself asking just when it was, exactly, that I became a bad guy.

For example, I believe in taxes, America and the commonweal. And I used to believe that I was doing what I was supposed to be doing: creating jobs (and sharing profits with my employees), trying to treat people fair and square and paying taxes. Lots of them.

In 1975, on the day I hired my first employee, I secured the best health insurance I could for her. The cost then compared to 1993 was small, but from my vantage point—sleeping on the floor in my sister's apartment, working 70 hours a week while generating a personal paycheck amounting to about zero—it was a lot of money. But I believed that if anyone was willing to dedicate themselves to the photo business I was trying to build, they shouldn't have to worry about health care. Now, with more than 100 employees, I have had to ask them to contribute. But I don't think we had to change as a result of my being a parasite. I think we had to change because even though I was doing my job trying to run a growing company on sound economic and ethical principles (and doing it pretty well, I think) the people in Washington weren't doing theirs.

I don't think, therefore, that it was precisely then that I became a bad guy.

Maybe it was two years ago when we took a tremendous risk opening offices in Europe and began bringing back foreign currency to this country. But, no, everybody says that's a good thing, so it can't be that.

Maybe it was when we started doing some hiring through "America Works," an absolutely terrific organization that provides welfare recipients with the support and training to enter the work force. But if that's what makes me a bad guy, then I'm willing to be one.

To tell the truth, I don't think it's any one of those things. I think I became a bad guy when Bill Clinton *needed* me to become a bad guy—for the same reason a pickpocket needs a "jostler"—to create a diversion.

No matter how much taxes are raised on folks like me, no matter how   10
many surcharges are imposed, no matter how many deductions are eliminated—it doesn't amount to a hill of beans in generating real dollars toward reducing the deficit. There are just too few of us. I know that, and Bill Clinton knows that. If you take $100 from 10 people, that's a lot less money than taking $1 from 10,000 people.

But if you can get the 10,000 to focus on the $100 you're taking from the 10, they might not notice the hand that's slipping into their own pocket. Or, better still, they won't care. Because they'll have the satisfaction of knowing the "fat cats" aren't getting away with it. As long as you keep thinking the problem with this country is that I don't pay enough taxes, you'll be diverted from demanding a solution to the real problem—the squandering and mismanagement of the taxes they already collect from all of us.

Positive contribution.   As a result of many years of hard work, not a little bit of luck, the help and support of a second-to-none staff of unbelievably dedicated people and the fact that I live in a country that I adore and whose principles I support unconditionally, I now make a tremendous amount of money—and pay huge amounts of taxes without complaining. (Well, at least I don't complain any more than anyone else.) Believe me, I know what it is like to earn $8,000 a year, or $30,000 a year. And I do not expect for an instant that anyone would or should care whether I like or I don't like the amount of tax I pay.

But I do expect this: I expect that after I have spent decades creating jobs, never cheating anyone, constantly trying to make a positive contribution to the society in which I live, doing everything I can to treat employees, customers and suppliers fairly, honestly and even generously, not only adhering to the founding principles of this country but actively trying to make an ongoing, positive contribution—I would not be spoken of by the president of my country as if I were a reptile.

I, like a lot of other members of the "economic elite," am ready, willing and able to support the Clinton initiatives for fundamental change. He and I are the same age, come from similar backgrounds and share, I think, some important core values. The only thing I ask is that he stop acting and talking as if anyone who makes more than $30,000 a year is the enemy and that we've all been prancing around gleeful in the knowledge that we're *getting away with it.*

I don't feel like I've been "getting away" with anything. Whether the   15
taxes I pay represent my "fair share" is a matter for debate. The ability to pay is only one prism through which to view "fairness." The ability to pay is essentially a practical issue—a valid one—but it is not necessarily an ethical one. By wrapping tax increases for the "economic elite" in an emotional mantle based upon a narrow and self-serving interpretation of the components of "fairness," Clinton fosters unnecessary and corrosive divisiveness throughout the economic spectrum.

While I claim no *greater* virtue for myself than any other hardworking man or woman in this country, I admit to no less. I don't consider myself the enemy of America. In fact, all in all, and on balance, I consider myself a pretty good guy. It would be nice if my president did, too.

QUESTIONING THE TEXT

1. Annotate the essay carefully, noting places where you find Scanlon working especially hard to make you either trust him or understand his feelings as a member of the "economic elite." What does Scanlon gain and lose by writing a first-person argument—talking about his own experiences and emotions?
2. About halfway through the essay, Scanlon compares Bill Clinton to a pickpocket who "needs a 'jostler'—to create a diversion." In terms of reaching or offending his audience, what risks does Scanlon take in suggesting that the president is acting like a common thief? In the context of Scanlon's argument, do you find the device effective or off-putting?

MAKING CONNECTIONS

3. Imagine that you are Scanlon reading the article and letter in "Young, Privileged, and Unemployed" (p. 566). Then write a letter as Scanlon might in reply.

JOINING THE CONVERSATION

4. If you belong to a group that is often the target of bad press or hostile criticism (for example, sororities, athletes, white males, pre-law students, homosexuals, fundamentalist Christians, liberals), write a defense of your group modeled after Scanlon's essay. Explain why you're not really the bad guy.

5. Watch the national news on the same network for at least a week and record all references to the wealthy or economic elite, particularly any that suggest a conflict between poor and rich. Then review your notes in light of Scanlon's claims and write a report for class.

W. MICHAEL COX and RICHARD ALM
By Our Own Bootstraps

*I*s THE GLASS *half full or half empty? Apply that question to the American economy and you've outlined the economic debate Americans have been having since the hyperinflation days of the 1970s. Ronald Reagan ousted Jimmy Carter in 1980 by asking the public, "Are you better off than you were four years ago?" Twelve years later Clinton bested Reagan's successor by suggesting that then President Bush didn't appreciate how bleak the economy actually was in 1992; the Clinton campaign's memorable mantra was "It's the economy, stupid!" When the "worst economy since the depression" bounced out of recession in mere months, the country should have been relieved (and suspicious). But the malaise has persisted, in part because the press has become far better at reporting bad news than good.*

The favored economic themes of the mainstream media are so familiar that most people regard them as facts, not claims: opportunity is vanishing in the United States; the middle class is disappearing; the wealthy control an exorbitant percentage of America's total wealth; no one can count on steady jobs at decent wages anymore. *Such analyses require villains, and these tend to be overpaid corporate CEOs and heartless corporations eager to ship American jobs overseas. Reported with far less fanfare are the robust mechanisms of American capitalism steadily drawing our standard of living upward, whether or not we notice the improvements. Is the glass half full or half empty? The question is important because how you perceive the economy may influence your ability to rise within it.*

So if you are depressed by dire economic forecasts or tales of dwindling job opportunity (for example, see p. 572), let me offer a more bullish analysis from the Federal Reserve, an independent agency of the U.S. government charged with managing money and credit. In the 1995 Annual Report of the Federal Reserve Bank of Dallas, W. Michael Cox and Richard Alm argue that "Today's American society is almost certainly more fluid than ever." Pointing to fascinating economic statistics and trends, they suggest that people who get an education and work hard still prosper: "Knowledge and effort alone can open doors, and both are available to all of us." From their collection of arguments and charts, I've selected Exhibits 3, 4, and 12 for you to examine critically, not taking their claims at face value, but as starting points for possible inquiries of your own into the state of the national economy and your own hopes for satisfying work. – J.R.

Exhibit 3   Inequality is not inequity

In the early 1970s, three groups of unemployed Canadians, all in their 20s, all with at least 12 years of schooling, volunteered to take up residence in a stylized economy where the only employment was making woolen belts on small hand looms. They could work as much or as little as they liked, earning $2.50 for each belt. After 98 days, the results were anything but equal: 37.2 percent of the economy's income went to the 20 percent with the highest earnings. The bottom 20 percent received only 6.6 percent.

This economic microcosm tells us one thing: even among similar people with identical work options, differences in talent, motivation and preferences will lead some workers to earn more than others. Income inequality isn't some quirk or some aberration. Quite the opposite, it's perfectly consistent with the economic laws that govern a free enterprise system.

Equality of opportunity doesn't yield equality of results. Inequality is not inequity.

In a complex modern economy, there are plenty of reasons for incomes to vary, and most of them have little to do with issues of fairness or equity. Among the most important factors are:

Education, experience.   The lifetime earnings profile tracks income for various age groups. As an economy becomes more advanced, there are usually increasing rewards for education and experience, so earnings rise faster over a typical lifetime. As that happens, there's increasing diversity in income.

Two-income households.   Obviously, two workers can earn more than one. The trend toward both spouses working creates some higher income households. As families choose different lifestyles, the income distribution will grow more unequal, even if individual incomes don't change at all.

Baby-boom demographics.   A bulge in the population can alter a society's income distribution. When the baby boom first enters the labor force, it floods the economy with lower income workers. As the generation ages, entering peak earning years, it provides a disproportionate number of high-income households. In both cases, the distribution becomes skewed, first toward lower incomes and then toward higher incomes.

A greater "churn."   A healthy economy grows by creating new, better and more affordable products. The process creates new industries and new jobs. They replace jobs in fading sectors. Economists call this the "churn." It makes society better off, and it produces big gains for entrepreneurs and higher incomes for most workers. For others, there will be spells of unemployment and downward mobility. When there are larger ups and downs in income, the distribution is likely to spread.

Longer retirements.   Individuals who anticipate longer periods of retirement will, on average, accumulate more assets during their working lives and earn more interest. The income of middle-aged workers will rise relative to that of the young, once again widening the distribution.

Higher rates of return on assets.   If accumulation of assets increases income disparity, higher rates of return on investment will do the same because those assets will produce more income.

A wealthier society.   Once a society progresses to the point where most people can afford food, clothing, shelter and other necessities, some people choose to work harder for luxuries, while others opt to enjoy more leisure. When people make different choices about goods versus leisure, the income distribution pulls apart.

No one ought to be surprised that these are trends that have reshaped the U.S. income distribution over the past two decades. Although most of them widen the income distribution, none necessarily entails lower income households becoming worse off.

Exhibit 4   Moving on up

Income Quintile in 1975	Percent in Each Quintile in 1991				
	1st	2nd	3rd	4th	5th
5th (highest)	.9	2.8	10.2	23.6	62.5
4th	1.9	9.3	18.8	32.6	37.4
3rd (middle)	3.3	19.3	28.3	30.1	19.0
2nd	4.2	23.5	20.3	25.2	26.8
1st (lowest)	5.1	14.6	21.0	30.3	29.0

Of individuals who were in the lowest income quintile in 1975, 5.1 percent were still there in 1991, 14.6 had moved up to the second quintile, 21 percent to the middle quintile, 30.3 percent to the fourth quintile and 29 percent to the highest quintile. Of those in the highest quintile in 1975, 62.5 percent were still there in 1991, while 0.9 percent had fallen all the way to the bottom fifth.

Exhibit 5   The poor are getting richer faster

Income Quintile in 1975	Average Income in 1975	Average Income in 1991	Absolute Gain
5th (highest)	$45,704	$49,678	$ 3,974
4th	22,423	31,292	8,869
3rd (middle)	13,030	22,304	9,274
2nd	6,291	28,373	22,082
1st (lowest)	1,153	26,475	25,322

Figures are in 1993 dollars.

Individuals in the lowest income quintile in 1975 saw, on average, a $25,322 rise in their real income over the 16 years from 1975 to 1991. Those in the highest income quintile had a $3,974 increase in real income, on average. The rich got richer, but the poor got richer faster.

Exhibit 9   Listen to your elders

Believe it or not, family fortune and luck aren't the way most Americans make their way toward the top. The experiences and choices of those who have prospered, as well as those who haven't, provide the basis for the following "secrets" on how to get ahead in life:

Get an education.   Nearly half of those in the top 20 percent of income earners graduated from college, compared with just 4 percent of people in the bottom 20 percent. Only 2 percent of those in the highest tier dropped out of high school, but a fifth of the lowest income group failed to get a diploma. In 1993, median income of households headed by someone with a professional degree was $87,666. It drops to $51,480 for an undergraduate degree, $28,700 for a high school diploma and $16,067 for dropouts.

Get a job.   Households in the top income quintile have, on average, 2.1 workers, compared with only 0.6 for the bottom fifth. Among the nonworking poor, only 13 percent say they are unable to find a job.

Work full-time, all year round.   In the lowest fifth of income earners, 84 percent worked part time, worked less than half the year or did not work at all. Four-fifths of the top bracket worked 50 or more weeks of the year. Only 7 percent of part-time workers say they are looking for full-time work and unable to find it.

Save money.   In the top income-earning quintile, median assets of households, excluding home equity, are $45,392. The bottom 20 percent has just $949. Not surprisingly, income from assets for the first group is 30 times what it is for the second. Savings can make a big difference, especially for retirement. For individuals 65 and older in the bottom quintile, 83 percent of income comes from Social Security and only 9 percent from savings. In the top bracket, earnings on savings account for 54 percent of income and Social Security for only 20 percent.

Form a family.   Only 7 percent of the top fifth of income earners live in a "nonfamily" household. In the bottom fifth, 37 percent do. People can live more cheaply together than they can apart.

Be willing to move.   The unemployment rate in McAllen, Texas, is 17.5 percent, whereas in Austin it is 3.5 percent. Wages can vary substantially, too, across regions. Geographical mobility is one way to close the income gap.

Be willing to retrain.   Average hourly wages for computer programmers are $20.64, whereas for textile workers they are only $9.51. Jobs come and go as the economy evolves, often requiring that workers learn new skills to keep up with economic changes.

Get a computer.   Workers who know how to operate a computer earn an average of 15 percent more than those who don't—and that's for doing the same job. The machine makes them more productive.

Stick to it.   Average income tends to rise quickly in life as workers gain work experience and knowledge. Households headed by someone under age 25 average $15,197 a year in income. Average income more than doubles to $33,124 for 25-to 34-year-olds. For those 35 to 44, the figure jumps to $43,923. It takes time for learning, hard work and saving to bear fruit.

Little on this list should come as a surprise. Taken as a whole, it's what most Americans have been told since they were kids—by society, by their parents, by their teachers.

Exhibit 12   Progress and poverty

Historically, economic growth, not welfare, has been the remedy for poverty. An expanding economy pays its dividends in rising incomes, lower prices and better products, all of which enable families to satisfy their basic needs with smaller and smaller portions of their income.

For households in the bottom income quintile, spending on food, clothing and shelter was 45 percent of consumption in 1993, compared with 52 percent two decades earlier, 57 percent in 1950 and 75 percent in 1920. As a result, today's poorest households have more discretionary income than ever before.

That helps explain why today's poorer households are more likely than those of a decade ago to own appliances and motor vehicles. Their consumption of these modern-day conveniences even compares favorably with that of all American households as recently as 1971.

	Poor Households*		All Households
Percent of Households with	*1984*	*1994*	*1971*
Washing machine	58.2	71.7	71.3
Clothes dryer	35.6	50.2	44.5
Dishwasher	13.6	19.6	18.8
Refrigerator	95.8	97.9	83.3
Freezer	29.2	28.6	32.2
Stove	95.2	97.7	87.0
Microwave	12.5	60.0	<1.0
Color television	70.3	92.5	43.3
VCR	3.4	59.7	0
Personal computer	2.9	7.4	0
Telephone	71.0	76.7	93.0
Air conditioner	42.5	49.6	31.8
One or more cars	64.5	71.8	79.5

*At or below the poverty line, as defined by the Census Bureau.

As consumption patterns show, many of today's poorest households have more than yesterday's, and more, even, than the general population had two decades ago. By today's consumption standards, the majority of Americans were once poor.

QUESTIONING THE TEXT

1. In Exhibit 3, Cox and Alm provide evidence to support their assertion that "inequality [of income] is not inequity," concluding that inequity is normal in a free enterprise system. Carefully examine the claims and evidence offered, and then generate a list of questions and concerns you'd like to see addressed in a longer essay on the same subject.
2. Exhibit 12 provides one way of looking at economic welfare—in terms of goods owned. In a group, discuss how well ownership of specific items serves as a measure of wealth and poverty. What objects might you add to such a list? What objects might you remove?

MAKING CONNECTIONS

3. How comforting would the material in this selection be to the writers in "Young, Privileged, and Unemployed" (p. 566)? How might either woman respond to the formula for economic success outlined in Exhibit 9?
4. Try turning the information in Exhibit 3 into aphorisms of the sort Benjamin Franklin's Poor Richard (p. 545) might compose. Can you find convincing ways to advise people to accept economic "churn" or the consequences of baby boom demographics on the distribution of wealth?

JOINING THE CONVERSATION

5. From Exhibit 9, choose one of the "secrets" of success and—working with several classmates—explore the library or World Wide Web for more information. After you've done your research, write a brief report explaining what you have learned.
6. Prepare for a class discussion on the question "Should economic equity be a goal of American society?" Using the library, examine as many points of view as possible. Read journals from different political and social groups. Then, in class, discuss various aspects of the issue more factually than argumentatively: how equity can be defined; where issues of equity become controversial; what mechanisms would be necessary to enforce or enhance economic equity. Finally, write a column for a local newspaper addressing the question.
7. Interview four or five people in your community about whether they agree with the four claims made in the second paragraph of the introduction to this selection. Then write a short report on your findings.

DOUGLAS COUPLAND
Microserfs

*T*HE RELATIONSHIP OF PEOPLE *to their work has been the subject of many novels in the capitalist era. In the nineteenth century, the French novelist Émile Zola chronicles the struggles of coal miners in his epic* Germinal *(1885), exposing the horrible conditions in the pits. In the Roaring Twenties, Sinclair Lewis casts a steely eye on the world of the conformist American businessman in* Babbitt *(1922). During the energy crisis of the late 1970s, John Updike's Harry Angstrom rises to middle-aged respectability by selling Toyotas in* Rabbit Is Rich. *And now, as our industrial century slides into an electronic millennium, Douglas Coupland (b. 1961), the novelist who named Generation X, depicts the lives of programmers and technicians creating that future.*

Coupland assembles a world of wealthy young geeks and techies in Microserfs *(1995), people adrift in the leftcoast soup of silicon chips and computer operating systems. Indeed, the book is virtually a catalog of 1990s icons and obsessions—foremost of which is Bill Gates, with his giant software empire. Gates defines American computers and electronics in the 1990s the way Henry Ford rode herd on the auto industry earlier in this century, his influence felt in areas far removed from computers and software programs. Early in the novel, the characters in* Microserfs *live worshipfully on Bill's Seattle campus, with its gray and plum carpets and finely honed lawns, wondering if and when they'll abandon their obsessions with Legos and junk food, encryption code and Microsoft stock options, to find what's missing in their lives. Theirs is an ancient quest in a new setting—pondering the meaning of one's daily labors—and they hope that someone, maybe Bill, knows the answer.*

The following selection from Microserfs *represents two days in the journal of danielu@microsoft.com, the narrator of the novel. −* J.R.

FRIDAY
EARLY FALL, 1993

This morning, just after 11:00, Michael locked himself in his office and he won't come out.

Bill (Bill!) sent Michael this totally wicked flame-mail from hell on the e-mail system—and he just wailed on a chunk of code Michael had written. Using the *Bloom County*-cartoons-taped-on-the-door index, Michael is certainly the most sensitive coder in Building Seven—not the type to take criticism easily. Exactly why Bill would choose Michael of all people to wail on is confusing.

We figured it must have been a random quality check to keep the troops in line. Bill's so smart.

Bill is wise.

Bill is kind.

Bill is benevolent.

Bill, Be My Friend . . . *Please!*

Actually, nobody on our floor has ever been flamed by Bill personally. The episode was tinged with glamour and we were somewhat jealous. I tried to tell Michael this, but he was crushed.

Shortly before lunch he stood like a lump outside my office. His skin   5
was pale like rising bread dough, and his Toppy's cut was dripping sweat, leaving little damp marks on the oyster-gray-with-plum highlights of the Microsoft carpeting. He handed me a printout of Bill's memo and then gallumphed into his office, where he's been burrowed ever since.

He won't answer his phone, respond to e-mail, or open his door. On his doorknob he placed a "Do Not Disturb" thingy stolen from the Boston Radisson during last year's Macworld Expo. Todd and I walked out onto the side lawn to try to peek in his window, but his venetian blinds were closed and a gardener with a leaf blower chased us away with a spray of grass clippings.

They mow the lawn every ten minutes at Microsoft. It looks like green Lego pads.

Finally, at about 2:30 A.M., Todd and I got concerned about Michael's not eating, so we drove to the 24-hour Safeway in Bellevue. We went shopping for "flat" foods to slip underneath Michael's door.

The Safeway was completely empty save for us and a few other Microsoft people just like us—hair-trigger geeks in pursuit of just the right snack. Because of all the rich nerds living around here, Redmond and Bellevue are very "on-demand" neighborhoods. Nerds get what they want when they want it, and they go psycho if it's not immediately available. Nerds overfocus. I guess that's the problem. But it's precisely this ability to narrow-focus that makes them so good at code writing: one line at a time, one line in a strand of millions.

When we returned to Building Seven at 3:00 A.M., there were still a few   10
people grinding away. Our group is scheduled to ship product (RTM: Release to Manufacturing) in just eleven days (Top Secret: We'll never make it).

Michael's office lights were on, but once again, when we knocked, he wouldn't answer his door. We heard his keyboard chatter, so we figured he was still alive. The situation really begged a discussion of Turing logic—could we have discerned that the entity behind the door was indeed even human? We slid Kraft singles, Premium Plus crackers, Pop-Tarts, grape leather, and Freezie-Pops in to him.

Todd asked me, "Do you think any of this violates geek dietary laws?"

Just then, Karla in the office across the hall screamed and then glared out at us from her doorway. Her eyes were all red and sore behind her round glasses. She said, "You guys are only encouraging him," like we were feeding a raccoon or something. I don't think Karla ever sleeps.

She harrumphed and slammed her door closed. Doors sure are important to nerds.

Anyway, by this point Todd and I were both really tired. We drove   15
back to the house to crash, each in our separate cars, through the Campus grounds—22 buildings' worth of nerd-cosseting fun—cloistered by 100-foot-tall second growth timber, its streets quiet as the womb: the foundry of our culture's deepest dreams.

There was mist floating on the ground above the soccer fields outside the central buildings. I thought about the e-mail and Bill and all of that, and I had this weird feeling—of how the presence of Bill floats about the Campus, semi-visible, at all times, kind of like the dead grandfather in the *Family Circus* cartoons. Bill is a moral force, a spectral force, a force that shapes, a force that molds. A force with thick, thick glasses.

I am **danielu@microsoft.com**. If my life was a game of *Jeopardy!* my seven dream categories would be:

- Tandy products
- Trash TV of the late '70s and early '80s
- The history of Apple
- Career anxieties
- Tabloids
- Plant life of the Pacific Northwest
- Jell-O 1-2-3

I am a tester—a bug checker in Building Seven. I worked my way up the ladder from Product Support Services (PSS) where I spend six months in phone purgatory in 1991 helping little old ladies format their Christmas mailing lists on Microsoft Works.

Like most Microsoft employees, I consider myself too well adjusted to be working here, even though I am 26 and my universe consists of home, Microsoft, and Costco.

I am originally from Bellingham, up just near the border, but my par-   20
ents live in Palo Alto now. I live in a group house with five other Microsoft employees: Todd, Susan, Bug Barbecue, Michael, and Abe.

We call ourselves "The Channel Three News Team."

I am single. I think partly this is because Microsoft is not conducive to relationships. Last year down at the Apple Worldwide Developer's Conference in San Jose, I met a girl who works not too far away, at Hewlett-Packard on Interstate 90, but it never went anywhere. Sometimes I'll sort of get something going, but then work takes over my life and I bail out of all my commitments and things fizzle.

Lately I've been unable to sleep. That's why I've begun writing this journal late at night, to try to see the patterns in my life. From this I hope to establish what my problem is—and then, hopefully, solve it. I'm trying to feel more well adjusted than I really am, which is, I guess, the human condition. My life is lived day to day, one line of bug-free code at a time.

The house:

Growing up, I used to build split-level ranch-type homes out of Legos.   25
This is pretty much the house I live in now, but its ambiance is anything but sterilized Lego-clean. It was built about twenty years ago, maybe before Microsoft was even in the dream stage and this part of Redmond had a lost, alpine ski-cabin feel.

Instead of a green plastic pad with little plastic nubblies, our house sits on a thickly-treed lot beside a park on a cul-de-sac at the top of a steep hill. It's only a seven-minute drive from Campus. There are two other Microsoft group houses just down the hill. Karla, actually, lives in the house three down from us across the street.

People end up living in group houses either by e-mail or by word of mouth. Living in a group house is a little bit like admitting you're deficient in the having-a-life department, but at work you spend your entire life crunching code and testing for bugs, and what else are you supposed to do? Work, sleep, work, sleep, work, sleep. I know a few Microsoft employees who try to fake having a life—many a Redmond garage contains a never-used kayak collecting dust. You ask these people what they do in their spare time and they say, "*Uhhh*—kayaking. That's right. I kayak in my spare time." You can tell they're faking it.

I don't even do many sports anymore and my relationship with my body has gone all weird. I used to play soccer three times a week and now I feel like a boss in charge of an underachiever. I feel like my body is a station wagon in which I drive my brain around, like a suburban mother taking the kids to hockey practice.

The house is covered with dark cedar paneling. Out front there's a tiny patch of lawn covered in miniature yellow crop circles thanks to the dietary excesses of our neighbor's German shepherd, Mishka. Bug Barbecue keeps his weather experiments—funnels and litmus strips and so forth—nailed to the wall beside the front door. A flat of purple petunias long-expired from neglect—Susan's one attempt at prettification—depresses us every time we leave for work in the morning, resting as it does in the thin strip of soil between the driveway and Mishka's crop circles.

Abe, our in-house multimillionaire, used to have tinfoil all over his   30
bedroom windows to keep out what few rays of sun penetrated the trees until
we ragged on him so hard that he went out and bought a sheaf of black construction paper at the Pay 'n Save and taped it up instead. It looked like a
drifter lived here. Todd's only contribution to the house's outer appearance is
a collection of car-washing toys sometimes visible beside the garage door.
The only evidence of my being in the house is my 1977 AMC Hornet
Sportabout hatchback parked out front when I'm home. It's bright orange,
it's rusty, and damnit, it's *ugly*.

SATURDAY

Shipping hell continued again today. Grind, grind, grind. We'll never
make it. Have I said that already? Why do we always underestimate our shipping schedules? I just don't understand. In at 9:30 A.M.; out at 11:30 P.M.
Domino's for dinner. And three diet Cokes.

I got bored a few times today and checked the WinQuote on my
screen—that's the extension that gives continuous updates on Microsoft's
NASDAQ price. It was Saturday, and there was never any change, but I kept
forgetting. Habit. Maybe the Tokyo or Hong Kong exchanges might cause a
fluctuation?
Most staffers peek at WinQuote a few times a day. I mean, if you have
10,000 shares (and tons of staff members have way more) and the stock goes
up a buck, you've just made ten grand! But then, if it goes down two dollars,
you've just lost twenty grand. It's a real psychic yo-yo. Last April Fool's Day,
someone fluctuated the price up and down by fifty dollars and half the staff
had coronaries.
Because I started out low on the food chain and worked my way up, I
didn't get much stock offered to me the way that programmers and systems
designers get stock firehosed onto them when they start. What stock I do
own won't fully vest for another 2.5 years (stock takes 4.5 years to fully vest).
Susan's stock vests later this week, and she's going to have a vesting   35
party. And then she's going to quit. Larger social forces are at work, threatening to dissolve our group house.

The stock closed up $1.75 on Friday. Bill has 78,000,000 shares, so that
means he's now $136.5 million richer. I have almost no stock, and this means
I am a loser.

News update: Michael is now out of his office. It's as if he never had his
geek episode. He slept there throughout the whole day (not unusual at Microsoft), using his *Jurassic Park* inflatable T-Rex toy as a pillow. When he

woke up in the early evening, he thanked me for bringing him the Kraft products, and now he says he won't eat anything that's not entirely two-dimensional. "Ich bin ein Flatlander," he piped, as he cheerfully sifted through hard copy of the bug-checked code he'd been chugging out. Karla made disgusted clicking noises with her tongue from her office. I think maybe she's in love with Michael.

More details about our group house—Our House of Wayward Mobility.

Because the house receives almost no sun, moss and algae tend to colonize what surfaces they can. There is a cherry tree crippled by fungus. The rear verandah, built of untreated 2×4's, has quietly rotted away, and the sliding door in the kitchen has been braced shut with a hockey stick to prevent the unwary from straying into the suburban abyss.

The driveway contains six cars: Todd's cherry-red Supra (his life, what little there is of it), my pumpkin Hornet, and four personality-free gray Microsoftmobiles—a Lexus, an Acura Legend, and two Tauri (nerd plural for Taurus). I bet if Bill drove a Shriner's go-cart to work, everybody else would, too.

40

Inside, each of us has a bedroom. Because of the McDonald's-like turnover in the house, the public rooms—the living room, kitchen, dining room, and basement—are bleak, to say the least. The dormlike atmosphere precludes heavy-duty interior design ideas. In the living room are two velveteen sofas that were too big and too ugly for some long-gone tenants to take with them. Littered about the Tiki green shag carpet are:

- Two Microsoft Works PC inflatable beach cushions
- One Mitsubishi 27-inch color TV
- Various vitamin bottles
- Several weight-gaining system cartons (mine)
- 86 copies of *MacWEEK* arranged in chronological order by Bug Barbecue, who will go berserk if you so much as move one issue out of date
- Six Microsoft Project 2.0 juggling bean bags
- Bone-shaped chew toys for when Mishka visits
- Two PowerBooks
- Three IKEA mugs encrusted with last month's blender drink sensation
- Two 12.5-pound dumbbells (Susan's)
- A Windows NT box
- Three baseball caps (two Mariners, one A's)
- Abe's Battlestar Galactica trading card album
- Todd's pile of books on how to change your life to win! (*Getting Past OK, 7 Habits of Highly Effective People* . . .)

The kitchen is stocked with ramshackle 1970s avocado green appliances. You can almost hear the ghost of Emily Hartley yelling "Hi, Bob!" every time you open the fridge door (a sea of magnets and 4-×-6-inch photos of last year's house parties).

Our mail is in little piles by the front door: bills, Star Trek junk mail, and the heap-o-catalogues next to the phone.

I think we'd order our lives via 1-800 numbers if we could.

Mom phoned from Palo Alto. This is the time of year she calls a lot.   45
She calls because she wants to speak about Jed, but none of us in the family are able. We kind of erased him.

I used to have a younger brother named Jed. He drowned in a boating accident in the Strait of Juan de Fuca when I was 14 and he was 12. A Labor Day statistic.

To this day, anything Labor Day-ish creeps me out: the smell of barbecuing salmon, life preservers, Interstate traffic reports from the local radio Traffic Copter, Monday holidays. But here's a secret: My e-mail password is *hellojed.* So I think about him every day. He was way better with computers than I was. He was way nerdier than me.

As it turned out, Mom had good news today. Dad has a big meeting Monday with his company. Mom and Dad figure it's a promotion because Dad's IBM division has been doing so well (by IBM standards—it's not hemorrhaging money). She says she'll keep me posted.

Susan taped laser-printed notes on all of our bedroom doors reminding us about the vesting party this Thursday ("Vest Fest '93"), which was a subliminal hint to us to clean up the place. Most of us work in Building Seven; shipping hell has brought a severe breakdown in cleanup codes.

Susan is 26 and works in Mac Applications. If Susan were a *Jeopardy!*   50
contestant, her dream board would be:

- 680X0 assembly language
- Cats
- Early '80s haircut bands
- "My secret affair with Rob in the Excel Group"
- License plate slogans of America
- Plot lines from *The Monkees*
- The death of IBM

Susan's an IBM brat and hates that company with a passion. She credits it with ruining her youth by transferring her family eight times before she graduated from high school—and the punchline is that the company gave her father the boot last year during a wave of restructuring. So nothing too evil can happen to IBM in her eyes. Her graphic designer friend made up T-shirts saying "IBM: Weak as a Kitten, Dumb as a Sack of Hammers." We all wear them. I gave one to Dad last Christmas but his reaction didn't score too high on the chuckle-o-meter. (I am not an IBM brat—Dad was teaching at the University of Western Washington until the siren of industry lured him to Palo Alto in 1985. It was very '80s.)

Susan's a real coding machine. But her abilities are totally wasted re-working old code for something like the Norwegian Macintosh version of Word 5.8. Susan's work ethic best sums up the ethic of most of the people I've met who work at Microsoft. If I recall her philosophy from the conversation she had with her younger sister two weekends ago, it goes something like this:

"It's never been, 'We're doing this for the good of society.' It's always been us taking an intellectual pride in putting out a good product—and making money. If putting a computer on every desktop and in every home didn't make money, we wouldn't do it."

That sums up most of the Microsoft people I know.

Microsoft, like any office, is a status theme park. Here's a quick run-down: 55

- Profitable projects are galactically higher in status than loser (not quite as profitable) projects.
- Microsoft at Work (Digital Office) is sexiest at the moment. Fortune 500 companies are drooling over DO because it'll allow them to down-size millions of employees. Basically, DO allows you to operate your fax, phone, copier—all of your office stuff—from your PC.
- Cash cows like Word are profitable but not really considered cutting edge.
- Working on-Campus is higher status than being relegated to one of the off-Campus Siberias.
- Having Pentium-driven hardware (built to the hilt) in your office is higher status than having 486 droneware.
- Having technical knowledge is way up there.
- Being an architect is also way up there.
- Having Bill-o-centric contacts is way, way up there.
- Shipping your product on time is maybe the coolest (insert wave of anxiety here). If you ship on time you get a Ship-It award: a 12-×-15-×-1-inch Lucite slab—but you have to pretend it's no big deal. Michael has a Ship-It award and we've tried various times to destroy it—

blowtorching, throwing it off the verandah, dowsing it with acetone to dissolve it—nothing works. It's so permanent, it's frightening.

More roommate profiles:

First, Abe. If Abe were a *Jeopardy!* contestant, his seven dream categories would be:

- Intel asembly language
- Bulk shopping
- C++
- Introversion
- "I love my aquarium"
- How to have millions of dollars and not let it affect your life in any way
- Unclean laundry

Abe is sort of like the household Monopoly-game banker. He collects our monthly checks for the landlord, $235 apiece. The man has millions and he rents! He's been at the group house since 1984, when he was hired fresh out of MIT. (The rest of us have been here, on average, about eight months apiece.) After ten years of writing code, Abe so far shows no signs of getting a life. He seems happy to be reaching the age of 30 in just four months with nothing to his name but a variety of neat-o consumer electronics and boxes of Costco products purchased in rash moments of Costco-scale madness ("Ten thousand straws! Just think of it—only $10 and I'll never need to buy straws ever again!") These products line the walls of his room, giving it the feel of an air raid shelter.

Bonus detail: There are dried-out patches of sneeze spray all over Abe's monitors. You'd think he could afford 24 bottles of Windex.

Next, Todd. Todd's seven *Jeopardy!* categories would be: 60

- Your body is your temple
- Baseball hats
- Meals made from combinations of Costco products
- Psychotically religious parents
- Frequent and empty sex
- SEGA Genesis gaming addiction
- The Supra

Todd works as a tester with me. He's really young—22—the way Microsoft employees all used to be. His interest is entirely in girls, bug testing, his Supra, and his body, which he buffs religiously at the Pro Club gym and feeds with peanut butter quesadillas, bananas, and protein drinks.

Todd is historically empty. He neither knows nor cares about the past. He reads *Car and Driver* and fields three phone calls a week from his parents who believe that computers are "the Devil's voice box," and who try to persuade him to return home to Port Angeles and speak with the youth pastor.

Todd's the most fun of all the house members because he is all impulse and no consideration. He's also the only roomie to have clean laundry consistently. In a crunch you can always borrow an unsoiled shirt from Todd.

Bug Barbecue's seven *Jeopardy!* categories would be:

- Bitterness
- Xerox PARC nostalgia
- Macintosh products
- More bitterness
- Psychotic loser friends
- Jazz
- Still more bitterness

Bug Barbecue is the World's Most Bitter Man. He is (as his name implies) a tester with me at Building Seven. His have-a-life factor is pretty near zero. He has the smallest, darkest room in the house, in which he maintains two small shrines: one to his Sinclair ZX-81, his first computer, and the other to supermodel Elle MacPherson. Man, she'd freak if she saw the hundreds of little photos—the coins, the candles, the little notes.

Bug is 31, and he lets everyone know it. If we ever ask him so much as "Hey, Bug—have you seen volume 7 of my *Inside Mac?*" he gives a sneer and replies, "You're obviously of the generation that never built their own motherboard or had to invent their own language."

Hey, Bug—we love you, too.

Bug never gets offered stock by the company. When payday comes and the little white stock option envelopes with red printing reading "Personal and Confidential" end up in all of our pigeonholes, Bug's is always, alas, empty. Maybe they're trying to get rid of him, but it's almost impossible to fire someone at Microsoft. It must drive the administration nuts. They hired 3,100 people in 1992 alone, and you know not all of them were gems.

Oddly, Bug is fanatical in his devotion to Microsoft. It's as if the more they ignore him, the more rabidly he defends their honor. And if you cherish your own personal time, you will not get into a discussion with him over the famous Look-&-Feel lawsuit or any of the FTC or Department of Justice actions:

"These litigious pricks piss me off. I wish they'd compete in the mar-   70
ketplace where it really counts instead of being little wusses and whining for
government assistance to compete. . . ."

You've been warned.

Finally, Michael. Michael's seven *Jeopardy!* categories would be:

- FORTRAN
- Pascal
- Ada (defense contracting code)
- LISP
- Neil Peart (drummer for Rush)
- Hugo and Nebula award winners
- Sir Lancelot

Michael is probably the closest I'll ever come to knowing someone who
lives in a mystical state. He lives to assemble elegant streams of code instructions. He's like Mozart to everyone else's Salieri—he enters people's offices
where lines of code are written on the dry-erase whiteboards and quietly op-
timizes the code as he speaks to them, as though someone had written wrong
instructions on how to get to the beach and he was merely setting them right
so they wouldn't get lost.

He often uses low-tech solutions to high-tech problems: Popsicle sticks,
rubber bands, and little strips of paper that turn on a bent coat hanger frame
help him solve complex matrix problems. When he moved offices into his
new window office (good coder, good office), he had to put Post-it notes
reading "Not Art" on his devices so that the movers didn't stick them under
the glass display cases out in the central atrium area.

QUESTIONING THE TEXT

1. In small groups, choose one section from *Microserfs* and annotate it, explaining all terms, allusions, or expressions—such as "Tandy products"
   or "Ich bin ein Flatlander"—that a stranger to the culture Coupland describes might not immediately understand. After several groups have
   completed their work, discuss the effectiveness of Coupland's technique. Is *Microserfs* too difficult to follow? Or do you enjoy mining its
   allusions?
2. Daniel defines himself and his friends in terms of categories from *Jeopardy!*—a television game show in which brainy contestants provide
   questions that fit a series of answers provided on a gameboard with

seven different categories. Try defining yourself according to seven *Jeopardy!* categories. Share your response with several classmates.

MAKING CONNECTIONS

3. In a short essay, try to reconcile the way Newt Gingrich (p. 576) paints the Third Wave technological revolution with the portrait Coupland presents of high-tech work at Microsoft. Are the visions of these two authors compatible?
4. Sven Birkerts (p. 279) worries that electronic books may produce "a souped-up cognitive collage" incompatible with careful habits of reading and thinking. Would you describe the passage from Coupland's novel as such a cognitive collage? In a brief critical response, define that term as you understand it and then explain why Coupland's novel is or is not such a collage.

JOINING THE CONVERSATION

5. Imitating Coupland's style, write a short piece about where you work or go to school. Describe the way people there behave, think, and dress; their backgrounds, dreams, and obsessions. A good subject for this portrait may be your writing class.
6. Write an essay describing the kind of work you hope to do (or may already be doing) and the satisfactions you expect from it.

MARGE PIERCY
To Be of Use

Marge Piercy (b. 1936) is remarkable by any standard: she is the author of over two dozen books of poetry (including To Be of Use, The Moon Is Always Female, *and* Mars and Her Children) *and fiction (including* Going Down Fast, Woman on the Edge of Time, Fly Away Home, *and* He, She, and It); *a political activist (she helped organize Students for a Democratic Society in the 1960s); an ardent feminist; and a constant social critic. Piercy writes with passion and a power that is hard to ignore. Often, her passion for justice and equity as well as for what she calls "work that is real" is born of hard experience. The child of often poor and working-class parents, Piercy (who is white and Jewish) grew up in a predominantly African American section of Detroit, where she learned firsthand about what she calls "the indifference of the rich, racism . . . the working-class pitted against itself." The first member of her family to attend college, she won a scholarship and graduated from the University of Michigan; she has contributed her prolific collection of manuscripts to its graduate library.*

Many of Piercy's poems get their power from a kind of pent-up rage that explodes on the page in front of her readers. In fact, I first got to know her work through just such poems, a number of which (like "Barbie Doll," which appeared in the first edition of this book) haunt me still. But Piercy can be hopeful, even celebratory, as well. And in the following poem, she is both, defining in vivid images and rhythmic cadences what she calls "work that is real." It is one of only four poems I carry with me always. — A.L.

The people I love the best
jump into work head first
without dallying in the shallows
and swim off with sure strokes almost out of sight.
They seem to become natives of that element,   5
the black sleek heads of seals
bouncing like half-submerged balls.

I love people who harness themselves, an ox to a heavy cart
who pull like water buffalo, with massive patience,
who strain in the mud and the muck to move things forward   10
who do what has to be done, again and again.

I want to be with people who submerge
in the task, who go into the fields to harvest
and work in a row and pass the bags along,
who are not parlor generals and field deserters   15
but move in a common rhythm
when the food must come in or the fire be put out.

The work of the world is common as mud.
Botched, it smears the hands, crumbles to dust.
But the thing worth doing well done   20
has a shape that satisfies, clean and evident.
Greek amphoras for wine or oil,
Hopi vases that held corn, are put in museums
but you know they were made to be used.
The pitcher cries for water to carry   25
and a person for work that is real.

IN RESPONSE

1. Piercy says work that is worth doing "has a shape that satisfies, clean and evident." Think for a while about examples you could give of such work. Reflect on them and on your relationship to and feelings about them. If you keep a reading log, record your responses there.
2. Try your hand at adding a stanza to this poem, after the second stanza. Begin with the words "I love people who. . . ." Bring your stanza to class to share with others.
3. Which writers in this chapter might Piercy see as doing "work that is real"? In a brief exploratory essay, give reasons for your choices.

OTHER READINGS

Baida, Peter. *Poor Richard's Legacy: American Business Values from Benjamin Franklin to Donald Trump*. New York: Morrow, 1990. Examines history of American attitudes toward enterprise and labor.

Berger, Peter L. *The Capitalist Revolution: Fifty Propositions about Prosperity, Equality, and Wealth*. New York: Basic, 1986. Argues that capitalism is demonstrably the most effective economic system.

Erdrich, Louise. "A Woman's Work: Too Many Demands, and Not Enough Selves." *Harper's* May 1993: 35–46. A writer and mother talks about the demands and conflicts she faces as she tries to balance her home responsibilities with her work.

Hochschild, Arlie. *The Second Shift: Working Parents and the Revolution at Home*. New York: Viking, 1989. Case studies that reveal the difficulties of balancing work inside and outside the home.

John Paul II. *On the Hundredth Anniversary of Rerum Novarum*. Boston: St. Paul, 1991. Considers relationships between business and labor.

Posey, Sam. "Ballet Mechanique." *Road & Track* July 1995: 134–39. Describes a symbol of America's past industrial greatness, Ford's River Rouge complex.

Snyder, Don J. "Winter Work: Diary of a Day Laborer." *Harper's* Nov. 1995: 34–45. Reflections of a man who lost his college teaching job and turned to construction work to support his family.

Snyder, Gary. "On the Path, Off the Trail." *The Practice of the Wild*. San Francisco: North Point Press, 1990. Uses paths and trails as metaphors for work, claiming that skills and work are reflections of the order in nature.

Sternburg, Janet, ed. *The Writer on Her Work* vol. II. New York: W. W. Norton & Company, 1991. Essays and poems by women who reflect on the work of writing.

ELECTRONIC RESOURCES

US Occupational Safety and Health Agency (OSHA):
http://www.osha.gov/
Provides information about the government agency concerned with on-the-job safety.

US Department of Labor:
http://www.dol.gov/
Provides information about the Department of Labor.

Free-market.com:
http://www.free-market.com/
Provides information about various groups committed to free enterprise.

Kathleen Norris, "Little Girls in Church" from *Little Girls in Church*. Copyright © 1995 by Kathleen Norris. Reprinted with the permission of University of Pittsburgh Press.

Sharon Olds, "Son" from *The Dead and the Living*. Copyright © 1983 by Sharon Olds. Reprinted with the permission of Alfred A. Knopf, Inc.

P. J. O'Rourke, "Review of *Guidelines for Bias-Free Writing*," *The American Spectator* (August 1995). Copyright © 1995 by P. J. O'Rourke. Reprinted with the permission of the author.

Paul Osterman, "Getting Started: The Great American Job Hunt," *The Wilson Quarterly* 18, no. 4 (Autumn 1994). Copyright © 1994 by Paul Osterman. Reprinted with the permission of the author.

Rosa Parks, "Role Models" from Rosa Parks with Gregory J. Reed, *Quiet Strength: The Faith, The Hope, and the Heart of a Woman Who Changed a Nation*. Copyright © 1995 by Rosa Parks. Reprinted with the permission of Zondervan Publishing House.

Marge Piercy, "To Be of Use" from *Circles on the Water*. Copyright © 1982 by Marge Piercy. Reprinted with the permission of Alfred A. Knopf, Inc.

Neil Postman, "The Word Weavers/The World Makers" from *The End of Education: Redefining the Value of School*. Copyright © 1995 by Neil Postman. Reprinted with the permission of Alfred A. Knopf, Inc.

Ayn Rand, "The Soul of an Individualist" from *The Fountainhead*. Copyright 1943 by The Bobbs-Merrill Publishing Company, renewed © 1970 by Ayn Rand. Reprinted with the permission of Simon & Schuster, Inc.

Adrienne Rich, "What Does a Woman Need to Know?" from *Blood, Bread, and Poetry: Selected Prose 1979–1985*. Copyright © 1986 by Adrienne Rich. Reprinted with the permission of the author and W. W. Norton & Company, Inc.

Matthew Rohrer, "Found in the Museum of Old Science" from *A Hummock in the Malookas*. Copyright © 1995 by Matthew Rohrer. Reprinted with the permission of W. W. Norton & Company, Inc.

Mike Rose, "Lives on the Boundary" from *Lives on the Boundary*. Copyright © 1989 by Mike Rose. Reprinted with the permission of The Free Press, a division of Simon & Schuster, Inc.

Henry Scanlon, "Suddenly, I'm the Bad Guy," *Newsweek* (March 15, 1993). Copyright © 1993 by Henry Scanlon. Reprinted with the permission of Henry Scanlon, Chairman, Comstock, Inc.

Jeremy Seabrook, "Family Values," *New Statesman & Society* 6, no. 282 (December 10, 1993). Copyright © 1993 by Statesman and Nation Publishing Company Ltd. (UK). Reprinted with the permission of the publishers.

Barbara Smith, "Home" from Barbara Smith, ed., *Home Girls: A Black Feminist Anthology*. Copyright © 1983 by Barbara Smith. Reprinted with the permission of the author and Kitchen Table: Women of Color Press.

Christina Hoff Sommers, "Figuring Out Feminism" from *Who Stole Feminism?: How Women Have Betrayed Women*. Originally published in *National Review* (June 27, 1994). Copyright © 1994 by Christina Hoff Sommers. Reprinted with the permission of Simon & Schuster, Inc.

Shelby Steele, "The Recoloring of Campus Life" from *The Content of Our Character*. Copyright © 1990 by Shelby Steele. Reprinted with the permission of St. Martin's Press.

Andrew Sullivan, "What Are Homosexuals For?" from *Virtually Normal: An Argument about Homosexuality*. Copyright © 1995 by Andrew Sullivan. Reprinted with the permission of Alfred A. Knopf, Inc.

David Thomas, "The Mind of Man" from *Not Guilty: Men: The Case for the Defence*. Copyright © 1993 by D T Productions, Ltd. Reprinted with the permission of Weidenfeld & Nicolson, Ltd.

Lewis Thomas, "The Hazards of Science" from *The Medusa and the Snail*. Copyright © 1977 by Lewis Thomas. Reprinted with the permission of Viking Penguin, a division of Penguin Books USA Inc.

Alice Walker, "The Place Where I Was Born" from *Her Blue Body Everything We Know: Earthling Poems 1965–1990*. Copyright © 1991 by Alice Walker. Reprinted with the permission of Harcourt Brace & Company.

Terry Tempest Williams, "The Clan of One-Breasted Women" from *Refuge: An Unnatural History of Family and Place*. Originally published in *Northern Lights* (January 1990). Copyright © 1990 by Terry

Tempest Williams. Reprinted with the permission of Pantheon Books, a division of Random House, Inc.

Cover Photo Acknowledgments

Mike Rose: Courtesy of the author; *Zora Neale Hurston:* Courtesy, Lucy Hurston; *Douglas Coupland:* AP/Wide World; *Lynne V. Cheney:* AP/Wide World; *Maxine Hong Kingston:* © Jerry Bauer; *Pope John Paul II:* Reuters/Corbis-Bettmann; *Joan Didion:* AP/Wide World; *Newt Gingrich:* AP/Wide World; *Martin Luther King Jr.:* UPI/Corbis-Bettmann.

Chapter Opener Photos

Chapter 3: Courtesy of The University of Georgia; *Chapter 4:* Kathy Tarantola/The Picture Cube; *Chapter 5:* This material was created with support to Space Telescope Science Institute, operated by the Association of Universities for Research in Astronomy, Inc., from NASA contract NAS5-26555 and is reproduced with permission from AURA/STScl; *Chapter 6:* Courtesy of Revlon Consumer Products Corporation; *Chapter 7:* Jean-Claude LeJeune/Stock, Boston; *Chapter 8:* Frank Micelotta/Outline; *Chapter 9:* Photofest; *Chapter 10:* Drawing by C. Barsotti; © 1996 The New Yorker Magazine, Inc.

Index

Notes for Teachers

Second Edition

THE PRESENCE
of OTHERS

*Voices That Call
for Response*

ANDREA A. LUNSFORD
JOHN J. RUSZKIEWICZ

Melissa A. Goldthwaite

NOTES FOR TEACHERS

Second Edition

To Accompany

■ **THE PRESENCE OF OTHERS** ■

Voices That Call for Response

Second Edition

NOTES FOR TEACHERS
Second Edition

Melissa A. Goldthwaite
Ohio State University

To Accompany

▪ THE PRESENCE OF OTHERS ▪

Voices That Call for Response

Second Edition

Andrea A. Lunsford
John J. Ruszkiewicz

St. Martin's Press
New York

Manufactured in the United States of America.

1 0 9 8 7
f e d c b a

For information, write:
St. Martin's Press, Inc.
175 Fifth Avenue South
New York, NY 10010

ISBN: 0-312-14831-3

Acknowledgments
Graff, Gerald. "What Has Literary Theory Wrought?" *The Chronicle of Higher Education* 12 February 1992: A48.
Hairston, Maxine. "Diversity, Ideology, and Teaching Writing." *College Composition and Communication* 43 May 1992: 179-193.
Jarratt, Susan C. "Rhetorical Power: What Really Happens in Politicized Classrooms." *Association of Departments of English Bulletin* 102 Fall 1992: 34-39.

CONTENTS

NOTES FOR TEACHERS

Second Edition

To Accompany

■ THE PRESENCE OF OTHERS ■

Voices That Call for Response

Second Edition

The Presence of Others is a college-level textbook designed for use in writing courses that emphasize the interrelatedness of reading and writing. Based on the principle that all language is social and that all reading and writing are done in a social context—in the presence of other readers, writers, and texts—this book is organized into chapters that present extended conversations about a wide variety of subjects that we hope will prove engaging to you and your students as you bring your voices into these conversations. The conversations this text presents are not unlike the "parlor conversations" Kenneth Burke discusses in *Philosophy of Literary Form*: "When you arrive, others have long preceded you and they are engaged in a heated discussion. . . . You listen for a while, until you decide that you have caught the tenor of the argument; then you put in your oar." These are the types of discussions we hope you and your students will engage in this term.

PLANNING A COURSE

The Presence of Others provides many more opportunities for reading and writing than students could take advantage of in a semester or even a year-long writing course. As a result, you will have the opportunity to choose which readings or chapters to focus on. Because the idea of an extended conversation is fundamental to this book, many of the questions following each reading ("Making Connections") as well as the commentary on the readings provided in this Teacher's Guide highlight links among readings within and across chapters. As you decide which readings to include in your syllabus, you may want to preview the "Making Connections" questions and the commentary in this Teacher's Guide to help you choose readings that are related in interesting ways and that illustrate a range of positions on a particular subject.

In addition to thinking about the relationships among individual readings, you should also think about the relationships among the chapters you choose to focus on or the subjects you choose to address, perhaps organizing your course around an overarching question that might initiate and sustain the conversation that you and your students and the voices in *The Presence of Others* will carry on throughout the term. Some questions you may want to consider include:

How do individuals represent themselves and others? This question encourages students to think about the ways in which particular writers (including student writers) represent themselves and others in their writing. You could organize your syllabus by chapter, asking students to think about how people represent themselves in terms of their education, faith, gender, home, or work. As an alternative, you could use selections from various chapters, asking students to consider how race, class, gender, sexual preference, and age affect the ways particular people represent themselves and others.

What is knowledge and what does it mean to know? This question can prove an important one for students just beginning their college educations. By using selections from **Chapter 3, Education; Chapter 4, Faith; Chapter 5, Science; and Chapter 8, Legends,**

you can invite students to investigate their relationships to various kinds of knowledge as well as the sometimes conflict-ridden relationships among these sources of knowledge.

America: the one or the many? This question would work well as the organizing principle for a course that focuses on diversity in American culture. In pursuing this question, it might be useful to start—or end—with **Chapter 3, Education,** which gives students a taste of the debate over how to make education more multicultural. As such, it invites students to reflect on the nature and purpose of the course you are teaching. Other chapters you might want to include are **Chapter 6, Gender; Chapter 7, Difference;** and perhaps **Chapter 8, Legends**.

What does popular culture mean? A course organized around this question would critically analyze subjects not usually thought of as scholarly or academic. You might initiate this conversation with **Chapter 3, Education,** which discusses implicitly and explicitly what American education ought to be about. Students could then subject to serious inquiry selections from **Chapter 8, Legends; Chapter 9, At Home**; and **Chapter 10, Work,** and perhaps some selections from **Chapter 4, Faith**.

Whatever individual chapters or readings you decide to assign, we recommend that you begin the course by asking students to read **Chapter 1, On Reading and Thinking Critically** and **Chapter 2, From Reading to Writing.** These chapters describe the kind of reading and writing that *The Presence of Others* asks students to do—reading and writing that are acts of meaning-making. These chapters can also provide you and your students with a common language for talking about reading and writing processes and with opportunities for self-reflection about those processes.

SPECIAL FEATURES

Each chapter in *The Presence of Others* includes special features designed to promote the idea of conversation among the various readings as well as among the students who join in that conversation. In addition, these features aim to make explicit that the reading and writing that people do is a product of their sometimes unique, sometimes socially shared positions. As you plan your course, you might want to think about how to use these special features to enhance students' understanding of not only the readings and the subjects they deal with but also of the acts of reading and writing.

Visual Texts
Each chapter includes one visual text that can be analyzed and studied in a variety of ways: in terms of who or what is represented (and how); what values are expressed; what effects the image has on viewers; the composition and purpose of the image; and how it relates to the written texts in the chapter. Visual texts can also be used as prompts for in-class writing exercises or response pieces. What associations do students have with the image? What emotions does it evoke? You could also ask students to write a short story, poem, or narrative essay in response to visual texts. Guidelines for "reading" visual texts begin on p. 6 of **Chapter 1, On Reading and Thinking Critically.**

Introductory Questions

Each chapter begins with a brief introduction to the subject of the chapter followed by general questions that invite students to explore the positions they already hold on the issue. You might want to ask students to write informally in response to these questions and to discuss their responses in small groups or as a whole class *before* they read the selections in the chapter. By discussing these questions, you and your class begin a conversation that the readings then contribute to, rather than the other way around. Answering these questions and exploring their initial positions on an issue can also help students gain insight into their responses to the readings and give them an opportunity to reflect on how the readings may have led them to change their positions.

Opening Quotations

Each chapter opens with a series of quotations, one from each reading. Asking students to respond to these quotations gives them another vehicle for exploring what they know about a subject before they read the selections. For example, you might have students read the quotations (which they might think of as snippets of a conversation that they have the opportunity to get in on) and to write a reading log entry or in-class response in which they describe or anticipate, based on the quotes, some of the important issues that will be addressed in the readings of the chapter. You can also ask them what they can guess about the author and the reading based on the quote.

Initial Readings

For each chapter, one selection was chosen to serve as the initial reading, the conversation starter, so to speak. In some cases, for example John Henry Newman's *The Idea of a University* and Mary Shelley's *Frankenstein*, these initial readings are well known or canonical texts which the other readings in the chapter might logically be said to respond to. But in other cases the initial readings were selected because they raise interesting questions the other readings seem to address. (Generally, for each selection, one of the "Making Connections" questions connects the selection to the initial reading.) In either case, it might be useful for students to recognize that the conversations in each chapter have been *constructed* by the authors of this book and to realize that an important critical reading skill is the ability to see—and to create—connections among seemingly disparate ideas.

A Range of Views

In selecting readings for each chapter, our first goal was to create an interesting conversation, and for us that meant presenting as many different points of view in as many different voices and discourse forms as possible. Although it may be tempting to ask students to read only those selections that you like and agree with (criteria that are often related), we encourage you to give students—and yourself—the opportunity to hear and to respond to even those voices that make you shake with anger or annoyance. If your classroom is like most, the text that you like least or find the least persuasive will be the one some students like most—and vice versa. Differences in response and the reasons for those differences can provoke important self-reflection and productive class discussion.

Opportunities for Questioning the Text, Making Connections, and Joining the Conversation
After each reading, students are invited to do a variety of kinds of writing in response to the text. In "Questioning the Text," students are often asked to do a close analysis of some aspect of the text—to define key terms or analyze the author's tone. Students are also often asked in these questions to describe their initial reaction to the selection or to the subject of the selection. "Making Connections" questions help students create links among various selections in the chapter, including the initial reading, readings that offer a sharply contrasting point of view, and readings that seem on the surface to share that selection's point of view. The final set of questions, "Joining the Conversation," invites students to articulate their own position on or ideas about issues raised in the selection, often giving suggestions for doing additional research (library research, interviews, surveys, observation). Many of these writing assignments encourage students to work together in small groups and to present their findings to the class, activities that further emphasize the importance of conversation in the making of knowledge and the collective nature of most intellectual inquiry.

Editors' Profiles, Annotations, and Responses
The editors' profiles and their annotations of and responses to one reading in each chapter can serve as models for how students might articulate their own responses to readings—and their reasons for responding as they do. Because the editors often take different positions on issues and have markedly different responses to readings, students can see that there is not just one correct interpretation of a text or one acceptable position on an issue. You may wish to begin the course by writing your own profile and asking students to do the same; such profiles can be read aloud in class early in the term and function as introductions and serve as a reminder that all voices (teacher, student, editors, authors) are important. Many of the questions at the end of readings invite students to write responses similar in form to the editors' annotations and afterwords (and to keep track of those responses throughout the course by putting them in a reading log). If you will be asking students to do this kind of writing, you might want to begin each chapter by assigning the annotated selection and asking students to respond to the annotations and editors' responses as well as the reading, perhaps referring back to the editors' profiles for some explanation of why they responded as they did. Although a few students may read this material carefully without explicit instructions to do so, many students may skim it or ignore it completely.

Other Readings
Each chapter ends with a bibliography of other readings related to the chapter topic. These books, articles, and Web sites can be valuable resources for students who wish to research the topic further, and serve as reminders that there are other voices in the conversation.

Sequenced Writing Assignments
We have provided one sequenced writing assignment for each chapter. These assignments ask students to pursue a sustained line of inquiry over a series of related writing assignments that usually include personal responses to the texts, critical analyses of the texts, an articulation of their own positions on an issue in light of their experiences and their reading, and a critical analysis of their positions.

Part One How We Learn

3 ■ Education: The Idea of a University (p. 35)

This chapter gives students a taste of the ongoing and frequently heated debate over what and who higher education is for. Consequently, it is a good chapter to do near the beginning of the course since it invites students to join a conversation about issues immediately relevant to them and that they may have already thought about. To give students the sense that they are familiar with the conversation articulated in this chapter, you might ask them to explore in writing their views on higher education before they read (and find themselves influenced by) the selections in this chapter. You might also ask students to talk in small groups about their responses to the questions at the end of the introduction to this chapter and to consider the ways in which (and perhaps the reasons why) their responses differ.

As you plan your discussion of this chapter, you might want to keep in mind some of the questions raised by the selections:

- Should colleges and universities serve to pass on to students the great traditions and values of Western culture? (Newman, Bloom, Rose)

- Do colleges and universities need to change to accommodate students once excluded from the university? (Rich, Steele, Rose, hooks, Brooks)

- Should colleges and universities emphasize a unified view of culture and the commonalties among people or should they emphasize people's differences? (Newman, Rich, Steele, Rose, hooks, Cheney)

- What is (and should be) the relationship between the university and society? (Newman, Rich, Bloom, Steele, Rose, Cheney)

- What should be the relationship between teachers and students in the classroom? (Cheney, Zawodniak)

- In what ways is knowledge acquired, passed on, or made in the university? Are some ways better than others? (Newman, Rich, Rose, Cheney, Zawodniak, Postman)

JOHN HENRY NEWMAN The Idea of a University (p. 39)

John Henry Newman's text argues passionately for what might now be called a traditional liberal arts education, one that teaches students to see humanity, culture, and the natural world as an intimately related and coherent whole. Newman also emphasizes the value of knowledge for its own sake and argues that universities are responsible for raising the intellectual tone of society. No matter what type of college students attend, though, they may have trouble getting beyond the difficulty of Newman's style to a consideration of his ideas.

Questions 1 and **3** ask students to deal with the difficulty of Newman's text by thinking about the contemporary relevance of his ideas. **Question 2** asks students to write explicitly about their experience of reading Newman, and thus gives them a place to talk about what they might have found boring or difficult about the text. All of these questions give students practice being self-reflective about their reading. These questions also introduce students to the idea that readers construct meaning from texts, in part, by considering the relevance of the text to their experience.

The relevance of Newman and the difficulty of reading him are good topics for a small group or whole class discussion that could lead students to see that their attitude toward Newman's text is a product of their history of reading, their attitude toward education, their personal experience, etc. By discussing these issues with others, students can see that their experience of reading Newman and their interpretation of him might be different from that of their teacher or peers and that the classroom itself can be seen as a site of conversation about particular texts and our reading of them.

Questions 4 and **5** ask students to reconsider Newman's idea of a university in light of two contemporary accounts of what a college education should be like. Although it may be fairly easy for students to see the similarities between Newman and Allan Bloom's idea of a university, students should be encouraged to consider how any criticisms they had of Newman (e.g. that his idea of a university may not be relevant to contemporary education) may also be true of Bloom. Similarly, if students find Bloom's idea of a university persuasive, you might ask them to reconsider any criticisms they had of Newman—are his ideas really as out-of-date as they might have seemed at first?

Students might be tempted to oversimplify Mike Rose's text by noting only the ways in which the diversity of the students he describes would make it difficult for them to fit into a university that emphasized a unified view of culture and the benefits of knowledge for its own sake. You might ask them to consider whether some of the specific students Rose describes (or marginalized or disadvantaged students in general) could benefit from an education that aimed to train people to be good members of society and to raise the intellectual tone of society. Either of these questions could be used as the basis of a longer or more formal writing assignment.

These questions invite students to use Newman's ideas as a means of evaluating the state of higher education today (**Questions 6** and **7**). To do so, students will need to draw on both their understanding of Newman's ideas of higher education and their own ideas about what higher education should be. Students could base their analysis of higher education on a variety of sources—an analysis of their own and others' educational experiences (the kind of material that **Question 8** might elicit), an in-depth analysis of their own college or university (based on a close reading of their college catalog or their college's core requirements), a survey of recent news stories and magazine and journal articles, or other readings in this chapter. Given that these questions ask students to take a position on such a large issue, you might ask students to write on one of these questions only after they have read several of the readings from this chapter.

ADRIENNE RICH   What Does a Woman Need to Know? (p. 44)

Although more contemporary than John Henry Newman, Adrienne Rich's text, a commencement address given in 1979, might also seem out-of-date to students—or conversely, they may find her too radical to be relevant. Many students respond negatively to feminist texts, and those students are likely to reject Rich's suggestions for what a woman needs to know. It may be helpful to spend some time discussing what the word "feminist" means to students and how Rich's text fits or doesn't fit the associations they have with feminism. As well, you may wish to spend some class time discussing the commencement address genre and Rich's audience, graduates of an all women's college. How might the genre and audience account for the content and tone of Rich's speech?

Question 1 asks students to consider the term "power" and the ways that term is used in Rich's speech. This question also asks students to compare Rich's understandings of power with their own understandings. The associations students have with the word "power"—negative and/or positive—are likely to affect their response to Rich. Question 2 asks students to identify the reasons and evidence Rich uses in arguing what women need to know. Before answering Question 2, students should list the three broad areas of knowledge Rich calls for; then they can identify her reasons and evidence. You may also wish to have small or large group discussions regarding whether or not students find Rich's reasons and support effective. Are the types of support Rich uses persuasive to students? Why or why not? What others types of support could she have used?

The "Making Connections" questions ask students to put Rich into dialogue with John Henry Newman and Lynne V. Cheney. Although Question 4 does not explicitly ask students to write a dialogue between Rich and Newman, that would be one way to get students to "respond" to Newman. (It would also be a good way to see how students interpret Rich and Newman as "characters," and would provide a basis for a discussion of the ethos or persona that writers create.) Another possibility would be to ask students to write a letter from Rich to Newman in which she responds to his understanding of students' basic needs.

Question 5 does explicitly ask students to write a dialogue between Rich and Cheney on the subject of "what a university should teach its students." While the students are given the topic to write on, you may wish to ask them to choose a specific place to set the dialogue—a coffee shop, at a university or political debate, in Cheney's office, in Rich's living room. In class, you could discuss how the place affected the conversation. What might these women say to one another if they were talking in private that they wouldn't say in a public forum?

In responding to Question 6, students will need to employ research techniques that many are unfamiliar with. They may need to work in groups or as a class to think of all the ways in which they can investigate how their university has changed to accommodate women. Since students new to the university will not have their own experience to draw on, they may need to interview women faculty members, read old campus newspapers or yearbooks, consider changes in curriculum by reading several years of sample syllabi, and so on. Students may also wish to consider whether different departments have accommodated women in different ways. Do some departments accommodate women better than others? Because of the demands of this kind of research, students may benefit from doing this project collaboratively. Since the second part of **Question 6** asks students to write an editorial for the campus newspaper, they may also want to bring in sample editorials from that paper so that, as a class, you can discuss the genre of editorial writing.

Question 7 will help students consider the types of knowledge they find important for women and men. It also encourages them to compare their essays and think about points of agreement and disagreement. You may want to encourage students to also include *why* they believe men and women need to know certain things.

ALLAN BLOOM The Student and the University (p. 52)

As J.R. notes in his introduction, Allan Bloom's text expresses many of the same sentiments expressed in John Henry Newman's text, particularly the idea that a liberal education should represent a unified view of the world and humanity's place in it and that such an education should raise the intellectual tastes of students. An important difference between the two texts is that Newman's is a proposal for a new university while Bloom's is a critique of existing universities; thus Newman's tone is hopeful, Bloom's somewhat despairing. **Question 1** helps students consider Bloom's tone.

Although it is interesting to compare Bloom to Newman, who shares his idea of what a university should be, it is important for students to consider in what ways students would not benefit from such a university (**Question 5**). The reading from Mike Rose's *Lives on the Boundary* provides a good source for students to use in testing the value of Bloom's idea of a university for specific students. (Students should also be encouraged to consider how they would fare in the kind of university Bloom advocates.) Of course, Bloom explicitly acknowledges that his critique is aimed at the most prestigious institutions—as distinguished from most state schools—and this acknowledgment (**Question 2**), which students may overlook, should lead students to consider once again whether there can be (as Newman implies) a single model of education that would benefit everyone, or whether, as Rose and Rich imply, the university must change to accommodate the needs of students once marginalized or excluded from the university. Questions to ask might include: Should different kinds of education be available, or is there a certain kind of education that all students should receive? One way to give students entry into this question is to ask them to think about the function of tracking students in high school, or they could talk in small groups about differences and similarities in their high school education.

Question 3 asks students to consider the strengths and weakness of an analogy Bloom uses and to come up with their own analogies. This specific question might be carried over into a more general class discussion about the uses of analogy and other types of metaphor in writing and linked to a discussion of Postman's ideas concerning metaphor, meaning, and how language shapes our understanding of the world.

Questions 7, 8, and **9** allow students to engage with Bloom's critique in a personal way by considering how their ideas about their own education might be like (or unlike) Bloom's. Although **Question 7** does not explicitly ask students to refer to their experience, it might be helpful for them to use their experience in college thus far (most first-year students take a variety of introductory courses) as an example of why Bloom is right (or wrong) in saying that "a smattering of introductory courses" gives students an inadequate perspective on learning.

Question 9 may prove intimidating to beginning students, especially those who think of themselves as poor readers. In addition to asking students to draw from books they have read, you might encourage them to list all the books or authors they read in high school (or college classes so far) and to talk in groups about which of these books should be considered "great" and why.

SHELBY STEELE The Recoloring of Campus Life (p. 63)

If this reading is the first annotated piece your students will be confronting, prior to assigning it you will need to think about how you want them to use the annotations and the reading responses. You may also want to use Shelby Steele's text and various editorial commentary on it as the basis of a discussion on the positioned nature of reading and writing. In particular, students could consider how the way Steele positions himself in this piece (for example, as a black man who every six months or so experiences a racial slur) affects them as readers (Question 3). Students might also compare the effect of Steele's positioning with that of Mike Rose, bell hooks (Question 5), or Christian Zawodniak, all of whom bring their personal experiences to bear on the subject of education, or compare the effect of Steele's text to those in which the authors do not talk about their personal experiences (Newman, Bloom, Cheney, Postman).

One of the reasons many readers find Steele's text persuasive is that he rejects the idea of entitlement programs as a means of redressing the wrongs done to African Americans in this country in spite of the fact that he continues to experience some of these wrongs—like hearing "nigger" being yelled from a passing car. Question 3 asks students to write about such an incident and/or to imagine how such an incident would make a person feel. If a student hasn't been a victim of a racial slur, he or she may wish to think about times when insults are the result of other kinds of hate—sexism, classism, homophobia. And they could also be encouraged to reflect on what it means to have never been the victim of these kinds of hate. It is also possible to extend the question and to ask students to write about an incident in which they uttered a racial slur or were in the company of someone who did.

Another reason students may find Steele's text persuasive is that he offers what seem to be clear and reasonable explanations for some of the more troubling manifestations of racism in the United States. By asking students to trace one of these cause and effect analyses (Question 2), for example, the argument that a politics of difference causes increased racial tension on campuses, they can better assess what makes Steele's argument persuasive—or not persuasive—for them as readers. Students would thus get practice in responding not just to the substance of Steele's argument but to the argumentative strategies he employs.

Like Newman and Bloom, Steele advocates an education that would stress the unity of culture and the commonalties among students rather than their differences. Question 6 asks students to consider how well Newman's concept of the university would work given the problems with "differences" that Steele describes. Is Newman's concept of the university a viable solution to the problem of difference?

Question 5 asks students to compare Steele's idea of education, with its emphasis on commonality, with that of bell hooks, who argues that students must find a way to preserve their ties to their home cultures, especially when those cultures are markedly different from the culture of school. Because both Steele and hooks are African Americans, it is interesting for students to note how the language and tone of their texts differ and to consider how these differences might be related to the different audiences each is hoping to persuade. Although Steele's text is from a book that might be said to address African Americans, his ideas have been enormously popular with conservative whites as well. And while hooks's text is aimed at black feminist women, her work has been popular with white feminists as well.

Questions 7, 8, and 9 give students the opportunity to articulate their position on some of the issues raised by Steele. Although many students have strong opinions about affirmative action, few have actually researched how specific affirmative action programs work; Question 7 gives them a chance to do so. Similarly, Question 8 gives students the chance to express their opinion about what may be a hot debate on their campus—the establishment of special dorms or cultural centers for specific groups. Question 9 asks students to consider whether Steele's analysis of black-white relationships is true of other groups on campus. Again, this is a good opportunity for students to explore their thinking about current campus issues and to consider the similarities (and differences) among categories of difference like race, gender, sexual orientation, and religion.

BELL HOOKS Keeping Close to Home: Class and Education (p. 85)

Although bell hooks's text focuses on her experience as a poor black woman from the rural south who attended a prestigious, predominantly white university, she also addresses the larger conflict many students feel between their alliance to their home culture and the pressure to assimilate to the culture represented by their college or university. Question 1 asks students to consider in what ways their college or university is pressuring them to assimilate, and students should be encouraged to reflect on how that pressure makes them feel. Questions 6 and 7 also ask students to use hooks's analysis of her experience to interpret their own experience, to consider how coming to college may have changed their relationship to their families or home communities (something most students feel the first time they return home for a visit), or to consider how their experiences with people who are different from them (which most colleges and universities provide in roommates, classmates, college professors) may have clarified or sharpened their sense of who they are.

One way in which students may feel pressured to assimilate is in their writing class. In order to make explicit the issue of what academic writing is and should be, students can look at both what hooks says about academic writing and also at how her text reflects or resists an academic style as she defines it (Question 2). Students might then think about their experiences with college-level writing and work together to come up with a definition of academic writing—both what it is and what it is not (Question 8). In doing so, students could be encouraged to keep track of the ways in which their individual definitions of academic writing might differ and to consider where their ideas of acceptable academic writing have come from.

By comparing hooks's ideas about education to those of Mike Rose and Shelby Steele (Questions 4 and 5), students will have to deal more directly with the particular difficulties faced by students who are from groups underrepresented in the university.

Although hooks does not describe having difficulty academically at Stanford, she does describe what it felt like not to fit in—and to not want to fit in. In this respect she is likely to agree with Rose (see **Question 4**) that a traditional Great Books education is inevitably exclusionary and that such an education should include an analysis of who it excludes and why. And she is likely to disagree with Steele's critique of a politics of difference and his idea that a university should emphasize commonalties among people. Given hooks's affirmation of differences (**Question 1**), especially those of race and social class, it will be interesting for students to imagine how she would respond to Steele's contention that a politics of difference reinforces the myth that African Americans are inferior (**Question 5**).

MIKE ROSE Lives on the Boundary (p. 97)

Like Adrienne Rich, Mike Rose is especially concerned with how to make the university more accessible to those students once excluded from it. The students who most interest Rose are those often thought of as "not college material" and labeled "remedial" or "underprepared," for example, immigrants, the poor, high school drop-outs, adults returning to the classroom after years of work or child-rearing. (**Questions 3** and **5** ask students to focus on individuals whom Rose describes.) Students are likely to have mixed reactions to Rose's text, depending on their own background and educational experience. For example, students from more privileged backgrounds may feel that students like those Rose describes don't belong in college, while students who share characteristics of Rose's students may be made uncomfortably self-conscious by his text.
  Although it is important to talk about what higher education has to offer underprepared students, it might be beneficial to first take up Rose's assertion that successful (and failed) educational experiences are more social than intellectual in nature. Is such a statement true for all students or more true for those who are intimidated by school? **Questions 1, 2,** and **6** ask students to think about their own experience in working toward an answer to this question. Adrienne Rich, Lynne V. Cheney, Christian Zawodniak, and Neil Postman also emphasize the importance of social and material conditions for learning while John Henry Newman and Allan Bloom describe education primarily in terms of books, academic subjects, and intellectual questions (**Question 4**).
  Questions 2 and **7** ask students to think about the relationship between home culture and school culture as illustrated both by Rose's text and their own experience. (The essay by bell hooks also explores the complex relationship between home and school.) By asking students to work together, **Question 7** gives students the opportunity to consider how differences in their own and their classmates' early literacy experiences may have affected their reading and writing in school. From a consideration of these differences, students may be better prepared to consider the differences of Rose's students.

LYNNE V. CHENEY PC: Alive and Entrenched (p. 112)

Depending on their own political (and personal) views, students are likely to respond to Lynne V. Cheney's piece in vastly different ways—some are likely to find her views affirming, while others may be deeply angered. But most students (and teachers) have probably felt silenced at one time or another in the classroom because their views differ significantly from the views of the teacher or other students—whether they support affirmative action or not, whether they consider themselves feminists or not. You may wish to begin discussion of this piece by asking students to relate times when they have felt silenced in the classroom because of their views—whether those views were liberal or conservative. You could begin by having students write in class in response to **Question 4,** which asks students to reflect on whether they usually feel free speaking in class, or whether they sometimes feel coerced into silence. Or students could begin by responding to **Question 7** which asks them to identify political currents and attitudes in the writing class and to decide whether their experiences reinforce or contradict Cheney's observations.

How you teach this piece will probably depend on whether you think all positions are political and how you interpret Cheney's understanding of "ideological teaching." It might be useful to spend some time thinking about the principles behind your own teaching practice, and consider sharing those principles with your students (and consider how sharing or not sharing your principles might silence your students or you). **Question 9** invites students to define how political a college instructor should be, and encourages them to think about how the context of a particular class might affect their definitions.

In **Questions 5** and **6**, students are asked make connections between Cheney's piece and two other readings in the chapter. **Question 5** asks students what values Cheney and Rose might share; attempting to find such common ground between seemingly disparate views concerning the nature of "truth" should also help students consider their own understandings of truth and how those understandings affect their educational expectations. **Question 6**, which asks students to read Rich's text in light of Cheney's criticisms and write a position paper on the politics in both essays, implicitly reminds students that while Cheney points to feminist and "liberatory pedagogy" as political and ideological, her piece is political as well.

You may wish to have students address **Questions 1** and **8** in the same assignment or class discussion. While **Question 1** asks students to compare an experience they have had with diversity training to the experiences of the students Cheney describes, **Question 8** allows students to go a step further and propose an event that might "foster greater community" among different people, an event that might avoid some of the pitfalls of diversity training Cheney describes.

CHRISTIAN ZAWODNIAK "I'll Have to Help Some of You More Than I Want To": Teacher Power, Student Pedagogy (p. 124)

Unlike the other pieces included in the education chapter, Christian Zawodniak's piece is written from the perspective of a student who is still in college. Like Cheney, Zawodniak deals with issues of power—the power teachers and students hold—in the classroom, but his tone is different. He seems to write for self-understanding and because he believes students' voices should be heard, but his essay also contains an argument, an argument for teachers to actively participate in the classroom and welcome students to do the same. **Question 5** asks students to consider how John Henry Newman would react to Zawodniak's call for "student-centered" pedagogy; it might also be interesting to ask students how they respond to such a call and if they have ever been a member of a student-centered class. If they have, how were issues of power negotiated? **Question 6** invites reflection on issues of power in the classroom and asks students if their experiences support Zawodniak's observations.

      Questions 1, 2, and **3** prompt students to think about Zawodniak's position as a student and his representation of "Jeff," the teacher. **Question 2** asks how in her headnote A.L. builds Zawodniak's credibility and asks students to consider what in the essay allows them to identify with the author and what keeps them from identifying. Does her headnote make the narrative that follows more authoritative? You may wish to ask whether or not students find Zawodniak as "authoritative" as other writers in the chapter—why or why not? Does his position as a student affect his persuasiveness one way or the other? **Question 3** deals with Zawodniak's use of his teacher's first name and asks what effect that has on the reader. You could ask students if they refer to their own teachers by first name; if so, what effect—if any—does this have on the way they view the teacher?

NEIL POSTMAN The Word Weavers / The World Makers (p. 133)

According to J.R.'s introduction, Postman suggests that schools don't so much as teach facts as provide perspectives on a world shaped by language, particularly the language of metaphor. As you begin discussing Postman's piece, you may want to ask students to think of their own metaphors or similes for education, teachers, and students. You could have students develop extended metaphors or analogies: If a teacher is like a coach and students make up a team, then what is the big game? Students will, no doubt, come up with more interesting similes—one of our students told us that "teachers are like Tupperware." Our puzzled response: "You have to press down in the center to get the air out?"

      Question 6 asks students to characterize the metaphors Postman uses to describe the process of learning, and they are encouraged to ponder whether and how metaphors shape the way we see things and how language shapes our understanding of the world (**Questions 3** and **6**). **Question 7** provides an exercise to show how similes shape descriptions of language, and **Question 3** invites students to consider the language of education. To emphasize that language in educational settings may not be monolithic, **Question 1** asks if students' experiences confirm or refute Postman's claim that each discipline has its characteristic way of speaking.

      Questions 2, 8, and **9** all point students to a consideration of technology—whether its history and implications should be taught in school (**Question 2**), how technology might be a kind of "Faustian bargain" (**Question 8**), and the advantages and disadvantages of particular technologies (**Question 9**). To answer these questions, students should be encouraged to draw from a variety of resources: their own experiences (some students have probably taken computer-supported classes; they might be asked whether the use of computers in the classroom enhanced or detracted from their learning); library research; Internet research (how does one become a critical reader of information on the Internet?); and so on. As a class, you might also make a list of some of the metaphors of modern technology: Internet metaphors—the information superhighway, the World Wide Web; space shuttles—*Challenger, Explorer,* missile names—Polaris, Poseidon.

GWENDOLYN BROOKS We Real Cool (p. 147)

Gwendolyn Brooks's short and well known poem describes the lives of a group of young men who "left school." As such, they are outsiders whose voices would not typically be heard in a conversation about the value of higher education. It is interesting then, for students to consider what those men, the speakers of the poem, might be saying about the relationship between education and "real life" (**Question 1**) and to imagine what the students described by Mike Rose, students who might also have been tempted to leave school, might say to the speakers of the poem (**Question 2**). **Question 3** invites students to write a poem on their own, perhaps in rap or some other contemporary form. In their poem, they might express their own or a fictional character's feelings about what school means to them.

Texts in Context: Sequenced Writing Assignments about Education

Assignment 1
Mike Rose and bell hooks both tell stories of moments in education that were particularly important to them. Spend some time thinking about the education you have received—the schools and classes you have attended, teachers you've had, books you've read, projects you've done. Then write a brief essay for members of your class telling them about a particularly important moment or event as concretely as possible, and explain why it was important to you.

Assignment 2
In recent years, the NBA and its players have mounted a large promotional campaign urging students everywhere to "Stay in School." The assumption of this campaign, as of a number of readings in this chapter (including those by Newman, Bloom, Brooks, Rose, and Rich) is that education provides a means to a better life. Reread several of these pieces and then reread the essay you wrote for assignment 1. Then draw up a list—with each item in complete sentence or paragraph form—of reasons to pursue an education, to "stay in school."

Assignment 3
Spend some time gathering and considering the metaphors several authors in this chapter use (or might use) to represent school or education. Newman, for example, might think of education as a lamp that illuminates or brings the light to us. What metaphors for education do you find in the essays by Shelby Steele, Mike Rose, or Adrienne Rich? Choose two or three readings and decide whether the metaphors associated with education and school are primarily positive or negative. Then spend some time brainstorming the metaphoric associations you have with education, noting whether they are primarily positive or negative. Finally, write a brief report intended for members of your class on "what a close look at metaphors reveals about attitudes toward education."

Assignment 4

Several writers in this chapter (including hooks and Cheney) explore ways in which educational institutions exert powerful pressures on students, pressures that are often oppressive or that favor conformity to certain ways of seeing the world and one's place in it. Look closely at one of the essays and try your hand at summarizing the argument it makes about the power of educational institutions to shape us in ways that may be harmful or counterproductive.

Assignment 5

Spend some time brainstorming about ways in which the educational institutions you have been part of have shaped or influenced you, have "written" you into your role as a certain kind of student. Then consider which influences have helped to give you a sense of personal power and which have perhaps given you a sense of helplessness or lack of power. Make detailed notes on these influences and be prepared to discuss them with your classmates, either in a small group or as a whole class.

Assignment 6

Read over your responses to and notes from assignments 1-5. Then prepare an essay for your class that presents your position on the place of higher education in American society and in your life. Consider the aims of education and how those aims do or do not carry out the larger goals of the United States as well as your own goals.

Assignment 7

Write a report to your instructor and classmates, explaining as much as possible why you took the stand you did in the essay for assignment 6, noting what in your experience has led you to that stance, and closing by reflecting on what you feel most confident about in that position and what you have some doubts about.

Part Two What We Believe

4 ■ Faith: One Nation, Under God (p. 150)

In this chapter, students are invited to join in a conversation about the importance of faith—faith in God, faith in traditional religions, faith in the American way of life, faith in stories—to individuals and to society. The introductory questions give students the opportunity to write about their own beliefs and values while also asking them to consider the relationship between faith and American society. It may be useful to ask students (individually, in small groups, or as a class) to come up with working definitions of "faith," "religion," and "spirituality"—key terms that recur in different contexts throughout the chapter. Students can also get a sense of the variety of approaches to "faith" that are represented in this chapter by asking them to eavesdrop on the conversation already in progress in the introductory quotes.

Some of the questions that recur throughout the chapter include:

■ What human needs does religious faith serve? (King, Elder and Wong, Brandt)

■ Do humans share in common a need to believe in something bigger than themselves? (King, Brandt)

■ What purposes do stories serve in relation to faith? (Elder and Wong, Carter, Brandt, Lee, Eliach)

■ Has America become secularized? Do Americans worship American god terms like "democracy," "individuality," "self-reliance," "prosperity" rather than some universal moral principle? (Herberg, Carter, Brandt)

■ Has faith in science replaced faith in God? (King, Herberg)

■ What should be the role of religion in the lives of children? (Brandt, Lee, Norris)

MARTIN LUTHER KING JR. Our God Is Able (p. 154)

One obvious example that students can use to respond to Martin Luther King's assertion that God is able to overcome evil (**Question 1**) is the civil rights movement itself. Although some students might see the advances made in civil rights as evidence that "God is able," others may want to argue that God had nothing to do with it, people did—people like Martin Luther King Jr. You might then encourage students to think about the relationship between people's faith in God, their belief that God supports their endeavors, and their subsequent commitment to those endeavors. More recent events motivated by religious belief include David Koresh's refusal to emerge from his compound in Waco, Texas, Sister Helen Prejean's work with death row inmates and her fight against the death penalty, and the anti-abortion activities of Operation Rescue.

After describing the view of life (which some might call cynical, others realistic) expressed in the Paul Laurence Dunbar poem King cites, students might be asked to discuss the consequences of holding such a view. They can also compare the view of life expressed in Dunbar's poem with that expressed by Martin Luther King Jr. (**Question 2**). Here, again, students may take up the question: What is the relationship between a person's view of life, a person's faith, and a person's actions?

Question 3, which asks students to consider what they already know or have heard about King, might be answered in class before students have read the King excerpt. As a follow up, students could write about how their view of King was affected by reading "Our God Is Able." What about the text affected them? Why were different people in the class affected differently?

The excerpts from Mary Shelley's *Frankenstein* consider the consequences of a science motivated only by human beings' desire for knowledge and power and carried out without concern for the larger forces that control the universe. (King would say "God.") For King, belief in science (or humanity's belief in itself) without an overriding belief in God can only lead to monstrous consequences (**Question 4**). Another reading in Chapter 5 that touches on the relationship between religion and science is Lewis Thomas's "Hazards of Science," which finds that religious arguments for limiting science are inappropriate.

Questions 5 and **7** ask students to think about faith in American society. Will Herberg's selection argues that what unites Americans is a shared belief in American values like democracy and individuality rather than a belief in universal moral principles (or God). King might very well label the America Herberg describes as one governed by a "man-centered" religion. King is also likely to question the degree to which the poor and African Americans living in the 1960s were invited to participate in this "common religion." As a follow up to **Question 5** (where students are asked to consider the relationship between what Herberg says Americans value and what King says Americans *should* value), students might find it useful to question whether Americans in the 1990s believe in the same god-terms Herberg identified in 1955. If not, what seem to be the current prevailing god-terms?

Question 8 raises the interesting issue of whether exclusionary language has different effects depending on the context. Given the subject of King's sermon, especially his concern for the oppressed and his belief in *universal* moral values, is his use of "man" to refer to all people more or less offensive? King's use of masculine pronouns might be compared to a more contemporary example, such as that of Allan Bloom in "The Student and the University" (Chapter 3).

WILL HERBERG This American Way of Life (p. 162)

Questions 1, 2, and **3** ask students to compare Will Herberg's view of American life—as illustrated by his definition of "democracy," his choice of key words, and particular sentences that now seem dated—with their sense of what America is like in the present. It might be interesting for students, working individually or in small groups, to attempt a "revision" of Herberg—write an updated definition of "democracy," if necessary, and define other key terms (perhaps keeping some of Herberg's, revising others, and adding new ones) that Americans in the 1990s seem to worship. You may also want students to consider differences in their views of America (and differences in their view of Herberg) and to offer explanations for those differences. These activities would give students some preparation in tackling the more extended writing they are asked to do in **Questions 6** and **7**.

Question 6 asks students to argue generally that the current American way of life (as they define it) is better or worse than the America of the 1950s. You may want to spend some time brainstorming with the class to come up with sources of evidence to support such an argument. What indicators do we use to judge how well off we are as Americans? **Question 5**, which asks students to compare the religious values espoused by Martin Luther King Jr. to the secular values described by Will Herberg, provides one way for students to talk about change in American culture. Is America more secular and less religious than it used to be?

Questions 7 and **8** ask students to consider their particular perspective on "the American way of life" by discussing either the degree to which they fit Herberg's definition of an American (**Question 6**) or by offering a description of a way of life with which they are familiar. You may want students to complicate their descriptions of "the Italian-American way of life" or "the Catholic way of life" by considering the relationship between the particular way of life they describe and the one described by Herberg. Is the Jewish-American or African-American or working-class way of life they describe compatible with the America Herberg describes?

Many students may have trouble pursuing **Question 9** on their own. If you ask them to write about the degree to which Americans' view of themselves may have changed as a result of national and world events, spend some class time discussing where our views of ourselves as Americans have come from and what sources they might use to give them ideas about how American views have (or have not) changed. The in-class preparation you do for **Question 6** would also be helpful here.

JOHN ELDER and HERTHA D. WONG The Creation (p. 166)

As A.L. points out in her introduction to this piece, "All cultures we know of tell stories that aim to answer the question of origin: where did we come from?" And most students will have an answer to that question, whether they believe in the big bang theory, the Genesis account, or some other story. **Question 6** asks students to write their own creation story—one they have heard before or one from their own imaginations. You could also encourage students to draw pictures to illustrate the story they tell; their own use of pictures might help them respond to **Question 1** which asks about the effect of the pictograms in the text and how they complement the words used to tell the story. If you have the students read their creation stories in class, you might also wish to have them reflect on how (or if) their stories reflect their values: If they've retold a traditional story, do they value tradition? Is the creative force in the story an individual or more communal? Does the story show process, ingenuity, patience?

You could also ask students what values are reflected in the Mohawk creation story and (using **Question 4** as a starting point) discuss the ways religious and spiritual values sometimes conflict with government regulations (on issues like the environment or even abortion or capital punishment). If you and your students agree that stories help reflect a culture's and/or a person's values, you could use this idea as a starting point for **Question 5**, a question asking what value Brandt might find in this Native American story. It may be helpful for students to answer **Question 6** in conjunction with **Question 7**, which encourages students to work collaboratively to find creation stories from religions and cultures they are not familiar with. In class, you could brainstorm resources for such an investigation and remind students that they can be resources for each other. Once the students collect a body of creation stories, you could analyze common elements in those stories or differences between the stories. **Question 2**, which asks students to list characteristics of Native American Earth-Diver myths, could help in the analysis, and students could also be asked to list characteristics of the stories they tell.

STEPHEN L. CARTER The Culture of Disbelief (p. 175)

The selection on "The Creation" invites you and your students to consider how stories and religious beliefs reflect both personal and community values. The questions concerning Carter's piece should help your class think about the complexities of expressing religious beliefs in public or political arenas—especially if and when those public arenas are centered more on secular values. This issue is taken up by **Question 8** in which students are asked to write about a time when they—or someone they know—experienced a conflict between religious and secular values.

Question 1 asks students to think about the personal tone of Carter's piece and to evaluate how this tone affects their consideration of Carter's argument. As you discuss this question, you can talk about different kinds evidence and which kinds of proofs you and your students find more persuasive and why. You may wish to refer to other readings in this chapter (as a way of comparing and contrasting) as you discuss tone and the use of personal narrative and examples.

In answering **Question 2**—about depictions of faith and religion in the popular media—you may wish to have students bring in examples for the class to analyze: clips from movies like *Dead Man Walking* or *Priest*, or television shows like *Touched by an Angel* or even soap operas or talk shows.

Question 3 also prompts students to analyze media attention to religion. In addition to searching for movie and television clips, students also should be attentive to what they see in newspapers or hear on the radio. As a class, you could brainstorm a list of events involving religion covered by the media--for example, the burning of predominantly black churches in the South or disagreements concerning prayer or religious symbols in public places. After an analysis of media representations, students can also test Carter's thesis by considering the presence or absence of religion in their immediate communities. They can draw upon their writing for **Question 8** and **Question 6** (which ask students to consider instances where professionals have been required to mute their expression of religious belief), consider the presence or absence of church-based community activities (like food drives, building or clean-up projects, street preachers or evangelistic outreaches, and so on), or look through newspapers noting both acclamations for and controversies surrounding behaviors based on religious belief. This discussion might also be linked to King's piece as you talk about the relationship between a person's faith and actions.

ANTHONY BRANDT Do Kids Need Religion? (p. 186)

If you are asking students to regularly annotate and/or write responses to the reading they are doing, you may want to begin each chapter with the annotated reading and ask students to read and write about the annotations fairly early in your discussion of the reading. **Question 3** explicitly asks students to respond to the editors' commentary on this text. In addition to comparing the kinds of questions each editor asks in his or her annotations, students might reread the editors' profiles and their annotations on other readings in an effort to explain why the editors have responded differently to Brandt's text. Students might then be asked to reread their annotations and/or their responses to Brandt and to reflect on why they responded in the way that they did.

Students could respond to **Question 1**, which asks them to describe the image of God they constructed as children, either before or after they read Brandt. In either case, it would be useful to have students read aloud and discuss their responses in small groups to give them the chance to consider how widely varying their religious backgrounds might be.

One way to organize a discussion of this reading would be to ask students to respond in several different ways to Anthony Brandt's question, "Do Kids Need Religion?" For example, students could write an informal response to this question before they read Brandt; they could then read and annotate Brandt with the purpose of answering **Question 2**, which asks them to describe how Brandt would answer this question. **Question 4** is a logical follow up to **Question 2** and asks them to answer Brandt's question either from the perspective of Martin Luther King Jr. or Andrea Lee. Finally, **Question 8** asks students to write a fully developed response to the question, one which could draw on their own experience, on the experiences of their peers (as revealed through small group or whole class discussions), on the readings in this chapter, or on additional research.

Another question that could guide discussion of this essay would be "What is the relationship between religion and spirituality?" Again, students could begin with their own definitions of those terms, then move to an explicit comparison of Brandt and King, for example, or Brandt and Carter (**Question 6**), or Brandt and Kathleen Norris (**Question 5**). This preliminary writing could lead students to a more extended exploration of the relationship between these two terms that might draw on several other readings from this chapter or other sources to help them reflect on the different ways religion, faith, and spirituality are reflected in various texts and lives.

ANDREA LEE New African (p. 196)

Since Lee's piece shows the place of religion in the life of the young character, Sarah, this might be a good story to link with Brandt's article. **Question 4** makes this link explicit in asking students to consider how Lee might respond directly to Brandt's question, "Do Kids Need Religion?" You may wish to have students assume Sarah's voice (either the voice of a child or an adult) in responding to Brandt and giving reasons for her answer to his question, or you can help your students make a distinction between author and character, asking them to consider whether Lee's answer to the question would be the same as Sarah's answer. Students could address a letter to Brandt from Sarah Phillips or Andrea Lee, or they could try to write a conversation between all three people. Another way to consider Sarah's perspective is to answer **Question 5**, which asks students to write a poem from Sarah's point of view about a little girl in church.

Of course, Sarah's point of view is important to an understanding of the story, and students should be encouraged to think about the ways Lee develops Sarah's character. One way that Lee develops Sarah's character is by showing how she responds to the religious symbols that surround her. **Question 1** should help students think about Lee's use of religious imagery; though the question doesn't specifically ask students to consider Sarah's role as narrator, as a follow up to **Question 1**, you might want to ask how Sarah responds to the religious symbols that surround her and how a child's understanding of religious symbols might differ from an adult's understanding. **Questions 6** and **7** ask students to consider further the relationship between children and adults in the New African Baptist Church and that relationship in the places of worship they might be familiar with. **Question 6** asks students to think about how particular religions view or represent children; in responding to this question, you could ask students to think about the ceremonies in which children are expected to participate in particular religious communities (bar mitzvah, baptism, confirmation, communion, etc.) and how those ceremonies welcome or alienate young people.

JOHN PAUL II A Minority by the Year 2000 (p. 208)

With the exception, perhaps, of Martin Luther King Jr., it is likely that John Paul II is the most well-known person represented in this chapter, and many students are likely not only to be familiar with the beliefs he represents, but also to have strong feelings about those beliefs. You may wish to begin discussion by asking your students what they already know about John Paul II and his beliefs and then move on to the specifics in this piece: the central themes, support used, positions represented.

Another way of talking about this selection is to make connections with other essays in the chapter: similarities and differences between John Paul II's attitude toward faith and the attitude expressed in Kathleen Norris's poem (**Question 3**); the similarity of a confident tone in both John Paul II's and King's selections and how that tone affects the appeal of their arguments (**Question 4**), and a continued exploration of issues Carter brings up concerning the difficulties people of faith encounter—or cause—in society (**Question 5**).

Questions 1 and **6** both deal with questions one might ask in an interview. In responding to these two questions, students should be encouraged to review the section on interviewing in Chapter 2 or even read Kevin Kelly's "Interview with the Luddite" in Chapter 5 to begin thinking about the types of questions one might ask in an interview setting. **Question 1** asks students to compose three questions they would ask the pope if they were interviewing him; you may also wish to ask the students why they would ask the questions they've composed and to imagine how the pope might answer those questions. **Question 6** helps students investigate attitudes toward the papacy by asking them to interview several Catholic friends and acquaintances. This question also points students to the library to do some research before generating the interview questions. The generation of questions could be accomplished effectively in groups, and if several members of the class administer the interviews, findings could also be compared and differences and similarities between attitudes could be discussed in class.

DIANA L. ECK In the Name of Religions (p. 212)

Many of the questions following Eck's article ask students, in one way or another, to consider religious diversity. **Question 1**, which asks students to relate the most surprising fact they discovered while reading Eck's article, is open-ended and probably a good question to have students to respond to in writing and/or in discussion. Discussion of such a question might reveal the religious diversity already present in the classroom and help students prepare to respond to **Question 2,** which focuses on working with others from different faiths to define key terms—Universalism, Fundamentalism, and Pluralism. In responding to this question, students could consider related questions like: Would an Islamic fundamentalist define fundamentalism the same way a Christian fundamentalist would? Would a Unitarian Universalist agree with Eck's representation of Universalism? Are the ideals of Pluralism likely to be supported by atheists, Buddhists, Jews, Christians? These questions should lead students to think about **Question 5**, which refers back to John Paul II's piece and asks them to think about how individual religious communities might react to Eck's call for "interreligious communication and cooperation." If there is religious diversity among the members of the class, students could be invited to answer this question by considering how they react to such a call, or students could try to imagine how other writers from the chapter—Eliach, King, Lee, Carter, or Norris—might react.

      Questions 6, 7, and **8** invite continued exploration of religious diversity by asking students to propose a college-level course in religious literacy (**Question 6**), to use various sources (the local phone book or World Wide Web sites) to explore religious diversity in their own communities (**Question 7**), and to write a paper on a religious community they were not greatly familiar with before their research (**Question 8**). While some students may find such exploration exciting, others may not be as open to exploring diversity (some people are likely to feel threatened by religious diversity). Before discussion, you may wish to consider how you will deal with differing positions in the classroom and how you will negotiate differing positions on the subject of religious diversity.

YAFFA ELIACH Good Morning, Herr Müller (p. 218)

As the questions following "Good Morning, Herr Müller" imply, stories and tales generally have a moral or lesson—though that lesson is not always explicit. **Questions 1, 2,** and possibly **4** should help students reflect on the lessons this tale teaches—lessons about proper titles and names (**Question 1**) and the importance of greeting one's fellow humans (**Question 2**). **Question 2** also invites students to make a list of additional lessons this story might teach. The list students make may help provide a foundation for answering **Question 4**: Would it be appropriate for students in public schools to read Hasidic tales like "Good Morning, Herr Müller"? Students' answer to this question might depend, in part, on the lessons they think this tale teaches.

Questions 5, 6, and 7 ask students to analyze the ways stories are constructed and told—and to consider the effects those constructions achieve. **Question 5** asks students to compare elements like tone, purpose, and length in the story Eliach tells and in Lee's story, "New African." In answering **Question 6**, students will share tales they've heard before, then write a tale structured like "Good Morning, Herr Müller." By telling tales and then writing one modeled after one they've read, students can see first hand how structure can affect content. This exercise should help students respond to **Question 7**, which asks them to research the way(s) "the history of the Holocaust has been recorded and told" and to write a report on some aspect of this story. Some students might choose to write about genre (Holocaust poetry, fiction, nonfiction); others might be interested in who tells Holocaust stories and how the story might change depending on who tells it.

The Qur'an Prayer (p. 221)

In her introduction to this prayer, A.L. points out the importance of reading it aloud. Before beginning discussion of this prayer, you may wish to have one of your students read it aloud in class—or you could read it aloud as a group. One way of discussing this prayer is to have students try to remember prayers from childhood (bedtime prayers, prayers before meals, or prayers spoken corporately in a place of worship) and then compare and contrast the Qur'an prayer to ones they already know.

Questions 1, 2, and 3 deal specifically with the prayer as text, inviting students to consider the most powerful line (**Question 1**), the characteristics that make it a prayer (**Question 2**), and the effect of the repetition of words in the prayer (**Question 3**). In addition to these considerations, you could also talk about the purpose of prayers and the functions they serve for people of various faiths. **Question 7** offers one possible purpose of prayer: to express wishes or needs; this question also invites students to write a prayer of their own. After writing their prayer, students could analyze their own prayers: To whom or what are various prayers addressed? Are there different kinds of prayers? Ones that make petitions, others that demonstrate thanks or praise? You could also ask your students why they think certain prayers have been recorded in writing, and you could discuss the differences between memorized and spontaneous prayers—do they serve different purposes?

To respond to **Question 8**, students must have a good deal of time—at least a week or more—in order to do the research, work with each other, and then work up a presentation for the class. If you have your students do group presentations during the term, this might be a good option for them. The presentation this question calls for would also provide the background for an even richer discussion regarding the prayer.

KATHLEEN NORRIS Little Girls in Church (p. 223)

The speaker in Norris's "Little Girls in Church" is an adult woman who, through her observation of and interaction with others, reflects on the condition of her own faith and shows concern for other girls in church. While the first six stanzas relate a series of experiences and memories, the final stanza is a direct address to little girls in church and a hope or prayer on their behalf. You may wish to ask your students to talk about the tensions between the spiritual (the Great Litany, icons, confession, prayer) and mundane (lace collars, church bulletins, sleeping, smoking) imagery in this poem and what that imagery says about the persona's faith. As well, you could ask how Kathy's drawing of "the moon, / grass, stars" functions as a metaphor for the wish the speaker expresses in the final stanza: that the girls may "find great love / . . . starlike / and wild, as wide as grass, / solemn as the moon." Or you could focus your discussion on the questions at the end of the poem, encouraging students to remember songs from their own childhood (**Question 1**) or asking them to relate their own beliefs in the form of a poem that they can then share with the class (**Question 2**). Perhaps students can create their own metaphors, metaphors grounded in concrete imagery, for their own expression of faith.

Texts in Context: Sequenced Writing Assignments about Faith

Assignment 1
Reread Kathleen Norris's poem (p. 223), and consider the place of song in her expression of faith. Then reread the Qur'an Prayer (p. 221). With several members of your class, brainstorm about songs you sang or prayers you said as a child. Try to remember them as exactly as possible and talk about each one in turn, noting what they imply we should have faith in. Then try your hand at writing the lyrics of a song or prayer you would like to teach your children or children close to you.

Assignment 2
Look at the prayer or song you or a classmate wrote and compare it to the Qur'an Prayer and to Martin Luther King Jr.'s sermon (p. 154). Start by listing the things the Qur'an Prayer suggests we have faith in. Then make similar lists for your own song or poem/prayer and for King's sermon. Do you find anything in common on the three lists? What differences are most striking to you? Write a couple of paragraphs about the similarities and differences you see in these lists of what we should have faith in and bring them to class for discussion.

Assignment 3
Andrea Lee's story shows how certain people can be very manipulative and coercive in the name of faith or religion. Reread Lee's story and then look through the Brandt piece to see if you can find any other suggestion of any negative effects of certain kinds of religious faith. Add any other examples you can think of that suggest ways in which religion or faith may have been harmful to some. Make notes on your explorations and bring them to class for discussion.

Assignment 4
Based on your thinking and discussions thus far, compose an extended definition of faith, including examples as well as positive and negative consequences you associate with faith. Make your definition at least one hefty paragraph in length. Then meet with several class members to compare definitions and talk about what the paragraphs do and do not have in common. Finally draw up a brief report of your discussions for the whole class (titled,

perhaps, "Current Thinking on Faith in America"), noting any points on which you and the other writers seem to agree and any on which you disagree.

Assignment 5

Return to your brainstormed lists in assignments 2 and 3 and your definition in assignment 4 and use them as the basis for coming up with 12 words or phrases that characterize your faith or religious beliefs. Be as free-wheeling as you want: just come up with 12 words or phrases as quickly as you can. Then return to the readings in this chapter and to one of the writers whose beliefs differ from yours. Make another list—again quickly—of 12 words or phrases that come to mind to characterize the other writer's belief(s). With a group of classmates, look at these lists of words and phrases, asking why you have chosen the words in each set and what those sets suggest about your attitudes toward the beliefs and faiths of others. Finally, write a letter to an author in this chapter whose beliefs differ from yours. In the letter, begin by noting any points on which you and the other writer seem to agree and then explain as clearly as you can why you hold the beliefs you do.

Assignment 6

Look at the letter you wrote in assignment 5, rereading the work of the author you were writing to. How would this author be likely to "read" your letter? Write the brief response that you think the author might well make to you. In what ways does the response help you think in new or different ways about what you said in your letter? Record your responses to this question in your reading log.

Assignment 7

Finally, work out an essay intended for your class and entitled "Do People Need Religion?" In the essay, make sure you define what you mean by religion along the way and also offer as many good reasons as possible in support of your answer.

5 ■ Science: O Brave New World (p. 227)

In this chapter, students are asked to think about the nature of science and the role that science has played in American culture and the world at large. In particular, this chapter explores Americans' seemingly contradictory attitude toward science. On the one hand, Americans revere science and are in awe of its power to discover what was once thought unknowable and to do what was once thought undoable. On the other hand, Americans fear the power of science to escape the control of human beings. The introductory questions invite students to explore their own ideas about and attitudes toward science as well as to consider the role that science has played in American culture. This chapter presents a number of different voices—scientists and nonscientists—conversing about science (as illustrated by the opening quotations) and students should be encouraged to consider why people—themselves included—express such different attitudes toward something that is not often seen as controversial. Some of the questions that the selections in this chapter address include:

■ Should the quest for (scientific) knowledge be boundless? (Shelley, Thomas, Kelly, Bishop, Birkerts)

■ What drives human beings to seek scientific knowledge of the world? (Shelley, Thomas, Kelly, Martin)

■ What is the relationship between religion (or faith) and science? (Thomas, Bishop, Rohrer)

■ Whose interests should science serve? (Shelley, Thomas, Martin, Kelly)

■ What is the relationship between science and reality? (Shelley, Rohrer)

MARY SHELLEY Frankenstein (p. 230)

Some students may find it strange that the initial reading for this chapter is an excerpt from one of the earliest science fiction novels written. Although "science fiction" contains the word "science," many students think of science fiction as escapist literature and think of science as a dry litany of facts to be memorized. Perhaps only those students actively involved in science will have thought about the relationship of the imagination to scientific inquiry. Mary Shelley's text foregrounds this relationship and highlights the human origins—as well as the human consequences—of science, something discussed by many of the other authors represented in this chapter. (See especially Lewis Thomas, Kevin Kelly, J. Michael Bishop, Emily Martin, and Sven Birkerts.)

Questions 1 and 2 draw attention to Victor Frankenstein's motivation and his single-minded pursuit of giving "life to an animal as complex and wonderful as man." As students respond to Question 1 by annotating the text and considering what motivates Frankenstein, they are likely to point to imagination, past successes and hope for future improvement, the desire to accomplish something great, and the pursuit of knowledge as some of Frankenstein's driving forces. As students consider another part of **Question 1**—whether these motives account for modern scientific development and technology—you can ask them to make connections with other readings in this chapter, having them point to others (**Question 5** points to Lewis Thomas and J. Michael Bishop) who might be motivated by these same forces. Are these motivations good ones? Do good motivations sometimes lead to negative consequences? If so, what should be the relationship between ambition and action?

Question 2 takes up the issues of ambition and behavior by asking what Frankenstein has to do to himself and others in order to create his monster, and this question asks students to write about the consequences, good or bad, of single-minded ambition. In considering this question, you may want to broaden the context beyond scientific pursuit, so students can think about others—athletes, entertainers, scholars, business people—who may be driven in similar ways. Does ambition always require sacrifice? How does one decide what (or who) is worth sacrificing? And what happens when a person realizes the goal he or she has set out to achieve and is disappointed? **Question 3** takes up the issue of Frankenstein's disappointment with his creation and asks students to explore the meanings and implications of Frankenstein's rejection of the monster.

Question 8 asks students to discuss the Frankenstein monster as being like a human being but also different, and then to compare the monster to others in our society who are considered "different." Students may quickly want to compare Frankenstein's monster to people with visible physical handicaps, but you may want to lead them to think about other kinds of differences like race, social class, and sexual orientation. Students who have read other parts of Shelley's novel will be aware that the monster is in no way responsible for his fate—and he uses his status as victim to defend his monstrous actions, including the murder of a child. To what extent are people whom society marks as "different" also victims? To what extent does their victimization lead them to act in monstrous ways?

The research project on the industrial revolution that is suggested in **Question 9** would likely take quite a bit of effort for students to complete, but if teaching them how to do library research and how to write up that research is an important goal for you, this question provides you with an opportunity to do so. If limited library resources or limited time are problems, students could do their report on the effects of industrialization collaboratively, by working in small groups to research different issues related to the industrial revolution. The class could then put together a single report.

LEWIS THOMAS The Hazards of Science (p. 236)

Thomas's essay is especially concerned with exploring the nonscientist's fear of and skepticism toward science. Thomas explores the relationship between scientific inquiry and the common citizen and concludes that scientific inquiry is natural and necessary and that decisions about its limits should be left up to scientists. By using the word "hubris" to describe the "problem" with science, as nonscientists see it (**Question 1**), Thomas both explains and criticizes that description of science. "Hubris" does have religious overtones—it is, after all, the pride that "cometh before the fall" of human beings, a belief in their abilities that leads them to reject the idea that they are limited or that they are dependent on forces beyond them. Thomas concludes that such religious feelings should not be allowed to interfere with scientific inquiry (**Question 2**). (Students who are interested in thinking further about the relationship between science and religion might be directed to some of the readings in Chapter 4, Faith, especially Martin Luther King Jr.'s sermon, "Our God Is Able.")

Question 3 asks students to reread A.L.'s introduction to Thomas's essay and point out the words and phrases that reveal her attitude toward Thomas. This activity could be linked to one in which students analyze the beginning of Thomas's essay for evidence of his attitude toward "hubris" and the way it is applied to scientists and science. Similarly, students might exchange their responses to any of these questions and point out words and phrases that reveal the writer's attitude toward Thomas. By doing this kind of multilayered analysis, students can see how writing can reveal a writer's position on an issue, even when the writer has not directly intended such a revelation. You might then raise the question of whether any kind of writing can be considered objective, using scientific writing as an example, perhaps.

Question 4 provides students with the opportunity to articulate what they see as Thomas's view of science by applying it to a "real" case—that of Frankenstein and his monster. Students may be tempted to approach this question by wanting to conclude that Thomas would either praise or condemn Victor Frankenstein, but it is just as likely that Thomas would give Victor a mixed review. For example, Thomas might respect Victor's drive for knowledge and grant him the right, as a scientist, to pursue his research, but he would certainly criticize him for failing to take responsibility for the consequences of his research, something Thomas believes should be left up to scientists. However students respond to the question, be sure that they explain both their evaluation of Victor (from Thomas's point of view) and their construction of Thomas's point of view.

Question 6 can easily serve as preparation for writing in response to **Question 7**. Students can first raise the issue of what humans have the right to know—about themselves and the natural world—in small groups. By doing so, they are likely to confront different points of view on the subject and thus help clarify (or complicate) their own. They may also generate, as a group, examples of knowledge we may or may not benefit from knowing, examples that students could use in the position paper they are asked to write in **Question 7**.

Once students have talked about the consequences of certain kinds of knowledge, as **Question 6** asks them to do, they are in an interesting position to consider what motivates humans to know about themselves and the world. Thomas argues that the desire to know is uniquely and inherently human. Students may readily agree. You might then want to push students to consider whether such a trait is always good and whether the desire for knowledge generally leads to good consequences (as Thomas seems to suggest). When the desire for knowledge leads to bad consequences—as it does for Victor Frankenstein—what is it that has gone wrong?

KEVIN KELLY Interview with the Luddite (p. 243)

While "Interview with the Luddite" is the only full interview included in this text ("A Minority by the Year 2000" in Chapter 2 is an excerpt from an interview), students are often asked to conduct their own interviews, so you may wish to point to Kelly's interview as an example for them. However, it will also be important to point out that there are different kinds of interviews, and Kelly's probably shouldn't be a model for every kind. Students should consider the purpose of their own interviews; the possible purposes are many: to gain information about a particular person, topic, or event; to take several viewpoints into account; to represent the voices of others—some voices they will agree with, others they won't. Students could initially look at the Kelly interview to consider purpose and tone, since the purpose—and the people involved—affect the tone of the interview. How does the fact that Kelly and Sale openly disagree affect tone? Would you describe this interview as more formal or informal? What is Kelly's attitude toward Sale? What is Sale's attitude toward Kelly? Before students conduct their own interviews, they should think about their own attitudes toward the person they are interviewing and how their attitude may affect the direction and tone of the interview. You could also ask whether students think interviews should be structured conversations or whether the interviewer should be somewhat distant, not offering his or her own opinions on the topic at hand.

Questions 1 and 2 ask students to point to the evidence Sale and Kelly offer for their views and to evaluate that evidence by deciding which speaker is more convincing. You could ask students to consider the ways opinions and evidence are presented in interviews and how they might be presented differently in an essay or article. Another way of asking this question would be, "How does form affect content?" Question 4 asks students to compare Sale's and Kelly's viewpoints to Birkerts's viewpoint as represented in the essay "Perseus Unbound" and asks whether Birkerts might be called a "neo-luddite." Responses to this question might prepare students to answer Question 6, a question that invites students to consider their own feelings—both excitement and fear—about new technologies. This question could also be linked to Question 2, which asks students whose position they most agree with.

Question 7 should help students think practically about how a particular technology has improved their lives and to write about what their lives were (or would have been) like without this technology. You could also ask students to consider the negative effects (if there are any) that technology has also had, inviting them to see the complexity of the issues Kelly and Sale discuss. While computers may make typing much easier, what is Sale trying to get across when he says computers have "poisonous insides"? Why does talking on the telephone give him physical pain and mental anguish? What does Kelly mean when he says, "Technology is a language of artifacts?" These questions should also help students respond to Question 5, a question concerning the images and metaphors for technology that Kelly and Sale use. Students could also be encouraged to make up their own metaphors for technology and share those metaphors in small or large group discussion.

J. MICHAEL BISHOP Enemies of Promise (p. 255)

Question 1 offers two choices for a writing assignment. The first part of the question asks students to write about the notion of a postmodern attitude toward science. To respond to this question, students will have to understand the term "postmodern" and how Bishop is using the term. Bishop claims that those from a postmodern "school of thought" consider "science to be wholly fraudulent as a way of knowing." It may be worth having your students consider whether those who believe science is socially constructed and that scientific principles are "useful myths" would truly believe science to be "wholly fraudulent." Before students begin writing, you could discuss as a class who might fit Bishop's definition of postmodern. Would Emily Martin—who discusses the use of metaphors to explain the immune system—fit Bishop's definition of postmodern? The second part of **Question 1** asks students to write about science as "the best way to learn how the world works." Then students are asked to work with each other to explore the differences between the two understanding of science. You might ask how scientific principles might be used in different ways, depending on how one views scientific knowledge. In addition to discussing differences between views of "science as a useful fiction and science as an ennobling fact," students could also discuss the similarities between these views. While some students will concentrate on the differences between fact and fiction, be sure also to discuss the modifiers "useful" and "ennobling"; what do those modifiers say about one's attitude toward science?

     Question 2 asks if there are any words, concepts, or examples in the piece that students don't understand. This question then leads students to the consideration of intended audience. Who is Bishop writing for? What textual clues help one decide the intended audience? In small groups, you could have students analyze elements like types of evidence, direct address to the audience, diction, tone, and place of publication in order to best decide Bishop's intended audience. You could also ask which elements of the essay students find most or least convincing and why.

     Question 7 should help students focus on the most important points of Bishop's article by asking them to write an abstract or summary of the piece. In preparation for this assignment, students should review the section on summarizing in Chapter 2.

     Questions 4 and **8** ask students to carry out different types of research (**Question 4** points them to the Internet and **Question 8** requires library research), research that will likely be conducted outside of class. But students will probably need suggestions and guidance before they take up these projects. For **Question 4**, you could point students to the Web sites at the end of the science chapter or ask if anyone in the class already follows a Usenet or listserv discussion on scientific issues. You may wish to prepare a handout for students that gives guidelines and suggestions on how to use such technologies. Since **Question 8** (a question dealing with an examination of technological change) requires library research, you could ask students to consider how the research methods they use have changed over the years due to technology.

     Question 6 asks students to write an imaginary dialogue between Bishop and a Luddite, encouraging the student to explore various sides of the issue. This assignment should help students think about some of the negative aspects of certain technologies and should prepare them to respond to **Question 9**, a question asking students to examine a technology they believe has caused more problems than it has solved. **Question 9** also pushes students to consider the cause of the problem and to also propose a solution. This assignment might be accomplished well in small groups where students can work together, sharpening the problem-solving skills by modifying their assessments and proposals collaboratively.

EMILY MARTIN The Body at War: Media Views of the Immune System (p. 264)

Before you begin discussing Martin's piece in particular, it may be helpful to start with a more general discussion of metaphor and its functions in language and how we see and understand the world. A.L.'s introduction to the piece might help focus such a discussion. **Question 7**, which could be assigned in advance, asks students to conduct an investigation concerning how a particular topic or entity (mothers, teenagers, nature, angels, men) is represented in words and images. This question leads students to an examination of the metaphorical power words and images can have. If two or more students choose the same topic, they could work together and present their findings before the class.

To focus the discussion on Martin's piece, you could ask students to discuss the images they associate with the immune system and then look to the images Martin describes, adding to the categories she provides (**Question 2**). **Question 1** points students to an analysis of the sources Martin uses in support of her thesis and asks students "to identify the major areas these sources come from." They are asked how Martin's examples work to support her argument and how credible the examples (and, by extension, the argument) are to the student. **Question 1** is complex, but responding to it should help students not only to analyze a reading they may find difficult but also to think about their own responses to Martin's argument and why they respond the way they do. After considering Martin's argument and their own responses, students should be prepared to do research that allows them to corroborate or challenge Martin's findings (**Question 8**).

Question 4 encourages students to complicate Bishop's definition of "postmodernist" views of science by asking how Martin might respond to Bishop's definition and discussion of such views; further, the question asks how Martin's analysis might support Bishop's claims for science. This question leads students to make connections between positions that might seem opposite, and it should help students read each piece more critically. You could have two students playact Bishop's and Martin's positions, putting the two in dialogue in a skit for the class. **Question 6** offers the opportunity for such dramatization by asking students to imagine that they, Thomas, the monster from *Frankenstein*, Birkerts, and Martin are on a talk show. While the question only asks students to define science for themselves and from the perspectives of the other talk-show guests, a discussion about science and its uses could be continued among the "guests" in front of the class.

SVEN BIRKERTS Perseus Unbound (p. 279)

Birkerts's text, like others in this textbook, is annotated by the editors. In some ways, the annotations illustrate the interactive nature of much of what one finds on the Internet or other electronic resources. As you discuss Birkerts's piece, you may wish to inquire about your students' access and relationship to interactive media. Does your college or university provide easy access to the Internet or World Wide Web? Do most students own their own computer and modem? Do you have computer access in the classroom? Such issues will probably affect not only how you discuss this piece but also how students feel about computer technology in general. **Question 1** helps students think about issues of technological ends and means even if they're not familiar with video technology by applying Birkerts's concerns to other technological changes—like the introduction of jet aircraft.

If your college or university has limited access to interactive media or if your students have little computer training, they may be perplexed by **Question 2**, which asks them to design an interactive video to support a subject from the school's course catalog. If you are teaching in a computer supported classroom or if students have Internet access on their own, you could have them look at several examples from Web sites (several Web site addresses are included at the end of each chapter). If your students don't have such access, they could design their interactive videos on paper, using words and pictures and objects to represent their ideas. Limited electronic access will also make **Question 8** difficult for students to answer; if they've never read something in hypertext, it may be hard to test Birkerts's claims. If you are not in a computer equipped classroom, it may be possible to visit one for the day, since many schools have a program for computer assisted learning.

A consideration of students' own relationships to electronic technologies should also help them respond to **Question 5** which asks whether technological change is manageable or if it is—like Frankenstein's monster—out of control. Students will likely hold differing positions on this question, but whatever their response be sure to encourage them to use specific examples to support their positions. As they answer this question, you could also refer students to **Question 6**, so that they could compare their own views to those expressed by Birkerts, Sale, and Kelly.

Question 9 allows students to assume a cantankerous tone as they criticize a technology, proposal, or organization that others seem to embrace. While you may wish to limit the topic to something dealt with in the science chapter (computers, e-mail, biotechnology, environmental concerns), this exercise could also be applicable to issues raised in other chapters. For instance, students could look at O'Rourke's book review in the Difference chapter as an example of another piece written from a curmudgeon's perspective.

MATTHEW ROHRER Found in the Museum of Old Science (p. 290)

Rohrer's narrative poem—like myths—tells a story. **Question 3** asks students to make connections between this poem and the Creation piece in the Faith chapter by considering the ways creation stories might be similar to old scientific texts. This question might also help students think about the connections between religious stories and scientific explanations—how both are often concerned with origins and how both seek to explain how the world works. Explaining how the world works is the focus of **Questions 1** and **2**. In **Question 1**, students are asked to explain to an imagined audience of young children—as clearly and technically as possible—how some natural phenomenon works. In responding to **Question 2**, students should take the phenomenon they explained technically and write an imaginative piece like Rohrer's. In might be interesting to have students analyze both their technical and imaginative explanations—which do they find more "true"? Which explanation do they find more effective and why? Do they use metaphors or similes in either or both of their explanations?

You might wish to discuss Rohrer's organization of his poem—how his first stanza functions as an introduction; the second stanza as an explanation of third, fourth, and fifth; and the sixth stanza as an explanation of the list that follows in stanza seven. In responding to **Question 4**, students will either add to Rohrer's list of famous raindrops or compose their own list of some other category. They could write their own list poems in response to this question, paying attention to their own organizational schemes and line breaks. These poems could be read to the class or even organized into a collection: "Famous Natural Phenomena from the Museum of Old Science."

Texts in Context: Sequenced Writing Assignments about Science

Assignment 1

Writing several decades ago, Professor Richard Weaver of the University of Chicago argued that we can learn a lot about the values of people by looking closely at what he calls their "God terms," by which he means those words or terms that represent what people believe in almost implicitly. In the United States, Weaver suggested, "progress" and "science" were such terms. Indeed, in many ways, people see science as that which brings about progress. Spend some time thinking about what associations you have with the term "science," reflecting on what you know about science that has changed, contributed to, or affected your experience. Then make a list of the words or phrases that immediately come to your mind when you think of science. Finally, write a one-page statement for members of your class in which you explain what your major associations with science are. You might think of this statement as a way of saying "where I stand on science as a God term today."

Assignment 2

Choose the reading in this chapter that most appealed to you. Read that selection again to see if you have the same response. Then draw out from the reading where the author seems to stand on the question of science as a strongly positive or God term. Compare your findings to the page you wrote for assignment 1. In what ways does your stand agree with that of the author whose work you have chosen to read? Do you note any differences? Write a brief statement for members of your class on "why writer X and I agree on the question of science and its status in our society."

Assignment 3

Emily Martin implicitly argues that science is far from objective or neutral, even though it presents itself as having these qualities. Reread Martin's selection, paying special attention to this claim. Then look at the J. Michael Bishop selection (p. 255) to see what you can find in their essay to support and/or refute Martin's position that science is not neutral. Does what you find lead you to rethink the statement that you wrote for assignment 1? Record your responses to this question in your reading log.

Assignment 4
Lewis Thomas, himself a distinguished scientist, clearly believes in the productive powers
of scientific endeavor. Might his essay just as easily be entitled "The Benefits of Science" as
"The Hazards of Science"? How might Thomas (p. 236) or Bishop (p. 255) respond to
Martin's concerns? Write an imaginary dialogue between Martin and either Thomas or
Bishop and bring the dialogue to class. Be prepared to read it aloud to your classmates.

Assignment 5
Return to the passage from *Frankenstein* with which this chapter opens. Then reread either
the Kelly or Birkerts pieces on contemporary technology. In what ways does Mary Shelley
anticipate some of the issues and ideas either of these writers raise? Assume you are going
to write a modern-day update of *Frankenstein*, probably for TV or video. Meet with several
members of your class to brainstorm about such an update. Then sketch out a plot line and
one or two main characters. Finally, compare your story to the statements you produced for
assignments 1, 2, and 3. Does the same picture or image of science emerge in each? Write a
brief report for your class on "My Different Takes on Science."

Assignment 6
Spend some time thinking about where your ideas about and attitudes toward science may
come from. Consider your family, school, and other institutions such as politics or the
church as well as the mass media. Decide which of these have most influenced your
thinking about science and make a page or two of notes on what those influences have been
and why they have been so significant.

Assignment 7
Now go back through all the work you have produced in the previous six assignments,
studying them for what they reveal about how you value or devalue science and for what
science in general means to you. Then prepare a brief essay (4-5 pages) for your class on
"The Hazards—and Benefits—of Science: Where I Stand on These Questions, Where My
Stance Comes from, and Where I Think It May Go in the Future."

Part Three Who We Are

6 ■ Gender: Women . . . and Men (p. 293)

In this chapter, students are asked to enter a conversation that has been going on in every culture for thousands of years. What are the differences between men and women, between masculinity and femininity, and how can we explain these differences? Are men and women naturally or instinctively different? What role does socialization play in the differences between men and women? For many years, this conversation (at least the public version of it) was carried on primarily by men, who talked mostly about the ways in which women were "different." This chapter presents a more diverse perspective on the subject and includes texts that discuss the nature of women and the nature of men, written by women and men. The questions at the beginning of the chapter give students an opportunity to explore their own thoughts and feelings on the subject of gender—thoughts and feelings that they may not realize are part of a long-standing conversation. As students engage with the selections in this chapter, you might encourage them to explore not just their reactions to the readings but their reasons for reacting as they do. How is their gender affecting their responses and the responses of their classmates?

Some of the recurring questions in this chapter include:

■   In what ways are men and women different? (Genesis, Truth, Thomas, Barry)

■   How does a person's society or culture affect his or her gender? (Truth, Sullivan, Kingston, Faludi, Sommers, Thomas, Olds)

■   How do differences between and among different men and women affect their ability to relate to one another? (Genesis, Truth, Sullivan, Kingston, Faludi, Sommers, Thomas, Barry)

GENESIS 1-3 (p. 297)

For many students, especially those brought up to believe that the Bible is the direct word of God, this text may be a difficult one to discuss. In addition to having students respond to the questions at the end of this selection, then, you might also ask them to write about their attitudes toward the Bible as a text, perhaps asking them to describe what they have been taught this passage from Genesis means and to comment on whether they accept this interpretation. This kind of self-reflection will give them (and you) a lens through which to read their responses to this selection.

Question 1 asks them to define "dominion" and to consider the meaning of the term as it is used in this selection; students are also asked to explain why Adam and Eve were unaware of their nakedness before they ate the forbidden fruit (Question 2). If your class is diverse, students should be able to offer differing interpretations of this text, but you may need to remind them that your purpose in discussing these interpretations is not to determine which are correct or incorrect.

35

Question 3 invites students to read the full text of Genesis, chapters 1-3 and to consider the excerpts A.L. chose and whether there are other passages from those chapters they would have included. The second part of the question, which asks students to reflect on why A.L. may have omitted certain passages, should encourage students to think about editorial choices and how context affects interpretation. Do interpretations of the passages included differ when the passages omitted are taken into account? You may wish to make photocopies of those chapters and pass them out to the class so that you and they can refer directly to the text in responding to this question.

Questions 4 and **5** allow students to make connections between an ancient story and modern day texts. **Question 4** asks whether the passages from Genesis support or refute the line from a calypso song that states "Man smart, Woman smarter." Of course, students' responses to this question will depend on how they interpret Adam and Eve's actions. **Question 5** asks how the serpent's interaction with Eve might be a form of victimization and refers them to Susan Faludi's argument. To explore many sides of the issue, you could encourage students to consider the question from differing perspectives: How would the serpent answer the question? What might Eve's position be? Is the serpent just doing what his nature compels him to do? Is Eve equally responsible for the consequences? Was Eve a helpless victim with no one to turn to? What was Adam's reason for eating the fruit? Does it make a difference that God told Adam not to eat the fruit of the tree before Eve was created, but there's no record in Genesis of God telling Eve this rule?

Question 6 gives students a chance to be creative in their own telling of the creation story. Writing this story can be another means by which students reflect on their own assumptions about what it means to be male and female, and writing about male-female differences humorously might help take the tension away from a particularly contentious subject. Be sure that students have a chance to share their stories with each other and to note the ways in which the writer's stories reveal their assumptions about male-female differences, something they will be invited to do with the other texts about gender differences presented in this chapter.

Having students conduct a survey on people's beliefs about gender differences (**Question 7**) is another way to give them exposure to a wide range of views on the subject. By having them do their research in groups, they will also have an opportunity to confront differences within the group as they work together to determine how to report the results of their findings. If possible, have them report on different group members' interpretations of the survey results as well as reporting a final consensus of the group, keeping in mind the role that gender differences might (or might not) be playing in their interpretations.

SOJOURNER TRUTH Ain't I a Woman? (p. 300)

Question 1 turns students' attention to the oral nature of Sojourner Truth's speech. The repetition of the rhetorical question, "And ain't I a woman?" is a feature common to oral discourse and one that might seem out of place in a written text. In considering the effect of this recurring question, students should consider both its effect in a written text and its effect when spoken; have a student read Truth's speech aloud to the class. Students might also point out other elements of Truth's text that mark it as meant to be spoken.

Much of the power of Truth's speech comes from its oral qualities as well as from our knowledge that Truth was a former slave who could neither read nor write. But does her speech represent a powerful argument (**Question 2**)? As students come up with possible criticisms of her speech (her lack of evidence beyond her own experience, her admission that she might have less intellect than a man, the absence of linear logic), be sure to have them make explicit their assumptions about what makes an argument effective.

By comparing Truth to both Christina Hoff Sommers and the passage from Genesis, students should be able to see how open to interpretation most gender issues are. For example, **Question 3** asks how Truth would respond to the idea that the oppression of women is a structural feature of society. How does Sommers respond to such an idea? For Truth, women have the power to "turn the world upside down"—clearly a revision of some traditional representations of women as weak and vulnerable—so certainly they would have the power to change the conditions in which they work, to rewrite the rules of the game.

In responding to **Question 5**, most students will take the position that men and women should have equal rights, and many believe that they already do, but others will recognize areas of life where there is still inequality. For example, why has the United States never had a woman president? Should men have equal responsibility for child rearing and care of the home? Again, students will benefit from having an opportunity to read and talk about each other's responses.

ANDREW SULLIVAN What Are Homosexuals For? (p. 302)

In his introduction, J.R. points to Sullivan's essay as a piece that "speaks quietly and eloquently to the entire political spectrum." **Question 3** asks students to assess whether "What Are Homosexuals For" is, as J.R. claims, an example of "civil argument," balanced and reasonable. Whether or not students agree wholly with Sullivan's discussion of homosexuality, they are likely to affirm and understand some of his claims: that American culture at large tends to define "normal" sexuality as heterosexuality (**Question 1**) and that gay people often feel like outsiders (**Questions 2** and **4**). **Question 1** encourages students to consider "how the cultural dominance of heterosexual marriage" affects society in general and people in particular. While Sullivan discusses how the ideal of heterosexual marriage affects young gay people, this question broadens this issue somewhat. How does the expectation of marriage—the power of heterosexual marriage as an institution—shape individuals and society? Some students will not be able to relate to Sullivan's feeling like an outsider because of sexuality, but **Question 2** invites them to describe a time when they have felt like an outsider because of gender, class, physical capabilities, or political preference.

Question 4 refers to Kingston's "No Name Woman" and brings up the issue of the constraints society puts on sexuality. Before asking students to respond to this question regarding the differences between constraints, taboos, and prejudices, you may want to ask students what particular constraints they think society does put on sexuality. Depending on their religious, political, and social beliefs and experiences, students are likely to answer this question differently. **Question 6** asks students to explore the appropriateness of an assignment asking students to write about a first date or first love. If you've already talked about sexual constraints and issues of people feeling like outsiders because of their sexuality, students may be particularly sensitive to how such an assignment might further alienate people. What if a person has never been on a date or been in love? What if a person prefers not to talk about his or her love life? What might be the advantages and disadvantages of such an assignment?

Some of the questions following Dave Barry's "Guys vs. Men" encourage students to think about stereotypes—about how they're used in humorous pieces of writing like Barry's and how they can also be limiting and not entirely true. **Question 5** asks students to consider "Barry's world of guys" and whether such a world has "room for homosexuals." While Barry doesn't explicitly talk about homosexual guys, are there any ways his essay implicitly offers a space for homosexuals? **Question 7** should help students explore the issue of stereotyping further by asking them whether one can making assertions or generalizations about any group of people "without engaging in harmful stereotypes." What are some reasons for arguing that certain groups of people—women, guys, lesbians, poor people, people with learning disabilities, the hard of hearing, the elderly—share some similarities? Are there ways of talking about similarities without confining people or negatively stereotyping them in harmful ways? **Question 7** asks students to explore these issues by writing a dialogue; have students think carefully about who they will represent in their dialogue and how identity and experiences might affect what position one takes on such issues.

MAXINE HONG KINGSTON No Name Woman (p. 313)

One interesting characteristic of this story that students may overlook is the impact of the story of "No Name Woman" on the author/narrator. Students may become so engaged by No Name's story that they will overlook the story's function as a lesson against the consequences of sex outside of marriage as well as an illustration of the ways in which stories can be appropriated by readers/listeners for their own purposes. **Question 1**, which asks students to consider the different versions of the story Kingston posits, can help them see that the story of No Name Woman is open to interpretation: the narrator/author tells the story differently than did her mother; A.L. interprets the story differently than would the villagers (**Question 3**); and the father of No Name's child would likely tell the story differently than did Kingston. **Question 7** invites students to rewrite one of Kingston's versions of the story from the point of view of a man and to consider this man's relationship to women; this question should help emphasize the point that a story changes depending on who tells it. **Question 4** explicitly invites students to interpret the lesson No Name Woman learned. Comparing these versions of No Name's stories should help students see how differently they might interpret the story. Perhaps a discussion of the openness of the story of No Name Woman will help students understand why the Genesis story—in spite of its status as a biblical text—has also been interpreted in various ways.

Kingston's text, like those of Sojourner Truth, Andrew Sullivan, Susan Faludi, David Thomas, and Sharon Olds, considers the ways in which gender roles are influenced by society. **Question 2**, which asks students to explore the narrator's—and their own—attitude toward the villagers who attack No Name Woman, can be an opportunity for students to think about society's power over the gender identity of individuals. Are we completely free to be the kind of man or woman we want to be? Although the villagers might seem to twentieth-century American readers to be irrational, superstitious, and vengeful, students can also see their actions as the product of cultural beliefs and values; they might also think about situations in which American beliefs and values have produced seemingly irrational behavior—the institution of slavery is an obvious example.

Having students interview older friends or relatives about the sexual norms that they grew up with (**Question 6**) will give students insight into the social constraints on gender identity and sexuality that those born after the sexual revolution may not be aware of. If students are reluctant to talk with their parents or others about sex, they might consult popular magazines and books written during the forties and fifties to try to get a sense of an older American society's views on men, women, and sex.

Comparing Kingston's telling of No Name Woman's story to Andrew Sullivan's discussion of homosexuality will allow students to consider the extent to which society continues to write the rules which men and women are expected to obey. In addition to considering the kinds of secrets people are often expected to keep, students might also compare the speakers in both of these pieces—Maxine Hong Kingston and Andrew Sullivan—and their motives for writing what they have written. What kind of lessons are Kingston and Sullivan trying to teach?

SUSAN FALUDI Whose Hype? (p. 324)

Both Faludi's and Christina Hoff Sommers's pieces deal with similar topics—feminism and the use and misuse of sources and statistics—from differing perspectives. While the two writers take different positions, their pieces implicitly prove a similar point: people often use and interpret sources differently depending on the point they wish to make. You could begin discussion by asking students whether they think the positions they already hold affect what types of sources they are likely to believe or value. Do students trust statistics? When trying to argue a point, what types of evidence do they use as support? **Question 2** takes up the issue of sources, asking students to identify the figures Faludi uses as correctives and to evaluate which of her sources seem most credible. In responding to **Question 7**, which asks students to collaboratively research violence against women on their campus, students will not only need to consider their own use of sources, but they will also see the ways in which the issues Faludi discusses affect their own campus community.

In her introduction, A.L. points to the dangers of "either/or" thinking, a kind of thinking that both Sommers and Faludi are sometimes guilty of. **Question 3** asks students to find examples of both "either/or" and "both/and" thinking (the kind A.L. favors) in Faludi's article. Sharon Olds's poem "Son" provides an example of "both/and" thinking. While the female speaker of the poem is probably concerned with issues affecting women, she is also concerned about the place her son will have in "any new world we enter." **Question 5** invites students to write a companion poem called "Daughter" from Faludi's perspective.

Questions 1 and **4** both deal with the concept of victim mind-sets. While some critics accuse feminists of having such a mind-set, Faludi turns the tables by claiming that while the media (movies, television, advertisements) may present women who are weak and whiny, the women she is talking about are feminists who "use wit, not whining" to make points. **Question 4** asks students to draw comparisons between the arguments

Sojourner Truth and Faludi make. Both Truth and Faludi are examples of strong women, and it should be interesting to see how students respond to these women and their pieces. Do any responses support Faludi's claim that there is a "hysteria" over forceful feminism, that there is a cultural fear of women becoming too aggressive?

Discussions about gender issues are likely to become heated, but **Question 6**, which asks students to write about how Faludi might differentiate between "women" and "gals," might provide a more lighthearted way of responding to the material. As a class, you could develop a chart—like the "Example Chart" Barry presents on p. 351—of women and gals.

CHRISTINA HOFF SOMMERS Figuring Out Feminism (p. 328)

As **Question 3** points out, A.L. and J.R. disagree about "gender politics," and the Faludi and Sommers pieces illustrate some of their disagreements. While the differences between Faludi and Sommers are clear, **Question 4** asks students to write a letter addressed to both Faludi and Sommers to suggest ways the two might find common ground. Although Sommers and Faludi may not agree on issues of gender politics, they probably would agree that it is important to check your sources. In fact, Sommers's article may be more about getting "facts" straight than it is an argument against gender feminism, although her position against "gender feminists" is also quite clear (**Question 2**). **Question 1** points students to the methods Sommers uses to undermine statistics she believes are incorrect and asks them to identify the grounds she offers to support her own statistics. This question, along with **Questions 5** and **6**, points to the complexities of using and interpreting statistics. **Question 5** invites students to reflect on how their own education has prepared—or not prepared—them to interpret statistics, and **Question 6** deals with the temptation to believe statistics—even false ones—that confirm what one already believes.

As an exercise to show how statistics—even ones that are technically correct—can be used to support different points of view, you could pass out a page of statistics about some social issue and ask students to interpret those statistics. Then, on the basis of their interpretations, have them write a page indicating what measures should be taken to respond to the issue as they see it, including their reasons for believing such a response is necessary. Most likely, students will not only interpret the statistics in vastly different ways, but they are also likely to call for differing responses. After reading Sommers's and Faludi's articles, some students may also be interested in where the statistics came from, who gathered them, and who funded such research. If students do call for different responses to some social issue—whether the issue deals with gender, class, race, or something else—they are likely to see how complex these issues are, and to realize that responses to complex issues are rarely easy or clear-cut.

DAVID THOMAS The Mind of Man (p. 337)

Thomas's essay focuses on differences between boys and girls and the ways boys may be treated differently from girls during elementary and secondary school years. As J.R. points out in his introduction—and reaffirms in **Question 3**—students may be more used to hearing about how differences and inequalities affect women. For instance, in the Education chapter, Adrienne Rich's speech deals with the inadequacies of the education women receive. **Question 5** asks students to compare and contrast the situation Thomas describes and the one Rich presents. One obvious difference is that Rich is talking primarily about college education, at a time when most professors were male and most of the books read by college students were written by men; whereas, Thomas is writing about boys who are taught primarily by women in elementary or secondary schools. Encouraging students to draw from their own experience, you could ask in what ways they think the sex of a teacher might affect education—for both males and females. (**Question 4**, which refers students to Olds's poem, also deals with the issue of women teaching boys.) Such a discussion will help students prepare to answer **Question 7**, which asks students to write a narrative about an experience that made them aware of how teachers or administrators treated girls and boys differently.

While Thomas makes clear that men and women do not differ in terms of "average overall intelligence," he claims they do differ in "the mental tasks at which they excel." **Question 1** asks students to research this claim and to decide whether these differences do exist, and if they do, "to determine the nature and quality of these differences." If students agree that there are differences, they may also wish to consider to what extent these differences are biological or the result of socialization. If males and females learn differently and/or have different educational needs, what would be the advantages and disadvantages of single-sex education (**Question 6**)? Some students have probably already experienced segregated education and will be able to discuss pros and cons from their own experience. As well, you could ask students why they chose to attend the college they are attending; did the presence or absence of the opposite sex affect their decision at all? Although **Question 2** has little to do with differences between men and women, it does deal with difference: differences between the British educational system Thomas describes and the one(s) students are familiar with. This question could also be broadened to include a consideration of the differences in American systems of education—private and public, same-sex and co-educational, religious, vocational, or military schools—and how males and females may be treated differently in other educational contexts.

DAVE BARRY Guys vs. Men (p. 343)

As the tone of J.R.'s introduction implies (**Question 3**), Barry's humorous piece is rather exaggerated and "plays off of gross stereotypes about men" (**Question 1**). Many of the questions following "Guys vs. Men" will help students take a closer look at Barry's piece to analyze the techniques he uses for effect. If your students aren't familiar with terms like "analogy," "parody," and "irony," you may find it helpful to bring in other writings that make use of such conventions or have them write their own analogies and parodies to demonstrate their understanding of how these conventions work. **Question 7** asks students to write an anecdote like the one Barry uses to illustrate the stereotypical competitiveness of guys, choosing their own stereotype of guys or gals as their subject. This question also gives guidelines to help students tell their story in a funny way. Before asking students to respond to this question, as a class, you could point to the places where Barry uses understatement ("considerable pain"), exaggeration ("twenty-three Advil in my bloodstream"), irony (the fact that Barry knew his coworkers were being "ridiculous" but joined them anyway and pulled a muscle doing so), and self-deprecation (quoting a typical fan letter: "Who cuts your hair? Beavers?").

Question 2 points to Barry's use of analogy and asks students to work in groups to discuss the features of Barry's extended comparison between his dog Zippy and the moral behavior of guys. How is Zippy's tendency to get into the garbage and, when scolded, to poop on the floor like the moral behavior of guys? Do students find such a comparison effective? As Question 6 points out, Barry's entire piece is an extended definition, and the question also names many of the techniques Barry uses to make his definition clear, giving students helpful suggestions for ways they can write their own extended definitions. As a class exercise, you and your students could write a chart on the board which shows contrasts between two similar terms: Kids vs. Children; Dads vs. Fathers; Maids vs. Housekeepers. (Question 6 provides other examples.) Such an exercise highlights how different words carry different connotations, and this exercise implies that the words we chose to use are important and have effects.

Issues of word choice are dealt with in O'Rourke's review of "Guidelines for Bias-Free Writing"; Question 4 highlights the differences between Barry's piece and O'Rourke's book review. While both are meant to be funny, there are significant differences in purpose, intended audience, and style. One important difference is that Barry's "mild mannered humor" is aimed at himself and other guys, whereas O'Rourke aims his invective at others, people he disagrees with. How might this difference affect the audience each piece is able to communicate with? Who is and who is not likely to think O'Rourke's review is funny?

Unlike many of the other questions, Question 5 deals more with content than style. It asks students to consider whether science is "really a male obsession with how things work." This question has at least two parts your students should consider: the use of the adjective "male"—since many females are interested in (even obsessed with) with how things work—and the idea that science is motivated by such an obsession. What other motivations might there be for scientific practice and inquiry? Do students see science as a primarily male interest?

SHARON OLDS Son (p. 365)

Olds's poem is short—just two brief stanzas—but it's certainly rich in description. Part of the power of the poem rests in the concrete images Olds uses to describe the sleeping boy: "freckled face / the scarlet lining of his mouth / shadowy and fragrant, his small teeth / . . . opal eyelids quivering / like insect wings." The close description of the son's face, in particular, prepares the reader for the next stanza which contains a list of some of the boy's other body parts and a kind of invocation: "Let no part go / unpraised." Question 1 points to the second stanza as a kind of prayer and asks students to consider how their hopes for their own children might be like or unlike the hopes Olds expresses. Question 2 continues with this theme of hopes and wishes for children by making a connection to Didion's piece and how she expresses wishes for her daughter. The question also asks students to consider what Olds might wish for a daughter; though the question doesn't explicitly ask them to do so, you could have students write a poem entitled "Daughter" in a similar form, using concrete imagery in the first stanza and an invocation in the second.

Texts in Context: Sequenced Writing Assignments about Gender

Assignment 1
Brainstorm for a while about some time(s) in your life when the fact that you were either a man or a woman (or a boy or a girl) was particularly important or significant to you. How did the fact of your sex affect you and the situation at the time? In a two- or three-page reading log entry, describe one of these times as thoroughly as possible: what happened, where you were, how you felt, how the event affected you both then and later.

Assignment 2
Imagine that you could change your sex for one week. With several members of your class, talk about what effects that change might create in your life and behavior. Then write a piece for your class exploring the advantages and disadvantages this change would mean for you. You may decide to compose an essay in response to this assignment, or a humorous sketch, or you may decide to try to create an imaginative experience: "A Day in My Life as a Man/Woman" presented as a play or short story.

Assignment 3
How would you characterize the man who impregnates No Name Woman? Make a list of words that come to your mind when you think of this character. Then make a similar list of words to characterize the guys and men Dave Barry talks about. What similarities and differences do you note in the two lists? Then write a brief analysis of the man in "No Name Woman" as you think Dave Barry would be likely to write it.

Assignment 4
If the views of men presented by Kingston and Barry differ substantially, so do the views of Faludi, Sommers, and Thomas on feminists. Look carefully at the particular words each writer uses to describe and characterize feminists. Working with several classmates, try to figure out why Faludi, Sommers, and Thomas draw such different pictures. What might account for such radically different interpretations? Try to decide which of the views is most acceptable to each group member—and why. Then try to identify as clearly as possible what in your own experience and value system leads you to prefer one of these characterizations over the other. Record your findings in a reading log entry.

Assignment 5
You have noted the varying ways in which writers in this chapter represent both men and women. Now, working with two other classmates, take some time to examine how women and men are represented in some other arena you are interested in investigating—in soap operas or car advertisements, for example, or in children's toys or clothes, or in a favorite book, movie, video, or song. To begin your analysis, ask yourself this question: "If all we knew about men or women was what we could learn from looking closely at how __ depicts them, what would we know?" Working independently, gather as much information as you can in response to this topic and bring it to the group. Then together, draft a report for your class on how women/men are represented in __. Finally, meet with your entire class to hear each group's report and to discuss the ways in which your own attitudes toward and valuing of gender may have been influenced by such representations.

Assignment 6
Return to your responses to assignments 1 and 2. In light of what you discovered in working through assignment 5, what can you say about how forces such as advertising, the media, or other representations have affected your own ways of thinking about and understanding of one sex or the other? Write a 2-3 page reading log entry exploring these issues.

Assignment 7
In an essay for your class, address the topic "Gender Differences Are Made, Not Born—or Are They?" Draw on the work you have done for assignments 1-6 as well as on the readings in this chapter (and the additional readings listed on p. 357 if you have time). In addition, consider those forces or societal, political, educational, and entertainment institutions that help to "make" or construct gender for us. Finally, draw on your own experiences of gender to help you respond to this topic.

7 ▪ Difference: E Pluribus Unum? (p. 358)

In this chapter, students are invited to participate in a conversation about the relationship between majority and minority cultures in the United States, a conversation that has recently taken on particular importance. The initial reading for this chapter, Hector St. Jean De Crèvecoeur's "What Is an American?", presents the traditional view of America as a cultural melting pot, a place where people of many origins come together to become members of a new culture. This view of America has been challenged by many groups and individuals who argue that assimilating to (majority) American culture can be difficult or impossible for many and that, instead, America should work to be a multicultural society, one that values the differences (rather than the commonalties) among its members. Opponents argue that an emphasis on cultural difference can only result in the kind of political tension and hostility that continue to plague Europe and the Middle East.

Some of the questions that recur throughout this chapter include:

▪ What are the consequences for America of emphasizing people's differences? (Hurston, Bernstein, Chavez, O'Rourke)

▪ What are the consequences for individuals in assimilating—or failing to assimilate—into (majority) American culture? (Crèvecoeur, Bernstein, Chavez, O'Rourke, Hughes)

▪ What is the relationship between majority and minority cultures in the United States? (Crèvecoeur, Hurston, Bernstein, Lassell, Kleege, Crouch, Chavez, Hughes)

▪ What do Americans have in common? (Crèvecoeur, Hurston, Bernstein, Lassell, Chavez, Hughes)

HECTOR ST. JEAN DE CRÈVECOEUR What Is an American? (p. 361)

Crèvecoeur's text offers unmitigated praise for the accomplishments of early America, accomplishments that might easily be overlooked by those focusing on the problems of American society today. **Questions 1-4** ask students to try to see the new America from Crèvecoeur's point of view, a Frenchman who was all too aware of the political and social problems the Europeans who came to America were seeking to escape. For example, **Question 2** highlights the opportunities for success that were available to the poor in America, opportunities unavailable in Europe where a person's economic status was determined by the social class into which a person was born. This economic opportunity was afforded, in part, by the availability of land in America for agricultural and industrial development, a scarce resource in Europe (**Question 3**). **Questions 1** and **4** ask students to compare Crèvecoeur's positive view of the accomplishments of the early European settlers in America to more contemporary views of these people. What less-than-positive aspects of their accomplishments were overlooked by Crèvecoeur (for example, their treatment of Native Americans and their importation of Africans as slaves)?

Crèvecoeur describes America as a place where differences in social class have been largely erased; Bernstein's piece, too, deals with issues of class. In his conclusion to "Dérapage," Bernstein claims, "The plain and inescapable fact is that the derived Western European culture of American life produced the highest degree of prosperity in the conditions of the greatest freedom known on planet Earth." While Bernstein seems to recognize class differences, both he and Crèvecoeur share optimism about what Bernstein calls "standards and modes of behavior that have always made for success in American life." **Question 5** asks students to compare the Americans Crèvecoeur imagines to the ones Bernstein depicts. You might ask students to try to imagine how Crèvecoeur would define multiculturalism and to consider how his position on the issues Bernstein raises would compare to Bernstein's position.

Question 6 asks students to compare two metaphors used to describe the mix of culture in the United States—Crèvecoeur's image of the melting pot and Hurston's image of "bags of miscellany." These two essays are especially interesting when considered together, since both emphasize commonalties among people, but they do so from radically different points of view. Having students discuss which metaphor seems most apt to them is a good prelude to answering **Question 7,** which asks them to come up with their own definition of "American" (which might take the form of an extended metaphor), taking into consideration the ethnic and racial diversity of the people in their classroom. Similarly, **Question 8** asks students to respond to Crèvecoeur's description of America as "the most perfect society existing now in the world." Their response might take several forms, including a refutation of Crèvecoeur's claims (arguing that his view of America was, in fact, wrong) or their own description of an ideal society, including evidence to illustrate why America does or does not measure up to this description. If students choose to come up with their own criteria for judging the success of a society, it might be useful for them to consider why Crèvecoeur's criteria no longer seem relevant.

ZORA NEALE HURSTON How It Feels to Be Colored Me (p. 366)

Like Hector St. Jean De Crèvecoeur, Zora Neale Hurston praises the commonalties Americans share—in spite of their differences. But unlike Crèvecoeur, Hurston acknowledges racial and cultural differences among Americans and suggests that American society is partially responsible for overemphasizing those differences. Hurston's references to color throughout her essay (**Question 1**) illustrate the ways in which a person's difference becomes apparent only when measured against his or her surroundings. For example, Hurston becomes "colored" only when she finds herself in a predominantly white environment, and she suggests that she stops being "colored" when she is feeling particularly self-confident. Making a connection with Georgina Kleege's "Call It Blindness," **Question 5** points out that color "depends largely on sight, or vision" and asks students to imagine "the world Hurston describes if vision were not so important."

Students will likely have different reactions to Hurston's essay, depending on their own attitudes toward racial difference and their experiences with people of different races. Some people may feel comforted by Hurston's ability to ignore or rise above her racial difference; other students might find her statements unbelievable or escapist. Be sure students have some opportunity to consider why they responded to Hurston's essays as they did and to discuss why various members of the class may have responded differently. In doing so, they might want to consider the ways in which A.L.'s introduction might have "colored" their reading of Hurston (**Question 2**).

As students discuss their responses to Hurston, you might encourage them both to sympathize with Hurston's point of view and to complicate it, perhaps by considering it along with Langston Hughes's poem, "Theme for English B" (**Question 4**). As students consider the similarities and differences in Hurston's and Hughes' attitudes toward racial difference, you might want to point out to them that Hughes and Hurston were writing at about the same time, that both were influential members of the Harlem Renaissance, and that Hughes openly criticized Hurston for what he felt was her failure to use her position to fight for the rights of African Americans.

Another way in which students might complicate Hurston's seemingly idealistic view of racial difference is to ask them to consider the various labels that have been used to refer to Americans of African descent. What connotations does the term "colored" have, especially in contrast to "white"? Why would the term "colored" be replaced by "black" and then "African American"? Ask students to consider the power of words, the power of naming. Hurston was certainly aware of the power of the majority culture to shape the minority culture's attitude toward itself—Hurston would not have become "a little colored girl" in her own mind if she had not known that she was thought of in that way by the white people she lived with. You might also ask students to consider O'Rourke's discussion of language and his position on how language shapes attitudes. What does O'Rourke's use of language say about his attitude toward others?

As students work to come up with their own explanation of the relationship between majority and minority cultures in the United States, they might begin by considering the ways in which they might be considered different from the "norms" of American culture. (**Question 3** provides one way for them to explore these differences.) **Question 6** asks them to read Linda Chavez's "Toward a New Politics of Hispanic Assimilation" and to consider explicitly the idea of "assimilation." Here they might also think about their own differences and the degree to which they are expected to assimilate to the "norm"—and then compare their own experience to that of people from different races and ethnic groups. Is the pressure to assimilate the same for all Americans? Are the benefits—and losses—the same for all? Students can draw on their responses to these questions as they construct their own metaphorical descriptions of their racial or ethnic identities (**Question 7**) and compare them to those of their classmates (**Question 8**). It might be interesting to work as a class to come up with a metaphorical description of an "American" that would take into account as many individual student's descriptions of themselves as possible.

RICHARD BERNSTEIN Dérapage (p. 372)

The annotations and afterwords for this piece provide a telling example of how different people can thoroughly engage in reading a text, read carefully and critically, and come to very different conclusions. A.L. and J.R. take almost opposite positions on the Bernstein selection, and students are likely to take widely varied positions as well. **Question 5** invites students to present their own positions on multicultural education in a position paper that supports, refutes, or offers a different perspective concerning Bernstein's thesis. Part of the disagreement about multiculturalism rests in definitions—how multicultural is defined and who is doing the defining (and for what purposes). Since definition is an important issue, you may wish to have students consider how and why A.L.'s definition—as reflected in her afterwords—differs from Bernstein's, and why J.R. tends to side with Bernstein. Both editors point, albeit generally, to their experiences; how might their experiences differ? (**Question 3** points to J.R.'s personal investment in Bernstein's book.)

Question 1 should help make students more sensitive to the various meanings of "multiculturalism" by asking them to think about the different contexts in which they've heard that term. This question also asks students to consider whether the concept of multiculturalism is as politicized as Bernstein suggests or if it's used in other ways as well. **Question 2** points to other terms that have become politicized in American society and asks students to explore terms like "family values" and "self-reliance" critically. What do these terms mean to your students? How are these terms used in political or public arenas—and for what effect?

Question 4 continues the theme of defining by asking students to review Neil Postman's essay and to consider the way Bernstein uses "Dérapage" to organize his argument. If students have difficulty wading through some of the historical allusions, it may be helpful for them to do a research report on one of the historical topics Bernstein alludes to. If your students are doing class presentations, you could ask a small group to research several historical topics and explain how they relate to Bernstein's argument.

MICHAEL LASSELL How to Watch Your Brother Die (p. 386)

This poem, which describes a heterosexual brother's experience of watching his gay brother die from AIDS, portrays the issue of sexual difference in terms most students should be able to respond to, regardless of their sexual orientation. **Question 4** asks students to describe their responses to the poem, and you may want to collect and respond to these responses before organizing small group or whole class discussions of the poem. This poem, like many of the selections in this chapter, takes up the issue of the relationship between majority and minority cultures in America. Tracing the uses of the term "forgive" in the poem will give students some insight into the poet's view of what these relationships are—and should be—at least between heterosexuals and the gay community (**Question 1**).

Comparing Lassell's poem to Langston Hughes's poem, "Theme for English B," will give students the opportunity to consider the similarities and differences between the positions of gays in American culture and the position of African Americans (**Question 2**). The narrators of both of these poems struggle to understand a culture that is different from theirs, but while the narrator of Lassell's poem is a member of the majority culture, the speaker of Hughes's poem is a member of a minority culture. How do the positions of these speakers affect their views of their relationship to the "other" culture? What effect do these speakers' positions have on students' responses to the poem?

Question 3 brings up the concept of "shared humanity and mutual acceptance" that Georgina Kleege discusses in "Call It Blindness." This question might lead to a discussion of relationships—the relationships among people who may not know each other at all, yet still care in active ways (like the people on the bus Kleege describes and the relationship between the speaker of Lassell's poem and the brother's lover); the relationship between doctors and a patient's loved ones (which seems distant in Lassell's poem); relationships between lovers, brothers, husbands and wives. All of these complex relationships are referred to in "How to Watch Your Brother Die" and should provoke interesting class discussions.

GEORGINA KLEEGE Call It Blindness (p. 390)

Like many other pieces in this book, Georgina Kleege's "Call It Blindness" deals both implicitly and explicitly with the power of words. **Question 1** deals with the positive connotations associated with vision and sight and the negative connotations associated with blindness, asking students to add to the words and phrases Kleege uses in her piece, considering the ways society values sight and blindness. **Question 4** reminds students how prevalent these words and phrases are by pointing them to O'Rourke's "Review of Guidelines for Bias-Free Writing" and asking them to list the ones he uses. Of course the use of such words and phrases is generally not meanspirited or malicious (though some might use these words to describe O'Rourke's piece), but it is still important to talk about the power language has to shape viewpoints (even the word "viewpoints" is a reference to sight). While people can't change every word or phrase some might construe as negative, students should be encouraged to consider the value of being more conscious about language choices—for this is one way to become a stronger writer and better reader.

Where, though, does one find the line between conscious and overly self-conscious? (This issue may be one that O'Rourke tries to deal with in his review.) Kleege talks about how some people—upon learning of her blindness—"become self-conscious about language, hesitant to say 'I see what you mean or 'See you later.'" **Question 5** helps address the issue of sensitivity—sensitivity to language and to people, expressing Kleege's hope for inclusion and the wish that someday the word "blind" will cease to be ugly and asking students to write a letter to O'Rourke or Bernstein explaining Kleege's point.

Fear is one of the themes of Kleege's essay—fear of the blind, fear of becoming blind (**Question 2**). A.L. expresses her own fear of losing her sight in her introduction when she talks about realizing that she "could no longer read the condensed version of *The Oxford English Dictionary* without using [a] . . . magnifying glass." **Question 3** asks students to consider the effects A.L. may have been trying to create by opening her introduction with this personal anecdote. One possible effect of the anecdote is a reminder that fear of losing one's sight is common. Kleege plays on this fear by acknowledging it in her essay and then inviting her reader to simulate blindness—she imaginatively takes her reader through a day of being blind, functioning as a guide (the blind effectively leading the blind?). **Question 6** urges students to follow Kleege's lead—to close their eyes and carry out the tasks she describes and to write a description of the experience to share with classmates.

STANLEY CROUCH Another Long Drink of the Blues: The Race Card in the Simpson Case (p. 410)

Since it would have been difficult to miss the media hype surrounding the O. J. Simpson trial, your students are probably quite familiar with the issues Crouch raises—and whether they agree or disagree, your class is likely to have some lively discussions concerning this piece. In his introduction, J.R. mentions his and A.L.'s apprehension about including a selection on the Simpson trial, and **Question 3** asks students whether such a piece should have been included. Your students' feelings about the trial, O. J. Simpson, racial tensions, domestic abuse, and media involvement in such issues will probably come out in their answers to **Question 3**; getting these reasons and feelings out in the open should help lay a foundation for discussion of Crouch's essay.

Question 1 points students to Crouch's piece in particular by asking them to annotate any sentences that make them uneasy. Some students may point to Crouch's use of name calling: "We make most-favored-victim laws, we hire separatist boneheads onto our university faculties, we tailor our history to self-flagellating theories, experience the national Peeping Tom craze for geeks on talk television. . . ." Others may be bothered by comments concerning affirmative action and "black street crime." Of course, other students are likely to agree wholly with Crouch's assessment, and helping students negotiate and voice their opinions may be a difficult task since many of the issues discussed are controversial.

Question 6 invites students to explain their own understanding of the Simpson trial by writing a letter to a friend who had no access to media accounts of the event. You could have students write this assignment before class discussion and have some students read their papers to the class; such an activity would bring differing interpretations to the forefront, allowing the class to discuss similarities and differences between those interpretations. Since the letter is to be addressed to someone who hasn't had access to media coverage of the trial, you might want to ask students how what they read or heard about the trial affected their viewpoints. What sources did they most trust? (**Question 7** deals more specifically with the part media played in the trial.)

Questions 4 and 5 ask students to compare Crouch's essay to other pieces in the chapter. **Question 5** makes a comparison between Crouch's claim that "black Americans are at the center of our national tale, functioning both as flesh and blood movers and metaphors in the ongoing democratic debate" and Chavez's belief that Hispanics should move closer to the mainstream of American life. In addition to the list of questions under the **Question 5** heading, you could also ask students to consider how the examples Chavez uses differ from or are similar to the ones Crouch uses and what position Crouch might take on issues of assimilation.

LINDA CHAVEZ Toward a New Politics of Hispanic Assimilation (p. 415)

Linda Chavez's position in relation to minority culture is much like that of Shelby Steele (see his essay, "The Recoloring of Campus Life," in Chapter 3, Education): a member of an ethnic minority culture, Chavez takes the unpopular view that the success of members of minority cultures depends not on special treatment like Affirmative Action policies or bilingual education, but on the ability of individuals to accommodate themselves to the standards set by majority American culture (**Question 2**). The power of Chavez's and Steele's argument comes, in part, from their status as members of a minority culture who have succeeded, and who have apparently done so without the special treatment that they feel harms members of minority cultures.

Knowing more about Chavez's own success story (**Question 3**) might make her argument more—or less—convincing, and it might be interesting for students to find out more about her and report their findings to the class with the purpose of exploring how a writer's personal history may affect his or her political position. Here it might be useful to compare Crèvecoeur's view of assimilation to Chavez's (**Question 4**). What are the similarities and differences in these two author's positions in relation to immigrant populations? In relation to majority American culture?

Langston Hughes's "Theme for English B" also deals with the problem of assimilation in relation to minority identity (**Question 5**). As students compare these selections, it might be useful for them to consider not just the argument that each writer seems to be making about the relationship between minority and majority cultures in the United States, but also the image of the writer that is portrayed by the text, and the relationship between the writer's argument, the image of the writer, and the writer's style. Encourage students to talk about which text they found more persuasive and why, taking into consideration the substance of the piece, the students' attitude toward the issue of minority assimilation, as well as their preferences for certain kinds of writing.

In considering why Chavez takes the position she does, students might also want to think about (perhaps even do a little research on) the current status of Hispanics in the United States, in particular the continuing influx of Hispanic immigrants (**Question 1**). This kind of research may also be helpful as students consider the responsibility of the government to minority groups (**Question 7**). As students work toward their own positions on "minority politics," encourage them to consider the issue both in the abstract—what ideally should be the relationship between majority and minority cultures in the United States—and more pragmatically—given the current state of the nation—what position can the government take toward minority cultures?

Because many students see education as the means by which any American, regardless of race or ethnic background, can succeed (**Question 6**), you may want students to focus on this aspect of minority politics. In addition to asking students to follow up on Chavez's argument, perhaps by researching the debate about bilingual versus English-only education, you might also draw on some of the selections from Chapter 3, Education, including Adrienne Rich's "What Does a Woman Need to Know?," Steele's "The Recoloring of Campus Life," and bell hooks's "Keeping Close to Home: Class and Education," and Mike Rose's "Lives on the Boundary."

P. J. O'ROURKE Review of *Guidelines for Bias-Free Writing* (p. 424)

J.R. makes clear in his introduction that he admires O'Rourke's use of language, his "splattering shots of ridicule." In fact, J.R. uses a similar tone to express his appreciation for O'Rourke's piece. **Question 2** asks whether students find the introduction offensive, whether they would prefer a more "neutral" introduction. Students who would prefer a

more neutral introduction would probably prefer that O'Rourke change his tone too.
Question 1 asks students to think about what O'Rourke gains and loses by the way he
presents himself and other in his review. While he may gain the enthusiastic support of
some, he is likely to alienate many others. It might be worth asking your students to
consider who O'Rourke is trying to communicate with. Will the members of the Task Force
on Bias-Free Language take his points seriously? Do students take his points seriously?
What is O'Rourke's argument? Does he have one that he effectively supports (**Question 6**)?

    Question 4 makes a comparison between O'Rourke's frankness and Kleege's frank
acceptance of her blindness and asks whether O'Rourke's blunt use of language "might not
offend those the Task Force . . . is eager to protect." Would Kleege find O'Rourke offensive
or refreshing in his directness? Is there a difference between referring to oneself as blind
and referring to others as "pointy-headed wowsers" "pokenoses" and "blowhards"? Is
O'Rourke functioning as an American in Crevecoeur's terms by writing in an "unfettered"
manner? (**Question 4**)

    A difficulty you may run into in discussing the issues brought up in O'Rourke's
review is that some students—despite O'Rourke's obvious exaggerations—may take him
too seriously, dismissing any consideration of sensitivity in language usage because of the
way O'Rourke presents the members of the Task Force on Bias-Free Language and their
text. While issues of language usage (like the avoidance of using "man" to refer to humanity
in general or "he" to refer to males and females—**Question 5**) are often controversial, many
people will be willing to discuss such issues reasonably, perhaps calling for a middle
ground between free use of language—no matter how offensive—and the supposed dictates
O'Rourke rails against. For instance, you might encourage students to consider the
difference between guidelines and rules, the difference between being needlessly offensive
and narrowly prescriptive. If you have access to a copy of *Guidelines For Bias-Free
Writing*, you could bring in a copy and see if students' interpretation of the book is similar
to O'Rourke's.

LANGSTON HUGHES Theme for English B (p. 432)

Hughes's poem, written from the perspective of a college student trying to complete an
assignment for his composition course, can serve as a poignant closing to the conversation
on difference represented by the readings in this chapter. For the speaker of Hughes's poem,
what it means to be an "American" (**Question 1**) is complicated by the fact that while he
shares many things in common with all Americans, he lives in a time when African
Americans are not free to live where they wish or eat in any restaurant or sit in any seat on
the bus. If students are reading this poem as the conclusion to this chapter, you might want
them to consider the ways in which the speaker's definition of "American" would—or
would not—be different now. Perhaps students could rewrite Hughes's poem from a
contemporary perspective.

    Question 2 asks students to think about a time when they had an experience
similar to the one described in Hughes's poem, perhaps a time when they have written
something that, consciously or not, represented both their own thoughts or feelings and
those of their teacher or of another person who influenced them. Although this activity
gives students one way of understanding Hughes's poem—a way that highlights the

common experience of college students regardless of their race or ethnicity (**Question 6**)—students should also consider the special difficulties faced by the student in Hughes's poem, a poor African American student attending an elite college at a time when segregation was legal in the United States (**Questions 3 and 4**). **Question 5** gives students the opportunity to reflect on how their own position—which is affected by gender, race, class, and family background—has affected their success in school.

Texts in Context: Sequenced Writing Assignments about Difference

Assignment 1
Write a one-page report for your class describing all the ethnic, national, cultural, and/or racial groups you can trace in your own family. Bring your report to class for a composite listing of all the peoples and cultures represented in the history of your class. Does anything about this list surprise you? What does it suggest about what an "American" is? Record your responses to these questions in your reading log.

Assignment 2
The readings in this chapter all speak in one way or another to the title and subtitle: difference and *e pluribus unum*, out of many, one. Look back at two or three of the selections (perhaps Chavez, p. 415, and Bernstein, p. 372) and reread them, asking what motto or saying each one of them might offer instead of or in addition to *e pluribus unum*. Choose one author, then write a brief profile from that author's point of view, putting forth the new motto and explaining why it could appropriately serve as a motto for the United States.

Assignment 3
The selections in this chapter take some very different perspectives on how to define a nation, some explicit like Crèvecoeur's, some implicit like Lassell's. Choose the reading that most appealed to you and then reread it. Then think for a while about why it appealed to you so much, about what in the author's argument or background or point of view allowed you to identify with that perspective. Consider also whether the piece you chose would also appeal strongly to your parents. What might account for their agreement or disagreement with your choice? Finally, draw up a list of reasons (in complete sentence form) explaining why you identify with this author's point of view. Bring your list to class for discussion.

Assignment 4
Imagine Crèvecoeur visiting the United States today. How might he describe the scene he would see now? In a couple of pages, and using Crèvecoeur's text as a model to get you started writing, write a brief essay on "What is an American—200 Years Later."

Assignment 5
Try your hand at describing the America or Americans you see reflected in or emerging from one of the following sources: MTV, the United States armed services, IBM, General Motors, current rap music, Disney, the films of Woody Allen or Spike Lee or the director of your choice. Imagining that all you knew of America or Americans you had to glean from

this source, write a page or so describing your findings. With several other members of your class, compare notes on what you have discovered. Do you agree with your classmates' depictions? If so, why? What might account for your agreement or disagreement over how one of these entities, say the army, represents America? Bring a report of your discussion to the whole class.

Assignment 6

Working with two or three other members of your class, form an editorial group charged with assembling a chapter for a book like *The Presence of Others*. The title of the chapter is to be "Difference: E Pluribus Unum," and it is to include between 8 and 12 selections. Bring in your own nominees for this chapter, being prepared to explain and defend your choices, to say where you are coming from in selecting these pieces, and to negotiate the final list. Together, draft a one-page introduction to your chapter. Then choose one of the selections you provided, or one you like very much, and write an introduction for it (see introductions for each entry in *The Presence of Others* as well as chapter introductions for examples). Finally, write a reading log entry in which you discuss your own introduction: where can you see your own agenda at work, your own biases and preferences present? What does your introduction suggest about what an American is or should be? In what ways does your introduction load the dice in favor of the selection or writer you are introducing?

8 ■ Legends: Larger than Life (p. 436)

The selections in this chapter present a lively and varied conversation on the subject of what it means to be a legend, and in particular, an American legend. The mix of people discussed in this chapter, from Ronald Reagan to Georgia O'Keeffe to Joe Louis, illustrates what makes defining a legend—and defining "American"—such a complicated matter.

Perhaps a good way to get students thinking about what it means to be an American legend would be to have them write an informal definition of the term based on the chapter's introductory quotes. Then as students read and respond to the selections in this chapter, you might have them redefine the terms "American legend" and "icon of popular American culture." Students might also consider the relationship between American culture and its pop icons. Do America's legends and celebrities change as American culture changes? Or do our legends represent enduring American values? How are today's celebrities different from some of those described in this chapter? How are they not different? Who determines whether someone will become popular or a legend? One way in which students can join the conversation presented here is to have them write about someone they believe deserves to be included in this chapter, giving reasons why that person deserves to be called a "legend" or "pop icon." Students might even want to frame this piece of writing as a proposal addressed to J.R. and A.L.

Some of the other questions taken up by the selections in this chapter include:

■ To what extent is American culture defined by its legends and popular culture? (Angelou, Rand, Noonan, Didion, Levy, Crouch, Costas)

■ What functions do legends/pop icons/role models serve for those who admire them? (Angelou, Parks, Didion, Crouch, Costas, Clifton)

■ What relationships are there among American political heroes, religious leaders, and celebrities of popular culture? (Angelou, Parks, Noonan, Johnston, Levy, Crouch, Costas)

MAYA ANGELOU Champion of the World (p. 439)

This selection, from Maya Angelou's autobiographical *I Know Why the Caged Bird Sings*, provides an interesting introduction to this chapter since it highlights an issue some of the other readings discuss only implicitly: the ways in which a person or celebrity can embody a culture's hopes and dreams (**Question 1**). Angelou's depiction of the townspeople's love and admiration for Joe Louis gains some of its power from the social and political context which Angelou provides. In addition to finding out more about Joe Louis (**Question 7**), students might also benefit from doing a bit of research on the social and political climate for African Americans during the 1930s. (They might also gain some insight into what life was like for African Americans then by reading Zora Neale Hurston's "How It Feels to Be Colored Me" and Langston Hughes's "Theme for English B" in Chapter 7, Difference.)

In a culture where African Americans were discouraged or prevented from competing with whites (and where the term "master" still had ominous connotations,

Question 2), Joe Louis represented an African American who dared to stand up to whites and who proved himself to be stronger than a white man. **Question 6** asks students to compare the triumphant scene after Louis's victory to the one Lucille Clifton describes in "malcolm," encouraging them to think about both triumph and sacrifice—joy and sadness. Angelou emphasizes Louis's value to the community: the champion of the world was some "Black mother's son." **Question 5** asks students to compare the elements Angelou points to in establishing Louis as a legend and role model with the qualities of an individualist described by Rand.

Students could also make comparisons between Louis and an heroic white athlete like Mickey Mantle, who was remembered by Bob Costas as a great teammate. Did Mantle symbolize to white fans the same things that Louis symbolized to African Americans? As an extension of this analysis, students might want to consider why sports figures hold such an important position in American culture. What contemporary athletes would they consider heroes today? Given that many of today's sports superstars are African Americans, is athletics one arena in which Americans have become "colorblind" or a sign that not much has changed since the 1930s? In discussing this question, you may need to help students see how even positive stereotypes—African Americans are good athletes—can be considered racist.

Question 4 asks students to think about why A.L. would describe Maya Angelou herself as a hero and a legend. In answering this question, students can certainly refer to the information about Angelou that A.L. presents in her introduction to this selection, as well as any other information they know or can find out about Angelou. But another approach to this question would be to reread A.L.'s profile and some of her introductions and annotations of readings and to imagine why a person like A.L.—a writer and teacher of writing, someone who loves the sounds of spoken language (**Question 3**)—would admire someone like Angelou. In a related activity, students might write about someone they admire and about why someone with their particular interests and background would choose such a hero.

AYN RAND The Soul of the Individualist (p. 443)

J.R., A.L., and T.E. disagree with the qualifications for a creative legend that Rand sets up in her work. The speaker of Rand's piece, Howard Roark, describes legends and creators as selfish, unsubmissive individuals who stand alone and against other people. How does this characterization of legends compare to students' understandings of what a legend is (**Question 1**)? Have students read *The Fountainhead* or Rand's other works like *The Virtues of Selfishness*? Since the annotators view Roark in a negative light, you may want to ask if there's any student who wishes to defend (especially since this excerpt is a defense speech from a trial) Roark? Is it significant that Roark gives a speech in his own defense? Is he functioning as an individualistic legend by doing so? Would he want anyone to come to his defense?

Question 2 points to Roark's argument that those who live to help other make suffering a priority in life. How would Roark feel about people like Mother Teresa? If Roark's understanding of legends is that they stand against others in achieving their accomplishments, would a sports figure like Louis or Mantle, who was loved and admired by many, be a legend in Roark's terms (**Question 3**)? What might have been Louis's or Mantle's motivations—selfish, altruistic, or some mixture of the two?

As J.R. mentions in his introduction, Roark's understanding of excellence differs significantly from Hannah Arendt's claim that the presence of others is necessary for excellence. **Question 5** asks students who they most agree with, Arendt or Roark. Another way of getting to this question might be to ask students who their own legends or role models are and how those people's accomplishments or qualities compare to Roark's understanding of what a legend should be. Can students think of film or television legends who fit Roark's profile (**Question 8**)? What impact do these figures have on popular culture? On individuals?

Roark claims that existing for no other person and asking no other person to exist for you is the only form of mutual respect possible. **Question 6** asks whether any other figure in the Legend chapter shares such an attitude. You might ask students to think about whether there is any difference between existing for others and requiring that someone else exist for you and caring deeply for the good of others and wishing to be cared about. How do students define mutual respect and brotherhood or sisterhood? How might other figures in the chapter define these concepts? Is altruism a form of slavery? **Question 7** asks students to consider the previous question in terms of their own civic, moral, and/or religious training. In answering this question, students might also consider differences between responsibilities, obligations, duties, and desires. What do they feel motivates themselves and others to do good for others?

ROSA PARKS Role Models (p. 452)

Parks's essay broadens the discussion of legends by encouraging students to think about the similarities and differences between what it takes to be a legend and a role model. Do the characteristics differ (**Question 3**)? Clearly, A.L. sees Parks as both role model and legend (**Question 2**): she points to Parks's "humility, her steadfast faith, and her commitment to young people everywhere," qualities which make her a role model for some. And A.L. also reminds readers of the act that made Parks a legend: her refusal to give up her bus seat to a white passenger. How might Ayn Rand's understanding of role models be similar to or different from Parks's (**Question 4**)? You could ask students whether Parks would be a role model in Rand's terms. Why or why not?

How do students define legends and role models? **Question 7** invites students to think concretely about what characteristics their own role models have and asks them to write an essay about the people they most look up to. Do they choose relatives, sports stars, friends, teachers?

Question 1 implies that Parks is a quiet, calm, woman who doesn't use any extra words and asks students to consider how these qualities are represented in Parks's writing. And there's also strength represented in Parks's writing—a quality alluded to in the title of the book this piece is excerpted from: *Quiet Strength*. **Question 5** ask students to consider how Parks's piece "illuminates Angelou's claim that 'we were the strongest people in the world.'" Indeed, this strength is illustrated by Parks's husband, who "refused to be intimidated by white people"; by her mother, who helped Parks feel proud of herself and other black people; by her grandfather, who taught Parks not to let anyone mistreat her; and by black leaders, who led fearlessly. **Question 6** encourages students to look beyond the piece in this chapter—to work in small groups to conduct further research on Parks, and this question gives several suggestions for places they may go to gather more information. This project would be ideal if you require students to do class presentations; if so, you could give the group assignment a week or two in advance of the day you plan to discuss Parks's piece.

PEGGY NOONAN Why We Already Miss the Gipper (p. 456)

It seems clear in his introduction that J.R., too, already misses "the Gipper"—he claims that Reagan will likely outlive his critics and "become the American who defines his era, a figure almost large enough for Mt. Rushmore." Similarly, Peggy Noonan offers high praise for Reagan, a man she claims was seen as "One of Us" by a variety of people (**Question 1**). Of course, not all students will share J.R.'s and Noonan's admiration for Ronald Reagan. One way to help students—those who admire Reagan and those who don't—share their assessments of Reagan is to assign **Question 6** before you discuss Noonan's piece. If students choose Reagan as the subject of their interviews and interview a variety of people, they are likely to hear many different assessments of Reagan and his work as president. Their own assessments will also come through as they respond to the second half of **Question 6** by writing an essay; those essays can be read aloud in class, and students can be encouraged to identify the ways other people's assessments are similar to or different from Noonan's.

As **Question 2** points out, Noonan structures her piece as a list of reasons why people miss Reagan. To consider the effectiveness of this stylistic choice, you could have students respond to **Question 5** by making a list as a prewriting activity of qualities they admire in a particular public figure and by reworking the information in their list into a more traditional essay form. What have they gained or lost by abandoning the list form in favor of the essay? What does Noonan gain or lose in her stylistic choice?

Question 4 makes a connection between Noonan's claim that Reagan held his beliefs not to be popular but because he believed his views were right and Rand's suggestion that creators act independently of public opinion. This question further asks students to consider whether Reagan—as Noonan presents him—would be a legend in Rand's terms. This consideration should remind students of the importance of making one's definitions clear, for different definitions—of "legends" and other key concepts—often reflect differing understandings of people and the world.

JOAN DIDION Georgia O'Keeffe (p. 461)

A.L. opens her introduction to Didion's essay with a discussion of heroes and legends, and **Question 3** asks students to distinguish between the two terms. It's clear that A.L. considers O'Keeffe a legend in the art world; would she also consider her a hero? Would Didion see O'Keeffe as a hero? **Question 2** asks students to consider Didion's attitude toward O'Keeffe, an attitude revealed in this essay by Didion's characterization of O'Keeffe as "hard, a straight shooter, a woman clean of received wisdom and open to what she sees." Didion also refers to O'Keeffe as "astonishingly aggressive," as one who fought against the estimations of men. **Question 5** points to Didion's admiration of O'Keeffe and Noonan's admiration of Reagan and asks if the traits each author admires in her subject are similar or different. The last part of the question invites students to record their own response to one of the essays, perhaps reflecting on what qualities they most admire.

Question 6 may alert students to the difficulties—and pleasures—of trying to "capture the life, personality, and importance" of a person they consider a legend in an essay. Such an assignment should function as an exercise in the process of selecting and ordering, a process that often reflects the writer's own interests. If two or more students choose the same legend to research, you could have them compare their essays, reflecting on how the choices they made were similar to or different from the choices of a classmate. Did they interpret events in a legend's life in the same way? Did they use similar sources? Did they ever disagree with the interpretations presented in sources they used?

Question 7 should also reveal how point of view affects interpretation. This question asks students to interview a member of the Art Department in order to identify the "men" Didion generally refers to in her essay. The question also prompts students to research these male artists and to write a version of Didion's fourth paragraph different from the point of view of "the men." In attempting to see from the point of view of the men, are students any more or less sympathetic to O'Keeffe as Didion presents her? What effect does Didion achieve by lumping all "the men" together? (**Question 1** asks students to consider the effects of Didion's use of quotation marks to emphasize certain words.)

GEORGE SIM JOHNSTON Pope Culture (p. 466)

Johnston's article discusses the impact Pope John Paul II has had—and continues to have—on the United States and Europe. It deals not only with politics and social issues but also with something more foundational: how people make decisions, what values are based on. **Question 1** sets up a dichotomy between "natural law, an antecedent moral sense implanted in man and written into the nature of things" and relativism. The question asks students to investigate the differences between the two and to discuss the consequences of accepting either of these "world views." After students have considered these terms, it might be helpful to discuss their understandings of them as a class: Who decides what is natural law (and by extension unnatural) when people disagree about a moral or social issue? Is relativism unnatural? On what does one base decisions if one is a relativist? Is committed relativism an option? How about relativistic natural law? You might also ask students what they base their decisions on and if they consider themselves relativists, proponents of natural law, or something else—and why.

Perhaps more fundamental than how humans make moral decisions is the question of the nature of human beings. **Question 5** points to John Paul II's belief that humans are specially created by God—in God's image—"to make a gift of self to another being." This view of the self can easily be contrasted with the view Rand presents in "The Soul of the Individualist," and **Question 5** asks students which view they find more heroic or challenging. You could also ask students to contrast the views Rand and Johnston present with views presented by other writers represented in the chapters. How, for instance, might bell hooks, Terry Tempest Williams, Andrew Sullivan, or Newt Gingrich define the nature and purpose of human beings? How might the Pope's understanding of humans affect (determine even) some of his positions on social issues like abortion or population control (**Question 2**)?

  Question 6 takes up the issue of the role of religious leaders in the political decisions of democratic societies. How much influence should they have? You could encourage students to not limit their thinking about this issue only to the role the pope should play but to also think about other religious leaders who have been involved in politics such as Jerry Falwell, Pat Robertson, Billy Graham. **Question 4** makes a connection between Ronald Reagan and John Paul II as actors, asking students to consider how their stage training may have affected their leadership qualities. **Question 7** also encourages students to think about influence—not just in a political sense, but more broadly—by asking them to consider how some leader (religious or not) has impacted the way they view the world. Or if they've not been impacted by a leader, whether they see the absence of such influence as negative or positive. While **Question 7** is structured as a writing assignment, you could also ask students to list on the board the leaders who have impacted their lives, noting what types of leaders (spiritual, political, popular, economic, etc.) are influential.

STEVEN LEVY Bill's New Vision (p. 474)

After reading Johnston's article, students may be surprised by Tom Brokaw's comparison: that walking with Bill Gates is like walking with the pope. They may also be surprised by how others view Gates—some regarding him as "nearly divine," others as "satanic." You may want to ask your students whether they also have strong feelings—whether good or bad—about Gates. What exactly is it about Gates that causes many people to view him with such strong feelings? Money? Power? Intelligence? Responding to **Question 7** might help students answer some of these questions as they research more about him. Perhaps, on the basis of their research, a small group of students could give a presentation on Gates. Did they find anything about Gates that surprised them? Anything that confirmed or contradicted Levy's article? If students follow the suggestion to write a response to Levy's article, you could ask them to analyze their own use of quotations from Gates, as **Question 1** asks them to analyze Levy's use of quotations.

  Question 3 asks students how they think A.L. views Gates, and what in her introduction leads them to the conclusion they come to. And how, **Question 4** asks, might Ayn Rand regard Gates? Would he be one of her heroes? What would Gates and Howard Roark have in common? **Question 5** shifts the focus from how others view Gates to a consideration of who in his viewpoint might serve as a role model. Students' nominations for Gates's role models—and their reasons for those choices—may also reflect how students view Gates.

  While many students depend heavily on computers and other forms of electronic technology, they may not be familiar with some of the terms Levy uses in his article. **Question 2** asks students to keep a list of words that are unfamiliar and bring them to class discussion. Those students with more familiarity may be able to lend some helpful insight concerning the more technical terms. **Question 6** asks all students, regardless of their comfort level with electronic technology, to monitor their activities for several days in order to determine how dependent they are on such technologies. Your discussion of these issues could be tied effectively to some of the articles in Chapter 5, Science—especially Kelly's "Interview with the Luddite" and Birkerts's "Perseus Unbound."

STANLEY CROUCH Blues for Jackie (p. 480)

Although most students in first or second year composition classes were not alive in 1963 when John F. Kennedy was assassinated (their parents, though, are probably able to locate in memory exactly where they were and what they were doing when they heard the news), they are likely to remember Jacqueline Kennedy Onassis—the news stories of her death, or perhaps even singer Sinéad O'Connor's "Jackie O." Stanley Crouch writes about the Kennedy era from the perspective of the "blue-collar Negroes [he] grew up among" and groups of domestic workers in his mother's kitchen; students will bring other perspectives to the conversation. **Question 1** asks them about the images they have of Jackie Kennedy. Where did those images come from—songs, parents, television, movies, history books? In class, you could encourage students to discuss the images of Jackie Kennedy they have. How do those images compare to the ones Crouch presents?

To extend the discussion of images, you could have students read the short papers they wrote responding to **Question 5**, which asks students to research a single aspect of Jacqueline Kennedy's life. If different students choose different aspects, a fuller picture of her should emerge as the students present their reports. Do the reports present her as a "real" person, or does she take on mythic or legendary—bigger than life—status? **Question 7** points to the Kennedy Administration's cultivation of associations with Camelot and asks students to consider the political power of such associations. You could also ask students to consider the power of the associations Crouch uses—his comparison between Kennedy at her husband's funeral and Mary seeing the body of Jesus taken down from the cross. What effect(s) does this association have? **Question 2** asks students to research two of Crouch's other allusions—his comparison between Jackie Kennedy and Bessie Smith or Mahalia Jackson. Once students understand Crouch's allusions more fully, you may want to ask them which allusions they find most effective and why.

Question 6 leads students in an examination of the "different roles first ladies that have played in recent presidential administrations" and then asks them to consider how such roles will develop in the future. Do students see any patterns of change? How do they view active/public spousal participation in the administration (like Hillary Clinton's participation)? What might the role of spouses of presidents be if the United States elects a female president? Are the people of the United States likely to elect an unmarried president? Why or why not?

Question 3 points to the form of Crouch's piece—eulogy—and asks students to look up its definition and etymology in order to describe how Crouch's and Bob Costas's pieces exemplify this genre. Does one piece more closely follow the form of a eulogy? Can students think of eulogies written for other popular figures?

BOB COSTAS Eulogy for Mickey Mantle (p. 483)

While Costas's "Eulogy at Mickey Mantle's Funeral" and Crouch's "Blues for Jackie" are both examples of eulogy, Costas's piece is more oral in tone—written to be delivered as a speech (**Question 1**). Costas makes reference, in his opening line, to the audience who are all thinking about Mantle. There is a collective "we" and reference to particular people in the audience (like Billy Crystal). What effect do these textual qualities have on the reader? Does he or she feel more a part of the funeral ceremony—or more excluded? Do students recognize the other baseball players Costas mentions?

Question 5 gives students the opportunity to write an eulogy about a figure they admire; more than a life history, a eulogy can be a form through which one expresses deep feeling and admiration—perhaps recalling memories and telling stories. If students write about a sports figure, they could tell a story about an important game they attended, a competition that was especially important (**Question 7**). Eulogies often limit the discussion of a person's life to the positive aspects of that personality, and if negative aspects are mentioned, they're generally not dwelt upon. As **Question 6** points out, Mantle did not live a perfect life; the question goes on to ask "how much of a legend's life the public is entitled to know and judge." Do students want to know the failings of public heroes? To what extent should a person's "private" life affect his or her legendary status? Given the fact that sports figures greatly influence young people (**Question 3**), to what extent should they be role models in ways that go beyond athletic records?

Question 4 asks students to make connections between Mantle's achievements and those of John Paul II. It may be helpful to remind students that George Sim Johnston opens his article by saying that "a senior writer at *Time* was advised to put the final touches" on the pope's obituary. In what way does an obituary differ from a eulogy? You could ask students to write a eulogy for John Paul II. In what ways is their eulogy similar to or different from Costas's eulogy for Mantle? **Question 4** also asks whether society gives "too much credit to sports heroes and other celebrities." Since it makes a connection with the pope, is the question implying that society doesn't give enough credit to religious leaders? Who might deliver a eulogy for religious leaders like John Paul II or Billy Graham? What would their accomplishments be?

LUCILLE CLIFTON malcolm (p. 488)

The briefest piece selected for this volume, Clifton's "malcolm" is just seven lines. In these seven lines, though, there are many concrete images that function in both literal and figurative ways: closed doors, women with saved heads, men in alleys, ambushed prophets, and black eagles. **Question 2** asks what these images suggest about Malcolm. Does Clifton, through her use of images, express any ambivalence toward him (**Question 1**)? While these two questions help students consider the content of the poem, you might also ask them to think about the form. What is the effect of the poem's briefness and the fact the every letter is lowercase (which is characteristic of most of Clifton's poetry)? What might it mean that every line except the last could function as a complete sentence, but no punctuation is used in the poem? Do students notice any tension between active and passive verbs? A consideration of the formal elements of this poem may help students consider the formal elements of their own writing, the choices they will make as they respond to **Question 3**, which asks them to compose a poem about another legend represented in the chapter. Encourage them to think about what images might best represent the legend they choose and how their use of line breaks and punctuation affect the way the poem is read.

Texts in Context: Sequenced Writing Assignments about Legends

Assignment 1
Write up a nomination for "Greatest Legend of All Time." You might choose a person, a character, or even an object as your nominee. In your nomination, explain why your particular nominee deserves "greatest legend" status. Be prepared to present your nomination in class.

Assignment 2
Some of the selections in this chapter are explicit about the legends they discuss, as in Angelou's description of boxing champion Joe Louis or Costas's eulogy for Mickey Mantle. Some are more implicit, however. What or who is the "legend" of the Rand piece, for instance, and how do you know? In addition, consider the ways in which some writers stress the positive aspects of a legend (Angelou), some negative (Levy), and some present a mixed view of the legend (Costas). Reread two essays in this chapter and write a statement concerning each writer's possible motivation for presenting his or her subject in a particular light. Bring your statements to class to share with two or three others. Then together, try to decide why the writers of these pieces see their subjects as legendary heroes, and whether or not heroes must always be role models. Make a list of reasons to support your decision and report them to the entire class.

Assignment 3
Would O'Keeffe be likely to be a "legend" for Rosa Parks? In a paragraph or two, explain why or why not. (You might choose to say whether Malcolm X would be a hero to John Paul II or vice versa, or you might consider the same question in regard to Mickey Mantle and Ronald Reagan.)

Assignment 4
Together with several class members, divide up the readings in this chapter and look at each one for clues it provides about what it takes to become or be a legend. Make a list of the items you identify in your selection(s) and bring them to your next group meeting. Together, draw up a description of "What Makes a Legend." Bring your description to class and be prepared to defend what you have said there.

Assignment 5
Spend some time after the work you and the class did on assignment 4 considering what the lists and descriptions you came up with suggest about what our society does and does not value in the way of legends. What kind of people, characters, and objects don't ever seem to get to be legends or heroes? Why don't they? Make some notes in your reading log in response to these questions. On the basis of your notes and the list you drew up for

assignment 4, ask yourself whether there are people in this chapter who don't meet the criteria you've established. Does the label of "legend" not fit some of them? Write a brief report to your class in answer to these questions.

Assignment 6
Do a bit of field research by asking six or eight people to nominate their first choice for greatest legend of all time and to give one or two reasons for their choices. Try for as much variety in your group of people as possible—go for different ages, different cultures or backgrounds, different personalities, and so on. Bring your list of nominees to class and assemble the entire group on the board. Then break into groups and talk for 15-20 minutes about what may account for the differences of opinion among the nominators. Together, draw up a report of your discussion to present to the whole class.

Assignment 7
Return to assignment 1 and reread it in light of the work you have done in the preceding six assignments and in the readings for this chapter. Revise your nomination for Greatest Legend of All Time. Then add to it a memo to your teacher and classmates. In this memo, reflect on what you have learned about your own values and preferences by looking at your choice of a legend. Consider what influences in your life led you to make the choice you did as well as what influences led you *not* to choose other possible nominees.

Part Four How We Live

9 ■ At Home: The Places I Come From (p. 490)

The readings in this chapter form a conversation about an issue all students have experience with but may have never analyzed: the idea of what a home is and what it should be. Although this chapter's more overt focus on what is thought of as personal experience makes it somewhat different from other chapters in this book, it also illustrates, as do many of the readings in other chapters, how personal experiences are related to political positions. The focus on the personal in this chapter also suggests in concrete ways how much is at stake when the government—and the public—debates about welfare reforms, gay parenting, teenage pregnancy, abortion rights, and the decline of the nuclear family.

As students work to enter the conversation about home and family presented in this chapter, you might encourage them to think about the issues from both the perspective of their personal experiences and from the perspective of American culture and American values. Although some students will welcome the opportunity to write about their own family and home experiences, others will be reluctant to reveal such personal information. Helping students to see that ideas of home and family are public as well as personal issues will allow them to engage with the subjects of this chapter without feeling that they must be self-revealing.

Some of the questions raised by the readings in this chapter include:

- What constitutes a typical American home and how has the typical American home changed as American culture has changed? (Didion, Seabrook, Smith, Frawley)

- To what extent should the American public or, specifically, the U.S. government, be responsible for providing homes for all its citizens? (Buckley, Himmelfarb, Frawley)

- How do issues of race, gender, and social class affect a person's home life? (Walker, Seabrook, Smith, Williams, Buckley, Himmelfarb)

- To what extent does the natural environment provide a sense of home? (Walker, Williams, Madden)

- In what ways does loss affect one's relationship to and understanding of home? (Walker, Smith, Williams, Madden)

JOAN DIDION On Going Home (p. 493)

Didion's essay, written from the perspective of a young married woman with a child, deals with the complicated relationships adults continue to have with the family they grew up with. In this respect, Didion's essay may describe an experience that many students just beginning college may not yet be familiar with. But in another respect, the experience Didion describes may seem uncomfortably familiar to students who have moved away from home for the first time, established in their dormitories and apartments their own homes away from home, and who are struggling to work out a new kind of relationship with their parents and siblings. **Question 3**, which asks students to analyze Didion's attitude toward "home," might be a starting point for their analysis of the relationship between the home they grew up in and the home they have established at college. It might be useful for students to compare their responses to Didion's essay (**Question 8**) and to consider how their experiences with their families and their feelings about being at college might have affected their response to Didion and then to consider how the differences in their experiences may account for differences in their responses.

Another issue raised by Didion is that ideas of home are changing—or by the 1990s, thirty years after Didion wrote this essay, have already changed (**Question 2**). One purpose of Didion's essay seems to be to express her mixed feelings about these changes rather than to analyze and comment on the nature of these changes, so students may want to gather additional information about the changing nature of American home life, some of which they can glean from the other texts in this chapter, such as the essays by Barbara Smith (**Question 5**), Alice Walker, and Jill Frawley, as well as through interviews with their own parents or older relatives or through library research.

In addition to reading Didion's essay as an essay about change, students can read "On Going Home" for the ways in which its representation of home and family may be true across generations. **Questions 1** and **7** ask students to focus on some of the "truisms" embedded in Didion's essay: the warring relationship between the mother and daughter, the idea that in marrying you betray your primary alliance to your family, or the feeling of being both similar to and different from members of your family. **Question 6** deals with a practice that is probably carried out by all parents—and by people who imagine they will one day be parents: making wishes on behalf of one's children. Students should be encouraged to consider the ways in which Didion's relationship to her family is both like and unlike their own family relationships and, perhaps more importantly, to consider why.

ALICE WALKER The Place Where I Was Born (p. 497)

In this piece, Walker uses both poetry and prose to demonstrate feelings of loss, longing, and love. A central figure in the piece is a tree with "old-growth pine nobility," one that functions as a metaphor for Walker's heart and symbolizes not only the destruction of nature but also a loss of Walker's childhood. **Question 1** points to the importance of the tree and asks students to consider what in the natural world they most love. Intimacy with the natural world is a theme in much of Walker's writing, and you could ask students to be especially aware of this theme as they respond to **Question 6** by researching Walker's life and work. Before starting more in depth research, students should reread A.L.'s introduction to Walker's piece (**Question 3**), which emphasizes Walker's education and work for civil rights, to begin thinking about some other possible themes of Walker's life and work.

Referring to the landscape of her birth in the first stanza of her poem, Walker writes, ". . . to save myself I pretended it was *you* / who died." Two couplets later, she says, ". . . now I can confess how I have lied." **Question 2** points to this passage, asking students what lie it is Walker has told. Because of her separation from her home—the landscape of her birth—Walker describes herself as a "displaced person." **Question 5** encourages students to consider what other people represented in the home chapter might be displaced. Surely the people in the nursing home Frawley describes would be displaced. Could Jeremy Seabrook also be described as displaced? What about the speaker in Barbara Smith's piece? In what ways might these people's displacement be similar and/or different?

Like Walker, Terry Tempest Williams feels a strong connection to the landscape of her birth—the deserts of Utah. And she, too, writes of loss. Didion's piece reflects her ambivalence toward home and a sense of longing for a certain kind of home. **Question 4** asks students to make these and other connections between the three pieces and then to write about which description of home is most compelling to them. The description students choose may be the one that reflects their own feelings about home—feelings of longing, peace, anger, ambivalence. These feelings may be reflected in their own writing as they respond to **Question 7** by writing their own essay and/or poem entitled "The Place Where I Was Born."

JEREMY SEABROOK Family Values (p. 502)

As J.R. mentions in his introduction, the concept of family values has been the topic of "intense political scrutiny" to such an extent that it's difficult, even, to know what such a phrase means. You may wish to start discussion by having students define "family values" for themselves and then to consider where their definition comes from: Are their understandings of this term shaped by their own experiences with family? The relationships they wish they shared with family members? A political position? Students could also consider how other writers represented in the chapter (like Gertrude Himmelfarb, who uses the phrase in her piece) would define family values. **Question 1** points to the cultural differences between "family life as Seabrook experiences it in India" and "perspectives on family values in the United States." In answering this question, students could compare their own values to the ones represented by Jagat's family.

If some students mention the equal treatment of men and women as one of their family values, they may be disturbed by Jagat's privileged status in his family in relation to his mother and sister, who both worked and waited on him (**Question 2**). Why was Jagat privileged, and how might he be a resource for family security in the future? How do students feel about the commitment to take family members—and extended family members—in and care for them when they are sick or old? (This question might be especially relevant if students have read Frawley's "Inside the Home.") What personal, political, and financial ramifications might this practice have if it were carried out widely in the United States (**Question 6**)? Another social difference between Indian and American cultures is the practice of arranged marriages. **Question 5** asks students to consider how the United States would be different today if parents chose their children's spouses. You could encourage students to think about this question in terms of their own experience: Would their parents be married today if their grandparents had been responsible for making the match? How would arranged marriages change their own dating practices? What space would arranged marriages leave for people who would rather not marry? What would be the position of homosexuals in such a culture (**Question 4**)?

Reading other essays in this chapter through the lens Seabrook's "Family Values" offers may be enlightening to students. **Question 3** asks how Jagat's mother or another Indian person might describe Joan Didion's relationship with her family. And if Jagat and his family were "shocked and disturbed" to learn that Seabrook was unmarried, what would their response be to Andrew Sullivan? You could also ask students to consider how writers like Williams, Buckley, Frawley, or Himmelfarb might respond to the family life and values Seabrook describes—would they find such family systems comforting, confining, or perhaps a little of both?

BARBARA SMITH Home (p. 507)

In her introduction, A.L. says that "home" in Barbara Smith's story is "not a specific place but rather . . . a location in the mind or heart, somewhere outside of time and space that signals rest and, most of all, acceptance," and **Question 3** asks whether students agree with A.L.'s statement. Indeed, students may have difficulty pinning down exactly what is the definition of home in this story, for it seems to shift and grow as the piece progresses. You could encourage students to read this story as a working and reworking of one woman's understanding of and need for home.

A multifaceted "home" is expressed through the narrator's need. Home is first defined as, "The house where I grew up," but the narrator quickly moves to a discussion of the women who reared her: her understanding of home cannot be separated from her desire for these women: her mother, grandmother, aunt. **Question 1** points to the importance of these relationships—the ways in which they are "passionate" and "complicated." The narrator imagines calling her aunt and telling her about her new home—the apartment she lives in and shares with her lover, Leila. She daydreams about talking with her aunt about making that vital connection between the past and her present, for without that connection, the speaker is displaced—not only physically but emotionally, like Alice Walker is in "The Place Where I Was Born" (**Question 4**).

Leila's talking with her mother is a connection to home, a connection the narrator doesn't have. Rather, she clings to objects—dishes, letters, a bank book—to maintain her connection. She sees her relationship with Leila as a way of loving passed down by her aunt, and the speaker wants to take Leila back to her childhood house, to her aunt, to find one of the necessities of home: acceptance. While Leila and the narrator are making a home for themselves, there's still fear—the fear of loss. **Question 2** asks students to consider that fear of loss and their own response to it. Another way of having students consider the issue of loss is to ask them to respond to **Question 5** by writing a poem called "Family Cemetery" from Smith's perspective, a poem peopled with the characters of her story.

Finally, it seems, home for the narrator resides in memory and imagination, for it's in her mind that she makes connections between her past and present loves—there she finds acceptance. **Question 6** should help students consider their own definition of home by writing down their associations with it and using those associations as a starting point for writing an essay.

TERRY TEMPEST WILLIAMS The Clan of One-Breasted Women (p. 513)

Unlike Barbara Smith, Terry Tempest Williams doesn't explicitly define home, but elements of her home—family and the Utah landscape—are central to her essay. Like Smith, Williams discusses loss—the loss of her mother, aunts, and grandmother to cancer and the destruction of the land she loves. A.L. ties these two losses together by invoking the metaphor "Mother Earth" to show how the destruction of our environment also affects mothers and others who people the earth (**Question 4**). Williams links these two losses to nuclear fallout from bomb testing in the 1950s and 60s. She admits that she can't prove that the women in her family developed cancer because of nuclear fallout, but she provides evidence to show the connections between the two. As A.L. writes in her Afterwords, "Williams is not writing a traditional academic 'argument,' in which she sets up building blocks of 'proof' to support her." Rather, she weaves stories together to evoke a response in her readers. **Question 1** asks students to identify the strategies and evidence she uses to support her belief.

       Williams's essay isn't only about loss; it is also life affirming, with death and birth images juxtaposed in evocative ways (**Question 2**). In spite of death and destruction, her essay ends on a hopeful note with a group of women "stranded" in the desert, knowing they were home. **Question 7** invites students to think about some environmental issue that affects their own home; such an assignment should help students relate Williams's essay concretely to their own lives and concerns.

       Questions 3 and **8** both deal with dreams—the dreams Williams includes in her essay and the dreams students have themselves Williams includes two dreams in her piece. a recurring dream of a flash of light in the desert night, which her father explains as the bomb they saw one night when Williams was a child; and the dream of women who trespass on contaminated land, the way Williams and others do later in the piece. The dreams seem to affirm and authorize Williams's beliefs and actions, emphasizing the importance of intuition. While **Question 3** asks students to consider why Williams includes her dream in her essay—what purpose the dream serves—**Question 8** asks them to further explore the relationships between dreams and reality by considering their own dreams.

       It could be argued that Williams's dreams help give her the courage to cross the line at the Nevada Test Site, an act of civil disobedience. **Question 9** asks students their own position on civil disobedience. If you discuss this question in class, you could have students think about others who have committed such acts—from Thoreau refusing to pay taxes to Parks, who refused to give up her seat on a bus. You could list other acts of civil disobedience (like blocking the entrance to an abortion clinic or freeing animals in laboratories), asking students when, if ever, such acts are justified. Students could also bring up times they have participated in acts of civil disobedience—and their reasons for doing so. Or as **Question 6** asks, What are a citizen's responsibilities when faced with social and environmental problems?

WILLIAM F. BUCKLEY JR. Should There Be a Law? (p. 525)

Whether or not students agree with Buckley, they—like J.R.—are likely to appreciate his direct, clear style and writing. **Question 2** points directly to Buckley's rational style and asks students to discuss other strategies a writer might use to address a problem comparable to the issue of children born out of wedlock. Terry Tempest Williams's essay offers an alternative—a personal narrative. Buckley could have written about the ways this issue has affected his personal life: Was he born to unwed parents? Did he ever impregnate a woman who wasn't his wife? Does he live next door to the people he writes about? **Question 4** turns the tables, asking students to imagine the problem Williams writes about written as an exploratory rather than personal essay. What might be gained or lost by such a recasting? **Question 5** invites students to use Buckley's form and style to write about some other local or national problem.

Unlike Williams's essay, Buckley's is a more traditional, logical argument. But for such an argument to be effective, the reader must share Buckley's assumptions and premises. **Question 1** helps students consider those assumptions and how—if they don't agree—they might modify or qualify them. If students can accept enough of Buckley's assumptions to enter the argument with him, they are invited by **Question 6** to respond directly to Buckley's challenge by offering their own suggestions about what might be done about the problem of births to unwed mothers. In small or large group discussions, these issues can also be debated: What might the consequences be of Buckley's suggested deterrents? Who would be responsible for enforcing such deterrents? Does Buckley take into account those individuals who want children and are not married? Do his deterrents take into account *why* women have children without being married? Of course, students will think of many more questions to add to this short list.

GERTRUDE HIMMELFARB The Victorians Get a Bad Rap (p. 528)

Himmelfarb, like Buckley, clearly takes a conservative stance in her op-ed piece. As **Question 1** mentions, she criticizes liberals who "jeered," "cackled," and "sneered" at conservative ideas that, in Himmelfarb's terms, turn out to be "right." The effectiveness of this short column depends, in many ways, upon appearances: characterizing liberal media people in such a way that they appear mean and foolish, showing that orphanages may not be as bad as they appear, making it appear that children in single or no parent families are responsible for most if not all social ills, and making Victorian ideals appear virtuous rather than oppressively confining. You may wish to ask students to look closely at the strategies Himmelfarb uses to make these appearances. (Some strategies include her use of adjectives and verbs and the examples she selects and carefully presents; as well, **Question 2** takes up the issue of Himmelfarb's authority on the subject of Victorianism.) Do students see the Victorian ideals Himmelfarb describes—chastity, cleanliness, orderliness, and shame—as virtues that are or should be returning to American life (**Question 6**)?

Question 3 asks whether Himmelfarb's proposal for more orphanages responds to Buckley's concern about out-of-wedlock births. While Buckley seems more concerned with punishing parents than with providing a space for children, both writers think shame and stigma should deter people from having children while unmarried. **Question 5** asks students to discuss the issue of re-attaching a stigma to out-of-wedlock births. Who would benefit from such a stigma? Who might be hurt?

Question 4 asks how orphanages would fit with the Indian family structure described in "Family Values." Since Seabrook describes an ideal in which members of a family take care of each other, would there be any place for orphanages? Any need for them? Yet Seabrook also describes a family that accepted him as an extended member of their family. Could orphanages be seen as a kind of family in which all members care for each other? How do you and your students define family? In what ways might an orphanage be a home?

JILL FRAWLEY Inside the Home (p. 533)

Jill Frawley's exposé of the nursing home in which she worked should prove thought-provoking to students whether or not they know people living in nursing homes. In addition to asking students to summarize Frawley's position on the degree to which nursing homes are what they claim to be (**Question 1**), invite them to bring their own experiences with and feelings about nursing homes to bear on their responses to Frawley, as A.L. has done in her introduction (**Question 3**). In addition, students can work in groups to do additional research on nursing homes, perhaps even researching such homes in their communities or the college community in an effort to determine whether Frawley's generalizations about the inhospitable and even harmful environments of nursing homes are accurate (**Question 7**).

Before answering **Question 4**, which asks students to look at a number of selections in this chapter and to try to write a definition of "home" that accounts for all of them, they may wish to respond to **Question 5** by writing a dialogue between Frawley and Seabrook about the definition and importance of home. How would Jagat and his family (characters in Seabrook's essay) respond to the kind of home Frawley describes—even the idea of a nursing home? In addition to complicating the idea of what constitutes a home in America, Frawley's essay raises the interesting issue of a person's relationship to her work and her employer (**Question 6**). Certainly some of the power of Frawley's description of the nursing home comes from the fact that she was an employee of that home, one charged with caring for patients but unable to do so because of the workload—something she ascribes to the greed of her employers. **Question 2** asks students to consider not only Frawley's attitude toward her employers, but also her attitude toward the patients and toward herself and where (and how) these attitudes are revealed in her essay.

ED MADDEN Family Cemetery, near Hickory Ridge, Arkansas (p. 537)

Ed Madden's poem provides a fitting ending to this chapter, not only because it is about the end of life and the ways in which the deaths of family members bring an end to family life as it once was, but also because it is about the complicated connections within families that manage to endure. Both "Family Cemetery" and Terry Tempest Williams's "The Clan of One-Breasted Women" are about the loss of family, and students may want to compare these two pieces for what they say about both physical and emotional losses—and connections. Both pieces also share an attention to nature, and students might benefit from considering the ways in which our relationship to the natural world is like or unlike our relationships to one another. To what extent is the natural world our home? To what extent is our extended family our home? **Question 1** asks students to read Madden's poem along with Seabrook's "Family Values." How are the ties between family members similar and/or different in the two pieces?

Question 3 asks students to write about an important moment in their own experience of family. You might have them compare the subjects of their descriptions or poems and discuss the range of topics they chose. Were there specific moments that several students chose to write about? Could those moments be considered archetypal or universal family experiences? What kinds of differences emerged in their choice of topics and how might they account for those differences? Based on this activity, and on the other reading and writing they have done for this chapter, would they say that families are generally alike or generally different?

Texts in Context: Sequenced Writing Assignments about Home

Assignment 1
The selections in this chapter offer some dramatically different definitions and representations of "home," from Didion's wish that her daughter's experience of home will be positive, to the nursing home in Frawley's essay, to the sense of home evoked in Ed Madden's poem. Begin this sequence by brainstorming a list of all those things you associate with home—including feelings, sights, smells, sounds, tastes, objects, and anything else that comes to mind. What picture of home emerges from this brainstormed list? Does that picture match your memories of home, or what you wish for in a home—or perhaps some of both? Using your notes and responses to these questions, draft a statement for what might become a class book on the concept of home. Perhaps begin by thinking about how you would finish this sentence: "For me, home means ____."

Assignment 2
Some demographic statistics and predictions suggest that the traditional American family, defined as a married heterosexual couple, one of whom is primarily at home to care for children, is already a thing of the past. What evidence can you find in the selections of this chapter to support or to refute such predictions? What can you offer from your own experiences and those of other people you know to add to that support or refutation? Bring your responses to these questions to class for discussion in small groups, particularly noting any differences of opinion that come up in your group. Based on your reading, responses, and discussion, prepare a brief essay, story, scene, or poem on "What American Families Will Look Like in 75 Years."

Assignment 3
Choose the selection in this chapter that is the most irritating or problematic for you and try to figure out where that writer's views and perspective on the home and family are coming from. To help you answer this question, think for a while about where your views come from, most likely your own experience with different kinds of homes and families. Beyond that personal experience, however, what other influences can you detect? Take a close look at the TV shows you like, the things you like to read, the movies you go to, the songs you listen to, and so on. What picture of home and family emerges from one or more of these sources? Is it the same picture of home and family you have? Make extensive notes on what

you find out from investigating one or more sources of possible influence on your ideas about home. Then go back and reread the selection you chose as most irritating or problematic. What does your investigation into where your own ideas about home and family come from suggest both about why you dislike the selection and what external forces might have influenced the ideas of home and/or family presented there? Prepare a 3-4 page report for your class called "Alternative Representations of Home (or Family) in ___ or ___."

Assignment 4

In class, divide into groups and work together on creating an exchange on the concept of home among the members of any of the following groups: Alice Walker, William F. Buckley Jr., and Jeremy Seabrook; Terry Tempest Williams, Gertrude Himmelfarb, and Barbara Smith; Ed Madden, Joan Didion, and Jill Frawley—or any other grouping you come up with. Try for a dialogue of 2-3 pages, and try to imagine what each writer might say as thoroughly as you can. Be prepared to read your dialogues aloud in class.

Assignment 5

After reviewing the readings in this chapter and your work on assignments 1-4, prepare a revision of your statement (assignment 1) on what home means to you, including reasons for thinking as you do about home and how your thinking has developed or changed. Gather these statements together for a publication called "Contemporary Perspectives on Home"—and consider asking your instructor to provide a preface for the class publication.

10 ■ Work: As Poor Richard Says . . . (p. 541)

Since many students view their college education as a means to more satisfying and/or better paying work, this chapter—with its emphasis on economic problems and opportunities—is likely to be of great interest to them. This chapter also interacts with other chapters in the text by helping students consider how education, science, gender, difference, and home affect one's work life. Although some selections, like Franklin's, emphasize the individual worker and his or her role in achieving success through work, many of the selections also emphasize the social forces that shape work conditions and the American economy. The questions in the introduction ask students to consider how Americans feel about work and the state of the economy, how workers should be treated, and how technology affects work. The questions following readings and in the sequenced writing assignments focus on particular selections and then invite students to consider their own experiences with and feelings about work.

Some of the questions raised by the readings in this chapter include:

- What counts as valuable or meaningful work? (Carlisle and Hoff, Coupland, Piercy)

- Are proper training and good work habits enough to "succeed"? To what extent do factors beyond an individual's control affect the work one can do? (Franklin, LeSueur, Carlisle and Hoff, James, Scanlon, Cox and Alm)

- Should young people be concerned or optimistic about the state of America's economy and the availability of jobs? (Osterman, Carlisle and Hoff, James, Gingrich, Cox and Alm)

BENJAMIN FRANKLIN The Way to Wealth (p. 545)

In his introduction, J.R. says, "Perhaps common sense and thrift never go out of style." Indeed, common sense and thrift are two qualities Franklin calls for in his piece—along with hard work, little rest, and no debt. In the voice of Poor Richard, Franklin seems to imply that anyone who lives by his maxims is certain to earn wealth. There are individuals represented in this chapter who would probably find Poor Richard's aphorism timely and true, but there are also those whose experiences would make them question the simplicity of some of his claims. What would America look like today if people followed the advice given in "The Way to Wealth" (**Question 8**)? Would there be a deficit? Who would own houses (without taking out loans)? Would anyone go on vacation? What jobs would no longer be necessary? What would the economy be like if people really spent little and saved and worked a lot? Would shopping malls be necessary? Who would have time to shop? **Question 1** asks students to identify any of the aphorisms they see as outdated, and **Question 9** gives them the opportunity to write maxims that are more up-to-date. What advice would Poor Richard give to Americans in the 1990s?

Although students may find some of the specifics of Franklin's piece outdated, some will find many of the principles behind his maxims sound advice. **Questions 2** and **7** point students to issues important to America's present-day economy—the role of government in the lives of citizens and the importance of staying out of debt. Students could be asked to consider what other writers in this chapter would be likely to agree with Franklin (or Poor Richard) on these issues and why. One way for students to compare and contrast the views Franklin presents with those held by other figures represented in *The Presence of Others* is to write an imaginative dialogue (**Question 6**). In this dialogue, students could imagine Poor Richard as one of Bill Gates's employees, imagine Poor Richard and Newt Gingrich talking politics or shopping for suits, or place Kirkpatrick Sale and Poor Richard together looking in the window of an appliance store.

In his introduction, J.R. points to Poor Richard's mistrust of leisure, and **Question 5** asks what role work-related maxims play in our lives. Do students feel guilty when they're not working? Do they work in order to finance leisure time? What factors influence their attitudes toward work and rest? Should a healthy lifestyle combine the two?

MERIDEL LeSUEUR Women and Work (p. 554)

The introduction to the work chapter discusses some of the tensions between capitalism and communism, and students who have studied American history are likely to understand what it meant—especially for someone, like a writer or actor, whose work was public—to be black-listed. Students should be encouraged to consider how social issues—like political associations, gender, and sexual orientation—can affect not only what one is allowed to do for work, but how that work is received. With her emphasis on community and being a voice for others, LeSueur's narrative may offer implicit qualifications to some of Franklin's neat aphorisms. **Question 5** invites students to write a few Poor Richard-like maxims in LeSueur's voice.

As a young girl in 1910, LeSueur knew that women had few career options and that those options were limited further for her because she was poor and could not afford an education. Of course, students are likely to rightly argue that times have changed and there are more options open to women, but LeSueur's narrative shouldn't be dismissed because times have changed. You could ask students to voice the changes that have taken place in LeSueur's lifetime and what things have not greatly changed. For instance, **Question 1** points students to LeSueur's discussion of "female stereotypes"—are some of those stereotypes still expressed today? And **Question 2** takes up LeSueur's assertion that the film industry was a "meat market" and asks whether that analogy holds today as well. Certainly there have been changes in people's experiences with work over the past eighty years. **Question 6** gives students an opportunity to interview people who are in their 80s or 90s about their work lives—recalling their earliest jobs and other memorable moments from work.

One important assumption behind *The Presence of Others* is that the positions an individual takes can be illuminated and better understood when seen in the context of the positions others take. **Question 4** asks students to assess who in the chapter LeSueur would have most in common with and who she'd most strongly disagree with—and why. One person with whom LeSueur would probably have very little in common is Henry Scanlon; **Question 3** gives students the chance to address Scanlon in LeSueur's voice, bringing up issues from a perspective different from Scanlon's. Putting people in dialogue together (even imaginatively as several questions encourage) helps show the differences and similarities between the stances writers take and makes students' understandings of the pieces more clear.

In reading and discussing the selections in this chapter, students will have many opportunities to consider the work others do—and the negative and positive aspects of that work. **Question 7** gives them an opportunity to consider the work they would most like to do and to explore their knowledge and feelings about such work. If you discuss this question in class, you could also ask students what they as children dreamed of doing for work, and whether they as college students are preparing to do that work. If not, why? What kinds of influences and pressures (finances, talent, parents, expectations, education) affect the work one ends up doing? What considerations do students take into account in preparing for a career?

PAUL OSTERMAN Getting Started (p. 558)

Osterman's piece, like Julia Carlisle's, points to some of the anxiety that young people feel about acquiring meaningful and secure employment. Many people—like Julia Carlisle—assume that those with college degrees are entitled to jobs in the field they prepared for in college, but the economic situation in America may leave young, educated job-seekers disappointed (**Questions 1** and **4**). While Osterman admits that even college graduates may have difficulty finding the jobs they desire, he offers evidence to prove that the situation is worse for those without a college degree (**Question 2**). As students reflect on these issues in relation to the readings, you could also encourage them to talk about their own expectations. Do they feel anxiety about the job market? Did they choose to come to college hoping to find a better job? In choosing a major, did they consider the employment situation in their respective fields? How do the college graduates they know compare to the "young people gainfully employed" represented in *Microserfs* (**Question 5**)?

Since Osterman makes a direct correlation between education and employment, students may wish to consider the ways in which their education has or has not prepared them for finding a job (**Question 7**). What experiences have students already had in the job market? Is preparing students for future employment the purpose of education? How would John Henry Newman (Chapter 3, Education) respond to such an idea (**Question 6**)? Do students see major differences between the type of education one receives in a liberal arts college and a vocational school? What is the relationship between book learning and practical experience? Are colleges responsible for providing both?

Question 8 asks students to consider the role the government should play in job training and school-to-job transition programs. What would the benefits be of such programs? Would the benefits be worth the price? Students should be encouraged to research Job Corps programs, perhaps even interviewing people who have been involved in such programs. Should there be options for students who do not wish to attend college (like internships or apprenticeships) to help them prepare for entering the work force? If students do not feel job training is a governmental responsibility, what other options do they see for preparing young people for the work force? Is education enough?

JULIA CARLISLE and FLORENCE HOFF Young, Privileged, and Unemployed (p. 566)

Carlisle and Hoff offer differing perspectives on work. Carlisle, who expects work to provide or reflect her self-worth, says, "Without doubt, we are our work." Her position raises an important issue: If we are our work and can't find or do the work we value, where then do we find self-worth? Hoff offers a different perspective on work; for her, work is a means to survival, even if one's job is "demeaning to the human spirit." How do students feel about work? Do they side with Carlisle or Hoff, feel sympathy with both or neither? To better articulate their own positions on what work is and should be, **Question 2** asks students to write definitions for work from Carlisle's, Hoff's, and their own perspectives. Using their definitions for work as a basis for response, they can then answer **Question 6** by writing their own letters-to-the-editor in response to Carlisle's article. In drafting their own letters, students should be encouraged to look closely at A.L's, J.R.'s, and T.E.'s responses. The writers of these responses use details from the texts they are responding to in order to illustrate and support the points they are trying to make. Students can further analyze details by responding to **Question 1**, which asks them to consider how Carlisle and Hoff use details in order to persuade their readers—students can use the same kinds of strategies in their own letters-to-the-editor.

      Question 7 helps remind students that attitudes are shaped largely by experiences, and this question encourages them to consider where either Carlisle's or Hoff's attitudes come from. What does it mean for Carlisle that she, as A.L. writes, is "privileged"? In what ways is Hoff not privileged? How did their backgrounds differ? In what ways have their parents' experiences helped shaped these women's views on work? Students should also be encouraged to consider how these factors shape other people's understandings of work. Why is Newt Gingrich, in *To Renew America*, so optimistic? How might Carlisle or Hoff respond to his claims—and why? (**Question 5**) If Hoff were to write to Coupland's "microserfs," what would she say? (**Question 4**) How do her experiences differ from theirs?

      Question 7 then asks students to consider the ways in which their own understandings of work have been shaped by their experiences and other external factors—from the media, to family, to school. In small groups, students could talk about their own educations and family backgrounds. Do students who come from similar socio-economic backgrounds share similar attitudes toward work? What roles do education, faith, gender, and home play in how they view work?

CARYN JAMES Pop Culture: Extremes but Little Reality (p. 572)

The two articles selected from *The New York Times* series "The Downsizing of America" illustrate why people like Julia Carlisle—and many others—feel anxiety about job security. Like the Carlisle and Hoff pieces, these articles show that downsizing affects both blue- and white-collar workers, but not necessarily in the ways popular culture media portray. **Question 8** gives students the chance to survey other students' feelings about downsizing and finding and holding a job. You could assign this question a week before you discuss these selections, urging students to bring in their findings so that the class can assess the feelings of their peers on these important issues.

In her introduction, A.L. challenges Franklin's Poor Richard, asking, "But what if those with both a 'trade' and a 'calling' can't find places to put them to good use?" A.L. voices concern on behalf of her students, students who "are plenty worried about getting and holding a job." **Question 1** asks students what stances James and A.L. take toward job insecurity and how these attitudes are revealed in their writings. While A.L. mentions her concern for her students' worries, how does James make her position clear? Are journalists supposed to let their own attitudes and biases show? In what ways are attitudes revealed even in seemingly objective forms of writing? How does James's article compare to "More Than 43 Million Jobs Lost"? While **Question 2** asks students to identify the points of agreement and disagreement between the two, it might also be instructive to have students think about differences in form. Does it make any difference that the writers of "More Than 43 Million Jobs Lost" are not cited by name? In what ways does the evidence they use differ from the evidence James uses? How do their sources and analyses differ, and what effect do these differences have on how their pieces are read?

Although "More Than 43 Million Jobs Lost" offers a largely bleak picture of job security, it is in some places hopeful: "Most workers who lose a job find another before very long . . . [and] more jobs usually are created than destroyed." (Of course, the article also points out that the new job will likely pay less.) If students have already read and discussed the Sommers and Faludi pieces in Chapter 6, Gender, they may be especially aware of how statistics can be used and interpreted. Does the statistic that says the total number of jobs is increasing affect the interpretation of lost job statistics? How do students interpret the information given in the sidebar? Do their interpretations agree with the article? Given the optimistic tone of Gingrich's essay, how would he respond to the "The Downsizing of America" pieces (**Question 4**)? Would he have any solutions to offer? Would he even agree there is a problem?

Questions 6 and **7** give students the opportunity to test James's thesis by analyzing the ways in which popular culture sources—television, film, music—represent work in America. If your students do class presentations, **Question 6** should prove to be an interesting prompt for them to respond to. You could ask them to bring in movie and television clips or songs—ones that they have analyzed or ones they would like the class to respond to in discussion. They could look closely at the examples James provides ("News Radio," "Falling Down," "Roseanne," "Grace Under Fire," "Dead Presidents," etc.) or find other examples from sources like documentaries, talk shows, or soap operas. What is the purpose of popular culture? Is it supposed to reflect social situations as they are? What other purposes might it serve? While James claims that popular culture does not clearly reflect the job situation in America, **Question 7** asks students to find an example from pop culture that does represent their own "view of the current jobs situation in the United States" and to explain why the example they've chosen seems to be a correct representation. Does it match an experience they or someone they know has had? If several students do this assignment, you could have them compare their sources and the images of work these sources portray. How are they similar or different? What might account for the differences in viewpoints?

NEWT GINGRICH America and the Third Wave Information Age (p. 576)

In his essay, Gingrich admits that technological change "inconveniences employees" and is "likely to put a few people out of work," but his assessment is far more optimistic than the one presented in "More Than 43 Million Jobs Lost." He argues that the world is entering a "Third Wave of Change," an age in which people can invent their own futures. The attitude toward technological change that Gingrich expresses in his essay is likely to make Kevin Kelly smile and neo-Luddite Kirkpatrick Sale (Chapter 5, Science) shiver. **Question 1** helps students consider change in concrete terms by having them list items and products that were not available just two generations ago. (If students have visited Disney World, they may remember some of the changes detailed in the attraction "The Carousel of Progress.") **Question 1** then asks them to categorize items on the list, identifying areas of significant change. How has travel, communication, or medical technology changed? What hasn't changed? While technology, indeed, may bring about many of the changes Gingrich expects, how people feel about those changes differs significantly (**Question 5**).

    Questions 6 and **7** allow students to consider their own expectations and frustrations with technological change. While **Question 6** gives them the opportunity to write a paper detailing their own vision of the future, perhaps describing some exciting advances or changes they think will be good, **Question 7** asks them to describe a time when they felt overwhelmed in dealing with change. Together these questions suggest that technological change can be both negative and positive—that one can look at both good and bad effects of change, weighing consequences and celebrating progress.

    Question 2 asks students to consider Gingrich's purpose and audience. Who is he writing to? Would students respond any differently to this essay if they did not know it was written by Gingrich? How is his ability to persuade affected by what students know and feel about his politics? Who is likely to benefit from the kind of competition and entrepreneurialism he advocates? How might valuing "entrepreneurialism and inventing" over "liberal social issues" affect society? Do Gingrich and Bill Gates (Chapter 8, Legends) share a similar vision of the future (**Question 4**)? Would Gates be a hero to Gingrich? Would Gingrich be a hero to Gates?

HENRY SCANLON Suddenly, I'm the Bad Guy (p. 585)

In his introduction, J.R. praises Scanlon's "sympathetic personal ethos—the kind that makes readers willing to listen." **Questions 1** and **2** deal with the ethos Scanlon establishes, as well. **Question 1** asks students to point to the places where Scanlon attempts to establish trust between himself and his reader and to consider what he gains or loses by writing in the first person. After his initial sarcasm, Scanlon establishes himself as merely confused, wondering when it was that he became a bad guy. He points to his own good qualities: hard work, fairness, willingness to pay taxes. But it's not only in praising himself that Scanlon tries to prove that he's a good guy; he also applauds his employees and the country he adores. **Question 2**, though, points to one place where Scanlon's strategy may be off-putting to some (especially those who are not already sympathetic to Scanlon): his comparison of Bill Clinton to a pickpocket. How does this device affect the ethos Scanlon tries to establish? Is the comparison a sly form of name-calling or a simile to illustrate a valid point? Why does Scanlon think the Clinton administration wants to set up conflict between rich and poor? Are there natural conflicts between the two groups? Is such conflict perpetuated by the media (**Question 5**)?

Name-calling, in fact, is central to this essay. Scanlon doesn't want to be considered a "bad guy" (or worse) any more than athletes want to be considered "dumb jocks." **Question 4** asks students who belong to some group that often receives negative criticism to write a defense, explaining why they are really not bad. One of the ways of getting people to understand that you're really not bad is to establish a compelling personal ethos—to have people look beyond ugly names and view you as a person with good motives and feelings.

While a few selections in this chapter offer implicit qualifications to some of Franklin's maxims, Scanlon seems a good example of how someone, through "many years of hard work, [and] not a little bit of luck," can find a way to wealth. But how would Scanlon respond to people like Carlisle and Hoff who haven't found such great success? Would he be sensitive to their problems? Offer either of them a position in his growing business? Tell them they're just not working hard enough? **Question 3** give students the chance to imagine Scanlon's response by writing a letter in his voice.

W. MICHAEL COX and RICHARD ALM By Our Own Bootstraps (p. 589)

In contrast to the bleak view of job security presented in "More Than 43 Million Jobs Lost," J.R. offers "By Our Own Bootstraps" and the claim that "how you perceive the economy may influence your ability to rise within it." **Question 7** gives students the opportunity to gauge how others in their communities feel about American economy by testing four claims made in Cox and Alm's introduction. As students conduct their surveys, they might also find it helpful to ask why the people they interview agree or disagree with the claims they are testing. What in people's experience leads them to the positions they hold concerning the state of American economy and opportunity? The Cox and Alm selection is a collection of exhibits, tables the students are invited to analyze. It should be interesting to see how students analyze these pieces, to see what conclusions they come to and why. Do their interpretations and conclusions differ?

Question 1 asks students to examine Exhibit 3 and to list questions and concerns they'd like to see addressed further. Some issues they may want to consider include: How does the opening example function as part of the argument Cox and Alm are making? Are the individuals and the economy they describe similar to American populations and economy? To what extent do students feel individuals control their own financial well-being? Is it primarily "differences in talent, motivation and preferences" that lead to income inequality? What factors—in addition to the ones Cox and Alm cite—do students think affect income inequality? Or, as **Question 6** asks, "Should economic equity be a goal of American society?" Like Poor Richard, Cox and Alm seem to be optimistic about an individual's power to succeed. In responding to **Question 4**, students can try to turn the information in Exhibit 3 into maxims or aphorisms like the ones Poor Richard offers.

Clearly, Cox and Alm offer a more optimistic view of the economy than Carlisle and Hoff seem to have. Would either of these women find the information offered in these exhibits comforting (**Question 3**)? Do Cox and Alm discuss work in terms of satisfaction and value? Does economic gain equal happiness? Should people like Carlisle and Hoff follow the suggestions given in Exhibit 9? What pressures might prevent people from following such suggestions? **Question 5** asks students to investigate the library or World Wide Web to further research one of Exhibit 9's recommendations, considering how people have exercised the option in the past and what the results were.

DOUGLAS COUPLAND Microserfs (p. 595)

As J.R. says in his introduction, "*Microserfs* is virtually a catalog of 1990s icons and obsessions." **Question 1** urges students to explore these icons and obsessions further by annotating the selection and explaining each popular culture allusion. After students have attempted this assignment on their own, they could work in small groups to compare their responses. Did they understand and define Coupland's allusions similarly? Do they see Coupland's novel as what Sven Birkerts (Chapter 5, Science) might call "a souped-up cognitive collage" (**Question 4**)? Do students know any people who are similar to the characters described *Microserfs*? One interesting strategy for quickly defining people and their interests is to do so in terms of *Jeopardy!* categories. Having students define themselves in such terms (**Question 2**) should be a fun class activity—and potentially enlightening too.

Students could also use this same defining strategy as they write about the place they work or go to school and the people they encounter in such settings (**Question 5**). In preparation for answering **Question 5**, you could spend some time in class discussion analyzing other elements of Coupland's style in this selection: first person journal entries from one character's perspective (including a self-introduction), short descriptive paragraphs, use of concrete details, use of both informal and technical language.

Coupland's characters may exist in the Third Wave age of information Newt Gingrich describes, but **Question 3** asks, "Are the visions of these two authors compatible?" Does the technology Coupland's characters use, in Gingrich's terms, "empower and enhance" them as people? Are these characters the innovative entrepreneurs Gingrich so admires? Would students like to do the kind of work these "microserfs" do? **Question 6** invites students to write a paper detailing the kind of work they hope to do and to share the satisfactions they hope to gain from such work. Implicit in students' discussion of the work they desire to do may be their assumptions about what work is and the types of rewards it should provide.

MARGE PIERCY To Be of Use (p. 607)

Two themes of the work chapter are the desire for work that is satisfying and the importance of working hard. Piercy's poem deals with both of these themes. In the first stanza, Piercy uses the metaphor of people jumping into water "head first" and becoming "natives of that element" to show the kind of worker she values. Another metaphor follows in the second stanza: people as hard working as oxen who demonstrate "massive patience" and "do what has to be done, again and again." These are the kinds of people the speaker loves best. **Question 2** asks students to compose their own stanza, describing the people they love best. Perhaps they could follow Piercy's example and use a metaphor in their own stanza to create a vivid picture. In addition to pointing to the kind of people they admire, **Question 1** asks students to identify work that is worth doing, the kind that "has a shape that satisfies." What kinds of work would (and would not) fit this definition? If the "work of the world," as Piercy describes it, "is as common as mud," what kinds of work might Piercy define as "real"? **Question 3** asks students this question and to give reasons for their answers. You could encourage students to use lines from the poem and information from A.L.'s introduction concerning Piercy's background to support their answers.

Texts in Context: Sequenced Writing Assignments about Work

Assignment 1
The selections in this chapter offer various viewpoints on "work," from Carlisle's desire for work that is meaningful and financially rewarding; to LeSueur's understanding of her work (her writing) as a way of bearing witness; to Gingrich's hope that changes in technology will transform work as we know it today. Begin this sequence by brainstorming a list of your own associations with work. Are they primarily negative or positive associations—or a mix of both? What viewpoint can you offer on the subject of work? Is it similar to one of the points of view represented in this chapter? Drawing from your list of associations and your answers to the questions above, draft a 2-3 page statement for your classmates that begins, perhaps, like this: "From where I stand, work. . . ."

Assignment 2
Choose the selection in this chapter that appeals most to you and try to figure out where that writer's views and perspective on work are coming from. To help you answer this question, think for a while about what has most influenced your views on work, most likely your own experiences with different kinds work or the work you've seen your parents or other family members do. Does the position the writer takes voice some of your own hopes or fears? Is that writer in a situation you've been in before or in one you expect to be in the future? What attitude toward work is expressed in the selection you've chosen? Imagine being a co-worker of the writer you've selected. What would it be like to work with him or her? Write a story, poem, or scene from a play, or a narrative essay entitled, "A Day on the Job with ___."

Assignment 3
Interview four people who do different types of work—perhaps a homemaker, lawyer, garbage collector, and factory worker (or any other grouping you can think of). Try for variety in age, gender, class, and profession. Talk with these people about the work they've done in the past and the work they do today. How do they feel about their work? Do they see the work that they do as, in Marge Piercy's words, "work that is real"? What are some similarities and differences between the people you've interviewed? Using the information you've gathered from your interviews, write a statement for your classmates on the topic "Kinds of Work That Are Real." (Of course, you'll also have to provisionally define what you mean by "real.")

Assignment 4

In class, divide into groups and share the information you gathered in your interviews and the statements you wrote. Are there any kinds of work you heard about that you wouldn't describe as "real"? Any that you wouldn't describe as "satisfying"? Working together, prepare a brief (10 minute) report of your findings for class, being sure to report on areas of disagreement as well as agreement.

Assignment 5

Review the work you've done for assignments 1-4, considering again the various perspectives on work people (you; your classmates; the writers, characters, and editors represented in the chapter) hold and the feelings associated with them: excitement, fear, hope, anxiety, weariness, satisfaction, ambivalence, disgust. Consider how these multiple points of view create a complex view of work, one that points out both the good and the bad elements of work and our society's views of work. Brainstorm alone or with several classmates about what you have come up with: In what ways can work be advantageous and "real"? In what ways is it disadvantageous or even harmful to the individual worker, to society, or even to the environment? Finally, using your notes as well as your responses to assignments 1-4 and selected readings in this chapter, prepare an essay (4-6 pages) in which you discuss this question: In what ways does work both constrain and free, enslave and liberate, people today?

A Conversation on the Composition Classroom: Exploring the Personal and Political

The essays that follow are intended to introduce you to an important conversation taking place among composition teachers and theorists about what it means to teach reading and writing at the college level. One issue that has provoked much public debate has been the question of bringing into the classroom what both advocates and critics call "politics," a term that invites a wide range of definitions. Since this conversation about the politics of writing instruction is one (among many) that has been in the background as *The Presence of Others* was being written, we thought it would be useful for you to consider how this book fits into that conversation.

As you read the following articles, we invite you to join the conversation represented by these texts by engaging with them in the ways you will ask your students to engage with the texts they read. First, consider your initial response to the question, "What is the relationship between politics and writing instruction?" Then, read these texts critically and analyze your responses. Enter into conversations with other teachers about the issues raised in these texts. Articulate your own position on the issue, one based on your experience as well as your reading. And finally, take some time to reflect on why you hold the position you do.

GERALD GRAFF What Has Literary Theory Wrought?

Recent literary theory has had many harsh critics, and I was once one of the harshest. Perhaps in spite of myself, however, literary theory has profoundly changed the way I teach.

Since the mid-1960s, I have frequently taught Joseph Conrad's *Heart of Darkness*. When I first assigned the novella in 1966 or 1967, I taught it in much the way that it had been taught to me in college in the late 1950s, as a profound meditation on a universal moral theme. I presented Conrad's story of the destruction of the idealistic trader Mr. Kurtz as a universal parable of the precarious status of civilized reason in a world too confident it has outgrown the seductions of the primitive and the irrational.

Recent literary theory teaches us that what we don't see enables and limits what we do see. My reading of *Heart of Darkness* as a universal parable of reason and unreason allowed me to see certain things in the novel that I still think are important. But it also depended on my not seeing certain things or treating them as not worth thinking about.

Of little interest to me, for example, was the fact that Conrad sets the novella in the Congo in the high period of European colonialism or that he chooses subjugated black Africans to represent the primitive, irrational forces that are Kurtz's undoing. That Conrad chose black Africa to represent primitive impulse was, I thought, incidental to his main intention, which was to make a statement about the human condition that transcended mere matters of geography and race.

It did not occur to me that black readers of the work might not have the luxury of dismissing the question of race so easily, and the small number of black students in my classes at that time helped guarantee that the question never came up. Political issues like the subjugation of black Africans might interest historians, sociologists, and political scientists, but in teaching literature such issues were at best of ancillary interest.

Today I teach *Heart of Darkness* very differently. One critical work that caused me to change was an essay by the Nigerian novelist Chinua Achebe, "An Image of Africa: Racism in Conrad's *Heart of Darkness.*" Mr. Achebe argues that Conrad's presentation of black Africa is thoroughly racist. And he is able to accumulate an uncomfortable number of quotations from the novel and from Conrad's letters and diaries that make it painfully clear how cruelly stereotyped Conrad's thinking about the black African is.

Mr. Achebe argues that Conrad reduces Africa to a mere "setting and backdrop which eliminates the African as human factor" and directs all our attention instead to the tragedy of the white imperialist Kurtz. As Mr. Achebe puts it, "Can no one see the preposterous and perverse arrogance in thus reducing Africa to the role of props for the breakup of one petty European mind?"

The real issue, Mr. Achebe says, "is the dehumanization of Africa and Africans. . . . And the question is whether a novel which celebrates that dehumanization, which depersonalizes a portion of the human race, can be called a great work of art." My answer is: No, it cannot.

After reading Mr. Achebe's essay, I could not teach *Heart of Darkness* as I did before. It was not that he convinced me that *Heart of Darkness* is totally racist—in fact, he didn't. What he did convince me of was that Conrad's assumptions about race are not simply an extraneous or nonliterary element of the novel, but something that the novel's literary and aesthetic effect depends upon. In this sense, Conrad's novel is not a disinterested work of art but a text that has played an active role in constructing the Western image of black Africa and in justifying the West's political and economic treatment of black Africa.

In short, Mr. Achebe's essay forced me to rethink my theoretical assumptions about literature. First, I was forced to recognize that I had theoretical assumptions. I had previously thought I was simply teaching the truth about *Heart of Darkness*, "the text itself." I now had to recognize that I had been teaching an interpretation of the text, and one that was shaped by a certain theory that told me what was and wasn't worth noticing and emphasizing in my classroom. I had been unable to see this theory as a theory because I was living so comfortably inside it.

When I assign *Heart of Darkness* to undergraduates now, I also assign the Achebe essay. I don't however, simply teach his interpretation as correct; I ask my students to weigh it against competing interpretations. Nor do I simply discard my former reading of the novel as a contemplation of universal truths about the human soul. I assign another critical essay that advances that interpretation. I also assign essays by critics who take issue with Mr. Achebe, conceding that he is right about Conrad's racism and colonialism but arguing—and I agree with them—that he overlooks the powerful critique of racism and colonialism that coexists in the novel with these more sinister attitudes.

After reading Conrad we read Mr. Achebe's novel, *Things Fall Apart*. When you come to this novel after reading his essay on Conrad, it is hard to avoid reading it—and the very different view of Africa it presents—as an answer to Conrad. It is as if the Nigerian writer were attempting to wrest the power to represent Africa away from the great European, testifying again to the way aesthetic representations are involved in struggles for power.

Finally, I supplement those materials with several short essays presenting opposing sides in the debate over the place or non-place of politics in art. I also invite conservative colleagues into my class to debate the issues with me and my students. To make sure that my students enter the debate rather than watch passively from the sidelines, I usually assign a paper or ask them to present their own positions in class.

In short, I now teach *Heart of Darkness* as part of a critical debate about how to read it, which in turn is part of a larger theoretical debate about how politics and power affect the way we read literature. With such an approach I think I am following the dominant trend in contemporary theory, which is not to reduce literary works to transparent expressions of ideology. That is the impression that has been given by critics, whose hostility to current theory exceeds their willingness to read it.

The most influential recent theories say that literature is a scene of contradictions that cannot be subsumed under any "totalizing" system or ideology. The only critic of literary theory I know who gets this right is Frederick Crews, professor of English at the University of California at Berkeley. In an essay called "The Strange Fate of William Faulkner," in the March 7, 1991 issue of *The New York Review of Books,* Mr. Crews accurately summarizes recent theorists as saying "that literature is a site of struggle whose primary conflicts, both intrapsychic and social, deserve to be brought to light rather than homogenized into notions of fixed authorial 'values.'" Mr. Crews presents a model of what a scrupulous critique of current theory should look like: He shows how at its worst this kind of theory simply replaces the clichés and predictable readings of earlier critical schools with a new set of clichés and predictable readings, but how at its best it has revitalized fields such as the study of William Faulkner's work.

What, then, has theory wrought for my own teaching of literature? Teaching *Heart of Darkness* as I now do does constitute a "politicized" way of teaching, for it puts ideological conflicts at the center of literary works and of the conflicts over interpretation. Yet contrary to the charge that such an approach lowers academic standards, introducing ideological conflicts seems to me to have made my course more challenging, not less. Theory seems to have raised the academic standards of my course considerably; my students now have to be more reflective about their assumptions than before, and they must take part in a set of complex debates that I previously hadn't expected them to.

Students don't seem to feel that the interpretive and theoretical debate distracts them from close reading of literature itself. On the contrary, I believe that the debate over the critiques of Mr. Achebe and others forces them to pay closer attention to the verbal and stylistic texture of *Heart of Darkness* than they would otherwise. Theory is not something *added on*, to talk about if there's time left over after you've finished teaching the work itself; it is a reflection on what is being assumed while you teach the work.

Nor has any student complained that reading Conrad alongside a non-Western writer "dilutes" the Western tradition, as so many conservatives charge. On the contrary, students have told me they felt Mr. Achebe's novel gave them a better grasp of Conrad's "Westernness," since they had something to compare it with.

I believe that all sides are being political in the dispute over literature, theory, and other educational issues today; the neo-conservatives' pretense that it is only their opponents who are acting politically is pure hypocrisy. The real question we should be addressing is not who is being political but whose politics are *better*—better grounded in truth and justice.

For it does not follow that once you say that a statement is "political" or "ideological," you have undermined its truth. What I have been arguing here is deeply political but no less true for that fact. Nor does it follow that raising political issues and taking positions on them in class means forcing my students to conform.

I believe the way to turn what is now an ugly scene of anger and recrimination into a useful and productive debate is to bring our present disagreements into our classrooms. The way to protect students from intimidation by dogmatists of the left, the right, and the center is to expose them to the debates among these factions. We are already implicitly teaching these conflicts every time a student goes from one course or department to another; we should start doing it in a way that enables students to experience and enter the debate.

I recognize how difficult this can be when there is so much hatred and acrimony in the air, but the hatred and acrimony seem to me all the more reason for channeling the debate into the orderly forums of the classroom.

Gerald Graff is professor of English at the University of Chicago. This article is adapted from a speech at a meeting of the National Association of Scholars.

MAXINE HAIRSTON Diversity, Ideology, and Teaching Writing

Where We Have Come From

In 1985, when I was chair of CCCC, as my chair's address I gave what might be called my own State of the Profession Report. On the whole it was a positive report. I rejoiced in the progress we had made in the previous fifteen years in establishing our work as a discipline and I pointed out that we were creating a new paradigm for the teaching of writing, one that focused on process and on writing as a way of learning. I asserted that we teach writing for its own sake, as a primary intellectual activity that is at the heart of a college education. I insisted that writing courses must not be viewed as service courses. Writing courses, especially required freshman courses, should not be *for* anything or *about* anything other than writing itself, and how one uses it to learn and think and communicate.

I also warned in my chair's address that if we hoped to flourish as a profession, we would have to establish our psychological and intellectual independence from the literary critics who are at the center of power in most English departments; that we could not develop our potential and become fully autonomous scholars and teachers as long as we allowed our sense of self worth to depend on the approval of those who define English departments as departments of literary criticism.

We've continued to make important strides since 1985. We have more graduate programs in rhetoric and composition, more tenure track positions in composition created each year, more and larger conferences, and so many new journals that one can scarcely keep up with them. In those years, I've stayed optimistic about the profession and gratified by the role I've played in its growth. Now, however, I see a new model emerging for freshman writing programs, a model that disturbs me greatly. It's a model that puts dogma before diversity, politics before craft, ideology before critical thinking, and the social goals of the teacher before the educational needs of the student. It's a regressive model that undermines the progress we've made in teaching writing, one that threatens to silence student voices and jeopardize the process-oriented, low-risk, student-centered classroom we've worked so hard to establish as the norm. It's a model that doesn't take freshman English seriously in its own right but conceives of it as a tool, something to be used. The new model envisions required writing courses as vehicles for social reform rather than as student-centered workshops designed to build students' confidence and competence as writers. It is a vision that echoes that old patronizing rationalization we've heard so many times before: Students don't have anything to write about so we have to give them topics. Those topics used to be literary; now they're political.

I don't suggest that all or even most freshman writing courses are turning this way. I have to believe that most writing teachers have too much common sense and are too concerned with their students' growth as writers to buy into this new philosophy. Nevertheless, everywhere I turn I find composition faculty, both leaders in the profession and new voices, asserting that they have not only the right, but the duty, to put ideology and radical politics at the center of their teaching.

89

Here are four revealing quotations from recent publications. For instance, here is James Laditka in the *Journal of Advanced Composition:*

> All teaching supposes ideology; there simply is no value-free pedagogy.
> For these reasons, my paradigm of composition is changing to one of
> critical literacy, a literacy of political consciousness and social action.
> (361)

Here is Charles Paine in a lead article in *College English:*

> Teachers need to recognize that methodology alone will not ensure
> radical visions of the world. An appropriate course content is necessary
> as well. . . . [E]quality and democracy are not transcendent values that
> inevitably emerge when one learns to seek the truth through critical
> thinking. Rather, if those are the desired values, the teacher must
> recognize that he or she must influence (perhaps manipulate is the more
> accurate word) students' values through charisma or power—he or she
> must accept the role as manipulator. Therefore it is of course reasonable
> to try to inculcate into our students the conviction that the dominant order
> is repressive. (563-64)

Here is Patricia Bizzell:

> We must help our students . . . to engage in a rhetorical process that can
> collectively generate . . . knowledge and beliefs to displace the repressive
> ideologies an unjust social order would prescribe. . . . I suggest that we
> must be forthright in avowing the ideologies that motivate our teaching
> and research. For instance, [in an experimental composition course he
> teaches at Purdue] James Berlin might stop trying to be value-neutral and
> anti-authoritarian in the classroom. Berlin tells his students he is a
> Marxist but disavows any intention of persuading them to his point of
> view. Instead, he might openly state that this course aims to promote
> values of sexual equality and left-oriented labor relations and that this
> course will challenge students' values insofar as they conflict with these
> aims. Berlin and his colleagues might openly exert their authority as
> teachers to try to persuade students to agree with their values instead of
> pretending that they are merely investigating the nature of sexism and
> capitalism and leaving students to draw their own conclusions. (670)

Here is C. H. Knoblauch:

> We are, ultimately, compelled to choose, to make, express, and act upon
> our commitments, to denounce the world, as Freire says, and above all
> oppression and whatever arguments have been called upon to validate it.
> Moreover our speech may well have to be boldly denunciative at times if
> it is to affect its hearers in the midst of their intellectual and political

> comfort. . . . We are obliged to announce ourselves so that, through the
> very process of self-assertion, we grow more conscious of our axioms.
> . . . The quality of our lives as teachers depends on our willingness to
> discover through struggle ever more fruitful means of doing our work.
> The quality of our students' lives depends on [it]. ("Rhetorical" 139)

These quotations do not represent just a few instances that I ferreted out to suit my thesis; you will find similar sentiments if you leaf through only a few of the recent issues of *College English, Rhetoric Review, College Composition and Communication, Journal of Advanced Composition, Focuses,* and others. Some names that you might look for in addition to the ones I've quoted are James Berlin, John Trimbur, Lester Faigley, Richard Ohmann, and Linda Brodkey. At least forty percent of the essays in *The Right to Literacy,* the proceedings of a 1988 conference sponsored by the Modern Language Association in Columbus, Ohio, echo such sentiments, and a glance at the program for the 1991 CCCC convention would confirm how popular such ideas were among the speakers. For that same convention, the publisher HarperCollins sponsored a contest to award grants to graduate students to attend; the topic they were asked to write on was "Describe the kind of freshman writing course you would design." Nearly all of the contestants described a politically focused course. All ten essays in the 1991 MLA publication *Contending with Words* recommend turning writing courses in this direction.

Distressingly often, those who advocate such courses show open contempt for their students' values, preferences, or interests. For example, in an article in *College English,* Ronald Strickland says, "The teacher can best facilitate the production of knowledge by adapting a confrontational stance toward the student. . . . Above all, the teacher should avoid the pretense of detachment, objectivity, and autonomy." He admits that his position "conflicts with the expectations of some students [and] these students make it difficult for me to pursue my political/intellectual agenda" (293).

David Bleich dismisses his students' resistance with equal ease:

> There is reason to think that students want to write about what they say
> they don't want to write about. They want a chance to write about racism,
> classism, and homophobia even though it makes them uncomfortable.
> But what I think makes them most uncomfortable is to surrender the
> paradigm of individualism and to see that paradigm in its sexist
> dimensions.

He cites his students' religion as one of the chief obstacles to their enlightenment:

> Religious views collaborate with the ideology of individualism and with
> sexism to censor the full capability of what people can say and write. . . .
> By "religious values" I mean belief in the savability of the individual
> human soul. The ideal of the nuclear family, as opposed to the extended
> or communal family, permits the overvaluation of the individual child
> and the individual soul. (167)

And here is Dale Bauer in an article from *College English:*

> I would argue that political commitment—especially feminist
> commitment—is a legitimate classroom strategy and rhetorical
> imperative. The feminist agenda offers a goal toward our students'
> conversations to emancipatory critical action. . . . In teaching
> identification and teaching feminism, I overcome a vehement insistence
> on pluralistic relativism or on individualism.

Bauer acknowledges that her students resist her political agenda. She says,

> There is an often overwhelming insistence on individualism and isolation
> . . . [They] labor at developing a critical distance to avoid participating in
> "the dialectic of resistance and identification."

Bauer quotes one of her students as saying in an evaluation,

> "The teacher consistently channels class discussions around feminism
> and does not spend time discussing the comments that oppose her beliefs.
> In fact, she usually twists them around to support her beliefs."

Bauer dismisses such objections, however, claiming she has to accept her authority as
rhetor because "anything less ends up being an expressivist model, one which
reinforces . . . the dominant patriarchal culture" (389).

Often these advocates are contemptuous of other teachers' approaches to teaching
or the goals those teachers set for their students. For example, Lester Faigley assails the
advice given about writing a job application letter in a standard business writing text:

> In the terms of [the Marxist philosopher] Althusser, [the applicant who
> writes such a letter] has voluntarily assented his subjectivity within the
> dominant ideology and thus has reaffirmed relations of power. By
> presenting himself as a commodity rather than as a person, he has not
> only made an initial gesture of subservience like a dog presenting its
> neck, but he has also signaled his willingness to continue to be
> subservient. (251)

In discussing Linda Flower's cognitive, problem-solving approach to teaching
writing, James Berlin calls it "the rationalization of economic activity. The pursuit of self-
evident and unquestioned goals in the composing process parallels the pursuit of self-
evident and unquestioned profit-making goals in the corporate market place." (What a
facile non-logical leap!) He continues in the same article to deride Donald Murray's and
Peter Elbow's approaches to writing because of their focus on the individual, saying

> Expressionist rhetoric is inherently and debilitatingly divisive of political
> protest. . . . Beyond that, expressionist rhetoric is easily co-opted by the
> very capitalist forces it opposes. After all, this rhetoric can be used to

reinforce the entrepreneurial virtues capitalism values most: individualism, private initiative, the confidence for risk taking, the right to be contentious with authority (especially the state). (491)

How We Got Here

But how did all this happen? Why has the cultural left suddenly claimed writing courses as their political territory?

There's no simple answer, of course. Major issues about social change and national priorities are involved, and I cannot digress into those concerns in this essay. But my first response is, "You see what happens when we allow writing programs to be run by English departments?" I'm convinced that the push to change freshman composition into a political platform for the teacher has come about primarily because the course is housed in English departments.

As the linguistics scholar John Searle pointed out in a detailed and informative article in *The New York Review of Books,* the recent surge of the cultural on major American campuses has centered almost entirely in English departments. He says,

> The most congenial home left for Marxism, now that it has been largely discredited as a theory of economics and politics, is in departments of literary criticism. And [because] many professors of literature no longer care about literature in ways that seemed satisfactory to earlier generations . . . they teach it as a means of achieving left-wing political goals or as an occasion for exercises in deconstruction, etc. (38)

I theorize that the critical literary theories of deconstruction, post-structuralism (both declining by now), and Marxist critical theory have trickled down to the lower floors of English departments where freshman English dwells. Just as they have been losing their impact with faculty above stairs, they have taken fresh root with those dwelling below.

Deconstructionists claim that the privileged texts of the canon are only reflections of power relations and the dominant class structures of their eras. Thus the job of the literary critic is to dissect Shakespeare or Milton or Eliot or Joyce to show how language reflects and supports the "cultural hegemony" of the time. They also claim that all meaning is indeterminate and socially constructed; there is no objective reality nor any truth that can be agreed on.

Marxist criticism echoes these sentiments. For example, Ronald Strickland writes in *College English:*

> Marxist critics have demonstrated that conventional literary studies have been more complicitous . . . than any other academic discipline in the reproduction of the dominant ideology. . . . Traditional English studies helps to maintain liberal humanism through its emphasis on authorial genius. . . . [Thus] there is a political imperative to resist the privileging

of individualism in this practice, for, as Terry Eagleton has demonstrated,
it amounts to a form of coercion in the interests of conservative, elitist
politics. (293)

All these claims strike me as silly, simplistic, and quite undemonstrable. Nevertheless, if
one endorses these intellectual positions—and sympathizes with the politics behind
them—it's easy to go to the next step and equate conventional writing instruction with
conventional literary studies. Then one can say that because standard English is the dialect
of the dominant class, writing instruction that tries to help students master that dialect
merely reinforces the status quo and serves the interest of the dominant class. An instructor
who wants to teach students to write clearly becomes part of a capitalistic plot to control the
workforce. What nonsense! It seems to me that one could argue with more force that the
instructor who fails to help students master the standard dialect conspires against the
working class.

How easy for theorists who, by the nature of the discipline they have chosen,
already have a facile command of the prestige dialect to denigrate teaching that dialect to
students. Have they asked those students what *they* want to learn? And how easy for these
same theorists to set up straw men arguments that attack a mechanistic, structuralist,
literature-based model of composition and call it conservative, regressive, deterministic, and
elitist when they know such models have long been discredited in the professional
literature.

But I think this is what happens when composition theorists remain
psychologically tied to the English departments that are their base. Partly out of genuine
interest, I'm sure, but also out of a need to belong to and be approved by the power
structure, they immerse themselves in currently fashionable critical theories, read the
authors that are chic—Foucault, Bahktin, Giroux, Eagleton, and Cixous, for example—then
look for ways those theories can be incorporated into their own specialty, teaching writing.

This, according to Searle's article, means that they subscribe to a view of the role
of the humanities in universities that is

> . . . based on two primary assumptions. 1. They believe that Western
> civilization in general, and the United States in particular, are in large
> part oppressive, patriarchal, hegemonic, and in need of replacement or at
> least transformation. 2. The primary function of teaching the humanities
> is political; they [the cultural left] do not really believe the humanities are
> valuable in their own right except as a means of achieving social
> transformation. (38)

Searle goes on to point out that this debate about what is "hegemonic," "patriarchal," or
"exclusionary" has been focused almost entirely in English departments.

I find it hard to believe that most English professors seriously hold these opinions
or that they are ready to jettison their lifelong commitment to the humanities, but evidently
significant numbers do. News releases and many professional articles suggest that these
attitudes have permeated the Modern Language Association, and the associate chair of the

English Department at the University of Texas recently said in a colloquium of the College of Liberal Arts that the "mission of English departments is always to oppose the dominant culture."

For those who agree, how natural to turn to the freshman writing courses. With a huge captive enrollment of largely unsophisticated students, what a fertile field to cultivate to bring about political and social change. Rhetoric scholars who go along will also get new respect now that they have joined the ideological fray and formed alliances with literature faculty who have been transforming their own courses.

Composition faculty who support such change can bring fresh respectability and attention to those often despised introductory English courses now that they can be used for "higher purposes." They may even find some regular faculty who will volunteer to teach freshman writing when they can use it for a political forum. Five years ago the regular faculty in our department at Texas tried to get rid of freshman English altogether by having it taught entirely in extension or at the local community college; this past year, many of those who had previously advocated abandoning the course were in the forefront of the battle to turn it into a course about racism and sexism. Now the course was suddenly worth their time.

The opportunity to make freshman English a vehicle for such social crusades is particularly rich: in many universities, graduate students in English teach virtually all of the sections, graduate students who are already steeped in post-structuralism and deconstruction theory, in the works of Foucault, Raymond Williams, Terry Eagleton, and Stanley Fish, and in feminist theory. Too often they haven't been well trained in how to teach writing and are at a loss about what they should be doing with their students. How easy then to focus the course on their own interests, which are often highly political. Unfortunately, when they try to teach an introductory composition course by concentrating on issues rather than on craft and critical thinking, large numbers of their students end up feeling confused, angry—and cheated.

I also believe that two major social forces outside the liberal arts are contributing to creating the environment that has given rise to this new model.

The first is the tremendous increase in diversity of our student population, especially in states like California and Texas and in all our major cities. With changing demographics, we face an ethnic and social mix of students in our classes that previews for us what our institutions are going to be like in the year 2000. These students bring with them a kaleidoscope of experiences, values, dialects, and cultural backgrounds that we want to respond to positively and productively, using every resource we can to help them adapt to the academic world and become active participants in it. The code words for our attempts to build the kind of inclusive curriculum that we need have become "multiculturalism" and "cultural diversity." They're good terms, of course. Any informed and concerned educator endorses them in the abstract. The crucial question, however, is how one finds concrete ways to put them into practice, and also how one guards against their becoming what Richard Weaver called "god terms" that can be twisted to mean anything an ideologue wants them to mean.

As writing teachers, I think all of us are looking for ways to promote genuine diversity in our classes and yet keep two elements that are essential for any state-of-the-art composition course.

First, students' own writing must be the center of the course. Students need to write to find out how much they know and to gain confidence in their ability to express themselves effectively. They do not need to be assigned essays to read so they will have something to write about—they bring their subjects with them: The writing of others, except for that of their fellow students, should be supplementary, used to illustrate or reinforce.

Second, as writing teachers we should stay within our area of professional expertise: helping students to learn to write in order to learn, to explore, to communicate, to gain control over their lives. That's a large responsibility, and all that most of us can manage. We have no business getting into areas where we may have passion and conviction but no scholarly base from which to operate. When classes focus on complex issues such as racial discrimination, economic injustices, and inequities of class and gender, they should be taught by qualified faculty who have the depth of information and historical competence that such critical social issues warrant. Our society's deep and tangled cultural conflicts can neither be explained nor resolved by simplistic ideological formulas.

But one can run a culturally diverse writing course without sacrificing any of its integrity as a writing course. Any writing course, required or not, can be wonderfully diverse, an exciting experience in which people of different cultures and experience learn about difference firsthand. More about that shortly.

Forces from Outside

The second major force I see at work is directly political. There's no question in my mind that this new radical stance of many composition faculty is in some ways a corollary of the angry response many intellectuals have to the excesses of right-wing, conservative forces that have dominated American politics for the past decade. Faculty in the liberal arts tend to be liberals who are concerned about social problems and dislike the trends we've seen in cutting funds for human services and for education. We're sick over the condition of our country: one child in five living in poverty; one person in eight hungry; 33 million people with no health insurance; a scandalous infant mortality rate; hundreds of thousands homeless. Yet we see our government spend billions on a dubious war. No need to go on—we all know the terrible inequities and contradictions of our society.

As educators of good will, we shouldn't even have to mention our anger about racism and sexism in our society—that's a given, as is our commitment to work to overcome it. I, for one, refuse to be put on the defensive on such matters of personal conscience or to be silenced by the fear that someone will pin a label on me if I don't share his or her vision of the world or agree on how to improve it. *Ad hominem* arguments don't impress me.

But it's entirely understandable that academics who are traditional liberals sympathize at first with those who preach reform, even when they sound more radical than we'd like. On the surface we share common ground; we'd all like to bring about a fairer, more compassionate society. But I fear that we are in real danger of being co-opted by the radical left, coerced into acquiescing to methods that we abhor because, in the abstract, we have some mutual goals. Some faculty may also fear being labeled "right-wing" if they oppose programs that are represented as being "liberating." But we shouldn't be duped.

Authoritarian methods are still authoritarian methods, no matter in what cause they're invoked. And the current battle is *not* one between liberals and conservatives. Those who attempt to make it so—columnists like George Will—either do not understand the agenda of the cultural left, or they make the association in order to discredit liberal goals. Make no mistake—those on the cultural left are not in the least liberal; in fact, they despise liberals as compromising humanists. They're happy, however, to stir up traditional liberal guilt and use it for their purposes.

What's Wrong with Their Goals?

Why do I object so strongly to the agenda that these self-styled radical teachers want to establish for composition courses and freshman English in particular?

First, I vigorously object to the contention that they have a right—even a *duty*—to use their classrooms as platforms for their own political views. Such claims violate all academic traditions about the university being a forum for the free exchange of ideas, a place where students can examine different points of view in an atmosphere of honest and open discussion, and, in the process, learn to think critically. It is a teacher's obligation to encourage diversity and exploration, but diversity and ideology will not flourish together. By definition, they're incompatible.

By the logic of the cultural left, any teacher should be free to use his or her classroom to promote any ideology. Why not fascism? Racial superiority? Religious fundamentalism? Anti-abortion beliefs? Can't any professor claim the right to indoctrinate students simply because he or she is right? The argument is no different from that of any true believers who are convinced that they own the truth and thus have the right to force it on others. My colleague John Ruszkiewicz compares them to Milton's "the new forcers of conscience." We don't have to look far to see how frightening such arguments really are. They represent precisely the kind of thinking that leads to "re-education camps" in totalitarian governments, to putting art in the service of propaganda, and to making education always the instrument of the state.

Those who want to bring their ideology into the classroom argue that since any classroom is necessarily political, the teacher might as well make it openly political and ideological. He or she should be direct and honest about his or her political beliefs; then the students will know where they stand and everyone can talk freely. Is any experienced teacher really so naive as to believe that? Such claims are no more than self-serving rationalizations that allow a professor total freedom to indulge personal prejudices and avoid any responsibility to be fair. By the same reasoning, couldn't one claim that since we know it is impossible to find absolute, objective truths, we might just as well abandon the search for truth and settle for opinion, superstition, and conjecture? Would that advance our students' education? Couldn't one also say that since one can never be completely fair with one's children, one might as well quit trying and freely indulge one's biases and favoritism? It's astonishing that people who purport to be scholars can make such specious arguments.

The real political truth about classrooms is that the teacher has all the power; she sets the agenda, she controls the discussion, and she gives the grades. She also knows more and can argue more skillfully. Such a situation is ripe for intellectual intimidation, especially in required freshman composition classes, and although I think it is unprofessional for teachers to bring their ideology into any classroom, it is those freshman courses that I am especially concerned about.

The Threat to Freshman Courses

I believe that the movement to make freshman English into courses in which students must write about specific social issues threatens all the gains we have made in teaching writing in the last fifteen years. I also think that rather than promoting diversity and a genuine multicultural environment, such courses actually work against those goals. Here are my reasons.

First, we know that students develop best as writers when they can write about something they care about and want to know more about. Only then will they be motivated to invest real effort in their work; only then can we hope they will avoid the canned, clichéd prose that neither they nor we take seriously. Few students, however, will do their best when they are compelled to write on a topic they perceive as politically charged and about which they feel uninformed, no matter how thought-provoking and important the instructor assumes that topic to be. If freshmen choose to write about issues involving race, class, and gender, that's fine. They should have every encouragement. I believe all topics in a writing class should be serious ones that push students to think and to say something substantial. But the topic should be their choice, a careful and thoughtful choice, to be sure, but not what someone else thinks is good for them.

Second, we know that young writers develop best as writers when teachers are able to create a low-risk environment that encourages students to take chances. We also know that novice writers can virtually freeze in the writing classroom when they see it as an extremely high-risk situation. Apprehensive about their grades in this new college situation, they nervously test their teachers to see what is expected of them, and they venture opinions only timidly. It is always hard to get students to write seriously and honestly, but when they find themselves in a classroom where they suspect there is a correct way to think, they are likely to take refuge in generalities and responses that please the teacher. Such fake discourse is a kind of silence, the silence we have so often deplored when it is forced on the disadvantaged. But when we stifle creative impulses and make students opt for survival over honesty, we have done the same thing. In too many instances, the first lesson they will learn as college students is that hypocrisy pays—so don't try to think for yourself.

My third objection to injecting prescribed political content into a required freshman course is that such action severely limits freedom of expression for both students and instructors. In my view, the freshman course on racism and sexism proposed at the University of Texas at Austin in the spring of 1990 would have enforced conformity in both directions. Students would have had no choice of what to write about, and the instructors who were graduate students would have had no choice about what to teach. Even if they felt unqualified to teach the material—and many did—or believed that the prescribed curriculum would work against their students' learning to write—and many did—they had to conform to a syllabus that contradicted their professional judgment and, often, their personal feelings. That course has since been revised and the freshman course in place since the fall of 1991 offers choices to both students and teachers.

New Possibilities for Freshman Courses

I believe we can make freshman English—or any other writing course—a truly multicultural course that gives students the opportunity to develop their critical and creative abilities and do it in an intellectually and ethically responsible context that preserves the heart of what we have learned about teaching writing in the past two decades.

First, I resist the effort to put any specific multicultural content at the center of a writing course, particularly a freshman course, and particularly a required course. Multicultural issues are too complex and diverse to be dealt with fully and responsibly in an English course, much less a course in which the focus should be on writing, not reading. Too often attempts to focus on such issues encourage stereotyping and superficial thinking. For instance, what English teacher wouldn't feel presumptuous and foolish trying to introduce Asian culture into a course when he or she can quickly think of at least ten different Asian cultures, all of which differ from each other drastically in important ways? What about Hispanic culture? Can the teacher who knows something of Mexico generalize about traditions of other Hispanic cultures? Can anyone teach the "black experience"? Do black men and women whose forebears come from Haiti and Nigeria and Jamaica share the experiences and heritage of African Americans? Is Southern culture a valid topic for study? Many people think so. What about Jewish culture? But I don't need to labor the point. I only want to highlight the concerns any of us should have when the push for so-called multicultural courses threatens the integrity of our discipline and the quality of our teaching.

I believe, however, that we can create a culturally inclusive curriculum in our writing classes by focusing on the experiences of our students. *They* are our greatest multicultural resource, one that is authentic, rich, and truly diverse. Every student brings to class a picture of the world in his or her mind that is constructed out of his or her cultural background and unique and complex experience. As writing teachers, we can help students articulate and understand that experience, but we also have the important job of helping every writer to understand that each of us sees the world through our own particular lens, one shaped by unique experiences. In order to communicate with others, we must learn to see through their lenses as well as try to explain to them what we see through ours. In an interactive classroom where students collaborate with other writers, this process of decentering so one can understand the "other" can foster genuine multicultural growth.

Imagine, for example, the breadth of experience and range of difference students would be exposed to in a class made up of students I have had in recent years.

One student would be from Malawi. The ivory bracelet he wears was put on his arm at birth and cannot be removed; he writes about his tribal legends. Another student is a young Vietnamese man who came to America when he was eight; he writes about the fear he felt his first day in an American school because there were no walls to keep out bullets. Another is a young Greek woman whose parents brought her to America to escape poverty; she writes about her first conscious brush with sexism in the Greek Orthodox church. One student is the son of illegal aliens who followed the harvests in Texas; he writes with passion about the need for young Hispanics to get their education. A young black man writes about college basketball, a culture about which he is highly knowledgeable. A young man from the Texas panhandle writes about the traditions of cowboy boots and the ethical dimensions of barbed wire fences. Another young black man writes about the conflicts he feels between what he is learning in astronomy, a subject that fascinates him, and the teachings of his church.

It's worth noting here that religion plays an important role in the lives of many of our students—and many of us, I'm sure—but it's a dimension almost never mentioned by those who talk about cultural diversity and difference. In most classrooms in which there is an obvious political agenda, students—even graduate students—are very reluctant to reveal their religious beliefs, sensing they may get a hostile reception. And with reason—remember the quotation from David Bleich. But a teacher who believes in diversity must pay attention to and respect students with deep religious convictions, not force them too into silence.

Real diversity emerges from the students themselves and flourishes in a collaborative classroom in which they work together to develop their ideas and test them out on each other. They can discuss and examine their experiences, their assumptions, their values, and their questions. They can tell their stories to each other in a nurturant writing community. As they are increasingly exposed to the unique views and experiences of others, they will begin to appreciate differences and understand the rich tapestry of cultures that their individual stories make up. But they will also see unified motifs and common human concerns in that tapestry.

In this kind of classroom not all writing should be personal, expressive writing. Students need a broader range of discourse as their introduction to writing in college. The teacher can easily design the kinds of writing assignments that involve argument and exposition and suggest options that encourage cross-cultural awareness. For instance, some suggested themes for development might be these: family or community rituals; power relationships at all levels; the student's role in his of her family or group; their roles as men and women; the myths they live by; cultural tensions within groups. There are dozens more rich possibilities that could be worked out with the cooperation of colleagues in other departments and within the class itself.

The strength of all the themes I've mentioned is that they're both individual and communal, giving students the opportunity to write something unique to them as individuals yet something that will resonate with others in their writing community. The beauty of such an approach is that it's *organic.* It grows out of resources available in each classroom, and it allows students to make choices, then discover more about others and themselves through those choices. This approach makes the teacher a midwife, an agent for change rather than a transmitter of fixed knowledge. It promotes a student-centered classroom in which the teacher doesn't assume, as our would-be forcers of conscience do, that he or she owns the truth. Rather the students bring their own truths, and the teacher's role is to nurture change and growth as students encounter individual differences. Gradually their truths will change, but so will ours because in such a classroom one continually learns from one's students.

This is the kind of freshman English class from which students can emerge with confidence in their ability to think, to generate ideas, and to present themselves effectively to the university and the community. It is a class built on the scholarship, research, and experience that has enabled us to achieve so much growth in our profession in the last fifteen years. It is the kind of classroom we can be proud of as a discipline. I don't think we necessarily have to take freshman English out of English departments in order to establish this model, but we do have to assert our authority as writing professionals within our departments and fiercely resist letting freshman English be used for anyone else's goals. We must hold on to the gains we have made and teach writing in the ways we know best. Above all, we must teach it for the *students'* benefit, not in the service of politics or anything else.

Freshman English is a course particularly vulnerable to takeover because English departments in so many universities and colleges refuse to take it seriously and thus don't pay much attention to what happens in it. They can wake up, however, to find that some political zealots take the course very seriously indeed and will gladly put it to their own uses. The scores of us who have been studying, writing, speaking, and publishing for two decades to make freshman English the solid intellectual enterprise that it now is must speak out to protect it from this kind of exploitation. It is time to resist, time to speak up, time to reclaim freshman composition from those who want to politicize it.

What is at stake is control of a vital element in our students' education by a radical few. We can't afford to let that control stand.

Maxine Hairston is a former chair of the Conference on College Composition and Communication and professor of English at the University of Texas.

Works Cited

Bauer, Dale. "The Other 'F' Word: Feminist in the Classroom." *College English* 52 (Apr. 1990): 835-96.

Berlin, James A. "Rhetoric and Ideology in the Writing Class." *College English* 50 (Sep. 1988): 477-94.

Bizzell, Patricia. "Beyond Anti-Foundationalism to Rhetorical Authority: Problems in Defining 'Cultural Literacy.'" *College English* 52 (Oct. 1990): 661-75.

Bleich, David. "Literacy and Citizenship: Resisting Social Issues." Lunsford, Moglen, and Slevin 163-69.

Faigley, Lester. "The Study of Writing and the Study of Language." *Rhetoric Review* 7 (Spring 1989): 240-56.

Harkin, Patricia, and John Schilb. *Contending with Words: Composition and Rhetoric in a Postmodern Age.* New York: MLA, 1991.

Knoblauch, C. H. "Literacy and the Politics of Education." Lunsford, Moglen, and Slevin 74-80.

_____. "Rhetorical Constructions: Dialogue and Commitment." *College English* 50 (Feb. 1988): 125-40.

Laditka, James N. "Semiology, Ideology, Praxis: Responsible Authority in the Composition Classroom." *Journal of Advanced Composition* 10.2 (Fall 1990): 357-73.

Lunsford, Andrea A., Helen Moglen, and James Slevin, eds. *The Right to Literacy.* New York: MLA and NCTE, 1990.

Paine, Charles. "Relativism, Radical Pedagogy, and the Ideology of Paralysis." *College English* 51 (Oct. 1989): 557-70.

Searle, John. "The Storm Over the University." Rev. of *Tenured Radicals,* by Roger
        Kimball; *The Politics of Liberal Education,* ed. by Darryl L. Gless and Barbara
        Hernstein Smith; and *The Voice of Liberal Learning: Michael Oakeshott on
        Education,* ed. by Timothy Fuller. *The New York Review of Books,* 6 Dec. 1990:
        34-42.
Strickland, Ronald. "Confrontational Pedagogy and Traditional Literary Studies." *College
        English* 52 (Mar. 1990): 291-300.
Weaver, Richard M. *The Ethics of Rhetoric.* Chicago: Henry Regnery, 1953.

SUSAN C. JARRATT Rhetorical Power: What Really Happens in Politicized Classrooms

The furor over educational change propelled by the new social movements arises from anxieties about power. Over the last two or three years, the popular press has been full of charges that teachers who call into question traditional knowledge and pedagogical methods are indoctrinating their students—using their authority as teachers irresponsibly. This same charge has been leveled against "rhetoric" in general over the centuries and against sophistic rhetoric in particular. One name for the accusation is *demagoguery*: the unethical manipulation of public opinion by a powerful speaker.

Along with the charge of demagoguery is a complaint that the so-called enforcers of political correctness limit free speech of others. Arguments over free speech always begin with rules passed by schools like Michigan, Wisconsin, and Brown restricting hate speech. But for the critics of curricular change, just about any successful challenge to the educational status quo counts as a threat to free speech. Articles in *Time, Newsweek,* the *New Republic,* and elsewhere describe the failures of attempts to reverse educational decisions expanding the canon and building programs in minority studies as evidence of "intolerance," "intellectual intimidation," and "taboos" rather than as what they really are—outcomes of struggles for control over curriculum, programs, and hiring that go on all the time in the academy. The language used is an artful rhetorical maneuver of reversal: accusing your adversary of your own wrong. What's missing or seriously muted in this discussion of free speech is an acknowledgment that at the very heart of the new educational transformations is the *freeing* of speech—bringing to voice knowledges, experiences, and histories for whole bodies of people previously unheard. But, as Foucault teaches, the powerful mechanisms of disciplinary knowledge operate by hiding themselves within institutions. And so disruptions of stable, traditional disciplines and their objects of study are read as "a decline in tolerance," when the critics know well that such "disruptions" are linked to the larger project of making social and economic conditions more "tolerable" for many citizens. But these material considerations are artfully ignored by the neoconservative critics of educational change.

It's difficult to get even well-intentioned but hard-line civil libertarians to acknowledge the link between social injustice and the limits, exclusions, and silences pervading discourses of all types—unwritten rules that let some voices in and keep others out. William A. Henry III, author of a 1991 *Time* article, has it right when he finds things being turned upside down. We hear Henry reporting with something between outrage and astonishment that educational changes "amount to mirror-image reversal of basic assumptions held by the nation's majority" (66). Precisely the point. The "outlandish" courses Henry names represent the perspectives of outlanders—those whose standpoint offers versions of rationality, aesthetics, and even science outside the parameters of the Euramerican heritage. Decisions at many levels making possible the restructuring of higher education to allow for those viewpoints have emerged out of struggle; the traditionalists focus attention on the struggle itself as indecorous, avoiding the real issues.

Even George Bush, in his commencement address at the University of Michigan in May 1991, has entered the fray, expressing dismay that "neighbors who disagree no longer settle matters over a cup of coffee." In evoking this homey scene, Bush insulted

103

those participants in the civil rights movement who, often denied the chance to live in neighborly proximity to their white oppressors, struggled courageously and at such great cost for the opportunity to sit down for a long-denied cup of coffee. But then Alexander Cockburn reminds us that "the will to retain a useful historical amnesia lies at the heart of the fury about PC" (690). In another moment of amnesia, Bush forgot his own campaign strategy of racial hatred and admonished that those "creating" divisiveness in our harmonious social system by insisting on change haven't successfully conquered the temptation to assign bad motives to people who disagree with them. It's worth noting on this point that the same edition of the *New York Times* that reported these remarks included an article about black high school students who organized a separate prom because of the climate of racial tension in their southwest Chicago school. Bush must be perceptive indeed to have guessed the motives of those who participated in racial incidents on 115 campuses in 1989. He must know more than meets the eyes and ears about the three thousand white students at the University of Massachusetts who chased and beat blacks in a mob attack in 1986, about the football players at the University of Connecticut in 1987 who spat on Asian American women, shouting "Oriental faggots" (Cockburn 690). Perhaps I should ask him about the motives of my students (more than one) who believe that homosexuals deserve to die of AIDS, who have proposed transporting "them" all to an island to die together, and who are not in the least interested in discussing this "disagreement" over a cup of coffee, or even over a beer.

Rhetoric in the Classroom: Indoctrination or Rhetorical Authority?

While I have been engaging here in an eristic rhetoric, sparring rhetorically with George Bush and others who have passionately resisted attempts to open the gates of the academy a bit wider, I believe that the classroom often requires a different rhetoric. The instructor who offers counterhegemonic explanations of reading and writing practices—like the feminist who teaches students to recognize the way language constructs knowledge on the lines of a gender system or the Marxist who examines the historical connections between social class and reading habits—forces an epistemic break from the comfortable paradigms of liberal humanism, positivist science, and capitalist progress. But these fundamental differences in pedagogical and epistemological theory are often misread—either willfully or out of ignorance. Those who hold to a view of teaching as the value-neutral transmittal of a body of objective knowledge accuse teachers who raise questions about how their subject matter has evolved within historical circumstances determined in part by the dominance of specific social groups of having dropped any disinterested attempt to present "content" and giving over the class to an unethical effort to force students to accept a set of opinions about race and gender difference. The popular press contributes to the process of blurring any distinction between taking up the politics *of* the classroom and offering up politics—that is, partisan issues—*in* the classroom. The media create the general impression that so-called politicized teachers use classrooms as platforms. Of course, any full discussion of "politicized classrooms" would take in every class, for the teacher who offers a Great Books survey course is no less entailed in issues of institutional power and social difference than a teacher offering the courses with "obfuscatory titles and eccentric reading lists" (Henry 66) named triumphantly as evidence of the corruptions of "politically correct" thinking. But here I wish to focus on instructors who introduce questions of power and difference in discourse—to counter the charge that teachers who acknowledge the political nature of their profession necessarily exercise demagoguery.

When David Laurence organized the ADE session from which this paper comes, he suggested, as a historical point of orientation for this question, an essay by Max Weber called "Science as a Vocation." In this 1918 analysis of the institutionalization of science, Weber outlines a distinction like the one I make above: between an approach to the subject of study through methods of cultural critique and the teacher's use of the lecture halls to act as prophet or demagogue. Weber acknowledges that students want more from their educators than mere analyses and statements of fact; they crave leaders and not teachers, he says. His formulation of the goal of critical teaching as responsible self-clarification approximates closely the critical pedagogy of today, but Weber's sensitivity to the pedagogical setting leads him to warn professors against the temptation to use the classroom to air their opinions about specific political or social issues. In the lecture hall, he explains, students are a captive audience; there is no possibility for critique or even response.

Even though most of us in English departments teach at least some of our classes to small groups of students, in which discussion is an essential element of the pedagogy, we are mindful of the complaint that the power wielded by the teacher—specifically, the power of the grade, but also the power of age, knowledge, the institution, the emotional power of giving or withholding approval and professional guidance—may mute dissent or criticism from students even when the classroom structure in principle provides opportunity for it. For some critics of political correctness there is little question about the domination of teachers' voices when they present their subject through the lens of sociological critique, only a question of how that power is wielded. On this model, two things can happen, both bad. In the first case, the teacher is overt about the political agenda of the course. Dialogue is impossible, critics say, because students are so intimidated by the teacher and so determined to get good grades that they won't risk expressing an opinion contrary to the teacher's. In the case of teachers who are more covert, the argument is that simply raising social issues in the current climate tips off students that you're "one of them." They will then respond by parroting a generally left position out of fear and without thinking through the issues on their own.

Certainly those things can and do happen. All kinds of things happen with our students: alienation and tune-out, but also resistance and opposition; dutiful reproduction, interested experimentation, even conversion. I heard recently of a kind of student manipulation that was new to me. Instructions are given by one male student to another about how to succeed in a feminist classroom: pretend to be a male chauvinist, then have a conversion. You're bound to get an A. This strategy raises an issue that the critics of political correctness never consider because it doesn't fit within their monolithic phantasm of the teacher: the ways teachers are positioned differently along multiple power axes within classrooms. For example, I sometimes have an easier time convincing my students in a composition class to try out unfamiliar pedagogical methods than my graduate-student teachers do, because of their youth and lower status in the institution, but perhaps I have more trouble than my male colleagues. Class and race offer more complications. The point is that there are more kinds of power than simply the institutional status of the teacher at work in a classroom at every moment. Indeed, everyone in the room—even at a mostly white, middle-class school like Miami—brings a rich history of diverse social relations. In my view, the aim of "politicized" teaching is to mobilize those histories into a complex interplay of authority and counterauthority in the classroom (see Graff). The pedagogy I advocate does not demand that students adopt a "politically correct" position; in fact, it argues against any fixed agenda in favor of a process of learning how technologies of discourse make possible the exploration of personally grounded and historically located knowledge. I'd like to offer two theoretical orientations for the exercise of rhetorical power in the classroom and then propose some suggestions for generating and sustaining dialogic classroom discourse.

Politics of Location and Dialogic Classrooms

In offering these ideas, I can't speak for everyone who claims to teach from liberatory or transformative pedagogical principles. The practices I describe have evolved out of my own experiences as a white, middle-class woman teaching first-year composition and graduate courses in rhetoric and social theory, from several years' work as a mentor and teacher of a pedagogy workshop for new graduate assistants, out of the feminist sophistics summer institute and seminar I co-directed in the summer of 1990 with Dale M. Bauer, and from ongoing collective work in feminist pedagogy at Miami. The pedagogy developed within these contexts advocates teachers' exercise of rhetorical authority toward ends of social transformation. In this pedagogy, English studies is defined along lines explored by Henry Giroux, Linda Brodkey, James Berlin, Patricia Bizzell, John Trimbur, Ira Shor, and many others as the development of critical literacies—one element in an education toward critical citizenship. While this goal may differ from the scientist's model of value-free knowledge transmission, or from the aesthete's aim of cultivating literary taste and sensibilities, I would argue that it shares with the humanism of William Bennett, Allan Bloom, and Lynne V. Cheney the goal of making students into certain kinds of human beings. I reject the charge that liberatory pedagogy is somehow more intrusive or manipulative than what it seeks to replace. When teachers make their own political and ethical commitments to social change a part of the course, students who have internalized a model of education as the transferral of "objective" knowledge may feel an uncomfortable dissonance. Speaking openly about ethics can create for students a painful awareness of the absence of a strong community consensus about right and wrong in our huge, diverse social system. But it can also provide a source of relief, pleasure, and challenge in confronting these anxieties.

Motivating students to locate themselves socially and historically in relation to the subject of the class can mediate institutional (teacher) authority and create the possibility for counterauthority to emerge within students' own discourses. This process takes place when students are led to describe their lives, especially their educational experiences, as socially and historically embedded—to articulate the self in history. It's a way to approach the understanding of differences without by exploring differences within. What's encouraged here is not political correctness but what I call a historical attitude. To have an attitude, one must have a position, a stance, instead of remaining undifferentiated. One must be situated not only in space but in time and social order, the last of these elements invoking "attitude" in its colloquial sense of "having an attitude" as an aggressive challenge to social hierarchies. I'm not suggesting we turn our students into little James Deans but rather that we teach them to see the act of speaking and writing as always relational. For writing classes, this view is a break out of the tyranny of the present; for literature classes, a break into tyrannically discrete historical pasts.

Having a personal investment or location in relation to class material protects students against indoctrination or coercion; further, it's the basis of any meaningful educational experience, as theorists from many camps would agree. But the process I'm describing needs to be attached to specific theoretical spheres; namely, cultural studies and feminist politics of location. It shouldn't be confused with self-satisfied psychologizing, with a purely confessional mode of consciousness-raising, or with a kind of composition teaching that uses narratives of student experience as a means of discovering the true self or unique voice. Nor does this approach represent a pluralistic embrace of all points of view as equally valuable and defensible. It's more aptly described in Nietzschean terms as a continual process of negating, consuming, and contradicting—enacted through the connection of singular with collective histories. Through this pedagogy students orient themselves as readers and writers within the asymmetrical power relations currently crisscrossing our society but also within their own specific histories as students, family members, and citizens. Further, this teaching method asks students to re-see those experiences in terms of social difference and power imbalance and within historically located disciplinary practices. It's not a demand that students express white or male guilt, nor does it participate in the race essentialism the critics of political correctness assume to be the theoretical basis of multicultural education. Rather, students identify their stances as provisional and dialogic and try on the role of transformative intellectual in their own historical moments and culture spheres.

The difference between classroom demagoguery and an alternative politics of the classroom depends on the theories of discourse underlying these competing accounts of language in the classroom. In a simple communication theory of language, one individual speaks to another, so that the speaker is an agent and the listener is characterized as a passive recipient of a reified message. This theory grounds narratives of indoctrination, coercion, or other manipulative rhetorical effects. But according to Marxist linguistic theorists like L. S. Vygotsky and M. M. Bakhtin, any discursive act involves a complex interplay of "voices," internal as well as external, present and past. When students use class materials to confront or re-create their own histories and present locations as social beings, they bring to voice internalized conflicts among authoritative voices as part of the dialogic classroom experience. Active engagement with language in the classroom shapes the consciousness of all the participants, teacher included. This shared linguistic experience is best described not in terms of communication—the delivery of the message from one, or even two, subjects to others—but rather in terms of a collective activity through which we are all constantly engaged in processes of semiotic transformation. Instead of conversion, the "politicized" teachers I know look for dialogic reflection in our students' writing and oral responses.

The practices of location and dialogism open a space for the teacher not as demagogue or prophet but as what Weber calls "leader" and Henry Giroux calls "public intellectual." The complex flow of language and interplay of power in the classroom calls for many different responses from the liberatory teacher; silent listener, supportive encourager, equal participant in debate, or, sometimes, advocate of a position that remains unrepresented or challenger of oppressive discourses generated by students. I think it's a mistake to advise teachers that they should never express opinions on vital public issues or to neutralize the composition teacher into the role of "facilitator." We should be able to demonstrate, when it is rhetorically appropriate, what our opinions are and, more important, how we derived them—how they may be connected to personal histories and social positions and how each of us will necessarily be limited in assessing those histories and views. These are delicate decisions, hard to generalize about. But that difficulty should not prevent us from taking seriously our role as public intellectuals to make the formation of political consciousness the subject of literacy education. Doing so within the theoretical parameters I've described is fundamentally different from using the lectern as a platform for partisan views on specific issues.

Classroom Practice

Moving from a descriptive to a prescriptive mode, I wish to suggest ways to foster a dialogic climate—to encourage the development of counterauthority—in English classrooms of all kinds: composition, literature, and theory. These are not all original ideas but draw on work—some of it unpublished, some in the form of lectures, discussions, and private conversations—by many colleagues, most significantly Patricia Bizzell, bell hooks, Steven Mailloux, and John Trimbur.

Mediating the conventional classroom dynamic. The most material way to effect counterauthority is to create an actual, physical intervention of another voice into the teacher-class dialogue (see Graff). Inviting former students or guest authorities to address the class members and team teaching in various forms (including simply trading off or combining classes for a day) are possible ways to accomplish this goal. The English department at Miami University allows advanced undergraduate majors to act as teaching fellows for faculty members, building in a triangulation of authority through the semester.

Foregrounding pedagogical decisions. Pointing out ways our teaching differs from traditional classes—making the educational institution itself the subject of the class—taps student resistance to authority but converts it into a collective critical inquiry. What does it mean to study writing, or literature, or rhetorical theory now, at this institution? What did it mean twenty years ago or two thousand? Such questions bring into focus issues of professionalization, disciplinary language, and paradigm change.

Making classroom discussion—how people talk—the subject of the course. Stepping out of the discussion from time to time to assess how language is working allows for reflection on power and difference in discourse. Rather than the "micro-management of everyday conversation" George Bush warns about, this practice encourages a microlevel attention to the way ideas are shaped. Readings on language and social difference—for example, Dale Spender on gender and Henry Louis Gates Jr. on Black English—build concrete knowledge about formerly unconscious practices. Audiotapes can help in this process in at least three contexts. In addition to bringing tapes into the classroom, teachers can use them to engage in self-critique or to work with other teachers interested in analyzing the complex play of power and difference in classroom discussion from day to day.

Using keywords. Each semester my students and I select and work closely with certain "keywords" (a concept created by Raymond Williams) that seem to emerge with some significance in public discourse from any of a number of spheres: within the class, on campus, in national or global news. We do a series of inquiries into each word, investigating its histories for us and the groups using it. For example, in work with sexist language in a composition class one semester, first-year students seemed really angry and resistant to a feminist critique of *lady*. While my analysis had emphasized economic dependence and class hierarchy, the students revealed, through discussions of how and where the word had entered into their experiences, the heavy weight of sexual socialization it had carried in high school and its use as a reward for "maturity." The point of these inquiries is not to resolve differences in liberal compromise but to gain a fuller understanding of the particular histories, differences, and powers language carries.

Taking advantage of the multiple sites for dialogue between teacher and student. While we may think of class discussion most immediately as the site of "politicized" teaching, a dialogic pedagogy exploits differences in rhetorical context provided by various opportunities for exchange between teacher and student and among students. Different kinds of exchange can occur in class (the most public context), in conference, on ungraded assignments, on graded papers. We should be aware of using different theoretical strategies for different occasions.

Reducing grade pressure where possible. Though students and teachers almost always work under the shadow of grades, doing a number of ungraded writing and speaking assignments allows students to perform the work of social and historical location in an exploratory mode without being measured and judged in the reductive terms of grades.

These suggestions concern the classroom instructor; on the departmental level, chairs can create a supportive climate for counterhegemonic teaching by looking carefully at student evaluations in dialogue with teachers' own accounts of their classes. This is not to imply that critical pedagogy always produces low student ratings, or that low student ratings can be explained simply by labeling the pedagogy "politicized." It is to point out that counterhegemonic teaching produces challenges to traditional ways of thinking and learning not often resolved within a quarter or even a semester. If the teacher's goal is to raise questions, to initiate new forms of reading and writing rather than to perfect old ones, and the effort is successful, the students' responses may be more tentative than effusive. In such cases, the best measure of success may not be high numerical ratings from students.

Another way to create a supportive climate is by organizing regular opportunities for faculty members to discuss the politics of the classroom. These discussions should not occur only when decisions have to be made about curriculum, program, or policies—situations in which various factions of the faculty have turf to guard or reputations to protect and when time constraints may create pressure to truncate discussion of complex questions. When teaching becomes an ongoing collective project, departmental practices reinforce the commitments of a critical pedagogy outlined above in terms of the single classroom.

Correctness Revisited

I'd like to end with a few more words about the phrase *political correctness*. My source is Geoffrey Nunberg, a linguist from Stanford, who in an editorial on National Public Radio's "All Things Considered" offered a historical perspective on the phrase. Nunberg sees the language of "correctness" today as a trivialization of political debate but reminds us of an earlier era when there was a more substantial connection between civility and civil liberties. As English teachers, we might be especially susceptible to the accusation of fussing over correctness and want to distance ourselves from that association. But it's the accusers themselves who frame the debate as one concerned with taste, manners, and propriety in the most reductive sense when it suits their purposes, though they sometimes turn the tables. For George Bush, manners become serious business when he depicts political debate in terms of lapses from neighborliness. Those of us invested in transformative pedagogy need to provide a vigorous counter-discourse to the characterization of our teaching as a faddish fixation on political correctness. The same rhetorical tradition that gives us the concept of demagoguery (as well as its critique) offers a long and venerable tradition of rhetorical instruction as a practice of civic responsibility. When we ask students and the public as well to engage in collective inquiry into language in society, we improve the prospects for progressive social change within and outside the classroom.

Note

In preparing this article, I used some ideas from "Feminist Sophistics: Teaching with an Attitude," which I cowrote with Dale M. Bauer. I'm also indebted to Patricia Bizzell's essay "Power, Authority, and Critical Pedagogy." Works by Paulo Freire, Henry Giroux, bell hooks, and Ira Shor are sources for my discussions of critical literacy, critical pedagogy, critical citizenship, and public intellectuals.

Susan Jarratt is the director of the Women's Studies Program and an associate professor of English at Miami University.

Works Cited

Bakhtin, M. M. *Speech Genres and Other Late Essays*. Trans. Vern W. McGee. Ed. Caryl
    Emerson and Michael Holquist. Austin: U of Texas P, 1986.
Bizzell, Patricia. "Power, Authority, and Critical Pedagogy." *Journal of Basic Writing* 10.2
    (1991): 54-70.
Bush, George, Commencement address. U of Michigan. Ann Arbor, 4 May 1991. *New York
    Times* 5 May 1991: 1+.
Cockburn, Alexander. "Bush and PC—A Conspiracy So Immense. . . ." *Nation* 27 May
    1991: 685+.
Downing, David, ed. *Changing Classroom Practices*. Urbana: National Council of
    Teachers of English, forthcoming.
Giroux, Henry A. *Schooling and the Struggle for Public Life*. Minneapolis: U of Minnesota
    P, 1988.

Graff, Gerald. "My Classroom Authority Problem." Downing.

Henry, William A., III. "Upside Down in the Groves of Academe." *Time* 1 Apr. 1991: 66-69.

Jarratt, Susan C., and Dale M. Bauer. "Feminist Sophistics: Teaching with an Attitude." Downing.

Nunberg, Geoffrey. Editorial. "All Things Considered." NPR. 15 May 1991.

Vygotsky, L. S. *Mind in Society*. Ed. Michael Cole, Vera John-Steiner, Sylvia Scribner, and Ellen Souberman. Cambridge: Harvard UP, 1978.

Weber, Max. "Science as a Vocation." From *Max Weber: Essays in Sociology*. Trans. and ed. Hans Gerth and C. Wright Mills. New York: Oxford UP, 1946. 129-56.

Williams, Raymond. *Keywords: A Vocabulary of Culture and Society*. New York: Oxford UP, 1976.